DATE DUE

DEMCO 38-296

INTO THE WEST

INTO THE WEST

The Story of Its People

WALTER NUGENT

Alfred A. Knopf   New York   1999

THIS IS A BORZOI BOOK
PUBLISHED BY ALFRED A. KNOPF

Copyright © 1999 by Walter T. K. Nugent
Maps copyright © 1999 by George Colbert

All rights reserved under International and Pan-American Copyright
Conventions. Published in the United States by Alfred A. Knopf, a
division of Random House, Inc., New York, and simultaneously
in Canada by Random House of Canada Limited, Toronto.
Distributed by Random House, Inc., New York.

www.randomhouse.com

Knopf, Borzoi Books, and the colophon are registered
trademarks of Random House, Inc.

Photo permissions can be found on page 495.

Library of Congress Cataloging-in-Publication Data
Nugent, Walter T. K.
Into the West : the story of its people / by Walter Nugent.—1st ed.
          p.   cm.
Includes bibliographical references (p.   ) and index.
ISBN 0-679-45479-9 (alk. paper)
1. West (U.S.)—History.   2. West (U.S.)—Population.
3. West (U.S.)—Ethnic relations.   4. West (U.S.)—Race relations.
5. Land settlement—West (U.S.)—History.   I. Title.
F591.N84   1999
978—dc21   99-18957   CIP

Manufactured in the United States of America
First Edition

For

The Other nÓg

CONTENTS

ILLUSTRATIONS

MAPS

PREFACE

When I was a teenager in northern New York in the late 1940s, soon to be shipped off to college in Kansas, I was talking with a few buddies. Someone asked, "Whatever happened to so-and-so?" and another said, "He went out west somewhere; Chicago, I think." In those days Chicago was still, in our eastern minds, the gateway to the Great West. When I arrived in Atchison, after changing trains in Chicago from the familiar New York Central to the exotic Santa Fe (now that was truly western!), I thought I had reached the edge of the earth. Anything west of Wichita was as mythical as the lands beyond Columbus's western ocean in the year 1500: full of demons, deserts, and Amazons.

Not until I was twenty did I lay eyes on the Colorado Rockies, not until thirty-one did I see San Francisco, and not until the late 1970s did I truly experience Los Angeles and Seattle. I knew that California existed because in B movies and on "Dragnet," cops and villains sped along streets lined with palm trees. But they were not places I had ever seen, and I accepted their reality only by willingly suspending disbelief.

This book may provide today's easterners, midwesterners, and southerners with eyes into the West and how it came to be—even though they may think they do not need enlightenment, because of their forays into Las Vegas, Vail, or the very uneastern megalopolis of Los Angeles. Such visits, while fine, cannot reveal the historical and present complexity of this most exciting region. During much of its history it was Indian or Spanish, essentially foreign to Anglo-America, and only in the twentieth century has it become a functioning part of it—a gradual and uneasy process in itself. In the coming century the West will doubtless play a crucial and leading role in the future of the American people, the billions who live across the Pacific, and the children and grandchildren of us all.

What may happen in the future, however, is not for this historian to prophesy. What I hope to show is what did happen. *Into the West* describes how the West got its people: why they came and mostly stayed. What myths, ideals, and dreams drove them there? Who were they? Why did they make the West more urban, earlier, than almost anywhere else in the country? How did it become more ethnically and racially diverse than any other region of the traditionally Anglo-Protestant United States? How did the West lead the nation's profound change from a farming people to city dwellers and suburbanites, for the West was the final, most concentrated cockpit of that transformation? Why has California become so large (over 12 percent of all the people), so productive (the seventh-largest economy in the world), and so diverse (more ethnicities than anywhere else in the country)? More people now live in California alone than lived in the entire United States when the Civil War broke out in 1861.

These are historical questions. My way of answering them is by providing a comprehensive narrative, a coherent story of a single, though hugely diverse, people. From prehistoric times to the present, many races and ethnicities have mixed and mingled in the West, and not always smoothly, as everyone knows. Usually the story of the West has been told without much reference to many of these groups because it has seemed more productive or patriotic to celebrate national progress, consensus, and unity and how the West has always promoted them. Indeed it has, but there is no blinking the conflicts. Nor does it do any good, conversely, to wallow in victimization and brutality. People are people, whatever their colors or national origins; some were heroic, others demonic, and most of them just lived as best they could. Perspectives have differed; learning to live together takes time. It would surprise the native-born as well as the European immigrants of a hundred years ago that their great-grandchildren live together so well. It may take another century, but the separations that seem large today among Asians, Latinos, Anglo-Americans, and African-Americans in the West may also abrade and fade. Class differences, though, may not go away that soon. Some appear here, but they deserve another book.

A social-demographic history like this one—a history of the people, not of their politics or other doings—divides up into periods that may seem somewhat unconventional. My chapter breaks will not be at changes of presidents or at familiar years like 1776, 1865, or 1945, but rather at 1848, 1889, 1913, 1929, 1941, 1965, and 1987, for reasons to be explained. Wars and depressions play major roles in whether people move about, but presidents, governors, and generals rarely do, and so those gentlemen rarely appear here. On the other hand, the Mexican-American War of 1846–1848, the many armed struggles between the United States and Indians, and the Vietnam conflict, to mention some major cases, certainly changed western population, as did the national depressions of the 1890s and the 1930s.

Still other events—so broad and pervasive as to deserve some bigger name, like megaevents—have been at least as important in the longer run. The rise and collapse of homesteading underpinned the entire history of the United States for over 200 years, from the Atlantic to the Sierras and beyond, and the West is where homesteading peaked and then died. The baby boom of the mid twentieth century was a major deviation from centuries-old reproductive behavior, and its effects will linger until midway through the coming century. The West led it and reveled in it, then was the first region to reject it. Federal immigration laws, determining who and how many could come to the United States, have had more to do with the shape and size of western population than anything political except the fact of American territoriality itself.

This book is not driven by any thesis. But it does have one continuing plot line, which is also a premise and a hope. The briefest way to phrase it is *e pluribus unum.* The peopling of the West is complex. Yet it is one story, just as western Americans are one people, sharing magnificent space and promise. You will find here a new, unified history of the people of the West from earliest times to the present. Before we get to it, however, "West" needs a bit of explanation. Where is it? Are there any overarching reasons why people went there? And what does the West have to do with the rest of the country?

August 1998

ACKNOWLEDGMENTS

As I look back on it, a great crowd of people have helped me on this book since I started sketching it out in the fall of 1986, and in a lot of different ways. Some suggestions I followed to the letter; others I didn't. In any case, the responsibility for how I used and interpreted all this help is mine alone.

Many people sent me copies of work-in-progress or conference presentations that I asked for. They were collegially most generous to do that. They are Michael Ebner, twice; Ellen Eisenberg; Myron Gutmann; Marilynn S. Johnson; Margo McBane; Dennis Moore; John Nieto-Phillips; Gail O'Brien; Emily Rader; Sandra Schackel; Carlos Schwantes; and Arthur Verge.

For all sorts of tips, cooperation, encouragement, room and board, and/or communications I thank James P. Allen, Judy Austin, James T. Carroll, William Cronon, Michael Ebner, Michael Engh, Jeri Echeverria, Ruth Hardin, the late Wilbur Jacobs, Mariam King-Cohen and Ed Cohen, Kathy Kobayashi, Paul K. Longmore, Rita Mendelssohn, José Moya, Douglas Nugent, Rachel Nugent, Terry Nugent, Roy Ritchie, Roberto Treviño, and D. H. Ubelaker. To Dick Etulain and Gerry Nash go my thanks for inviting me in 1985 to write an essay on the peopling of the West that was published in a book of theirs in 1989; it showed me that the subject really required more than an essay. To Martin Ridge go my thanks for suggesting back in the 1980s that I write a book on the demographic history of the twentieth-century West for our series. This is a different, broader book, but his suggestion helped start the process.

Archivists and librarians all over the West helped me along with unfailing courtesy and cooperation. I particularly thank State Archivist David Hoober in Phoenix; Willa K. Baum, director of UC-Berkeley's Regional Oral History Office; at the oral history collection at California State University in Long Beach, Kristie French and Professor Sherna Berger Gluck; the Chicago Historical Society, especially Corey Seeman; the Denver Public Library's Western History Department; the First American Title Insurance Company of Santa Ana, especially Barbara Blankman; the Henry E. Huntington Library, especially Jennifer Watts and Alan Jutzi; Judy Austin at the Idaho State Historical Society; the photographic division of the Library of Congress; Carolyn Kozo Cole at the Los Angeles Public Library; the Massachusetts Historical Society; the Center for Southwest Research at the University of New Mexico, especially Nancy Brown; the Newberry Library; the Oklahoma Historical Society, especially Chester Cowen, Rodger Harris, and Judith Michener; Jim Strassmeier at the Oregon Historical Society; Texas Tech's Southwest Collection, especially Vicky Jones; Special Collections at UCLA; the Regenstein Library at the University of Chicago; the University of Notre Dame's Hesburgh Library; the Utah State Historical Society, especially Phil Notarianni; Special Collections (especially Claudia Rivers) and the Institute of Oral History at the University of Texas-El Paso; the University of Washington (Karyl Winn at Manuscripts and University Archives, as well as the Pacific Northwest Collection and Special Collections); David Hastings at the Washington State Archives; Cassie Chinn and Ruth Vincent at Seattle's Wing Luke Asian Museum; and Yale University's Beinecke Library.

Notre Dame gave me a full-year research leave in 1996–1997 to draft much of the book, time that was utterly essential. My gracious and diligent student assistants between 1988 and 1994—Brad Birzer, Drew Buscareno, Emily Mily, Bruce Smith, and Jolene Smith—saved me incalculable shlepping. The Huntington Library provided access to its collections and a much-needed, much-sought-after work space in 1987. Yale awarded me a Beinecke Fellowship in May 1990, and there I found scads more sources, thanks very importantly to George Miles.

Several colleagues and friends did me the honor of reading drafts. Their comments have improved the book enormously and saved me from a grand stack of bloopers and infelicities. Bill Deverell read chapters four through ten. Jim Gregory read seven and eight. Patty Limerick read one through six. Dean May read three and four. John Nickerson and Richard Jackson read part of nine. Mac Rohrbough read one through four. Carlos Schwantes read five and six. Dave Weber read two and three. All of these contributed their exceptional expertise in particular periods and in very special ways.

Three people read it all. Martin Ridge, my former colleague at Indiana University and career-long friend and collaborator, brought to bear his characteristic incisiveness at many points. Suellen Hoy, who as always is my editor-of-the-first-instance, best friend, and sustainer, chased dirt from every nook and cranny of the manuscript. Bernie Weisberger, with his unique talents as a historian and with his inexhaustible *Menschheit,* produced dozens of pages of guideposts to follow and gaffes to avoid. To these friends not only I, but my readers, owe a very great deal. Gerry McCauley, friend and agent since we were tads, has been ever supportive and ingeniously helpful. Thanks also to my editor, Ashbel Green.

Finally, and above all, I thank Suellen, for innumerable instances of support in addition to her readings and comments. Without her, it would not have been completed.

INTO THE WEST

1

WHERE THE WEST IS AND WHY PEOPLE HAVE GONE THERE

The West is a thing of imagination, not of boundaries.
—Shirl Henke, Youngstown, Ohio,
western writer

I follow the regions of the U.S. Census. . . . [The West's defining characteristics are] latitude and longitude.
—Allan G. Bogue, Madison, Wisconsin,
western historian

The Mysterious West

In 1976 the cartoonist Saul Steinberg drew a famous cover for the *New Yorker* showing the locals' mind's-eye-view of the United States. Looking westward from midtown, the Manhattanite saw, close up, Ninth Avenue, then Tenth, then the Hudson, and then, in fast-closing perspective, vagueness, error, and finally dismissal.

If Steinberg had drawn for the *Los Angeles Times,* he would have produced a much different map. It would have highlighted the Big Bear Lake ski area, Las Vegas, and Lake Tahoe; Sacramento and San Francisco; Phoenix, Denver, and Seattle; Washington, D.C.; and not much of New York except Wall Street and the theater district. But the map would certainly have shown London, Paris, and Rome and, looking west, Hawaii, Australia, and Japan. Mexico, definitely.

Even in the West, however, people have strange ideas about their own region. Sophisticated and case-hardened editors of metropolitan dailies on the Pacific Coast do not believe that anything east of the Rocky Mountains is really part of the West. Conversely some residents of Billings, Boulder, or Boise—the interior West—think that California, Oregon, and Washington are outside the West. Such people would prefer that any place west of the

Sierras should break off and float out into the Pacific. They think that the "real" (meaning, ideal) West no longer exists, that it has already gone to metropolitanized hell. For them, what is left might as well be strip-mined, deforested, overgrazed, desertified, and paved over because the "true West" can never be found again except in the pages of writers like Louis L'Amour, Larry McMurtry, and the earlier Zane Grey and Owen Wister. To this way of thinking, the West is myth, memory, imagination, not a place at all, because the place that is now there has too many cities, too many people, and hardly any buffaloes or cowboys.

But it is a place, with people more diverse in race or class than those of the other great regions of the United States: the Northeast, the Midwest, and the South. They are more varied today than they used to be, but they have always been a mixed lot, not just cigarette-smoking cowboys or hippies on beaches. This book is one story about the people of the West: who they are and have been, how they got there, what myths motivated them to go there, and how they have interacted. Some were in what we now call the West at least fourteen thousand years ago, and others, from Europe, Africa, and Asia, have been arriving from that day to this. They are all part of this story.

The Five Motivators of Migration into the West

Demography measures births, deaths, marriages, and migrations and what speeds or slows them, like health and disease. Demographic history traces these phenomena over time. Among them migration is especially crucial for the western story because in the long run it has shaped the West most. Millions of migrants mean millions of stories. But it would be impossible, and for that matter meaningless, to tell every tale. A few motives, broadly defined, account for western (and most other) human migration.

First, the hunger for land has been well-nigh universal, from ancient times in Europe, Asia, or Africa to the present. In American history, land hunger has taken the form of the Agrarian Myth, codified by Thomas Jefferson into an ideal society of independent, individualistic smallholders, or homesteaders. (Indians, to the contrary, usually considered land a "free good," like air, owned by everybody; land privately owned was a foreign concept to them, and in that difference of attitude rested much of the problem between whites and Indians.) Homesteading was crucial for pulling the land-hungry across the Overland Trail to Oregon in the 1840s and 1850s and in settling the Great Plains from the 1870s to the 1920s. It was not at all crucial, and in fact almost marginal, in populating California. Whatever its name—the Homesteading Ideal, or the Agrarian Myth, Jeffersonian or otherwise—it reflected a profound attachment to the idea of getting and keeping some land of one's own and thus creating a "family farm."

Second, contrasting with the ideal of settling, is the idea of finding a valuable resource, taking it, and exploiting it for its value. Natural resources have been targets of exploitation since before King Solomon had mines. In the American West this motive first exploded in the California Gold Rush of 1849–1852, reappeared in Colorado and Nevada in the late 1850s and again in dozens of later strikes of gold and silver across the West. It operated in the twentieth century when entrepreneurs sought fossil fuels and more exotic substances like molybdenum or uranium. Homesteading inspired people to find a place to settle; the gold rush idea caused people to migrate to find and extract resources. The two overlap in one respect: Land itself has sometimes been an exploitable resource, especially for grazing animals, but it is often renewable, with care, while minerals are not. In the twentieth century the gold rush idea has underlaid migrations to find more abstract forms of wealth, as when corporations merge and hopscotch from place to place, seeking the best returns. This is attenuated gold rushing, but the basic motive is similar.

A third historic reason for migrating is simply the search for a better quality of life, specifically in California. The California Dream has been the motivator of health seekers, retirees, entrepreneurs, hedonists, hippies, escapees from Jim Crow or foreign repression, looking (with or without much accurate information) for a land of opportunity and "the good life."[1] The California Dream has taken many forms. Its earliest expression was the legend floating around Europe in the early sixteenth century that California was an island where a race of black Amazons lived, ruled by their queen, Calafia. It took two centuries to convince mapmakers that California is not an island. The dream became anglicized with the American takeover in 1846.[2] Since then California has attracted millions of people with its "Hedonistic Middle based on the desire of ordinary people to get a little more out of life, to have more fun."[3] The modern California Dream began in southern California as early as the 1870s and became possible, affordable, and achievable for millions in the twentieth century. The more the area became Anglo-American, the more the California Dream attracted people from the rest of the country, particularly the Middle West. The dream had Spanish and Mexican origins, but they were modified and romanticized after the 1870s into something quite new.

A fourth motivator of migration is nostalgia. It urges people to return home, or to what they think is home, either as a lost place or a lost time, a "golden age." It brought Ulysses back across the wine-dark sea, and it made sojourners rather than settlers out of roughly half of the tens of millions of Europeans and Asians who came to the United States by sail and steam between the 1820s and 1914. A great many of those "immigrants" (so defined not by themselves but by the America they were entering) came not to stay but to improve things at home, to which they intended to return. In the American West the nostalgia motivator is the newest of these four. It is the one now most vivid in people's minds, in the United States and around the world, thanks to media saturation, beginning with Buffalo Bill Cody. It actually brings far fewer people to the West except as tourists, than the other three, although it has recently prompted tens of thousands to leave the coastal and metropolitan West (especially California) for the interior West, where the myth remains strongest.

According to one of its defenders, this myth reaffirms and seeks out "Cowboy Code traits of individualism, democracy, equality, ingenuity, and courage," makes a hero out of the cowboy because his "individualism, stoicism, common sense, adaptability, courage, and democracy" are "consummately American," and clings to "the epic story of an American people crossing a continental frontier and taming its wild forces."[4] That "epic," however, rests far too much on about twenty-five years of Indian-white struggle on the Great Plains, ignoring four hundred years of deeper history. Yet its imagery strongly affects western life today, including demography, and therefore must be taken into account. Call it the Old West/Golden West mythology.

The fifth motivator is the most historically universal of all. People have always migrated to improve themselves and their families, materially or spiritually. Southern Europeans went north for centuries before steamships and railroads opened North and South America to them as targets of opportunity.[5] Contract workers from China, Japan, and the Philippines sailed east for similar reasons. In the American West, migration for wages (not land) brought Mexicans to *El Norte* throughout the twentieth century, African-Americans from Texas and Louisiana to Los Angeles after 1940, Asians ever since the Gold Rush, Indians from the reservations to the cities, and whites from Europe and the eastern and midwestern United States throughout western history.

These five motivators—homesteading, gold rushing, California dreaming, nostalgia for the Old West/Golden West, and sheer betterment—overlap in individual cases because people always have, of course, mixed motives. These reasons do not explain everybody (political refugees, for example), but they cover the great majority. Of the five, however, the most important in terms of the number of people who directly responded to it is today, ironically, the most forgotten: homesteading.

Where Did the Buffalo Roam, Anyway?

What "the West" means has changed radically over the course of American history. Where and when are we talking about? The Census Bureau defines the West as the thirteen Mountain and Pacific states, from Montana south to New Mexico, and everything west of them, including Alaska and Hawaii. It does not include the Great Plains tier from North Dakota to Texas. Yet Texans and Oklahomans (and many Kansans, Nebraskans, and Dakotans) vigorously insist that they are western. The commonsense definition of the West is the area where the people who live in it think they are western. This today includes everything west of the 98th or 100th meridian: the Great Plains, the Rocky Mountain subregion, the Great Basin, the Pacific Coast, and Alaska and Hawaii. (To look ahead, this is the West as I shall use the word in this book: essentially the Census West, plus the Great Plains.) But what makes one place western and another not? Should the definition consider not just where we are talking about but when? Has not "the West" shifted over time?

Also, "frontier" and "West" have often meant the same thing, though they are not. This confusion goes back far, but its most powerful expressions appeared about a century ago from Owen Wister, the novelist whose *The Virginian* (1902) set the formula for hundreds of novels and films since; Frederic Remington, who glorified the macho cowboy in oils and bronzes; William F. "Buffalo Bill" Cody; Theodore Roosevelt; and Frederick Jackson Turner. Cody's long-running road show, *Buffalo Bill's Wild West* (1885–1911), reenacted the victory of American bluecoats and buckskins over the "savage" Indians, employing some of those very same ones (including, briefly, Sitting Bull) to replay their defeat. Roosevelt's multivolume *The Winning of the West* (1889–1896) told the story, chiefly, of white-Anglo conquest of the buffalo, the plains, and the Indians who lived there.[6] Turner drew a much broader picture in his epochal essay "The Significance of the Frontier in American History," which he presented as a lecture in Chicago in 1893. Rather than "the West," he described "the frontier," from Massachusetts and Virginia in the early 1600s to his own time, from the Atlantic to the Mississippi Valley, a zone of settlement that shifted westward as time went on. It made Americans uniquely what they are. And that, he said, was finished. He rested his case on the 1890 Census, which stated that a true frontier line could not be drawn any longer because white settlement had scattered so widely across the West.

"The frontier," however, was not the same as "the West." Except for the Great Plains with its then-recent Indian wars, these mythmakers ignored most of the region we are defining as West. The western half of the continental United States hardly figures in their stories, was as yet sparsely populated, remained a mystery to most Americans, and still contained millions of acres available for settlement—or, more in line with what later happened, for city building. The "West" was still to be won, and would be, by a much broader spectrum of people than the Anglo-Americans of whom Turner, Roosevelt, Cody, Remington, and Wister were representative.

The West deserves a more inclusive history than the traditional frontier "epic." It has become much more important in the national and international scheme of things than it used to be. In 1890 the western census region contained only 3,000,000 of 63,000,000 Americans, less than 5 percent. By the late 1990s it was home to nearly 60,000,000 of the nation's 270,000,000. In 1890 fewer than 1 of 20 Americans lived in the West. To the other 19, it was an exotic place that was distant, unknown, dreamed about, and mythified. Many today who live in other regions have never lost their innocence about the West. They still think of it in ways learned from Buffalo Bill's theatrical Wild West, or the art of Remington and Russell, or western novels and films, or even Steinberg's *New Yorker* cover. It is time for the mystery to end.

Plains to the Pacific or Just Dodge City to the Sierras?

Just where the West is, and what it is, have puzzled Americans for some time, not least because they have confused it with "frontier" for so long. Both have been central to Americans' thinking about their history from the beginning. Are they places on the map or constructions in the mind? Are "frontier" and "West" the same, or is one the present echo of the now-dead other? If the West is a place, exactly what does it include: the thirteen states so defined by the Census Bureau, or only parts of them, or more?[7] If it is a mental construction, is it Thomas Jefferson's Agrarian Myth, or Buffalo Bill's Wild West, or Frederick Jackson Turner's frontier, or the California Dream, or a mixture of these and other ideas?

According to a poll I conducted in 1991,[8] most historians and other experts agree that the borders with Mexico and Canada delimit the West on south and north. Most said that the western edge is the Pacific (though they usually admitted Alaska and Hawaii) and they put the eastern edge at the 98th or 100th meridian, where the Great Plains begin. This includes the western halves of the Dakotas, Nebraska, and Kansas, all of Oklahoma, and Texas west of Austin; call it the Plains-to-Pacific West. A minority of the experts voted for a tighter West running from the High Plains—about at Dodge City—to the Sierras, including the Rockies, Great Basin, and the deserts—in effect, the arid region. This West specifically excludes the Pacific

Coast and its great metropolises, with the view that such places are nonwestern or at best postwestern. Washington, Oregon, and California west of the Cascades and Sierras are not part of this Dodge-to-Sierras West. Dodge-to-Sierras can be regarded as the interior West, or the exclusive West, because of what it leaves out.

People who actually live in the three Pacific Coast states, however, regard their own states plus all of the Rocky Mountains, Texas, and Oklahoma, as western. Those who live in Kansas, Nebraska, and the Dakotas see their states as partly western, partly midwestern. Texans and Oklahomans usually want their states wholly included in the West, though some draw a line between Dallas (no) and Fort Worth (yes) or are uncertain about Texas south and east of Austin.

Somewhere in Kansas and Nebraska, the Midwest becomes West. The *Almanac of American Politics* describes the Third Congressional District of Nebraska, which runs from Grand Island and Hastings to the Wyoming line, as "geographically and politically . . . where the Midwest becomes the West," rancher and wheat grower Republican like western Kansas just south of it.[9] Some Nebraskans make Omaha the border point; others, North Platte or Grand Island. Dakotans both North and South name the 100th meridian, which cuts most of those states into the West. Kansans are sure that the West begins *somewhere* in their Sunflower State.

So where is the eastern edge of the West? A writer in *Time* in 1989 affirmed that "Signs of America's Old West start as far east as Adair, Iowa [seventy-five miles east of the Missouri River], where an old railroad wheel marks the spot on which Jesse James held up his first moving train in 1873. . . . By the time you reach Al's Oasis at Oacoma, S. Dak., on a bluff over the glistening Missouri River [and just thirty-four miles east of the 100th meridian], all doubt vanishes. . . . The proud sign at Al's . . . unabashedly announces WHERE THE WEST BEGINS."[10]

By the 1990s, many towns on Interstates 70 (across Kansas), 80 (across Nebraska), and 90 (across South Dakota) were recouping their waning agricultural fortunes by claiming to have had significant roles in the shaping of the historic West. Minden, Nebraska, between Kearney and Grand Island, boasted a Pioneer Village theme park "Showing Man's Progress since 1830" and "The Story of America and How It Grew." Visitors could see "Elm Creek Fort": "The first log cabin in Webster County, Nebraska, both as a dwelling and as a community fort against Indian attack, built in 1869. The interior is authentically furnished. An original Pony Express mailbox is on the wall [even though the Pony Express ceased in 1861]. A replica general store . . . [is] completely stocked with by-gone items [including] a glass cat on the cracker barrel." Also visible were a relocated land office, an "authentic replica" sod house, and much else. The Stuhr Museum "of the Prairie Pioneer," at Grand Island, Nebraska, with a main building designed by the architect Edward Durell Stone, honored actor Henry Fonda's birthplace (1905), although Fonda was at best a highly attenuated frontiersman. It displayed a "re-created" prairie town that told the story of "community development in Nebraska during the last decades of the nineteenth century."

North Platte celebrates Buffalo Bill Cody, who built a ranch there in 1886, although he spent most of his life elsewhere. But who could argue when North Platte asserts that "No one personifies the frontier better than Buffalo Bill Cody . . . [whose] legacy lives on today"? Visitors tour the eighteen-room ranch house and the horse barn, "all preserved in the finest detail," and then partake of a "genuine buffalo stew cookout."

On I-90 in South Dakota, 1990s travelers visited "Deadwood's Broken Boot Gold Mine" from the 1890s ("Give a Hoot—See the Boot") or, at Mitchell, the extraordinary Corn Palace, first opened in 1892 and refitted in 1937 with "moorish-designed minarets, turrets, and kiosks." The exterior is replaced every September with "thousands of bushels of corn, grain, and grasses, which are native and of natural color." Dodge City, Kansas, perched exactly on the 100th meridian, strives harder for accuracy than most of these Great Plains frontier sites. Dodge literature states frankly that the original Front Street burned down in 1885 and the present Long Branch saloon and other attractions have been reconstructed three blocks away from the original site. Yet Dodge lives on as "the most western town of all, beautiful bibulous Babylon, the Cowboy Capital of the world."[11]

But was the West mostly bluecoats and "redskins," gunslingers and marshals? Was (and is) it really violent? Historical truth scarcely justifies its reputation and belies the mythology of western violence. In 1920 the leading seven states in homicide rates were not in the West but in the South. California was ninth, Washington thirteenth, but no other western state (even Texas) placed in the top twenty-four of the then–forty-eight states. By the mid-1990s the relative positions of South and West had not changed greatly. Of the nineteen states we are counting as western, thirteen had homicide rates below the national average, but nine of eleven southern states were above it.[12] Montana, Idaho, and Wyoming, despite the Unabomber and the anarchistic militias within them, were among the ten least afflicted by murderers, rapists, and robbers. Western violence never remotely compared, except in myth, to southern violence.

Should Hawaii, Alaska, Canada, Mexico—and California—be included in a history of the people of the West? The English novelist David Lodge says yes to Hawaii: "One day Lewis came back from a big convention in Philadelphia and said he had been offered a good job, associate professor with tenure, at the University of Hawaii. . . . To me the idea of moving to Hawaii seemed bizarre—I mean, it didn't sound like a serious place, where anyone would do serious work. It was somewhere you went for vacations, or your honeymoon, if you were kind of corny and had the money and didn't mind long airplane trips. It was a resort. The last resort. It is, you know. This is where America ends, where the West ends."[13] The census agrees with Lodge, and so do I. Hawaii has volcanoes, like the Pacific Coast. Aside from the Parker Ranch on the Big Island, it lacks cattle and cowboys, and its spaces, except for the ocean, are not wide open. Never did it have homesteaders, forty-niners, long cattle drives, or mountain men. Yet it has hotels, condominiums, visitors, racial mixture, and seekers of the good life, like southern California. So by nineteenth-century criteria Hawaii might not qualify, but by twentieth-century ones it certainly does.

Alaska is less problematic. Despite its long Russian past and much longer habitation by native peoples, it hardly had any *American* history until the late 1890s, when Klondike gold pulled thousands of wealth seekers up through its panhandle. Since the 1970s oil from Prudhoe Bay has created another resource exploitation frontier. In its gold rush and oil-drilling traditions, its concentration of population in urban oases separated by vast stretches of raw and beautiful wilderness, its native peoples, and its economic ties to Seattle and the Pacific Northwest, Alaska has several claims to westernness, negated only, if at all, by its separation from the lower forty-eight.

Western Canada and the western United States are of a piece. The Great Plains cross the forty-ninth parallel for hundreds of miles, so that Montana and North Dakota blend imperceptibly with Alberta and Saskatchewan. The Rockies are as important a feature of Alberta and British Columbia as they are of Montana, Idaho, and Colorado. Vancouver is as much a Pacific Rim city as Seattle. Canada certainly had a settlement frontier, which closed officially in 1930. By then western Canadians had developed a distinct region, containing cities as different as Vancouver and Winnipeg and such contrasting landscapes as Alberta's mountains and glaciers and Saskatchewan's flat prairie. The region was united by "affable contempt of Toronto and a serious hatred of Ottawa."[14] Western Canadians have also been united by a sense of difference from the United States, for many good reasons. But despite the continuities, we will leave western Canada out of this story except when Americans migrated to the Canadian prairies after 1901.

Physiography joins southeastern California and southern Arizona with Sonora, Mexico, and west Texas with Chihuahua. It is the same desert. Spanish place-names and Hispanic people appear all along the border from Brownsville to San Diego and well north of it. Nevertheless, the boundary

line of 1848 that means so little physiographically means too much politically to include Mexico. In the demographic story it provides people for the
American West but is separate from it.

Finally, what about California? Those who would exclude it always seem
to live elsewhere. It admittedly does not fit the Dodge-to-Sierras stereotypes:
hardly any cowboys or gold miners, at least not for a long time; never many
homesteads; no buffaloes. Indians, yes, but without horses and feathers. It is
not like Kansas, or even Colorado, and never was. It does have several
mountain ranges, including the Sierras, highest in the continental United
States. It has naval and military bases and defense-related industries galore
and other federal property and agencies; they make it very much part of the
post-1940 West, though many nostalgists do not believe that such things can
really be western. It is the leading agricultural state. It has several of the
world's greatest universities. It contains three of the fifteen largest metropolitan areas in the United States, all of which grew much faster than the
national average since 1980, as well as ten of the fourteen fastest-growing
American cities of over a hundred thousand. It elects more representatives
to the United States Congress, spread more widely across the political spectrum, than any other state. Its people speak more languages and represent
more ethnic and racial groups than anywhere else in America. Of the ten
congressional districts in the United States with the highest median household value, eight are in California.[15] None of these fits well into the Old
West/Golden West stereotypology. But in respect to three of the migrant-
motivating myths—gold rushing, general betterment, and of course California dreaming—the state was and is fundamentally western. It is, as often
said, at the edge of the West and at its center, all at once.

The Agrarian Dream vs. the Old/Golden West

Although California inaugurated two of the motivating myths of western
migration, gold rushing and California dreaming, and is a major target of
hoped-for betterment, it has never had much to do with the oldest motivator (the Agrarian Dream), or the newest (Old West/Golden West nostalgia).
In the mountain and plains West, however, these have been crucial. They
have also been fundamental to Americans' national self-images, though at
different times: the Agrarian Dream for the first centuries of nationhood,
the Old/Golden West idea much more recently.

In his *Notes on Virginia* (1784), Thomas Jefferson derided Europe, where
"lands are either cultivated, or locked up against the cultivator," and "manufacture must therefore be resorted to of necessity. . . . But we," this planter
wrote, "have an immensity of land courting the industry of the husband-

man. . . . Those who labor in the earth are the chosen people of God, if ever He had a chosen people. . . . Corruption of morals in the mass of cultivators is a phenomenon of which no age nor nation has furnished an example." Twenty years later, from the White House, Jefferson bragged to the French political economist Jean-Baptiste Say that, again unlike Europe, "Here the immense extent of uncultivated and fertile lands enables every one who will labor, to marry young, and to raise a family of any size." Malthus had no purchase on America; here population would never outrun food.[16]

Jefferson spoke often along these lines, and his Americans, 95 percent of whom lived on farms or in country villages, never doubted him. He had, and the people had as well, a "nearly mystical sense of the American West." Enriched by the Louisiana Purchase, opened by Lewis and Clark, the West was for Jefferson "a self-renewing engine that drove the American Republic forward . . . boundlessly prolific . . . America's fountain of youth." He was "a westerner."[17] Jefferson himself drafted the bill that became, revised, the Ordinance of 1785, by which the United States public domain would be surveyed and sold to settlers. In all subsequent land legislation, through the Homestead Act of 1862, which gave the land away to actual settlers, and beyond into the twentieth century, the Jeffersonian vision and the agrarian, homesteading ideal were inseparable.

Besides the California Dream, gold rushing, and the Agrarian Myth, Americans have manufactured the mythology of an Old (or Golden, or Wild) West, the wide-open–spaced, manifestly destined, now-threatened West. Such a mythical West is held to have shaped Americans into free individuals and to have been no less than the story of American progress itself. Threats to it, which some perceive, signal American decline. As Turner said of the frontier, it made Americans who they are; to lose it is to lose ourselves. For cowboyphiles, it has become a creation myth, an explanation of the primal, and not to be messed with.

What has really declined, however, is the traditional Agrarian Myth. The Old/Golden West Myth, often framed in ranching and cowboy icons and heroes because they seem the most emblematic of individualism, has in the Cold War and post-Vietnam years been most resurgent. In the late twentieth century the ancient Agrarian Myth that motivated much of the nation from the 1600s to the early 1900s has been entirely overwritten by this very different myth of the Old West, even though that myth is not old at all.

But myths come and go, ebb and flow, as people seek a usable past, even an invented one. John Wayne and the Marlboro Man are icons of the Old West Myth, and they are recent ones. Wayne was Marion Morrison, a refugee from Winterset, Iowa, working as a Hollywood stagehand before the director Raoul Walsh began molding that tall putty into a star.[18] The Marlboro Man emanated in 1954 from the minds of Chicago admen Leo Burnett and John Benson, who were trying to devise a more macho pitch for Philip Morris's filter tip cigarette and agreed that "the most masculine figure in America" was the cowboy. In the next forty years the smoking cowboy traveled the world (and two actors who played him died of lung cancer).[19]

The search for the usable, if mythical, past manifested itself in a special issue of *Life* magazine of April 1993, describing "The Wild West, Yesterday and Today."[20] Reviewing the mythology, it also propagated it: "There were giants in those days. The men and women who tamed the Wild West were brave, fierce, ambitious, violent sometimes but implacably determined to build a new world and to live there in complete and glorious freedom. They dreamed a mighty dream and in a few extravagant decades made it come true. Born during the Gold Rush of 1849, the Wild West of wagon trains and Indian raids and range wars and fast-draw artists faded into history as the 20th century arrived with its civilized amenities: government regulations, special interests, local, state and federal taxes—and lawyers." But Buffalo Bill's *Wild West* kept the legend going, as did dime novels and then films and television. The result, according to *Life*'s writer: "[T]he spirit of the Wild West is still alive. You can find it if you take the trouble to look. Come along with us to sagebrush country."

In short, we are drenched with clichés: the golden age is now gone; there were giants then; people were once free but now are ridden by government and lawyers. The narrative is entirely Anglocentric. Was the West born in 1849? What about the Overland Trail and the Mormon migrants of the mid-1840s, the mountain men of the 1820s and 1830s, the Texan rebellion of 1836 against Mexico, the Lewis and Clark Expedition (1804–1806)? What about the Spanish colonization of the Southwest? Plenty happened before 1849; in fact Santa Fe was already 240 years old. Were there no lawyers in the nineteenth century? What about the monumental case of *Lux* v. *Haggin* (decided 1886) that laid down the law on who controlled California water, or the Santa Fe ring that euchered *nuevomexicanos* out of ancient Spanish royal land grants? In fact lawyers had argued Indian rights for centuries, beginning with the great debate between Bartolomé de Las Casas and Juan Sepúlveda in Valladolid in 1550 to help the Emperor Charles V decide whether Indians were fully human. (Las Casas convinced him that they were, and Spanish law took that position.)

Nor was any West ever innocent of government. Congress created the U.S. public domain in 1785, and the federal government sold and distributed it to settlers and speculators thereafter. The Northwest Ordinance of 1787 laid out the procedure by which newly settled areas became full-fledged states of the Union, rather than malcontent colonies of the original thirteen.

Did not the government provide military forces to protect settlers and miners, resettle Indians on reservations, and subsidize much of the transMississippi railroad system? Where, in this mythology, are the Hispanics and the Indians, who were there before the Anglo-Americans; or the Chinese and Japanese who arrived in the late nineteenth century; or the European immigrants, who made western industrial mining (not just the flash-in-the-pan gold rushes) as ethnically diverse as Pennsylvania's?

After this stirring and entirely misleading introduction, *Life* presented a photo of seven riders—perhaps Indians, but one can't be sure—passing beneath the thousand-foot-high cliffs of Arizona's Canyon de Chelly. Caption: "This is the essence of the West: the grandeur of nature, the insignificance of human beings. Great cities have sprung up all over the region, but between them lie vast stretches of magnificent wilderness like the Canyon de Chelly. In such settings, man seems no more than an ant." Such a dehumanized definition claims that the real West is where people aren't and that where they are, they are insignificant. It absurdly contradicts the previous assertion that the West never amounted to much until the "giants" of "those days . . . tamed the Wild West."

Life gave lip service to the brutality of Indian removal in the 1830s, but then fell back into a cliché anecdote about the valor of "Indian fighting" and the supertough Texas Rangers. Then, with a photo of the Dust Bowl, readers learned: "It wasn't the plow that broke the plains. It was greedy, ignorant farmers who in less than 50 years turned 87 million acres of the richest soil on the planet into a great Dust Bowl centered in Kansas and Oklahoma. The land simply blew away, and with it went thousands of Okies, who piled into jalopies and hit the road to California."

This is a fascinating comment, inadvertently marking the eclipse of the Agrarian Myth and Jefferson's ideal. The yeoman, the prairie schooner family heading west full of hope in a new homestead and a fresh start, Daniel Boone leading settlers through the Cumberland Gap (as in George Caleb Bingham's famous painting) were *the* all-engrossing American conception of the frontier West throughout the nineteenth century and well into the twentieth—not the big sky cowboy symbolism of the likes of Buffalo Bill, Theodore Roosevelt, and John Wayne. *Life*'s blatant disrespect for agriculturists, homesteaders in fact, would never have seen print in the same magazine even as late as the 1960s, when millions of farm families still existed and the homestead idea still resonated. *Life* could have mentioned "greedy, ignorant ranchers" whose cattle and sheep—once called "grasshoppers with hooves"—overgrazed the public domain the ranchers leased at subsidized rates. No doubt there have been greedy farmers, and greedy ranchers. Many were not greedy, however; just hard pressed to make a living. *Life*'s inaccu

rate insult reveals that the Agrarian Myth, motivating two centuries of settlement, has been thoroughly supplanted. By 1993 hardly any farmers were
left to complain.

Nevertheless, *Life* presumably told a mass readership much of what it
wanted to believe about a topic with which it continues to be fascinated.
Americans won nearly all the Nobel prizes in 1993. One of the chemistry lau-
reates, Kary Mullis of San Diego, explained why: "We're a frontier society. All
of us are all still a product of a culture which rewarded people who were
mavericks and who thought of new things." Superior funding and the
United States' abundance of researchers (compared, for example, with Germany, which consistently led other countries in Nobels before the 1930s)
explained less to Mullis than the mystical frontier did.[21] The term "last frontier" has been a mantra of the NASA rocketry programs, although they have
all necessarily been carried out by teams rather than by lone individuals, as
was true of most things throughout western history. "Stay the hell out of my
nostalgia," a reader wrote to *Montana*'s editor, protesting a piece critical of
western mythology:[22] a howl of a wounded man, but rare only in its frank-
ness. A college teacher reported in 1993 how difficult it was to teach "the
truth about the history of the American West." Since Turner, she concluded,
it had become "the frontier," the "national myth," and thus "resistant to
knowledge." Her students wanted their "stereotypes about Indians confirmed, not torn away."[23]

Yet in recent years critiques of the myths of the frontier and West have
come from many quarters. The sheer weight of demography has eroded
what lingers of the homesteader-frontier mythology on the Great Plains.
Depopulation since the 1920s steadily lengthened the list of counties with
fewer than two people per square mile. Frank and Deborah Popper, social
scientists at Rutgers University, argued that "settling the prairies . . . was the
largest, longest-running agricultural and environmental mistake in United
States history" and that the region should revert to "buffalo commons" since
in any case "almost two-thirds of today's Plains farms and small communities may vanish by 2020." Plains people responded by cussing the messenger,
insisting that "Our landscape is a powerful source of spiritual renewal." The
Poppers named this reaction "Prairie Zen." As a National Park Service veteran observed, "For many Plains people, deep down inside, it's still 1870.
Self-reliance and caution are profoundly important to them; outside interference, profoundly suspect."[24] But the facts have long been clear to those
young enough to vote with their feet. For decades now, population has
fallen, and median ages have risen. Few remain even to remember the Agrarian Myth and homesteading.

Several fault lines distinguish people's ideas about the West. One separates those wedded to the victory narratives of Buffalo Bill, Turner, or novelist Zane Grey, from demythologizers who are more aware of "the manifold ways in which one people's ambitions are fulfilled at the expense of another's."[25] A parallel fault line divides those who see the frontier narrative as progressive and ennobling from those who stress conflict, conquest, and environmental depletion. Another line splits those who define "the West" as myth or state of mind from those who anchor it in historical and geographical fact. Still another separates those who define the West as the interior, exclusive Dodge-to-Sierras country, from those who see it extending from the Great Plains to the Pacific. The former think it really ended around 1915. The latter will tell you that it is still happening.

The Angeleno's view of the world is certainly more cosmopolitan than the 1970s' perspective from midtown Manhattan in Saul Steinberg's cartoon. But neither says much about history or about the migrations that have peopled the West. It is time to get to the story, keeping in mind that the West in question here is the Plains-to-Pacific West, the census's West plus the Great Plains, the left half of the map of the United States. Millions of people went there, motivated in most cases by homesteading, gold rushing, California dreaming, nostalgia, or unembellished wage earning. That is the where and the why. *Who* peopled the West, and when? Those are questions for a demographic history, which is as follows.

2

FROM TIME IMMEMORIAL TO 1848

[Mission Carmel has] about thirty Christians, not counting various babies who had winged their flight to God.

—Fray Junípero Serra to Viceroy Antonio María de Bucareli, Mexico City, 1773

The object of your mission is to explore the Missouri River, and such principal streams of it, as, by its course and communication with the waters of the Pacific ocean . . . may offer the most direct and practicable water-communication across the continent.

—President Thomas Jefferson to Meriwether Lewis, Washington, D.C., 1803

At the beginning, ancestral Indians first appeared in, or migrated to, what is now the West. They left no voices and not much record. Yet they were certainly in the area twelve thousand years ago and likely arrived much earlier. Whenever they came, they speak to us now only through a few bones, arrowheads, and pot shards, a little architecture, and a few petroglyphs. After about 1540, when the Spanish and then other Europeans entered the American population story, the voices multiplied. We hear Coronado, then Oñate, Kino, Serra, Micheltorena, Pío Pico, and others with Spanish names; a Russian or two, up the California coast and in Alaska; Black Kettle, Chief Joseph, Sitting Bull, and more Indians; Queen Liliuokalani and her dynasty in Hawaii; James Cook and George Vancouver, the English argonauts; Manuel Lisa and fur traders on the upper Missouri; and finally the Americans like Meriwether Lewis and William Clark, Abel Stearns, Stephen Austin, Narcissa Whitman, John C. Frémont and Stephen Kearny, Phil Sheridan and George Custer, Brigham Young, Mark Twain, James J. Hill, and Leland Stanford. Many others, women and men, remaining virtually silent, were there too.

Arrowheads, Large Animals, and Cliff Dwellings

Drive out Wilshire Boulevard from downtown Los Angeles toward Santa Monica and the sea. About halfway along, you will cross an unobtrusive bridge over the corner of a pond. The sun shimmers across its surface, but no ducks or gulls alight there; no ripples disturb it, for the pond is made not of water but asphalt. This is La Brea, the tar pits, which for thousands of years trapped small animals that mistakenly came for a drink, as well as the predators that tried to catch them and were caught themselves. At least one human became entombed there, and her embellished skeleton is displayed today at the Page Museum, adjacent to the tar pits, a branch of the Los Angeles County museum system. Along with her are the bones of American lions, saber-toothed cats, horses, dire wolves, camels, giant sloths, huge short-faced bears, and many lesser beasts that roamed southern California at the time humans arrived.

Exactly when that was is uncertain. Where these humans came from and how many they were are also unknown. The conventional wisdom (not unchallenged) is that the first ones crossed a land bridge from Siberia to Alaska and wandered southward along the Pacific Coast, or along the east face of the Rockies, eventually populating North and South America. The land bridge, which is called Beringia because the Bering Strait now covers it, appeared when the enormous glaciers covering North America as far south as present Illinois and Indiana sucked up enough seawater to lower the oceans hundreds of feet below their present level. When the glacier melted, Beringia became submerged. But by then—11,000 to 14,000 years B.P., before the present—humankind had come to stay. Not long after, many of the large animals became extinct (though not all; bears, moose, elks, cougars, bison, wolves, and others still roam). Whether the humans' skillful predation caused the extinctions is vigorously debated. In any case, spearpoints and arrowheads were discovered near Folsom and Clovis, New Mexico, in 1927, arranged amid buffalo bones in such a way that only human hunters could have been responsible. Twenty some years later carbon 14 dating established these sites to be around 11,500 years old. Since then, many Clovis sites have emerged in the present United States and Canada.[1]

Certainly Paleo-Indians, as archaeologists call these people, were living there at least that far back. Possibly they came to the Americas much earlier or in several stages. Recently discovered sites in Brazil and Chile, far from the reach of any glacier, may go back more than thirty or forty thousand years. These people almost had to have migrated from Asia by some route, because there is no New World fossil evidence of primate ancestors, nor were the Paleo-Indians a different species from modern Indians or other people. Certain Native American creation stories, however, say that people came up out of the earth itself.[2]

The Beringia theory of human entry into the Americas remains plausible but problematic. Canadian and American geographers and geologists in the 1990s discovered human remains and evidence of a narrow but sufficient corridor along the present coasts of Alaska and British Columbia to permit migrations. Sea level, they demonstrate, was a few hundred feet lower in 14,000 B.P. than today. Analyses of mitochondrial DNA indicate some migration from Siberia to Alaska and southward about thirty-four thousand years ago, perhaps by the ancestors of the Pimas of Arizona, the Mayas of Mexico, and the Yanomamis of northern Brazil. Migrations between 15,000 B.P. and 9500 B.P. brought others.[3]

The Beringia thesis does not fully explain puzzles such as South American sites that are perhaps much older yet more developed than the Clovis culture. Nor does it answer why newly discovered sites of human habitation in Alaska, which should be the oldest if people first arrived from nearby Beringia, are younger than many others thousands of miles to the south. Alternative explanations include long, eastbound voyages across the southern Pacific Ocean forty or fifty thousand years ago (technologically possible, but highly unlikely and irritatingly implausible to most archaeologists), migration of at least some peoples from Africa or northern Europe, or the likelihood that migrants arrived from Asia in batches, on many occasions, over a long time, between glaciers earlier than the last one.

Whatever happened, we need to keep in mind only a few certain points: these humans were very often migrants; they subsisted at first on large animals but rather quickly developed agriculture and a vegetarian diet; they built a bewildering range of cultures and languages; and they experienced war, disease, and brief lives just as Europeans, Asians, and Africans did.

The development of agriculture likely slowed migration, although soil exhaustion and shifts in water supplies no doubt forced some moves. Many foods appeared, some (like avocados) requiring several years of irrigated cultivation before bearing fruit. Corn, a human contrivance and no simple gift of nature, became the mainstay of many peoples' diets. Developed by natives of Mexico, corn spread by trade, conquests, or other means to the Mississippi Valley and eastward, revealing an agricultural, stable basis of Native American civilizations several thousand years before Europeans arrived. Squash, beans, chilis, and many other foods greeted the Spanish and very soon enriched European diets, while tobacco added to their indulgences.

In the present Southwest, highly ingenious agriculturists—the Hohokams, Anasazis, and Mogollons—developed elaborate methods of cultivation. The Mogollon people had appeared by 300 B.C.E. in the forested mountains east of Phoenix, developed horticulture and potmaking by 300 C.E., and expanded to southeastern New Mexico by 950. The Hohokams created a 150-mile irrigation system in present Arizona between 800 and 1400. The cliff dwellings at Mesa Verde and villages at Chaco Canyon and Bandelier in New Mexico were Anasazi monuments to intelligent survival, built between 900 and 1250. While these southwestern groups produced the most elaborate architecture, economics, and agriculture, other peoples sustained themselves more simply through the prehistoric millennia: the Plains Indians (as yet horseless), the maritime fishing peoples along the Northwest Coast, the densely settled Californians, and the hardy tribes of the Rocky Mountains and Great Basin.

They traded with one another, warred on and enslaved one another, pushed one another from place to place, lived, reproduced, got sick, and died. For eleven thousand years—at a very minimum—prior to Coronado's incursion in 1540, hundreds of thousands of people lived in the future American West. Their lives were peaceful at times, not peaceful at others; not changeless, timeless, or Edenic. Some built canals, others a city for fifteen thousand people. The most complex cultures north of present Mexico—at Cahokia, Mesa Verde, and Chaco Canyon—peaked in the thirteenth or fourteenth century, two hundred or more years before Europeans had any contact with them. Cahokia, in present day western Illinois, following five hundred years of agriculture-based civilization, had passed its apogee by 1300 and disappeared after 1400, although it "had the largest and densest pre-contact population north of the Rio Grande and was bigger than contemporaneous London."[4] When French missionaries arrived three hundred years later (1698–1699), its most impressive visible remnants were nothing but huge burial mounds. The Hohokam irrigation system and the Anasazi cliff dwellings fell into disuse long before Spaniards saw them. Why? Silt? Drought? Too many people for the crops to sustain? Enemies? Perhaps religion: "every Pueblo origin myth is a history of a people wandering from one place to another, spurred to move by water shortages, soil infertility, disease, or factionalism."[5]

Drought and warfare are reasonable possibilities. The Southwest and California have undergone cycles of rainfall and aridity throughout historic times. Sedimentary evidence indicates that "epic drought" bedeviled California from 892 to 1112 and again from 1209 to 1350 and caused the Anasazis and Hohokams, despite their public works efforts, to move every generation or two in search of water.[6] The Anasazis abandoned their well-constructed

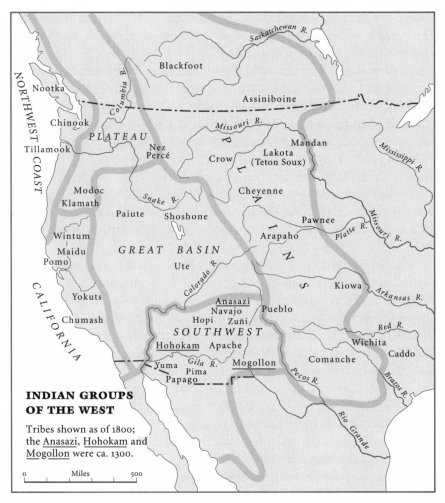

INDIAN GROUPS
OF THE WEST

Tribes shown as of 1800;
the Anasazi, Hohokam and
Mogollon were ca. 1300.

0   Miles   500

villages around 1250, perhaps because of drought and soil exhaustion, but
their Pueblo descendants explain that "the serpent, their rain and fertility
deity, mysteriously departed one night," and they had to move on in search
of the god's new place.[7] The Mogollons too retreated by 1400 from the Rio
Grande and Pecos valleys. From the Mesa Verde, Pueblans may have
migrated up the San Juan River valley to the Santa Fe area, virtually empty
until 1200. Yet the droughts may have been only the final disruption in
Anasazi life. Cultural traumas such as civil wars over religious heresies,
fights over water rather than the sheer absence of it, and spiritual disillusion
may have been more important than simple environmental changes.[8]

Warfare seems to have been constantly present. Apachean peoples, ancestors of the historic Apaches and Navajos, pushed southward from Utah

between 1150 and 1250, scattering the Anasazis in the Four Corners and San Juan Valley areas. Violence from some source—internal?—ruined part of the Hohokam heartland, south of Phoenix, about 1340. On the plains, nations were muscling one another about at that time and were to do so for another half millennium, at which point the U.S. Army played one group against another, divided them, and conquered.[9] Mandans in the fourteenth century, then Hidatsas and Arikaras in the seventeenth pushed westward into the plains, in turn pushing out the Apacheans. Ojibwas did the same to Siouxians in the eighteenth.[10] Between 1400 and 1600 Kiowas and Apaches apparently forced the Southern Plains Village Indians, ancestors of the Wichitas, in the direction of the Caddos.[11] Along Puget Sound, Haidas raided Makahs and other tribes, enslaving captives; Tlingits and Tsimshians also warred aggressively.[12] It was a human world, not an ideal world. Migration, as always, was sometimes voluntary, sometimes forced.

Disease was no stranger. European and African diseases laid low the Amerindians more effectively than any arquebus, steel sword, or horse. But long before Europeans arrived, tuberculosis, spirochetes, bacteria, viruses, trauma, malnutrition, genetic malformations, and degeneration of body organs all limited human life in the Americas. The life expectancy of American natives, whether in 5000 B.P. or 1000 C.E., is a mystery, but an unmedicated, uncontacted Brazilian Indian today might expect to live thirty-five years. Surely her ancestors would not have lived any longer. The entry of Europeans on this not-so-pristine scene greatly lengthened the list of causes of death, but the list preceded them.

How many Indians were there at the time of European contact? We can only make educated guesses, and the estimates by responsible archaeologists have varied considerably. Just before the Spanish arrival, the population north of central Mexico may have been just under 2,000,000.[13] If so, the area now within the American West supported about 1,155,000 of these. Nearly half, 454,000, lived in the Southwest, with another 221,000 in California. On the Great Plains were 189,000, along the Northwest Coast 175,000, and in the Great Basin and Colorado Plateau 115,000.[14]

Among the Plains Indians, to take one group as an example, decline in numbers from the time of first contact with Europeans to their nadir point may have been as high as 98 percent for the Arikaras, 97 percent for the Pawnees, 70 percent for the Crows, and 43 percent for the Arapahos.[15] A few tribes may have remained roughly stable (Cheyennes at 3,000, Kiowas at 1,000). A very few, the Crees and the Teton (Western, Lakota) Sioux, fell steeply after first contact, bottomed out after smallpox epidemics in 1780–1782, and then recovered in the nineteenth century. In 1840, after decades of shifting alliances, competition for turf, and bloody struggles, the major groups on the central plains—the Cheyennes and Arapahos, the Kiowas and Comanches, and others—resolved their differences at a grand conclave on the upper Arkansas River. In the years from 1820 to 1860 these groups probably increased from around 8,000 to 20,000.[16] Before white settlers arrived to squeeze the Plains Indians relentlessly, demographic upheaval had been going on for two or three generations; "the plains had never seen such movement and displacement of people in such a blink of time."[17]

Why did Indian groups have such different demographic histories? Because some had met and survived smallpox and other European diseases early, some much later. The Teton Sioux apparently increased from 8,500 in 1805, when Lewis and Clark met some of them, to 16,110 in 1881, when after three wars the U.S. Army confined them to reservations. (Throughout the nineteenth century, children outnumbered women, and women outnumbered men, suggesting that warfare among Indians was very destructive before the army ever got there.) Hard-won immunities allowed the Tetons to increase in number just as their rivals for space in the northern Plains were suffering their worst epidemics. The Ojibwas had pushed the Tetons to the west between 1736 and 1768, accelerating the Tetons' swing into the prairies and plains, displacing several disease-weakened groups between 1680 and 1750, and then the Mandans, Hidatsas, and some Cheyennes by 1800 and the Crows in the 1850s and 1860s. The Sioux's battles with the army had "immense political effect," but the "demographic impact was comparatively minor."[18]

Some anthropologists estimate precontact Indian population in the West to have been higher than 1,155,000. Whatever the original number, it declined steeply and unevenly to 300,000 or fewer by 1900. Since then Indian numbers have recovered to somewhere near their precontact level. Southwestern Indians suffered their worst declines in the seventeenth century, Northwest Coast groups in the eighteenth, Plains and (most terribly) California Indians in the nineteenth. After twelve to thirty thousand years, whatever the vicissitudes had been, change sped up bewilderingly when Europeans entered the American West.

Cortés, Oñate, and New Spain

However indefinite the arrival of Paleo-Indians to the Americas, and however hidden their motives for migrating might be, European appearances are certain. Norsemen (and women) placed a small colony on the northern tip of Newfoundland around 990 C.E. and left after a few years. Columbus and his successors began colonizing the Caribbean islands beginning in

1493, and Cortés landed on the coast of Mexico in 1519. The future American West was first visited by Europeans on Coronado's expedition in 1540–1542, and the earliest intentionally permanent settlement came in 1598, when Juan de Oñate, "the last conquistador," founded El Paso del Norte (now part of Ciudad Juárez, on the Mexican side of the Rio Grande) and then pushed upriver into what thus became New Mexico.[19]

More than half the four hundred years of European presence in the West has been Spanish. After Oñate, two more centuries passed before Spain had any significant European competition. A few French traders and missionaries ventured onto the Great Plains in the eighteenth century, and a few British in the plains and along the Pacific Coast shortly before 1800. But not until after 1805 did English speakers consistently foray into the West. No firm Anglo-American presence existed west of the ninety-fifth meridian as late as 1804, when Lewis and Clark set out from St. Louis up the Missouri River into terra truly incognita to satisfy President Thomas Jefferson's curiosity about the Louisiana he had just bought from Napoléon and to ascertain whether the dream of an all-water route to Asia might yet be true. After Lewis and Clark, fur traders entered and mapped parts of the plains and the Rockies. Permanent American settlements were still another forty or fifty years in coming.

During the 206 years between the expeditions of Oñate and Lewis and Clark, Spanish missionaries, soldiers, and ordinary people penetrated the Southwest and California, converting, decimating, interacting with, marrying, and transforming the lives of those already there. Spanish horses revolutionized every aspect of the lives of the Plains Indians. Spanish friars brought the Catholic form of salvation to the Pueblos, the Pimas, and many California groups. Spanish Baroque style, tinged with indigenous statuary and altarpieces, graced the churches at Mission San Xavier del Bac, near Tucson, at Ranchos de Taos and at Acoma Pueblo, and in California at Missions San Juan Capistrano and Carmel. And all that time Spanish diseases observed no color line and devoured Indians by the tens of thousands.

What motivated their migrations? The five-point pattern of homesteading, gold rushing, California dreaming, nostalgia reinforcement, and wage seeking obviously does not explain anything about the Paleo-Indians, and it also fits poorly into the history of colonial Spain and northern Mexico before 1848. The timeworn textbook trilogy of "God, gold, and glory," as the aims of the Spanish, still does not capture what they were about. Many true settlers, looking for land and a better life than in Spain or, by 1598, in central Mexico, were in some sense homesteaders, although the ways in which they organized their lives and property differed so much from Anglo homesteaders in the later United States that the term misleads more than it explains.

Some, especially soldiers, did seek gold, though none had the luck of their predecessors in central Mexico in the 1520s and Peru in the 1530s. (Coronado tried and failed.) Some had a sort of California Dream—the legend of Queen Calafia and her Amazons—but that was not the later one. As for wage seeking, it was seldom part of the plan on the northern frontier. Wage-work was by no means unknown in a Spanish Empire whose products and trade networks were far-flung even in the sixteenth century,[20] but insofar as it existed, it was not attractive enough to bring many migrants northward. It also goes without saying that the Wild West/Old West had not yet happened.

The colonial Southwest was therefore a prelude to western history from the standpoint of motivations for migration. In the Spanish and Mexican eras the region certainly had settlers (though "homesteaders" they were not) and California dreamers of a primeval sort. Whatever motivated people to proceed to the northern frontier, however, did not motivate enough of them. Underpopulation dogged it throughout its entire 250 years, from its beginning in 1598 to its end in 1848.

From Spain, slightly more than 16,000 people migrated to Mexico before 1600, most from Seville and Andalusia. Of these, 25 to 30 percent were female, who came principally to join husbands or to become servants.[21] About 400 or 500 people followed Oñate from central Mexico north toward the Rio Grande in the spring of 1598. Of these, 129 were grown men, mostly in their twenties, the rest women, children, and a few older men. Ten Franciscan friars joined them.[22] A few may have been pure-blooded Spanish, though criollos born in Mexico; at least 8 were African-blooded, part of the 200,000 who went to Mexico from Africa before 1821; most were probably descended from Spaniards, Africans, and Indians alike.[23] Their basic intention was not to explore, to intimidate, or to convert (though those results occurred) but to settle.[24]

The Spanish conquest of the Southwest began with Oñate, but the Pueblos already had a long history before he came.[25] Taking shape by 1300, Pueblo culture elaborated through 1450 and might have become as complex as the great cultures of central Mexico if the Spanish had not arrived when they did.[26] Oñate was well aware from the Coronado expedition of 1540–1542 and later ones that large numbers (in fact tens of thousands) of people already lived along the upper Rio Grande. He may not have known that they had already been weakened by waves of epidemics, carried not only by Spanish interlopers but by Indians who had been exposed to "Spanish breath," by animals, even by disease-bearing air and water. Typhus, smallpox, and measles killed many natives in Sinaloa, just south of the future New Mexico, in 1593,[27] and diseases spread northward, erupting periodically in the decades before the Pueblos rebelled against the Spanish in 1680.

Innocently armed with this devastating weapon, Juan de Oñate y Salazar, a third-generation Mexican of Basque ancestry, led his group cautiously up the Rio Grande beyond the "North Pass." After several days of a straight but waterless trek through the Jornada del Muerto ("Dead Man's Route") east of the river, they reached a cluster of settlements just south of present Socorro. Here began the pueblos, homes to perhaps forty thousand,[28] a hundred for every Spanish man, woman, and child, stretching up the valley another two hundred–plus miles to Taos and beyond. The Spanish passed several pueblos already five to seven hundred years old, a basket-weaving, pottery-making, agricultural society, part of a trading network extending across the San Juan Valley and including the Hopi and remnants of Hohokam people in present Arizona. Apachean peoples, including the then-emerging Navajos, had been moving westward from the plains toward the Rio Grande pueblos since about 1550. They continued migrating westward into Arizona for another century, never becoming Hispanicized, never quite sedentary.[29] Different languages and traditions separated the pueblos themselves; they were less a unified culture than a group of city-states. But all were forever on tenterhooks with the Apacheans.

Except for the mesa-top pueblo of Acoma, about sixty miles west of the river, the pueblos generally capitulated without great struggles. The first ten years were problematic. Oñate stepped down under pressure in 1607. But after Franciscan missionaries proudly reported several thousand baptisms to Mexico City, the viceroy agreed to reinforce New Mexico. In 1609 or 1610 the new governor, Pedro de Peralta, established the province's capital at Santa Fe. The next seventy years brought periodic epidemics, great batches of baptisms yet a persistence of Indian customs, some increase in Spanish population, and a drop in Indian numbers to perhaps only ten thousand.[30]

In 1680 most of the pueblos united for once and threw out the Spanish. Blaming disease (and even drought) on the Spanish and revulsed at contemptuous treatment of their religious leaders and their culture, the Indians rose in fury. They had long since learned how to use Spanish guns and horses and used them well in 1680.[31] About 20 missionaries and 380 colonists out of 2,500 perished. The rest (along with many loyal Indians) retreated to El Paso, creating Ysleta and several other villages, eventually more Hispanic than Indian, that are still there.[32]

The Spanish returned in 1692 and painfully reestablished themselves within a few years. They created new towns, notably Albuquerque in 1706. The subsequent history of Spanish New Mexico was by no means simply blood and gore. A peculiar grafting of Catholicism and Indian religion, wholly satisfactory to neither side, gradually worked itself out. Parallel accommodations evolved in trade, services, and agriculture. As in Mexico, intermarriage occurred between "Spaniard" and Indian. Colonial New Mexico was a place of conversion, forced if necessary, but not of pure conquest or displacement. Compared with what was going on in the English colonies on the Atlantic seaboard at about the same time, "the Spaniards look very good indeed. New Mexico saw none of the English mixture of hypocritical piety and ruthless underlying policy that had as its final aim the destruction or removal of all native groups. The reconquest [of the 1690s] was far from being a reenactment of New England's King Philip's War (1675–76) and its aftermath, the devastation of regional Indian groups."[33]

After the reconquest, Indian population stabilized and perhaps even gained, in contrast with the decimation from 1598 to 1680. From a possible 100,000 Indians in 1598, perhaps only 10,000 survived by 1680, but the number crept up to around 20,000 by 1764.[34] By 1800 New Mexico's population consisted of about 25,000 Spanish and mestizos (people of mixed Spanish and Indian blood) and 9,000 pure Indians,[35] and slightly more on the eve of Mexican independence twenty years later.[36] At that point New Mexico was not only much the oldest but much the largest and the most racially mixed of Spain's northern frontier provinces.

Some of the Spaniards may have been Jews. Columbus set sail from Cádiz in 1492 on the next day after the deadline Ferdinand and Isabella had set for the expulsion of unconverted Jews and Muslims from Spanish territory on pain of death. Many left, many converted, and many only seemed to convert. In New Mexico, stars of David on tombstones, surreptitious ritual circumcisions, the lighting of Sabbath candles, and Jewish genealogical fragments have appeared for centuries. Observance of *el día grande* (i.e., Yom Kippur) was sworn to in Inquisition records before the 1680 revolt. To Spanish crypto-Jews, the Inquisition's long arm had to be weaker and surveillance lighter on the ultimate colonial frontier, New Mexico, many months distant from Mexico City.[37]

Spain entered three other parts of the future American West in colonial times: Arizona in the 1680s, Texas in the 1710s (effectively), and California in 1769. None of these provinces became as large or as complex as New Mexico during the Spanish period.

No border divided present Arizona from northern Mexico until 1848, and to Indians and Spaniards alike, the area before then was Pimería Alta, the upcountry where the Pimas lived. North of that, in a series of mesas, lived (and still live) the westernmost pueblo people, the Hopis, their few thousand augmented by refugees from New Mexican pueblos who stayed away after the Spanish returned in 1692. The Hopis successfully resisted Christian conversion, Hispanic culture, and European diseases. Newcomers defining themselves as Apaches or Navajos filtered into Arizona and New Mexico from the Great Plains in the sixteenth and seventeenth centuries, only slightly before the Spanish. Together they may have numbered some tens of thousands; they too resisted Christianity; predictably they and the Hopis did not get along.

South of the Gila River lived the Pápagos, today known as Tohono O'odham; the Pimas, likely the descendants of the Hohokams, who had lived close by until the 1400s; and (near the Colorado River) smaller groups, including the Yumas, Yavapais, Mohaves, Havasupais, and others. Among the Pimas and Pápagos the Spanish Jesuits had the most success (or met the least resistance). Pimería Alta was a small Jesuit enterprise. Its great missionary was Father Eusebio Francisco Kino, a northern Italian who arrived in 1687, converted many Pimas, and in the process traveled widely through present southern Arizona and mapped it between 1691 and 1702. Kino built the missions; after he died in 1711, they languished. The chief ones were Tumacácori and Guevavi near present Nogales, and San Xavier del Bac just south of Tucson. Presidios of a few dozen Spanish soldiers protected them. The latest and largest, though with seldom more than a hundred soldiers, was Tucson Presidio, created in 1775 to protect San Xavier.

Very unlike New Mexico, Arizona was never a settlement frontier in Spanish colonial times. By 1766 it probably had no more than 600 Spanish and mestizos, including civilians, soldiers, their families, and missionaries. About 2,000 Christianized Indians also lived there.[38] By then the total Pima population north of the present border may have been about 5,000—a drastic drop from the 15,000 that Kino estimated in 1696—and an unknown number of Pápagos.[39] In the missions themselves an Indian population of about 8,600 in 1690 fell to 4,000 in 1761, 2,000 in 1774, and 1,100 in 1820. Epidemics, worst in the 1760s and 1770s, caused the steepest declines.[40] By 1819, on the eve of Mexican independence, Tucson may have had 62 "Spanish" settlers, and all of Pimería Alta, about 550, raising sheep, cattle, and crops, cut off from New Mexico to the east by Apaches, from California to the west by Yumas (who rebelled in 1781, interdicting the route), and from everybody else by the Sonoran desert. Of the four Spanish probes among the southwestern Indians—New Mexico, Texas, Alta California, and Pimería Alta— the latter was the smallest and least successful, leaving only a minimal Spanish presence in Arizona. Its one major monument is Kino's Mission of San Xavier, whose present church, built in the 1780s, continues to display its two-tone Baroque façade to the brilliant desert sun.

Spain's initial move into Texas was defensive, underfunded, undermanned, and brief. In 1690 a few priests and soldiers trekked several hundred miles north of the Rio Grande to eastern Texas, then chiefly occupied by the agricultural Caddos, and founded two missions. The Caddos were

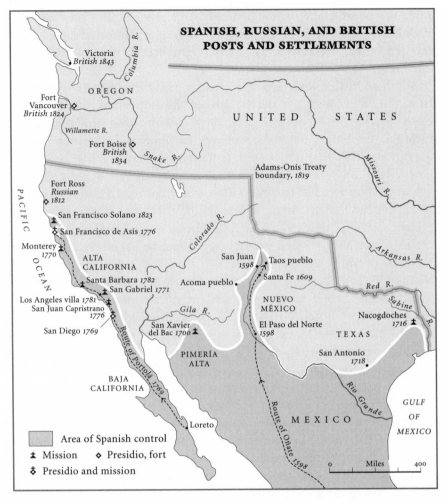

SPANISH, RUSSIAN, AND BRITISH POSTS AND SETTLEMENTS

Victoria *British 1843*

Columbia R.

OREGON

Fort Vancouver *British 1824*

Willamette R.

Fort Boise *British 1834*

Snake R.

UNITED STATES

Missouri R.

Adams-Onís Treaty boundary, *1819*

PACIFIC

Fort Ross *Russian 1812*

San Francisco Solano *1823*

San Francisco de Asís *1776*

Monterey *1770*

Colorado R.

Arkansas R.

ALTA CALIFORNIA

San Juan *1598*

Taos pueblo

Santa Fe *1609*

Red R.

OCEAN

Santa Barbara *1782*

San Gabriel *1771*

Acoma pueblo

Los Angeles villa *1781*

San Juan Capristrano *1776*

Gila R.

NUEVO MÉXICO

Sabine R.

Nacogdoches *1716*

San Diego *1769*

San Xavier del Bac *1700*

El Paso del Norte *1598*

TEXAS

Route of Portolá 1769

PIMERÍA ALTA

San Antonio *1718*

BAJA CALIFORNIA

Route of Oñate 1598

Rio Grande

GULF OF MEXICO

Loreto

MEXICO

Area of Spanish control

✝ Mission   ◇ Presidio, fort

☗ Presidio and mission

0   Miles   400

reputedly hungry to become Christians. Franciscans would convert them, and Spain would get, on the cheap, a buttress against French expansionism in the lower Mississippi Valley and the Gulf of Mexico. (The Sieur de La Salle had in fact landed at Matagorda Bay in 1685, though both he and his visit were short-lived.) The military went back to Mexico. The Caddos were less pious than had been hoped, and the missions closed in 1693. The only demographic impact was a smallpox epidemic that the Caddos correctly blamed on the Spanish. This episode happened very close in time to the Pueblo revolt in New Mexico and Kino's missionizing in Pimería Alta. But the Texas probe was not primarily intended to be either a group of settlements, like New Mexico, or a missionary effort, like Arizona. In Texas an entirely new motive prompted the Spanish: the need to create a defensive barrier to offset another European power—namely, France. This drove Texas's early colonial history and meant more emphasis on settlement than in Arizona, as well as more emphasis on geography and strategy in creating missions and presidios than in New Mexico.

In 1716 a new group of Spanish missionaries and soldiers (several of whom brought their wives) arrived in east Texas, close to the 1690–1693 location. Two years later, along the way, others established the mission of San Antonio de Valero (better known later as the Alamo) and the *villa* of San Antonio de Bexar. By 1722 the Spanish built ten more missions and four presidios, and settled several hundred people, in east Texas and San Antonio. In the 1730s and 1740s *pobladores*—settlers—created livestock ranches and several towns south of San Antonio, between the Nueces and the Rio Grande. (In the 1850s the Nueces/Rio Grande corridor would be taken over by Anglo ranchers who misleadingly became known as the "pioneers" of the area, when what they really did was to displace the *tejanos* who had been there for over a century as, in effect, homesteaders.)[41] The Spanish tried to create more outposts until the late 1750s but succeeded poorly even in east Texas and not at all farther north. Missionaries almost never converted nomadic tribes, and the huge region north and west of San Antonio, the *comanchería*, or land of the Comanches, was full of nomads.

Attempts to missionize the Comanches, or anybody else (such as Apaches) only infuriated them. In 1757 missionaries with more than two hundred soldiers and their families betook themselves to the San Saba River, about 120 miles northwest of San Antonio out on the Edwards Plateau. A year later they were either dead or back in San Antonio, pushed aside by a much larger, well-armed force of Comanches, Tonkawas, and other inhospitable Plains Indians. Aided by French supplies, the Indians confined the Spanish close to San Antonio and also closed the route from there to El Paso.[42] The Spanish northern frontier, thin enough anytime, met its limit.

By 1759 about twelve hundred non-Indians lived in the province of Texas, half of them in San Antonio. Because of a half hour battle that year in far-off Quebec and events in farther-off Europe, the Treaty of Paris in 1763 removed France from North America, turning over New France to Britain and Louisiana to Spain. No one except Indians prevented Spain from expanding throughout east Texas. But, except for Nacogdoches in 1779, little expansion took place because the fundamental raison d'être of Texas had always been defense rather than settlement. During the 1770s, no longer worried about the French, Spain let its frontier presidios languish, not only in Texas but in New Mexico and Arizona. The aim was to pacify, not populate. The redoubtable governor of New Mexico in the 1780s, Juan Bautista de Anza, did just that, winning military and diplomatic accommodations from the

U. S. A.

MEXICO

ARKANSAS TERRITORY

Adams-Onís Treaty
boundary, 1819

Sabine R.

Brazos R.

*Anglo
migration*

Waco Village •

Nacogdoches •

• Los Adaes

COAHUILA Y TEXAS

LOUISIANA

Austin •

San Jacinto R.

San Jacinto
Apr. 21, 1836

*AUSTIN'S
COLONY*

San Antonio •

San Felipe
de Austin •

• Brazoria

• Galveston

Goliad •

Lavaca R.

Rio Grande

*Nueces
R.*

• Matagorda

San Patricio •

GULF OF MEXICO

• Laredo

TAMAULIPAS

NUEVO
LEÓN

• Matamoros

**MEXICAN TEXAS
1821–1836**

0   Miles   150

Comanches, Navajos, and other Indians. Peace broke out across the entire
northern frontier from Tucson to San Antonio and continued until the
struggle for Mexican independence from 1810 to 1821 reshuffled all decks.[43]
Population increased slowly.

Texas's Indian population in 1779 was just under 11,000—Caddoans,
Wichitas, and others—900 of whom lived on the five missions around San
Antonio and the two in east Texas.[44] Spanish numbers rose from 1,200 in
1760 to 2,500 in 1790 to about 3,500 by 1821, most of them settlers rather than
soldiers, raising cattle or plying the usual crop and cattle-related trades of a
frontier town. Although outnumbering Pimería Alta, Spanish Texans were
only one-eighth as numerous as New Mexicans in the 1790s, while Mexico
City's 100,000-plus dwarfed them all.[45] Like one of its own coastal islands,

sunny and calm, Texas could abruptly be overwhelmed by a demographic tidal wave. Not many years later just such a wave inundated the Hispanic Texans, what remained of the French, and even the Comanches and Apaches.

The fourth and final Spanish probe northward began in 1769, when Fray Junípero Serra led several Franciscan confreres into Alta California. Spain had laid claim to the region ever since its ships sailed by in 1533, 1602, and later. But none had made a landing. By 1769 British navigators and Russian seal hunters had begun to show an interest in the Pacific Coast, and Spain responded as it had in east Texas when the French appeared: with a good offense as the best defense. Madrid's strategy in the late 1760s was to take effective possession of the Pacific Coast as far north as it could. The initial target was Monterey Bay, sighted and claimed by the navigator Sebastián Vizcaíno in 1602 and regarded ever since by the Spanish as a potential harbor base. Exploring and controlling the hundreds of miles of coast from Baja California to Monterey was part of the preemptive strategy, and again, Franciscan missionaries were the inexpensive means to do that. In California the missions succeeded as nowhere else: as the linchpin of Spanish presence and as the baptizing agent of many thousands of Indians. Presidios and *villas* accompanied them, presidios with soldiers to defend the crown's interest and *villas* with farmer-settlers (often retired soldiers) to raise crops and livestock to feed them. Indians soon became crucial additions to the agricultural labor force, often preferring to work for the *pobladores* than for the stricter missionaries.[46]

Spanish California's population history resembles New Mexico's in certain broad outlines. Indian numbers fell steeply; white and mestizo numbers rose gradually. White contact with southern California Indians began in 1769 and reached those in the Sacramento Valley and farther north only by 1849—a long time, 250 to 320 years, after Cortés conquered Mexico. Estimates vary on how many California natives there were in 1769. One says 310,000 (64,000 in the mission areas); a more recent one is 221,000. Most agree on 200,000 at the end of the Spanish period in 1821, reflecting substantial mortality (especially infant mortality) among mission Indians. The number slid to perhaps 150,000 by the time the Gold Rush began in northern California in 1849.

Then it plunged to around 30,000 by 1860, from "disease, starvation, homicide, and a declining birthrate."[47] If the missions were distinctly unhealthy, the gold rush was lethal. On the other hand, the "Spanish" increased from about 150 missionaries, soldiers, and settlers who came from Mexico and Baja California in 1769 to about 1,000 in 1790 and 3,270 by 1821, living in *villas* or presidios near the coast.[48] They in turn were to be completely overwhelmed by more than 200,000 gold seekers from "the States," Europe, and elsewhere after 1848.

In 1769 the California tribes may have been the most densely settled Indians in North America. Although they lacked the architectural talents of the Pueblos, they invented languages in profusion, speaking well over a hundred. Usually organized in rancherias of less than a thousand people, they hunted, gathered, fished, and sometimes farmed. They were not confederated for self-protection. They seldom gave the Spanish the open, armed resistance that Indians threw at them at Acoma, or in the 1680 revolt, or in Texas time and again, or by the Hopi continuously. But "hidden resistance," cultural preservation, never ceased, and occasional uprisings occurred, notably the one of 1828–1829 led by the Indian Estanislao at Mission San José. Against smallpox and malaria, which struck in the 1830s, they were defenseless.[49]

Spanish California and Its Missions

North of the Baja lay the harbor of San Diego, long known but never colonized. Two ships and an army of sixty under Gaspar de Portolá, accompanied by Serra, reached San Diego on July 1, 1769. Serra created his first mission, San Diego de Alcalá. Portolá proceeded overland toward Monterey. He missed it but found San Francisco Bay, and on a second trip in 1770 he established the presidio of Monterey. Within the next dozen years Portolá's military successors (notably Pedro Fages and in the mid-1770s Juan Bautista de Anza) created presidios and towns, while Serra created missions, all along the coast of California from San Diego to San Francisco. The best known were the missions and presidios at San Diego (1769), Monterey-Carmel (1770), San Gabriel (1771), San Francisco (1776), and Santa Barbara (1782).

Serra died in 1784, but other Franciscans kept on missionizing. They established almost two dozen, seven in the 1790s alone, although only three after 1800, the last and northernmost near Sonoma (at the foot of the Sonoma Valley, north of San Francisco) in 1823. Besides the presidios and missions the Spanish founded the *villas* of San José (1777) and Los Angeles (1781). A revolt of the Yuma Indians at the head of the Gulf of California in 1781 cut off Alta California from Mexico except by sea, and because it was so hard to get to, few migrated there. Natural increase was fairly rapid, but immigration slight.

By the early 1800s native peoples still vastly outnumbered the few thousand Spanish-Mexicans. Imbalance persisted through the Spanish (1769–1821) and Mexican (1821–1848) periods, though Indian numbers fell. A recent estimate of population "in the coastal portion of Alta California that Spain controlled" puts "soldiers and settlers" at 150, and Indians at 59,700, in 1770, with "Spanish" increasing and Indians decreasing steadily, to 3,400 "Spanish" and 21,750 Indians in 1820.[50] Thus more than 21,000 still lived on missions in 1821, but if 59,700 (or 72,000 by another estimate) actually had lived in the mission area in 1769, then many had died during the previous half century.[51]

Much has been written about the California missions. A romantic legend of tinkling bells, smiling friars, docile Indians, and peacefully grazing livestock predominated through much of the early and mid-twentieth century. More recently historical demographers have taken note of the unromantic but unarguable die-off that befell Native Americans after contact with Europeans. One of the prominent examples has been the reduction of the California Indians after 1769. What happened, why, and was Serra paying attention?

The Franciscans built twenty-one missions between 1769 and 1823. They were "secularized" by Mexico in 1834. So the actual mission period lasted sixty-five years. All the missions were along or near the coast from San Diego to Sonoma. None was north of that, none in the Central Valley, the Sierras, or the desert. They were thus limited in time and place. If the total California Indian population was 200,000 in 1800, and if the mission population was about 22,000, then obviously the great majority of Indians did not live under mission conditions. This does not mean that the other 178,000 were completely unaffected by them. Many "neophytes" remained briefly and then ran off to resume tribal life. They could and did transmit communicable diseases. So did white explorers, traders, birds, and ground animals. But before the 1830s, except for syphilis, epidemics rarely ravaged the nonmission majority. From that point, just as the missions closed down, contagion swept into virgin territory. Epidemics in 1833, 1837 (smallpox), and the 1840s together carried off more than 10,000.[52]

Despite this decline during the mission period and the epidemics following it, California's Indians probably numbered around 150,000 by 1848. If we accept the estimate of 310,000 in 1769, the reduction was half; if we accept 221,000 as the base, it was about a third. In either case it was serious and real. But it did not destroy entire tribes and cultural systems. The great devastation came not during the Spanish and Mexican periods but with the Gold Rush, which began in 1848: "Deterioration was vastly intensified by the invasion of the Americans, whose desire for farms, timber, and gold took them into those precise localities which hitherto had formed a more or less secure refuge. Thus the population decline became catastrophic between 1848 and 1860. The number of Indians fell from the order of 200,000 or 250,000 in twenty years to merely 25,000 or 30,000."[53]

With this context in mind—that the mission population was never more than a small minority of the entire California Indians and that the Gold

Rush, not the missions, brought most of the destruction—we can move to the question of mission mortality.

To live on the missions was to court disease and a short life. Birthrates were not much different from those of any preindustrial society. But death rates were frightfully high, especially in the northern missions, where the Franciscans housed converts in adobe barracks, ideal for spreading contagion. Deaths among infants and children were extremely common. The death rate at Mission San Francisco has been calculated at 127 per 1,000, high by any standard.[54] Much mortality resulted from overcrowding and poor sanitation; polluted water, promoting dehydration and thus diarrhea among children; syphilis; chronic respiratory ailments; and the locking up of women and girls in unhealthy dormitories at night. Cultural upheaval produced psychic stress, then physical debility.[55]

In the southern California missions, death rates were more like sixty-seven per thousand. Closest to normal (for those days) were the mixed-blood residents of the presidios of San Diego, Monterey, San Francisco, and Santa Barbara, where death rates were generally in the thirties and birthrates higher than among the mission Indians. Since the climate and the locally prevalent infections were the same for presidios and missions, living conditions were probably at the root of the missions' lower birth and higher death rates. Both presidios and missions suffered from time to time from epidemic smallpox, measles, diphtheria, influenza, and other unidentified diseases. Syphilis (possibly present before contact with the Spanish) appears to have been common, and because it depresses fertility, it made Indians less able to reproduce themselves.[56] The high death rates, however, seem to have resulted less from occasional epidemics than from chronic dysentery, tuberculosis, and other respiratory diseases, transmitted and intensified by poor ventilation and sanitation. By 1810 or 1815 the inland Indians were becoming streetwise about epidemics and mission life, and new recruits became scarce; more Indians ran off; mission population slid further.

By then the missions had accumulated hundreds of Indian converts, thousands of head of livestock, and tens of thousands of acres of land. As early as 1784 Governor Pedro Fages of Alta California began to repeat the centuries-old practice of kings, viceroys, and governors in Old Spain and New, and granted three requests from soldiers of the San Diego presidio for land around the three-year-old *villa* of Los Angeles. These first grants, to Juan José Domínguez, José María Verdugo, and Manuel Nieto, included much of what are now Los Angeles and Orange counties. Verdugo got 36,503 acres (much of present Glendale, Burbank, and Eagle Rock); Domínguez, 75,000 (San Pedro, Carson, Dominguez Hills, and the Palos Verdes peninsula); Nieto, 158,000 (Long Beach and south along the coast into Orange County).[57]

Spanish crown officers made about thirty-three more grants before 1821 along the coast to San Francisco Bay and, in a few cases, inland to north of Sacramento. The idea was to promote colonization. Grantees were obliged to improve their tracts by building permanent ranch houses, keeping at least two thousand head of cattle, and employing enough hands (with families) to take care of them and raise crops. The grants would reward the soldiers' services to the crown, and the soldiers would supervise California's settlement by *gentes de razón*—i.e., people of at least nominally European stock.

Mexican authorities, after independence from Spain in 1821, continued the land-grant policy, making about three dozen grants prior to secularization of the missions in 1834. Women were eligible under Spanish and Mexican law to own land, and of the eight hundred grants made during the entire 1769–1846 period, fifty-five (7 percent) went to women, a proportion not disgracefully below the 13 percent of Los Angeles households headed by women as of 1844.[58] In 1827 a woman, Doña Eulalia Pérez de Guillón, received a grant of the Rancho San Pascual, consisting of fourteen thousand acres formerly belonging to the Mission San Gabriel, including what are now Pasadena and South Pasadena. Failing to improve it satisfactorily, she lost it to Coronel Manuel Garfías of Governor Manuel Micheltorena's staff. Although Garfías became an American citizen and a Los Angeles councilman after the American takeover, he too lost it. According to a later account by Anglo real estate agents, in 1856 "the opportunity presented itself[!] to Dr. John S. Griffin of Los Angeles to foreclose on the 14,000 acres, and it passed forever from the possession of the Spaniards."[59] Seventeen years later Indiana investors bought it, as we shall see.

Secularization came, by decree of the Mexican Congress, in August 1833, effective in 1834. The Catholic Church was to retain the church building, rectory, schools, and shops—enough to conduct normal parish activities. The resident Indians were supposed to get about half the land and then settle down. The governor would grant the rest of the land "to bona-fide colonists."[60] Governors Juan Bautista Alvarado, Manuel Micheltorena, and Pío Pico gave more than seven hundred tracts to friends, supporters, Anglo Californios, and other "bona-fide colonists" between 1834 and 1846. Most ranged from 1 to 11 square leagues, or about 4,400 to 49,000 acres. A few were larger. Alvarado presented two parcels totaling over 133,000 acres, formerly part of Mission San Luis Rey, to Pico and his brother Andrés; much later it became the Camp Pendleton marine base in northern San Diego County. Mariano Vallejo, far to the north in Sonoma, received even more.[61]

As for the Indians, after secularization they left the missions, melted into the countryside, moved to nearby towns, became farmhands on the ranchos created out of mission lands, or in some cases received and farmed their own plots carved from mission holdings. The religious functions of the Franciscans fell to diocesan clergy, and the missions became ordinary parishes. The mission Indians got free of the Franciscans but were less protected than ever from disease and exploitation.[62] Epidemics raged during the 1830s and 1840s. Secularization ended the mission regime and "freed" both the land and the mission Indians.

As early as 1780, long before the 1834 secularization, the Franciscans realized that the mission Indians were not reproducing themselves.[63] They understood what their own records of baptisms and deaths meant. Serra himself, dead fifty years before secularization and before most of the missions were established, was already fifty-five, an old man by his day's standards, when he arrived in San Diego in 1769. With years of mission work behind him, he had a single purpose: to save Indian souls. It is almost impossible, in the 1990s, to get inside the mind of a 1760s missionary like Serra. He was so strict, single-minded, and penitential in his own life that he might have fitted better in the 1560s at the height of the Counter-Reformation. For such men this world does not ultimately count. Its purpose is to earn a good place in the next and eternal one. From this perspective the death of an unconverted heathen was tragic, while the death of a baptized convert was joyous.

Death rates were simply not Serra's major concern. From Monterey in 1772 he described the Carmel mission's first days: "It was hardly founded two months when it sent to heaven the souls of three little ones; the number has increased since, as well as the number of little children who give glory to the name of God on earth."[64] In 1773 he wrote Viceroy Antonio Bucareli that Mission Carmel "had about thirty Christians, not counting various babies who had winged their flight to God." Early in 1775 he sent Bucareli an inventory of the five existing missions, reporting 833 baptisms, 124 marriages (a few between soldiers and Indian women, which he encouraged), 74 deaths, and thus 759 live converts.

From Carmel he reported in 1779 an eight-year total of 575 baptisms, 139 marriages, and 98 deaths, 46 of them children. Produce, livestock, furnishings, tools, the church appointments, were enumerated, but causes of death and treatment of the sick hardly mentioned. Writing Governor Felipe de Neve, he insisted in 1780 on the right to punish Indians physically: "That spiritual fathers should punish their sons, the Indians, with blows appears to be as old as the conquest of these kingdoms; so general, in fact, that the saints do not seem to be any exception to the rule." Cortés himself was "flogged by the Fathers, in full sight of the Indians" to teach everyone that even he was "subject . . . to this humiliating treatment." Such methods, Serra believed, made clear to the Indians "that we, every one of us, came here for the single purpose of doing them good and for their eternal salvation." Truly this was invincible paternalism. Mortality, child or adult, did not enter in.

Spanish California lasted fifty-two years, from 1769 to 1821. Mexican California continued for twenty-seven more, to the Treaty of Guadalupe Hidalgo of 1848, which ratified American control. Long before the Franciscan mission era ended in 1834, the Spanish had also created presidios and *villas* with names familiar today. Because of its future, not because of its beginnings, a word is in order about the *villa* of La Reina de los Angeles de la Porciúncula.

Los Angeles was planted on September 4, 1781, near an Indian village on a small river some miles from the sea. The Yuma uprising had closed the only overland route to Mexico three months before. Encouraged by royal authorities and the military, though not by the friars less than ten miles away at Mission San Gabriel, the new *pobladores* were to provide agricultural produce so that the presidio could avoid having to import it by sea from Mexico. Other than Indians, who were to be displaced, absorbed, or married into, the settlers and their families numbered forty-six people of various ages, sexes, and colors. Only two were completely Spanish; the rest were mestizo, mulatto, or African; perhaps twenty-six of the forty-six were African in whole or in part.[65] After the first year few new migrants arrived in Los Angeles (though Monterey and other settlements had better luck, recruiting orphans from Mexico City).[66] Spanish-Indian intermarriage was frequent, especially in the early years. Females, on average, married at about twenty, males at thirty or later (a little later than elsewhere in the northern Spanish colonies), and couples usually had from three to seven children, although large families (nine or more children) were not unusual.[67] The 850 who lived in Los Angeles when Spanish control ended in 1821 were the grandchildren of those first settlers.[68]

Soldiers, settlers, and their families received a modicum of land and livestock. The *villa*'s plat included a plaza and other common lands as well as town and farm lots. People as well as their horses, cattle, and sheep multiplied rapidly. Few of the *pobladores* led anything more than hand-to-mouth lives, most of them focused close to home, although ships came and went, and padres and officials shuttled back and forth to Mexico, bringing delayed reports from the outside world to this close-knit community.[69] Some settlers managed later to acquire substantial acreage and were to acquire more when the mission lands were secularized and granted out after 1833. Retired soldiers joined *pobladores* and their descendants as holders of extensive properties, and many of their names still designate streets and districts of Los Angeles: names like Pico and Sepúlveda, Verdugo and Domínguez.[70]

The first Sepúlveda, the "patriarch" Francisco Xavier, age thirty-eight in 1781, came from Sinaloa as a soldier with his wife and six children. He died a civilian in 1788, but his prolific offspring, through good marriages, good business, and betting on the right sides in political upheavals during the 1820s and 1830s, became masters of estates of more than eighty thousand acres.[71] But by 1880, in less than a century after Domínguez, Verdugo, and Nieto had received the first land grants, most of these families had lost their land and power in southern California, their counterparts in northern California sooner than that.

Between 1598 and 1821 the Spanish created a thinly peopled, defensive frontier stretching from east Texas to the Pacific coast. The oldest of these provinces, New Mexico, was decidedly the most populous, and in 1817 it contained 36,579 persons.[72] At that moment, to take an ominous peek ahead, Anglo-American Missouri already had 67,000, and some of them started heading westward along the trail to Santa Fe just as soon as Spanish prohibitions on trade lifted in 1821.

The Also-Ran Empires: France, Russia, and Britain

During the 1600s and 1700s three European powers besides Spain sailed by, touched, or entered the future American West. None had Spain's impact on native peoples, nor did any of them leave permanent settlements. But they are worth noting, both to complete the early record and to ratify the point that without a self-sustaining and fairly large population, imperial outposts disappear sooner or later.[73]

The French presence was never properly part of the West as we are defining it. Marquette and Jolliet in the 1670s, La Salle in the 1680s, and later Frenchmen explored the Mississippi, founded bases at Cahokia (1699), New Orleans (1718), Ste. Genevieve (1725), and St. Louis (1764, before news arrived of the Treaty of Paris) and elsewhere. From these posts the French traded with Indian tribes, explored rivers, and thereby—without many people or settlements—laid claim, in the European way, to the vast area they called Louisiana. Along the Gulf Coast and into east Texas they frightened the Spanish into situating defensive garrisons and missions, as we have seen. In 1763 this entire Louisiana came under Spanish "control." (Caddos, Comanches, and many other Indians probably laughed at that idea, but it satisfied the courts of Europe.) French power ended in North America in 1763; French people and culture, however, stayed. Louisiana was French again in 1800, but only technically, and just long enough to be turned over to the United States after Jefferson bought it in 1803. French continued to be spoken for some time in New Orleans and St. Louis and still is in Cajun Louisiana. But the French impact on the present West was brief and marginal.

The Russians lasted in California for 32 years (1809–1841) and in Alaska for 126 (1741–1867). At the other end of Europe from Spain, Russia was no less expansionist from the sixteenth century to the eighteenth. But its frontier was overland and eastward to Siberia, not overseas and westward to America. Before Peter the Great died in 1725, Russian settlers and sable traders had passed Yakutsk and reached the Kamchatka Peninsula. Tsar Peter authorized further eastward exploration of the north Pacific and its coasts, a world region as yet completely unknown to Europeans. He also commissioned an experienced Danish sailor, Vitus Jonassen Bering, to captain an expedition. Peter died, but the plan survived. In 1728 Bering found the strait separating Siberia from Alaska; it thereafter bore his name, as eventually did the Pleistocene land bridge it submerged (Bering Strait, Beringia). On a second voyage, in 1741, Bering traced the Aleutian chain and the Alaskan coast. There the Russians discovered sea otters, whose pelts made Alaska as attractive as sables made Siberia, and as beaver skins were soon to make the northern plains and the Rockies to French and English traders.[74]

In the next several decades Russians made scores of voyages from Siberia to the Aleutians and Alaska. Landing parties forced the native Aleuts to harpoon sea otters from kayaks. A trader named Grigorii Shelekhov drove off the natives on Kodiak Island and built a base there in 1784. In 1799 he helped create the Russian American Company, which, like the Hudson's Bay Company in future Canada, became the surrogate operator for the distant imperial government. The Russian American Company forced all Aleut males from eighteen to fifty to hunt sea otters for them. Because of such serfdom and European diseases, as many as four out of five Aleuts died off within two generations.[75]

In 1799 the company's new manager, Aleksandr Baranov, established a "capital" in Alaska that he named Novo-Arkhangel'sk (New Archangel, later renamed Sitka). The indigenous Tlingits resisted fiercely, capturing the base in 1802, burning it, and killing more than 400 of its 450 residents.[76] Baranov reconquered it in 1804 with heavier firepower, and a visit in 1805 from his managing director, Nikolai Rezanov, eventuated in Rezanov's sailing to San Francisco, reassuring Spanish officials of his solely mercantile intent, winning the heart of Concepción Argüello, the commandant's daughter, and then sailing off never to return. (He died at Krasnoyarsk in Siberia on the trip home to St. Petersburg; she died, faithful to hope and memory, in a Benicia convent fifty years later.)

By the 1790s Spanish, Russian, British, and American vessels were crossing one another's paths all along the Pacific Coast from San Francisco to Sitka. Russians were firmly based in Alaska, on the lower Yukon River as well as at Sitka, and on the Aleutians.[77] Unlike Russia's Siberian settlements, Alaska was a typical resource exploitation frontier, 90 percent male; Russian women were not brought in to settle. Consequently a "creole" population evolved, mixed-blood Russian and native, making up a fifth of the population by the 1830s. Contact beginning in the 1770s brought smallpox, measles, dysentery, syphilis, and other plagues and eventually a great smallpox epidemic that devastated the Queen Charlotte Islands Indians in 1862–1863. Some Tlingits and others were vaccinated and survived. Among the fierce but untreated Haida, mortality approached 90 percent.[78]

Russian Alaska existed to harvest sea otter pelts, not to convert the natives. Nevertheless Russian Orthodox churches, some still there, did appear. Father Ivan Veniaminov (who went on to become the metropolitan of Moscow) and other priests ministered to the Russian residents and also missionized among the native peoples.[79] The population of Sitka and the other Russian outposts never grew beyond a few hundred, and the continuing presence and competition from British and American ships and hunters persuaded St. Petersburg, fitfully, to pull back.[80] The tsarist government signed treaties with the United States in 1824 and Britain in 1825 limiting Russian America to the coast above 54° 40′ north latitude (although Russians lingered in California until 1841). After the Crimean War of the 1850s, Russia decided to concentrate its efforts on Central Asia, and in 1867 it sold its American holdings—Alaska—to the United States.

Before that happened, Russians lived on the California coast for more than thirty years. Rezanov, after his romantic and diplomatic visit to San Francisco in 1805, recommended creating a base nearby, not to threaten the Spanish but to trade with them, to catch more sea otters, and, above all, to provide fresh food for scurvy-prone Alaska. In 1809 Ivan Aleksandrovich Kuskov sailed a Russian American Company ship to Bodega Bay, roughly fifty miles north of San Francisco, and stayed for eight months. His crew demolished hundreds of sea otters, whales, and elephant seals and lost five members, who ran off to live with local Indians. Kuskov made another hunting trip in 1811 and returned in 1812 to found another base, which he called Rossiya, now known as Fort Ross, eighteen miles north of Bodega. A nearby stream he named Slavianka, now the Russian River. By 1818, 26 Rus-

sians and 102 Aleut fishermen lived at Fort Ross, and its population later stabilized at 200 to 400 during otter hunting.[81]

Yet it was not a success. Spanish (and, after 1821, Mexican) authorities in
San Francisco limited trade; the Russians overtrapped the sea animals; crop
yields faltered. Governor Mariano Vallejo ousted the Russians in 1841. They
sold the company's properties not to Vallejo (holder of a huge grant just east
of them) and the Mexicans, who had never recognized their legitimacy in
the first place, but to Johann August Sutter, a German-born trader based at
his fort at present Sacramento. The price was thirty thousand dollars for
land, livestock, buildings, and movables. Sutter resold it for a loss in 1859. By
then, of course, the whole area had been American for over a decade.[82]

South of present Canada, the British left no more marks than the Russians. Before 1846 they dominated the Pacific Northwest from Fort Vancouver, the Hudson's Bay Company base on the lower Columbia River.[83]
Although from 1670 it represented Britain in western Canada (and there are
still HBC department stores in Canadian cities), it never operated in the
present United States except in the Oregon Country. As of 1790 or 1792, however, a sensible prophet would have guessed that the future of the Pacific
Coast north of San Francisco would be Russian or British. James Cook in
1778 had sailed along much of it, and his former midshipman George Vancouver in 1792 explored the Strait of Juan de Fuca, landed at present Everett,
Washington, and circled the large island later named for him. The United
States' only good claim rested on the voyage of the Boston sea captain
Robert Gray, who found the mouth of the Columbia River in 1791–1792.

Overland, however, the Americans were first on the ground. Meriwether
Lewis and William Clark traveled down the Columbia River to the sea in
1805, passing the spot where the Hudson's Bay Company was to establish
Fort Vancouver twenty years later. Moreover, John Jacob Astor's trading post
at Astoria, also at the mouth of the Columbia, lasted from 1811 to 1813, when
the (British) North West Company forced its surrender as a trophy of the
War of 1812. The only European-stock people—and they were few—actually
to inhabit the Pacific Northwest before the early 1840s were Canadians
(English or French), scattered in outposts from Okanagan (founded by
Astorians in 1812), Walla Walla (1817), and others south to Fort Vancouver
itself, much the largest, enclosing five acres and nineteen buildings inside its
stockade.[84]

The Hudson's Bay Company never attracted people to these posts. It
operated vigorously north of the forty-ninth parallel, which the United
States and Britain agreed in 1818 to define as the international boundary east
of the Rockies, leaving the area to the west under a kind of joint sovereignty

for the time being.[85] The company lingered for some years south of the forty-ninth but retreated after 1841. That year, coincidentally, was the first in which Americans struggled along the Overland Trail from Missouri to the Oregon Country, joining a few Catholic and Protestant missionaries who came in the mid-1830s. In 1844 Dr. John McLoughlin, the Hudson's Bay manager at Fort Vancouver, reported to London that the Oregon Country was home to 6,000 Americans but only 750 British.[86] The next year the company moved north to a new deep-water base to be called Victoria, on the southern tip of Vancouver Island. In 1846 the British and American governments agreed by treaty to extend the border along the forty-ninth parallel to the Pacific, except for Vancouver Island. Oregon was American.

America's Empire for Liberty

The French, British, and Russians thus departed the future American West respectively in 1763 (the Treaty of Paris), 1818 and 1846 (the agreements setting the American-Canadian boundary along the forty-ninth parallel), and 1867, the American purchase of Alaska. None of the three empires had created much more than trading posts, nor had any of them left anything like the number of place-names, people, or settlements that the Spanish had bequeathed. By tactical retreat and by treaty, the European empires departed the West, sometimes politely, sometimes rudely jostled by what proved to be the continent's greatest imperial power of all, the United States. By 1848, by one means or another, the United States had taken over the Great Plains, Rocky Mountains, Great Basin, and the Pacific Coast.

In 1803, back in Monticello, having bought Louisiana from Napoléon, President Jefferson wondered what it contained. Officially or privately Americans had had virtually no contact with their future West before 1804. Exceptions were Robert Gray's cruise to the Columbia in 1792, a few merchant vessels illegally stopping at Monterey or San Diego, some visitors to St. Louis or New Orleans, and the flight of Daniel Boone and a few dozen Americans (invited and newly naturalized) into Spanish Missouri in the late 1790s.[87] The United States in fact did not exist even in its own eyes until it declared independence from Britain in 1776, or in the world's until the 1783 Treaty of Paris, which placed the new nation's western boundary at the Mississippi River. The treaty was generous in doing so, because hardly any Americans, except thousands of Indians, yet lived between the Appalachians and the Mississippi hundreds of miles farther west.

America was then an infant nation, but Americans were already a numerous people. In 1700 about 250,000 lived in the English-speaking settlements hugging the Atlantic coast. From immigration, but more from a vigorously maintained fertility rate, these multiplied to 1,000,000 in the 1740s, 2,500,000 by 1776, and about 5,500,000 by 1803. The "Spanish" and mestizos from Texas to California were far fewer, as were the French and English in Canada. Native peoples greatly outnumbered white Americans west of the Appalachians, but they had become scarce east of them. The surge of several hundred thousand white Americans through Cumberland Gap and other routes between 1780 and 1810 was a crystal-clear foretaste of the demographic future.

Jefferson's purchase included all the territory that France had ever claimed (and that Spain admitted was French) west of the Mississippi. It included the port of New Orleans and the west bank of the Mississippi, along with the drainage basin of the Missouri River, which extended to the still-legendary Rocky Mountains. Jefferson argued that Louisiana also included Spanish Texas, but Spain rejected that unhistorical claim. As the ink dried on the purchase agreement, Jefferson immediately dispatched a Corps of Discovery under Meriwether Lewis and William Clark to explore the Missouri to its source and to determine if any easy route to the Pacific existed—in short, the Northwest Passage that explorers from Columbus to Cook had looked for. Of course there was none. Lewis and Clark crossed the Rockies with extreme difficulty and learned that the Snake and the upper Columbia rivers were wilder than they and Jefferson had ever imagined.

The extent of Jefferson's (and everyone else's) ignorance about the interior leaps out from his instructions to Lewis and Clark. He not only hoped they would find an easy portage from the Missouri to a westward-flowing river but also provided them with letters of credit that would be honored, if need arose, by American consuls in the South Seas and the Cape of Good Hope, half a world away. No such need arose, and Lewis and Clark managed to deal with the Mandans and Shoshones without such letters. They succeeded in reaching the Pacific and returning. Subsequent expeditions explored the sources of rivers that rose in the Rockies and trickled across the Great Plains, whose aridity inspired explorers and geographers to call the area the Great American Desert. After 1821, when Mexico lifted Spanish commercial restrictions, American traders followed the Arkansas River to the Rockies and then proceeded south to Santa Fe. Particularly eager parties risked Indian confrontations and took a shortcut across the future Dust Bowl. By the time of the American conquest in 1846, the Santa Fe Trail between Missouri and New Mexico was well known and well traveled in both directions.[88]

Santa Fe became American without bloodshed. Its leaders valued American trade more than their link, by then only dubiously defensible (or even desirable), to Mexico City. During those years from 1807 to 1840 American fur trappers—several hundred of them, never a great number—infiltrated the Rocky Mountains in search of beaver skins and in the process explored many areas that Lewis and Clark and other government expeditions had missed. Their most important find was the South Pass, between the east-flowing Platte and the west-flowing Snake rivers in Wyoming. This barren plateau between the northern and southern Rockies became the critical link in an Overland Trail from Independence and Council Bluffs to the Oregon Country.[89] Emigrants—some dozens in 1841, a few thousand by 1846—followed this trail west. Brigham Young led Mormon emigrants (the first of a great many) along the Platte and across the South Pass to Utah in 1847. Two seasons later the Gold Rush began, crowding the trail with scores of thousands of young men. All told, probably 350,000 emigrants followed one or another branch of the trail between 1841 and 1866.[90]

But much of that came after 1848. Before then two consequential migrations to the West took place. One was involuntary: the forced removal of about twelve thousand southeastern Indians to Oklahoma, and of a smaller number to Kansas from Indiana and Illinois, in the late 1830s. The other, the earliest true settlement migration of Anglo-Americans into what is now the West, was the voluntary surge of white southerners into Texas beginning in December 1821. Without it, New Mexico and California would not have fallen into American hands in 1846. As American frontier settlers inched toward the Mississippi and gingerly crossed it—Illinois and Alabama became states in 1819, Missouri in 1821—Texas suddenly received a demographic onslaught that brought the United States not just to the Rio Grande but to the Pacific.

Ever since La Salle's expedition down the Mississippi in 1682, Spain had defended Texas, its northeasternmost province in America, from French incursions. In the 1819 Adams-Onís Treaty with the United States, Spain protected itself again by defining the eastern boundary of Texas as the Sabine River (still the boundary between Texas and Louisiana). It is ironic that just as its 140-year-old policy of defending the east Texas border seemed most assured, Spain invited a voracious American fox into the Texan chicken coop.

In the spring of 1821, during the last weeks of its three-hundred-year rule over Mexico, the Spanish parliament debated a plan to strengthen Texas with new settlers. Land grants would be the bait. Although the discussion revealed a healthy suspicion of its aggressive American neighbor, the Spanish appreciated that Americans (including Moses Austin, who had already applied for a grant of Texas land) had lived peaceably and law-abidingly in Louisiana when it was Spanish. If potential settlers agreed to Spain's conditions, why not invite them into Texas? The conditions included the clear provisions that immigrant settlers be (or become) Catholic and that they bring no slaves with them. An elaborate Mexican government report on immigration, drawn up several months later, incorporated these points:[91] Americans were already seeping into Texas; filibustering marauders had already tried to take over; an officially controlled immigration of the right people, Americans among them, would secure the province. At that time the population of Texas, not counting Indians, was around 3,500, of whom 1,500 lived in San Antonio.[92]

Stephen F. Austin, son of Moses (who died in 1821), received a grant of land for 300 families who were to be Catholic and without slaves. They arrived by late 1823 and two years later numbered more than 2,000, including over 400 slaves. The central government could not or would not enforce its antislavery requirement, and the state government of Coahuila y Texas in 1825 enacted a further land-grant law whereby *empresarios* could bring in a minimum of 100 families and would receive extensive farm and grazing land. The floodgates were open. By 1830 about 8,000 Americans outnumbered the Mexicans 2 or 3 to 1.[93] Mexican officials correctly feared that Americans privately, and the U.S. government officially, regarded Texas's future as other than Mexican.[94] A tougher colonization law in 1830, restricting American immigration, came too late and only stirred up Anglo-Texan resentment that the factionalized government in Mexico City could not suppress. In Anahuac, for example, founded on a land grant in 1831 by Mexican Colonel John Davis Bradburn, Anglo settlers clashed with Mexican soldiers almost immediately. When the garrison left, more settlers (some German) arrived and raised the population to 124 in 1834. The soldiers returned only to be chased out in 1835 by Anglo-Texans led by the firebrand William Travis, soon to die famously at the Alamo.[95]

The Anglo-Texans' successful drive to become independent in 1836, followed by annexation to the United States in 1845, stimulated further immigration. Most of it came from nearby, particularly Mississippi and Alabama, Kentucky and Tennessee, Missouri and Arkansas. The natural tendency was to replicate, on more and better land, the cotton-growing and slave labor economy of the lower South. Alabama and Mississippi were going through their own "flush times" of very rapid growth in the 1820s and 1830s, and east Texas from the Sabine to the Brazos was in many ways of a piece with them. A few large plantations mixed with many smallholdings; most settlers farmed or raised livestock, while some shaped dozens of new towns. Some hundreds of free blacks fled the slave South for Mexican Texas after 1821, and as the slavocracy overtook them by the mid-1830s, free blacks and slaves alike—perhaps four thousand by 1855—moved south into Mexico.[96]

After independence and annexation, the Texas settlement frontier attracted Europeans as the Missouri Valley was doing farther north. Over five thousand Germans arrived and founded New Braunfels in 1845 and Fredericksburg in 1846, in what was still Comanche country; Fredericksburg is about halfway between San Antonio and San Saba, where the Spanish probe had been wiped out in 1758, less than ninety years before. But through diplomacy (smoothed by neighborly Delawares and Shawnees), gift giving, and mutually beneficial trade, the Germans got on reasonably well with the Comanches and other Indians. Relations worsened during the 1850s, but smallpox and cholera among the Indians, and an ever-growing white population, tipped the balance against the native peoples as the Spanish had never been able to do.[97]

Swiss, Poles, and other Europeans arrived in the 1840s and 1850s. From fewer than 4,000 Spanish and perhaps 20,000 Indians in 1821, the population of Texas shot up to 142,000 by annexation time in 1845. The census of 1850 counted 213,000 Texans (59,000 of them slaves): 53.5 percent male, 95 percent rural, with a median age well below twenty. Somewhere between 14,000 and 23,000 were Spanish-speaking. Texas—Mexican, Anglo-American, European immigrant, black, and Indian—tripled during the 1850s and passed 1,000,000 in the early 1870s. In all these respects except the large slave minority and the still-small Spanish-speaking community, Texas's demographic profile in its early decades mirrored the other frontier rural states and territories north and east of it. Between 1850 and 1900 another 40,000 Anglo-Americans and probably 50,000 Mexicans migrated to Texas, the Mexicans fleeing the reactionary Porfirio Díaz regime and growing poverty, settling south of San Antonio and along the border to El Paso. Of the 2,261,000 Texans in 1900, 165,000 were Hispanic, many of them recent immigrants.[98]

The annexation of Texas of course touched off war between the United States and Mexico. The result was to detach New Mexico, the former Pimería Alta, and Alta California from Mexico and add them to the United States. With the Hudson's Bay Company and the British crown vacating the Oregon Country by treaty in June 1846, the United States gained in three years (1845–1848) more land than Jefferson had bought in 1803 and became in the fullest sense a two-ocean continental nation. Between 1783 and 1848 its western boundary shifted from the Mississippi to the Pacific, it acquired the northern half of Mexico at Mexico's expense, and it retained Michigan, Wisconsin, Minnesota, the Dakotas, and the Pacific Northwest, which in 1783 and for a long time afterward could easily have remained under British control. The new boundaries, moreover, were secure. The United States could spend the rest of the century and part of the next filling up its new space with mostly European-stock people without fear of foreign interference.

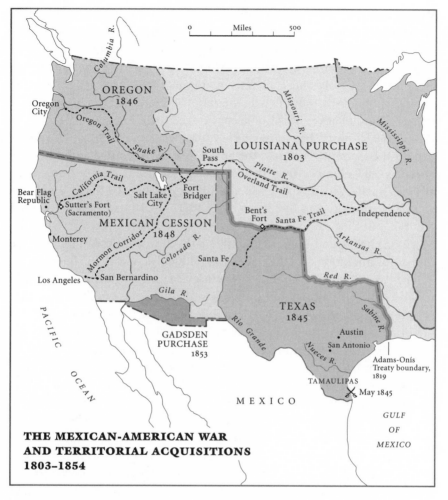

**THE MEXICAN-AMERICAN WAR
AND TERRITORIAL ACQUISITIONS
1803–1854**

The Texas story from 1821 on is a classic case of a demographic inundation leading to complete political and cultural change. Oregon too was a
demographic story, though on a smaller scale. Missionaries, both Protestant
and Catholic, began working to convert Indians in the Northwest in the
mid-1830s, and by 1840 about five hundred Americans were farming along
the Willamette River valley.[99] The natives, for example, in the Calapooya Valley, which runs down the Cascades into the Willamette River between
Eugene and Albany, disappeared because of disease, displacement, and
destruction; 90 percent of them died in the 1830s from malaria and "had all
but vanished by the commencement of extensive white settlement in the
1840s."[100]

Information and interest in this nubile Oregon land spread quickly. Joel

Walker and his family came overland from Missouri in 1840, and by 1841 perhaps 100 Anglo-Americans and French-Canadians had arrived. True wagon trains began in May 1842, when a party of 112 migrants left Independence, Missouri, for Fort Vancouver. More than 1,000 made the trip in 1843, establishing the Overland Trail as the main route west for nearly three more decades. In the usual way of chain migration, emigrant letters from Oregon to friends and relatives back home encouraged them to come. From 1844 to 1850, as the Hudson's Bay Company left, another several thousand made the trip up the Platte River, across the South Pass in Wyoming, and down the Snake to the Columbia. By 1850 over 12,000 Americans, people from virtually every state, most notably Missouri, Illinois, Ohio, Kentucky, and Indiana,[101] lived in Oregon. By then 11,000 Latter-day Saints had also followed the trail, but they stopped on the eastern shore of the Great Salt Lake; the Mormons had found Zion. In addition, a third, very different, much more numerous migration—to the California goldfields—was in full flood.

The American acquisitions of New Mexico and California were not at root demographic stories, but preludes to them, because military conquest preceded Anglo population. Mexican independence from Spain in 1821 did not bring a great many changes to New Mexico, although a few were important. Instead of being captured and jailed (the Spanish habit), Missouri traders found themselves welcomed in Taos and Santa Fe in 1821. From then on, despite local disruptions, thousands of traders and millions of dollars crossed the trail both ways between the upper Rio Grande and St. Louis. Population surged; New Mexico probably increased by 10,000 between 1835 and 1845.[102] Santa Fe and El Paso reached 5,000 (other than Indians) each, Albuquerque 2,000 plus, and Taos 700. New Mexico probably held between 30,000 and 40,000 Spanish-Mexican-mestizos and perhaps 180,000 Indians, not far below the eighteenth-century peak.[103] The scarcity of water and arable land limited the carrying capacity of the upper Rio Grande Valley to not much more than that, given mid-nineteenth-century technology. Anglo-Americans were about to enter that valley in some numbers and assume political control. But they never obliterated either Indian or Spanish presences, nor did they fully in Texas and California.

During the fifty years after 1821 *nuevomexicanos* gradually expanded their agricultural domain in all four compass directions, eventually bumping up against Mormon settlements pushing down from Utah and against Texas cattlemen on the High Plains by 1870.[104] In Texas south of San Antonio the *tejanos* increased from 10,000 in 1850 to around 70,000 by 1900.[105]

The Plains Indians were about to undergo a fiercely contested but ultimately unhappier experience. Stephen Watts Kearny led a U.S. Army force of about seventeen hundred across Kansas to Bent's Fort on the Arkansas River in mid-1846, headed for Santa Fe. With another several hundred traders and hangers-on waiting for the military situation to clear, the trading post entertained more white people than had ever gathered before on the Great Plains. The spectacle was not lost on Yellow Wolf, leader of the Cheyenne, and other Plains Indians witnessing it; seventeen hundred soldiers' tents and twenty thousand horses and other livestock caused the Indians to remark "over and over that they had never supposed there were so many white people."[106]

Yellow Wolf realized that Indian population was decreasing. Unfamiliar diseases were reducing or wiping out whole bands of hitherto remote and protected Plains Indians. The Taos traders had made inroads on the buffalo, as the Indians themselves were doing.[107] The future of the Plains Indian cultures was already dark (despite their own peace treaty of 1840), even before the 1850s, when wars with the U.S. Army seriously erupted and white homesteaders pushed the Anglo-American settlement frontier into Kansas and Nebraska.

California's largest towns were anything but large in 1846. Los Angeles's population was 1,250, Santa Barbara's 1,000, and Monterey's 750.[108] Spain and Mexico, prior to secularizing the missions, had made several dozen grants of land to soldiers and settlers, but from 1833 to 1846 the Mexican governors granted nearly seven hundred more, bearing now-familiar Los Angeles names like Tujunga, Cahuenga, and Malibu.[109] Ranchos replaced missions, and Californios replaced missionaries. Indians who should have received allotments from mission lands either did not get them or soon lost them. By 1846, 800 grantees *each* controlled over ten thousand acres in California, at least nominally. At that point California's population consisted of 5,000 to 6,000 Spanish speakers (the majority of them working-class Mexicans) in the south and along the coast, over 70,000 scattered Indians, and perhaps 1,500 English-speaking migrants in the north, around the Sacramento Valley.

A few of the English speakers became upper-class Californios themselves. Joseph Chapman, William Hartnell, and William Gale were probably the first Americans to appear, coming in 1822. General George S. Patton's grandfather B. D. Wilson arrived at San Gabriel Mission in 1841 and bought twenty-two-hundred acres around future San Bernardino and Riverside for a thousand dollars. He married Ramona Yorba, daughter of the owner of what became the town of Yorba Linda and environs. She died in 1849 at age twenty-one, and Wilson later married his Anglo housekeeper, Margaret Hereford, whose daughter became the general's mother.[110]

The most successful of these Yankees, Abel Stearns, joined the group in 1829. "Don" Abel, born in Lunenburg, Massachusetts, in 1798, spent three years in Mexico in the mid-1820s and then came to Monterey and soon after

that to Los Angeles, where he married Doña María Arcadia, daughter of the
wealthy Don Juan Bandini. Don Abel rose "from modest beginnings in hides
and wines at Los Angeles and San Pedro" to become the leading businessman in southern California and lord of Rancho Los Alamitos, 28,000 acres
in present Orange and Los Angeles counties.[111] Unlike Pío Pico, the last
Mexican governor, who lost his own extensive holdings before he died in Los
Angeles in the late 1870s, Don Abel held on. When he died in 1871, he left
130,000 acres to Doña María Arcadia. He and men like him became true Californios. They spoke Spanish, raised Catholic families, dressed like hidalgos,
and behaved as, indeed were, local grandees.[112] They supported Mexican
authority and grew nervous at the upheaval an American takeover could
bring. Stearns was involved in July 1846 in an application by an Irish priest,
Eugene McNamara, to Governor Pico, for a land grant to create a colony for
up to ten thousand Irish famine refugees, to counter the *ambición* of the
United States.[113] But it was too late. The Americans were already inside California's door.

Some dozens of fur traders crossed the Sierras in the late 1830s, but the
outstanding non-Hispanic in northern California was Johann August Sutter. Sutter's famous fort at present Sacramento employed many Indians,
produced food and livestock, and, most important for this story, welcomed
American settlers. The first overland group came in 1841 from near Independence, Missouri: 32 persons, including women and children, led by John
Bidwell and John Bartleson. Some went to work for Sutter. Another 25
Americans arrived that same year via Santa Fe. A few hundred more trickled
into northern California in the next five years. In 1845 the head count was
680, and by the summer of 1846, perhaps 1,500 were living there.[114] These
formed an Anglo-American vanguard, an embryonic settlement frontier of
the United States, decidedly unlike the assimilated Yankee Californios and
hostile in every way to Mexico and Mexicans.

Among these were the people who at that moment heard rumors of war
between the United States and Mexico. They trembled that Mexican authorities would move against them and were inflamed in those thoughts by the
newly arrived and politically ambitious American officer John Charles Frémont. They declared themselves an independent Bear Flag Republic at
Sonoma in June 1846. The roving bear and the words "California Republic"
still grace the state flag. An American naval force, acting not on behalf of the
settlers but as part of the overall strategy of the just-declared Mexican-
American War, captured Monterey on July 7 and quickly replaced the Bear
Flag with the Stars and Stripes. Further naval and overland actions in August
captured Los Angeles and thus all of Alta California by January 1847.[115] Now

ruling California politically, Anglo-Americans were about to dominate its population.

Trading posts and missions had not preserved the Russian presence in California, the British one in Oregon, or the Spanish ones, however ancient, in Texas, New Mexico, or California. The Hudson's Bay Company prudently withdrew when it became obvious that Americans were outnumbering British along the Willamette and Columbia and soon were to do so near Puget Sound. Mexico was forced out of Texas by overwhelming numbers of Anglos, rising in armed rebellion. Their presence was ratified by the Polk administration's military belligerency, which soon extended to New Mexico and California. The Guadalupe Hidalgo Treaty in 1848 and the Gadsden Purchase in 1853 formalized the "Manifest Destiny" of U.S. borders, but those events could never have happened without the unceasing migration of Anglo-Americans. The military conquest in Texas followed the population conquest.

Since "Manifest Destiny" also assumed racial and cultural superiority, except for the few formerly Anglo Californios who were rich enough and white enough to get away with it, Mexicans and Indians (and soon Chinese and other "others") began to be treated as if they were not fully human.[116] California would always be multiracial, but never comfortably.

3

THE UNITED
STATES
CAPTURES
ITS WEST,
1848–1889

> *California is a new unfinished country, and hasn't a*
> *Presbyterian church on every corner and a sidewalk*
> *and a serving society in front of every house. . . . If one*
> *waits for Eastern improvements before coming land will*
> *be so dear that few can buy it. So I am willing to take the*
> *country barefooted and wait for shoes & stockings.*
> —Daniel Berry, Pasadena, January 1874

The Gold Rush Flood

James W. Marshall's discovery of gold in the creek by Sutter's Mill in the
Sierra Nevada foothills in January 1848 was quickly shouted about the streets
of San Francisco (the few there were). Mexicans, suffering the injury of the
loss of half their national territory in the 1846–1848 war, now witnessed with
frustration the insult of the discovery of gold within that territory even
before the peace treaty of Guadalupe Hidalgo was signed. Land, not gold,
and mainly in Texas, not California, was the Polk administration's design
when it provoked war in 1846. But some Mexicans suspected otherwise.
Even without such a plot they had plenty to resent.

People began arriving in the summer of 1848 in northern California and
invaded in great numbers through 1852, by which time the easy pickings of
nuggets from the streams became scarce. Many followed the Overland Trail
to Mormon Country, then struck across the Great Basin to the Sierras and
descended the western slope to the mother lode. Thousands more arrived by
sea, around Cape Horn (one clipper ship made it from New York in eighty-
nine days) or across Panama, either on foot or, by the mid-1850s, on an
American-built railroad. Across the Pacific came a few from Australia and
many from China. Most were Anglo-Americans, but Irish, Germans,

French, Portuguese, and other Europeans appeared too, and a few thousand African-Americans and South Americans. San Francisco and northern California were ethnically and racially diverse from the start. Evidence of the Spanish-Mexican missions and presidio virtually disappeared. So did most of the northern California Indians.

From 1848 through 1852 about 200,000 migrated to northern California. From 1769 to 1842 the European-stock population of all Alta California, chiefly Spanish-speaking, had crept up to around 5,000. By 1848, just before the Gold Rush began, it may have reached 14,000—perhaps 7,500 Spanish speakers, mostly in the south and around former missions, and at most 6,500 Californios, men from "the States," and other Europeans in the north.[1] San Francisco with 800 people, San Jose with 700, and Monterey with perhaps 600 were northern California's main centers.[2]

Suddenly swollen by these Anglo-Americans and others, the total rose to 26,000 by the end of 1848 and to 100,000 by the end of 1849. The federal census of 1850 found 93,000 non-Indians in California, certainly an undercount; the true figure was at least 112,000. A state census in 1852 revealed 255,000, and the federal census of 1860, 380,000, despite something like a 10 percent defection in 1858–1859 to join a new gold rush along the Fraser River in British Columbia and the first Nevada silver rush.[3]

The 1860 census listed 38.5 percent (146,528) of California's population as foreign-born, far beyond the proportion "back in the States." Much more diverse than states farther east, California's people very early included Chinese, Irish, Germans, Hawaiians, Filipinos, Peruvians, African-Americans, Australians, Mexicans—more a cross section of the world than of the United States up to that time.[4] The Indian population was falling precipitately; it sank to 23,000 by 1880. From 10 Indians to every white in California in 1848, the ratio had swung to 2 whites per Indian by the early 1850s.[5]

The California Gold Rush exploded within five years and continued to attract not only miners but people who sold things to miners, plus newspapermen, including Samuel L. Clemens and Bret Harte, lawyers, missionaries (from Ireland, not Spain), investors, and even a few farmers. Many failed to get rich, but some did; Patrick E. Power, who had left Cork, Ireland, "about twenty years since" to work on canals, returned in 1852 bringing "with him some thousands of pounds worth of gold."[6] It was a uniquely large and varied migration.

It also deviated from the usual pattern of American relocations, such as to Texas or Oregon, in a very crucial and radically new way. The Gold Rush was not a frontier of farm settlement, of land seekers, of stayers, but of gold seekers, resource exploiters, and others who made a living from them. It was not quite urban, but it was certainly not rural in any traditional sense. A

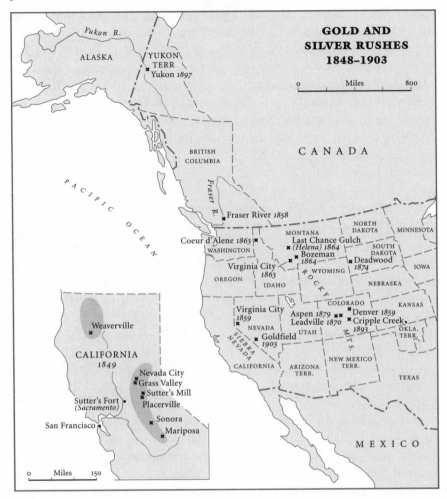

GOLD AND SILVER RUSHES 1848–1903

"frontier" it undoubtedly was; it brought many new people to a new place, and it was an *American* frontier, making California a state in 1850. Some who failed to strike enough gold stayed to become homesteaders, but that was just a more prosaic form of enterprise; the capitalist motivation was the same.

The Gold Rush had well-defined characteristics unlike any farm settlement frontier. Its profile reappeared in a whole series of freshly discovered gold and silver bonanzas that bobbed up around the West for the next fifty years. The Fraser River rush of 1858 was next. Then came the first Comstock boom at Virginia City, Nevada, in 1859; gold near Denver, also in 1859; Last Chance Gulch (soon renamed Helena), Montana, in 1864; the second Comstock strike in 1873; the Black Hills gold rush (setting off war with the Teton

Sioux) in 1874; and more and more until the Klondike rush in 1897. In all of them, at least in the first stages, men greatly outnumbered women. In California the ratio was 12:1 in 1850,[7] when back in "the States" males held only a 104:100 edge. As others arrived, the ratio fell sharply to 256:100, males to females, in 1860, and to 138:100 by 1890. Only gradually did women come to California, by way of Panama or overland.[8]

As early as 1860, when 107,000 females and 273,000 males lived in California, women were no longer the utter rarity that they were in the early 1850s. In *Roughing It*, Mark Twain described how a group of miners in those first days stopped a passing settler's wagon and demanded an appearance from the farm wife. "Bring 'er out!" they shouted. She stood there for a bit, the miners gazed, thanked her for the look, and the wagon went on. Only among the Chinese did the male imbalance actually increase: from 19:1 in 1860 to 22:1 in 1890. The Chinese suffered the most severe and lasting gender imbalance of any immigrants ever to come to the United States.[9]

Another striking feature, the preponderance of young adults, contrasted this mining frontier not so much with farm settlements as with the broad age spectrum of cities. In 1850, 92 percent of white Californians were between fifteen and forty-five. It was a society of restless young men. Like the sex ratio, the age structure veered toward normality as time went on. Women appeared, families formed, children were born, people aged. By 1890 only 52 percent were fifteen to forty-five, with the rest divided almost equally between younger children and older adults.

The profile proved to be typical of precious metal mining frontiers. Colorado's immigrants in 1860 were 97 percent male, 97 percent aged fifteen to forty-five; Nevada's in 1870 were 86 percent male, almost all fifteen to forty-five; Idaho, Montana, and Alaska (not counting Inuits and Indians), in their mining boom beginnings, roughly the same. In Helena, Montana, whose mining heyday began in the mid-1860s and boomed from thirty-six hundred in 1880 to thirteen thousand in 1893, four to five young, unattached males outnumbered every female. Among them, prostitution "constituted the largest single women's employment outside the home."[10]

Frontiers of farm settlement, on the other hand—because they attracted families and not freebooting young fortune seekers—invariably included a fair balance of sex and age-groups. The Utah farm settlement frontier in 1860 was 50 percent male, Kansas's in 1870, 55 percent, and Oregon's in 1890, 58 percent, and in all three exactly half the population was between fifteen and forty-five, the other half children or older adults.[11] Mining and farming frontiers were demographically polar opposites and usually remained so for twenty to forty years after a territory had first begun receiving migrants. By then the ages and sex ratios of the people became much more balanced.[12]

Industrial mining—not for gold and silver but for copper, lead, coal, or other less precious minerals—was yet another matter; Butte, with its strong families and social stability, is a good example. The California Gold Rush, however, was virtually a pure type of a precious metals mining frontier, a society (if that is the appropriate word) of unattached young men. A little later in the West, cattle drives, large ranches, lumber camps, and wildcat oil boomtowns also had a preponderance of young men and an absence of women, children, and older fellows.

Forty-niners came from everywhere. Except for Missouri, however, which many migrants claimed as home simply because the Overland Trail started there, their origins were northern rather than southern, not only during the Gold Rush but long after it. In 1860, 45 percent of Californians reported birthplaces in the Middle Atlantic, New England, and Old Northwest states, but only 14 percent from the South. By 1890, when California natives were already a majority of the state's population, the out-of-state sources remained northern (28 percent) rather than southern (6 percent).[13] Much later the South (particularly Texas, Oklahoma, and Louisiana) sent two large groups to California: whites (the inaccurately named Dust Bowl migrants) in the 1930s and African-Americans in the 1940s. They did not reverse the general northern and midwestern cultural predominance, including speech patterns, which have made most Californians sound midwestern rather than southern. Early settlers in the midwestern prairies came from the middle colonies and to a lesser extent from New England and New York, rarely from the South.[14] Those who later moved from the plains to California carried their folkways a long step farther.

The Gold Rush as Melting Pot

California's ethnic and racial diversity was already high in 1849 and has remained so ever since. Its 38.5 percent foreign-born in 1860 came from several dozen countries, with China (34,935) and Ireland (33,147) followed by Germany (20,919), England-Wales-Scotland (17,262), and Mexico (9,150). Among them also lived 8,000 French, 5,000 Canadians, 5,000 African-Americans, 3,000 Italians, and others. Irish and Chinese remained the two largest foreign-born groups forty years later, ahead of Germans, British, Canadians, and Mexicans.[15] The proportion of foreign-born in California in 1860 was three times the United States' 13 percent. The gap narrowed a little but always remained wide; in 1910, when the national foreign-born population reached its all-time peak at 14.7 percent, California's was still 24.6 percent.

Being early on the ground helped many groups get along. Although California has always had its nativists, it also has included enough Irish, Jews, and Italians since Gold Rush days to integrate these Europeans much better into mainstream economic and cultural life than east of the Mississippi, where they arrived relatively late. Contrast, for example, the early success of the Irish in northern California with the "No Irish need apply" nativism of New England in those same 1850s.

Nonwhites, however, were ghettoized early. The several thousand blacks in California in 1852 were all free, some operating businesses, churches, and a newspaper. But they were excluded from juries, voting, homesteading, and intermarrying.[16] The large Chinese population also found that early settlement in no way helped them. Migration to California, the *Gum Saan* or Gold Mountain, was a small part of a much larger relocation from southeastern China in the mid- and late nineteenth century to Southeast Asia, the western Pacific, and beyond. Those who went to California came from a few districts around the Pearl River delta in Guangdong and Fujian provinces in the south, not from a broad cross section of China.[17] Most sailed with the Pacific Mail Steamship Company from Hong Kong to San Francisco (clipper ships to the late 1860s, then steamships), paying a hefty fifty dollars for the four- to five-week voyage. By 1850 a few Chinese merchants had appeared. Large-scale migration—20,000—began in 1852. The number fluctuated greatly over the next thirty years, until the Chinese Exclusion Act of 1882 cut off most of the traffic. By that time around 136,000 Chinese (the most until well into the twentieth century) lived in the United States: 90 percent in the West, 68 percent in California.[18]

The Chinese usually arrived as contract laborers. They worked first in the mining counties of the Sierras, more often in service trades than as miners, then in railroad building, in construction work, and by the 1870s and 1880s in all sorts of occupations and at every level from owner-operators to tenant farmers to wage laborers. The 1882 Exclusion Act and its successors, together with male skewedness, gradually reduced their bachelor society to a low of 29,000 Chinese-born Californians by 1920, less than 1 percent of the state population compared with over 9 percent in 1860.[19]

Carried eastward by railroads, Chinese gravitated to other gold strikes after California's had turned more capital-intensive. In Idaho Territory nearly half the miners and one-third of the total population in 1870 were Chinese, 4,300 of them, but by 1900 they had dwindled to 1,467.[20] In Arizona Territory 1,419 Chinese were recorded in 1900, all but 32 of them male. Most arrived as railroad workers, and a few managed to lease land for irrigated truck farming along the Santa Cruz River near Tucson in the 1880s.[21] Chinese miners appeared at Nevada's Comstock Lode in 1859, but when Tonopah and Goldfield boomed around 1909, they were kept out. Chinese numbers in Nevada peaked in 1880 at 5,416, partly because of "periodic racist violence, and scapegoating for economic depressions." Their unbalanced sex ratio and the restriction laws guaranteed their decline.[22]

Anti-Chinese riots broke out in San Francisco in 1871, killing twenty-one Chinese; in Denver in 1880; and other places throughout the period. One of the worst sullied Rock Springs, Wyoming, in 1885. The Union Pacific had hired Chinese strikebreakers to work its coal mines in 1875. When it took on more in the summer of 1885 at three-fourths the whites' wage, a riot erupted, leaving twenty-eight Chinese dead and many homes burned to the ground. Union Pacific and Wyoming officials persuaded President Grover Cleveland to send army units to restore the peace and protect the Chinese (and the mine operations). Quiet resumed in Rock Springs, with few white miners left.[23]

The Irish migrants to California included more men than women, but in much closer balance than the Chinese. The very poorest Irish could not go anywhere, and more than a million starved at home in the Great Famine of the late 1840s. Those with a little land to sell, or a trade to practice, were able to buy passage and sail to some port between Quebec and Baltimore and then drift west. Others came by way of Australia. Some did very well. In 1834, before the famine, the Irish-born Californio John Thomas Reed, received from Mexican authorities the eight-thousand-acre Rancho Corte de Madera del Presidio, which included sizable portions of present Marin County, including Corte Madera and Tiburon. Two years later he married Ylaria Sánchez, daughter of the commandant of the San Francisco presidio. Reed died in 1838, leaving several heirs, including a daughter, Hilarita. In 1872 she married a former U.S. Army physician from Vermont, Benjamin Franklin Lyford. With a brother-in-law and fellow heir, Hugh Boyle, and the help of the wealthy Colonel Peter Donahue, they began dividing and developing the rancho. Soon they built railroads, ferries, a health spa named Hygeia, mansions, and a Catholic chapel, St. Hilary, whose first pastor was Father Hugh Lagan of County Derry and Dublin's All Hallows College. From the 1830s well into the twentieth century, the north shore of San Francisco Bay was a Californio-Irish-Yankee enterprise.[24] Names such as Dillon, Conness, Fallon, O'Sullivan, O'Farrell, and Donahue appear prominently in its early history.[25]

By 1859 San Francisco and the northern California Gold Rush region included a hundred thousand Catholics, most of them Irish, served by fifty-seven churches and sixty priests. Irish nuns of the Presentation order and Sisters of Mercy began operating hospitals and schools in San Francisco in 1854, and in 1863 the Mercy Sisters arrived in Grass Valley to teach school and "to establish an orphanage for the children of the miners who were killed in the accidents which occurred so frequently."[26] In 1860 Eugene O'Connell, head of All Hallows College in Dublin, became vicar apostolic of the territory, which included the Sacramento Valley and western Nevada. He found plenty of work. One-third of the population, O'Connell reported to Rome in 1866 and 1871, was Catholic: seven thousand in Virginia City and an equal number in the Sacramento Valley. Though population stabilized in the Gold Rush area, it exploded on the other side of the Sierras when the Comstock Lode opened in 1859. O'Connell's priests, parishes, and people expanded fourfold during the 1860s, and by 1871 five congregations of nuns were teaching school and caring for the sick and orphaned.[27]

Jews appeared in northern California from 1849 on, enough to establish themselves in Sacramento, San Francisco, the mother lode towns in the Sierras, and Humboldt, Shasta, and Siskiyou counties close by Oregon. In 1849 and 1850 the Edinburgh-born Gabriel McCohen helped organize the Hebrew Benevolent Society and raised funds for a Jewish cemetery in San Francisco. Moses Hyman's home in Sacramento hosted High Holy Day services by 1850, and the first synagogue in the Far West was dedicated there in 1852. In Mokelumne Hill, Jewish women had formed a Hebrew Ladies Benevolent Society in 1860, by which time scores of Jews were carrying on community life in many places and were already numerous enough to splinter into Polish or German, Orthodox or Reform, or Sephardi congregations. Cauffman Mayer wrote from San Francisco in 1853 that fifty families observed Pesach (Passover) that spring. McCohen's society in 1854 sponsored a Purim ball that "about 200" ladies attended, and so many people observed Pesach the next month that "one man has sold $160 worth of horseradish" for the seder.

An extraordinary improvisation was the "quasi-rabbinical career" of Ray Frank, "Girl Rabbi of the Golden West." She was born in San Francisco in 1861, graduated from Sacramento High School in 1879, and taught at the silver town of Ruby Hill, Nevada (where the mine owner was Jewish), and then at Eureka. When the mines played out in the 1880s, Ray moved to Oakland, took courses at the University of California, became a tutor and principal of a Hebrew school, and then surfaced at High Holy Days in 1890 in Spokane. It was without a synagogue or rabbi, so she did the preaching. Except to the Orthodox, she was a wonder. She preached in August 1895 at Temple Emanu-el, the Reform congregation in San Francisco, led High Holy Day services at Congregation Emanu-el in Victoria, British Columbia, a few weeks later, preached at the Stanford University chapel early in 1896 and at the Stockton congregation for Pesach in 1897.[28]

Jewish charities and commerce also flourished in San Francisco by the end of the 1850s. Some Jews joined the Gold Rush as miners, but more typically they served San Francisco, Sacramento, and the mining towns as clothing and dry goods merchants, jewelers and watch repairers, and manufacturers. The most famously successful Jewish entrepreneur in the Gold Rush, Levi Strauss, had arrived from Bavaria in 1850, aged twenty, with "a considerable stock of merchandise," including duck and denim cloth. By 1853 he and his two brothers in New York had formed Levi Strauss Work Clothes. It prospered even before he began copper riveting the pockets of blue denim work pants in the late 1860s; from that point Levi's achieved worldwide success and many imitators.[29]

The ethnic mix of San Francisco and the Gold Rush region was as rich as a tub of cioppino, the local bouillabaisse. "Sydney Ducks" from Australia transferred the skills they learned in the Victoria goldfields to the mother lode. The French government ran a lottery to pay for emigration to California, and it may have sent as many as three thousand people.[30] More than six thousand Germans had populated San Francisco by 1860, many after paying the Hamburg-America line's one-way fare of eighty-two dollars. In 1851 the local Germans organized the Pacific Ocean Singers (*die Sänger an Stillen Meer*), and in 1852 they formed the San Francisco Turnverein. Newspapers and a German-language hospital followed, as did other accoutrements of German-American life similar to those in places like Cincinnati or Chicago: breweries, restaurants, saloons, churches, musical groups, and benevolent societies.[31]

Italians had cut a *bella figura* in northern California ever since a few Genoese settled in San Francisco's North Beach, then "the Latin Quarter." Northern Italians continued to arrive, to become commercial fishermen at nearby Fisherman's Wharf. Some came to prospect for gold, but others brought enough capital to start small businesses, thus becoming part of the establishment, such as it was, in the city's first American decade. Spectacular successes in the twentieth century, such as Amadeo Pietro Giannini's Bank of America and the great wineries like Gallo and food concerns like Del Monte, should not distort the fact that most Italian migrants were fishermen, farmers, small tradesmen, or laborers. In certain respects, especially its "distinctly northern character from the beginning" and its wider spread across the spectrum of occupations and wealth, California's early Italian community was less like those that developed in the northeastern United States after 1900 than the one then arising in Buenos Aires.[32]

Conspicuously missing from the ethnic and racial groups that participated in the Gold Rush were Hispanics and Indians. The Spanish presence was never strong north of Monterey and increased little. As for the California Indians, the Gold Rush has been accurately called a disaster for them. They virtually disappeared from the Bay Area and the mother lode country.

What happened to them? At first (1848) several thousand were recruited or forced into mining, while others (especially in the mountains north of the Sacramento Valley) managed to trade with whites and continue tribal life for a time. But white numbers and aggressiveness defeated them. By late 1849, writes Rohrbough, "they largely had disappeared from the gold camps, and the influx of gold seekers (many of them also hunters) had devastated their fragile economic base. In the [hard] winter of 1849–50 . . . their isolated raids in search of subsistence aroused the fury of the Americans [who] organized a series of raids against [them] in the mountains."[33] After California became a state in 1850, Anglo-American ranchers and settlers pressured the U.S. Army and formed volunteer militias to attack and kill Indians or press them into indentured servitude, as state law permitted.[34] Miners "vehemently and brutally objected to competition from cheap Indian labor," state government responded to white citizens, and through the 1850s Indians went unprotected.[35] The belief that Indians should be removed so that the land could be put to better use justified an ethnic cleansing in California no less complete than in the valleys of the Ohio and the Mississippi a generation or two earlier.[36] The Indians of California, as a result of Gold Rush demographic change, experienced disease, economic deprivation, enslavement, and outright massacre, retail or wholesale.

The Gold Rush in a very few years brought to California a great many people new to the country. Nativists from "the States" resented any "foreigner" digging for "American" gold and pushed aside the foreign-born as well as Indians if they could.[37] Of the 380,000 counted by the census in 1860, fewer than 50,000 lived in southern California or along the coast. The majority inhabited the Sacramento Valley, the mining counties, and the shores around San Francisco Bay.[38] The mining communities quickly stopped growing, some turning into ghost towns, but San Francisco kept on. It reached 100,000 by 1870, becoming one of only fourteen American cities that large, just after the transcontinental railroad opened to Oakland. Los Angeles remained tiny; its great expansion did not begin until the late 1880s and had an entirely different dynamic.[39]

The California Gold Rush quickly devolved into a continuously growing population center in the Bay Area and the Sacramento Valley. But most western mining booms did not. They were firecracker communities, exploding with great noise and brilliance but fast subsiding into ashes after prospectors had exhausted the surface ore. Mark Twain and Bret Harte helped make the western prospector a folkloric figure, but the great majority of western miners were something else entirely. Western miners mainly dug for zinc, copper, or lead, not gold or silver. Such mining was industrial, requiring deep shafts, drainage and exhaust systems, and technologically complicated smelting and refining. Its work was organized through company managers and wage workers, not freelance prospectors. It soon acquired a demographic profile very different from gold rushes but not greatly different from eastern coal-mining towns. (In fact thirty-three thousand *were* mining coal in the West by 1889, and nearly a hundred thousand by 1910.[40]) Butte, Montana's copper-mining capital, became a stable and thoroughly industrialized community by the 1880s. Irish dominated it at every level, from Marcus Daly, Con Kelley, and John D. Ryan, the early presidents of Anaconda, to the lowest-on-the-scale mine hands.[41]

Other hard-rock mining sites dotted the West after 1860 from the Tanana field near Fairbanks, Alaska, south to Tombstone, Arizona, and from Nevada City and Grass Valley, California, east to Park City, Utah; Telluride, Leadville, Georgetown, and Idaho Springs, Colorado; and Lead, South Dakota. Socorro, New Mexico, jumped from 1,272 people in the spring of 1880 to around 2,500 by late fall, after silver ores (and the Santa Fe Railroad) appeared. A minor boom elevated real estate values and population to 5,000 by 1887; a smelter employed almost 400 men. The collapse of the silver market in 1893 ruined all that.[42] Western industrial miners became, in historian Mark Wyman's phrase, "the advance agents of the Industrial Revolution" in the region.[43]

Native Americans benefited even less from these developments. Before 1848 Mexican settlers and French fur traders often married Indians, but no such mixing graced the mining booms. Indians became integral parts of colonial Spanish and Mexican society, but very seldom of American or northern European; they had to go.[44] In northern California, beginning with the Gold Rush, Indian numbers dropped to 15,000 by 1900. In the same fifty years Indians in the Great Basin and Colorado Plateau mining regions declined from 72,000 to 33,000.[45] A rush for gold into the San Juan Mountains in southwestern Colorado in 1860 did not produce much gold, but it opened up northwestern New Mexico, beyond Abiquiu and Tierra Amarilla, for white settlement—by expelling the Utes.[46] The sudden appearance of 100,000 "fifty-niners" trampling the plains on their way to the Colorado goldfields in 1859, more than went to California in 1849, made an already desperate situation worse for the Plains Indians, beset by drought, epidemics, and shrinkage of the buffalo herds.[47]

The story repeated itself in many places between the Pacific and the High Plains; gold seekers and settlers (often the same people), usually backed by the army, "opened" Indian areas, fighting many engagements. The best known are the Modoc War of 1872 in northern California and the Nez Percé War of 1877 in Idaho and Montana, but blood flowed even more freely in other conflicts. Pacific Northwest Indians were disarmed and confined to reservations by 1880. Despite the fig leaf of treaties between equals, the realities of disease, force, and demographic inundation dispossessed them.[48] Sometimes there was not even a treaty. In 1875 Congress decreed unilaterally the takeover of 737,000 acres of Indian land along the Oregon coast. The Tillamooks and other tribes living there were removed to reservations by 1881.[49]

On the High Plains the discovery of gold in western Montana in 1862–1864 prompted the opening of the Bozeman Trail, also known as the Powder River Road, from Fort Laramie on the upper Platte to Montana gold sites. Unfortunately it ran directly across the hunting grounds, protected by treaty, of the Northern Cheyennes, Arapahos, and Sioux. About a thousand whites followed the trail in 1864 and in 1866, despite some fatal skirmishes. The numbers of migrants astonished the Indians, but for once they were able to stop the white onrush for several years. A treaty at Fort Laramie in 1868 traded peace for Indian control of a large area including the religiously significant Black Hills.[50] But gold appeared there in 1874. Despite the treaty guarantees, gold seekers began drifting in. The Indians resisted, the whites demanded protection from the army, and after initial hesitation a protective force under George A. Custer opened the gates. The episode began a tale whose next to last chapter was Custer's annihilation at the Little Bighorn in June 1876. The very last chapter soon followed. The army confined the Plains Indians to reservations by 1881. The High Plains were now open to miners, migrants, and before long homesteaders.

The Settlement Frontier: Kansas, Nebraska, and Dakota Territory

In 1848 the traditional westward movement, the frontier-rural settlement process of Anglo-Americans, had not yet crossed the Missouri River. Exceptions, to be sure, were the migrants to Texas in the 1820s and 1830s and the few thousands crossing the Overland Trail to Oregon or Utah in the 1840s. But homesteading was yet to come to the plains. The process had begun in the early 1700s in the piedmont of Virginia and the Carolinas and the river valleys of Pennsylvania and New England. Homesteaders had reached the Appalachians by the 1750s, paused for the French and Indian and Revolutionary wars, and then surged through the Cumberland Gap, across Pennsylvania's military roads, and along the Mohawk River. In central New York, the upper Ohio River, Kentucky, and Tennessee, farm settlement was well under way by 1790. By 1835 settlers were crossing the

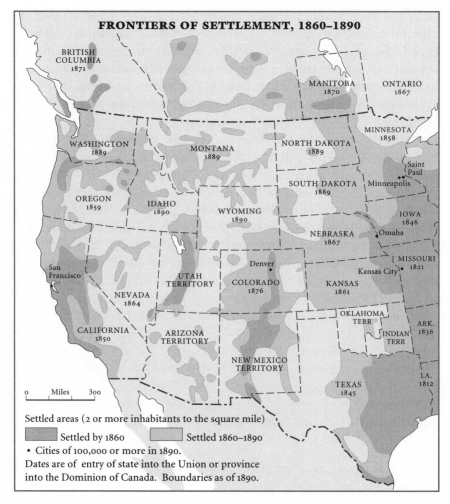

FRONTIERS OF SETTLEMENT, 1860–1890

BRITISH
COLUMBIA
1871

MANITOBA
1870

ONTARIO
1867

MINNESOTA
1858

WASHINGTON
1889

MONTANA
1889

NORTH DAKOTA
1889

Saint
Paul

OREGON
1859

IDAHO
1890

WYOMING
1890

SOUTH DAKOTA
1889

Minneapolis

IOWA
1846

NEBRASKA
1867

Omaha

San
Francisco

UTAH
TERRITORY

Denver

COLORADO
1876

KANSAS
1861

MISSOURI
1821

Kansas City

NEVADA
1864

CALIFORNIA
1850

ARIZONA
TERRITORY

OKLAHOMA
TERR

INDIAN
TERR

ARK.
1836

NEW MEXICO
TERRITORY

TEXAS
1845

LA.
1812

0   Miles   300

Settled areas (2 or more inhabitants to the square mile)

Settled by 1860   Settled 1860–1890

• Cities of 100,000 or more in 1890.
Dates are of entry of state into the Union or province
into the Dominion of Canada. Boundaries as of 1890.

Mississippi River. By 1848 they were poised to cross the Missouri, and by
1860 they had reached the ninety-eighth meridian in Kansas, the edge of
the West by our definition.

Accelerated by railroad building, farm settlement sped across the Great
Plains. Anglo-Americans, augmented by land-seeking European immigrants beginning in the 1840s (mainly British, Irish, Germans, Scandinavians, and Bohemians) displaced the Plains Indians. This frontier was one
gigantic land boom from the late 1850s to 1887, with late outliers probing
into the Dakotas, Wyoming, Montana, and the Pacific Northwest.

The settlement frontier bore no demographic resemblance to the California Gold Rush and its successors. Instead of unattached young males, families were the norm. Ages and sexes were much more evenly distributed.

People over forty-five remained rare until an area had been settled for a decade or two, but children, hordes of them, were as omnipresent as they were absent on mining frontiers. Young men and women brought forth children almost as fast as pregnancy and weaning permitted. Death rates (except among infants and children) stayed below those in older areas since so many of the migrants were young and in the healthiest times of their lives.[51]

The sons and daughters of Anglo-Protestant farm families in the Ohio and Mississippi valleys hurried by the thousands to Kansas, Nebraska, and a little later Dakota Territory after Indian titles had been, in the day's legalese, "extinguished." A few had the cash to pay their own start-up costs, many more combined cash and credit, and some (both young men and women) hired themselves out until their nest eggs were large enough to begin on their own. Congress intended that the land be settled, and it passed law after law to hasten that result. The most famous (though by no means the first) was the Homestead Act of 1862, which gave away 160 acres of public domain to anyone who paid a ten-dollar filing fee and actually lived there for five years. Congress also encouraged settlement by granting land to help build transcontinental railroads, creating the Department of Agriculture, promoting agricultural colleges, and providing the funds whereby the army forced the Plains Indians onto reservations.[52] When the settlement line reached the 100th meridian and aridity in the 1880s, further laws encouraged settlers to keep on homesteading, although risks multiplied. Railroads also unabashedly hawked their land grants to young settlers.

Up to the early 1880s farms begun under the Homestead Act generally succeeded, because they were in well-watered parts of Iowa, Minnesota, Kansas, and Nebraska. But when settlement crept west of the arid line in the mid-1880s, the chances of surviving economically for five years on 160 acres dwindled with each passing meridian. Eighty acres, even 40, could support a family in Ohio or Kentucky, while 240 could bring starvation in western Kansas. By 1910 or 1920 this truth was plain. From the 1860s to the late 1880s it was not yet appreciated. Compounding the problem, the western line of farm settlement reached the 98th and 100th meridians just at the crest of a heavier-than-normal rainfall cycle, persuading otherwise prudent people that central Kansas was as rainy as Illinois or Indiana. In some years it was, but in others the migrants tasted the bitter dust that hid the afternoon sun. Recently, in the drought year of 1988, less than two inches of rain fell in parts of eastern Montana, rather than the average fifteen or so. Western rainfall was just as capricious a century ago.

The pace of settlement was extremely fast, abetted by the spreading network of railroad lines. North of Indian Territory (now Oklahoma) lay the territories of Kansas, Nebraska, and Dakota. By 1870 most of Kansas was ethnically cleansed (of Indians), as were the entire northern plains by 1881. In Nebraska the Pawnee found themselves ground between white pressure to behave like homesteading farmers and their own traditions of horticulture and buffalo hunting. Pressed further by encroaching white settlers to sell their reservation lands, and by enemy Brulé and Oglala Sioux who killed their hunting parties, the Pawnee voluntarily moved to Indian Territory in 1874 as "a last, desperate, and ultimately abortive attempt to preserve a way of life."[53] Great Lakes Indians (Shawnees, Miamis, Pottawatomis, Osages, and others) who had been removed to eastern Kansas in the late 1830s were "persuaded" to give up their new homes in the 1850s. At least ten million buffaloes that had roamed virtually all of Kansas and the entire region north of it from the Rockies to Lake Superior were destroyed; only about a thousand survived in 1884.[54] Many were slaughtered for their skins, their tongues, or just "sport." Many others died from brucellosis and anthrax carried by newly arrived domestic cattle.[55] Exit the buffalo, exit the Indian. Earlier fears about the "Great American Desert" were forgotten.

With just over 100,000 white inhabitants in 1860, the eastern third of Kansas was settled as far as Manhattan on the Kansas River. The settlement line reached Salina, about the ninety-eighth meridian, by 1870. By the mid-1880s every county west to the Colorado line was in place. At the crest of the 1885–1886 boom (the last one for a while), Governor John A. Martin exulted that "to populate a county thirty miles square within six months . . . may seem like fiction, but they have been realities in Kansas."[56] There population soared by 240 percent in the 1860s, by another 174 percent (to about 1,000,000) in the 1870s, and by yet another 44 percent (to 1,428,000) by the end of the 1880s. Growth halted abruptly in 1887 for about a dozen years, but the three-decade era of Kansas's settlement frontier sowed people throughout a landmass over four hundred miles wide from the Missouri River to Colorado.

Such rapid growth was in no way extraordinary for American farming frontiers in the nineteenth century. Nebraska started later but expanded by 324 percent in the 1860s, 267 percent in the 1870s, and 135 percent in the 1880s, from no white population to about 1,000,000. A little later still, Dakota Territory, not split until 1889 into North and South, grew 300 percent between 1880 and 1890 to more than 500,000. In 1860 the three northern plains territories (Kansas, Nebraska, and Dakota) contained 136,000 people; in 1890, 3,031,000—twenty-one times as many. South of Indian Territory, Texas more than tripled in the same thirty years from 604,000 to 2,236,000.

The homestead ideal of a land dotted everywhere with industrious and fecund farm families appeared to be the new reality in Kansas and the rest of the plains. More than half the Kansans of 1865 had been born in Missouri, Ohio, Indiana, and Illinois, most of them on farms when those states were in their own frontier phases twenty to thirty years earlier. Kansas's foreign-born were then chiefly Irish, German, Canadian, or British.[57] In the 1870s and 1880s substantial groups of Scandinavians, ethnic Germans living in Russia (Catholic, Lutheran, and Mennonite), blacks from Kentucky, Tennessee, and the lower Mississippi Valley, Italian miners, Bohemians, Swiss, French Canadians, and others also arrived. Kansas was never more than about 13 percent foreign-born, but the immigrants were visible culturally and politically; there were over fifty thousand Germans in 1890, for example.

Why these people came has often, and accurately, been ascribed to railroads, relatives, and state governments. In a famous case the land-poor Santa Fe Railroad, trying to sell off its land grant, in 1876 sent a German-speaking recruiter named C. B. Schmidt to Russia. There Schmidt happened upon several thousand Mennonites very upset by the tsar's reneging on his ancestor Catherine the Great's guarantee in the 1760s—in order to recruit them *to* Russia—that they would be forever exempt from army duty. In short order they arrived in central Kansas, bought land from the Santa Fe, and started growing wheat better than anyone. The Kansas Pacific's emigrant handbooks in Danish, newspapers in Swedish, German, Italian, and other languages (even Welsh) all helped boost Kansas; ticket agents advertised the place throughout Europe.[58]

Minorities had their own special reasons for establishing enclaves on the plains. Newly freed or escaped slaves rushed into Kansas and other parts of the West during the Civil War. With Texas not allowing black homesteading, and Indian Territory as yet too unstable, Kansas was the nearest available place with "free land."[59] From only 627 in 1860, black Kansans increased to over 12,000 by 1865, most of them in eastern towns like Topeka but some out in homesteading country.[60] African-Americans founded Nicodemus, near the 100th meridian in northern Kansas, in 1877, and despite many vicissitudes, it lasted through the twentieth century. Founded by white and black townsite promoters, Nicodemus attracted blacks from Kentucky and Tennessee who hoped to homestead. Some succeeded, despite a sore lack of capital and experience.[61] Another colony of black emigrants from Lexington, Kentucky, began in Hodgeman County north of Dodge City virtually without resources in 1877 and nearly failed but weathered the drought and depression of the late 1880s and early 1890s.[62]

Seven Jewish agricultural colonies, named Beersheba, Montefiore, Lasker, Leeser, Touro, Gilead, and Hebron, "were born, grew, and perished" along the 100th meridian in the 1880s. At Beersheba in 1882 Russian Jews were living in sod houses as so many first settlers did in that treeless region, and they were reading Torah portions in a possibly unique sod synagogue. The pogroms of 1882 triggered a great wave of Jewish emigration from Russia. One of its many outlets was agricultural colonization, which promised economic and cultural self-sufficiency. At that moment western Kansas had available land, and thus, almost inevitably, some Russian Jews went there. Two tough winters followed by drought in the late 1880s snuffed out these efforts, as they did a great many others in that time and place.[63] The Jewish agriculturists were no more inept, and no more lucky, than their Christian neighbors. The Jews who survived and prospered in Kansas usually did so operating dry goods stores in county seat towns.

From about 1855 to 1887 Kansas was a settlement frontier, the latest place to brand the hoary homestead ideal into the American brain. Jane Carruth, who emigrated with her husband and children from Watertown, New York, to Osawatomie, Kansas, in 1856, enthused about "this land of promise" in a letter to a friend back home: "I wish that you and many more could see with you[r] own eyes; you would almost think that you were in the same garden that our Mother Eve was in." They ate bread, hasty pudding, butter, tea, coffee, and fruit; "If we always have as good we shall not get very lean." Even the Kansas summer pleased her: "The thermometer stands, at eleven, at 104 in the shade, but I like it. . . . The country and climate are very delightful. On our claim you can see twenty miles or more. . . . How I wish that thousands of our poor but worthy people could be transferred here; what homes they could have." Her enthusiasm survived even the burning of Osawatomie that August by proslavery marauders from Missouri: "I look back and compare the present with three years ago this time with perfect horror. Such a prison as I was in!"[64]

Jane was writing about her new realities, and she stressed the positive. That is what her friends in northern New York read. A New England woman who moved in 1854 near Manhattan, Kansas, kept a private diary that revealed many more workaday problems: cholera, typhoid, and snakebite; hot summers, harsh winters, and cloudbursts; Wyandot Indian rights clouding title to their claim; skirmishes and raids between free staters and slave staters. There was loneliness: "Heard of the death of Mrs. Carol of Wildcat, the only woman who visited me in my lone two months residence and sickness here. This dear woman walked three miles to comfort [me] in my affliction. A Mormon by profession and fared hard." Accidents too: "Mr. Green was killed in a well by a stone falling on him. . . . John [a son] cut his foot with an ax. Abbie [a daughter] fell down the ladder. . . . The wolves are becoming troublesome, they bite calves so that they die, we have lost one, wild animals catch the poultry." Always sickness: "Dr. Adams visits me, called my disease Intermittent fever. Charged two dol." Nevertheless, she concluded, "I love to think and trust in an over-ruling Providence. . . . Let us be thankful that we are yet an unbroken circle since our sojourn in Kansas, with health improving and prospects brightening. We will ever trust in and praise the Great Ruler of all things."[65]

A newlywed from Illinois arrived at her new sod house near Cimarron, in southwestern Kansas, in early 1887. "I really can't say I am pleased with first impressions," she wrote, but "I think I can make ours seem home-like." Hailstorms destroyed their crops and killed their chickens, coyote howls depressed her, prairie fires threatened them, and two years later her young husband died in a shooting accident. She returned to Illinois, taught school, married again, and died herself a year later.[66]

By no means were all attempts at homesteading so grim. Of the 249,100 homestead claims filed between 1873 and 1880, 140,400 (56.3 percent) "proved up"—i.e., the original settlers stayed for the five years required by law and gained clear title. (What they did with it after that—kept it or sold it—is another matter.) Between 1881 and 1890, when much homesteading was taking place west of the ninety-eighth meridian, 487,000 hopefuls filed claims and 210,600 proved up, a ratio of 43.2 percent.[67] In short, the overall success and failure rate of Kansas homesteads was close to fifty-fifty.

Heads of families qualified as homesteaders. That excluded married women but included single women, both never-marrieds and widows. Pre-1862 laws had not allowed them to file. After that, under the Homestead Act, upward of 18 percent of filers in Colorado and Wyoming were female, and they apparently proved up at a higher rate than men did. Along the South Platte in northeastern Colorado, nearly 12 percent of the filers before 1900 were women, about half of whom stayed the five-year course.[68]

Kansas of course was only the beginning of Great Plains farm settlement. Nebraska followed, then Dakota Territory, and finally the plains portions of the Front Range states—Montana, Wyoming, Colorado, and New Mexico. Quickly they became home to settlers who either busted the sod and planted corn or (increasingly) wheat or brought in cattle and sheep to feast on the grass where the buffalo had recently roamed.

The settlement surge to Dakota Territory in the 1880s culminated in 1889, when Congress split it into two states: South Dakota, bisected almost per-fectly by the 100th meridian and the Missouri River, and North Dakota, nearly all of it west of the 98th. From 14,000 whites in 1870, living amid a larger number of Yanktonai and Teton Sioux and other Indians, Dakota Ter-ritory appeared safe for whites by the late 1870s. It thereupon swelled to 135,000 in 1880 and more than 540,000 in 1890. Through the Sioux Agree-ment of 1889, over nine million acres west of the Missouri in South Dakota shifted to the U.S. public domain. The majority of the Sioux signed the agreement.[69] The Dawes Act of 1887 and several subsequent laws encouraged the leasing and sale of tribal lands to whites for farms, ranches, and mines. Many Indians did practice agriculture and stock raising, but with no more success than their white neighbors. The allotment policy opened much remaining tribal land to fee simple sale before 1920.[70]

In Dakota Territory in 1885 new settlers typically arrived young, married young, and had children young. Men, especially in their twenties, outnumbered women, but the roughly 60:40 male-female imbalance of 1880 eased to 55:45 by 1890. Fertility began high in the first frontier years. On average, Russian-German couples raised seven or eight children, Norwegians six or seven, and those of American parentage about four. These young settlers of the 1880s were themselves the products, very often, of settlers of Illinois or Wisconsin in the 1850s or of European peasants. Their children in turn helped settle eastern Montana and the Canadian prairies after 1905 or moved to cities like Chicago, Minneapolis–St. Paul, Seattle, or Los Angeles.[71]

The Northern Pacific Railway, completed as far as Bismarck by 1873 and then west through the Yellowstone Valley a few years later, protected and patronized by the U.S. Army, carried American and foreign-born migrants from Duluth, Chicago, and the Twin Cities to North Dakota. Railroad publicists trumpeted the reputedly moderate climate and great agricultural promise of Dakota Territory, and believers flooded in. Dakota's spring wheat output soared from 1,700,000 bushels in 1879 to 36,000,000 in 1887. Then, abruptly, the whole region from Kansas northward careened into economic depression. Settlement stalled.[72] The Northern Pacific eagerly unloaded parcels from its large federal land grant for as little as a knockdown $2.50 an acre.

Because steam engines required water and coal, small towns sprouted around watering stations every fifteen to thirty miles across the prairie in Dakota and Montana. Jamestown, Dakota Territory, "is all alive with emigrants," wrote a new arrival from Iowa in April 1882. "Last year it had two hundred inhabitants, and now two thousand, every hut and even all old stables are occupied." He and his wife were among the first in their county, but one year later she wrote her sister: "Every quarter [160-acre tract] in Dickey County will be entered this spring." The Chicago, Milwaukee & St. Paul Railroad built a line near their farm in 1886, bypassing their village. It folded immediately, but its businesses moved a few miles away to a stop on the railroad and resurrected themselves. "Land has doubled in value in the last 5 months," claimed the farmer. Yet when the boom ended in the late 1880s, the couple returned to the 78 acres in Iowa that they had wisely kept, not risking their future on a full 640-acre section in Dakota.[73]

Far and away more characteristic, however, were new arrivals who stayed and multiplied. States and territories across the northern plains shipped boatloads of promotional advertisements to European prospects. Lutheran, Mennonite, Hutterite, Catholic, and other Christian groups from Europe formed congregations and parishes that used languages other than English and served as safe havens for potential emigrants still in Europe. The myriad weekly local newspapers (some county seat towns in Kansas had five or six) displayed unabashed, unmitigated boosterism. Any "kicker" would be seriously ostracized for failing to agree that the climate was the most salubrious and the crop yields the highest.[74]

The size and speed of the in-migration were astonishing. Boosters outran even the settlers sometimes; many towns were surveyed, platted, and sold as speculations, but little or no development ever happened. If a railroad bypassed an existing settlement, it often blew away in a season.[75] Yet the seemingly inexorable westward advance of the settlement line in the 1870s and 1880s mothered village after village, most of them unremittingly ugly but essential as supply points, rail stops, post offices, courthouses, and centers for churches and schools.

Abilenes and Tombstones: Cattle Drives and Cattle Towns

Among the many mythical golden ages of the American West, the 1870s and 1880s provided more than their share of the best legends, among them Custer vs. Sitting Bull, the long cattle drives, the flawed but heroic lawmen of Abilene, Dodge City, and Tombstone, the Long Branch Saloon, the gunfight at the OK Corral. The myths glorify rugged individualism. The history, however, much more often reveals communities and civic cooperation rather than the extremely rare shoot-outs.

The Kansas land boom that began before the Civil War concluded somewhere up in the Arkansas River valley in Colorado in late 1887. Until then speculators platted towns and sold lots, the state organized new counties, and people everywhere waited for the railroad to come. The boom extended well northward from Kansas. James J. Hill's Great Northern Railroad, intended to link St. Paul with Puget Sound, reached Grand Forks on the Red River in 1880 and proceeded to Minot and the Montana-Dakota line in 1887, only ten years after Crazy Horse surrendered. West of the 100th meridian, the railroad gave would-be settlers animals, seed, and even loans.[76] Paris Gibson, a Maine man who early visualized the potential of interior Montana, platted Great Falls in 1883 and saw it reach almost four thousand by 1890 on a relatively drought-resistant base of sheep raising and copper mining.[77]

The 1870s and 1880s also brought settlers to Manitoba and Saskatchewan, although their greatest land booms (and Alberta's) came after 1900. Canadian land seekers often migrated to Minnesota and Dakota Territory in the 1870s, but after railroads reached Winnipeg and beyond between 1878 and 1883, the Canadian migration shifted north of the border.[78] Eastern Canadians, Americans, Irish, Scots, English, Poles, Lithuanians, and various Scandinavians marched behind the Canadian Pacific Railway into southwestern Saskatchewan in 1882 and 1883 to become ranchers.[79] The Canadian homestead law of 1872 copied the American one of 1862 but bettered it by reducing the proving-up period from five years to three and making a second 160-acre tract available on credit for "preemption." Settlers could acquire even more from nearby Canadian Pacific grant land.

Manitoba, the first western province, had known the fur trade. Until the 1870s its people were largely métis, French and Indian mixed-bloods. In the 1880s Anglophones from Ontario and Europeans of at least fourteen different ethnicities overwhelmed them. By 1886 Manitoba's population was 109,000, already a third of Dakota's; only 7 percent were métis. Winnipeg battened on the presence of the Canadian Pacific and reached 20,000 people by 1886. The Indian and métis village of 1870 had turned into a "Protestant, conservative, and very British" city by the late 1880s.[80] The Canadian Pacific reached Calgary in 1883 and opened southern Alberta first to cattle ranching and then to farm settlement; ranchers poured in, fences breached the open range, and by the 1890s farmers were crowding the ranchers.[81]

Much the same was happening below the border in Montana. The "long drives"—the escorting of herds of semiferal Texas cattle up the Chisholm and other trails to the Kansas railheads of Abilene, Ellsworth, Wichita, Caldwell, and Dodge City—began in the late 1860s, bringing about the short-lived, but mythically eternal, era of the cattle towns. The drives to Kansas continued until 1873, when a national depression began, and resumed from 1879 to 1886 with a different objective, the stocking of the grasslands of Wyoming and Montana. There, cattlemen mused, their animals would roam unfenced, fattening and multiplying just as buffaloes had done for so long.

Whether in Abilene, Kansas, in 1867 or Calgary, Alberta, in 1890, the newcomers were transient young men, as in a Gold Rush camp, with women almost absent except for a few to entertain and do laundry.[82] There may have been thirty-five thousand young men riding on the long drives in those twenty-some years. The majority were white, often from Texas, where the drives began, but sixteen hundred (as of 1890) were black, also from Texas or nearby, many of them former slaves, looking for a new life, like the black mountain men of the 1820s and 1830s.[83] Some of the cowboys, white and black, settled down on Great Plains farms; others got jobs on railroads or in the many new small towns; some remained ranch hands the rest of their lives. Abilene and Dodge City had even more ephemeral populations than early mining camps because the drives were seasonal. Most cattle towns quickly withered away when more accessible railheads replaced them. One, Wichita, survived to take on more diverse economic functions; others, like Abilene and Ellsworth, were engulfed and given second lives by the westward progression of farm settlement.

Cattle towns boomed and busted so quickly that censuses usually missed their peaks. Most did not even appear until after their cattle town phases were over and they had become something else, usually county seat towns servicing the surrounding farms. Abilene, whose cattle town heyday lasted from 1867 to 1872, soon became a farm town. By 1890 the county around it contained over twenty-two thousand people, many of them Germans or Swedes, raising corn and wheat. Its rambunctious days were long done; it had become the very plausible boyhood home of Dwight D. Eisenhower.[84]

By the mid-1880s cattle and sheep overpopulated the northern plains from western Kansas and eastern Colorado north to Canada. A disaster impended. A Forest Service inspector wrote some years later: "Not an acre of the land was left unoccupied, and ranges that for permanent and regular use would have been overstocked with a cow to every 100 acres were loaded until they were carrying one to every ten. . . . No one provided any feed for the winter, the owners preferring to risk the losses. Gradually the native grasses disappeared."[85]

In early January 1886 a fearsome blizzard pounded western Kansas, Indian Territory, and the Texas Panhandle, building enormous snowdrifts. Temperatures plunged fifty or sixty degrees to sub-zero within an hour. Of an estimated 2,500,000 cattle on the northern plains, at least 10 percent drowned, froze, or starved. "Piles of dead cattle," one rancher recalled, "were stacked so high along the fences [that] succeeding waves of drift cattle could cross to the other side on the frozen carcasses and hard-packed snow."[86] In the immediate aftermath of this disaster, everyone got hurt. Stockmen and farmers went broke; towns stagnated and shrank. Depression beset ranching and farming in the plains until the late 1890s.

Arizona and New Mexico were touched by both mining and farm settlement between 1846 and 1890, but only lightly. *Nuevomexicanos* spread out in several directions from their traditional base in the Rio Grande Valley. Sheepmen from Santa Fe headed east to Las Vegas (New Mexico) and from there crossed the plains into the Texas and Oklahoma panhandles. From Taos they pushed up the Rio Grande into Colorado, founding Trinidad. They took sheep westward from Albuquerque and southward from Belen. By the 1870s and 1880s they had begun to meet Anglo ranchers and settlers, and their expansion halted. By 1900, however, the *nuevomexicanos*, descendants of Oñate's band of 1598, had created scores of new settlements throughout the area and grown to more than 140,000 people in New Mexico, Colorado, and eastern Arizona.[87] Anglo drovers, then ranchers and cowboys arrived in eastern New Mexico and Colorado with the long drives, and many stayed. The army squeezed the Navajos onto reservations in the 1860s and the Apaches in the 1880s, and after the Santa Fe and other railroads had laid their tracks across the desert, white settlement followed.

Over in Arizona, Prescott began in 1864 as the Union administrative center, and Phoenix in 1870 as a mining camp. Unlike other places in Arizona and New Mexico, they were devoid of any Hispanic past, although Prescott did have one Chinese pioneer and received more Chinese in the late 1860s.[88] Anglo-Americans arrived in Arizona by various routes. Virginian Andrew Ruffner and his wife appeared in 1867, after losing their farm in the Civil War. Ruffner first tried mining and found some rich lodes but had no way to bring out the ore. He arrived in Maricopa in 1882 and Prescott shortly after that and then invited three of his brothers, who visited, stayed, and ultimately brought out the ore or sold it to companies that did.[89] In 1872 "Big Mike" Goldwater appeared in Phoenix, one of the first Jews there, and opened a dry goods store. Others followed and started tailor shops, pharmacies, pawnshops, and jewelry stores.[90] Isaac Isaacson, a partner in a San Francisco pawnshop, homesteaded near Nogales in 1880, not to farm but to put a store on his claim. He succeeded, sold the store, and moved to Los Angeles in 1883, while his brother Jacob remained as postmaster.[91] In 1879 Tombstone popped on the scene as a mining boomtown, and within three years upward of four hundred Jews among its fifty-three hundred people were running newsstands, barbershops, restaurants, and all sorts of stores. Among the better-known Tombstone Jews, Josephine Marcus became Marshal Wyatt Earp's third consort in 1882, and A. H. Emanuel ran a blacksmith and haulage business and was elected mayor in 1896, 1898, and 1900.[92] In greater numbers, homesteading Mormons filtered south into northern Arizona from Utah during the 1870s and 1880s.

But the weight of tradition and population remained in New Mexico, where the territorial government created a Bureau of Immigration in 1880 just as the eponymous railroad reached the city of Santa Fe. Over the next thirty years the bureau assiduously distributed hundreds of thousands of promotional blurbs to all takers.[93] Often, with laws and traditions of Hispanics and Anglos clashing, the former lost land and the latter gained it.[94] Litigation and political finagling over the 1835 Mora land grant in the mountains of northeastern New Mexico, for example, home to several thousand *nuevomexicano* sheepherders, alienated it to the Santa Fe "Ring" and other

Anglos.[95] In Santa Fe and elsewhere in New Mexico, however, the Hispanic elite were often able to preserve much of their position and property. Santa Fe, virtually stable for a quarter century after the American takeover in 1846, rose between 1870 and 1880 from 4,765 to 6,635, mostly from new Anglos. But the city peaked in the early 1880s, and by 1910 it had reverted nearly to its 1850 level. New Mexico, despite the railroads and the ranchers, was not yet fully part of the settlement frontier.[96]

The New Northwest

The historic Old Northwest between the Great Lakes and the Ohio River opened to American settlement in the late eighteenth century, and the new Pacific Northwest of mining, ranching, and farming (and combinations of them) opened in the late nineteenth. The arrivals of the 1860s were (as usual) young, and about three out of five male. Many were refugees from the Civil War, not necessarily from combat itself but from avoidance. Going west avoided the draft; it also avoided the anguish of having to fire on a brother or cousin or dying for a cause not heartfelt. For some the struggle was culturally too unbearable.[97]

By the 1880s railroads connected Portland, Tacoma, and Seattle with San Francisco to the south and with the Twin Cities two thousand miles to the east. The United States' purchase of Alaska in 1867 "hemmed in" British Columbia, already depressed after the Fraser River gold rush had exhausted itself, shrinking B.C.'s population from 13,624 in 1861 to 8,631 in 1866.[98] In a curious way, this led to more rapid homesteading in Saskatchewan and Alberta, some of it by Americans. Fearing another American takeover, Canadian lawmakers devised a "National Policy" to connect Vancouver with eastern Canada by railroad and also to populate the intervening prairies. By 1887 Vancouver had its railroad, and its population jumped from 2,000 to about 14,000 in the next four years.[99] Similarly in Washington Territory, the Northern Pacific linked St. Paul with Portland (with a branch to Tacoma) in 1883. Seattle, temporarily disadvantaged, connected with Vancouver in 1891 and to St. Paul in 1893 via the Great Northern. Thereafter Seattle's lead over Tacoma, Portland, and Vancouver as the largest city in the region never faltered.

Before these rail lines opened, settlers came by wagon, the final voyagers on the Overland Trail. By 1880 farms covered the Willamette Valley south of Portland, the original objective of the migrants; the eastern littoral of Puget Sound, shared with loggers; and the Walla Walla Valley and Palouse country of southeastern Washington. Oregon and Washington each had a hardworking Bureau of Immigration, broadcasting pamphlets in German, Danish,

Norwegian, and Swedish with great success, to judge by the origins of the immigrants who responded. At the same time, in northern Idaho, mining became thoroughly industrial; soon Coeur d'Alene and Kellogg suffered fights between miners and mineowners as bitter as any in the East.[100]

The railroads greatly augmented the population and economic growth of Idaho, Oregon, and in particular Washington, which soared from 75,000 in 1880 to 357,000 in 1890, taking it past Oregon's 318,000.[101] Oregon attracted Swedes and other Europeans, though its base was the earlier arrived and highly reproductive Overland Trail settlers from the Missouri and Ohio valleys. Several thousand Chinese lived in Portland by 1890, most of them, as usual, men.[102] By 1885 3,200 Chinese miners lived in the Tacoma-Seattle coastal strip, unnerving white workers. In early November a white mob forced several hundred Chinese to leave. Army units deployed to protect the Chinese. The episode paralleled the anti-Chinese outbreak at Rock Springs, Wyoming, two months earlier.[103] In 1887, 31 Chinese miners were murdered near Hell's Canyon in northeastern Oregon for the fifty thousand dollars in gold they reputedly possessed. A gang of whites shot 10 Chinese with rifles one day, and 21 the next, in one of the worst racial atrocities in the mining West. Three men were arrested but ran off, 3 others were tried and acquitted.[104]

Over two million acres in the Columbia Valley and southeastern Washington went under the plow. Sheep grazing started in earnest in arid eastern Oregon, and lumbering in the Cascades. Southeastern Washington, centering in Walla Walla, attracted "predominantly Anglo newcomers" from the upper Midwest and elsewhere. Population exploded at a typical frontier 400 percent rate during the 1870s, trees tumbled and wheat flourished, and the area soon began calling itself the Inland Empire.[105] Manufacturing— sawmills, food processing, farm equipment, clothing and housing materials, and the like—had sprung up by 1890 in Portland, Tacoma, and Seattle. A new rail and wheat center in eastern Washington, which began as Spokane Falls in 1873, had only 350 residents by 1880 but 5,000 in 1885, after the Northern Pacific arrived, and 12,000 by 1890; a year later it dropped the "Falls" and became simply Spokane.[106] It overtook Walla Walla as the dominant trade center of the inland Northwest by 1883.[107] By 1890 farms dotted eight counties of southeastern Washington from Spokane to Walla Walla, the lower Columbia River valley, a strip northward from Vancouver (Washington) and up the eastern shore of Puget Sound to Canada, and for the first time the Yakima Valley.[108] Washington, booming since the 1870s, was developing a diversified population, both rural and urban, by the time it achieved statehood in 1889. Native groups, such as the Spokanes and Coeur d'Alenes, were displaced or forced into individual land allotments despite good title but in accord with the assimilationist policy of the time.[109]

Much of Idaho and Nevada remained mining frontiers, sparsely popu-lated. Mines and miners came and went so quickly that the decennial cen-suses recorded only some of them. Even so, the official figures for Nevada reflect part of the roller coaster: 7,000 in 1860, just after the first Comstock Lode silver strike; then 42,000 in 1870, despite the Comstock's collapse in 1864 and the departure of many to new strikes in Idaho and Montana. The second Comstock boom began in 1872 and lasted until 1878, and during those years there may have been as many as 20,000 people in Virginia City and Gold Hill. Over 15,000 were still there in 1880, when the census counted 62,000 in the state. After that, its mines failing, Nevada became the first state to lose population in two successive censuses: 1890, down to 47,000, and 1900, down further to 42,000. The male-female balance—76:24 in 1870 and still 64:36 in 1890—reflected a bonanza society, too transient for wives and children. Roughly half the people present in the 1870s were Irish, English, German, Chinese, or of some other foreign birth. Eureka, in almost the exact center of Nevada, was an explosive example: 7,000 in 1880, only a few hundred a century later.[110]

Some grazing and a little farming began to happen in eastern Nevada. For the most part, however, the "great rotten borough" remained an economic and political appendage of northern California, a demographic yo-yo dependent on mining bonanzas and the Californian and eastern money required to develop them. Lacking groundwater or rainfall, Nevada could not sustain a farm settlement frontier. Without a Yellowstone or a Grand Canyon, it also lacked tourists. The railroad ran through it, not to it.

Idaho, like Nevada, was arid, high, with volatile precious metal mining and a transient four-fifths-male majority, strongly foreign-born in 1870. Chinese worked in mines, Basques in high desert ranges. Southern Idaho, northern Nevada, and eastern Oregon attracted Basques by 1870, coming from their home in the Pyrenees and by way of Argentina and Chile, at first bedazzled by the California Gold Rush. Better at herding sheep than at min-ing, most of them intended to return home, and many did. Some, however, stayed to become owner-operators of sheep farms, marrying the few Basque women in the area, raising families, and making homes in Boise, Reno, and Winnemucca.[111]

But distinguishing Idaho from Nevada was one crucial difference: the Snake River. In southern Idaho the Snake River valley quickly became much more a farm settlement frontier than a mining one like Nevada. Many mid-westerners arrived in the 1860s, hoping to strike gold near the old fur trade post of Boise, and soon found themselves farming. (Central Idaho, with its tree-covered mountains, became mining and timbering country, while the northern panhandle opened to both mines and small farms a little later.) Of the 667 towns in the West in the 1870 Census, 270 sprang up during the 1860s, with a spirit almost as unstable and acquisitive as cattle towns of that era.[112] The youths who left the Midwest in the 1860s became the young adults of the 1870s in Idaho and its neighbors. Their exodus marked the end of frontiers in states like Indiana and Illinois and the beginning of Idaho's. White population, in typical frontier fashion, rose from very few in 1860 to 15,000 in 1870, then doubled to 33,000 in 1880, nearly tripled again to 89,000 in 1890, and doubled and redoubled to 326,000 in 1910—while Nevada's population shrank.

Creating the Mormon Culture Area

Farther up the Snake River valley lived Mormons, not midwesterners. Much has been written about the 1847 trek of several hundred Latter-day Saints under Brigham Young from Council Bluffs, Iowa, along the north bank of the Platte River through the South Pass to the shore of the Great Salt Lake. It was a major part of the overland exodus of the 1840s.[113] Also well recorded is the subsequent gathering of thousands of converts from the East and from northern Europe (especially Britain and Denmark) to Salt Lake City and Utah's Wasatch Front stretching north and south of it. In the 1850s the "Mormon Corridor" probed southwest as far as California, founding San Bernardino. Wagon trains in the 1860s brought more new Mormons across the plains.[114] This initial settlement, rounding out the "apostolic age" of Mormon history, gave Utah thirty thousand people by 1856 and eighty-seven thousand by 1870, almost exactly balanced between males and females, normally distributed as to age-groups. More than any other of that day, theirs was a family migration.[115] Also, early Utah achieved an ethnic and religious homogeneity very unlike the West that surrounded it.

The Mormon core settlement area stretched north from Salt Lake City through Ogden on the transcontinental railroad to Logan (founded 1861) in the Cache Valley, and south through Provo and Manti to St. George (also 1861). It was replete with towns, farms, and ranches by the time the pioneer generation aged and died in the 1870s and 1880s. Agriculture was difficult, but the Mormons learned early to irrigate and kept irrigation under church control. From an economic or engineering standpoint alone, the Saints' irrigation of the Wasatch Front was remarkable, and its theocratic aspect made it unique.[116] Marketing cooperatives also flourished within the encompassing structures of church and community.[117]

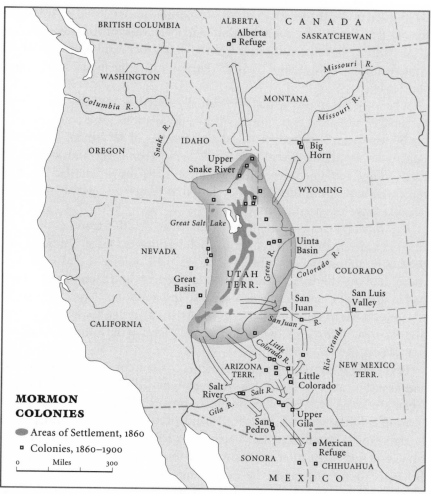

By then the less known expansion of the second generation was well under way. Mormon women were marrying early (half before their twentieth birthdays) and were having many more children than American mothers generally.[118] Even within the fecund Mormon context, marriages happened sooner and more often in the 1860–1880 period than ever again. Polygamy—plural marriage—was not primarily responsible since only a small minority could afford to practice it; moreover, Mormon birthrates have remained high although the church revoked the doctrine in 1890. The theological duty to provide bodies for waiting unborn souls has always played a more direct demographic role.

The expansion of the second generation involved more people than the first migration, and it combined a fast-reproducing, fast-settling farm family frontier, under theocratic guidance, to a degree unparalleled in American history. The Puritan "Great Migration" and its expansion in eastern Massachusetts in the seventeenth century is the only other significant case of an American theocratic frontier. But the Puritan experiment was smaller and shorter-lived.

Where the Mormons settled, they usually stayed. From Salt Lake City to the smaller cities and agricultural villages, populations were unusually stable by American standards, especially by frontier of settlement standards. Religious commitment ensured the settlers "a unifying and stabilizing force." Some settlements were the result of "calls" by church leaders, but most were not. Mormons simply preferred to preserve their way of life by keeping to their own communities.[119]

But what of their many children? As happened on other frontiers of settlement in nineteenth-century America, high fertility and large families—and they were almost never higher and larger than among the Mormons—meant that the children, as they grew into teenagers and then young adults, had to spin off to some new region of cheap Indian-cleared land. In the small Mormon town of Kanab (1871) near the Arizona border, for example, land and water became scarce almost immediately, forcing the founders' children to move on.[120]

Beginning about 1865, Mormon colonies of the second generation spread southward into the Arizona Strip, the region between the state line and the Colorado River, extinguishing the Indian presence.[121] The immense Grand Canyon kept the strip culturally independent of the rest of Arizona, while being below the Utah state line encouraged some of its Mormons to continue polygamy long after the church had forsaken it. In 1877, urged on by Brigham Young just before he died, Saints founded Mesa, Arizona, and planned colonies in Mexico, which began in Chihuahua and Sonora in 1885, partly to avoid federal prosecution under antipolygamy laws. But the main arena of expansion was to the north. In other directions, a geographer points out, they were "hemmed in by a girdle of wastelands [that] could be gleaned at their margins by herds and flocks but were barren and impenetrable by the agricultural colonist." Northward they went into Utah's Cache Valley, then crossed into Idaho for the first successful time in 1860 and in 1863 created sixteen communities near Bear Lake. In a second and larger wave from 1879 through the 1880s, Mormons settled Rexburg, Pocatello, Idaho Springs, and Lewisville along the upper Snake River plain and valley. "Beyond the reach of United States marshals," they founded Cardston, Alberta, in 1887.[122] By 1900 probably twenty thousand Mormons lived in Idaho, Alberta, and southwestern Wyoming.[123]

The Mormons did not have this great region to themselves for long. The

Utes and other native tribes were small and dwindled after the Saints arrived, but non-Mormons quickly appeared. The first were transients on their way to California and the Gold Rush, some as settlers but most as miners, refitting themselves at the Mormon "Halfway House" in Salt Lake City (halfway, approximately, between Missouri and California). With the Golden Spike completing the transcontinental railroad in 1869, Ogden was born, and soon several railroads crossed the Great Basin, spraying watering stations and division points (Pocatello became one) all across Zion. Mines and smelters rose throughout the Wasatch Front, clustering industrial miners and their families, not at all like the nearby Mormon villages.

By 1890 the Great Basin—Utah, southern Idaho, Nevada, and eastern Oregon—was dotted with Mormon communities, railroad hamlets, mining towns, and some villages around which were scattered farms and ranches. A place like Middleton, Idaho, a few miles west of Boise, started in 1864 as an agricultural base for nearby gold miners. At first it had a young male–dominated, strongly foreign-born population. It evolved in the next thirty years toward families and farming, a way of life best characterized as "agri-mining."[124] It was typical, certainly, of many small communities in the Great Basin and beyond, a cash basis kind of place. Not all western towns were like that. Aside from the many Mormon settlements with their strong communitarian theology, examples abound of orderly, nonviolent towns like Sublimity, Oregon, where Upland South (indeed Scots-Irish) traditions of the clan persisted into the twentieth century, and Butte, Montana, with its intricate net of Irish Catholic families, parishes, and labor unions.[125]

California Latifundia

> Latifundia: "great landed estate[s] . . . often held by an absentee owner and typically employing servile or semi-servile labor and primitive agricultural techniques."
> —Webster's Third New International Dictionary

California had some small farmer settlers as far back as Sutter's time and, of course, its Gold Rush. But the striking thing is how the state became an immense producer of crops and livestock, yet *had almost no frontier of settlement in the eastern or midwestern sense.* The state that became in the twentieth century the largest in population *and* in agricultural output did not seriously participate in the frontier-rural, homesteading process that was the experience of so many Americans from the early 1700s to the early 1900s. The geography of rural California is marked typically by large landholdings, not by homesteads and other family farms. It has been so ever since the Spanish and Mexican land grants. The large holdings also very often employed migrant workers. California's technology of production and marketing has been far from "primitive," but otherwise it neatly fits the definition of "latifundia."

Alexis de Tocqueville wrote in 1831 that compared with Europe, the United States was democratic and fast-moving because it was unencumbered by a feudal past. Analogously, California has been faster-moving than the rest of the United States because it was never encumbered with a homesteading past. Instead it moved directly after the American takeover to a more modern, incipiently twentieth-century, form of capitalism. Except for some Indians and Californios, no one there lived as a subsistence farmer. The American Californians found a land system that was latifundist and a class system that was not egalitarian, and when they breathed a raw capitalistic spirit into them, the result was a society very different from that east of the Rockies. Despite antimonopoly feeling as strong as elsewhere in the United States, writes land historian Paul Gates, "Capitalists continued to have their way," concentrating landownership and backing prolatifundist state laws. The federal Timber and Stone Act (1873) and Desert Land Act (1877), hyped as encouragements to homesteaders in the semiarid plains, actually helped lumbermen and monopolists in California, "under the guise of easing the path of the small man to landownership."[126]

The contrast is stark between California and the Great Plains from 1860 to 1890 with regard to landholding and land use. In Kansas and Nebraska a new farm then was typically 160 to 320 acres, a quarter or half section either bought from a railroad or deeded by the federal government or the state from the public domain to an "actual settler" (or someone pretending to be one) under the Homestead Act or some other coexisting land law. The cost of the land itself might well be just a few dollars an acre or nothing at all.

No provision in the law, however, helped settlers break the sod, build a dwelling, plant seed, erect a windmill to pump water, or dig a well. It did not help them fence the garden, the pasture, the cornfield, or the corral and survive until the first crops were harvested and sold. The region had not yet produced. It had not yet generated anything. Its people therefore had to bring their own capital or, more commonly, borrow it. These settlers were small producers—whether of corn, wheat, hogs, or cattle made little difference—and no small producer was significant enough to have any impact on market prices or costs. Typically the family did the work, assisted at harvest by neighbors or hired hands. Laborers from outside the family were not unusual; they were often young people trying to save enough to start their own farms and families. Thus, though land may have been cheap, capital and labor were not. Warts and all, however, the settlement process bore enough resemblance to the Jeffersonian Agrarian Myth that people kept believing in it.

In California, on the other hand, holdings of hundreds or thousands of acres, though mixed with small holdings, were common enough to dominate. Families, individual entrepreneurs, and corporations (led by the Southern Pacific Railroad) owned these domains. The Southern Pacific defended and extended its claims against squatter-settlers by force and through the courts. Farm workers were not future homesteaders but people drawn from a succession of "outsider" racial groups, beginning with Indians in the mission period, Chinese during the Gold Rush and railroad-building phase, then Mexicans, Filipinos, and Bengalis, later the Okies and Arkies of the 1930s, and other Latinos later still. Much of the wealth from the Gold Rush stayed in California, permitting bankers, railroad nabobs, and other wealthy men to invest in cattle, sheep, and wheat and raise them in the Central Valley with the most efficient machinery and methods of the time.

In short, California began and remained a land of efficient, well-capitalized, industrial agriculture, much of it organized in large holdings employing an ethnically second-class contract labor force. It was aggressively capitalistic from the start, whereas settler farmers in the Great Plains were only then beginning the painful shift from traditional semisubsistence life to market-oriented agriculture. Whether we speak of land, labor, or capital, California's rural development differed dramatically from what was happening on the Great Plains at the same time or on settlement frontiers farther east a bit earlier.

No one planned this. Instead Spanish custom, the missions, their secularization, the Gold Rush, and confirmation of land titles by American courts combined to produce it. From 1848 through the 1850s American officials, as the Treaty of Guadalupe Hidalgo required, investigated the validity of the Spanish and Mexican-era land grants, some dating back to the 1780s, others as recent as 1845 or 1846. A claims commission created by Congress in 1851 confirmed many of them. But the hazards and costs of stock raising, heavy land taxes, and protracted litigation kept most of the California dons from enjoying ownership for long.[127] By the time Pío Pico died in the late 1870s, he was broke and "depended on family and friends for his unpretentious subsistence."[128] Don Abel Stearns, the leading Anglo Californio, nearly lost his land too but managed to keep Rancho Santiago de Santa Ana after a two-year lawsuit (1866–1868). To succeed in this, he had to take on partners, one of them James Irvine, a northern Irishman who had joined the Gold Rush in 1849. Irvine's share of the Santa Ana judgment became the basis for the Irvine Ranch, which still owns much of Orange County.[129]

Few of the Californios held on to these grants, and often the Anglo-Americans who took them over either lost them or broke them up. But that was a long process, long enough to avert a rush of Great Plains–type home-steaders. Would-be settlers led their covered wagons into California in the 1840s and early 1850s but could not get title for lack of an official survey; the Land Office was slow in opening for business and slow in deciding anything. It could not act until the claims commission had sorted out the validity of the Mexican grants, and the commission moved with very deliberate speed. As a consequence, the federal government did not survey any California land until 1853, did not sell any until 1858,[130] and accordingly preserved many large holdings against homesteader encroachment.

Except for the lands granted to the Southern Pacific by the U.S. Congress, California's largest holdings began as Spanish or Mexican grants.[131] The 813 claims based on them added up to about 14,000,000 acres, excellent for grazing or crops, much of it in or around Los Angeles, San Francisco, and the Sacramento, San Joaquin, and coastal valleys. The American commis-sioners and courts in the 1850s and 1860s confirmed nearly 9,000,000 acres of these ranchos, and the other 5,000,000 were only partially subdivided.[132]

Regardless of whether the tracts remained in the families of the original grantees or, through sale or litigation, fell to new owners, they remained very large by the usual standards of settlement frontiers. California had 3,000,000 cattle and 1,000,000 sheep by the early 1860s. Although a devastat-ing drought in 1863–1864 ruined many cattle ranchers, huge tracts of over 100,000 acres still existed. Disease-ridden, the cattle herds in southern Cali-fornia dwindled to 13,000 by 1869, but 3,000,000 sheep quickly replaced them.[133] Major examples were the Miller and Lux partnership in the San Joaquin Valley with 700,000 acres, and William S. Chapman's 1,000,000 acres around Fresno in the 1870s. Some of the land barons converted to wheat after 1870, but that too was done on a large scale, using gang plows, steam tractors, combines (by 1886), and other technology new for the time. All this required considerable capital and a migrant labor force, a very dif-ferent enterprise from the smallholding homesteads of Kansas and Nebraska.[134] Nobody went to the Central Valley for anything but enterprise and profits. Sometimes foggy, it gained a reputation for "miasmas," those mythical inventions of nineteenth-century medicine, and a well-founded one for malaria. Health seekers shunned the place as "inherently insalubri-ous" and headed for Los Angeles instead.[135]

When Isaac Lankershim rode into the San Fernando Valley just north of Los Angeles in 1869, it was covered with wild oats. Lankershim bought half the valley for $115,000 ($2 an acre) from Andrés and Pío Pico, put it out to wheat, and hired Isaac N. Van Nuys to manage it. Lankershim died in 1882, but by then Van Nuys had married his daughter and took over the immense wheat farm that almost from the start was a mass-production operation, where "giant combines, drawn by thirty-six horses [or mule teams] and manned by four men, cut a twenty-foot path through the fields—harvesting, threshing, winnowing, and stacking grain in a single operation."[136] Many of the large ranchos continued to flourish in California in the late twentieth century, renamed agribusiness.[137]

As for the Southern Pacific, its story began in Sacramento in 1861. Four storekeepers and an engineer incorporated the Central Pacific Railroad Company. Leland Stanford, Collis Huntington, Mark Hopkins, Charles Crocker (soon to be dubbed the Big Four), and the engineer Theodore Judah, all in their thirties, secured a grant of land and credit from Congress to construct the western segment of the proposed transcontinental railroad.[138] They built it, while keeping control. The Southern Pacific, as the company was renamed after 1865, remained a California entity not beholden to eastern capital. It became the largest single landholder in California by falling heir to federal grants, including the Central Pacific's from Ogden to Sacramento, the yet unbuilt Atlantic & Pacific's from San Francisco to Yuma, and the Oregon & California's route northward to Portland.

The law authorizing the Oregon & California grant provided that the land be sold to actual settlers in 160-acre tracts for no more than $2.50 an acre. But the General Land Office never enforced that provision, and only 128,000 of the grant's 3,728,000 acres were sold as such.[139] All told, the federal government granted in California, either directly to railroads or to the state for railroad building, 20,440,766 acres of public domain, the most given within any state except Montana.[140] The Southern Pacific aggressively sold land to individuals and colonizing groups for small farms.[141] (At least one African-American colony, Pettyville near Stockton, began in the 1880s, but it did not survive long.[142]) Nonetheless it remained an enormous landholder and a leading contributor to California's radically distinctive landholding pattern.

Fresno County, created in 1856, marked the start of the commercialization of the San Joaquin Valley. In the 1860s the Southern Pacific and the federal government sold blocks of land at $2.50 an acre to syndicates. One, the San Joaquin Valley Land Association, by 1875–1877 started building irrigation canals and platted 192 twenty-acre lots selling for $1,000 ($150 down and $12.50 a month with no interest). Other colonies followed, and homesteading never happened. Outside the irrigated tracts, bonanza (latifundist) wheat ranching continued.[143] The city of Fresno began as a four-block plat in 1872 and gained a post office in 1874. By 1880 its eight hundred people lived in "a dusty, straggling village, loosely clustered about the railroad depot." During the 1880s, however, it boomed, reaching more than ten thousand in the 1890 census. In late 1887 the last of the railroad lots were sold.[144] Fresno's future—indeed the whole San Joaquin Valley's—was already in place: irrigated crops, produced by the newest technology, picked by contract labor, and sent to market by the Southern Pacific that ran through it.

Students of California ranching and farming universally agree that the dominant, if not typical, holding, from Spanish times to the present, was and is large. Claimants to land—whether Californios, miners and their successors, or squatters—arrived earlier than the federal land surveyors. The normal method by which the United States conveyed its enormous public domain to "actual settlers," Jefferson's agrarians and their families—by surveying it section by section and then selling it (or, under Homestead, giving it away) through land offices—hardly took place in California. Instead of a frontier of settlement, where young people simultaneously started farms and families, California "largely bypassed the self-sufficient, general farming state of development" and set itself up for large-scale agribusiness from the beginning.[145] Ironically, the process began with Father Serra's mission bells.

Not that there were *no* homesteads in California. There were, and they were sharply contested for. As a result, a higher proportion of attempted homesteads (63 percent) succeeded than in any other state before 1885. From 1866 to 1878 homestead entries of public domain in California totaled 2,250,000 acres, and private individuals bought another 7,000,000 acres, reflecting strong demand.[146] Between 1860 and 1900, 147,000 homesteads and preemptions were filed for in California. Many, however, were never true homesteads but dummy entries soon combined into large holdings. Thus by 1900 almost 5,000 California farms averaged 4,000 acres each, a far cry from the homestead of 160 or 320 acres. Farms larger than 1,000 acres accounted for almost two-thirds of California's 28,000,000 acres in farmland.[147]

Amid these huge numbers and the upheavals that rent California's history between 1848 and 1890, Indian dispossession persisted. The government ignored their presence and treated the land as empty, surveying it, putting it up for homestead or sale, and transferring it to white settlers. If any Indians lived there, they were out of luck.[148] One such case arose when whites began homesteading the San Pasqual Valley near Escondido in far southern California in the late 1860s. They convinced officials to leave the valley open to homesteading instead of creating a reservation for the Kumayaay band of Mission Indians who had lived there beyond memory. The settlers built houses, thus satisfying the law as "actual settlers," and they had the sheriff serve an eviction notice on the Indians. Then, ever so generously, they employed a few Indians in odd jobs and let them keep 40 acres to live on, as well as their old church and cemetery. With towering audacity, they pleaded that "we only took 120 acres" rather than the 160 they were "entitled" to. Only in 1911 was the San Pasqual reservation created on 1,400 acres "not claimed by any settlers"[149] (because the land was worthless). The reservation would not grow much.

The Future and It Worked: Creating Pasadena and Los Angeles

If the eviction of the Kumayaay was one microcosm of California history, the creating of Pasadena was another. Pasadena, tucked under the San Gabriel Mountains about eight miles northeast of downtown Los Angeles, just north of Mission San Gabriel, has had several claims to fame: as the site of the New Year's Day Rose Bowl football game and occasionally the Super Bowl, in the 1940s for the Pasadena Playhouse, and in 1910 as "the richest city per capita in America," a "millionaire's retreat." Since the 1890s several opulent resort hotels served as winter homes for well-heeled New Yorkers and Chicagoans, who were perhaps the first snowbirds, Florida still being naught but swamps and sand.[150]

Pasadena began in 1873 as an investment or speculation idea. Boom and bust, and occasional quiet success, typified hundreds of towns in Kansas, Nebraska, and the rest of the West through the 1880s. But Pasadena was not Abilene, or Dodge City, or Ogden, or Coeur d'Alene. It got rich in a hurry and stayed rich. Its very first months displayed an aura of fast-track enterprise that set it apart from all those county seats and mining towns in the plains and basin and defined it as peculiarly, prototypically Californian.

The future Pasadena, as explained earlier, devolved between the 1830s and 1850s from part of Mission San Gabriel to the large Rancho San Pasqual and then to John Griffin, an army doctor, to whom "the opportunity presented itself" to foreclose on thousands of acres. In 1873 a group of Indianapolis men with money to invest had been impressed by Charles Nordhoff's popular new book *California: For Health, Pleasure, and Residence*. They also considered Texas and Louisiana but decided that "Southern California was the spot unifying the blessings of the tropics without their heat, malaria, or enervating influences."[151] Forming the "California Colony of Indiana," they sent Daniel M. Berry as their agent, probably on the new transcontinental railroad, to scout for land.

Arriving in San Francisco in mid-August 1873, Berry consulted with a rich Californio and another man knowledgeable about ranchos. They recommended he look around San Diego.[152] Berry sailed there and noted that the "spacious and beautiful bay of San Diego . . . is destined to form an important feature in the future trade of the United States." It was inevitable because "it is the only safe and spacious harbor for seven hundred miles of the coast of Southern and Lower California, and is the terminus of the great Texas and Pacific railroad which is now being rapidly built from Shreveport to this place."[153] (As it happened, Los Angeles got a railroad first, in 1876.)

Berry liked San Diego, but after sailing up to Los Angeles, he was even more impressed with the San Fernando Valley—except that it would need expensive artesian wells and irrigation. "We are told that grain has been raised in the valley, (wheat, barley, rye, and oats) in abundant crops without irrigation; but we saw no stubble of this year's growth . . . and hence conclude that these great grain crops grew there previous to 1869, and not since the dry years came on." Fruit trees, especially orange trees, were the investors' preference. But in the huge, dry San Fernando Valley, trees would require artesians.[154] Berry kept looking.

A week later he was writing his Indianapolis principals about a 2800-acre tract just east of a "wooded canyon" (where the Rose Bowl now sits) and just below the San Gabriel Mountains. "By judicious management the wood can be made to pay the cost of the land entirely in three years," he claimed. A railroad depot was already nearby, and "it is likely that the great through railroad" from San Bernardino to the San Fernando Valley and on to San Francisco "will go right across our tract." Crucially, "the streams from deep in the mountains are turbid with fresh rainwater." And the germ of speculation: "I think we can get out water enough to sell to parties on the south [of the tract, now South Pasadena] who have no water." The bottom line: "For humanity's sake let us buy the 2800 acres and be happy. . . . I hope you will telegraph me to take it all. . . . It is better to pay $10 per acre here right in town as it were than to pay $1 per acre 60 miles off." The prospects were exceedingly attractive: "The fruit growers here are a much more prosperous class than the commercial men. The same time and labor devoted to fruit here that we give at home to business would make us happy and rich in a short time."[155]

The California Dream—capitalistic but with a permanence missing in the Gold Rush—was taking a new shape. Berry wrote, "The aristocracy here work and raise fruit. People who come here expecting to have a social status and a good living from their antecedents in the East, will find they are d——— fools." When his wagon broke down one night, four men helped him fix it:

> The chap who [repaired?] the wagon was a lawyer once . . . and a graduate of Harvard with the consumption, and rich besides. He runs a vineyard. The chap who went for a wrench at a ranch was nephew of Edward Atkinson the great Free-trader, a graduate of Harvard, and

keeps sheep for a living. The chap who owned the old wagon, is an ex-judge, was a student of Judge Storey and Parsons at Harvard Law School, once an editor in Missouri, now runs a vineyard. The chap who lifted the wagon was a Senator 4 years in Nebraska. The chap who fixed the wheel and killed a tarantula was myself. All jolly crew, and all spoiling for work. Raise little orange plants to sell, raise grapes the third year to sell, raise limes in two years to sell, it will take about two years to conquer an income from unimproved land.[156]

The national financial panic of 1873 struck at exactly this time, throwing the Indianapolis investors into a bearish crouch. The California Colony dissolved. Although Berry kept pleading for funds, no money came. Instead one investor, Calvin Fletcher (of Indianapolis's Fletcher bank), went out and saw for himself. Fletcher agreed with Berry. "We have a good tract well located in every respect and healthful. . . . The climate is all that could be desired so far."[157] Five surviving shareholders went ahead with the purchase of 3,962 acres from Griffin in late December 1873 and incorporated themselves as the San Gabriel Orange Grove Association.[158]

Berry was smitten with California. He wrote Helen Elliott, wife of investor Thomas Elliott, "California is a new unfinished country, and hasn't a Presbyterian church on every corner and a sidewalk and a serving society in front of every house. All is new, romantic, rude, quaint, peculiar. The wants of the people are fewer than in a rigorous climate. . . . If one waits for Eastern improvements before coming land will be so dear that few can buy it. So I am willing to take the country barefooted and wait for shoes & stockings."[159] Berry and associates paid $25,000 for the land and another $25,000 for improvements over the next twelve months. In early 1874 they renamed the place "Pasadena, an Indian name for the Key of the Valley."[160] Later that spring Berry told his more conservative colleagues in Indianapolis to forget about the gold standard, support greenbacks, and "let corn alone." He exhorted them to buy another thirty acres "of orange land inside city limits at $40 an acre. Cheap . . . cut it into 5 acre lots and make a good thing out of it."[161]

In a matter of weeks other Hoosiers arrived. They and Berry wanted nothing to do with corn and bought more orange tree seedlings. They also purchased and soon were selling real estate. The shifts from corn to oranges to urban development happened in their case within a season. By June 1874 they had laid out Orange Grove Avenue, replete with a water main and lined with orange trees. A month later Berry identified himself as a partner in the "Los Angeles Real Estate Agency," selling "Lands of Every Description, and City Property . . . Money Loaned, and Colony Lands Selected." Within two

years the group had built forty houses, subdivided the tract, planted thousands of trees and grapevines, and begun one of the most commercially successful land developments yet done in the United States. Their speed, scale,
and success were no longer Midwestern, no longer at the pace, frenzied
though it sometimes was, of the settlement frontier. In 1886 Pasadena incorporated as a municipality, and in 1890 the first Tournament of Roses
marched along Orange Grove Avenue.

Though Pasadena did become the "Key of the Valley" by 1890, Los Angeles made some critical moves of its own in the forty-four years after the
American takeover of 1846. Founded as a Spanish *villa* in 1781, a center of
hide and tallow trade and the home base of Californios like Don Abel
Stearns during the Mexican period, Los Angeles was still a "sleepy pueblo," a
"nondescript village of less than 3,000," in 1846, by Anglo-American
accounts. Change came slowly. The action was in northern California. As
San Francisco passed the metropolitan threshold of a hundred thousand
people by 1870, Los Angeles remained a minuscule town of six thousand
huddled around a plaza, like Santa Fe, still mostly Mexican, Indian, black,
and mestizo.[162] The ranchos were losing their competitive place, and Mexicans who arrived from Sonora in the 1850s remained, for the most part,
landless and transient. Neither landlord nor peasant should have been confident. Theft of cattle and horses, and other criminality, increased. Although
Anglos did their share of it, Mexicans were disproportionately blamed.[163]
The last Mexican mayor left office in 1872.[164]

Population jumped to 11,000 in 1880 and during the 1880s burst to 50,000
in the city and 101,000 in the county. Its Hispanic character was suppressed
into the barrio under the Anglo inundation, well under way when the
Southern Pacific arrived in 1876. That made the area's climatic and entrepreneurial charms accessible, and the coming of the Santa Fe in 1885 made them
doubly available. By then, as someone long ago remarked, Los Angeles was
"a real estate boom waiting to happen." Happen it did in the late 1880s.
Competition for passengers between the Santa Fe and the Southern Pacific
produced a rate war in early 1887. Prior to that, a round-trip ticket between
Kansas City and Los Angeles cost $125, almost four months' wages for an
eastern factory worker. In 1885 the fare fell to $30, in 1886 to $10, then to $5,
and on one day in March 1887 to a ludicrous $1. Fares rose again, but not for
some time above $25 from St. Louis and only a little more from Chicago
or New York.[165] Freight rates and steamship charges dropped similarly.[166]
The result was a migration to southern California not as sudden as but
ultimately much larger than the Gold Rush forty years earlier to northern
California.

As the townsite boom collapsed on the Great Plains in the winter of

1886–1887, southern California became a safety valve for midwesterners, townspeople and countryfolk alike. No one has figured exactly how many merchants, promoters, farmers, lawyers, engineers, and others who were facing drought and failure in Kansas and Nebraska bailed out to Los Angeles. Certainly many "professional boosters" and "the townsite sharks of the Middle West" alighted from westbound trains.[167] But not every immigrant took in his neighbor's mortgage; not everyone was rapacious or foolish. One town near Corona was "laid out by a party of Methodist men from Halstead, Kansas, who after buying 30,000 acres, returned to Kansas to fetch their wives and children and settle the land."[168] And just in time, for Halstead, on the treeless prairie between Wichita and Hutchinson, had already peaked. Edward L. Doheny arrived in 1892 with mining experience and promptly brought in the first of Los Angeles County's great oil fields. Less spectacularly successful but soon to be comfortable were the thousands of midwesterners who began organizing state societies in the 1880s. Hamlin Garland found the Iowa Society people "incredibly unaesthetic and yet they were worthy, fine serious folk."[169]

Real estate sales in Los Angeles topped one million dollars in January 1886, rose to three million in December, then soared to twelve million in July 1887. Developers platted dozens of new towns. Some came to nothing, but others succeeded famously: Riverside beginning in 1886, Hollywood in 1887, then Inglewood, Redondo Beach, Long Beach, Sierra Madre, Claremont, Ontario, Azusa and Cucamonga, Glendale, Burbank, and many others. The state carved Orange County out of southern Los Angeles County in 1889. Subdivisions multiplied within Los Angeles and Pasadena. Twenty-five new towns appeared in the thirty-six miles from Los Angeles to the San Bernardino County line along the Santa Fe and the Southern Pacific.[170]

The boom lasted about eighteen months and was clearly over by early 1889. The usual detritus from expired land booms appeared all over the county: unsold lots; townsites without people; uncollected taxes; some personal fortunes wiped out. But the difference between this "crash" and those of town builders and homesteaders on the Great Plains was that southern California had a solid base. Kansas and Nebraska had only land, wheat, corn, and livestock, and when their values and prices collapsed, nothing remained except an interminable wait for recovery. That took more than ten years.

Southern California survived its crash and went on its way. Though failed real estate speculations hit Pasadena hard, the low Santa Fe fares and the resort hotels continued to attract "wintering health seekers."[171] Climate and capitalism combined again. Following the lead of Isaiah Hellman's Farmers and Merchants Bank, the Los Angeles banks had lent conservatively and on farmland valuations rather than anticipated rises.[172] As a result, the worst of the paper speculation occurred outside the established financial structure. Southern California before, during, and after the boom produced millions of gallons of wine from 150,000 acres of vineyards, and the citrus industry had become even larger; no droughts or hailstorms there.[173] Los Angeles hurried to build its streets, waterworks, sewerage, schools, and other civic infrastructure.[174] Although fourteen million dollars in property values may have evaporated in 1888–1889, as the county government estimated, "a substantial deposit of wealth and population" remained nonetheless. People were surviving, someone said, on "faith, hope, and climate."[175]

In direct contrast with what was happening on the Great Plains, the southern California bust of 1887–1889 was a shakeout, not a disaster. The railroads kept unloading travelers—the middle class in the city and the wealthy at the Green and Raymond hotels in Pasadena and the huge, opulent Hotel del Coronado (1887) next to San Diego Bay. In Los Angeles newcomers found two cable rail lines operating in 1885 and 1886 and an electric railway by 1887; electric lights, it went without saying, were also in place.[176] The Southern Pacific and the Santa Fe had vigorously promoted migration and settlement, and they redoubled their efforts when the boom deflated.[177] In Santa Ana, "all speak in unmistakable language of the dawn of an assured and brilliant future," and for once the boosters were right.[178] Travel books whetted emigrants' dreams of the good life: "the fact that hundreds of those who were deemed hopeless invalids on their arrival here are to-day enterprising, energetic and successful capitalists, merchants, manufacturers, farmers and orchardists, attesting the effects of this sun-kissed land and health-renewing climate on the human system; and so long as there are any sufferers from the blizzards, cyclones and other life-destroying elements east of the Rocky Mountains, just so long will Southern California, and Los Angeles in particular, continue to receive thousands annually of the best citizens of the republic, until it becomes the most densely populated portion of the United States."[179]

Salubrity, freedom from extremes of heat or cold, the promise that the climate would cure diseases—especially tuberculosis, the leading killer at that time—had been bringing health seekers to California since the 1870s. Perhaps a third of the migrants primarily sought health, not wealth, and among the health seekers were professionals, writers, and people of means.[180]

Health seekers were not the only California dreamers. Emigrant colonies of different sorts, individuals united for a common purpose, became a feature of California life as early as the 1850s. The Indiana investors who founded Pasadena came together to make profits. Others were secular utopian groups, organized around a variety of socialism or cooperation.

Some were religious; many simply sought health or leisure.[181] Helen Hunt Jackson's best-selling 1884 novel *Ramona* rang the mission bells and romanticized the Indian past beyond reality, evoking a sense of "spiritual awe . . . peacefulness . . . a place of relief from the pressures of modern urban existence."[182] The Los Angeles Chamber of Commerce in 1890 rejected any idea that a serious "bust" had slowed down the city; taxes were rolling in, the ranchos still had abundant land to subdivide; the "best all-the-year-round climate in the United States, if not in the world," remained "wonderfully salubrious and equable. . . . Mad dogs and sunstrokes are never known here."[183] By 1892 Doheny's oil strike had opened another huge source of wealth to Los Angeles.[184]

The promotional literature of the 1870s to 1890s stresses several themes. First, the climate: health is preserved; indeed, desperately ill patients recover. Second, southern California is frontier no longer. Agriculture flourishes. Third, living costs are reasonable; the scenery is wonderful and (hear the mission bells) picturesque. Hope and opportunity abound.[185] The result: regardless of boom or bust, southern California had come to stay. The Californio past, the big ranchos, and (long since) the missions and the Indians had essentially been superseded, and by 1890 the region had more than weathered a storm. It had taken shape as a new kind of American frontier, unlike the ongoing frontiers of settlement, unlike the Gold Rush, even unlike northern California.

There were costs. The rancho-mission culture expired. Less than a century after Serra died, "only a trace of the original settlers' descendants or lifeways survived, hidden away in the city. The Mexican community was segregated in Sonoratown. . . . The few remaining Indians lived on reservations or married Mexicans."[186] But southern California had graduated from backwater. Different from the Gold Rush or San Francisco and northern California, Los Angeles already, by 1890, embodied the idea that "California as the ultimate west was a land of no limits."[187] Its modern history had just begun. So, we can now see, had America's twentieth-century way of life.

The West as an Urban Frontier

A final word about western cities.[188] The West between 1846 and 1890 included both the frontier of settlement, moving westward across the Great Plains, and the mining frontiers, beginning with the northern California Gold Rush. It also comprised cities, what some liked to call an urban frontier. As early as 1880 the West's people had become more urban than rural, despite all the farmers, stockmen, miners, and wide-open spaces. At that early point 30 percent of the population of the mountain and Pacific States lived in cities, compared with 28 percent across the nation. After 1890 the West was to be increasingly more urban than the national average.[189]

A list of western cities as of 1890 must include a few that lie outside our strict definition of the West (the ninety-eighth meridian to the Pacific), starting with Chicago. It was then usually considered western and behaved like it. Between 1880 and 1890 Chicago doubled from half a million to one million, as Los Angeles did in the 1920s. It functioned, Janus-like, as the interface through much of the nineteenth century between the settled United States and the yet unknown West. At Chicago began the railroad trails—the Union Pacific, the Santa Fe, the Burlington—leading to the plains and the Pacific. Though its westernness was fading fast, it could still claim to be the West's gateway, if not its capital.[190]

Beyond the ninety-eighth meridian, only two cities reached a hundred thousand, true metropolitan size, in this period: San Francisco in 1870, two decades out of the Gold Rush, and Denver in 1890, up from forty-eight hundred in 1870. Still a volatile, overgrown, male-skewed mining town, Denver remained for some time about as strong or weak as the ranching and mining within the hinterland it served. But it also became a stable administrative and commercial center. Its foreign-born population was 25 percent, lower than most American cities outside the South, but it offered unusual opportunities. Easily reached by rail, it gained a reputation as a healthy place for tuberculars.[191]

West of the Front Range, Leadville and Aspen rose and fell with silver mining and the roller coaster of federal demand for silver to coin.[192] From south Texas westward across New Mexico and Arizona, the largest places seldom exceeded 10,000. Anglos and *tejanos* uneasily shared San Antonio (38,000 in 1890), while El Paso, after the Southern Pacific and Santa Fe had arrived in the early 1880s, boomed from 736 to more than 10,000 in 1890, serving as an oasis, a health center, and an arrival port for Mexicans beginning to come north by rail from Chihuahua.[193] Albuquerque and Tucson retained a strong Hispanic life around their old plazas, diluted only a little by the railroads passing through them by 1890. Tucson also remained vulnerable to the ups and downs of nearby mining, though it continued to be the largest town in Arizona until 1920.[194] Phoenix managed to become the territorial capital in 1889. Soon the Santa Fe Railroad brought health seekers there too.[195]

Other than Salt Lake City, which reached 45,000 in 1890, the only sizable cities in the West by then, outside California and Denver, were Portland (46,000), Tacoma (36,000), and Seattle (43,000). Seattle did not look promising. Its railroads were still essentially branch lines, and a fire, "caused by the upsetting of a glue pot in a cabinet-maker's shop on Front and Madison Street" in June 1889, destroyed its business district. But its real estate activity was leaving Tacoma and Portland far behind, and the as-yet-unforeseen Alaska gold rush was to decide the rivalry conclusively in Seattle's favor.[196]

It had taken "from time immemorial," through the Spanish and Mexican periods and the forty-three years since the American takeover, to create the West as it was in 1889: a panoramic fifteen-hundred-mile-wide region of farms, ranches, mines, cities, and still mostly magnificent space. The native peoples, the sole and uncontested occupants before 1598, declined in numbers slowly during the fur trade and mission years and then disastrously fast with the Gold Rush and the arrival of the army and settlers on the plains. They were effectively confined to reservations by 1886. In 1889 and 1890 the entire northwestern quarter of the United States—the Dakotas, Montana, Wyoming, Idaho, and Washington—ceased to be territories and became states of the Union. In every state and territory Anglo-Americans and their culture predominated, making a very different region from 1848.

The Census Bureau in its introduction to the 1890 census stated that no meaningful frontier line—meaning a western line of settlement—could be mapped any longer. The young historian Frederick Jackson Turner in 1893 took that to mean that "four centuries from the discovery of America, at the end of a hundred years of life under the Constitution, the frontier has gone, and with its going has closed the first period of American history."[197] Much frontier activity had in fact taken place by 1890: settlement, mining, exploitation of timber or livestock resources, even the creation of cities. But Turner jumped the gun. The frontier, by any definition, was not over. His frontier, the settlement frontier, lived on for more than two decades. By the 1880s, however, a new kind of western living had appeared in southern California. For the next quarter century the story was to be how *both* the settlement frontier *and* this new way of life played themselves out in tandem across the West.

$$4$$

DEFYING
THE
DEPRESSION,
1889–1901

> *Rain follows the plow.*
> —Popular irrigation slogan, 1890s–1900s

> *I fear it's lost.*
> —F. Morris Lookout, Jr., speaking
> of Osage culture, 1983

Depression, Frontier Persistence, and the New West

The notions of a bygone West and a closed frontier were already vivid in 1889. Buffalo Bill was packing audiences in, and in 1893 the genteel, academic version of the same idea was to issue from the pen and voice of Frederick Jackson Turner. The reality was different. The process of frontier settlement, of European-stock people displacing the natives, turning prairies into farms, and buffalo ranges into cattle and sheep pastures, paused in 1889. The settlement frontier had moved west from the Atlantic for nearly two hundred years, capturing and converting ever more land and in the process (helped by railroads) tying the lives of midwestern and western farmers ever more closely to distant markets. A young person looking west from Chicago at that time, thinking of "free" land, might well see in the mind's eye thousands of square miles out toward the Rockies, just waiting, it seemed, for homesteaders' plows.

Homesteading was deeply ingrained. By 1889 it was a long-sanctioned, traditional American behavior pattern. It had to end someday, and that day finally arrived in the 1920s. But for another thirty years or more, hundreds of thousands of people pressed westward beyond the 100th meridian toward the mountains, filling the High Plains of Montana, Wyoming, Colorado, and New Mexico with their farms and ranches. Why they did so and whether they were wise to try are good questions, but try they did. As of 1889, the traditional settlement process remained not solely in the past but decidedly in the present and future, even though the Northeast, Midwest, and South were long beyond their settlement days.

In truth, two great dramas were running simultaneously in much of the West in 1889. The traditional settlement frontier narrative was playing itself out on the Great Plains, at the same time that a new, metropolitan story had already begun in southern California and a few other places. On the Great Plains, from Texas to the Dakotas, people were in an uproar about farm problems that were essentially nineteenth-century matters: currency in circulation; mortgages; freight rates; the Populists' triad of money, land, and transportation. In California people were exercised about water, fruit growing, Pacific trade, and urban real estate, a constellation of concerns appropriate to the twentieth century, a new world of possibilities just opening up.

And so for most Americans the West remained remote and mysterious, the region where the last chapter of the country's traditional frontier story was winding down but where the first chapter of the twentieth-century metropolitan story was revving up. A vast area with as yet a tiny population, it was as future-oriented as any American region ever was. The Agrarian Myth of Jefferson and all those homesteaders, so strong still, would shrink in the next hundred years to *Life*'s "greedy farmers," while other myths, notably the California Dream and the cowboy culture, were to continue to enthrall and inspire action.[1]

The "Gay Nineties" were not gay at all, even in the traditional sense. The image of bicycles built for two, overdressed bathers on boardwalks, early ragtime, and general frivolity may describe a few of the people some of the time. For most Americans the decade brought economic stringency, even misery. On the settlement frontier of the Great Plains, the boom had already burst by 1888. The agrarian South was doing no better. For the industrializing Northeast and Great Lakes, prosperity and high employment overheated into a shaky inflationary phase in the early 1890s and then collapsed utterly in the spring and summer of 1893. The Panic of 1893 ushered in the worst depression the nation had seen up to that point, and the Great Depression of the 1930s, though it lasted longer, was hardly more severe. In 1894 the official unemployment rate passed 18 percent (the real rate was higher) and did not fall below 10 percent until 1899.[2]

As the word quickly reached Europe that jobs in America had dried up, immigration fell drastically. An upheaval in politics reflected the downheaval in economics: in 1894 and 1896 Republicans won sweeping victories that installed them as the majority party for most of the next thirty-five years, until hapless Herbert Hoover presided over the 1929 crash and the onset of the Great Depression.[3] The 1890s—as it turned out, sandwiched between the two prosperity decades of the 1880s and the 1900s—were a depressed and difficult interlude.

The West by no means escaped these events. Parts of it, however, especially the intermountain states, did not do badly during the 1890s. Nevada lost population, but every other western state or territory expanded faster than the nation, the whole region almost twice as fast.[4] The "frontier" most definitely did not close in 1890.

These were times of which myths are made. The "Old West" of present memory reaches back for many of its icons to the 1870s and 1880s. In fact most of the mythic West derives from the brief time of 1865–1890 and the confined space of the Great Plains and Rockies, which are just a small part of the long history and vast realm of the American West. Yet as that moment closed, many signs pointed toward the metropolitan twentieth century. In 1889 Crazy Horse's destruction of Custer was only thirteen years back, but the first Tournament of Roses was soon to take place in Pasadena. The gunfight at Tombstone's OK Corral was only eight years past, but Stanford University was about to begin classes, and the University of California had been operating for over twenty years. Stagecoaches and freight wagons were still a common sight, but railroads crisscrossed the region and connected all major points. Geronimo gave himself up only in 1886, and the "Battle" of Wounded Knee was still ahead in 1890; but Native American armed resistance had collapsed for all practical purposes, after four hundred years of European pressure. (That, not the frontier, was what really ended in 1890.) And Indian Territory was about to be opened, in salamilike slices, to white settlers.

The story of western settlement from 1889 to 1901 is not so much one of occupying new areas as of preparing to do so when prosperity returned. Except for the Oklahoma land rush, the 1890s were not remarkable for new settlement. But the decade did bring serious, broader than local efforts to control water resources through public works and irrigation, a process that became a major theme of western development in the twentieth century. Industrial mining and mining exploration continued prosaically through the 1890s; the silver market crashed when Congress repealed silver purchases in 1893; the gaudy episodes of the Cripple Creek (1893) and Klondike (1897) gold strikes captured most of the attention. Seven new western states entered the Union between 1889 and 1896, and Hawaii became an American territory in 1898. Amid all this, the West's urban proportion kept increasing. Its cities continued to attract health seekers, the idle rich, the middling hopefuls, the improvement-searching immigrants from Europe, a few from

Asia, and a good many from mid-America. For the nation, it was a depressed decade, but for the West, not a dull one.

Indian Territory Becomes Oklahoma

Kansas has had 105 counties since 1886. In each one is a Register of Deeds Office. In central and western Kansas these offices date back to the 1870s and 1880s, and from those years remain heavy, elephant-folio volumes, their stiff rag pages covered with ornate Gilded Age handwriting entering every sale, purchase, mortgage, sheriff's deed, cemetery lot, or quitclaim. In some counties the furious rate of transactions from 1883 to 1888 required a book a year. After that, however, the big books bespeak quiet grief. A single volume suffices for several years until well into the 1890s, and most of the entries are foreclosures and sheriff's sales. It takes no skill to pinpoint the end of the Kansas land boom, county by county; it happened in late 1887.

Only in Indian Territory could a boom continue. Surrounded by white-settled land on three sides, in Kansas, Texas, and Arkansas, Indian Territory increasingly looked like the protected salient it was. In the 1830s the Five Civilized Tribes of southeastern Indians had been removed there from Tennessee, Georgia, and Alabama, presumably placed out of the harm's way of white encroachment and conflict. Cherokees got the northeast corner, Creeks and Choctaws the southeast corner, and Chickasaws and Seminoles west of them in what became south-central Oklahoma.[5] Within thirty years, however, white settlement approached again. By the late 1880s, pressed by settlers disgusted with Kansas but still eager for land, Congress contrived to open these Indian lands to whites.

By the mid-1880s many white Americans believed the time was ripe for a major change in federal Indian policy. The era of warfare was about over; the Plains Indians had been subdued and concentrated on reservations, and the Apaches soon would be. Indian numbers continued to dwindle, and the more Darwinian of the whites convinced themselves that since only the fit survive, the Indians would either disappear before long or be absorbed into the general population. Humanitarians in effect agreed: the only salvation for the remaining Indians was to acculturate them in special schools and to promote their shift from tribal to individual property ownership, or "severalty." Hundreds of whites already lived in Indian Territory, many married to Indians. Why not put them all on an equal footing?

In 1887 Congress passed the General Allotment Act, better known as the Dawes Severalty Act. Under it, tribal lands would be "allotted" to Indian heads of families, who would then farm their allotments and, after a few years, receive title, just like white homesteaders. The Five Civilized Tribes

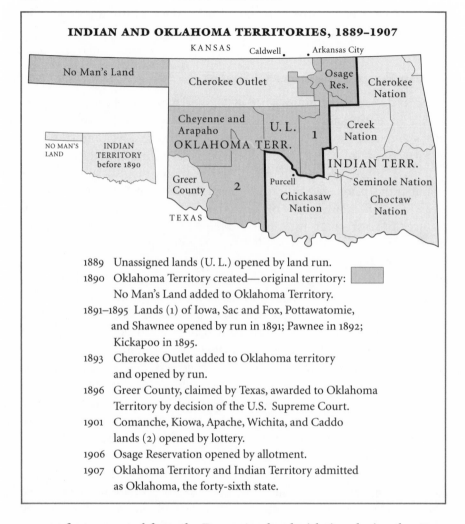

INDIAN AND OKLAHOMA TERRITORIES, 1889–1907

1889 Unassigned lands (U. L.) opened by land run.
1890 Oklahoma Territory created—original territory:
      No Man's Land added to Oklahoma Territory.
1891–1895 Lands (1) of Iowa, Sac and Fox, Pottawatomie,
      and Shawnee opened by run in 1891; Pawnee in 1892;
      Kickapoo in 1895.
1893 Cherokee Outlet added to Oklahoma territory
      and opened by run.
1896 Greer County, claimed by Texas, awarded to Oklahoma
      Territory by decision of the U.S. Supreme Court.
1901 Comanche, Kiowa, Apache, Wichita, and Caddo
      lands (2) opened by lottery.
1906 Osage Reservation opened by allotment.
1907 Oklahoma Territory and Indian Territory admitted
      as Oklahoma, the forty-sixth state.

were at first exempted from the Dawes Act, but legislation during the 1890s included them. Beginning in 1896, the Cherokees and other Indians were "enrolled"—in effect, registered as bona fide members of the tribe, eligible for allotments from tribal lands—and in 1898 tribal governments, courts, laws, and landownership were abolished. Oklahoma Territory, created in 1890 out of the western part of Indian Territory, then absorbed the eastern part.[6]

Potential settlers, impatient and landless in Kansas or Texas, coveted the area. Border town merchants and the railroads foresaw new customers if it opened. Indians, however, expected that allotments and white settlement would mean the final disruption of tribal life and organization. Their improbable allies were white ranchers, who, accustomed to grazing their cattle on western Oklahoma's open range, wanted no farmers coming in and plowing it up. Thus railroads and dirt farmers were eager to open the land, but cattlemen, Indians, reformers, missionaries, and even "whisky peddlers and outlaws" opposed it.[7]

A century later it is easy to disparage the Oklahoma land rush. "At the worst," writes one historian, "the run can be viewed as an act of conglomerated human greed, where citizens dashed frantically about to grab land that had once been faithfully promised to the Indian forever. At the best it can be seen as a fulfillment of God-fearing citizens who wished to build homes for themselves and for future generations. In truth the Run of 1889 was much of both."[8] In larger terms, one white western myth collided with another: homesteader-agrarianism versus rancher-cowboyism. This time the agrarians won. Settlement was still a sacrosanct ideal. As for Indian rights, the new idea of severalty supposedly protected them, while treaties and purchases made U.S. acquisition legal.

White settlers were already pressing hard to get into Oklahoma. They did so in stages, through several land rushes stretching across fifteen years. The earliest, in 1889 and 1893, were incredibly chaotic. In 1889, after the army had surveyed and divided central Oklahoma's 2,000,000 acres of "Unassigned Lands"[9] into 160-acre farm tracts and some town lots, the government opened all of it at noon on April 22. From Arkansas City and Caldwell, just above the Kansas line, tent cities holding impatient thousands shifted forty miles south during April to the edge of the target area. Travel agents in Liverpool and other European ports enjoyed jumps in sales to land seekers. The Santa Fe Railroad sold more than seven thousand tickets from Kansas City to Guthrie and Oklahoma stations, and at Arkansas City, upward of ninety-three jammed coaches awaited the signal to move south. Trains at Purcell in Chickasaw country were filled with Texans and others eager to move north. Phalanxes of young men on horseback dashed hell-bent at the signal, reins in one hand and claim stake in the other.[10]

A few "sooners" sneaked in early, actually jumping the gun. At least fifty thousand legal boomers—one-fourth of the estimated number in the entire California Gold Rush from 1849 through 1852—walked, rode, or took the train into central Oklahoma on that single day.[11] By sundown Guthrie, Kingfisher, Stillwater, Oklahoma City, El Reno, and Norman—nonexistent the day before—were surrounded by a sea of homestead stakes.[12] Congress neglected to establish any territorial or local government until the next year, but it did provide some army units, which kept most contests over land claims from developing into homicides.[13]

With variations, the scene of instant whitening of Indian lands repeated itself as the government opened piece after piece of the new Oklahoma Territory for settlement. In September 1891 Iowa and Sac and Fox country, enough for seven thousand homesteads, became available; in an afternoon all were staked out, disappointing two-thirds of the twenty thousand seekers.[14] Cheyenne-Arapaho land, 3,500,000 acres in western Oklahoma, opened in April 1892. But this time only twenty-five thousand takers appeared. Homesteaders knew that rainfall became palpably scarcer mile by mile west of Oklahoma City.

For the same reason, the greatest of the Oklahoma land rushes, the 1893 stampede into the Cherokee Outlet[15] along the Kansas border, concentrated in its eastern portion. The outlet ran from the 97th meridian (fairly well watered) to the 100th (semiarid), and from the Kansas border forty miles south into Oklahoma. After Indian and public school allotments had been left aside, more than six million acres became available, enough for forty thousand homesteads. The government bought it all from the Cherokee Nation for about $8,500,000.[16]

On September 16, 1893, some hundred thousand people raced across the line seeking their 160 acres each.[17] Five years of drought had anathematized western Kansas and shrunk its population. The Garden City, Kansas, Land Office, which opened in 1883, was overwhelmed for the next few years by crowds of homesteaders (truly doing a land office business), but it closed in 1894.[18] Over a hundred thousand who had tried life in western Kansas in the mid-1880s found it impossible by 1890. For them the Cherokee Outlet was "a godsend . . . a place to escape from big mortgages and bad memories."[19]

In 1901 a lottery rather than another land run distributed much of southwestern Oklahoma to settlers, because far more would-be homesteaders wanted land than the next two million acres could hold.[20] During the late 1890s, and concluding in 1906, further Oklahoma lands, most important the Osage lands just west of the Cherokees in northeastern Oklahoma, were opened by lottery, but only to Indians. The Osages, under Chief Big Heart (1875–1906), kept not only their land but the rights to the minerals beneath it, including oil, "in order to distribute Osage wealth among all the enrolled." Decades later Sylvester Tinker, Jr., the principal chief from 1966 to 1978, managed to have the mineral rights confirmed in perpetuity, so that "as long as there's one drop of oil left, it belongs to the Osages."[21] The Osages kept their land and their oil, but they also chose to keep their language and religion secret and succeeded so well that they transmitted neither to younger generations. Their early decision "to follow the white man's road" in education, adoption of English, and economic practices took them farther from their original culture than they had planned. Another Osage leader lamented in 1983, "I fear it's lost."[22] But Osage County, northwest of Tulsa, still remains their country.

Population always soared on settlement frontiers. Oklahoma Territory was a mighty example. It went from theoretically nothing before the first land rush on April 22, 1889, to 61,000 in the 1890 census to 400,000 in the 1900 census. East of it Indian Territory, at 197,000 in 1890, rose in 1900 to 390,000, many of them whites or mixed-bloods. By 1907, when the former two territories became the state of Oklahoma, over 1,414,000 people lived there, far more than any previous newly entering state.[23] As in Kansas and Texas, the majority of the whites were native-born of native stock, but immigrants were everywhere. Germans, German-Russians, Bohemians, Irish, and Britons took up homesteads in the land rush areas. Italians and Poles showed up in the 1870s and 1880s to work in newly opened coal mines in the Choctaw Nation in southeastern Oklahoma.[24] Jewish shopkeepers started stores in small Oklahoma towns in the 1890s as they had been doing all across the West.[25] Transients took advantage of Oklahoma Territory's short ninety-day residence requirement and obtained quick divorces, before the law tightened in 1896.[26]

Oklahoma also attracted and kept a substantial African-American population from the end of the Civil War onward. Besides the emancipated slaves of the Cherokees and Creeks and their descendants, blacks took part in the 1891 and 1893 land rushes, and black migrants from neighboring southern states populated thirty-two all-black towns in Indian and Oklahoma territories as well as many homesteads.[27] The black population of the territory jumped from three thousand in 1890 to fifty-five thousand in 1900.[28] A year later, despite school and other segregation, Oklahoma was home to more African-Americans than to European immigrants.[29]

The Nadir Period for Indian Population

Native Americans reached their lowest numbers since 1492 sometime around 1890 or 1900, causing population historians to call the 1890s the Indians' nadir.[30] After 1900 their numbers rose, and life improved slowly in other ways as well. By 1900 the situation was bad, but not hopeless. Oklahoma Indians did not disappear and in fact increased and multiplied. But by 1901 allotments to individual Indians from tribal lands had easily and frequently shifted to white owners. Native American population was about to start recovering, though not necessarily on tribal lands. Indians, until then a malevolent foe or a noble savage to whites, were about to begin their role (in white eyes) as another underprivileged minority within the dominant society.

What happened in the awful quarter century leading up to 1890 has been told so often, from Buffalo Bill to recent films, that the impression is widespread that those events are the whole story of Indian-white relations. Depredations abounded, yet Indians managed to survive. True, they were defeated everywhere and forced onto reservations. For example, Kit Carson and the army force-marched eight thousand Navajos (three-fourths of the tribe) from their Arizona home three hundred miles eastward to Bosque Redondo on the parched Pecos in 1864. In 1868 they escorted them back, the misery searing the Navajo historical memory as deeply as the Civil War did that of white Americans.[31] Yet from then on the Navajos, their sheep herds, and their land area expanded.[32]

Another example: the army continually defeated Sioux, Cheyennes, Kiowas, and others up and down the plains in the 1860s and 1870s, except for a blip (militarily, though not mythically) like the Lakota-Cheyenne wipeout of Custer in 1876. By 1880 virtually all western Indians were confined on reservations. Several treaties, the last in 1889, shrank Sioux lands from fifty-nine million to thirteen million acres and decreed they would live on allotments.[33] Yet the military defeats scarcely affected Sioux population size, which continued to rise.[34]

Meanwhile, the Nez Percé and Shoshoni in Idaho, the Modocs in northern California, and the Apaches in New Mexico and Arizona all were, even the holdout Geronimo, reduced to reservations in the 1870s and 1880s. Yet the Apaches did learn how to farm, did learn English, and did adjust despite demoralizing punishments. "Many Apaches developed a hatred for Anglo ways," writes an observer, but others "became devout Christians and devoted pursuers of the Anglo way of living."[35] Life was grim but not hopeless; traditional culture was severely disrupted, but the Indians adapted and lived on, contrary to social Darwinian predictions that the unfit (such as Indians, according to the Darwinians) would not survive.[36] Crows and other northern Plains Indians managed to preserve their horse culture, despite efforts by Anglo officials to suppress it, by developing fairs and rodeos, which grew and flourished in the twentieth century.[37]

Reservations and allotments had a mixed impact on Native American population and health. Though Lakota population had already bottomed out, California Indians continued to decrease until 1925 or later. Nationally Indians numbered somewhere between 237,000 and 466,000 in 1900, depending on who and how one counts.[38] In any case, they then constituted less than 1 percent even of the West's population.

White medical care, such as it was in the 1890s, gradually came to the reservations. Infant and maternal sickness and death remained prevalent. Among Northern Cheyenne mothers and children, for example, mortality remained high.[39] Only in the twentieth century did high birthrates outpace infant deaths sufficiently to grow Indian population. Smallpox vaccination was a boon, but the germ theory and sanitation only gradually gained acceptance. Smallpox epidemics devastated the Pueblos and Hopis in Arizona and New Mexico in 1898 and 1899. Entering New Mexico from old Mexico in late 1897, smallpox hit Isleta Pueblo in January 1898, and by August it had infected 385 people, 85 of whom died. Every Hispanic settlement and Indian pueblo south of Santa Fe suffered outbreaks; among them, over 600 more died by early 1899. The death rates far exceeded those of major eastern cities at the time. Among the Hopis in Arizona, many preferred traditional medicine. Of 220 Hopis who refused vaccination or simply missed it, 163 died; of the 412 who were vaccinated, 24 died. Often well-meant but inept public health care on reservations reflected underfunding and widespread public indifference.[40]

In many parts of the West whites were openly hostile. They feared and hated no group more than Apaches for several reasons: their legendarily effective leaders like Cochise, Victorio, and Geronimo; their bewildering lack of hierarchy and loose political organization, which made a general settlement (except by force) impossible; and their terrifying and frustrating elusiveness in the desert mountains. Apache resistance to white takeovers of land and resources was especially stubborn, once they understood what white occupation meant.[41]

White settlers in New Mexico sometimes demonized Apaches. Agnes Meader Snider, born in 1860, recalled Victorio's reputation; he "murdered everything and everybody he come to." She said at one time he "killed 35 or 40 Mexicans that had sheep up in there; you could walk on dead sheep where they just went and cut their throats. You know they were that mad, the Indians did [that] just for spite." Between Victorio's resistance in 1880–1882 and Geronimo's in 1882–1886, Mrs. Snider recalled, "There was six years that we had no peace. That is when we got up in the morning we didn't know whether we'd have a scalp at night or not." She also believed the story of the mutilation of a scout named Cooney: "they said that his [penis] was taken off and put in his mouth. . . . Of course that's only hearsay. But I guess it must have been true."[42] Henry Brock, born 1867, a cowboy and part-time sheriff, claimed he had seen a corpse mutilated in just that way. According to him, "Any time that you saw an Indian you either run or did your best to kill him [or] he waylaid the white man. He's a cowardly scamp. . . . He'd never come out and fight if he could help it."[43]

Some whites empathized with Indians and Mexicans. In 1886 Marietta Wetherill was a small child freshly arrived in New Mexico from Kansas with her family when Geronimo himself and some companions passed by their camp. Alone (her parents were over the next rise looking for Anasazi ruins), Marietta bantered with Geronimo as his men watered their horses. One said, "We'll take her with us," but Geronimo reminded him that "we're in a hurry to get away, we can't take a child, we'd be in more trouble." They left her some beef and rode away. In 1904 Geronimo was on exhibit at the St. Louis World's Fair, and Marietta reminded him of the encounter. He remembered her and agreed in detail with her account. When she was interviewed in 1953, she declared: "I was never afraid of an Indian"; they were more to be pitied than feared. "Oh, nobody knows what those Indians have gone through!" she said.[44] For some whites, contact confirmed prejudices; for others, it encouraged tolerance.

The Farm Depression: Irrigation as Salvation

Drought did not end on the plains until 1901. During the 1890s, except for Oklahoma, new settlement languished while theorists, scientists, dreamers, and boosters promoted irrigation, if possible with federal assistance, as a solution to the chronic water shortage. Without water, no development. With it, endless possibilities and new life for the frontier.

John Wesley Powell, the head of the U.S. Geological Survey in the 1880s, lost an arm at the Battle of Shiloh but left the Union army as a major and with his enthusiasm for western exploration unquenched. In the late 1860s he led an expedition, certainly the first by white Americans, down the Colorado River through the Grand Canyon. Then in the 1870s he explored other parts of the Great Basin. His famous *Report* of 1878 urged the country to realize that the Great Basin, and for that matter the High Plains, could never be settled with 160-acre farms. Instead Powell urged that the public domain become either livestock ranches of four entire sections (2,440 acres), equal to sixteen homesteads, or 80 to 100-acre irrigated plots. Either irrigate crops or graze sheep and cattle, because nothing in between would work.[45] Even so, he warned, "within the Arid Region [the parts of the United States getting less than twenty inches' annual rainfall] only a small portion of the country is irrigable,"[46] and irrigation should be done cooperatively, through the formation of "irrigation districts" made up of self-governing local landowners.

Congress and development-minded westerners listened to Powell selectively. The idea of irrigation districts caught on. Irrigation congresses subsidized by railroads and developers met at Salt Lake City in 1891, Los Angeles in 1893, and Denver in 1894, drumbeating the booster message of development by irrigation. But at the Los Angeles congress, an associate of Powell's, Richard J. Hinton, threw his mentor's caution to the winds and advocated extensive federally sponsored irrigation projects.[47] Congress followed in 1894 with the Carey Act, which transferred up to a million acres of federal land to states willing to irrigate them. The results were disappointing. In 1902, however, the Newlands Reclamation Act passed Congress with bipartisan support and the backing of President Theodore Roosevelt, and it placed the main responsibility for irrigation on the federal government.[48]

The Newlands Act empowered the Interior Department to lend money for irrigation works to settlers on homestead-size tracts of 160 acres (and limited to that). Settlers had to organize themselves into irrigation districts. They were to repay the loans with the abundant proceeds earned from the irrigated crops. The secretary of the interior, through a Reclamation Service (which Roosevelt quickly created), would decide what public lands should be irrigated and authorize projects on them.

These would include what normally went with irrigation projects: dams, catchment basins, canals, laterals, pumps, and valves, all presumably on a scale that a farmer could walk across and operate. By the 1920s and 1930s, however, the irrigation districts and catchment basins of the Newlands Act had exploded into enormous structures like Boulder Dam and the 115-mile-long Lake Mead behind it. The Newlands Act became the charter for massive nature control. Historians rank its importance to the West with the 1862 Homestead Act and even with the 1785 Land Ordinance, which had set up the ground rules for distributing the public domain.[49] The historical path ran—with some twists—from Powell's *Report* of 1878, to the exigencies of the Depression of the 1890s, to the Newlands solution in 1902, to the gigantism of the 1930s' New Deal.

Enthusiasm drowned Powell's restrained view of how much of the West could be irrigated. State laws concerning water rights already were a contradictory jumble, often promoting monopoly. The 160-acre limitation in the Newlands Act and the payback provision were almost never enforced. Unquestionably, however, the act vastly extended the possibilities for irrigating. Private and state support had done about all they could by 1900. Newlands demonstrated how federal resources and power can change things. Like the huge railroad land grants of the 1860s, the federal government underwrote the West's development in a wholly new way. For demographic history, irrigation guided the direction of settlement, and *federal* support for irrigation expanded those directions not just toward farm settlement but toward huge cities sitting amid deserts. No water, no people. If water, then people. Irrigation, which through its Newlands Act incarnation came to include long-distance aqueducts and enormous dams, made possible the peopling of much of the West.

Irrigation in the West was already an old story, of course, in 1890. The prehistoric Hohokam aqueducts in Arizona, the acequias of colonial New Spain, the Mormons' capture of melt-off cascading down the Wasatch

Front, Hispanic villagers' trenches along the Rio Grande in the 1850s, and Anglo-American irrigators of places like Anaheim, California, in 1857 and Greeley, Colorado, in 1870, are early cases.[50] On the High Plains in 1880, at the spanking new settlement of Garden City, Kansas, on the Arkansas River, farmers dug their first irrigation ditch and kept digging despite upstream diversion by Colorado farmers and the unpredictable maleficence of nature in limiting rainfall and Rocky Mountain snowpack to trickles and trifles. Garden City later boasted "the largest public swimming pool in the world." But not often was it full of water; nature and neighbors were not always reliable.

Yet projects often succeeded, at least locally. Mormons built irrigation works from 1887 on, near Cardston and Lethbridge, Alberta, and along the Snake River in Idaho; sugar beet growers along the South Platte in Colorado, using immigrant workers, irrigated after 1900.[51] Optimism was unkillable. Many would-be homesteaders believed in the insidious notion that "rain follows the plow." The theory assured them that if they dug enough furrows, clouds would appear; then rain would fall and be absorbed into the thirsty soil instead of running off the hard prairie surface. Evaporation would foster more rain. First heard in the 1880s, the slogan sounded again after rains resumed in the early 1900s, reinforced by the hype for dryland or dry farming. Both worked fine—if it rained.[52] Why people risked their futures in this way is hard to comprehend, apart from the combined strength of previous (and misleading) experience in better-watered places, boosterism and propaganda, and the still-invincible homesteading dream: the combination of irrelevance, misinformation, and faith.[53]

Irrigation in California's Central Valley was a much surer thing because its water source was melt-off from the snowy west face of the Sierras. California's irrigation system, now the world's largest, began in the late nineteenth century. North of Stockton is the Sacramento River valley, a low plain prone to sudden flooding depending on how fast winter snows in the Sierra Nevada melt and flow down through the Sacramento's many tributaries. South of Stockton the San Joaquin Valley was (before irrigation) an arid basin a hundred or more miles wide between the Sierras and the Coast Ranges, fed by few streams, useful mainly for animal pasturage and wheat fields. Dryness increases from Stockton southward through Modesto to Fresno to Bakersfield to the Tehachapi Mountains, which separate the valley from the Los Angeles Basin. Thus, in the north the problem was keeping too much water under control, while in the south the problem was spreading scarce water over abundant land. In either case, manipulation of water had to come before the Central Valley could be populated or used "effectively" (that is, for large-scale agriculture).

Waterworks began controlling the unpredictable Sacramento Valley and refreshing the arid San Joaquin Valley in the 1870s. Rain never followed any plow, but people always followed irrigation and flood control in California. The Central Valley's dusty whistle-stops became towns, then cities, and in the twentieth century the whole valley became an enormous factory of metropolitanized agribusiness. The small semisubsistence homesteader, so typical of plains settlement, seldom had a chance there, because of both latifundia and the ways in which water policy emerged in late-nineteenth-century California. In 1868, after local attempts at flood control had failed, the state passed a flood control act (the Green Act) that defined flood-prone tracts—and much dry acreage—as swamp. It thereby made state land available to buyers in effectively unlimited amounts for a dollar an acre or less. Large tracts of so-called swampland (in one case 250,000 acres) became the property of private monopolists, once again squeezing out the small-holder.[54]

In the San Joaquin Valley, irrigation began with a forty-mile canal from the San Joaquin River in 1874, spreading ditches that by 1880 watered about three hundred thousand previously dry acres and by 1890 a million. Around Fresno twenty-one irrigation colonies opened by 1886, many of them large-scale speculations by developers.[55] In 1887 another state law, the Wright Act, created a peculiarly Californian unit of governance that, yet again, kept the homesteader away and benefited the middle-wealth family farm and, though unintentionally, the large landholders. Under it, two-thirds of the farmers and other residents of an area could vote themselves into communal existence as an irrigation district. Once formed, this body could tax everybody and all land within its boundaries and then issue bonds for the irrigation system on the security of property taxes. The San Joaquin Valley would be marked off into irrigation districts (at least where latifundias did not already exist), rather than into townships, sections, and homesteads, as in Iowa or Kansas. The thrust of the idea was to democratize landholdings, and for a time it did so; but it made no fundamental reversal of latifundia creep.[56]

Irrigation districts were a mixed success. Less than 10 percent of a potential twenty-eight million acres became irrigated under the Wright Act, and the average farm decreased only 5 percent across the state, though more so in Fresno and Los Angeles counties.[57] The act could do nothing to prevent droughts, and bonds never sold unless buyers had confidence in the tax base they rested on. Nonetheless, farmers had "easier access to credit and capital, large-scale technological resources, far more political leverage, *a common labor pool*, and cooperative marketing strength."[58]

"Labor pool" needs emphasis because the Wright Act, for all its supposed

democratization, reinforced California's seasonal wage labor system. Homesteads on the Great Plains gave everyone, at least in theory, a chance of independent success. The California irrigation district system solidified the
property-owning status of those lucky enough to get into it early. It drove up
the average per acre cost of land in California far beyond what the Kansas or
Nebraska homesteader faced or could afford. It therefore meant that farm
workers and their families were in most cases consigned to become a rural
working class rather than an aspiring lower middle class. The San Joaquin
Valley soon divided between property owners—ranging from huge to quite
small (in acreage, not value)—and the propertyless.[59]

Irrigation also fructified southern California. Riverside, east of Los Angeles, began irrigating in 1873. In the Imperial Valley, the southeast corner of
the state, canals brought Colorado River water to nearly two hundred thousand desert acres by 1900,[60] and most of California's irrigation was yet to
come. Wheat, barley, and cattle still occupied much of the landscape at the
turn of the century, but irrigation, with its class and political concomitants,
was firmly in place.

From 3,600,000 acres in 1890,[61] the irrigated farming area of the United
States expanded tentatively in the next dozen years, then swiftly after 1902,
when the Newlands Act passed. Private efforts, except the Mormons', faced
too many obstacles before that, and 90 percent of them went under.[62] After
Newlands, however, federal funds became the underwriter of new settlement, which could not survive without "reclamation," the buzzword for
irrigation.[63]

Riding the Railroads—and the Rails

The West of the 1890s was full of contrasts, its population already extremely
diverse, some westerners struggling along in nineteenth-century patterns,
others already in new-century ways. While "tramps" rode the rails and
empty boxcars, passenger trains brought tuberculars to New Mexico and
southern California and wealthy eastern tourists to Pasadena and Yellowstone. Cowboys and Basque sheepherders chased livestock over lonely
steppes, while Irish copper miners in Butte and Mormon farmers in Utah
and Idaho led lives centered in family, church, and ethnicity. The dream of
owning a family farm still obsessed many, while irrigated waterworks, steam
tractors, and oil wells pointed toward the mechanized new century. As Indians ceased to compete for turf, the region's ethnic spectrum widened to
include all sorts of new Asians and Europeans.

Stagecoaches still made the hair-raising three-hour journey from Ironton
to Ouray in southwestern Colorado, while railroads brought in immigrants

from the East and Europe and carried away the mineral and timber wealth of the mountains. Many mining camps lacked running water or sewerage, while at the same time in the Mormon town of Provo "water for irrigating purposes flow[ed] down each side of the streets, and shade trees in abundance and of luxuriant growth render[ed] the walks cool and inviting."[64] Los Angeles, San Francisco, Seattle, and Denver had infrastructures the technological equal of Chicago's or New York's. Already the varieties of western experience were many.

Robert Porter and Henry Gannett made no mistake when they declared in their prologue to the 1890 census that "up to and including 1880 the country had a frontier of settlement, but at present the unsettled area has been so broken into by isolated bodies of settlement that there can hardly be said to be a frontier line."[65] To buttress their point, they provided a set of maps showing white population at each census since the first in 1790, with the newest one, for 1890, revealing a welter of curved lines and density blotches scattered without pattern from the 100th meridian to the Pacific. Even the "empty" salient of Indian Territory revealed settlers occupying its center. Settlements appeared all along the Pecos and Rio Grande rivers in New Mexico, along Colorado's Front Range and sprinkled around Rocky Mountain mining towns, in southern Wyoming rangeland, in South Dakota's Black Hills, in the Yellowstone and Missouri River valleys in Montana, in Mormonland, in mining towns in Nevada and Idaho, and up and down the Pacific Coast. Yet a surprisingly large potential area remained to be ranched, put to the plow, or townsited.

When drought and depression ended in 1901, a boom greater than that of the 1880s began. Even during the unpleasant 1890s western population kept growing. The Oklahoma boomers, the assorted Indians, the refugee homesteaders from western Kansas, and the irrigators were only some of the cast.

Others included unattached young men who wandered the West looking for work, and they formed a new American underclass. Most had been forced to become migrants because of the 1890s' depression. Many were blacklisted by employers because of union activity in mines or lumber camps. Coxey's Army of 1894, marching on Washington, D.C., to protest unemployment, is usually thought of as an eastern affair because Jacob Coxey was from Ohio. But it really began in California and the Northwest.[66] The depression of the 1890s was the first in the nation's history to generate tramps, the bedraggled roving unemployed who had been reduced to begging or odd jobs. The People's Party governor of Kansas, Lorenzo Lewelling, enraged his Republican opponents in 1893 when his "Tramp Circular" announced that members of "a standing army of the unemployed numbering . . . not less than one million able bodied men" should not be prosecuted for vagrancy in Kansas just because they were unemployed.[67] The less sympathetic journalist Josiah Flynt portrayed them in 1899 as loafers and incipient criminals: "I have met in [Denver], at one time, as many as one hundred and fifty bona-fide tramps, and everyone had been in the town for over a week. The people, however, do not seem to feel the burden of this riffraff addition to the population; at any rate, they befriend it most kindly."[68] The newly built rail network allowed tramps to get around the West as they could not do in the preceding depression of 1873 to 1878. Hopping freights and "riding the rails" afforded mobility for the seasonally or chronically unemployed, who formed a male-skewed population—Seattle was two-thirds male in the 1890s—living in a society "of urban enclaves of employment agencies, cheap hotels and lodging houses, soup kitchens, saloons, and brothels."[69]

Such individuals did not have the leisure to write many autobiographies, and their stories were seldom considered edifying enough for a middle-class readership. These men were certainly not all alike, ethnically or otherwise. We do know for certain that a large migrant churning of unattached, mostly young men and (Flynt suggests at one point) some women as well, a proletariat too elusive and unrespectable to merit middle-class notice except when they threatened disorder, emerged in the 1890s in the West and did not disappear from sight until World War II. They reproduced themselves, culturally, if not biologically, reinventing a haven for the marginalized. It was not a part of society that boosters cared to dwell on, even though tramps continued to be part of the western (and eastern) scene. Their numbers swelled greatly during the Great Depression of the 1930s. Since then the word has fallen into disuse; instead we hear and see "homeless," who do not seem to travel as much.

In both the United States and Canada, railroad cars that carried tramps underneath carried settlers up above. The Canadian Pacific was already selling off its grant lands when it opened coast to coast in 1885, while the Union Pacific and the Northern Pacific extolled the glorious potential of the High Plains. The Northern Pacific advised that "millions of acres of good agricultural land are awaiting development, but, owing to the light rainfall, irrigation is generally necessary." (How to irrigate all those acres remained an unsolved question.) The railroad also proclaimed the Yellowstone River "navigable during a good state of water for more than 250 miles from its confluence with the Missouri . . . by steamboats of two or three hundred tons." (If they had wheels.) Of Glendive, in eastern Montana, 692 miles west of St. Paul, a railroad guidebook assured readers that "the soil in the neighborhood is a rich, sandy loam, and the gardens of the inhabitants yield fine vegetables. The valley produces wheat, barley, corn, rye, oats and other crops. Wherever the land has been broken, young trees have appeared spontaneously. . . ." Trees, it seems, followed the plow too. Seventy-five miles farther up the Yellowstone River from Glendive, Miles City was a former "flourishing frontier trading post" where, "after the extermination of the buffalo, the immense grazing country surrounding it was rapidly occupied by stockmen." On the other side of the Rockies in Washington, "the Yakima Basin greatly resembles many of the California valleys. The winters are short and mild and the summers long and sunny. The soil produces, under an inexpensive [!] system of irrigation, very heavy yields. . . ."[70]

The Union Pacific and Northern Pacific aggressively sought the tourist trade to Yellowstone Park and other scenic wonders. The Missouri Pacific touted Denver as the "most delightful city in the world to live in, with its pure mountain air, faultless climate, cosmopolitan appointments and all that is needed to make life enjoyable. All the transcontinental railways center at Denver [patently untrue]. The finest opera house west of New York, the Tabor Grand, is located in Denver."[71] The Southern Pacific and the Santa Fe promoted the resorts of southern California, and the Great Northern those of Glacier Park, discovering that despite the depression of the 1890s, enough well-off people still lived in Chicago and other eastern points to fill many a train and hotel. The West remained the dream of would-be homesteaders throughout that depressed decade. It also remained an exotic, wild Eden that revealed itself safely to the ambulatory bourgeoisie through the windows of Pullman Palace cars.[72]

Thanks to the railroads (despite such misleading advertising) and people (rich, middling, or poor) eager to use them, the settlement frontier stumbled on during the 1890s despite drought and depression. A whistle-stop tour of the West demonstrates what was actually happening. We begin on the plains, cross the Rockies into the Great Basin, and go to the Pacific.

Whistle-Stops: The Great Plains

Kansas and Nebraska, each of which gained over a half million people during the boom of the mid-1880s, welcomed almost no one in the 1890s. High birthrates on farms compensated for outflows of emigrants, so the states did not actually show negative balances. Kansas also benefited slightly from the start of oil and natural gas production, which enticed hundreds of Italians, Greeks, Austrians, and other Europeans to Allen, Crawford, and Montgomery counties in the state's southeast corner.[73] Kansas's and Nebraska's stasis in the 1890s was unique in the West, and they fell irretrievably behind in the state-by-state rank order. Second in population only to Texas in 1880 and 1890 among western states, Kansas's 3 percent growth during the 1890s placed it forever behind California. Nebraska gained even less, only 0.3 percent, thirty-six thousand people among a million. Nearly every county in Kansas and Nebraska west of the ninety-eighth meridian lost people in the 1890s. By 1890 the boom years of the two states were behind them, and seldom again would they grow in double figures in any decade.

From 234,231 in 1887, the western third of Kansas slipped to 140,959 in 1897 and recovered to just 154,019 in 1900. The foreign-born aged and died off and were not replenished by new arrivals, while their children matured and moved on. The Kansas frontier of settlement that had moved irresistibly westward from the 1850s to 1887 met the immovable obstacles of drought and depression, abruptly stopped, and retreated. Kansas started exporting its young people to Oklahoma, Colorado, and the Pacific Coast as well as to Kansas City and St. Louis. Farms in western Kansas doubled, on average, from 226 acres in 1890 to 521 in 1900, as leavers sold out or abandoned land to stayers.[74]

In the Dakotas the story was less bleak. Despite the collapse of the 1880s boom, statehood in 1889 and railroad promotion continued to lift the former territory from 540,000 to 721,000 during the 1890s, a 34 percent gain. The boosterish *Dakota Farmer* kept hammering away about "the experience of the successful farmer," and with so much cheap land still available, people listened.[75] Above the Canadian border, settlers in Manitoba and Saskatchewan had similar experiences. A homesteader could double 160 acres on the Dominion Lands (Canada's public domain) by buying another tract reasonably from the Canadian Pacific Railway or the Hudson's Bay Company. Tens of thousands of Europeans of a dozen different ethnicities availed themselves of prairie province land, even in the difficult 1890s, although British immigrants, Canadians from Ontario, and Americans outnumbered the rest. The Canadian and American occupations of the northern plains were very much of a piece.[76]

Oklahoma's land rushes tripled its population in the 1890s. Every county outside the panhandle at least doubled. Texas beyond the 100th meridian was also a settlement target in the 1890s; within a triangle from Abilene west to Odessa and north to Amarillo, thirty-six counties each grew 50 to 100 percent or more, collectively from 58,000 in 1890 to 108,000 in 1900. The old *comanchería,* where the Comanches bedeviled and repulsed the Spanish for so long, was about to be overrun with Anglo farms and ranches. Ominously, however, small-farm counties that had been settled a little farther east in Texas in the pre-1887 wave, near the ninety-eighth meridian, including Lampasas, where the Texas Farmers' Alliance was born, lost people.

To the west, the Front Range states and territories all grew at husky rates during the 1890s: New Mexico by 22 percent, Colorado by 31, Wyoming by

48, Montana by 70. The actual numbers were not huge; scarcely any of them gained what western Kansas alone lost in the late 1880s. But increase they did, all from mining, ranching, farm settlement, and town growth.

Industrial mining, well under way by 1890, tripled the populations of Butte, Anaconda, and Great Falls during the 1890s.[77] Two transcontinental railroads, the Great Northern just below the Canadian border and the Northern Pacific along the Yellowstone River, brought in ranchers and Montana's first homesteaders. In Helena single men continued to predominate, and the fairly sparse female population worked mostly in service occupations, including perhaps a hundred prostitutes. Over four hundred black men and women arrived after the Civil War, first for gold prospecting, then as domestics or service workers.[78]

Helena's bawdy women were a small share of the estimated fifty thousand who operated between St. Louis and San Francisco between 1849 and 1900. Places with male-skewed sex ratios—cattle towns, mining and lumber camps, army bases, any resource exploitation frontier in its early days—predictably had prostitute populations, as did the larger cities, notably "wideopen" San Francisco, where boisterous Gold Rush traditions were a matter of subterranean civic pride.[79]

Butte was a different story. Its mines opened in the mid-1870s, part of the eastward-moving mining frontier, just as the Sioux were surrendering to the army and to reservation life in the flat eastern part of the state. The town in 1879 elected its first mayor, a Jew named Henry Jacobs, and through the 1880s it became about one-fourth Irish. One of them was Marcus Daly, who with George Hearst's support bought the Anaconda mine in 1880 and converted it from silver to copper. From that point on Butte was a union town and family town, replete with Irish Catholic parishes, an Ancient Order of Hibernians chapter, and the Robert Emmet Literary Association, a nationalist and fraternal benevolent organization. Butte was extremely stable; until World War I it had no strikes.[80]

Wyoming's ranching country around Casper and Sheridan expanded in the 1890s, as did the coal-mining towns of Rock Springs and Evanston along the Union Pacific. Grim and businesslike, Rock Springs was (according to a visiting Yankee mining engineer in 1898) "a hopeless town of the regular railroad type, full of tramps and drummers, not to mention a large assortment of Chinamen, whom the population occasionally use for amusement by killing off a few,"[81] as in fact happened to twenty-eight Chinese in 1885, when the railroad substituted them for white workers who cost more.[82]

In Colorado plains farming counties just west of Kansas shared its depression, and silver towns in the Rocky Mountains virtually collapsed when Congress repealed silver purchases for the mint in 1893. But Teller

County, home of the 1893 Cripple Creek gold rush, popped from nothing to 29,000, and the newly irrigated Arkansas River valley jumped by thousands. So did Colorado Springs, Boulder, and Denver. Denver boasted telephones by 1880, electric lights by 1882, streetcars by 1886, and over 100,000 people by 1900.[83] By then 30 percent of its adult males were foreign-born, just about the national average for larger cities and higher than Brooklyn, St. Louis, Cincinnati, or Milwaukee. Among them was Dr. Charles David Spivak, a Russian pogrom refugee of 1882 who moved to Denver in 1896 because of his wife's "incipient tuberculosis" and founded a home for Jewish tuberculars.[84] It flourished for years. In silver-mining Aspen a boom from 1885 until the crash of 1893 raised its population of miners from 650 to 2,500, many with families. Houses tossed up four a day cost twelve hundred dollars, with lot, and rented for twenty-four dollars a month. For miners and their families, "it was home . . . families poured into these clapboard dwellings the energy and love necessary to make it a special place with flowers, curtains, paint, and whatever furnishings the[ir] tight budget would allow."[85]

But Colorado was moving out of the raw frontier stage. Its early attractions, gold and silver, leveled off after 1900, just as oil, coal, and natural gas, the minerals of the future, began commercial production. The state's mining camp–like sex ratio of 70 percent male in 1880 eased toward 56 percent male by 1900 because of newborns, a shift to industrial miners and farmers with families, and an outflow of jobless single silver miners.[86] Before the depression knocked the bottom out of the silver market, Italians and other Europeans flocked to Denver to become gardeners, grocers, peddlers, masons, musicians, and tailors as well as miners.[87] The city boasted a fine opera house and the elegant hotels and restaurants redolent of sudden riches. The collapse of silver in 1893 made it the stuff of tragedy; composer Douglas Moore used the rise, romance, and fall of the silver and real estate tycoon Horace Tabor as the basis for his opera *The Ballad of Baby Doe.*

Cripple Creek, a few miles above Colorado Springs, boomed in 1893 with one of the last classic gold rushes. For a season or two it was another roaring gulch. But it changed fast, from a camp of prospecting young men to a town of wageworkers, living with their families in company housing and buying in company stores. "In less than twenty years," writes one historian, "with particular rapidity in Cripple Creek, small-scale placer mining (panning ore from streams or gravel beds) was replaced by lode, or quartz, mining (deep shaft operations which removed rock from which the ore had not been separated and which was later milled and refined). The profitable development of such mining required railroads, advanced technology, large refining facilities, a specialized work force, and considerable capital."[88] Besides copper, coal continued to employ miners, despite explosions that killed a hundred of them in Krebs, Oklahoma, in January 1892 and two hundred in Scofield, Utah, in 1900.[89]

In population dynamics, the difference between prospecting and mining was stark. Mining towns like Cripple Creek became real communities with families, schools, courtships, and marriages. Economically the men depended on their jobs and on their union, the Western Federation of Miners, and wives depended on their men. The few unmarried women taught school, clerked in stores, cooked and waited on tables, entertained in dance halls, and kept boardinghouses for unmarried miners.[90]

In New Mexico, High Plains ranching and farming provided more than half the territory's population gains, with the rest coming from Albuquerque and the southwest mining areas around Silver City and Lordsburg. Albuquerque and Las Vegas continued as trading centers, each with about six thousand people in 1900, both being "dual towns," twinning the old *nuevomexicano* plaza and a new Anglo settlement about a mile east on the railroad. Although rails reached Santa Fe in 1887, the capital (with fifty-six hundred people in 1900) hugged the plaza and the Palace of the Governors, approaching their 300th anniversaries. Archbishop Lamy's new French-style cathedral was rising down the street, and the philanthropist nun Katharine Drexel had already established St. Catherine's School for Indians.

El Paso, where the Southern Pacific crossed the Rio Grande, had sixteen thousand by 1900. On the Mexican side of the border, Oñate's old village of Paso del Norte had been renamed Ciudad Juárez, the northern terminus of the Central Mexican Railway that would soon bring thousands into the United States. Texan El Paso, 56 percent Mexican-American and largely segregated in 1900, battened on its border situation, on adjacent Fort Bliss, and on mining activity in nearby New Mexico.[91]

The Great Basin

Already in the 1890s, this dry mountain and desert subregion was filling with a diverse population. Arizona had attracted more than one hundred thousand whites by 1900, scattered around mining sites, ranches, and a few towns. Railroads were making copper, zinc, lead, and coal mining more profitable than gold and silver, and thus Jerome, Globe, Clifton-Morenci, Santa Rita, and Bisbee sprang up around smelters and mine shafts. The farm villages of Tempe, Glendale, and Mesa encircled Phoenix. In Tucson, the new center of southern Arizona's mining region, the University of Arizona started classes in the fall semester of 1891.[92] Health seekers were hearing of

Arizona too. In Chicago's Catholic newspaper a reader praised the Sisters of Mercy's "charming sanitarium" in Prescott, with its "fine airy rooms . . . and all that neatness and universal cheerfulness that the good sisters seem to have the secret of. . . . I saw a number of people who had come to this district with various forms of lung disease, now cured wholly or partially and carrying on business in this thriving little city. Others had come to die, but seemed to be as far from that event as ever. . . . In the south is Phoenix, a city of tropical luxuriance and a popular winter resort."[93]

Theocratic Utah was not quite depression-proof, but it survived the 1890s better than most parts of the West. Cultivated acres tripled from 1,300,000 in 1890 to 4,100,000 in 1900 from St. George in the south to the Idaho border, while a new Mormon salient stretched westward across desertlike Tooele and Juab counties toward Nevada. Cache County in the northeast, around Logan, led the shift from self-sufficient to commercial farming.[94] Mines opened in the Wasatch Range around Price and Helper and in the Uintah around Vernal, as well as on the Colorado Plateau at Moab. All employed east European immigrants. Largely from Mormon fecundity, the heartland around Salt Lake City and Provo expanded steadily at about 3 percent per year. By 1890, however, 44 percent of Utah's people, especially the miners and railroad workers, were *not* Mormon. The adult population may even have had a non-Mormon majority, since the high Mormon birthrate meant that many Saints were children.

In the Pacific Northwest refugees from the depressed Great Plains appeared in Idaho, Oregon, and Washington.[95] Howard Mason migrated in 1896 to New Plymouth, Idaho, from Clay Center, Kansas, where "three years in succession . . . we didn't get the seed back." His father worked one summer on a cattle ranch in Oregon, made enough to pay for a cabin on a homestead entry, and brought his wife, five children, and mother to Idaho, there to stay and raise apples and alfalfa.[96] Virginia Slavin, born in 1892 at Hays, Kansas, arrived in Lemhi County, Idaho, with her French Canadian father and family as a four-year-old and spent her life there.[97] Israel Bromberg went from Russia to Philadelphia and then to a Jewish agricultural settlement in North Dakota in the 1880s. According to his daughter, he had "never been a farmer, he was a real scholar. . . . They just couldn't make a go of it and the blizzards in the winter and the heat waves in the summer were just more than they could reckon with." And so, as others did, he moved to Portland, Oregon, and succeeded as a retail merchant.[98] Another Jewish couple left Ukraine in 1881 and soon arrived in New Odessa, North Dakota, to grow tobacco. Neither they nor anyone else managed to do that, and they moved on to Albany, Oregon, to design and sell woolen goods. In 1910 they landed in Portland, "where there were more Jews so we could be exposed to our 'contemporaries' "—i.e., to avoid intermarriage.[99]

In 1898 or 1899 a black couple arrived in northern Idaho, near Moscow. According to their son, Eugene Settle, who told their story almost eighty years later, the area was "Scandinavian country," except for "quite a few Chinese" and one "Negro man" named Crissman who ran a small diner. Settle's parents took a train from Fort Smith, Arkansas, headed for Seattle, but were "so amazed about the open spaces, . . . the open land for homesteading," that they got off at Moscow and took over an abandoned homestead. Settle claimed never to have suffered racial discrimination except in his segregated unit in World War I, although his daughter, "the first black student that ever graduated from the University of Idaho," met racism as a teacher in Berkeley, California. Settle later worked for sixteen years as warehouse superintendent for the Latah County Graingrowers. "I had as high as 25 or 30 [presumably white] men working for me at one time."[100] However typical Settle's experience may have been, without question Chinese and Japanese suffered severely from discrimination after they arrived as laborers on the Oregon Short Line. By the 1890s they already had trouble holding land or finding anything other than segregated living space.[101]

Women encountered other prejudices. The Homestead Act permitted single women to file land claims, but in at least one case a federal inspector in Idaho disallowed two women's claims on the grounds that no female had the strength to cope with homesteading conditions there.[102] Women, however, played central economic roles on Montana homesteads, "making every minute count," stretching egg and chicken money to run the kitchen so as to leave stock and crop income for the farm itself. Farm wives also of course cooked, laundered, sewed clothes, and minded the children until they were old enough for chores.[103]

Europeans, Africans, and Asians abounded in Idaho. The forebears of Idaho's black community arrived with the railroad around 1890, and many stayed to make their lives in the division point of Pocatello. John Nasi, a second-generation Finn born in northern Michigan in 1893, arrived in a covered wagon with his family, bent on farming near McCall, which they did although his father returned to mining in winter. Bill Hallberg's father trekked from Sweden in 1885 to Caldwell, Idaho, drove a mule team for five years, mined in DeLamar, and finally became a farmer: "he wanted to be free. He didn't want to be tied up like they were back there [in Sweden]. They couldn't go no place." Frank Bottinelli's parents came in 1889 from Italy to Kellogg; they saw the Bunker Hill mine explosion in 1899 and subsequent Industrial Workers of the World (IWW) troubles.[104] Boise's first synagogue opened in 1895.[105] To the south, though Reno swelled from sixty-four hundred to ninety-one hundred, it could not make up for the collapse of silver towns like Virginia City, already well on its way to ghost town status.

The Pacific West

West of the Cascades the Great Basin's mines, ranches, and sheep herds were virtually unknown. The coast was already a subregion of cities and towns, sprinkled with small farms and lumber camps. In the entire West from the ninety-eighth meridian to the Pacific, the parts least tied to the nineteenth-century homesteading past best defied the depression of the 1890s. In Oregon, Portland (which about doubled to ninety thousand) and surrounding Multnomah County accounted for about 30 percent of the state's growth in the 1890s, the rest coming from nearby farm counties and a few others along the Columbia River.[106] Similarly, in Washington and California, the incipient metropolises led population expansion, even in the 1890s depression.

In California irrigation was developing rapidly but was not yet decisive for population change. Large-scale, mechanized grain growing and livestock raising flourished, and while much rangeland was changing into orchards and vineyards, the conversion was expensive and not yet general.[107] California agriculture struggled through the 1890s, employing seasonal workers in fits and starts, marginalizing many settlers.[108] Mining counties shrank, like Nevada's and Colorado's. As gold and silver veins played out, copper and coal did not replace them as they were doing in Montana and Idaho. The next California mineral boom—and it was huge—was in oil, awaiting not beneath the Sierras but in the south, under Los Angeles and Santa Barbara.

California's largest increases during the 1890s came in the East Bay around Oakland and Berkeley and in southern California. San Francisco, the oldest and greatest western city, increased 65,000 during the 1880s (from 233,000 to 299,000) and "only" 44,000 during the 1890s (to 342,000), more than Nevada's entire population.[109] Insulated by distance and its own demands from the agricultural depression in the plains and the industrial depression of the Midwest and Northeast, California surged ahead. In the south, Ventura and Orange counties rose by nearly 50 percent, and Los Angeles County nearly 70 percent, from 101,000 to 170,000. The Los Angeles Chamber of Commerce, created in 1888 in the wake of the real estate bust, sent a train called *California on Wheels* on a two-year tour of the country. It visited every fair and every major city it could, making Los Angeles "the best advertised city in America."[110] During the 1890s developers laid out streets and suburbs, Edward L. Doheny struck oil within the city limits, and electric trolleys replaced horsecars. Frederick Rindge paid three hundred thousand dollars in 1892 for 13,330 acres and 23 miles of Pacific beachfront known as Rancho Topanga Malibu Sequit (now known simply as Malibu, where a single house or lot has long been cheap at that price).[111]

The railroads never ceased bringing people to see the California Dream being realized: health seekers, wealth seekers, people looking for "the cutting edge of the American Dream . . . a balance of physicality and intelligence, perhaps even an escape from the Puritan past . . . the hope for a special relationship to nature."[112] The Southern Pacific Railway published a new promotional booklet in early 1894, defining and selling the bottom-line attractions of California. It appealed to "those who find pleasure in seeing the beautiful and majestic creations of Nature, and . . . the strange and picturesque pursuits of a people; . . . those whose health might be improved; . . . [and] those who wish to better their material condition by engaging in new, delightful, easily learned and profitable pursuits, in which the hard conditions imposed by competition in the older industries are practically unknown."[113] Other California dreams surfaced. Agrarians founded a "cooperative commonwealth" at Winters' Island near Stockton in 1893; Christian Socialists influenced by William Dean Howells formed a utopian colony in 1894 in the Sonoma Valley and called it Altruria; Theosophists created their own colony, Point Loma, near San Diego in 1897; Carmel, first appreciated as a fledgling resort in the 1880s and then by David Starr Jordan and other Stanford grandees in the late 1890s, became reincarnated by 1905 into a colony for artists and writers.[114] California seemed heaven-sent for experimental living of all sorts. In fact, it has been such a site for two hundred years, in radically different ways, from Serra's missions of the late 1770s to the Mormons' San Bernardino in the 1850s to the communes and ashrams of the 1970s.

Los Angeles's foreign-born population in 1890 lagged well below the average for American cities, while San Francisco's was well above. Yet L.A. retained some Hispanics from its pre-Anglo days, and a new stream of migrants from Mexico began appearing in the 1890s after the Southern Pacific built rail connections deep into Mexico.[115] The railroads also brought black people, so that by 1900 Los Angeles had become the largest black city on the West Coast, with over two thousand.[116] It was also the tuberculosis cure capital, outstripping Denver and Colorado Springs. California in the 1890s reputedly had more physicians per capita than any other state, and Los Angeles County more than any other in the nation.[117]

The Jewish community included both the obscure and the prominent. Among the latter was Herman Silver, born in Prussia in 1830, a migrant to Illinois in the 1850s, to Denver in the 1870s (where he worked at the federal mint), and finally for his health to "the paradise of turn-of-the-century, smog-free California" in 1887. He joined the Los Angeles Chamber of Commerce in 1891, was elected to the L.A. City Council in 1896, was named its president in 1899, and ran (unsuccessfully) for mayor in 1900. Silver died in 1913, much honored.[118] In the 1890s many other Jews had come, as he had, for their health, especially to cure tuberculosis.[119] As was true in Portland and San Francisco, the other western cities with sizable Jewish communities in 1900, the Los Angeles group concerned itself with garment making, wholesale and retail trade, and finance; there were few of the "proletarians" so evident in New York.[120] European origins may have guided American destinations: Jews from the southern parts of the Russian Pale were often less traditional and more commercially experienced than others and were more likely to proceed to Portland and perhaps the other West Coast Jewish communities than to stay in New York.[121]

Doheny's new oil well, which began producing at Second Street and Glendale Boulevard in 1892, was the first of a great many in and around Los Angeles. In a region where coal and wood were scarce and expensive and had to be shipped in, local oil became the fuel for heating homes and factories. In a grand example of Los Angeles luck, having its own oil abruptly demolished a major barrier to massive population expansion. (Another, the lack of natural water, was to be removed soon.) Doheny himself became a plutocrat and philanthropist, buying European art treasures for the Catholic archdiocese. Another beneficiary was Emma Summers, a piano teacher who came to L.A. in 1893 and lived near Second and Glendale. She bought a half interest in a well near Temple and Court streets for seven hundred dollars, borrowed more to keep the digging going, and kept reinvesting as wells came in. By 1900 she was known as "California's Petroleum Queen," controlling "half of the production in the original Los Angeles Field," selling barrels by the thousands to utilities, railroads, and office buildings.[122]

California closed out the 1890s having gained 179,000 people, more of them migrants from other parts of the United States than foreigners or newborns. Whites accounted for 94 percent, Indians under 1 percent (about 15,000). Chinese, still the largest foreign-born group in 1890 at 71,000 (19 percent of all foreign-born), dropped to fourth in 1900 at 40,000 (11 percent), behind Germans, British, and Irish. Italians and "Austrians" (actually southern Slavs for the most part) each increased by a few thousand during the decade. But the new group of the 1890s were the Japanese, who surged from 1,224 in 1890 to 10,264 in 1900. California acquired fewer people in the 1890s than in the 1880s, but it nonetheless easily passed Kansas to become the second most populous western state, trailing only Texas.[123]

Cities carried Washington's growth as well. Seattle and Spokane took the new state past the 500,000 mark. Seattle, stimulated by the arrival of the Northern Pacific in 1893 and the Alaska gold rush in 1897, nearly doubled from 43,000 to 81,000 as it shifted from an isolated local retail supplier to a regional manufacturing and services hub. Spokane, rising from 20,000 to 37,000, was becoming the economic focus of northern Idaho and eastern Washington. Tacoma moved slowly during the 1890s, from 36,000 to 38,000, despite its earlier railroad link and its great smelter on the shores of Commencement Bay, which opened in 1889; Seattle was getting the growth. Bellingham, just over 10,000 by 1900, led a group of lumber-processing and shipping towns around Puget Sound and Grays Harbor. Lumbering and farming opened Okanagan and Stevens counties on the Canadian border, and the first large-scale irrigation began around Yakima, east of the Cascades.

Across the entire West, except for Kansas and Nebraska, whose boom times were behind them, growth—not rapid, but steady and endemic, from diverse causes—marked this otherwise depressed decade of the 1890s. Cities expanded, faster than rural population, from Kansas City to Seattle and Los Angeles. Homesteading, ranching, and mining all pulled lone opportunity seekers as well as growing families westward. The West's people were young, birthrates were high, death rates low. When prosperity returned, as it did by 1901, the West was poised for one of its greatest booms.

State Making and the Offshore West

This great multitude of whistle-stops, from the Great Plains to the Pacific, inevitably coalesced into states of the Union, if they had not already done so between 1850 (California's admission) and 1876 (Colorado's). Not until 1889, however, were the northwestern territories brought in, with others entering later still. Politics much more than population determined statehood.

No firm number established a cutoff point at which a territory became a state. The Northwest Ordinance of 1787, when it outlined structures of governance for the Old Northwest, required a territory to have 60,000 people in order to petition for statehood. But that number had gradually risen. California had more than 93,000 when it became a state in 1850; Kansas had 107,000 when it entered in 1861. As of 1888, the states straddling or west of the ninety-eighth meridian included Texas (admitted in 1845), Kansas (1861), Nebraska (1867), Colorado (1876), Nevada (1864), California (1850), and Oregon (1859). Much of the rest, organized as territories, had populations large enough to bring them to the threshold of statehood. But how to cross?

The deep currents of demography did not always coincide with the surface waves of politics. Otherwise the Census Bureau could simply have notified the secretary of state that Territory X had reached sixty thousand, or whatever the law specified, and the secretary could simply have ratified the fact. Instead the Constitution provides only that Congress has the power to admit new states and that they must have "a republican form of Government."[124] Congress thus acted, in its own way and in its own good time, on petitions from territories for statehood. Each new state meant two new senators and at least one representative. If the balance in House or Senate between the political parties was close, new members might upset it. To confer statehood could thus have national consequences. And between 1876 and 1889 the balance in the Senate was usually within two or three votes.

In February 1889 Democratic President Grover Cleveland was preparing to turn over the White House on March 4 to Republican Benjamin Harrison, elected the previous fall. Republicans held the Senate by only thirty-nine seats to thirty-seven. The House was Democratic, but only through March 3. The next House, already elected in the fall of 1888 but not to take office until December 1889, was to have a Republican majority. Several territories had ample population to justify statehood, but whom would they elect to Congress? After much negotiation Congress passed and Cleveland signed, just before they all left office, a bill permitting the territories of Dakota, Montana, and Washington to enter the Union later in 1889, without further review by Congress. If Dakota Territory was split into two states, then the eight new senators were expected to fall roughly four each to Republicans and Democrats. In November 1889, a month before the new Republican-controlled Congress took office, North and South Dakota, Montana, and Washington did become states, with no question about their having sufficient populations; they ranged in the 1890 census from 142,900 for Montana upward to 357,200 for Washington.

In December 1889 newly seated Republican majorities in both House and Senate felt no great need to compromise any longer with the Democrats. They sent a bill to an agreeable President Harrison authorizing the admission of Idaho (with 88,500) and Wyoming (with 62,600, just a whistle over the minimum that the Northwest Ordinance had required 102 years earlier). Wyoming and Idaho became states in July 1890 and forthwith elected Republicans. Several other territories, with substantially larger populations, remained territories: Utah (210,800 in 1990), New Mexico (191,000), Arizona (88,200), and Oklahoma (258,700 boomers already). None was safely Republican. (Nor was Nevada "decommissioned" to territorial status. Although its population fell to only 47,400 in 1890, its senators were Republicans.)

The chief objection to Utah, besides doubt about how it would vote, was the Mormon doctrine of plural marriage. Republican reformers for two generations had condemned it, along with slavery, as one of the "twin relics of barbarism." In 1890, however, Mormon President Wilford Woodruff announced the end of plural marriage. Mormon leaders pressed national Republican decision makers to admit Utah, threatening that Saints living in already admitted states such as Idaho and Colorado would vote Democratic en bloc if Utah were kept out any longer. The Republicans gave in, and Utah joined the Union on January 4, 1896. (It voted 83 percent Democratic anyway in the fall.) Oklahoma, New Mexico, and Arizona—all predictably Democratic and in New Mexico's case with a large electable Hispanic population—had to wait eleven to sixteen years longer.[125]

Two other future states, Alaska and Hawaii, enter the West's story at this point, although their real importance came later.[126] Alaska, bought from Russia by Secretary of State William H. Seward in 1867, became nationally visible with the Klondike gold discoveries of 1897. The 1890 census counted 32,052 persons in the whole territory. Of these, about 19,000 were male and 13,000 female, a frontierish sex ratio of 150:100. About 74 percent were Indian and Inuit native peoples, with the rest distributed among whites (13 percent); "Mongolians" (i.e., Chinese; all were males), 7 percent; and "descendants of intermarriage between Russians and natives," about 6 percent. Half the whites were "temporary," working on whalers or in salmon canneries.[127] By 1900 the total had exactly doubled to 64,000, and the newcomers were mostly men, 30,000 of them white, with a median age around thirty, a typical population for a gold rush frontier. With 46,000 males and 18,000 females, the sex ratio ballooned to 256:100.

The Klondike gold rush involved considerably more people than these numbers indicate. Many came and left before the 1900 census takers made their count, and much of it took place over the line in Canada's Yukon Territory rather than in American Alaska. The best routes to the goldfields were in Canada, from Whitehorse to Dawson and then down the Yukon River into central Alaska. To get to Whitehorse, you traveled to Seattle or Vancouver, sailed up to Skagway in the Alaskan Panhandle, and then took a horse or wagon (or, by 1899, a narrow-gauge railroad) about 110 miles over a mountain pass to Whitehorse. From there you had your pick of several gold-yielding sites, all remote.

The news of gold traveled fast. When the steamer *Portland* docked in Seattle from Alaska on July 17, 1897, with sixty passengers, "every one of them seemed to have struck it rich."[128] Fortune seekers by the thousands invaded Dawson in the summer of 1897. Improvident, like the California forty-niners of a half century before, they traveled light. Dawson and other outposts virtually ran out of food the next winter. Many left, and others barely managed to survive in the several small boomtowns that sprouted along the river. These in turn emptied when a new gold strike at Nome pulled prospectors there in late 1899. The Klondike rush lasted into 1900, long enough to disrupt native peoples and their cultures; as in California in the 1850s, some were wiped out.

The last major strike occurred at Tanana, near Fairbanks, in 1902.[129] By then Alaska was already settling into more prosaic industrial mining of non-precious as well as precious metals. Its population rose very slowly for decades, from the sixty-four thousand of 1900 to just seventy-three thousand by 1940. Agriculture, despite hopes, never took off; farms peaked at a negligible 623 in 1940. Alaska, writes a geographer, was "one of the exceptional areas in the United States where the cherished yeoman farmer tradition was not implemented."[130] Remote and sparsely settled, Alaska awaited another boom. It came, but only after World War II.

Hawaii received its first humans, a Polynesian people, sometime before the year 900 C.E. Europeans did not bother them until Captain James Cook's third voyage in 1778 stopped on the Kona coast of the "Big Island." Cook was well received at first, but the Hawaiians ceremonially killed and ate him on an ill-timed return visit. Subsequent European navigators visited the islands sparingly until American Protestant missionaries arrived in 1820. As the saying goes, they came to do good, and instead they did well. By the late nineteenth century their descendants were planting and shipping cane sugar, using Hawaiian labor and immigrant Asian workers. In 1893 they overthrew the native ruler, Queen Liliuokalani, and petitioned the United States for annexation. President Cleveland turned them down, but a more imperial-minded Republican Congress voted Hawaiian annexation in 1898.

The native Hawaiians meanwhile had not done well. Captain Cook's sailors introduced them to European diseases, and by the early nineteenth century they were dying off from syphilis, gonorrhea, influenza, measles, mumps, chicken pox, smallpox, and other infections. All these killed directly and also reduced fertility, sterilizing both men and women and raising infant mortality. More than 400,000 Hawaiians died within twenty-five years of Cook's visit, and they kept on dying. Estimated at 800,000 in 1778, the Hawaiians numbered 37,000 at the American takeover in 1898. In 120 years a "virgin soil" population declined by 95 percent. It is worth noting that this disaster took place in a limited space, over a limited time, and is reasonably well documented. The destruction of native populations of North and South America, which happened in a much larger space, over a much longer time, from less verifiable starting points, has been debated for just those reasons. But the Hawaiian case is collateral evidence that the mainland kill-off, for 400 years after 1492, was indeed catastrophic.[131]

The native Hawaiians in 1898, by then a minority in their own country, protested the annexation to President William McKinley, but fruitlessly. By then they shared their islands with 45,000 whites (including about 12,000 Portuguese sugar workers from the Azores), 30,000 recently arrived Japanese contract laborers, and thousands of Chinese, who had held relatively privileged positions under the Hawaiian monarchy.[132] Immediately following annexation, some of the Portuguese left for California, and Japanese more than replaced them. In the 1900 census, Hawaii reported 154,000 persons, more than two-thirds of them male, three-fourths of them Asian or Polynesian, with whites a small minority.[133]

This racial distribution worked against the statehood that the American elite wanted and expected. The Chinese Exclusion Acts of 1882 and later disqualified Asians from citizenship, so for statehood purposes, they did not count. Without them the white minority was too small to provide enough voters for statehood. Hawaii did not become a mass settlement target for Americans, instead remaining a colony and resource exploitation frontier whose white Americans consisted of planters and their families, naval and military forces, a small number of businessmen, and a cadre of public officials. As with Alaska, a rather somnolent early twentieth century was followed by massive changes during and after World War II. Among those postwar changes came statehood for both, at long last, in 1959.

Westerners did defy the depression of the 1890s, but in many different ways. On the Great Plains and parts of the Great Basin, they hunkered down where they had to and rushed into new settlement turf where they could. Still others, who were incurably infected with the homesteading virus, talked and thought of the wonders that irrigation and dry farming could bring, believing that the dream would come true as soon as rains began again and crop and livestock markets revived. To them the depression was just another cyclical glitch, signaling only a pause, not a fundamental refiguring. They had no compelling reason to think differently. "Frontier anxiety," what was to become of America after the frontier ended, was worth worrying about, but it was an abstract and general worry. Anyone closer to the ground knew very well that millions of farmable acres still awaited settlers.

The new story, however, had begun. Mining was already just another industry, the railroad network was largely in place, and cities led the population surge in state after state. California in 1900 had an urban majority of 52 percent. The transformation of America from the frontier rural society of the eighteenth and nineteenth centuries to the metropolitan society of the twentieth was *the* major change in American history. So great a change did not and could not happen in a year or even a decade. In the West it began developing in Pasadena in the 1870s and Los Angeles in the 1880s, and the contrasts of the old story and the new sharpened in the 1890s. In the first dozen years of the new century the two stories spun out side by side. But by 1913 the older story of homesteading had reached the end of its long American season.

5

THE GOLDEN TWILIGHT OF THE SETTLEMENT FRONTIER, 1901–1913

That bugbear of the eastern farmer—the weather—is forgotten and irrigated farming becomes almost an exact science, crops never fail. . . .
—Big Horn Basin Development Company, 1908

I was raised in Chicago without so much as a back yard to play in, and I worked 48 hours a week for $1.25. When I heard you could get 320 acres just by living on it, I felt that I had been offered a kingdom.
—Montana homesteader to Marie MacDonald, 1986

Homesteading's True Heyday

Between 1862, when the Homestead Act passed, and 1900, 1,400,000 people applied for its quarter section family farms. Between 1901 and 1913 another 1,000,000 filed—over twice as many per year.[1] Those first thirteen years of the twentieth century were the true heyday of homesteading. Compared with them, Kansas and Nebraska in the twenty years after the Civil War were a prelude, and Oklahoma for all its explosiveness was only an overture. The first dozen years of the century brought an extravaganza of settlement, from Texas north across the High Plains into the Canadian prairies. The peak was 1913. From then on the possibly farmable land became ever scarcer, and Turner's statement of 1893, that with the end of the settlement frontier "came the end of the first great period in American history," finally fitted the facts.

In truth, these first years proved absolutely pivotal. As the new century opened, American society turned away from its rural past, the lifeways that had been most people's common experience in Anglo-America since colonial days, and faced a new metropolitan future. The shift signaled a change far larger than simply a move from farm to city, from raising crops and livestock to working in factories and offices. Rather, it was a shift in lifestyles and worldviews, one that required decades to complete. These were the last years in American history when *both* cities and new farms would proliferate. New York emerged in the 1880 census as the first million-plus metropolis, to be joined by Philadelphia and Chicago in 1890. At every census throughout the nineteenth century, city people took a greater share of American population, from one in twenty in 1800, to one in seven in 1850, to two in five in 1900. Yet farms and farm people multiplied too. In 1913, 59,363 final homestead entries, covering 10,885,000 acres of land, were proved up—that is, deeded over from federal to private ownership. Never before or since did proved-up acres exceed 10,000,000 in one year.[2]

This parallel pattern of both farm and city growth continued to about 1913. After that cities kept developing, but rural America began leveling off. New homestead entries averaged over 83,000 every year from 1901 through 1910, but slipped to 53,000 a year between 1911 and 1915, and below 24,000 from 1921 to 1925. Fingers of new settlement probed into certain isolated areas after 1913, to be sure. But after that peak year American farms and farm population stopped expanding, stabilized for twenty-five years until the late 1930s, and then started to shrink and have shrunk ever since.

This of course was not evident in 1901. The western horizon was not cloudless, but there were plenty of reasons why land seekers should have been optimistic. Vast lands remained "open"; railroads were eager to sell their grants; Congress kept inflating homestead sizes to try to accommodate High Plains aridity. Experts insisted that irrigation and dry farming were the answers to the devil of drought. So the frontier of settlement, stalled since the outset of the Great Plains farm depression in 1887, started moving west again. Simultaneously cities and industries proliferated. Mining, more than ever an industry involving substantial capital and wage labor, attracted migrants as multiethnic as in the Northeast; Serbs, Croats, Greeks, and others did not fear to cross the Mississippi. In Arizona, Bisbee with its mines and Douglas with its smelters, almost unpopulated in 1900, topped nine thousand a dozen years later; Price, Utah, attracted several thousand. Northern Idaho communities from Lewiston to Coeur d'Alene nearly doubled. Mexicans and Japanese were much more visible than before 1901.

Several cities small in 1901 easily passed 100,000 by the 1910 census or by 1913. Salt Lake City rose from 54,000 in 1900 to more than 100,000 by 1913, and by the 1910 census Spokane had gone from 39,000 to 104,000; Oakland from 67,000 to 150,000; Portland from 90,000 to 207,000; and Seattle from 81,000 to 237,000.[3] Several counties in California's San Joaquin Valley more than doubled their populations because of irrigated crop raising and intensive stock farming. California's "hydraulic society" had begun. Los Angeles

County became the population leader of the entire West, exploding from 170,000 in 1900 to 504,000 in 1910 and nearly doubling to 936,000 in 1920.

With drought and depression behind it, the West became briefly a rare and clear case of simultaneous urban and rural growth, the dual expansion of both the very customary and the very new. This was nearly the final hour of the traditional, Jeffersonian, homestead-seeking America, yet also a time of headlong rush into a new kind of world. By the early years of the century the West was already resistant to generalization. Texas was not Montana; Idaho was not Wyoming. In the following pages we shall look at each part, beginning with Texas, proceeding north through the plains to Dakota, down the Front Range and across the Rockies and Great Basin into the mining West, then to the Pacific Northwest and finally California. We move from homesteaders to miners to city dwellers, including the incredible diversity of ethnics, from Asia as well as Europe—an even greater range than in Ellis Island–era New York. We shall also look at the metropolitan West in 1913, the year when homestead entries reached their never-again-equaled peak, when the San Francisco Exposition celebrated the West's maturity, and when engineering brought virtually limitless water to Los Angeles and San Francisco and thus assured their futures.

In the first thirteen years of the century the Great Plains west of the 98th and 100th meridians truly opened up. Homesteads, railroad lines, whistle-stops, grain elevators, churches, courthouses, and all the trappings of commercial farming and stock raising filled the treeless, sunbaked sea of grass from south Texas to the middle of Alberta and Saskatchewan. No part of the region lacked migrants. The most startling increases took place in Texas and Oklahoma, which between them added 1,715,000 people in 1900–1910 and another million or more by 1917. Expansion in the four plains states north of them (Kansas, Nebraska, the two Dakotas) was also considerable: 787,000 between 1900 and 1910, 300,000 in 1910–1920.[4]

So strong was the optimism, so confident the people, so reassured were they by scientific theories of dryland farming and the possibilities of irrigation that they surged beyond the 100th meridian, beyond the 102d into Colorado, the 103d into New Mexico, the 104th into eastern Montana. In 1890 two giant counties occupied all Montana between Wyoming and Canada for about 125 miles west of the Dakota line. Only 7,400 people rattled around in them. By 1920 they had calved off into sixteen counties with 117,700 people, settled on farms or ranches or in small towns sprinkled along the routes of the Great Northern and the Northern Pacific. None of those towns came near having 10,000 people, or ever would. Similar county chopping took place in eastern Colorado and New Mexico, as scores of thousands homesteaded the grasslands and sprinkled them with little towns marked from miles away by their tall white grain elevators.

Wheat Country, from Texas North

The entire High Plains became an enormous wheat field and cow pasture. We shall follow the harvest route from Texas northward.

Nowhere were changes greater than in Oklahoma and west Texas. Railroad building, sod busting, cotton and wheat growing, Hereford ranching, town forming, and oil drilling transformed the old *comanchería* into capitalism. In 1901 the western line of farm settlement in Texas crossed the 100th meridian past Abilene, Wichita Falls, and San Angelo. Towns of 2,000 or 3,000, no larger, appeared only in the late 1890s. Lubbock County had fewer than 300 residents; Amarillo and Potter County under 2,000. Only four panhandle counties exceeded 1,000, and most were still looking for 500. Texas, however, was already the sixth-largest state in population in 1900 and was poised for a new demographic surge, which it had, growing by 28 percent (848,000) by the census of 1910 and another 20 percent (766,000) by 1920.

Almost every part of the Texas Gulf Coast from Mexico to the Louisiana line grew faster than the state average. This area included Brownsville, Corpus Christi, Houston, Galveston and other ports, and Beaumont, after the Spindletop oil field opened in 1901. Dallas, Fort Worth, and San Antonio (as well as Houston) passed the hundred thousand mark in 1910, El Paso in 1920, with Waco, Beaumont, and Wichita Falls following soon after. Texas was never just cowboys and cattle ranches. But big cities and the Gulf Coast aside, the demographic action in early-twentieth-century Texas happened west of the 98th meridian. Railroad building and friendly land laws from the legislature in Austin had much to do with guiding the paths of population advance, which formed two westward-thrusting prongs: first, a string of twenty-two counties from just east of Abilene, south to San Saba, and west to Odessa, focused mainly on cattle ranching, then cotton, and soon oil; second, about thirty-one counties north of Lubbock through the panhandle, opening to cotton around Lubbock and, north toward Amarillo and beyond, winter wheat and beef cattle. Around Odessa, west of the 102d meridian, stock raising beat dry farming, as the law permitted a rancher to claim four sections (of 640 acres each) for himself as well as to find cowboys "to take up more, then buy them out" and hire them on the ranch.[5]

In this fashion, when Lucy and Olive Tubbs's father and his three brothers found land too expensive in Kaufman County, southeast of Dallas, in 1890, the father took up four sections near Lubbock, exchanged one for a mule, paid up the others, and claimed four more farther west, while the brothers

1. Pío Pico, last Mexican governor of California, with his wife and nieces.

2. Don Abel Stearns, most prominent of the ex-Yankee Californios.

3. Daniel M. Berry, emissary of Indiana investors and founder of Pasadena, 1873.

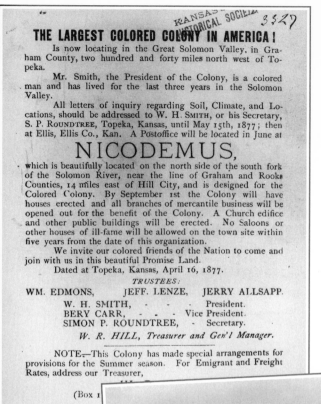

THE LARGEST COLORED COLONY IN AMERICA!

Is now locating in the Great Solomon Valley, in Graham County, two hundred and forty miles north west of Topeka.

Mr. Smith, the President of the Colony, is a colored man and has lived for the last three years in the Solomon Valley.

All letters of inquiry regarding Soil, Climate, and Locations, should be addressed to W. H. SMITH, or his Secretary, S. P. ROUNDTREE, Topeka, Kansas, until May 15th, 1877; then at Ellis, Ellis Co., Kan. A Postoffice will be located in June at

NICODEMUS,

which is beautifully located on the north side of the south fork of the Solomon River, near the line of Graham and Rooks Counties, 14 miles east of Hill City, and is designed for the Colored Colony. By September 1st the Colony will have houses erected and all branches of mercantile business will be opened out for the benefit of the Colony. A Church edifice and other public buildings will be erected. No Saloons or other houses of ill-fame will be allowed on the town site within five years from the date of this organization.

We invite our colored friends of the Nation to come and join with us in this beautiful Promise Land.

Dated at Topeka, Kansas, April 16, 1877.

TRUSTEES:

WM. EDMONS,   JEFF. LENZE,   JERRY ALLSAPP.
W. H. SMITH, - - - President.
BERY CARR, - - - Vice President.
SIMON P. ROUNDTREE, - Secretary.
W. R. HILL, Treasurer and Gen'l Manager.

NOTE.—This Colony has made special arrangements for provisions for the Summer season. For Emigrant and Freight Rates, address our Treasurer,

(Box 1

4. Poster advertising Nicodemus, Kansas, a settlement colony for freedpersons, 1877.

5. The first Oklahoma land rush: "ready for the race," April 22, 1889.

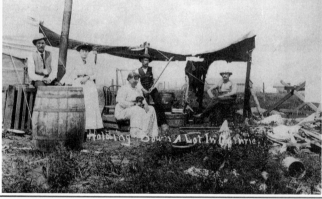

6. The Oklahoma land rush of 1889: "holding down a lot in Guthrie."

7. The Cherokee Outlet rush of September 11, 1893: men waiting to register and proceed.

8. African-Americans picking cotton, Oklahoma, 1890s.

9. "Miss Blanche Lamont with her school at Hecla, Montana, Oct., 1893." Lamont appears here as a typical teacher of the one-room schools that dotted the Great Plains through the 1940s. Two years later she and another young woman were discovered "nude, mutilated, and dead on Easter Sunday" in the belfry of a Baptist church in San Francisco. A Sunday school superintendent protested innocence as he was hanged for the murder in 1898.

10. Three modes of transportation in Los Angeles, 1906: buggies, an auto, and a Pacific Electric interurban streetcar at Sunset Boulevard and Micheltorena, still open country.

11. Indians at Muskogee, Indian Territory, enrolling for land allotments under the Dawes Severalty Act, about 1898.

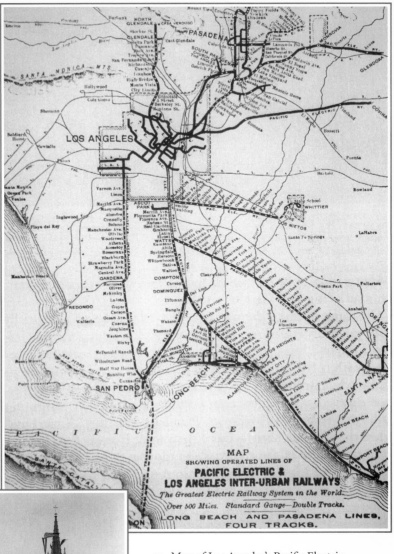

MAP
SHOWING OPERATED LINES OF
**PACIFIC ELECTRIC &
LOS ANGELES INTER-URBAN RAILWAYS**
The Greatest Electric Railway System in the World.
Over 500 Miles. Standard Gauge—Double Tracks.
**LONG BEACH AND PASADENA LINES,
FOUR TRACKS.**

12. Map of Los Angeles's Pacific Electric interurban system, about 1907. In the next few years it reached farther, to Santa Monica and Venice and elsewhere throughout the county.

13. Multiethnic crowd dedicating St. Mary's Church, Mount Angel, Oregon, 1912. But American flags fly highest.

14. The California Dream, 1911: a bungalow in Glendale.

15. The California Dream, 1913: first day of a land auction at Montrose, near Los Angeles.

16. The Mexican Revolution, April 1914. A middle-class woman at El Paso, expelled from Torreón after Francisco Villa's forces captured it, about to register as a refugee at the U.S. Migration Office.

17. January 1914: a refugee march to Presidio, Texas, of Huertistas defeated by Villa.

18. Children and burro escaping across the Rio Grande.

20. Nisei children: Hiroshi Ikeda and Aiko Kuromi on wooden tricycles at Redondo Beach, Los Angeles, 1921.

19. Soonkee Thee, interpreter, with a group of Korean contract workers in Maui or Oahu, 1903.

21. Katharine Drexel (r.), founder of the Sisters of the Blessed Sacrament and philanthropist to Indians and African-Americans, with Navajo leaders in New Mexico, 1928.

23. Americans now: Reina and Jacob Touriel in Los Angeles, 1929.

22. Not yet Americans: Reina and Jacob Touriel, Sephardic Jews, on Rhodos, 1921.

24. Nathan Krems, son of Polish-Russian immigrants, dressed for his third birthday party, Seattle, 1918.

claimed six sections more—among them, 8,320 acres. They were part of the first intensive settlement. By 1901 they were growing feed for the area's many cattle.[6] Cotton took over soon after, attracting "trainloads of prospectors, speculators, and investors . . . eager to buy land at from twelve to twenty-two dollars per acre" in 1908, a state official reported—probably a higher price than long-term returns justified, because several of these counties lost much of their new population by 1920.[7] Water gushed upward as improved windmills, some gasoline-powered, began to tap the apparently inexhaustible underground sea of the Ogallala Aquifer, which extended from near Pecos hundreds of miles northward into South Dakota.[8] Most of the panhandle, tied by rail and wheat markets more to Kansas City than to Dallas, kept gaining people. In both prongs of west Texas settlement, oil and gas wells sprouted following the Wichita Falls strike of 1911.[9]

The one other growth area in Texas in those years was along the Rio Grande. El Paso (always more Mexican and New Mexican than Anglo-Texan), Brownsville, and some *tejano* majority areas near the border gained well above the state average. Population dynamics in this area had little to do with cotton, wheat, and oil, but much to do with the Hispanic urban growth more typical of the borderlands of the future, from south Texas to California. Revolution (Mexico's, after 1910), not rainfall or the lack of it, primed the expansion of El Paso and other border towns.[10]

In Oklahoma the invasion of the 1890s continued with some new twists, bringing the population to more than enough to justify statehood in 1907. Despite the history of severe drought in Kansas west of the 100th meridian, homesteaders started quarter section family farms in western Oklahoma. Some sold out fairly quickly to cattle ranchers or tried to become ranchers themselves rather than wheat farmers; others doggedly stuck to farming, even through the Dust Bowl of the 1930s. Severalty—privately owned allotments—effectively shrank Indian holdings in eastern Oklahoma as whites bought them up. The first of Oklahoma's prodigious oil and natural gas discoveries took place early in the century, and two dominant cities, Oklahoma City and Tulsa, quickly appeared. Each exceeded a hundred thousand by 1920. Hopeful homesteaders more than doubled several rural Oklahoma counties between 1901 and 1913, but thousands had retreated by 1920, causing losses in about a third of the state's counties.

As the century opened, Oklahoma headed toward statehood as homesteaders sought safe havens in its red-soiled windy west. C. L. Alley, born in 1894, later described how his young parents (his father from Des Moines, Iowa, his mother from Hoisington, Kansas) went to Colorado looking for land, bore him, and then homesteaded south of Alva in the Cherokee Outlet two years later. They traded that place to a neighbor, rode a wagon to

Arkansas, and returned in December 1900 to join the homestead rush around Woodward, in the northwest corner of the territory. The family lived there in a one-room dugout, sixteen by twenty-four feet, until 1909, when they took a train to Oregon and tried life at Oceanside, just west of Tilla-mook on the sea; they "thought it might be a better place than Oklahoma." But, said Alley, it was too rainy for Oklahoma people, so they returned to Woodward, built a four-room house of cement blocks in 1911, and there they stayed. They broke the sod—with a good team, two acres in a day—and grew broom corn, kaffir corn, and regular corn to keep going. The school-house, a dugout built in 1902, provided him and another twenty or so stu-dents an eighth-grade education by the time he was sixteen.[11]

Russell Adams's young parents—his father a Missourian and his mother a Russian-born German from Kansas—homesteaded on a quarter section near Fargo, Oklahoma Territory, in 1901: "Just like other people . . . land was terrible high where they were living; they heard about this land here, being given 160 acres," and so they came.[12] Robert Kohler's father, a German who arrived in western Kansas in 1897 at age eighteen, knew blacksmithing and became a "windmill man" on a ranch. In time he took care of forty-eight windmills, filed and proved up on a homestead near Boise City in the tip of the panhandle in 1907, and eventually bought out twenty-seven homesteads in the area. With horses, he built a 320-foot dam and 8 miles of irrigation canals along the Cimarron River, employing his sons and other men. In later years the younger Kohler served on the High Plains Council to advise on the shrinkage of the Ogallala Aquifer.

Oklahoma had many black homesteaders. Mary Wyatt arrived in 1902 by train with her parents, children of slaves, from Mount Airy, North Carolina. Her father sold his farm there, and homesteaded 80 acres, then another 160, near the South Canadian River at Hinton, Oklahoma. Mrs. Wyatt attended grade school there, then high school nearby and Langston University, and became a teacher. They chopped (weeded) cotton, pulled it, and picked it, and "raised everything on the farm they needed to eat . . . all they had to do when I was growing up was to raise their own chickens, their own beef and pork; they'd kill about seven or eight hogs, and my mother would even make the sauces." Leaving at 4:00 a.m., they took garden vegetables twenty-five miles to El Reno and sold the produce on the street.

The Hinton area had nearly filled between 1902 and 1906, when Fern Behrendt's parents came to Oklahoma with fourteen other families who had rebelled at farming for half shares in Huntington County, Indiana. "The owners . . . had had the property from the Civil War on, and the young folks didn't have any place to get started on, only just rent . . . they heard about this land being open for filing," 160 acres in the Oklahoma Panhandle, with nothing on it but grazing cattle.[13] The old frontier story of young people settling, land prices rising over the next generation, and new young people moving off to a new area of "empty" land repeated itself for about the last time. This family moved from tent to dugout to frame house. A subscription school opened for six months a year; "the men gathered at the store . . . and decided they'd pay $1 a month for each child to the teacher." Country post offices proliferated, and in a few seasons beginning in 1906, Cimarron County filled up as much as it ever would. Twenty-five years later it became the heart of the Dust Bowl.

Oklahoma's creation of new counties, reflecting population increases, shifted after 1913 from the homesteading western part to the eastern. There Indian land that opened to severalty in the 1890s was leased, rented, or sold to whites, without the necessity of tribal approval. The announced purpose of the Dawes Severalty Act of 1887 had been to assimilate Indians into white society by making them homesteaders on 160-acre "allotments" rather than members of a tribal group with communal land. When land shifted from Indians to whites, the assimilation goal lost immediacy. But rather than change the policy, the Indian Office continued to promote ownership and development of Indian land by non-Indians.[14] Opened as a refuge for the major tribes of southern Appalachia in the 1830s and 1840s, Oklahoma after 1913 had become no safe home for either Indians or homesteaders.

Kansas and Nebraska, where drought and depression pulled settlers back from their western counties from 1887 until rains returned in 1901, revived during the next dozen years. The westward movement in these states was sedate compared with that of west Texas, but it was still considerable. Following the railroads' energetic promotions and colonizing efforts, settlement ventured west of the 100th meridian again. Irrigation and dryland farming were touted as the scientific answers to aridity—irrigation much less vocally than before, dryland farming more and more confidently.[15]

But then the entire decade from 1901 to 1911 turned out to be one of those cycles of above-average rainfall, like 1879–1887, and in fact reasonably provident rainfall continued in Kansas and Nebraska with few serious interruptions into the 1920s. When "knockers" reminded their neighbors of the crash of the late 1880s (in rainfall, crop prices, and real estate values), they were soberly advised that agricultural science, primitive in the 1880s, was now competent to guide prudent settlers. Consequently western Kansas and Nebraska were resettled: not densely—western Kansas averaged five or six persons a square mile in 1910[16]—but with a continuous blanket of farms and people. Farms were about three times the size of those east of Topeka and

Lincoln and concentrated on winter wheat and cattle raising, plus sugar beets for those irrigating from the South or North Platte River under New-lands Act provisions.[17]

Population shifted in Kansas and Nebraska from 1901 to 1913 much like in Texas, though on a smaller scale. Many of the rural counties in the eastern third or half of these states, places that had been themselves the settlement frontier in the 1860s and 1870s, lost population. The major cities—Kansas City, Topeka, and Wichita in Kansas, Omaha and Lincoln in Nebraska—gained population faster than the state averages. Scottsbluff, North Platte, Salina, and Dodge City, though with only a few thousand people each, had high growth rates. In Kansas the strongest migration flowed into the hith-erto almost uninhabited ten southwestern counties clustering between Dodge City and the Oklahoma and Colorado lines. There the growth much resembled that of the Texas Panhandle just thirty-five miles to the south.

All this area more than doubled in population from 1901 to 1910 and kept drawing people for several more years while wheat markets continued strong. Railroad spurs and grain elevators multiplied.[18] Indeed all of the westernmost sixty to ninety miles of Kansas bordering on Colorado enjoyed such growth. A few counties overreached their carrying capacity by 1917, los-ing a few thousand by 1920. But the retreat was minor compared with that of the late 1880s. High fertility among farm families partly offset the out-migration.[19]

Farther north the Dakotas were undergoing their most intense frontier development: the land office business, the clattering new railroads, and young couples tossing together farms, fences, and families. With the turn of the century came fifteen boom years, bringing a half million new settlers and those who served them with dry goods stores, banks, implement dealer-ships, churches, schools, railroads, and grain elevators. Well over one hun-dred thousand were foreign-born,[20] just over half (53 or 54 percent) were male, and nearly all lived on farms or in country towns.[21]

Some oversettled places, however, started retrenching by 1911 in South Dakota and by 1917 in North Dakota and eastern Montana. The Dakotas grew 61 percent between the 1900 and 1910 censuses, but only 11 percent from 1910 to 1920, most of it in the early part of the decade, and they slowed further to a flat 7 percent in the 1920s. Later years would be even less kind. Land policy, Indian policy, and railroads enticed people into the Dakotas after 1900. Twelve or fifteen years later, low rainfall and falling wheat prices persuaded them to leave or stay away.

Nowhere on the Great Plains were climatic conditions more precarious, extremes of temperature greater, theories about how to get around them more contrived, and hope higher than in the Dakotas and eastern Montana.

From well over a hundred degrees Fahrenheit in the summer—lethally high in an enclosed space like a sod house—the temperature could drop to forty below in winter, sometimes plunging sixty degrees in an hour or two. Wind was (and is) almost always present, seldom less than fifteen knots; it could bring snow, hail, searing heat, or even a cooling breeze. Some of this treeless, fuel-scarce region had long been considered the Great American Desert, forever unfit for settlement. Its Canadian segment, the arid area north of Montana from about Lethbridge, Alberta, east to Moose Jaw, Saskatchewan, had been marked for avoidance when Captain John Palliser surveyed it in the late 1850s. Nevertheless settlers swarmed into the dreaded Palliser's Triangle as well as the American northern plains.

The irrigation panacea, reinforced by the federal Newlands Reclamation Act in 1902, attracted multitudes of new preachers and believers. In 1904 Colorado boomers touted irrigated land along the Arkansas and Platte rivers, the mountain-bound San Luis Valley, the western slope of the Rockies, indeed just about anywhere, claiming that Colorado already had 12,000 to 15,000 miles of main canals plus uncounted laterals, covering 4,500,000 acres, of which more than 1,000,000 were "actually irrigated. . . . When a farmer can look up at the snow banks whence comes his water supply; when he can see the moisture stored in great reservoirs, ready for use; when he can direct and control its application, day by day, by means of canals, laterals and ditches, almost at his very door, he can sleep soundly at night, without troubled dreams of burnt up crops or consequent financial losses. The Colorado farmer, with his forty, eighty or one hundred and sixty acres of land, and a water right, is the most independent producer on earth. . . ."[22]

The Denver Reservoir Irrigation Company in 1907 advertised irrigated land only nine miles from the State Capitol, promising fifty to sixty bushels per acre of winter wheat: "Farming by irrigation is becoming more and more a business because it offers an ample field for the use of scientific knowledge, good judgment, alertness and energy, the qualities that successful business men possess. There is less risk in farming by irrigation than in any other business. We want people—lots of them. We have blazed the way for thousands of happy homes and thrifty families. You may become one of the beneficiaries." The company offered land, including a water right, for $75 to $125 an acre, far above the homestead commutation price.[23] But so close to Denver, the investment was indeed safe, if you could afford it. (That land has long since been subdivided into suburbs.)

In Montana, hucksters promised, in essence, opportunity and freedom. For example, the Big Horn Basin Development Company opened 245,000 acres of irrigated land to purchase and settlement in 1908. Here, its creative writers claimed, "that bugbear of the eastern farmer—the weather—is forgotten and irrigated farming becomes almost an exact science, crops never fail, and the tiller of the soil can sow with pleasure and reap with profit— *verily irrigation is crop insurance.*"[24] Also in 1908, the U.S. Reclamation Service, created to carry out the Newlands Act, promoted a new irrigation district about to be formed around Klamath Falls, Oregon. The area, at forty-one-hundred-foot elevation with fourteen inches' annual rainfall, had "abundant" water for irrigation. "Perhaps 80 per cent of the land is at present only roughly dry farmed or unoccupied," wrote a Reclamation Service official; 80 acres "will make a fine farm in the district"; it took, he claimed, only $1,500 to buy the land and get through a year before crops came in. "Before the project is completed, several million dollars will have been expended by the government, in the proper installation of a complete irrigation system."[25] No objection to federal aid here.

In Wyoming, north of Cheyenne, the "Wheatland Colony" in 1913 offered land from $35 to $60 an acre, zero to 20 percent financing, with start-up costs estimated to total $897 for horses, harnesses, a wagon, a grain drill, a milk cow, a plow, a harrow, and a drag leveler. A house, fencing, seed, a well, and access roads were not mentioned, though they were unavoidable. In a slightly pleading tone rather than uninhibited boosterism, the promoters promised that "any man who is willing to work and understands farming, can prosper in the Wheatland Colony."[26] Others beware. New Mexico, after some false starts in the 1880s and 1890s, acquired substantial irrigation works on the Pecos and Rio Grande through federal and private investment, underpinning a surge of farm settlement by 1912.[27] Arizona, California, Utah, Nevada, Idaho, and Washington also fostered irrigation and settlement through this period, with and without federal help. In 1905 the Chicago, Burlington, & Quincy Railroad advertised four projects planned by the U.S. Reclamation Service, under the Newlands Act, in Wyoming and adjacent Montana and South Dakota, another case of federal-railroad cooperation in economic development.[28]

By 1905 a new solution to aridity promised to settle many more people than irrigation ever could. This was dry farming, defined as "agriculture without irrigation in regions of scanty precipitation."[29] Its early and greatest apostle was a Vermonter named Hardy Webster Campbell, who homesteaded near Aberdeen, South Dakota, in 1879. Through the 1880s his success was at best moderate. With Yankee-like observation and invention, Campbell developed methods and machines by the 1890s that he claimed would capture and preserve soil moisture even in the driest years. His basic principles included deep plowing (six to twelve inches), packing the subsoil, mulching the topsoil, cultivating it frequently, and planting wheat (and occasionally other crops) on only half the land in a given year, leaving the other half fallow, rotating the fields biennially.[30]

Campbell fine-tuned these practices and applied them a little differently depending on time and place. The basic idea, however, stood: careful, clever methods would permit settlement far beyond the limits of irrigability. Faith in his own ideas helped make him an enormously effective propagandist for them. Periodicals, his book *Campbell's Soil Culture Manual,* which first appeared in 1902 and went through several editions, Dry Farming Congresses, and demonstration farms all popularized his program. Campbell's prediction that the plains would become "the last and best grain garden of the world" precisely matched the spreading folk belief that "rain follows the plow"—that plowing the prairie sod would permit moisture to seep in and nourish grain, instead of running off wastefully.

Campbell's homespun methods had given way by 1910 to more refined better farming movements connected with state agricultural experiment stations and the Department of Agriculture, all of which fitted neatly into the Progressive Era's faith in education, science, and experts. Commercial progress was part of it too. Irrigation, dry farming, and better farming received support from railroads, real estate developers, bankers, local and regional merchants, grain elevator operators and millers, politicians, and editors, who all equated progress, development, and capitalism.[31]

This was no cynical conspiracy but a deeply felt value system in play, one that incorporated and went beyond the simpler Agrarian Dream of Jefferson. Nature would be manipulated and the plains yield to productive settlement. And so hopeful settlers who were convinced that they could defeat aridity, as eager as Americans and Europeans had ever been to own and farm their own land, careered into the Dakotas, eastern Montana, southern Saskatchewan, and Alberta, in the dawn years of the new century.

Dakota the Multicultural

Begun in the late 1870s, crowned by statehood in 1889, and slowed through the 1890s, the land rush into the Dakotas resumed massively by 1901, carrying settlers westward across the 100th meridian and the Missouri River into semiarid and often difficult terrain. Drought returned from 1910 to 1912, ending the rush in South Dakota, although western North Dakota continued receiving people until 1917. Montana's rush started in force in 1909 in the Yellowstone Valley, peaked in 1910, but also lasted until 1917. North of the border about a million migrants entered Alberta and Saskatchewan from 1901 to 1913, smaller numbers from then through the 1920s.[32]

Of these settlers, some were born in the United States (either of American or Canadian parents), others in Canada, and many in Europe. The Great Northern Railroad carried about 13,000 of them *a year* into western North Dakota in the late 1890s and 35,000 by 1900. By spring 1903 both the Great Northern and the Northern Pacific had to add extra trains to bring 6,000 to 10,000 there *daily*. By 1905 the western edge of settlement had reached Minot, just west of the 101st meridian, and ran south past Bismarck to Fort Yates in the Standing Rock Sioux Reservation and along the 100th meridian to the South Dakota/Nebraska line.

A great many of these new settlers and their communities began precariously and continued that way. Tens of thousands proved up their homestead claims, but as many or more did not. The attempt could often be called a triumph of hope over inexperience because the settlers sometimes lacked any farming background that they could adapt to the plains, or any at all. Of the many determinants of the flow of migration, two stood out: recurring drought, which cut it off, and the railroads, which kept it happening.

Settlers often preceded the railroad into a new area, but they seldom stayed long without one. The Northern Pacific, the Soo Line, the Great Northern, and the Canadian Pacific farther north brought migrants west; sold land to them; platted and created country villages around coaling and watering stops and grain elevators; carried their wheat to Minneapolis–St. Paul for sale and milling; brought their brides and relatives from Europe; imported their mail orders from Chicago; pushed irrigation and dry farming alike; and performed many functions that tied the homesteader, however lonely or without means, to a larger society and economy. Pioneers they truly were, but not in the same autonomous way that settlers in 1820s' Indiana or 1720s' Virginia had been, because the railroad was now vital.

After the quiescent 1890s the railroads began laying track and platting towns prodigally: from 1901 to 1913, usually 50 to 100 miles of new track a year (in 1905 alone, over 300 new miles of track and nearly forty new towns). The Northern Pacific, confident that farmers would keep coming, started selling tracts no larger than 320 acres. Wheat farmers were occupying former rangeland, pushing out the stock raisers.[33] The Great Northern not only promoted irrigation and dry farming but also backed the Good Roads movement, the campaign in the Midwest and West to create a network of all-weather paved roads. The railroads sent demonstrator trains to educate settlers in home economics and better farming methods, and they began in 1911 sponsoring dozens of demonstration farms.[34]

Bowman County, for example, in the southwestern corner of North Dakota, opened up in 1905. Most of its settlers arrived by train, took up 160-acre homesteads often on former Indian reservation land, and hired gasoline and steam tractors to break the sod prior to wheat planting. The county's stockmen sold out or moved to Indian reservations in the face of such strong demand for farmland. Newly built railway branch lines kept the land boom going until 1917, when drought triggered departures.[35]

The settlers were an extremely multicultural lot. Ethnicity was more mixed the farther one looked north on the plains, and North Dakota became especially polyglot. In the years of heaviest European migration to the United States and Canada, roughly 1901 to 1925, the railroads carried many to the plains, first as wageworkers and then as passengers. Italians, Greeks, Chinese, Japanese, and others helped build the roads, and though most moved on, a few stayed to settle. Norwegians, followed by Germans from Russia and Germany, Canadians, and many less numerous groups crowded into North Dakota, making it one of the most heavily immigrant states in the nation. South Dakota and Montana were nearly as mixed, Alberta and Saskatchewan more so. North Dakota's Bureau of Immigration competed with the Canadian Ministry of the Interior in promoting and propagandizing aggressively. In North Dakota, railroads, Realtors, merchants, journalists, and other boomers complained that Canada was outspending and outpersuading them, and that was probably true. Nonetheless, a quarter million foreign-born, many of them European peasants for whom freeholds were dreams now within reach, arrived in North Dakota between 1898 and 1915.

By 1914 free homesteads were about gone, and World War I squelched recruitment within Europe. The themes of state immigration literature and newspaper editorials began dwelling more on community and personal values than on the quality of soil and climate, as had earlier propaganda. The new keynotes were not future rewards but achieved worthiness. A Pembina editor observed in 1915: "This land so far has been settled by the cream of creation. . . . Immigrants, particularly [those accustomed] to cold climate, are the strongest, best and most energetic as well as the bravest of their home communities. The weak of body and mind don't emigrate. It has been youth and vigor that has [*sic*] made these prairies blossom like a rose." Others lauded Horatio Alger–esque clean living, patriotism, and hard work, as well as "the special quality of North Dakotans and their society idyllic"—a list of self-administered backpats very much in accord with the "Prairie Zen" that Frank and Deborah Popper confronted decades later when they suggested that the plains had been overfarmed and ought to revert to buffalo commons.[36]

Poles, Ukrainians, Greeks, and Italians helped lay and maintain Soo and Northern Pacific track. Ukrainian section hands stayed to mine lignite, along with Romanians, Bulgarians, and some of the Scandinavian, German, and Czech farmers already in the area who needed winter income. Migration patterns varied but within the usual range: the railroad workers and miners were often unattached young men, recently arrived in the United States, recruited in the East or the old country as work groups, usually intending to make money and take or send it home to improve life there. Some did; others stayed and in time managed to acquire farms—often quarter sections that had been abandoned or sold for unpaid taxes, rather than fresh homestead entries, which required a declaration of intention to take on U.S. citizenship.

Not all newcomers to North Dakota were tenderfeet. Half or more of first-time homesteaders, however, in some fairly extensive parts of the Dakotas and Montana had no relevant farming background. That inexperience, combined with their chronic lack of capital, the cost of increasingly complicated farm machinery necessary to compete, and the wickedly unpredictable climate, made successful homesteading difficult no matter what the effort put into it. Remarkably few of the surviving letters, diaries, and oral histories about the settlement years say anything upbeat about the whole process, only about its outcome. They talk about hardships, calamities, heartbreaks, and ultimately, in most stories, hard-won triumph through tenacious self-reliance and, in many cases, the protection of Providence. Among all those millions of settlers, at least a few must have been sufficiently well capitalized and experienced to have avoided dire hardship and mortal peril. But if any of them had it easy, they have kept quiet about it.

The Norwegians and German Russians, who were the majority of North Dakota's ethnics, have said very little at all about their settlement experience. One family whose story we do know are the German Russians descended from Ludwig Neher and Fred Martin, as recorded years later by Pauline Neher Diede, a daughter of Ludwig's. She writes of a "desperate journey . . . from conscription and poverty in Germany to even more harsh and primitive conditions" in Russia in the 1760s. Ludwig and others were drafted to fight in the Russo-Japanese War in 1904 despite Catherine the Great's pledge not to conscript them. The trip to North Dakota in 1909 included a terrifying sea voyage from Hamburg to Montreal, the illness of a child en route, and nobody able to understand their dialect of German. They arrived in the wrong Dakota, in the wrong town, in the early fall—the wrongest time of the year.

Then, she writes, came the first winter living in a railroad boxcar, "worse than a coyote hole," with little food and the death of the sick child. Yet Ludwig and Fred made it to Bismarck and filed for public land, an abandoned homestead. They built a sod house; they planted oats, wheat, and garden vegetables, with help from some neighbors and snubbing by others; they also suffered "excruciating poverty" and work that "strained the limits of physical strength" of women and children as well as men. But after a few years of that the families' sheer survival was no longer at risk. Both ran moderately successful farms during the 1920s. The Nehers lost theirs in the 1930s, but their children, the story goes, "attained the American Dream—a place in the middle class."[37] Like many others, the Neher-Martin tale is a horror story, dystopic, the polar opposite of the booster propaganda, mitigated only by a measure of success in the next generation. One consolation, though the German-Russian immigrants could not have known it, was that Joseph Stalin would probably have murdered them, as he did most Volga Germans, if they had stayed in Russia another three decades.

Though few stayed long, some scores of Japanese, Russian Jews, and Syrian-Lebanese Arabs also homesteaded in North Dakota, though not always for long, often moving to county seat towns to operate laundries, restaurants, or dry goods stores.[38] About seventy Muslim Lebanese men homesteaded in Mountrail County, on the 102d meridian between Minot and Williston, from 1902 to 1929, when they built themselves a mosque on the prairie. That, and the homesteaders named Mohamed, Ali, and Abdullah who attended it, were uncommon even in North Dakota's ethnic mosaic. A colony of Yiddish-speaking Russians homesteaded about twenty-five miles from Bismarck, and Sophie Truppin recalled that her father built a cement mikvah (ritual bath) for her mother, who kept kosher very closely under impossible conditions and carefully observed the Sabbath. "On the day preceding Yom Kippur," Sophie wrote, "all the Jewish homesteaders, who were scattered over many miles, gathered their families and started on a journey to a common meeting place in order to observe the holiest day of the year. The farmhouse that could accommodate the most worshippers was the house of the Weinbergs. It was to be our *shul.*"

But as happened to Jewish farmers in Kansas in the 1880s, homesteading in North Dakota lasted only a short time. Sophie's parents made aliyah (emigrated) to Nahariyya in northern Israel in 1953.[39] Rachel Calof, born in Kiev in 1876, made her way in 1894 with her new husband to a homestead north of Devils Lake, where they persevered until 1917. Forced to live with in-laws she couldn't stand in "shanties" twelve by fourteen feet (to satisfy the homestead requirement), she survived incredibly tough winters, which "dominated our lives." Yet by 1910, sixteen years and seven children later, she and her husband proved up 320 acres clear, plus another 120 held jointly with her brother-in-law. By 1917, despite having "tamed the land and made it fit for humans," they left for St. Paul and eventually Seattle.[40]

Did these people fail as homesteaders? The Norwegians, German Russians, and Anglo-Americans whose descendants are still there four generations later would likely define success by persistence and failure by departure. But the Truppin and Calof memoirs define success another way. For them the homestead meant no peasant symbiosis with the land but a route to a capitalist stake. By 1910 twelve hundred Russian Jewish colonists were living on 250 North Dakota farms, many with proved-up titles.[41] Then, having improved the land, they sold out, turning their hard-earned homesteads "into capital by selling their land to . . . larger wheat farmers who had the technology, capital, and labor to realize an economy of scale." By the late 1920s virtually all of North Dakota's two thousand Jews lived in urban areas; many had taken the railroad to Portland or Seattle. In Janet Schulte's trenchant phrase, "proving up meant moving up."[42]

Anglo-American frontier farmers had often traded improved farms for fresh land, building the kind of wealth most common in a rural society. Rarely, however, had they homesteaded as a way of raising enough capital to own a store. The European peasant's binding with land may have differed in its feudal source from the American Agrarian Myth, but the practical result was the same: persistence. Anna Langhorne Waltz, a Philadelphia woman who arrived in South Dakota as the bride of a Baptist missionary in 1911 and lived by herself for almost a year and a half with a small baby on an isolated sod house claim, went through a grueling and life-threatening experience in order to gain title. In a lottery Anna and her husband won the dubious right to homestead in a remote and droughty area. "Nearly 54,000 people applied for 8 to 10,000 homesteads," and the Waltzes were among the lucky ones. Anna later wrote:

> Excitement was running wild . . . there was to be a land opening for homesteading! The government had decided to open another section of the rosebud [sic] Indian Reservation to the white man. . . . In the post office and stores and wherever there happened to be a group of people, all the talk was "homesteads," such as, "Hey, you goin' to register?" or, "Got your name in the pot?" Some of the families were going out there to the new section in wagons to camp, hoping to get a choice piece of land—some for themselves or for a son or daughter or, perhaps, for some relative or friend. They had me all stirred up about it until I persuaded my husband to give his consent to my entering my name in the drawing.

Not long after, she and her new baby rode out to the claim, its sod hut, an outhouse, and a small cave for food storage and tornado protection. She realized "that there was much more to this homesteading than simply being given permission by the government to acquire a title to 160 acres with fourteen months of residence . . . there is the problem of building a place to live.

There are absolutely no roads, only Indian trails; no fences; no trees except along the river and these mostly scrawny cottonwoods; no shelter of any kind, just the vast expanse of land and sky stretching out in endless distance, broken only by canyons here and there. . . . Many who came out here thinking they would have a life of ease soon discovered their mistake. . . . This is truly a land of Indians, coyotes, prairie dogs, rattlesnakes, sage brush, and tumbleweed."[43]

Anna and the thousands like her in the lottery, despite the snakes, blizzards, drought, and all the rest, followed an ancient American path. William C. Allen, who became editor of the *Dakota Farmer* in 1910 and promoted scientific farming and "a happy, balanced partnership within the farm home," kept the Dakota dream alive devotedly for three more decades. Even through the Great Depression, he preached the evangel of "optimism, confidence, and 'never say die. . . .' "[44] Prairie Zen again, faith trying to trump climate.

Down the Front Range

Settlement in Montana, and northward into Alberta and Saskatchewan, was much like North Dakota's, except that it took place a few years later and less often switched to wheat from sheep and cattle. Railroads were vital there as well. They brought people in and took their products out, dropping hamlets every score or so miles along their boundary-hugging "high line" and the Yellowstone Valley like great ambulant egg-laying ducks. The many-thousand-acre cattle ranches of the 1880s and the competition in the 1890s between big cattlemen and big sheepmen ended when the railroads, the government, and many of the large landholders started selling or giving quarter and half section tracts to farmers and keepers of small herds.[45] Only then did eastern Montana, Canada's Palliser's Triangle, and Wyoming begin to be seriously populated. Faith in dry farming persuaded bankers and railroad men—not just overeager settlers—that central Montana could become wheat country. In 1903, according to one old rancher, stockmen could drive a thousand sheep seventy-five miles across the Judith Basin east of Great Falls without hitting anything except another herd. But by the fall of 1907 they "began to encounter scattered homesteaders . . . [and] saw the writing on the wall. . . . The public domain with its open range and free grass was all but done."[46] People, not livestock, were about to occupy it.

James J. Hill, creator of the Great Northern, seems really to have believed that a quarter section could support a family in northern Montana through careful dry farming. One of his 1908 promotional booklets promised forty bushels of wheat to the acre and asserted that homesteaders had been filing a

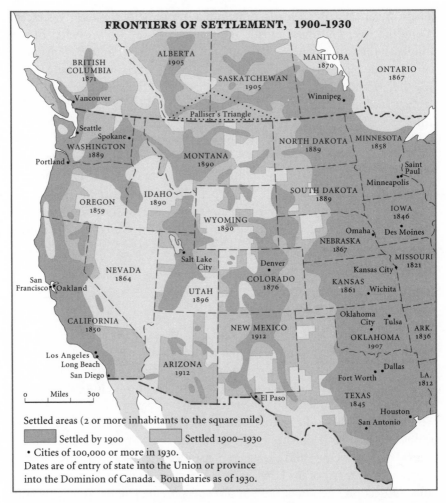

FRONTIERS OF SETTLEMENT, 1900–1930

Settled areas (2 or more inhabitants to the square mile)

Settled by 1900   Settled 1900–1930

• Cities of 100,000 or more in 1930.

Dates are of entry of state into the Union or province into the Dominion of Canada. Boundaries as of 1930.

hundred to two hundred claims a month for the past year, while "real estate dealers from . . . as far as Chicago have been buying up the big ranches and preparing to sell them in small tracts." The Judith Basin, it said, had averaged seventeen inches of rainfall a year for seven years, mostly in the "growing months" of May, June, and July: "*There has never been a crop failure from lack of sufficient moisture.*" (Nor had any crops ever been planted there more than seven years back, so that was a safe statement.) The best land in the basin was "bringing $20 to $35 per acre," state land $10 and up.[47] Boosterism and Babbittry were by no means limited to towns. The enticement of would-be yeomen to prairie paradises—which turned out often to be predicaments—was equally artful.

Congress, prodded by the roads, doubled maximum claims from 160 to

320 acres in the Enlarged Homestead Act of 1909. Thousands of young people, men and women, single and married, rushed in. One of them told Marie MacDonald, a teacher and historian in the area, "I was raised in Chicago without so much as a back yard to play in, and I worked 48 hours a week for $1.25. When I heard you could get 320 acres just by living on it, I felt that I had been offered a kingdom."[48] Despite the drought that put the quietus on homesteading in North Dakota in 1910, land seekers flocked into even drier Montana. Land salesmen called locators met the newcomers, known as honyockers, scissorbills, or simply the less pejorative homesteaders.[49] "By 1913," writes one Montanan, "the land was fully homesteaded, and a new era had begun." Living in sod houses or tar paper shacks, sending off their children, trailed by coyotes, to one-room schoolhouses, these young families attended Catholic or Protestant churches, increased and multiplied despite all difficulties, and together created more than twenty-two hundred school districts, community clubs, two dozen new counties and the requisite public officials.[50] Rural eastern Montana went from almost no white population in 1901 to nearly sixty thousand by 1917, when the weather changed and the golden twilight of homesteading faded into dark.[51]

Southward the flat, grassy eastern halves of Wyoming, Colorado, and New Mexico also enjoyed an influx of settlers in the first dozen or so years of the new century. The main lines of the Union Pacific in Wyoming and the Santa Fe in New Mexico had already had their major impacts before 1890, but spurs and branches opened new counties assumed to be irrigable or dry farmable. Wyoming's bureaucrats in 1901 played several cards: farming, stock raising, tourism, climate, health seeking, even jobs for carpenters and masons ($3 to $5 a day), railroad trackmen ($1.50 to $1.75), coal miners ($35 to $75 a month), and cowboys ($25 to $40 a month with board). The state proclaimed an "estimated" ten million acres to be "suitable for agricultural purposes by irrigation." The high altitude (five to seven thousand feet in much of the state) promised "cure for special maladies," especially "pulmonary affections" (tuberculosis, the greatest killer of the time), and, for the healthy, a "vacation resort for tourists and hunters." Sheep raising? Well. A man hardly needed any capital at all: "A sheep man needs no ranch, and makes no preparations in the way of harvested feed for the winter, but, like Abraham of old, moves about with his flocks, in the summer living in tents in the cool shades of the mountains and in winter in a 'sheep wagon,' which is fully equipped with a spring bed, stove and kitchen outfit. Sheep are subject to no disease except scab, which is easily cured. . . . The wool, at ten cents per pound, a little more than pays all the costs of running the sheep a year, so that the increase and mutton are the accumulated net profit."[52]

Led by Nebraskans and Iowans, Colorado's surge peaked in 1910. It continued for a few more seasons but was definitely over by 1920. Generally the homesteaders married at about twenty-five (men) and twenty (women) and over the next two decades averaged about five children per couple, figures similar to those for homesteading couples on other post–Civil War settlement frontiers. About one mother in four saw a child die, but more than nine in ten children lived to age eighteen. Four out of five homesteaders lived past sixty, almost half to over eighty.[53]

Did homesteading drive women crazy, as happened to the pitiable heroine Beret of Ole Rölvaag's 1927 novel *Giants in the Earth?* Some perhaps, but not likely many. Rölvaag created something of a myth. Women filed 10 to 20 percent of the claims on federal land in Colorado, either under Homestead or other laws, sometimes as individuals and sometimes to add to family holdings, and they succeeded about as well as men.[54] Homesteading not only put single women on a legally equal footing with men but produced many independent female homesteaders who probably were role models.[55] As one Colorado homesteader explained years later, "What made things go was the woman helped the man to make things go. If it wasn't for the woman, you couldn't survive on one of these mountain ranches. And all the women around here were about the same way."[56]

To read the promotional blurbs, one would think that women or men hardly had to work at all. A 1911 advertisement showed wheat that "threshed out 64 bushels to the acre." Artesian wells gushed water "soft and as pure as crystal." Problems? "We have no waste land. We have never had a failure. We have fine churches and schools. We have no cyclones or severe storms. We have the best artesian wells in the world. We have 350 days of sunshine during the year. We have a complete telephone system covering the entire valley. We have the best wagon roads and the cheapest fuel and the purest water in the world. . . . We hold the world's record on . . . potatoes, sugar beets, wheat, oats, barley, alfalfa, field peas, and onions. . . . We have the best irrigation and also the cheapest and the best soil and climate in the world. . . ."[57]

Another effusion in 1915 insisted that millions of acres of first-class land remained open for homesteading and noted, not quite in the Jeffersonian spirit, that "the easiest money a farmer can make is what he can make out of the increase in the value of his land. Every $10 per acre increase on 320 acres amounts to $3,200. Colorado's cheapest lands today will rapidly increase in value as they are cultivated."[58] The old idea—get land almost free, work hard (or bet well), and end up a rich farmer—still beckoned in Colorado.

New Mexico also created county after county in the first decade of the century, when the state's population jumped 68 percent. The eastern half, where the plains extend from Oklahoma and Texas until they become near desert around Albuquerque and mountains near Alamogordo, opened up after 1900 to ranching and farming in a big way. The southeastern counties containing Roswell, Hobbs, Artesia, and Carlsbad, especially the irrigated Pecos River valley, soared by over 250 percent in the decade, while the dry-farmed northeastern counties did almost as well. Texans predominated in southeastern New Mexico; Kansans and other midwesterners, farther north.

The former People's Party congressman from Kansas, Jerry Simpson, moved to Roswell in 1902 as a probable tubercular and actively promoted the Pecos Valley's possibilities for stock raisers, irrigators, and health seekers.[59] State guides advised that Colfax and Union counties, in the northeast corner of the state (county seats: Raton and Clayton), had "ideal" climates for "the pursuit of agriculture and horticulture," as well as "ideal conditions for the cure of consumption [tuberculosis] and throat trouble," although they had been "one vast range [for] the cattle and sheep raiser" up to that point. Almost four million acres "are still subject to entry" in Union county, and in Colfax County, "[t]here are splendid opportunities . . . for men with big and little capital, for miners, horticulturists, agriculturists and stockmen and also for all whose lack of means is compensated for by intelligence, energy, and a strong determination to win out in the battle for independence and wealth." Thirty years later Union and Colfax were Dust Bowl.

In Eddy County (county seat: Carlsbad) in the southeast corner, irrigation of the Pecos River was the great draw, together with health: "Eddy County is the Riviera of New Mexico. It is a garden spot of the great lower Pecos Valley. . . . To the average consumptive, Eddy County holds out greater promise of relief and cure than either Arizona or California. . . . The man or woman who cannot recover from tuberculosis in Eddy County by outdoor life and observing simple rules of hygiene and dietary [sic] cannot recover anywhere else. . . . [Its] magnificent irrigation system is at the foundation of its prosperity, yea, its very existence . . . there must be maximum crops and there can be no crop failures." Irrigated land could be had from $25 to $100 an acre; "patented lands without any water rights" for $2.50 to $5.[60] Another government publication promised results from both irrigation and "the Campbell method of soil culture," which solves "the real difficulty in the arid region—not a lack of rainfall, but the loss of too much water by evaporation." The Campbell method, it claimed, worked with only eight inches of rain a year, and New Mexico had sixteen or even more; dry farming promised to convert "the arid plains and mesas of New Mexico . . . into fertile farms." Opening his arms to all, this publicist announced: "New Mexico wants more people; it needs them; it has room and resources for them. . . . It is to the home seeker, to the farmer, to the stock raiser, to the miner, to the merchant, to the manufacturer, to the capitalist, that New Mexico is an undeveloped empire of magnificent resources, which throws a peerless cli-

mate in to the bargain with the rich returns that are offered to the man with
capital to invest, or with brain and brawn to apply."[61] It would be presump-
tuous to call this propaganda fraudulent and their salesmen authors liars.
Very likely they believed much of it and thought a little exaggeration in a
good cause was excusable. But, as John Wesley Powell told Congress in 1890,
and as a Canadian historian of homesteading judged later, to misrepresent
and mislead so many people into such misery, hardship, and so many wasted
years was morally criminal.

Homesteading amid the Mountains

The desert Southwest (much of New Mexico and Utah, virtually all of Arizona and Nevada) had almost no settlement frontier because not even
Hardy Campbell and the railroads could convince anyone that dry farming
would work there. As for irrigation, it required *some* dependable sources of
water. The desert had few, and Nevada almost none. Yet the Southern Pacific
trumpeted that "the digging of great canals and the taking up of irrigable
tracts" will make Nevada "the homes of thousands of prosperous and enterprising farmers." Nevada's future lay in agriculture: "Miners come and go,
but the land abides, and to the soil we must all go for our supplies of daily
bread." The mining towns would become "a promising home market" for all
those future farmers.[62] Another dreamer-promoter averred: "Had prince
[*sic*] de Leon sought the elixor [*sic*] of life in climate, instead of a spring,
he would have found his quest in the healthfulness of this region." The
same writer, in a paroxysm of untruth, declared: "Nevada is second to no
other state in the conditions favorable to dairying [which] is as yet in its
infance [*sic*], but is coming to the front with long strides. . . . This is but
the beginning!"[63]

Irrigation never transformed Nevada, but in a few oases it underpinned
solid population growth in the Southwest. In Arizona between 1900 and
1910, by combining federal reclamation money and early agribusiness organization, the Roosevelt Dam (1905–1911) on the Salt River and other works
on the Gila and lower Colorado rivers nourished enough irrigated cotton,
dairy farming, and fruits and vegetables to feed Phoenix.[64] Another Reclamation Bureau project, the Elephant Butte Dam and Reservoir on the Rio
Grande, built 1910 to 1916, ensured that El Paso and its Mexican twin, Ciudad
Juárez, would have the water they needed to grow.[65] Elsewhere in the Southwest, as Powell predicted, useful irrigation was rare.

Like so many things, irrigation could have unintended consequences. It
could occasionally subvert homesteading rather than promote it. Bruce
Babbitt, when he was Arizona's attorney general, once spoke about "subdivi-

sion frauds [that] really got going with the advent of irrigation of the Salt River Valley," the first major project under the Newlands Act of 1902. The law's intent was to encourage homesteading by guaranteeing a water supply. Instead, existing landowners and speculators subdivided and offered land they already owned, making it "better to buy into a development than to simply go out and homestead. . . . [At] the point that you got irrigation water, the business really got going." Babbitt referred to a valley west of Phoenix where in 1920 Los Angeles developers promised future water from Boulder Dam (far in the future indeed; the water eventually rushed straight through to Phoenix). He called it "an integrated swindle" because they "sold half the valley to blacks, half the valley to Anglos." However, the Anglos managed to escape during the 1920s, while "several hundred families" of blacks "are still hanging on, working [as] farm laborers," fifty years later.[66] Irrigation here became not the hope of homesteaders but the cash cow of developers.

The Southwest was simply not the country for 160-acre homesteads. Irrigated tracts, yes. In California just across the lower Colorado River from Arizona, the Imperial Valley Farm Lands Association around 1910 advertised tracts "up to 640 acres at $65 to $100 an acre; ten-acre tracts close to town $125 to $150 an acre . . . $15 per acre for perpetual water rights."[67] By 1915 boosters in Yuma County, Arizona, offered unimproved land for $75 to $125 an acre, improved land for $100 to $300. For them, the Yuma Project was "the premier project of the United States Reclamation Service" and "will carry the waters of the Colorado River to 150,000 acres of desert land as rich in agricultural possibilities as can be found in the world." But public domain land was seldom available; "none . . . is open to entry at this time."[68] In other words, Yuma had private land for sale, irrigated by federal money—a far cry from traditional homesteading and a long step toward agribusiness.

Utah's increase in farm and ranch population was very steady and thus slightly off pattern; no slump, boom, slump in the 1890s, 1900s, 1910s, but moderate, inexorable growth. Even so, Utah had impressive moments, as in 1905, when twenty-five thousand would-be settlers drew lots for land appropriated from the Utes in the northeast corner between Wyoming and Colorado; or after 1910, in southeastern San Juan County, when cattle companies sold subdivided ranches to Mormons for farms; or when would-be dryland farmers patented more than a million near-desert acres south and west of Great Salt Lake.[69] "A myth of success in making formidable deserts bloom was widely accepted," according to one historian; "alkali flats were confidently promoted as good land, water was blithely promised, and the miles between farm and market were brushed aside with the stroke of the developer's pen."[70]

In 1907 entries jumped under the Desert Land Act of 1877, which gave
away 640 acres of public domain—on condition that it be irrigated within
three years, an impossibility for small farmers.[71] A Jewish colony at Clarion,
virtually in the center of Utah, opened in 1911 and grew to two hundred families, but by November 1915 only seventeen of them remained. The colony
closed because of aridity, leadership conflicts, lack of capital, lack of experience, and arguments about religious observance.[72] Much of Utah's population growth early in the century happened in Salt Lake City and, more
precariously, in mining communities. But the Mormon farms and small
towns continued their quiet fertility, producing another generation to send
into the expanding Mormon culture area. That included Colonia Juárez,
Colonia DuBlan, and Colonia Deis in northern Chihuahua, Mexico, where
Mormons from central Utah settled in the 1880s to escape American laws
against plural marriage. The Mexican Mormons returned to the United
States in 1912, when revolutionaries demanded "that we give them all of our
guns and ammunition," killed their cattle, and pillaged them.[73] Armond
Jackson later described how Mormons fled Mexico: "First the women and
children came out on the trains. And then the bridges were burnt and the
men were left down there. . . . At one time, my father and my two brothers
were the only people left in the Mormon colony because they had missed the
company that they were supposed to come out with [and] every time they
would try to come out . . . they were picked up and taken back . . . to grind
wheat for the revolutionaries." But finally they made it to El Paso.[74]

Idaho was more diverse than Utah. Mormons lived there, but so did
many a non-Mormon farm family, either American or European born. Mining, lumbering, and some farming brought a mix of people to the northern
panhandle. Only one Idaho county had more than ten thousand residents in
1890, but eight did in 1900, fifteen in 1910, many of them double or triple
their 1900 size. Rather like neighboring Montana, about two of five Ida-
hoans or their parents had been born abroad, chiefly in the Scandinavian
countries, Germany, England, or Canada. But Italians, Finns, Greeks, and
many others were visible in the northern mining towns; Japanese, Chinese,
and blacks in the Snake River valley; and Basques on the ranges south and
west of Boise.[75]

There is no way to know how many Basques lived in Idaho, Nevada, and
northern California in those years because they were counted in the census
not as Basques but as Spanish or French. From the first few who arrived
around 1870, Idaho's Basques multiplied to twenty-five hundred or three
thousand by 1922, most living in Boise by then. Before 1913 the majority
herded sheep in southeastern Oregon's high desert, a dry plateau where at
the five-thousand-foot level snow squalls can strike in May or June and

which merges imperceptibly into Nevada. Basque boardinghouses and restaurants popped up from Winnemucca to Reno and over the Sierras into the San Joaquin Valley, where a Basque hotel opened in east Bakersfield in 1893.[76]

Nearly all were Catholic single young men between fifteen and twenty-five. A few women also arrived, so that young Basques very often married each other, often someone from the same village, suggesting a pattern of nuptial chain migration. In Winnemucca, of seventy-three Basque marriages registered between 1895 and 1915, seventy were Basque on both sides.[77] Philip Uberuaga and Marie Belaustequi married in their early twenties at Boise in 1933. His parents (and perhaps hers) came from the Spanish province of Guipúzcoa, part of Basque country. They and those of "all the Basque kids in Boise" ran boardinghouses, fifteen or twenty of them, each home to a dozen or more sheepherders, enough to engender a job market: "A Basque always had a good chance of getting a job in Boise stores 'cause they'd look for somebody to speak Basque to help the Basque people."[78] Like the beet-picking German Russians in Colorado, the Basques in Idaho and Nevada carried on their traditional seasonal migration of sheep flocks and shepherds much as they had in their Pyrenees homeland for centuries.

The irrigable Snake River valley in the early years of the century remained a highly active settlement frontier. Farming near Twin Falls boomed around 1905, thanks to irrigation under terms of the Carey Act of 1894 and then the Newlands Act,[79] making the valley population much more stable than dry-farming areas east of the Rockies. The Great Feeder Dam system, built there in the mid-1890s, was the world's largest at the time, and it helped Mormon farm families expand into Idaho. Historian Leonard Arrington recalls that his parents came from Oklahoma by freight train to near Twin Falls "shortly after the tract was opened in 1905. . . . My father raised sugar beets, potatoes, beans, and of course wheat and alfalfa in rotation. Irrigation was a way of life with us." Around Twin Falls, Snake River water irrigated 240,000 acres. The nearby Minidoka project, built with Newlands Act funds in 1907, opened another 120,000.[80] Rexburg, Idaho, advertised itself as "the largest irrigated district in the world[;] the richest soil; the most wonderful water supply; the most productive country of the last great West," with land selling by 1913 at $25 to $30 an acre "for outlying non-irrigated farms" and "$60 to $150 for choice . . . irrigated lands lying close to the larger towns."[81]

Experiences varied, to judge from later interviews of settlers. Betty Hitt came with her family to Idaho in 1903, following family members who had farmed in Kircudbrightshire in the Scottish lowlands and "got into the sheep business" in Idaho, encouraged by a local sheepman. "I don't know what they [her parents] did it for—[her mother] was 49 years old . . . we were pretty well fixed. We had a maid and a housekeeper and a cook. She never had to do anything, dirty work"—but in Idaho, eight miles from any neighbors, she did plenty.

Jessie Ettles, born in Keith, Scotland, in 1890, quit school at thirteen and in 1913 borrowed the passage money from her father ("at that time it cost very little—few dollars") and married John Allan, another Scot, five years later. They had known each other in grade school, "but I didn't pay no attention to him over there, til I came here. . . . He came out [to Idaho] in 1909, the same way; he had a lot of cousins here . . . worked here to Mr. Brown the place where we were living then and he finally bought it. Bought the place, had the sheep and we lived there."

The migration chain was a long one. First, "an aunt and uncle that came here to some friends that they had . . . they did make a trip home in 1911 . . . and that is when my brother, he was seventeen, came out with them . . . and that was the start probably of *my* coming out."

For these and thousands of others, the routes to landowning were many. But neither farming communities nor mining towns were particularly stable. Homesteaders might stay, or they might commute and sell; miners could leave, or they could form families and grow roots. The "reclaimed" Snake River valley, with its sugar beets, potatoes, beans, and peas requiring stoop labor, began to attract migrant farm workers well before World War I.[82] Even then, simple traditional homesteading was being overlaid by an expensive, technological kind of agriculture.

Northern Idaho is really part of the Pacific Northwest rather than the Great Basin. Around Lewiston and Moscow, it abuts the rich farm country of eastern Washington, one of the last great farm settlement areas of the West. Ever since the 1880s Washington State was a demographic success story second only in the West to California. Just after 1900 people spread throughout the timberlands of the Cascades, some working in the paper mills of Hoquiam, Tacoma, and Everett. To the superb all-year harbors of Puget Sound, especially the metropolis of Seattle, they came, and to the soil-rich farms around Walla Walla and the Palouse Country in the southeast, and to the increasingly irrigated Yakima Valley.

Homesteading began in eastern Washington in the 1870s and 1880s, languished in the 1890s, and flourished from 1901 to about 1913, in some places to 1917. Dry farming had much less to do with it than irrigation. Between 1901 and 1915, the number of farms in Washington closed in on its historic peak.[83] By 1904 irrigation systems already watered 36,000 acres along the Yakima River, and in 1905 the Newlands Act encouraged the Interior Department to begin the Yakima project, ten times as large. Despite only seven inches of annual rainfall, the valley sprouted fruit trees, alfalfa, and other thirsty crops abundantly,[84] matched only by the voluminous boosterism that announced all the fecundity. By 1910 irrigated farms in the Yakima Valley averaged only 96 acres, but each acre cost $126, while wheat farms in southeastern Washington averaged 384 acres at $47 each. Some wheat land could still be had in 1910 for as little as $10 an acre, and railroads sought farmers to buy it; but in less than a decade it brought $30 to $50.[85] Most Washington land therefore was already becoming far more valuable than homestead or railroad land on the High Plains. Irrigated fruit orchards dominated central Washington around Yakima and Wenatchee, winter wheat the east and southeast, where Spokane outfought Walla Walla to become the regional metropolis. The Great Northern and other railroads performed their by now usual functions of promoting irrigation, bringing in settlers and farm workers, and carrying produce away to markets.[86] Washington east of the Cascades had become, by 1915, the staple crop region that it still is.

Enriched by migrants from Illinois, Iowa, Wisconsin, Missouri, and Minnesota, east-central Washington from Spokane west to the Columbia Valley enjoyed its greatest rural growth in this period; it thinned out later.[87] Contrariwise, a few west-central counties, notably Yakima, kept growing through the 1910s and 1920s. Typical of settlement frontiers, as well as places requiring unskilled nonfarm workers, Washington's people in this period continued to be disproportionately young and male. The vast majority were white, with Scandinavians, Germans, British, and Irish well represented. Blacks rose from two to over six thousand, arriving as railroad workers and then staying, and Japanese tripled from around five to fifteen thousand.[88] Most of these minorities concentrated around Seattle, not east of the Cascades.

The Cascades similarly divide Oregon, and the dry, high country of central Oregon received many a hopeful homesteader for several years following 1901. There reality checked the inflow of settlers sooner than almost anywhere in the West. Cousins of the 1990s' radio commentator Rush Limbaugh left their native Cape Girardeau, in southeast Missouri, to homestead in north-central Oregon around a town called Madras. They paid the statutory dollar and a quarter an acre. Women of the family filed claims adjacent to the men, to make the largest contiguous holdings they could; families borrowed from one another to keep going; teenagers hired themselves out to work on wheat harvest crews; couples married, bore children, and buried some of them. But despite fidelity to the homestead ideal, these families never made it. They had either died or moved on by 1910, unfortunately only a year before a railroad came to Madras, prolonging its hopes through the war years. A few managed to farm elsewhere in Oregon, and others retreated

to Portland, Boise, and other northwestern cities.[89] Perhaps raising sheep
would have saved them, as it did some of the more successful in that area.
Established sheep ranchers, as a local woman said, "bought lots of homesteaders' places after they found out they couldn't make it on 160 acres."[90]

And so, while American agriculture continued its historic growth in the
years from 1901 to 1913, all the expansion took place in the West.[91] The
Northeast and South lost farms and farm acreage, but the West far more
than made up for them.[92] After 1913, however, rural development was spotty
even there. The "pioneers" of 1901–1913 were already relying on the railroads
and distant urban markets in ways that nineteenth-century settlers seldom
knew. Despite the myth of individualism, the more they produced, the more
dependent they were. For many farmers, the economic Indian summer of
the World War I years, effectively 1916 through 1918 in terms of demand for
wheat and other foodstuffs, prolonged prosperity, but seldom longer.

To all intents and purposes homesteading was already over in some
places, like central Oregon by 1909 or western South Dakota by 1911. North
Dakota and Montana soldiered on through 1916, and some isolated places
even into the 1920s, especially western Canada, where the promotional campaign and European recruitment by government and railroads continued
relentlessly. Yet by 1913, that all-time peak year for proved-up final entries of
U.S. public domain land, the very nature of homesteading had changed in
almost every key respect from its eighteenth- and nineteenth-century past.
Few frontier farmers in the Jacksonian or Revolutionary years ever troubled
their minds with scientific methods of cultivation. They did not need to.

But the semiarid West required a Hardy Campbell and irrigation congresses and the backing of them by railroads, banks, and publicists to persuade people to try to make a living in it. Settlers, and the hamlets that
served their needs, rarely lived long in a place without a railroad. Railroads
dictated the pace and direction of settlement even though they generally did
so with no civic consciousness beyond their own profitability. When irrigation succeeded, it put the recovery cost of the land it watered far beyond the
means of the young would-be homesteader, as these several examples—the
Imperial Valley, Idaho, Washington—all show. The capital required for
farming had begun either to divide rural population into owners and workers (again, not what Jefferson had in mind) or simply to drive people off the
land and into towns and cities.

Mining as an Industry, Miners as Communities

Farming was becoming thoroughly capitalistic. Mining was so already, and
the arrival of corporate mining provoked the West's most explicit class con-

flict. The Great Railway Strike of 1877 gave relations in America between capital and labor, management and workers, a sharper edge than ever before. The Haymarket riot in Chicago in 1886, the Homestead strike near Pittsburgh in 1892, and the Pullman strike south of Chicago in 1894 (which reverberated all across the West) convinced many observers by the close of the 1890s' depression that a class war was imminent. Western mining was hardly exempt. When silver miners struck in Kellogg and Coeur d'Alene, Idaho, in 1892, state militia and federal troops dispersed them. Strikes involving shifting ethnic coalitions and the Western Federation of Miners erupted in 1903 in Clifton-Morenci and in 1909 in Jerome, Arizona, in 1912 at Bingham Canyon, Utah, and, most famously, in 1914 among coal miners and their families at Ludlow, Colorado, where a dozen women and children burned to death. In 1917 unionized copper miners at Bisbee, Arizona, suffered a historic, crushing defeat, and vigilantes (with company and sheriff's cooperation) summarily railroaded two thousand miners and stranded them on the desert 175 miles east in New Mexico.[93]

These are all well-known events in American labor history. Less known is the quiet development of stable industrial towns in the intermountain states, nothing like the legendary mining camps at all. Men dug for the more prosaic copper, zinc, lead, and coal, not gold and silver. Families, not free-floating young prospectors, were the social norm. Accidents, not strikes, accounted for most of such violent deaths as there were.

Goldfield, Nevada, was an exception, an economic and personal free-for-all, not calm or corporate, a place with the same firecracker quality and homicide-driven death rate as earlier gold and silver rushes. Mining began there in 1903. By 1907, 18,000 people crowded Goldfield, but the 1910 census found only 5,435. In those seven years 779 died there, most from typically young-person causes: infectious diseases (especially pneumonia or influenza), accidents, homicides, deaths in childbirth, infant and childhood diseases, typhoid and other results of poor sanitation. As the gold veins petered out (the main company shut down in 1919), suicides and homicides increased.[94] Goldfield folded quickly, as did other Nevada rush towns of the period, like Tonopah (opened 1900), Rhyolite (1904), and Rawhide (1906). It is a bit of an exaggeration to say, as one Nevada historian did, that in these towns "the happy-go-lucky miner was gone, his place taken by the proletarian radical."[95] His place was taken, if at all, by family men. Moreover, soon not much was left to be radical about.

The ethnic variety of the early-twentieth-century industrial mining towns was as great as anywhere in the United States. Bingham, in the Utah mountains, for example, had 1,210 Greeks, 639 Italians, 564 Croats, 254 Japanese, 217 Finns, 161 Englishmen, 60 Bulgars, 59 Swedes, 52 Irish, and 23 Germans in 1911.[96] These were the top years of European migration to the Americas, and the West got its full share. Railroad agents recruited and sold land to farm families and also recruited wageworkers. Labor padrones, like the Greek Leonard Skliris, contracted their countrymen's labor (for a cut) to mining companies and other employers. After years of being exploited, Greek workers broke his hold in 1912.[97]

Greeks and Italians soon outnumbered all other Europeans and Americans in Carbon County, Utah. In 1915 Greek miners in Price, the county seat, petitioned their bishop in Crete to send them a priest, and a year later young John Petrakis, with his wife, mother, and four children, arrived. A thousand miners from all over the Utah mountains greeted their train when it pulled into Salt Lake City "with a celebratory thunder of gunshots fired into the air." Men who had not seen women or children from Crete since leaving home "knelt and prayed in gratefulness, and some wept and reached gently to touch the hem of my mother's dress as she passed," writes the novelist Harry Mark Petrakis of his parents' arrival in Utah.[98] Greeks earned a reputation as fighters for workers' rights. One, Louis Tikas, took part in the overthrow of the grafter Skliris and then gave his life in the infamous Ludlow Massacre.[99]

In Wyoming the Colorado Fuel and Iron Company bought up a copper camp named Hartville in 1899, and in a year the area's population boomed to around fifteen hundred. The majority were recent immigrants, led by hundreds of Italians and Greeks, scores of Swedes, English, Lebanese, Japanese, and others. By 1910 Greeks and Italians were running bakeries, grocery stores, saloons, and construction firms. Hartville had become a family-oriented working-class community.[100] In Helena, Montana, there were over four hundred African-Americans. Blacks had first come there during its gold rush and remained to operate restaurants, hotels, and retail stores, some becoming rather substantial as early as the 1880s.[101]

Butte's maturation from mining camp to community continued. The censuses of 1910 and 1920 counted about forty thousand, and in 1917, at the height of wartime copper demand, it was doubtless higher. Irish men and women had been arriving since the 1870s, and as happened in San Francisco, early arrival meant easier assimilation. Irish were not the only ethnics; before 1903 even more miners from Cornwall were there, and by 1910 Croatians, Germans, Italians, and Finns contributed fifteen hundred to three thousand each.[102] Yet Butte had more of an Irish flavor than any other for half a century. Only in 1917, when worsening labor conditions set off its first real strike, did its social edifice start to crack. The gradual, inevitable exhaustion of the copper ores made the decline irretrievable.[103]

Hard-rock industrial mining towns lasted longer than the old prospectors' camps. Women and children were more evident; teachers and housewives decidedly outnumbered prostitutes and dance hall girls. The union man and his family were what are called today social conservatives; in an Irish Catholic town like Butte this was certainly the case. Wives created homes as havens; husband and wife were head and heart of the home, as traditional marriage theology prescribed. It actually worked that way in a great many cases.

Hazards lurked. The risk of injury to the miner and therefore disaster to the family, immigrant and native-born alike, was always present. The records of the North Star Mining Company, of Grass Valley, Nevada County, California, provide a glimpse into mining's social system. Year after year the secretary of the Western Federation of Miners local wrote the company to thank its officers for "their kind donation of $100" or "your very liberal Donation" to the "Widows & Orphans Fund." For there were definitely widows and orphans. One letter of June 1, 1908, from a miner's wife, Mrs. J. H. Phillips, to the mine manager, A. D. Foote, explains itself: "I will write and ask if you will do me a favor.

"If I was kind enough not to sue the North Star Company as the people wanted me to do for the death of my husband, John H. Phillips, why cant they be kind enough to donate me some money. I have not had good health myself and my baby has been sick a great deal which makes a great expense, I do not like to depend on my brothers for everything as they have expenses of their own. They have cared for baby an I ever since."

Foote evidently did do something for Mrs. Phillips, but he was not his own master. On August 3, 1909, a Mr. Pagan wrote Foote from corporate headquarters in Wall Street noting that Foote's June statement included "a payment of $60. for pensions, included in which is the amount you have lately been paying to Mrs. Phillips under the pay-roll. Mr. Agnew [the new company president] desires me to enquire of you as to the nature of these pension disbursements and the principle on which they are to be made." The previous president, James D. Hague of Calumet, Michigan, had authorized Foote two years earlier to set up a company hospital, "guaranteeing for five years the support of two beds . . . at $100 per month each to be used for the injured men." Records do not show if the new president continued this practice. At least the company did authorize the usual Christmas allocation of six thousand dollars to the miners in December 1909. The windows of scrutiny thus looked upward from miners' wives (or widows) to the union local to mine manager Foote to Wall Street and even beyond. Hague notified Foote in December 1906 that the Aetna insurance company was balking at claims by North Star and needed Foote's records.[104] No doubt Aetna, in turn, had to face its stockholders.

These towns, though more stable than earlier ones, nevertheless could dwindle and die rather quickly. The veins played out, or the ore became too low-grade to bother with. Management sometimes overbuilt a site, bringing in too many workers only to dismiss them quickly, as at Florence, Colorado.[105] In Marble, Colorado, west of Aspen, marble mining raised the population by thousands in three years (1910–1913), supporting schools, newspapers, a hospital, and movie theaters. But two avalanches, tram runaways, and other accidents killed people and damaged the mill; corporate debt and low demand closed operations for a time, and the mill finally burned down in 1926.[106]

Through these years, despite wild gyrations of population and the mixture of class struggle and conservatism, mining and miners shrank in regional importance. In Colorado mining generated 25 percent of the state's income in 1880, but by 1920, only 5 percent.[107] Grass Valley, California, slipped from 4,719 in 1900 to 4,006 in 1920; Aspen, Colorado, from 3,303 to 1,265; Virginia City, Nevada, from 2,695 to 1,200. Throughout this interior West, cities and homesteads provided the growth.

The Ethnic West

Homesteaders and miners were not the only ethnics; every city and town had its Europeans and Asians. Young Greeks escaped poverty and military service in San Francisco after 1890, and by 1910, eight thousand lived in Greektown, part of the South of Market district.[108] Others found work around Pocatello and Boise on the Oregon Short Line Railroad and then stayed.[109] Gus Demus came from a small town in Greece to Spokane in 1909, when his father, already there, sent him a ticket. As so often happened, the decision to migrate was made, or clinched, in America rather than in Europe. The son worked on the railroad for $1.30 a day, then in a sawmill in Potlatch, Idaho, among "Greeks, Italians, Austrians, all them countries . . . from the south of Europe. . . . They were bachelors, most all of 'em." Three to six men would rent a house and "batch"; eventually they brought over Greek women, married, "and now it's quite a community."[110]

Nearly 3,000 Italians were living in Nevada in 1910, the state's largest ethnic group, many of them northern Italians working as truck farmers.[111] Through chain migration, dozens of Croatian stonemasons settled in Great Falls and then Lewistown, Montana, after 1898; women and children followed, raising the "Austrian" (actually the Croatian) population of Lewistown to 373 in the 1910 census.[112] Los Angeles's Jewish community swelled from 2,500 in 1905 to 10,000 by 1912, many of them hoping that the salubrious air would cure their tuberculosis, others for clerical or retail jobs.[113] Portuguese contract workers appeared on sugar plantations in Hawaii beginning about 1878, and many migrated to California's East Bay (Oakland, Milpitas, and San Leandro) after 1897, the men to work primarily on farms and the women (who made up an unusually high 40 percent of the group) also on farms and as domestic servants.[114]

Italians, two-thirds of them from the north (in contrast with New England, New York, and New Jersey, where most Italians were southern), did all sorts of work: as farm laborers or truck gardeners in California, as section hands on the Southern Pacific, as fishermen, as masons, carpenters, and general construction laborers, as restaurateurs and bakers and in many other trades. They were especially visible in the San Francisco–Oakland–San Jose triangle and rural northern California and in Los Angeles. Names like Gallo, Franzia, Cella, Petri, and DiGiorgio became nationally known for food and wine, as did Giannini in banking.[115] In San Francisco most of the 7,508 Italians in 1900 lived in North Beach, where the 1906 earthquake hit very hard. But the Italians had resources. Elsewhere ruptured gas and water mains spread the fire, but in North Beach bucket brigades hoisted seawater from the bay, and blankets soaked in wine from the Italian Swiss Colony warehouse protected many a roof.[116] Italians farmed all over the Bay Area, the lower Sacramento Valley, and down the coast through Monterey as far as San Diego. Commercial fishing became largely a family business, conducted by Italian-style dragnet fishing in the bay, augmented by relatives and friends brought over from Italy to help.[117]

San Francisco was the Italians' western capital, but other cities had their Little Italys. Reno's flourished for thirty years or so after 1910; Italians owned fourteen hotels there in 1920. Phoenix's included more than fifteen hundred in 1910, operating restaurants, saloons, grocery stores, and candy shops. Oregon had five thousand by 1910, running restaurants, fruit and vegetable markets, and bakeries, working in construction, functioning as priests, physicians, and lawyers. As in the Bay Area, Portland's first Italians came from the north, but the great wave of Italian migration to the United States from 1905 to 1914 brought many southerners. Italians spread over Portland's east side, growing vegetables and fruits in small plots much as they were doing along the Platte in Denver or in South San Francisco. Mostly single men at first, the Italians soon developed families and became property owners. Among the three thousand Italians and twenty-two hundred eastern European Jews in Portland in 1910, the Italians were more often laborers, the Jews more often proprietors. But proportionately more Italians owned their own homes, stayed in their original neighborhoods, and had smaller families. Jewish wives averaged 2.5 live births; Italian 2.1.[118]

The Jewish presence in the West, going back to the California Gold Rush or earlier, strengthened and diversified with the 1881–1914 wave of eastern European immigrants. Though the agricultural colony at Clarion, Utah, failed in 1915, other groups succeeded, like the new Congregation Agudath Achim, founded in Pasadena, California, in 1907 with "thirty members, besides a Ladies Auxiliary Society. . . . The attendance, on the first day especially, considering the small number of Jewish residents; was excellent, and so, the ancient flag of Judaism was planted in what is conceded to be the most beautiful and serene spot in the world, replete with retired millionaires and magnificent hotels."[119] From 1907 to 1914 the financier Jacob Schiff sponsored a migration called the Galveston Project, which brought upward of nine thousand Jews from all parts of the Russian Pale through the port of Galveston to several Colorado cities: Denver, where they quickly founded yeshivas and Orthodox synagogues; Colorado Springs, whose first synagogue duly appeared in 1909, with mikvah and shochet; Pueblo; and Cripple Creek. Few, however, proceeded even that far west. Kansas City received the largest part of the Galveston migrants, and the total amounted to only about 2 percent of all the Jews who came to the United States in those years.[120]

The Irish also ranged widely in class and purpose, from millionaires to Butte miners to missionary nuns. A Kerryman named Tom Walsh came to the United States in steerage after the Civil War, made his way to Central City, Colorado, in 1874, and then, in 1876, to the Black Hills (Dakota Territory) gold rush. There he "cleaned up 75,000 or 80,000 dollars," moved to Leadville, and "built and ran the Grand Hotel until 1880." He later relocated to Denver, where he made a much larger fortune. With far different objectives, Sisters of Mercy from Dublin opened a hospital, chiefly for tuberculars, at Silver City, New Mexico, in 1893. They replenished themselves by recruiting trips to Ireland, bringing back young women who spent their lives working among the sick and poor in the Southwest. Katharine Drexel's nuns, mainly Irish too, meanwhile continued to teach and staff their schools for Indians in the plains and Southwest, living their lives and being buried there, a different kind of migration of women to the West.

Dominican sisters in Lisbon, Portugal (though mostly Irish), were exiled in 1910 by an anticlerical government, and some landed in Oregon in 1911 following an invitation from the short-handed local bishop at Baker City. There they built a convent, a hospital, and schools in "a growing town, no city, some . . . very fine buildings, but in many parts no streets as yet, just opening up the roads . . . a very nice little Cathedral," as one young nun wrote back to Ireland.[121] The local Commercial Club wanted a hospital, and the nuns, ten of them and a laywoman, opened one in April 1912. Sheepherders with spotted fever from sheep ticks, typhoid victims who drank untreated water from the Snake River, and hungry tramps received their help. Anti-Catholic attitudes surfaced sometimes; in the 1920s the local Ku Klux Klan, strong in Oregon, occasionally burned a cross. In 1914 several of these nuns who spoke Portuguese accepted a call to Hanford, California, on the Southern Pacific near Visalia, and operated a hospital and school for its sizable Azorean community. They opened several more in the Central Valley during the next two decades.[122]

Colorado received more African-American migrants than any other mountain state. In 1900 about eighty-five hundred were living in Denver, Colorado Springs, and Pueblo, or on homesteads and the black colony of Dearfield, east of Greeley, which persisted into the 1930s.[123] Denver also attracted eastern Europeans. Poles from the Płock district first settled in the Globeville section in 1889, around the Globe and Grant smelters. In 1900 they founded St. Joseph's, joining existing German and Italian Catholic parishes. St. Joseph's soon served Slovenes, Croats, and Slovaks, although not, over the years, without ethnic frictions. After World War I immigrants' children began marrying across ethnic lines. The community persisted as primarily Polish, however, until the construction of Interstate 70 bisected it in the 1950s and the new Denver Coliseum then supplanted the Grant smelter.[124]

Issei and Nisei

The most significant new ethnic presence in the 1901–1913 period was the Japanese, who began arriving in sizable numbers after 1901. Most gravitated toward the land, where they had lived at home. But they had little to do with traditional homesteading and instead concentrated in intensive, often irrigated specialty farming, not far from urban markets and consumers. In this respect they fitted well into California agriculture as it was already taking shape, and they played an increasingly important role in it, despite laws beginning in 1913 against aliens owning land. The Japanese immigrants also provided West Coast xenophobes with a new supply of Asian targets just as the Chinese were fading. Their appearance amid the regional ethnic mosaic further established the West as the America of the twentieth century before the rest of America realized what that was.

International migration usually begins when people start believing that they would be better off in another country than in their own. Life in Japan in the 1880s was, for people without much property, at least as intolerable as for those in the Russian and Austrian empires and southern Italy. Japanese began seizing chances to emigrate on labor contracts for Hawaii, where twenty-nine thousand went to work on sugarcane plantations between 1884 and 1894. Some of these people (and others coming directly from Japan) traveled on to the North American West Coast.

The first Japanese in Los Angeles arrived in 1885. They were *wataridori*—sojourners, like the Italian *golondrini,* birds of passage. Seasonal labor migrants, *dekasegi,* were already commonplace, within Japan and overseas, and to extend the route to Hawaii or even North America indicated no intent to leave permanently; "a return home within a few years was regarded as a foregone conclusion."[125] By 1900, however, showing no signs of returning, about five thousand were living in British Columbia, and more than twenty-five thousand in the United States.[126] Quite likely "they were not of the poorest or the lowest class of society"[127] but, like a great many mobile Europeans, intelligent and ambitious, though not propertied. One analyst suggests that those who adjusted best in the United States had been "relatively disadvantaged in Japan" and hence more flexible about changing their ways,[128] which also describes many European migrants.

From 1900 to 1907 migration was "free" (voluntary rather than through prearranged labor contracts), and numbers swelled. Thirty thousand came to the United States in 1907, the year of the Gentlemen's Agreement between Tokyo and Washington. This exchange of diplomatic notes provided that Japan would issue no more passports to the United States for laborers, unless they had already been there; wives, parents, or children of Japanese already living in the United States remained eligible, as did students. Steamships charged $25 to $30 for the trip from Japan to Seattle, Portland, or San Francisco, besides which the migrant needed $30 to $50 as "show money" to avoid looking to American port authorities like a possible public charge and being sent back. In all, he needed around $100, perhaps $150 after 1910. That was still a lot of money, but many raised it by selling land or borrowing.[129]

The census counted 24,326 Japanese in the United States in 1900, 72,157 in 1910, and 111,010 in 1920. Seattle had 2,990 Japanese in 1900, far outstripping San Francisco (1,781) or Los Angeles (150), probably because of lower steamship fares. But in the next ten years Los Angeles County became home to 9,000. The number rose to 20,000 in 1920, making L.A. "the metropolis of Japanese America," with Seattle second and San Francisco third, always more Chinese than Japanese. Oakland and Sacramento each had over 1,000 Japanese by 1910, as did Fresno soon after.[130] The Japanese surge in Los Angeles was "spectacular" in the several years prior to the Gentlemen's Agreement and continued to grow at about 10 percent a year for several years, creating "an imposing and visible colony."[131]

The pre-1908 migrants to Hawaii and the mainland were mostly men, so that while the gender imbalance was never so great as among the Chinese, it was certainly skewed. Los Angeles's Little Tokyo, just east of downtown, with 300 businesses and nearly 100 boarding and lodging houses, was seven to one male at that point. (At least it survived. Los Angeles' pre-1930s China-town was torn down to make way for Union Station; its successor lives around Hill Street and North Broadway.[132]) The 1907 Gentlemen's Agreement, meant to keep out Japanese but more face-savingly than the rigorous and insulting Chinese Exclusion Acts of 1882 and after, did limit male arrivals, but permitted female. The unintended effect was gradually to balance the Japanese-American sex ratio and permit families to form.

From 1910 to 1924 more than thirty thousand Japanese women came to the United States. Many of them were "picture brides" in marriages arranged by parents in Japan and unseen by their grooms in America except in photographs. Arranged marriages were common enough in traditional Tokugawa Japan but regarded in romantic, individualistic (and nativistic) America as barbaric. Ise Kato, born in Hiroshima Prefecture, became a picture bride at eighteen to a twenty-nine-year-old railroad foreman in Utah and lived her life in Ogden, bearing six children, returning once to Japan in 1962.[133] Michiyo Kanegai's husband, on the other hand, worked at various jobs in Salt Lake City and Los Angeles before he returned to Japan to marry her. They went back to Salt Lake City and ran a restaurant.[134] Alice Kasai, herself born in Seattle in 1916, recalled that her grandmothers arranged her parents' marriage, and because one family were samurai and the other farmers, they could not cross class lines in Japan. They married in Nagasaki but immediately sailed to live in Seattle.[135] By several routes, besides picture brides, the immigrants' sex imbalance dropped to two or three males to one female by 1920, not greatly different from many European immigrant groups at the time. In 1924 Congress passed a law restricting much immigration from Europe and virtually stopping any at all from Asia. By then, however, enough women had arrived to avoid among Japanese the aging and shrinking that befell the Chinese in America until the exclusion law ended in 1943.[136]

This first generation—literally translated Issei—lived, worked, and aged from the opening of the century until the World War II years, marrying and having children. The children became the second generation, or Nisei, who by 1930 were about as numerous as their parents. The arrival of women and the establishing of families ended the *dekasegi,* or migrant worker, phase of Japanese migration to the United States. From 1908 on more and more Japanese took up truck farming and other intensive agriculture. By 1910 Los Angeles County had 531 Japanese farms totaling 6,173 acres; on average, 11.6 acres each. By 1916 the county had 1,321 Japanese farms and nurseries, nearly all under 100 acres, producing poultry, vegetables, flowers, and berries (though rarely citrus or grapes) for the local produce market, which other Japanese increasingly controlled as middlemen.[137] Whether Japanese farmers owned, leased, or contracted for land, their holdings rose from 62,000 acres in 1905 to 282,000 in 1913, most of it in California and Washington and a little in Colorado sugar beet country.[138]

Oregon's first Japanese person—the wife of an Australian professor of animal husbandry who had lived in Japan—arrived in 1880 with her brother and adopted daughter. Others trickled in, getting jobs on the Oregon Short Line Railroad or operating farms or small businesses. By 1910 Portland had fifteen hundred Japanese, about to settle permanently. By 1920, despite several alien land acts for which the American Legion and the Ku Klux Klan were "major endorsers," the community had established itself firmly.[139] The arrival of women and the creation of family life had profound consequences, underpinning better enterprise as well as families.[140] Though the Japanese-born were excluded from U.S. citizenship, their Nisei sons and daughters possessed it by birthright under the Fourteenth Amendment.

In May 1913 the California legislature passed the Webb-Heney Act, better known as the Alien Land Law, with few dissents. Japanese could no longer lease agricultural land for more than three years, nor could they buy any more on the grounds that they, as "Mongolians," were not eligible for citizenship. (By that reasoning, European immigrants were not affected.) Here the Nisei proved crucial. As native-born citizens they could own or lease land. Issei parents thereupon transferred much acreage to them. Corporations with Issei stockholders also could hold titles. Through such devices the 1913 act could be circumvented. But in 1920 California voters passed a referendum measure, by three to one, preventing anyone from acting as guardian for a native-born minor who owned land that immigrant Japanese could not legally hold themselves. Washington State passed a similar measure in 1921. Thus Japanese who wanted to farm had to wait until the Nisei reached adulthood. Many went into other work.[141] The law reduced Japanese-American–held acreage until Nisei children reached adulthood and could serve as trustworthy mediators.[142]

The Asian dimension has always made race relations different in the West, and for more reasons than economic competition.[143] In the case of the alien land laws, Anglo nativism was obnoxiously obvious. *Grizzly Bear,* the publication of the Native Sons and Daughters of the Golden West, in its first issue (1907), ran an article, "The Asiatic Peril," that pointed out that while the Chinese had been successfully kept out in 1882, a new threat, the Japanese, had arrived. "If we, the sons of California, remain sluggish and inert at this crisis, our State in not many years will become as Hawaii is—a

Japanese colony with a small minority of white Americans." By 1921, advocating a stringent land law, it demanded "aggressive action within the law . . . if California is to get anywhere in the Jap crisis . . . [we want] none of the mikado's worshipers holding land in California."

The Native Sons also wanted Issei to stop commercial fishing, and they urged a boycott of Japanese-Californian fish and fish products. Further examples are easy to find.[144] Not every Californian was a nativist. Neeta Marquis published a protolerance, pro-Japanese piece in the church progressive magazine the *Independent,* affirming that through "Christian love and mutual toleration of differences most of the difficulties arising from the mingling of races disappear entirely."[145] But too often such people were in short supply.

Yoshisawa Kawai, born in Hiroshima in 1889, told his story in Seattle when he was eighty-one. He came to the United States in 1906, at seventeen, with a high school education. "At that time there was [in Japan] an enthusiastic immigration movement, and two or three persons who graduated before me, and my own teacher . . . had already come." This was not precisely chain migration, but it was migration by example. Disembarking in San Francisco, he quickly hired on at an apple-canning factory in Watsonville, picked fruit, took and passed an auto mechanic's course, and became "an established mechanic" in Culver City at the Hal Roach studios.

Henry Fujii, son of a farmer, born in Tottori-ken in 1886, was interviewed at age eighty-five. He came first to Seattle by ship for "around fifty or sixty dollars," then went to Montana as a railroad section hand. After proceeding to Emmett, Idaho, he picked sugar beets, "just like Mexicans . . . now," and lived in a house with fifteen other young Japanese men. He too had a high school education, and he knew some accounting. He saved enough to buy his first farm, for six thousand dollars. Then he hired other Japanese men as hands until they, like him, could get established: "Very first Japanese [who] came to Nampa, Idaho, was hired by Oregon Short Line Railroad Company. . . . Railroad company like Japanese so well they make him go back to San Francisco and get more Japanese and send man to Hawaii, bring more Japanese here, and one time about 3,500 Japanese working for the Oregon Short Line Railroad Company. And time I come to Nampa, 1907, about 500 people were working for the railroad around here, and some for the electric carline, some working for sugar beets; we must of had [sic] about 800 Japanese working around Nampa." He met his wife of sixty years in Japan: "I went back to Japan to visit my folks and get married, she come with me to Idaho." They visited Japan in 1926 with four children to show the grandparents. "When Japanese quit the railroad," he recalled, "they wanted to go into business . . . either farmer or restaurant." He had no problem with whites until 1915, when agitators from California tried "to make anti-Japanese land laws in Boise." Although Idaho did pass an alien land law in 1923, Fujii had already bought his land in 1918 and thus had "no trouble." After 1923 Japanese leased land in Idaho.[146]

These are typical stories in most respects: young men arriving, not intending to stay; starting work on railroads and moving into farming as soon as they could; marrying, usually to a woman from Japan (picture bride or otherwise), though occasionally to a white; moving up through tenancy to cash renting to ownership or leasehold as the law permitted. In Oregon, in the 1901–1913 period, one-fourth worked on railroads, one-third farmed, and the rest were cooks, house servants, lumberjacks, or cannery hands. Several hundred women arrived after 1910, and marriages multiplied. Not all Japanese in Oregon succeeded in creating small farms and stable families; the state's alien land law was a difficult obstacle. Utah's 2,110 Japanese in 1910 (of whom only 89 were female) were either farm workers or renters near Salt Lake or lived in mining towns like Price and Bingham; some still worked on the railroad. By 1920 the total number had risen to about 3,000, over a third female; Utah's Issei community was taking shape.[147]

The West in 1913

By 1913, as homestead entries reached their highest number ever, images of the twentieth-century West were resolving into clear black and white, while the nineteenth-century figures of the stagecoach driver, the prospector, the cowboy on the long drives, the marshals and the gunmen were fading into sepia. They were to linger in mythology but count for nothing in reality. The peopling of the West rested no more on old-style gold rushes or wagon trains. More and more visibly, it depended on water. In this too 1913 was a crucial year because then—in politically unconnected but parallel moves— Los Angeles opened its aqueduct and San Francisco secured a federal law assuring water for itself. Later in the century San Diego, Phoenix, and Las Vegas also constructed themselves on imported water.

How Los Angeles captured the water of Owens Lake, 233 miles north of the city and several thousand feet higher, just below the east face of the Sierra Nevada range, has been told as an engineering achievement, a political coup, and a drama of conspiracy (in the film *Chinatown*). Similarly, San Francisco's taking and damming of the Hetch Hetchy Valley (about 20 miles north of, and parallel to, the Yosemite Valley) for its water, is familiar because the environmental prophet John Muir tried to stop it and could not.

The stimulus was great. San Francisco already had 343,000 people in 1900 and expected to continue adding at least 50,000 a decade—if it could find more water. The private company then supplying the city could not provide enough. Choices, distant and costly, confronted the city. Its 1900 charter called for more water. The city engineer recommended damming the Hetch Hetchy Valley and building a gravity flow system of reservoirs, aqueducts, and power plants to the city over 150 miles away. For another dozen years contending political forces, including the old water company, proponents of other routes, and Muir and his Sierra Club, got in one another's way. Even the earthquake of 1906, when the water lines broke and fires spread out of control, failed to galvanize agreement. Finally, Congress in 1913 authorized construction to begin. (It helped that the new secretary of the interior under Woodrow Wilson, Franklin K. Lane, had supported the project for years when he was San Francisco's city attorney.) Piece by piece the project got built. San Francisco and its neighbors began receiving Hetch Hetchy water in 1934.

The Bay Area had been growing since 1900, but not nearly as fast as Los Angeles. There the water shortage was more pressing. The San Gabriel, Santa Ana, and Los Angeles rivers, available groundwater, and seasonal rainfall were hopelessly small. Large bond issues in 1905 and 1907, backed by a virtually unanimous power structure and supported by the people's votes in referenda, raised the money. Engineer William Mulholland frightened voters when he predicted that existing water could supply no more than 200,000 people (the city had already reached 102,000 in 1900), but he did not exaggerate. With the new aqueduct, Mulholland declared that the city could grow to 2,000,000, including the newly annexed San Fernando Valley, hitherto fit only for sheep and wheat.

The annexation doubled the size of Los Angeles, making it geographically the largest city in the country and eliciting different judgments. In one view, taking on the valley "doomed [the city] to become a huge, sprawling, one-story conurbation, hopelessly dependent on the automobile."[148] In another, the water and the valley, together with the interurban transit system, reinforced the city's character well before automobiles began appearing in numbers, and that character was "horizontality . . . the fundamental orientation of the urban settlements filling the coastal plain between mountain and sea."[149] Whether blunder or boon, the water arrived on November 6, 1913, "delivering four times as much water as . . . Los Angeles was then capable of consuming."[150]

Aqueducts and irrigation systems were also under way by 1913 in central Arizona and in the Central Valley of California. The Salt River project, authorized under the Newlands Act, watered 125,000 Arizona acres by 1907, and its centerpiece, Roosevelt Dam, completed in 1911, helped raise the state's irrigated acreage to 400,000, raising crop yields, land prices, innovations like ostrich farming, and water to let Phoenix grow far beyond its 5,544 of 1900.[151] In California the same A. D. Foote who superintended the North Star Mine in Grass Valley published an article in 1910 proposing an irrigation system to include the entire Central Valley from Chico to Bakersfield, rearranging everything on the model of the ancient Egyptians, whom he frankly admired. The true worth of the valley, Foote contended, had been obscured by "fifty years of mishandling natural riches." Just seventy-five million dollars of state money and a few years' work would bring water to "not only the lands in the basins, but also the cities and towns, and the mines, [and] all property in the Valley."[152] Much of this came to pass.

In these first thirteen years of the new century the population of the West surged by two-thirds. For all the homesteading, irrigating, dry farming, and mining, it was in cities that the major action took place. They grew twice as fast as farm and ranch country. In 1910 San Francisco's 607,000 towered above other western metropolises, but Los Angeles with 319,000, Seattle with 237,000, and Denver with 213,000, plus Portland, Oakland, and Spokane, made seven with populations over 100,000 compared with only three in 1900. Already nearly 5 of 8 Californians lived in cities, a proportion not far behind the East's and well ahead of the Midwest's.[153]

Western cities all had Anglo-American majorities, mostly from the Midwest, but they also were mixing races and nationalities just as eastern and midwestern ones were doing. Seattle, for example, found its "early Scandinavian flavor . . . strongly reinforced" by 15,000 recently arrived Swedes, Norwegians, Danes, and Finns and seasoned with "about 10,000 Russians, Hungarians, Italians, and Greeks," besides 3,000 Japanese and 2,000 African-Americans, whose housing was better—albeit segregated—than that of their counterparts in Chicago and New York.[154] Denver's blacks, together with those in Portland, Denver, San Francisco, and Los Angeles, numbered over 18,000 in 1910, far more than the black cowboys, homesteaders, or even soldiers in the West. San Francisco had the longest-established black community, dating back to the Gold Rush; Oakland perhaps the most popular, though Denver was also favored; and Los Angeles, with 7,600, the largest west of Texas.[155]

Los Angeles throve on everything: health seekers, tourists, oil fields, the eclectic and appropriate new bungalow style of homebuilding, the "big red cars roaming over nearly 1,200 miles through four counties," the never-ending sunshine, and its own excitement. Pasadena, by 1913 almost stodgy, still flourished as a resort where, sniffed the *Chicago Record-Herald*, "a large part of the community are spenders, living in costly houses and giving up their lives to rest and enjoyment." On the growing west side, according to a much later magazine advertisement, "as the Old West slowly faded into the sunset and the star of Hollywood peeked over the horizon, a new hotel found a superb way to welcome visitors to California. It was named the Beverly Hills Hotel."[156] A Philadelphia visitor in 1909 waxed eloquent about the fine trolley that whisked him from downtown to the ferry dock at San Pedro for the boat to Catalina Island; the Hotel Green in Pasadena; and the inclined railway lifting him to the Alpine Tavern, five thousand feet above the city in the snow-covered San Gabriel Mountains.[157] A thirty-five-year era of wheat harvests closed in the San Fernando Valley, as developers began subdividing it for family homes, with water provided by the new aqueduct.[158] Suburb after suburb spread the city across the Los Angeles Basin, giving it a density of just over three thousand people per square mile, compared with over sixteen thousand in Boston or New York.[159]

Los Angeles was by then producing several million barrels of oil a year, obviating imported fuel, providing export income. Its first auto show drew admiring crowds in 1908. In 1909 a southward annexation assured it a harbor. In 1910 the filmmaker D. W. Griffith brought Mary Pickford to town, and Glenn Curtiss brought the airplane to the Dominguez Hills air fair. Energy, cars, ocean trade, motion pictures, and airplanes all had arrived. As had enough water.

So far California's urban workers devoted themselves to trade and services, not heavy industry. Its oil, water, and climate apparently assured, its agriculture a great productive success, the Golden State was never more golden. If California in its rural aspect never had a homesteading past to overcome, it also has never had a bowl to rust. Both industrially and agriculturally, it rumbled into the twentieth century without that baggage of the past.

Across the entire West, these years from 1901 to 1913 continued the dual narrative. The ancient American story of homesteading and settling reached its historic peak from Texas to the Dakotas and through the Plains and Northwest. The new story of the metropolitan West already framed the daily lives of many more people.

6

TOURISTS, HONYOCKERS, MEXICANS, AND MORE, 1914–1929

Poor Montana! . . . We met hundreds of families driving out, in old "prairie-schooners," with all their household furniture and their cattle. . . . They had lost everything.
—Beatrice Larned Massey, auto tourist, 1919

I'm going to tell you about a bubble that never broke, about the most beautiful bubble in all the world. This bubble . . . is called Los Angeles.
—G. Allison Phelps in *Southern California Business*, 1926

World War I and the 1920s

The bifurcation between the old, homesteading West and the new, urbanizing West widened further through the 1910s and 1920s. After Europe collapsed into war in the summer of 1914, American farmers benefited from high demand for their wheat and corn as the United States joined the Allies first economically and then (in April 1917) militarily. But the stimulus was temporary; the end of the war in late 1918, coupled with another drought, forestalled further homesteading and forced the retreat of many who had tried it earlier. Yet the West, especially its towns and cities, continued to expand, enriched by new elements, among them a developing rail and highway system that made the region accessible; a series of oil booms; and above all, from the demographic standpoint, the arrival of Mexicans fleeing revolutionary upheaval and seeking opportunities. In many ways the West became not just an exotic curiosity but an integral part of the United States between 1914 and 1929. It led the nation's fundamental change from rural to urban, it reveled in the expansion of the 1920s, and it took a much weightier place vis-à-vis the Northeast, Midwest, and South, tipping the national balance toward the Pacific. World War II was to magnify this shift, but it had well begun by 1929.

In 1914 the Panama Canal opened, greatly pleasing California boosters and business interests who foresaw how it would increase naval and commercial ship traffic. San Diego and San Francisco with their marvelous natural harbors were sure to benefit, and did. Los Angeles, busy since the late 1890s promoting a deepwater harbor, seized the moment to open one at San Pedro. Chambers of commerce and newspapers like the *Los Angeles Times* applauded the "growing partnership of the city and the sword," and voters approved, "frequently by stunning majorities." The Panama Canal and World War I initiated these military-municipal-commercial complexes; World War II was to augment them.[1]

The canal also stimulated two grand expositions in 1915, world's fairs in all but name. The Panama-California in San Diego opened at Balboa Park, while the Panama-Pacific in San Francisco memorialized the Gold Rush and previewed the diesel engine ("California's Destiny") and other futuristic devices. California's frontier days, the expositions proclaimed, were history; a new and recast California Dream lay ahead.[2] On January 25, 1915, Alexander Graham Bell phoned San Francisco from New York, and coast-to-coast service began. Plans for the Lincoln Highway, also between New York and San Francisco, became definite in 1914, and the actual road materialized a few years later. By 1929 curious tourists and hopeful migrants could drive to the West Coast along several routes.

In its levels of public health and afflictions the West had achieved national standards by 1914, for better or worse. Except for Indian reservations generally and Hispanic districts in the Southwest, and the lag in more remote rural areas, demographic indices like infant mortality and morbidity from diseases and accidents did not deviate greatly from the rest of the country.[3] The germ theory of disease transmission was just then becoming widely accepted, and western public health authorities, like those elsewhere, were promoting sanitation, clean water, and personal hygiene as never before. Viruses, however, were still a mystery. The West suffered thousands of deaths in the great pandemic of "Spanish" influenza, which killed at least thirty million people globally and six hundred thousand in the United States in 1918 and 1919. The West's contribution was to start it, not to cure it. The earliest identified cases appeared at Camp Funston, Kansas, a tossed-together training ground for army recruits on the edge of the Flint Hills near Fort Riley, a nineteenth-century base too small to handle the sudden manpower surge. Recruits from Funston carried it to other bases and then to France in early 1918.[4]

The West fared no better than anywhere else. Quarantines, gauze masks, patent medicines, and more frequent street sweepings availed nothing. A man in the Texas oil boomtown of Ranger remembered: "I saw the time when . . . you couldn't hardly look up and not see a casket. [We] made them just out of lumber and buried them . . . by the dozens here every day."[5] Despite being on the cutting edge of modernity, the West and the rest of the advanced world could do no better in 1919 than to let the epidemic burn itself out, like the Black Death of the fourteenth century and viral epidemics before and since.

In another way, however, the American West was demographically ahead of the country. Immediately before 1920 the American people became more than half urban, in the sense that by then just over half were living in towns and cities (of 2,500 or larger), just under half on farms and in country villages. By this definition, the West was more urban than the national average (and had been since 1870), slightly more so than the Midwest and much more than the South.[6] Most western cities, whatever their size, grew or at least held steady between 1914 and 1929. Butte was one of the rare decliners in the 1920s, down about 5 percent following a spate of labor trouble during and just after World War I.[7] Some small places scattered around the West enjoyed big percentage gains, among them wheat town Hays, Kansas; ranching and irrigation Carlsbad, New Mexico; Burns, Oregon, in the sheep range; Fort Stockton, Texas, in cattle country; and the mining towns of Price, Utah, and Rawlins, Wyoming. Dwarfing them, however, was Los Angeles. The city exploded twelvefold from 102,500 in 1900 to 1,238,000 in 1930, half the increase coming in the 1920s, and by 1930 nearly another 1,000,000 lived in Pasadena, Long Beach, and dozens of other municipalities in Los Angeles County but outside the core city limits.[8]

Smaller families and more balanced sex ratios developed during the 1920s in the West. As the coastal and mountain states urbanized, all except for Mormon Utah and Idaho and Hispanic New Mexico fell below the national average of 3.4 people per family, while the Great Plains farm states exceeded it. The sex ratio of formerly frontierlike Seattle, Spokane, and Tacoma drew about even, and San Francisco's became much closer than before. The same happened in Denver, Los Angeles, Oakland, and Portland on the coast. Outside the larger cities, especially among the foreign-born, males still predominated; while the West's overall sex ratio hovered just above the balance point, foreign-born males still outnumbered females 144 to 100 in the mountain states, 132 to 100 on the coast.

Though the federal immigration laws tightened in the 1920s, "nonwhites" (the census's term) increased—not only Chinese and Japanese, Filipinos and Asian Indians but, most strikingly, Mexicans: up 74 percent in Texas, 77 percent in the mountain states (to 249,000, mostly in Arizona and New Mexico), and 113 percent on the coast (from 122,000 to 370,000, mostly in California).[9] This was the great age of European immigration in the East and Midwest and in California and the West as well. But Mexicans seized first place after 1910. California also attracted hundreds of thousands from Illinois, New York, Missouri, Ohio, and Iowa, and other states, and like every western state except Utah, the majority of its people had been born elsewhere, either in the United States or other countries. Most of the American-born newcomers continued to come, as they had for decades, from the Midwest and Northeast, not from the South. In the plains states, however—even Texas—immigration had slowed or stopped; births, not migrants, provided such growth as there was; most people were locally grown.[10]

The Tourist Vanguard: The West Becomes Terra Cognita

Besides its demographic convergence, the West joined the rest of America in another way in these years. It became geographically accessible because of automobile tourism. Beginning in the 1900s, it was often abetted by the nonchalant railroads, which discounted the thought that the unreliable gas buggies might ever compete with them. As a railroad trade journal mused in 1908, "First came the parallel electric [trolley] line, next the development of the long-distance telephone line, and now the automobile. The future will tell whether the airship is to be a fourth. But the first two of these the railroad has overcome, the third is comparatively a minor factor, the fourth a commercial nebulosity as yet."[11]

The Santa Fe, the Burlington, and other roads vigorously promoted excursions to Yellowstone Park, Glacier Park in northern Montana, and above all the Southwest. The Santa Fe laid on a free overnight trip to the Grand Canyon from its main line through Arizona beginning in 1901, including a stay at El Tovar, its faux rustic, elegantly appointed hotel on the south rim.[12] Fred Harvey built El Tovar and a string of other inns from Kansas City to Los Angeles and staffed them with the gracious Harvey Girls, the functional predecessors of flight attendants but serving rather better food. In the same era the Canadian Pacific constructed its massive luxury hotels all across Canada from the Château Frontenac in Quebec City to the Empress on Vancouver Island, all with their steep green-coppered roofs, all establishments that did Britannia proud.

The Rock Island Railroad advertised in 1903 that "a month in California will do you more good than all the medicine in Christendom." Another ad in 1906 exalted Pasadena and its resort hotels as "a sun-kissed jewel," a place "where every sense is gratified," and "where Italy and California join hands." The rancher Zach T. White spent $1,500,000 to open the Hotel Paso del Norte in El Paso on Thanksgiving Day, 1912, resplendently marbled and glowing beneath its sapphire blue twenty-five-foot glass dome designed by

Louis Tiffany himself.[13] The usual patrons of these trains and hostelries were people of means, looking to relax safely amid the exotic yet perhaps to "find" America, a "final haven for the regeneration of the nation's Anglo-Saxon heritage," as one historian suggests.[14]

For the truly wealthy and truly Yankee, a private railway car was the way to travel. The old-money Bostonian James Murray Forbes (1845–1937) attached his luxury car, the *Black Hawk,* to a passenger train in Burlington, Iowa, in October 1903 and headed west. In Albuquerque he found "a large station and hotel in the Old Mission style, a museum and large store, with all kinds of Indian and Mexican things, blankets, baskets, etc.; said to be the best of its kind in the country, and we saw the Indians weaving their blankets and at other work." The next day, at the Grand Canyon, "none of our party was disappointed . . . in spite of all we had read and heard." The *Black Hawk* took them on to California, then back through Tucson to El Paso, where they hooked on to the Mexican Central Railroad. Forbes talked with "Mr. Allen, Trainmaster of the Mexican Central R.R.," and "learnt from him that the average Mexican is five times as lazy as the negro [*sic*], and twice as clever as the best New York pickpocket." Mexico City discomfited them, and they returned ahead of time, reaching Burlington, Iowa, "after an absence of 40 days and 40 nights (largely in the wilderness)."[15] Forbes, as his log shows, took his biases as well as his millions with him. For him the West remained, after his lavish trip, as foreign as Patagonia.

But by means of railroad excursions, and later by cross-country auto trips, the West was becoming part of the national experience, its reality filtering slowly down from the leisure class to the masses. Extreme cases on either end of the spectrum are Forbes's private railroad car of 1903 and the flivvers of the Dust Bowl refugees of the 1930s. Most visitors were at neither pole, but a definite democratization of touristic experience took place from the beginning of the century to World War II.

The first cross-country car trips, much like train travel by Pullman, were not for those with shallow pockets. Auto travel required plenty of time and money and a vehicle more substantial than the utilitarian Ford Model T. The removal of the West's mystic veil began with railroad excursions to West Coast resorts like Pasadena or Monterey or to the great national parks. The veil dropped further with the first tentative, gutsy auto trips from New York and Chicago to the Pacific, and it dropped completely in the 1920s and 1930s, when the newly developing national highway system made cross-country trips almost commonplace. By 1929 they had changed the once-exotic West from a place as unreachable as the tents of Araby or the court of the Great Khan into a familiar, almost quotidian region. "The auto tourists of 1913 to

California were prosperous Eastern city types, the mainstays of the big hotels—bank directors, corporation presidents, 'young bloods, without hats and in white flannels, talking golf, polo, and motor cars . . . elderly ladies of comfortable embonpoint, with lorgnettes and lapdogs.' "[16] A good many of these early voyageurs kept notes or diaries and later published them, sometimes privately for their friends' amusement and occasionally for mass marketing. Some are inevitably self-praising and gee-whizzy, but the rigors and risks of trips before 1920 (and some after that) come through clearly, along with how these travelers overcame obstacles with ease (i.e., with money). These accounts are true travel books; they describe adventures and places that the reader visits vicariously, not expecting ever to go there in person.

Primitive, prehighway conditions were merely a challenge for Alice Huyler Ramsey in the summer of 1909. Aged twenty-two, with a stay-at-home husband willing to buy her cars and outfits, with three women friends happy to make the trip (though only Ramsey could drive), and with the Maxwell motor company eager to subsidize her for the publicity, Ramsey and companions made it from New York to San Francisco in forty-one days. They crossed the Mississippi River on a bridge "of wooden planking and just wide enough for passing"—a tense moment. But once on the Iowa side they rejoiced: "Now, at last, we were West!" The Iowa mud nearly defeated them, and after thirteen days of slogging they put the Maxwell on a freight car for the last hundred miles to Omaha. As they crossed Nebraska, their nemesis was sand. Not a road was paved, and the "highway" was "a mere trail . . . into Cheyenne as it crossed the ranches and hills." Ranchers, not expecting much auto traffic, had fenced in the range with gates that "we had to open and close behind us as we passed through." But at Rock Springs, Ramsey "saw on a neighboring rise a coyote yowling his blood-curdling cry. There was no doubt I was truly in the West." After a harrowing climb over the Sierra's cliffs and switchbacks, on a road "heavy with sand [and] in truth no automobile highway [but] an old wagon trail," they reached a third epiphany, the ultimate West, the Golden Gate.[17]

Six years later, in 1915, ballyhoo about the new Lincoln Highway from New York to San Francisco encouraged Emily Post to make the trip with her son. No less intrepid than Ramsey, the tsarina of etiquette found road conditions hardly improved. The Lincoln Highway was "a disappointment . . . a meandering dirt road that becomes mud half a foot deep after a day or two of rain!" In Iowa, "twenty-five minutes of drizzle turned the smooth, hard surface of the road into the consistency of gruel . . . [mud] lurks in unfathomable treachery, loath to let anything ever get out again that once ventures into it."

Omaha disappointed her by its familiarity: "Where, oh, where is the West that Easterners dream of—the West of Bret Harte's stories, the West depicted in the moving pictures? . . . We have gone half the distance across the continent and all this while we might be anywhere at home. Omaha is a big up-to-date and perfectly Eastern city."

Colorado Springs she "had imagined . . . a sort of huge sanatorium [with] long lines of invalid chairs on semi-enclosed verandas." Though there were plenty of tubercular patients, the place proved to be a lively resort. After crossing Raton Pass and "washed-out roads, arroyos, rocky stretches, and nubbly hills [that] just about smashed everything" between Las Vegas and Santa Fe, she found Albuquerque "a surprisingly modern city." But the car was the worse for wear, and in Winslow, Arizona, she put it on a freight to Los Angeles and went on by train. The Lincoln Highway, she decided, was "an imaginary line." For California she had the highest praise; from Los Angeles to Santa Barbara "never, never was there a more beautiful drive . . . not the Cornici of France—not even the Sorrento to Amalfi of Italy."[18]

In 1919 Beatrice Larned Massey drove 4,154 miles in thirty-three days from New York to San Francisco via Chicago, Yellowstone Park, Salt Lake City, and Reno, together with her engineer husband and another couple in a Packard twin-six touring car. The Masseys carried all manner of cables, tow-lines, spark plugs, tires, pumps, wrenches, and other auto first-aid equipment. They also took their tennis rackets and golf clubs but no camping gear, for they preferred to stay in good hotels. Conditions had improved since Ramsey's trip; Utah had some real cement roads, the best since the group left the East. But California, "the beautiful land of sunshine and flowers," had miles of roads "smooth as marble, with no dust."

Mrs. Massey noted many things, but one was truly remarkable: her encounter between Glendive and Miles City, Montana, in the Yellowstone River valley, with "hundreds of families driving out, in old 'prairie-schooners' "—eastward.[19] These were people who "had tried to raise crops, and were literally driven out. The children looked pinched and starved. The women and men were the color of leather, tanned by the scorching sun of the plains, the dust, and the dry, hot winds. They had lost everything."

This meeting in 1919 of upper-middle-class westbound tourists with dirt-poor failed honyocker homesteaders retreating eastward must be one of the great symbolic encounters in recent American history, though neither side recorded it that way. The valley of the Yellowstone River in eastern Montana opened to homesteaders about 1909. Auto travel across Montana became commonplace by 1929. Massey was, in 1919, one of the first auto tourists, and she met some of the last of the homesteaders, headed in the opposite direction. If ever two Americas—a threadbare nineteenth century and a plush twentieth—greeted each other, that may have been the time.

The agreement in 1914 between state and local governments and private enterprise to create the Lincoln Highway, followed by the 1916 Federal Highway Act authorizing joint state-federal road building, made travel less an adventure and more a lark, though still mostly for the well-off. Sinclair Lewis, who wrote a series on "Automobumming" for the *Saturday Evening Post* in 1919–1920, found cars much improved but roads that "would have been a disgrace to the Balkan States in A.D. 1600." Mud, sand, ruts, silt, and hills defeated him; too rare were hot meals in decent restaurants, and reliable "autohobo hotels," gas stations, and garages.[20] A few years later he would have found all these at reasonable intervals.

Car tourists' accounts from the 1920s still belong to the travel book genre, but they record constantly improving roads and facilities. Another Federal Highway Act in 1921 forced states to spend their cost-sharing money on a real intercity network, and in 1925 Interior Secretary Hubert Work proclaimed the system of numbered roads, including U.S. 1, U.S. 40, and many more. Macadamized and concrete roads, not yet created in 1921, carried thousands of Model Ts four years later. A family who drove from New York to San Francisco in 1926 found that "not more than ten percent of the thoroughfares we traveled were uncompromisingly bad," and auto camps with showers, charging a half dollar a car per night, presented themselves in many places west of the Mississippi. In Wyoming, "Times have changed. . . . No bleaching skulls, no wrecks of prairie schooners lie beside the reincarnations of the old overland trails. Instead, the roadside is adorned with burst tubes, worn-out tires and now and then the rusted remnants of a car which its apparently disgusted owners left in a ditch to perish." Yellowstone's camps were "overcrowded" despite an entrance fee of $7.50 for the day (or the season); motor camps in Oregon and California were "comfortable and clean."[21] By 1929 the infrastructure of mass tourism was in place: cabins, rest stops, restaurants, service stations, oil company road maps, national brands of gas and oil, motorists' associations (the AAA and others)—the immediate precursors of the post-1945 motels and fast-food chains.[22]

The highway network and mass-marketed cars, as well as intercity buses and trucks, had in little more than a decade transformed auto travel to the West from an upper-class preserve to a fairly common experience. In the 1930s travel books changed into guidebooks, from accounts of adventures to be read for vicarious pleasure by the fireside to lists of tips for soon-to-be travelers. Class and color bias still infected some travelers; Herbert Carolan's account of his trip from Chicago to California in the early 1930s advised his no doubt relieved readers that they could ship their cars through the

Panama Canal and from San Francisco to Seattle while cruising to music and dancing, with "colored attendants . . . available and willing . . . to aid your pleasure and comfort."[23] But car travel was available to the masses by the 1930s, permitting many thousands to drive west to California on U.S. 66 to escape the farm depression.

Honyockers' Hell

Not every honyocker retreated out of Montana in 1919, nor did home-steading cease suddenly after the all-time peak year of 1913, when more than 59,000 final entries transferred title from the government to men, women, and families for nearly 11,000,000 acres. The next year was almost as prolific, with 53,308 final entries for 9,941,000 acres. Original filings continued through 1917 to range between 59,000 and 65,000, though a smaller percent-age of them ever proved up. Homesteading (and the urge to try it) slowed almost imperceptibly. Except for 1918 and 1919, when World War I and the flu epidemic brought a brief pause, original and final entries continued.

But the long-term trend gradually revealed itself. By the 1930s there could be no doubt that 1901–1913 had been the golden years. From 1901 through 1910 every year averaged over 83,000 original claims and 37,000 final entries, almost double the rates of the 1880s and 1890s. From 1911 through 1920 new claims averaged only about 51,000 a year, final entries 44,000. Then came real slippage: from 1921 to 1925, 24,000 new *and* 24,000 final claims, on aver-age, each year; from 1926 to 1930, 11,000 new and 8,000 final claims each year. Homesteading withered away, already over with when the Taylor Grazing Act closed the public lands to new entries in 1934.[24] In the 1910s and even the 1920s it was not always easy to see what was happening: the beginning of the end of the small family farm as well as the end of homesteading. More Americans lived on farms in 1916—32,530,000—than ever before or since. The number slipped below 31,000,000 through the late 1920s, picked up for a time during the early 1930s, when there was no point in going to a city and joining the job lines, but then began falling again in 1935 and has never stopped since.[25]

Mechanization assuredly played a role; farming required ever fewer peo-ple. Russell Adams, of Woodward, Oklahoma, recalled that he saw his first combine about 1921 or 1922. His family did not have a tractor yet, and to plow two and a half acres was "a pretty good day's work." A neighbor, C. L. Alley, might do five acres on a good day on a sulky plow behind two horses. But then things changed, with gas-driven combines and tractors that could fertilize an entire 160 acres in two hours: "I don't know how to tell you, but it's undescribable to me."[26] New young farmers, who in wave after wave had been replenishing America's farm population since the seventeenth century, were simply redundant. The farms no longer needed them.

Increasingly, especially in the South, farmers found themselves tenants on the land they worked, no longer the owners. Rural life appeared strong from 1914 to 1929, and by some statistical measures in fact it was; but its future was behind it. The occupying and cultivating of new farmland, whether acquired from the public domain or the railroads or another source, sputtered during the 1920s and in many places began retreating. The retreat began well before the Great Depression and the Dust Bowl. The problem was oversettlement based on overinvestment in the oversold homesteading ideal.

The railroads, interestingly and not coincidentally, were peaking too. Every year between 1866 and 1916 American railroads added at least a thousand miles of track, but they never did so again. Main track mileage rose a few thousand miles every year up to 1916 but then stabilized, added less than a thousand more, and started declining irreversibly in 1931.[27] In both the United States and western Canada, "retrenchment" was the railroads' watchword, and from 1921 to 1935 they closed down or actually tore up more track than they built.[28]

Railroads were still crucially important, but after World War I they no longer led the way west or anywhere else. The story of Coburg, Montana, typifies what happened in the 1920s—and later in the century, many times more—to country towns that the railroads called into existence, to be snuffed out later by weather and economics. Coburg began life as a rail siding on the Great Northern in the late 1880s. By World War I fifty families lived there in an apparently successful settlement. Life was not plush; a dry summer in 1918 devolved into a "brutal" winter, "as disastrous as the winter of 1886–1887" for cattle herds, and "for homesteaders huddled in tarpaper shacks, it was agony." Still, homesteaders kept arriving; banks kept extending credit into 1921. Then came a sharp national recession. Credit dried up; auctions proliferated; "horses were a drug on the market . . . left to run free on the deserted homesteads" and finally "rounded up in large herds to be shipped out for dog food and glue." "Tangible disintegration" started in 1921, when "one cold morning, as I rode across the valley to get the mail, I could see that Coburg's skyline was short one [grain] elevator and thin columns of smoke rose from the spot." By 1922 "the Farmers' elevator and the frame boxes that had housed the pool hall, real estate office, and post office had also vanished. By the late 1920s all that remained of Coburg were the depot, the section house, the hotel, one store building, and an isolated shack or two. Everything else had either burned or . . . been torn down and hauled away. There were just three families [left]." The Great Northern pulled out early in the 1930s, the remaining buildings were razed, and "Coburg was no more. . . . Where once there was a farmstead on every 320 acres there is not now a sign of human habitation in two hundred square miles."[29]

Another Montana town, Rudyard, did better. On the Great Northern and U.S. 2, about halfway between Shelby and Havre, Rudyard began in 1910 with a railroad station, then a post office, a saloon, two general stores, a hotel, a school, churches, a newspaper, and an electric power plant. In the midst of the great prairie that extends up into Palliser's Triangle in Alberta and Saskatchewan, the country around Rudyard had been cattle range until homesteaders started arriving in 1909. In a year Rudyard incorporated, claiming a population of 598. That turned out to be its high point. Intense boosterism kept it going. By the 1940s it was half as large, but by 1980 it crept back to 500. It does not long deter the driver along U.S. 2, but it has survived. The railroad created the town and preserved it, becoming a better citizen as the years went on. Larger than Coburg and more strategically situated, Rudyard had just enough critical mass and capital for precarious survival.[30]

The organizing of new counties by state legislatures had been a sure mark of the settlement process ever since colonial Virginia created Kentucky well before 1800. Governor John Martin's remark in the 1880s about wonderful Kansas, spawning a new county every six months, was accurate. From 1910 to 1917 (nearly all by 1915), eighty-three new counties split off from existing ones as fast as ever, forty-four in Idaho and Montana, thirty-nine in every other western state except Kansas and California. During the 1920s, by contrast, only eight new counties appeared, five of them in Montana. Their glory was often brief; twenty-one counties created between 1910 and 1920 lost up to half their populations by 1930.

Since 1930 only three counties have been created in the West, and three others have been deorganized. (One of the new ones was Los Alamos County, New Mexico, formed early in World War II to isolate the atomic scientists from surrounding local governments; it had nothing to do with homesteading.) County creating, another time-honored indicator of settlement frontiers, was basically over by 1915, completely so by 1930. By all three indices—new homesteads, new railroads, new counties—the West completed its rural settlement phase in the three or four years immediately after 1913.

That is the regional big picture. Even through the 1920s, however, many far western counties of all the plains states, from North Dakota south through Texas, kept and attracted people. The ninety-eighth meridian divided losers to the east and gainers to the west. South Dakota, for example, gained only 9 percent statewide during the 1920s, but almost a third of its counties—nearly all on or west of the Missouri River—rose between 20 and

112 percent. Corson and Dewey, farm counties in north-central South Dakota just west of the Missouri, gained about a third—i.e., about 1,500 to 2,500 people. Pennington (seat: Rapid City) rose 58 percent to 20,079, followed by other Black Hills counties, where mining was still important.

The map of Texas shows dozens of counties gaining far more than the state's 25 percent average during the 1920s. The panhandle, the area south of it from Lubbock eastward to Fort Worth, the Permian Basin (Odessa, Midland, Abilene), and a scattering of counties south to the gulf were the major gainers, while dozens of east Texas counties, many of them gainers a decade earlier, lost people. Hockley County, containing Lubbock, increased almost 7,000 percent, from 137 people in 1920 to 9,298 in 1930. The Lubbock area was shifting to cotton, attracting some dozens of young black couples like D. C. Fair and his wife, who came to pick cotton, work on the new gin, and become servants who lived "out behind the big houses"; the Klan, they recalled, was not as strong as it was in east Texas.[31] About a hundred miles north, Amarillo's Potter County grew 176 percent in the 1920s, from 16,710 to 46,080. The economic bases for much of this increase were wheat, cotton, cattle, and often oil—extractive enterprises all. But despite Texas's Stetson and boots image, major cities—Dallas, Houston, Fort Worth, and El Paso—accounted for the bulk of the new people.[32]

All over the plains, in fact, and in most of the West, cities led growth: Oklahoma City and Tulsa; Topeka, Wichita, and around Kansas City in Kansas; Omaha and Lincoln, Sioux Falls, Fargo, and Bismarck on the northern plains; Denver, Albuquerque, Phoenix, Tucson, Boise, and north and south of Salt Lake City in the mountain West. Dry farming or irrigation kept, or occasionally even attracted, people to western Kansas and along the Pecos in New Mexico, the South Platte in Nebraska, and the Snake in Idaho.

For many people the times were auspicious and reassuring. Changes as fundamental as those taking place in this period were too deep to be seen or heard. Rarely did they make headlines or even books, but they, not surface events, were the deep history of that time. When the 1920 census revealed an urban majority, wrote the demographer Calvin Beale, "the shock was so great that Congress, for the only time in its history, found itself unable to reach any consensus on congressional reapportionment and ignored its constitutional requirement to reapportion," the basic reason for having a census in the first place. "Distrust of urban society and disbelief in the permanence of the out-movement from farming" underlay Congress's dereliction.[33]

The power of the homesteading ideal—and the propaganda of railroads, land companies, and state immigration bureaus—overwhelmed caution. Railroads did sometimes warn the unprepared; a longtime agent for the

Northern Pacific, H. W. Byerly, advised land seekers swarming toward Montana in the peak period of 1910–1919 that they needed capital and experience: "We started our greatly increased advertising for homeseekers in January, 1910, and for a long time thereafter received an average of over 200 letters a day. Too many . . . were not qualified to make a success in western Dakota and eastern Montana. I wrote hundreds of them that unless they had enough capital, and the grit to stick it out till they could prove up, they should not consider the adventure. However, you could not stop most of them, even with a club."[34]

Homestead experiences in Montana, Nebraska, Kansas, and North Dakota followed similar broad outlines but varied somewhat according to the age and economics of the specific area. Before 1916 honyockers poured into Montana, following the railroad lines (the Northern Pacific, the Burlington, and the Great Northern), their cheap lands, and their accessibility. Marie MacDonald, a teacher and librarian, interviewed 175 "survivors of the boom" of pre–World War I days some decades later. She reports that they "were not the Joads of their day" but brought anywhere from one to five thousand dollars from savings, inheritances, or proceeds from farms or businesses farther east. Perhaps a third lacked such capital but earned money from some skill such as teaching, doctoring, and carpentering. "They were men and women in the prime of life, in their twenties and thirties."

The height, she learned, came in 1916, and "thereafter, war, drought and twenty years of depressed farm prices drove thousands of homesteaders, many of them almost starving, into softer climates." Some stories were tragic. But other "old-timers that I talked with recalled with gusto the comfortlessness of their early years" and the wonder of being the first ones to farm a new country.[35] In the 1910s, and by 1920, despite shakeouts, some areas continued to attract people and fulfill traditional dreams. In Nebraska farmers on the plains lived better after 1919 than those in the eastern part of the state, by most measures. They shifted from traditional methods faster, took to irrigation quicker, got into less debt, and were more willing to "mobilize the federal government" through farm support legislation.[36] In Kansas good harvests and good prices continued nearly every year from the 1910s well into the 1920s, keeping people on the land. In the remote, treeless, and nearly townless southwest corner of Kansas, population quadrupled between the state censuses of 1905 and 1925 and rose further when natural gas fields opened late in the 1920s. But in only a few years this was the epicenter of the Dust Bowl.[37]

Fortunately the thirty-county area of western Kansas never contained more than thirteen people per square mile, except in and around Dodge City; much of it stayed at two to six. Frontierlike population densities, age and sex distributions, and high numbers of children per family had all but disappeared, though the birthrate in western Kansas remained higher through the period than in eastern Kansas. Conversely, mortality was lower. Average farm size in western Kansas doubled between 1890 and 1900 from 226 to 521 acres but then stayed there. Throughout the 1914–1929 period, small towns in western Kansas quietly developed, and though decline became a fear, it still lay in the future. Farm tenancy increased during the 1920s, but more as a statistical category than from any real hardening of class lines; as farmers aged, they often leased land to their sons or other relatives, creating a "kinship type of tenancy" that actually meant greater rural stability rather than less.[38] Rural western Kansas remained a viable, if not prosperous, place to live before 1929.

In North Dakota railroads imported workers—not all of them seasonal and temporary—into the 1920s to repair, replace, or double-track their lines. By 1915 the attractive homestead land had mostly been taken up, and World War I closed down promotional offices in Europe. But the state continued advertising land for sale, tried to bring buyers and sellers together, and raised appropriations for its state immigration board.[39] The inflow of Poles, Ukrainians, and other eastern Europeans slowed from pre-1913 levels (though it did not stop, since many of these people had already arrived in other parts of the United States before war broke out in 1914). By the 1920s intermarriage across ethnic and even religious lines began to happen, signifying real assimilation of people to each other and to the country.[40]

Some people were pass-throughs. Wanda Sankary later told of her girlhood on a farm south of Scranton, North Dakota. Her parents emigrated from Poznan, in Prussian Poland, first to Pennsylvania in 1901 and then to North Dakota "when there wasn't a village or a neighbor or a human being within sixty miles—no roads, nothing but buffaloes and Indians" (or so she had been told). Wanda's father was an experienced coal miner and kept the farm going by part-time work as a miner. Wanda's five older siblings left for San Diego, Spokane, and other points west. Her parents stayed on the farm until 1926, when Wanda was seven. She remembered rattlesnakes, "the wind howling *every* day.... Army Worms [crop-eating moths] [where] the ground would be just covered . . . and frost, and droughts, and rust on the crops." A tornado struck their place, crippling her father, forcing a move to town and then, in 1930 when Wanda was eleven, to San Diego to try to cure his "arthritis." Yet "I was very happy out there. When I learned to walk, I'd follow the other two kids to school . . . so by the time I was three, I was in the Christmas programs, saying poems . . . getting up there when I was a little kid saying those silly little Christmas poems up there on the stage." "One of the fondest memories of my childhood," she said, was "harvest time when

we went in to the railroad depot and picked up a truckful of 'bums.' Some of
the men came back year after year. They just rode the freights to the various
states wherever seasonal work was available. They slept on the ground and
sang around the guitar player. My mom was very busy cooking huge meals
for the crew of about ten to twenty. I fell in love with one blond very young
man and followed him over all the fields and was broken hearted when he
left. I was five, about." As with many others, however, the city, not the homestead, became home.[41]

Through the 1920s, Montana lost people, while North Dakota started
losing, then picked up, and South Dakota gained several thousand.
Saskatchewan and Alberta, truly the last farming frontiers in North America, each increased by about twenty thousand in the late 1920s, as wheat
prices and rainfall remained sufficiently high to permit a decent return.
After 1930 prices fell and rain did not.[42] In the Canadian prairies drought
and low postwar prices pushed some settlers out between 1919 and 1924, but
immigration resumed from 1925 to 1930. Settlement meant not so much
settling down as swarming for an advantage or just a foothold: "Prairie people were on the move, from farm to city, construction camp to coal mine to
homestead, southern prairie to northern parkland, and most of all, out of
the region entirely. They migrated to the Pacific, to the United States, or
back to Europe." Of more than two million in the Canadian prairies in 1921,
probably only eight hundred thousand of them remained ten years later,
others having taken their places.[43] Farms in western Canada and the United
States often changed hands several times in a few years. The underlying
insecurity, fretfulness, and gamble of homesteading, either Canadian or
American, were pervasive; gone was the headlong exuberance of the century's first dozen years.

Defeat and Retreat: Case Studies

By the early 1920s many recently homesteaded parts of the Great Plains and
Great Basin were seeing retreat and defeat. Mrs. Massey's Montana strag-
glers had plenty of company. It is difficult to date the close of the settlement
frontier precisely because the peak and decline happened over a considerable time, from 1908 or 1909 well into the 1920s, depending on where one
looks. When west Texas was just beginning to prosper, parts of South
Dakota, Montana, and Oregon's high desert had already suffered hardship
and depopulation. Turnover sometimes began "almost as soon as settlement," as a geographer has written.[44]

Two stories of failure happened before 1914: one in Oregon and one in
South Dakota. Each underscores Dayton Duncan's summary of home-

steading in Nebraska: "The whole story of this beautiful country . . . is the American Dream in reverse."[45] Or, to put it another way, when a hundred thousand people tried to settle South Dakota west of the Missouri River between 1900 and 1915 and failed, "Daniel Boone had become Sisyphus."[46] People did not learn from the Kansas and Nebraska experience of the late 1880s and tried to outwit aridity in a new place west of the 100th meridian. Drought struck them in 1910 and 1911. Nearly half of them retreated, defeated.

Sporadically farms emptied in late 1911; one country store and post office that had sixty patrons in January had four the next December. Rural poverty took many forms: searching for cow chips to keep stoves burning; walking over a hundred miles in sub-zero weather to find a job to feed a family; boiling thistles for vegetable soup. Wells and creeks dried up, livestock died, and drinking water became dangerously scarce. The drought persisted from 1911 to 1915. Irrigation had never been an option, and dry farming never worked without water. Editors and other boosters praised the persisters and condemned the "quitters" and "misfits" who had no business attempting so demanding an enterprise. Among the families who stayed were often sons old enough in 1917 for the army, and after they had seen, if not "Paree," some place better than western South Dakota, these young men did not return. Machinery and consolidations of old homesteads into larger units in the 1920s kept the population barely stable. From an outside perspective, this settlement frontier meant failure for thousands. The stayers, however, "saw heroic struggle," a "new frontier myth that prized endurance, self-reliance, and irony rather than quick success, manifest destiny, and the march of progress."[47]

The Oregon story involved fewer people but is in many ways similar. East of the Cascades the state is high and dry, four thousand feet or more in elevation with a few lakes, some with water, some without. Basque sheepherders made a lonely living in part of it. In another part, Lake County, over 1,000 would-be homesteaders tried to realize their dream of independence beginning in 1905. Nearly 300 filed homestead entries in 1912, the peak year. Through this period and until 1916, rainfall averaged just under ten inches each year—actually a little above normal—and the growing season (days without frosts) lasted about three months (though in 1909 it was only thirty-nine days). Never was this a land of milk and honey. After 1916 it became sheer desert. Rainfall in 1917 was four and a half inches; oft-tilled soil turned alkali; jackrabbits devoured green shoots; frost came in July. Sawmills that opened in Bend (the nearest city, about eighty miles northwest) in 1916 drew men off the farm. So did World War I. Between 1916 and 1920 a fourth to a half of the homesteaders retreated, including some who had fully proved up.

In one district, where 1,200 people lived in 1912, 360 remained in 1920. In another, 842 taxpayers in 1915 dwindled to 169 in 1920. Twenty public schools, opened between 1907 and 1915, shrank to five in 1919. The 1920s and 1930s did not improve matters.

Why did so many people "go too far"? Why, asks this Oregon frontier's historian, Barbara Allen, "did the homesteaders undertake such a futile venture?" She gives several reasons: some wanted land to "provide a living for themselves and their families," even if they had never farmed before; some wanted to prove up and sell at a profit; some thought landownership meant security; a few did it just as "a lark." Like South Dakotans, they put themselves at a level of risk that nature would not sustain, and like them, those who stayed condemned the leavers as fainthearted rather than realistic and praised themselves as courageous and patriotic rather than stubborn. In their own minds, as later interviews showed, they saw themselves as "like-minded, hardworking, nobly motivated individuals, pitting their strength and desire and will against the wilderness to create an ordered society in true American pioneer fashion." Thinking this way, they remained adamant that the frontier experience was good and, because it steeled the character of those who persisted, even glorious.[48]

Many people migrated to the homesteading frontier because they received letters from relatives or friends telling them that despite the hard work, they should come. The phrase "the best poor man's country" occurs again and again in these letters. Migrants were not being gulled by the railroad flacks and state immigration promoters, or at least not entirely. They trusted their friends and relatives on the scene. The letters did not intend to deceive; the homesteaders who wrote them believed things were working out, or soon would; they wanted company, but they also wanted to share the improvement in quality of life they were experiencing. They were very often young, optimistic, eager, putting the best face on things, not yet desiccated in both property and personality by lack of rainfall, not yet tempered by failure. They believed they were acting out the dream of personally owning land and being their own bosses. Little wonder that they wrote home with enthusiasm. Little wonder that those back home believed them.

The South Dakota and Oregon cases were early failures. In other places around the West too the lid closed on the settlement frontier. In 1909 a Mormon-led group planned to build a dam on a creek running into the Humboldt in northeastern Nevada large enough to irrigate twenty-five thousand acres, but their company went into receivership in 1912. A Salt Lake City consortium built a canal the next year to irrigate fourteen thousand acres about forty miles south, but it never brought "a drop of water. . . . As late as 1917 about fifteen families were still huddled on the flat, trying without much success to raise potatoes, alfalfa, and small grains by dry farming methods."[49]

Louie Blevins recalled homesteading near Weiser, Idaho, in 1916. Nearby thirty-nine people had tried it in the preceding two years, but only two families survived until the late 1920s. "It was prevalent more or less over the West at that time to homestead the land," he said, "but there was a time in the late twenties when they were more or less forced out of that. They were encouraged to come and work for wages. . . . That's when the big change was from the country to any kind of job."[50] Reams of history and thousands of homestead stories add up to exactly that.

A Methodist minister named Luia ("Louie") Barnes took his family in September 1912 from Gregory, South Dakota, where his pastoral three hundred dollars a year would not feed his wife and six children, to a 640-acre homestead near Oyen, Alberta, two hundred miles north of the Canadian border. Snow was already falling, and Barnes "could not guess that the snow-covered wilderness he would call home for ten years was covered with stones and almost totally unsuitable for crops or cattle." No buildings graced the place, only a root cellar built by "past inhabitants who had abandoned the land." Miseries multiplied: food shortages, a physician who refused to ride thirty-five miles to treat a child with pneumonia, tornadoes, hail, dust storms, grass fires. The family left for Calgary in 1922 and then for British Columbia.[51]

David Love, a government geologist whose parents settled near Lander, Wyoming, records how his father shipped cattle to the Omaha stockyards and got back a bill for twenty-seven dollars, which was how much the shipping cost exceeded what the cattle sold for. Blizzards killed their sheep, the local bank failed and devoured their savings, and in the winter of 1918–1919 they nearly died of the flu.[52]

In eastern Montana "serial failure is the driving theme in the family narrative of a great many," records the travel writer Jonathan Raban. Near Miles City the well-watered years of 1910–1912 seemed to ratify Hardy Campbell's dry farming methods, and settlers rushed in for another three seasons. Then "the winter of 1916 . . . gave the settlers their first taste of the pitiless, extreme character of the Montana climate." Blizzards, lightning-set prairie fires, tornadoes, capricious hail, grasshoppers, rainfall below twelve inches for four years from 1917 through 1920 convinced thousands to leave. Those "who survived into the 1920s found that their attachment to the land had grown beyond reason, as love does."[53] Railroad propaganda, the Enlarged Homestead Act of 1909, and a little rainfall persuaded people to enter 30,000,000 acres of new homesteads in eastern Montana from 1910 to 1919; drought from 1918 and lower wheat prices in the early 1920s pushed them back from much of that land.[54] The Stock-Raising Homestead Act of 1916 further led inexperienced, undercapitalized, ill-equipped people to try to raise cattle on 640 acres. After "the inevitable drought" began, half or more of these homesteaders left, and ranchers bought the abandoned land for taxes or less. Settlers well enough fixed to survive extended their mortgages and only postponed failure.[55]

In his 1935 Pulitzer prizewinning novel *Honey in the Horn,* H. L. Davis writes of how once-eager settlers in eastern Oregon's high desert finally admitted they had to leave. Their artesian wells ran dry in 1919. "It was pure unfounded faith in the benevolence of nature that had led the settlers to depend on those wells to start with. They could come only from drainage water. . . . There had been an abundance to start with, because it had been storing up underground since the dawn of creation, but now they had drained it all out, and it would require another 5,912 years for it to fill up again." Jobs, not fresh homesteads, were their alternative. "There was likely to be competition for railroad work, for the starve-out that year was general, and people emptied out from dozens of new settlements, hurrying to change their status from landholders to payroll hands. Nobody ever counted up how many dry wells got left for cattle to fall into, how much good grass got plowed up and left as worthless stubble, or how much lumber was abandoned. . . ."[56]

In *Dancing at the Rascal Fair* (1987), the novelist Ivan Doig portrays homesteaders through the eyes of a young Scottish-American sheep rancher: "Was this what that dry land was meant for—plowed rows like columns on a calendar, a house and chicken coop every quarter of a mile? In homesteading terms, it indubitably was. But when can land say, *enough?* Or *no, not here?* . . . Here were people straight from jobs in post offices and ribbon stores, arriving with hope and too little else. . . . Winter waited four or five months away yet. Nonetheless I began saying a daily prayer to it: be gentle with these pilgrims." Winter wasn't, and life got worse. "The summer of 1918 had been dry. This one of 1919 was parched. . . . By the first of August, the wagons of the 'steaders and their belongings were beginning to come out of the south benchlands."[57]

It was people like these, eastbound, who met Mrs. Massey and her touring car on the way to California. By 1922 some 75 percent of the post-1909 Montana homesteaders had retreated. Drought in the worst-hit places lasted six straight seasons, from 1916 through 1921. In Montana and the western Dakotas it was "lost hopes and abandoned effort."[58] On the northern plains, farms were liquidated, tenancy rose, legislators pondered and passed credit relief bills. Farm life even when "successful" was primitive; few farmhouses had bathrooms, furnaces, indoor running water, electric lights, telephones, or appliances before 1930 (although pianos, radios, and periodicals graced many of them).[59]

In southern Canada, between Moose Jaw and Calgary (including the arid Palliser's Triangle), watered land had been taken up by 1908. But the Canadian Pacific kept promoting settlement, and Ottawa then opened up the dry lands to homesteading. Between 1901 and 1916 southwest Saskatchewan swelled tenfold from 17,700 to 178,000 people, and cropland from 124,000 to 4,473,000 acres. Then came drought, and "from 1917 to 1925 the [area] underwent distress equaled only by the worst years of the great depression." Summer fallowing, a key dry farming technique, depleted nitrogen and let soil blow away. Desperate farmers hired rainmakers in 1921; others, "penniless families, often from the United States," sold what they could and "absconded" south, leaving their debts behind.

By 1925 some districts had lost a third of their people. Saskatchewan had over forty-nine hundred abandoned farms; Alberta was in "much worse" shape. A farmer in Saskatchewan despaired that "we are not able to abandon our places, neither are we able to stay," and a Peace River homesteader predicted: "We'll all be buried down here in this dry belt, if we wait for the government to get us out . . . and parts of it are pretty desolate places to be buried in."[60] One settlement, Carlstadt, begun with optimistic boosterism in 1906, peaked in the 1910s, declined from 1921 to 1926, and had become a ghost town by the early 1940s.[61] In Idaho, land values fell by two-thirds from 1919 to 1922, potatoes from $1.51 to 31 cents a bushel, sheep from $12.20 a hundredweight to $5.30. Farms failed; banks failed.[62] A Mormon woman recalled that the "trend . . . of one neighbor buying out their next door neighbor and making a larger spread [began] in the twenties somewhere. . . . Some of 'em got discouraged and wanted to get out and somebody else would buy them out. Nobody else would come in and that's the reason in later years there wasn't enough out there to keep the roads open. We had to move into Driggs here to get our children to school."[63]

A German-born old-timer who had migrated to Kansas, Canada, Montana, and finally Idaho reminisced in 1973 about the 1920s: "Of course, '29, '30, and '31 there, it took a lot of farmers, they went broke. Lost their places. . . . You take the Potlatch Ridge there, when we came here . . . there were all the first settlers. They all disappeared. Every one of 'em sold out for a little or nothin' and they didn't make nothing here . . . it happened the same way in Canada, the same way in Montana, the first ones that got in there, why they all went broke. But excepting I didn't, I got out in time and just by nip and tuck."[64]

In central Nebraska out-migration began in the 1920s and never stopped. The 1990 population was less than half of 1930's.[65] In Montana the temptation was to blame nature and James J. Hill, who "built his Great Northern Railroad across the Montana Highline . . . claiming 320 acres would support a homestead farm; settlers . . . built shacks, they tried to farm, most of them failed and left, having wasted years in dirt-eating poverty."⁶⁶ The daughter of a honyocker sheepman remembered: "From 1910 until 1918 [nature] chose to play Jim Hill's game. . . . But in 1919, nature grew tired of her benevolence. . . . By 1924 many homesteaders were leaving—leaving with despair and bitterness in place of the eager confidence and hope with which they had come." Her epitaph for Montana's settlement frontier can stand for all the others: "So the covered wagons rolled again—eastward."⁶⁷

It is hard to pinpoint just when reality caught up with the homesteading dream and started reversing the population flow, but in most places the retreats began between 1914 and 1921. If it must be reduced to a single year, 1916 is as good as any, because the numbers of the nation's farms and farm people then peaked forever. From the 1920s on new settlements and new births on the American and Canadian plains no longer countered the outflow. The activity that had engaged the spirits and dominated the lives of tens of millions of Americans since colonial times was over. Farming and crop raising have continued, but homesteading as a way of life ended. From then on rural life has not been settlement or frontier life, but simply agriculture, with its own history and dynamics, one sector of the economy among several and, though an important one, not the genius idea energizing American development. Other disasters, notably the Dust Bowl and the Great Depression, were to strike the rural West in the 1930s, but these were exclamation points to a tale already written. When these farms failed, the answer was not to try another homestead farther west, as so many generations had done, but to find a wage-paying job. If the Oregon high desert dried up on you, your next stop was a job on the railroad. Cities kept growing, rural areas stopped, and with that the North American frontier process ceased.

Lack of water, either from the sky or from the ground, was not the only reason for the end of homesteading. Mechanization was another. Beginning with McCormick's reaper in the early nineteenth century, machinery continuously raised a worker's ability to produce wheat or corn, until by the 1920s one man produced as many bushels, in the same time, as three could do in 1840. Mechanization was only one part of a larger system of agricultural economics. The quarter or half section dry land homestead simply could not compete with irrigated agriculture. The homestead was no match for latifundia, and by the 1920s both big and small producers were competing for much the same urban consumers. Despite the nobility of the homestead and family farm ideals, together with the traditional American dislike of anything that looked like a monopoly, the small farm was just not competitive and never would be again.

Center stage in the West was filling with new activity: oil and gas booms, bringing a new sort of gold rush demography; unprecedented immigration of Mexicans; and increasing dominance of cities. Even on the Great Plains, from Texas to Canada, cities provided the nodules of growth, outstripping the farming and ranching counties. Farther west, and above all in giant California, it was hardly any contest. Cities dominated.

The Oil Patches

But first the oil patches. From southern California in 1892 and the Texas Gulf Coast in 1901 until the 1930s, oil and gas transformed communities small and large, flooding them suddenly with residents and capital, much as gold and silver rushes did beginning in 1848. Oil affected people and places much like precious metals mining. A gold rush motivation drove migration. Success or failure usually came quickly, rather than protractedly, as in homesteading. Petroleum geology developed into a science, but never a certain one. Consequently the demographic impact on specific localities often proved momentary, although the whole Southwest, particularly from southern Kansas to western Texas, was permanently and substantially affected by oil people and oil culture.

Edward Doheny's oil strike near downtown Los Angeles in 1892 exploded to twenty-three hundred wells by 1897 and over nine million barrels a year by 1902. Eight years later California oil production reached seventy-eight million barrels, largely for home and industrial fuel, before serious automobile demand even began. Exploration continued frantically, with storybook success. Huge strikes at Huntington Beach in 1920 and at nearby Santa Fe Springs and Signal Hill in 1921 were so great that they depressed the national retail price, which was already falling from the rivers of oil pouring out of Texas and Oklahoma.[68]

The demographic impact in southern California was not as profound as it was farther east. Oil was just one more element among many making up the metropolitan eruption of Los Angeles. But in Oklahoma and Texas oil discoveries—one after another from 1894 through the 1920s—created instant communities where very often nothing but cattle and cotton had stood. Oil drilling required capital and luck. It cost thousands to drill a well, and although a man could raise enough money to syndicate a drilling, he could easily lose it down a hole that produced then-useless natural gas, or salt brine, or nothing at all. Oil towns thus had all the impermanence (and at

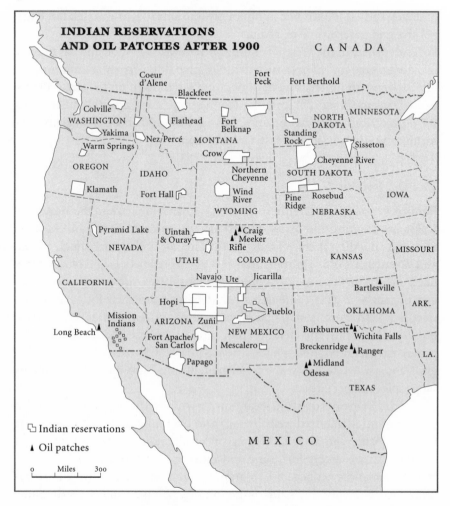

INDIAN RESERVATIONS
AND OIL PATCHES AFTER 1900

Indian reservations
▲ Oil patches

0   Miles   300

first the male-skewedness) of gold and silver mining camps. In a rare case
the oil field proved large enough to last for several years, giving the locale
some of the stability of an industrial mining town. But most of them went
from nothing to thousands to nothing again in a few years.

Texas opened its early oil patches with the Corsicana field near Dallas in
1894, then Spindletop near Beaumont in 1901, and a succession of others. The
era closed in the early 1930s with the development of the enormous east
Texas field, so large that it required huge corporate financing that pushed out
the still-eager wildcatters.[69] All these fields lay east of the ninety-eighth
meridian and were only marginally, though culturally, western. Oil, however,
accounts for the growth of many a west Texas county between 1901 and 1929,
in some places being much more important than cotton, wheat, or cattle.

Along the Red River the first boom in 1911 came at Wichita Falls, and then an amazing one at nearby Burkburnett lasted from 1912 to 1918. These strikes engendered startling but spotty growth, so that some Red River counties registered large population gains while adjacent ones, with no oil but only beaten-down homesteaders, actually lost people. Between Fort Worth and Abilene a substantial field developed from 1918 to 1921, only to wither by 1925; within it, however, one previously inconsequential county seat, Breck-inridge, produced thirty-one million barrels of oil and claimed thirty thousand residents in 1921 alone. The Permian Basin field, in the heart of the old *comanchería* around Odessa, Midland, and Fort Stockton in southwest Texas, stretching into southeastern New Mexico, began its long and happy history in 1923. It produced hundreds of millions of dollars of endowment money for the University of Texas system, to which the state legislature had once dedicated the land (and the then-unknown oil beneath it).[70]

Midland began as a spot on the Goodnight-Loving cattle trail. Its first town lots sold in 1884, and it remained a quiet cattle- and sheep-raising community until 1923, when the first oil well came in, after two years of trying. The county's population jumped from twenty-four hundred to eight thousand during the 1920s, as oil people revamped the place. By 1927 tents for oil crews were dotting a landscape recently scattered with the line camps of cowhands.[71]

Ranger, a minuscule place sixty miles west of Fort Worth, became drenched with oil in 1917. Before then it consisted mostly of two cotton gins and a couple of drugstores.[72] Its eight hundred people had arrived with the railroad in the 1880s, and by 1917 Ranger was a country village surrounded by cotton and cattle. Oil transformed it in the next two years. Lloyd Bruce left in 1917 to go to college in Kansas, but when he returned a year later, he "couldn't hardly recognize it" for the mud, people, "cabarets and everything else." A mule pulling a wagonload of pipe fell in the sea of mud and drowned. Truckers tore out fences to drive through plowed fields because the roads were even more muddy and rutted.

The census of 1920 reported 20,000 people in Ranger. Bruce worked at the post office, where "people lined up for blocks to get their mail—couldn't get any boxes, you know." Land that leased for twenty-five cents an acre before the oil strike leased for thousands of dollars after a successful drilling anywhere near it. Bruce stayed and ran an insurance agency for many years. He believed that if the field had been regulated at all, if the gas had been saved and the oil wells plugged correctly, Ranger might still be producing oil. But the boom ended in the 1920s. Banks and businesses folded; in one place "an old bank vault [sits] out in the mesquite bushes," nothing else around it. "Like any other town," Bruce reflected, "they was good people, and the worst—all together."[73] In the federal censuses, Ranger's population went from 586 in 1910 to 16,205 in 1920 to 6,208 in 1930.[74]

In Oklahoma oil started flowing just before statehood in 1907. The Phillips brothers made their first strike at Bartlesville, in 1905, and were in on many others, forming Phillips Petroleum—later the sellers of Phillips 66, named after the highway—in 1917. Strikes in the Cherokee, Creek, and Osage lands sent "oil men scrambl[ing] to persuade the Indians to sign leases and allow drilling to begin." The Osages, who controlled their own mineral rights by treaty, "found themselves among the richest people in the world," receiving $12,400 per headright by 1923. Tulsa proclaimed itself, justly enough, "oil capital of the world," with eight hundred oil companies and 140,000 people by 1930. Many were transient, or seemed so. Herbert Feis, the future State Department official and historian, visited Tulsa in 1923 and saw "crowds of men" on "the street corners day and night . . . who look as if they had just come to town and had no place to go. Many are in khaki shirts, army breeches and high boots—the ordinary dress of the oil fields and the plains. . . . The oil industry is, after all, one which keeps its people on the move without notice."[75] As many perceived, "the wildcatter had replaced the Forty-niner."[76] Often, after the first rush, workers traveled with wives and children, who "showed up in school any day, at any point in a semester."[77] Companies moved their employees whenever and wherever their skills were needed, all over the oil patch, a bridge, of a sort, to the corporate culture of the late twentieth century.

The Entrada of the Mexicans

The close of homesteading coincided with a population movement far more consequential than the oil patch. From Texas to California—part of Mexico until 1848—Mexicans began arriving after 1910 in numbers that would have been the envy of the Spanish and Mexican colonial authorities who had tried so vainly to populate their northern provinces. This migration was to provide the basis for the Southwest's largest minority by the close of the twentieth century and probably the nation's by the year 2010.

Homesteads did not particularly concern Mexicans coming to the Southwest before 1910. Their American Dream was not westward but *El Norte*, and very few of them had ever heard of Thomas Jefferson and his Empire for Liberty. The United States attracted them for a different reason—wages for work—and it became accessible when railroads connected central Mexico to the Southern Pacific at El Paso, Nogales, and Laredo around the turn of the century. The Mexicans who surged northward in large numbers not only for wages but for a wide range of reasons in the 1910s and 1920s formed a true international migration, similar in many respects to the Asians and Europeans then crossing the Pacific and Atlantic. Their intentions had far more in common with the labor-seeking migrants of 1880 to 1924, who moved west across the Atlantic from southern Italy, Poland, and the Balkans to American mines, factories, and construction sites, and much less in common with the land seekers from Scandinavia, Britain, and Germany, who mostly came earlier. Thus Mexicans were never considered potential inheritors of the land, in either their own minds or those of their often surly hosts.

Mexicans had always moved back and forth across the Rio Grande and the southwestern deserts, before and after 1848. After 1890 the coming of the railroads seriously increased migrant numbers. Well before 1910 the Southern Pacific and the Santa Fe, vigorously recruiting young Mexican men, employed them throughout the Southwest and as far afield as Kansas City and Chicago. From an estimated 78,000 in 1890, Mexicans living in the United States increased to 103,000 in 1900, most of them working in Arizona mines or Texas farms and ranches. Railroad recruitments pulled the number of Mexican-born residents to 220,000 in 1910, and by then about 160,000 children of Mexican or Mexican-Anglo parents brought the total to 457,000, according to the census of 1910. These included only people born in Mexico or those born in the United States whose parents, one or both, were natives of Mexico.

But add the descendants of people of Spanish or Mexican stock, American-born of American-born parents, some with forebears present in the Southwest as far back as 1598 in New Mexico, the early 1700s in south Texas, or 1769 in California, or add the American-born grandchildren of Mexicans who had arrived as recently as the 1870s or 1880s. Then the total community may have numbered 500,000 in 1900 and three times that (around 1,650,000) by 1929.[78] By this definition, "Hispanics" (the somewhat inaccurate census term for all of them) in 1910 numbered 845,000, nearly twice the census count. The great majority, as later, lived in border states: the largest group in Texas (293,000), then the *nuevomexicanos* (166,000), Californians (108,000), and Arizonans (74,000). In those states the sex of Hispanics (53 percent male) nearly matched non-Hispanics (51.5 percent male), unlike the much more male-skewed European immigrants of the time. They were somewhat younger than the non-Hispanic population—more children and young adults, fewer people over forty—and they produced children at rates slightly above African-Americans and well above neighboring Anglos. On average Hispanic literacy levels were lower than Anglo, but not uniformly; among those born in the United States of Mexican parents (the second generation), only about 55 percent in Texas were literate, compared with nearly 90 percent in California. Like African-Americans, a greater proportion of the adults were farm laborers or wageworkers, and fewer were farm owners, artisans, or in middle-class jobs, compared with Anglo-Americans.[79]

Up to 1910 Mexican migration was almost purely labor-seeking. From 1910 to 1921 the massive turmoil of the Mexican Revolution and aftershocks, such as the Cristero revolt of 1926, swelled immigration from perhaps 24,000 between 1900 and 1909 to 427,000 (not counting any illegals) in the 1920s.[80] Texas was home to the majority of Mexicans of all birth categories until 1930, when California began leading among states, and Los Angeles, with 97,116, among cities.[81] Women and children accompanied male workers to railroad and cotton field jobs and to cities, constituting perhaps half the migrants of the 1910s.[82] The migrants were young, with a median age of twenty, compared with twenty-six for the U.S. population in general; they often came as families, so that their sex ratio was close to even, like the rest of the people in border states; and despite their largely rural origins in Mexico, over half by 1930 were settling in American cities, not on farms or in migrant worker camps.[83]

From every standpoint the Mexicans brought change to the four states and territories of the Southwest (Texas, New Mexico, Arizona, and California) and beyond. The main concentration of Spanish speakers shifted from New Mexico to Texas and California. The newcomers quickly overlaid smaller, much longer-rooted communities along the Rio Grande and a few other places. The migrants became strangers in their homeland yet never quite at home in the new. They were also anything but uniform, despite Anglo-American stereotyping that lumped all "Mexicans" together just as it lumped all "Indians" together. The Mexican newcomers came from different places, at different times, for different reasons, and they varied in class, occupation, literacy, and every other characteristic.

As of 1900, probably seven-eighths of the Spanish-speaking population of the Southwest lived in New Mexico, where their ancestors first appeared in 1598. Most of the rest were in southern Colorado, with a few clusters in Arizona and the panhandles of Texas and Oklahoma. In the nineteenth century, despite the American takeover of 1848, these people had expanded vigorously in numbers and area well beyond the original Rio Grande Valley communities. The "Hispano Homeland" in 1900 included most of New Mexico and contiguous parts of Colorado, Texas, Oklahoma, and Arizona.[84]

The Hispanos, or *nuevomexicanos,* embodied a culture that in 1900 was older than Boston or the Tidewater. They were proud of the ancestral colonial conquest and stressed their Spanish heritage (in contrast with Mexican) during the decade-long campaign leading to New Mexico's statehood in 1912.[85] In their core areas, where they had strong majorities in 1900, they controlled law enforcement and land distribution. Control weakened when

Anglos successfully challenged large colonial land grants, and the Hispanos did not easily "set forth along new cultural paths, under a new economy, and under a foreign . . . administration."[86] In the San Luis Valley of southern Colorado, where Hispanos had lived since the 1850s but found themselves outnumbered by Anglos after 1900, their culture became subsidiary. Anglo commercial farming overwhelmed their subsistence agriculture and absorbed young Hispanos as wageworkers picking potatoes, lettuce, and other garden crops.[87]

But old and new "Hispanics" were not alike, even in their own eyes. The long-settled group had adjusted to the Anglos, sometimes despite itself; in 1924 a "leading Spanish-American of Trinidad [Colorado]," J. M. Madrid, stated that the "old Spanish ways," still conserved in New Mexico, were no longer functioning in Colorado. "You would be surprised," he said, "at the assimilation which has taken place in the last ten years. Since 1905 or 1910 there has been a great increase in the use of English . . . it is the language of the country, and . . . must be used."[88] But the new wave had not yet adjusted. J. J. Guerrero, an elected official in Huerfano County (Walsenburg, Colorado), also in 1924, complained: "The Americans think we are no good; they class us with this trash that comes over from Mexico; we are greasers and nothing more. We have suffered much from these Mexicans, for the Americans lump us all together because we speak Spanish."[89] Moreover, the new presence was sizable. Mexicans were not among the top six foreign-born groups in Colorado in 1910 but they ranked fourth in 1920 and first (with 13,144) in 1930, with a birthrate double the Anglos'.[90] Prejudice was strong in New Mexico too; Belle Eckles, a settler who was disgusted by it, remarked that in Roswell, "They don't want to serve them in restaurants and things like that. It makes you sick."[91] In Texas many worried whether Mexican immigration threatened "white Civilization . . . in the Southwest" and regarded "practically all Mexicans as unambiguously nonwhite."[92]

The Hispanos of New Mexico and Colorado were no more ready for the Mexican immigration than were the Anglos of Texas and California. But come it did, in increasing numbers after 1900, from a series of factors on both sides of the border. The railroad network built in Mexico during the 1880s and 1890s allowed people from the densely populated central plain to reach El Paso and other border points. The reduction by the Porfirio Díaz government of the ejidos (the traditional communal landholdings) and their absorption by large haciendas forced great numbers of Mexicans to choose between debt peonage or emigration. When American companies started recruiting them for wages far higher than anything available at home, the preference was clear.

The first migrations took campesinos from the central states to the north, where the Díaz government was promoting development through free trade. From the northern states the move across the border was simple and quick. As in Europe, peasant attachments to the home village loosened first with seasonal migrations and then ranged more widely across the international boundary. An American law of 1885 prohibited contracting workers in foreign countries, but recruitment at the haciendas went on anyway, and employment companies legally greeted migrants as soon as they crossed the bridge in El Paso and signed them up for railroads, mines, or irrigated fields. By 1910 thousands of Mexicans—many young men alone but dependents as well—were working and living in Trinidad and Pueblo in southern Colorado, around Gallup, New Mexico, and in south Texas, mining coal to keep the locomotives running. One company transferred more than two thousand Mexicans from its mines in Sonora fifty miles north through Naco into Arizona in 1908. Very soon border officials were no longer counting the migrants in the hundreds but in the tens of thousands.

What was happening was a nearly pure wage labor migration, very much like that of Poles to the Rhineland in the nineteenth century, or Turks to Germany in the twentieth, or southern Europeans to the United States from the 1880s to World War I. All were heading from low-wage, low-opportunity areas to richer ones. Word of mouth and letters from brothers and friends, as well as paid recruiters, directed the flow to eager employers, and the sojourns might be for a week, a season, or a lifetime. In every major way but one, these Mexican migrants were doing the same thing as young Greeks, Slovaks, Sicilians, and Poles. The difference was that home was not very far, and it was over land, not water, so that the cultural bonds to home could be easily refreshed, and conversely, acculturation into America would be less complete and quick. In this respect migration from Mexico to the United States was more like the migration inside the United States (soon to start) of African-Americans from the rural South to the urban North. All these, however, were migrations not in search of homesteads, or to transplant European peasant villages to the prairies, but to find higher-paying jobs, to earn money to spend or invest back home.

The Mexican Revolution

From 1910 into the 1920s the northward Mexican migration included a distinctly new element, one that was almost singular among the many flows into the United States in that era because it consisted of refugees more than of wage seekers. The revolution that overthrew Porfirio Díaz in November 1910 spawned enormous upheaval and random violence. Mexico did not stabilize until a faction from the northern state of Sonora, led by Álvaro

Obregón, smothered most of the flames in late 1920. Emigration followed closely the undulations of guerrilla warfare and temporary truce. It crescendoed in 1912, then subsided when Francisco Madero established a government; it rose again in 1917, when Venustiano Carranza formed another; and it curved upward a third time until Obregón took over in 1921. This third cycle of migration strengthened from a virtual open-border policy by the U.S. government from 1917 to 1921, in response to growers in California and Texas who pleaded for more farmhands for the "war effort." The population of Mexico should have risen from 15,200,000 to about 16,800,000 had the rates of 1900–1910 continued. Instead, after the civil war, the flu epidemic, and emigration, it fell to 14,300,000.

The revolutionary migration of 1910–1921 certainly contained many land-poor and job-seeking peasants. But it also included "*un grupo muy diferente*" from the peasants, a middle class of landholders, professionals, and managers who were displaced or in danger because they were on the wrong side of local or national politics.[93] The slightest evidence of cooperation with partisans of Francisco Villa or Pascual Orozco or the *federales* of the moment, even at the point of a rifle, could mean death or dismemberment by the next faction fighters to come along. Danger could ride up from many miles away or from partisans down the street.[94]

In Zacatecas, for example, one young campesino couple left the hacienda where they worked and walked to Durango because "the revolutionists would not only raid the haciendas but also raid the peasants themselves."[95] With or without property, everyone was at risk. To leave was prudent. So leave they did—whether wealthy ranchers, village merchants, skilled artisans, clerics, nuns, peasants, accountants, or physicians. Americans consequently received a people with a highly structured and differentiated class structure but mistakenly took them to be just another mass of unlettered proletarian immigrants.[96]

An emigration in which highly factionalized political and cultural-religious divisions overlay all the "normal" economic difficulties produced all sorts of experiences. For María Barrionuevo (born Zacatecas, 1904), school closed and her rancher father lost his herd because of the upheaval. Abigail de Zayas's father, a Porfirista and landowner, escaped to El Paso in 1910 with the help of the Mexican consul there. Fred Ponce (born 1870 near the city of Chihuahua) had a shoemaking business and inherited some land from his father, but as Villa moved in, he "silently phased out," retrieved his buried money, made it to Juárez and then to El Paso in 1916, where he started a macaroni factory and lived past ninety.

María de la O. (born in Chihuahua, 1905) escaped with her family to El Paso in 1916, when "Francisco Villa was going to attack . . . our house at 4 in the morning." Her father "had a very good position and we never had to go without anything. . . . My mother . . . had maids and a lot of help." Adjusting to two rooms in El Paso was difficult; they were "not used to seeing [or being] poor people."

Louise Gates, born in Mexico in 1902 of an American father and Mexican mother, grew up in Coahuila mining towns, where her father worked for the American Smelting & Refining Company. When the revolution began in late 1910, Maderistas burned the railroad trestles, isolating rural places like theirs and cutting off cities from supplies from the country. The local garrison of Díaz soldiers had no support and walked out. The Maderistas "seemed to be a friendly bunch at the time, [but] there was no way of knowing . . . [and] by then the whole country was in an uproar. There were not only Maderistas between Sierra Mojada [their village] and Torreón, there would also be the Orozquistas [partisans of Pascual Orozco]. I believe that the Carranzistas came in later." What to do? "So we just started out . . . you couldn't pack more than a couple of trunks . . . it rained . . . we slept on the floor. . . . We would run into occasionally some armed men . . . they were friendly enough. They were kind of frightening because they were always armed and sometimes drunk. [But] there was not a trace of ill feeling towards Americans as such. They had a particular enmity for what they, the people, called *los científicos* and that just meant the rich to them. Being rich was a crime to them." The family made it to Presidio, Texas, and on to El Paso.[97]

Border formalities hardly existed. According to Gates, since "there were many, many people coming into the United States fleeing from the *revolucionarios,* the United States [had an] open arms policy . . . they simply could walk across the bridge anytime because they were coming here . . . in danger of their lives."[98] The flu epidemic presented yet another danger. "I remember it was terrible" (María de la O.). "As time went by even the doctors wouldn't go to the homes; they would just send medicine. I would see the people loaded on the wagons, like trash, when they were dead."[99]

Violent, migrant-expelling political shifts continued through the 1920s.[100] Whoever the people in power were, they were ineffective land reformers. Smallholders and peasants, particularly from the northwest states and the crowded central plateau around Mexico City and Guadalajara, gained little but further misery. Guanajuato, Michoacán, and Jalisco in the center and Chihuahua, Sonora, and Durango in the northwest provided most of the migrants. Few came from the gulf states just south of Texas.[101] More and more, El Paso and rail points west of it received the new arrivals. The Mexico of 1910–1921 almost forced a choice of emigration or destruction: "Armies and bands of marauders numbering in the hundreds of thousands marched, countermarched, robbed, and killed over the face of the country. In the process, the civilian government was destroyed [several times] and the agriculture and other economic activities were disrupted. The resultant inflation, starvation, unemployment, and lack of personal security forced upwards of 10 percent of the Mexico's population, probably in excess of 1,000,000 people, to flee to the United States . . . [and] perhaps 1,000,000 people, military and civilian, had been killed."[102] Hundreds of Mexicans, many of them middle class, fled Sonora for Arizona (notably Tucson and Nogales) in 1910–1911. The parents of essayist Richard Rodriguez, San Francisco–born, came from a village too small to show up on a map and were certainly not urban middle class. But they were "prominent, conservative, Catholic in the Days of Wrath—years of anti-Catholic persecution in Mexico. My father saw a dead priest twirling from the branch of a tree. My father remembered a priest hiding in the attic of his uncle's house."[103]

In Agua Prieta, Sonora, opposite Douglas, Arizona, in April 1911, the "entire noncombatant population . . . came across the border," running headlong into a southbound wall of some 2,000 American men, women, and children eagerly lined up to see the fighting. Federal [Mexican] forces, hopelessly outnumbered, fled also to Douglas."[104] In 1912 a whole village of 358 people in Coahuila appeared in Del Rio, Texas, with a homicidal army—not Pancho Villa's but one like it—at their heels. In 1912 and 1913, 1,500 Mormons escaped Orozco's troops.[105] Eagle Pass, Texas, received 8,000 people from Piedras Negras, Coahuila, in 1913. Tens of thousands arrived in 1916 in border towns from Brownsville to San Diego.[106] American railroads, sugar beet growers, mine operators, irrigators, and other employers were eager to get them, especially after August 1914, when World War I ended European migration. Eagerness by no means ensured good treatment; shantytowns, company stores, strikebreaking, ID cards, deportation threats, and the other customary antilabor practices of the time, exacerbated by racist contempt, greeted the Mexicans. From Texas to California "the border was transformed from an open frontier to something resembling a war zone" filled with "civil war, ethnic revolts, and exploitation."[107]

Mexicans' Destinations

Those who survived to make new lives in El Paso then had to swim uphill against Anglo prejudice, the "*stereotipe del mexicano como un peón.*" Guillermo Balderas, who arrived in 1917 at age seven, was the only Mexican in his elementary school but proceeded to junior high. There a teacher told him that "as a rule your people are here to dig ditches, to do pick and shovel work. But I don't think any of you should plan to go to high school." Rodolfo Candelaria, born not in Mexico but in the *segundo barrio* in El Paso, went to a Catholic grade school where "they wouldn't even let us speak Spanish. We were there to learn English. . . . Well, among ourselves . . ." the kids spoke Spanish.[108]

By 1920, although Obregón and his successors imposed a shaky peace on Mexico, the habit of migration to the United States was almost ingrained among Mexicans. Life, limb, and land titles remained insecure; faithful Catholics resented government anticlericalism; jobs continued to beckon. Young men could make six times the wages in the United States (though it cost more to live there), and they sent home many a postal money order.[109]

The strongest demand shifted to California.[110] There the Mexican-born population in 1920 ranked second among the state's foreign-born groups, just behind the Italians and ahead of the Japanese. The majority (54,000) lived in Los Angeles County, and nearly all the rest in the other six southern-most counties plus agricultural Fresno.[111] The true number of Mexicans in California in 1920 may have been 121,000. It rose to 368,000 in 1930.[112] Women accompanied young men, if not on the first trip, then on a later one, and (as with European immigrant women) fertility rates were relatively high among those coming from more rural areas; California birthrates rose and fell when migration rose and fell.[113]

Los Angeles took over from El Paso in the 1920s as the leading Mexican-American city, with around 200,000 or perhaps even 250,000.[114] The numbers are less interesting than the fact that contrary to wide belief, only a minority (37 percent) of California's "Mexicans" were farm workers. Almost as many worked in factories, 17 percent worked for the railroads or else-where in transportation, and a good many were small-business people or artisans: metalworkers, carpenters, masons, construction workers, tilemak-ers, and the like.[115] Among the 51 percent who lived in cities by then, many owned land or houses—a third of those in San Antonio, Tucson, and Fresno, and one-fifth of those in Los Angeles.[116] No doubt undocumented migrants were not doing so well, and much rootlessness continued. But clearly a per-manent Mexican-American community, with its own class structure, had taken shape.

By 1929 Mexican-Americans formed a large, distinct, undoubtedly per-manent minority, internally diverse although perceived monolithically by a dominant culture that considered them nonwhite outsiders. They differed from European and Asian migrants in that many of them regarded, with much justification, the Southwest and California their own country, ripped from Mexico in the war of 1846–1848. While Anglos thought of them as "always the peon laborer and never the potential citizen,"[117] Mexican migrants considered themselves wageworkers, family builders, and oppor-tunity seekers, and if seldom "homesteaders" in the American tradition (and not many Anglos were homesteading by then), nevertheless homeowners. California grower-irrigators viewed them very often as replaceable migrant seasonals and, ironically, as instruments making possible *their* American Dream of the "family farm"—their families, their farms.[118]

Throughout these years it was a simple, nonbureaucratic matter to cross the Mexican-American border in either direction. Before 1924 there were no passports and no border patrol. The federal immigration restriction law of 1924 created one, but enforcement was sporadic until after 1929 and the onset of the Great Depression, when it became very tight. Growers could then no longer afford hired hands, local governments balked at paying for services or relief, and the federal government chose to enforce the 1885 law against contract labor together with the 1917 requirement that immigrants pass literacy tests.[119] Despite these obstacles, back-and-forth travel continued through family and personal networks that eased migration, helped job seeking, and preserved Spanish speaking. Particularly for people close to the border, in Baja California, Sonora, or Coahuila, the result was "a social landscape" that strengthened and supported northbound migrants and their families.[120]

Family solidarity, intermarriage among young Mexicans north and south of the border, *compadrazgo* (godparenting, close friendship) all promoted kin networks around the region.[121] Family life remained central and possible because of these connections and the short distances between homes, although young men often migrated alone or with each other, as in any labor migration. But women soon arrived. As early as 1911 the congressionally sponsored Dillingham Commission's *Report* found that wives accompanied 58 percent of Mexican railway and streetcar workers. Vulnerable to childhood diseases and afflictions resulting from poor nutrition and sanitation, like European immigrants and the Anglos themselves, the Mexicans managed to preserve and extend their folkways, language, religion, code of honor to women, and families.[122]

During the 1910s and 1920s Mexicans appeared in many western sites. In Oklahoma after statehood in 1907 they labored in coal mines, cotton fields, and ranches.[123] In Ventura County, California, they worked alongside Japanese and other citrus pickers, living in segregated housing, with their children attending segregated schools, bombarded with pleas to Americanize (i.e., speak English and Protestantize), and in Oxnard in 1903 joined with their Japanese coworkers to strike against miserable conditions despite anti-immigrant hostility from the American Federation of Labor.[124] The leading social work periodical lamented substandard living conditions of Mexicans in Los Angeles and advocated special well-funded but segregated schools as the best way to hasten their "greater Americanism."[125] By 1930 nearly seven thousand "Mexicans" and their children were living in Denver, though more were from the native-born Hispano people of rural Colorado than actual Mexicans. In the blinkered eyes of the dominant culture, they were not distinguishable from the true Mexicans working in sugar beet fields in Colorado and in western Kansas, around Garden City and Lakin.[126]

The Mexican community had become by 1929 the seventh-largest ethnic group in the United States. In Kansas the Mexicans were second only to Germans. Much more urban than the state average (60 percent versus 39 percent), their principal barrio was in Kansas City, with smaller ones in Topeka, Wichita, Emporia, and Garden City. Typically the men—five thousand of them in 1930—worked for the Santa Fe Railroad, which began recruiting them through El Paso around 1905, in machine shops as well as along the tracks. Another thousand worked in the salt mines, coal mines, oil fields, and meat-packing plants of Kansas. From railroad camps in 1905 they created permanent communities, barrios, by the 1920s, seeking education for their children despite segregated and inferior schools.[127]

The late 1920s found middle-class Mexicans living in all the southwestern border towns. Mexican farm workers constituted one-third of the population of California's Imperial Valley, the "Inland Empire" west of Yuma irrigated with Colorado River water. Labor demand held very strong from the 1910s through the 1920s, and Mexicans chiefly met it. African-Americans from Texas occasionally appeared, but more often they headed for midwestern factories; Mexicans outnumbered blacks twelve to one in Imperial County. As always with migrations, easy routes fostered movement. When U.S. 99 crossed the Tehachapi Mountains north of Los Angeles in 1927, as part of the new national highway network, forty thousand Mexicans headed for Bakersfield and the rest of the irrigated Central Valley during the next two seasons.[128]

Los Angeles was the emerging Mexican-American metropolis. The city's image as the mecca for transplanted Anglo midwesterners was fostered assiduously by the Chamber of Commerce and the *Los Angeles Times,* but in truth the barrio was an equally historic story. Mexicans spread from the old plaza area south to Watts, east to Boyle Heights and Belvedere, attracting newcomers from the central plateau of Mexico but also adding a new generation of native-born Mexican-Americans. Wages on the railroads, the streetcar system, and other service and manufacturing jobs remained low, and so did the naturalization rate, reflecting the peculiar cultural strength of the community.[129] Its internal class divisions, from migrant workers to upper middle class, have yet to be described in all their richness.[130] From 1929 on the east side of Los Angeles became the greatest of American barrios.

In late 1929 the stock market crash struck this community with great force. With the onset of the Great Depression, demand for Mexican labor plummeted. Employer-producers had, through political pressure, stayed the hand of immigration enforcement despite the law of 1924. No longer. All Mexican migrants, not just field hands, were cut off from *El Norte*. Instead of easy immigration, not only was the border closed, but tens of thousands already in the United States were "repatriated"—sent back to Mexico, citizens or not—in the early 1930s.

The Pot Thickens: Europeans, Blacks, and Asians

The Mexicans were not the only "new" ethnic immigrant group to enter and become permanent fixtures in the West between 1914 and 1929. Italians, Portuguese, Armenians, and Japanese entered agriculture at every level from wageworkers to owner-operators and in everything from wine making to dairying to fruit growing to running feedlots, and the stoop labor of picking cabbages and figs.[131] By 1915 California's Central Valley was home to Punjabi Sikhs (centered in Yuba City and Marysville), Armenians (Fresno), Germans (Lodi), Filipinos (Stockton), Italians, Dutch, and more.[132] A Basque named Juan Arriaga, born in Viscaya, Spain, in 1902, came to Idaho in 1920 after a twelve-day sail from Bordeaux to New York and four days on the train because "a friend of mine—my closest neighbor—he had a brother here. And he send him money to come over here and that big fella was makin' a hundred dollars a month. So he, he was goin' to come. . . . I decide to come, and my folks they didn't want to come. . . . I ain't goin' to stay very long. Four or five years and I'll go back I told him. I've stayed forever. Lucy [the American he married in 1938] and I, we need to go back. . . . But the folks is gone." He stayed first at Uberuaga's boardinghouse, run by a woman called Grandma whose husband was a section hand on the railroad. At Sunday night dances, where "there would be dancing, all the Bascos, girls—there wasn't too many single girls came from there. Most of them got married pretty quick. But there was some," and some American girls. Sheepherding was "the way you make the most money" though "it wasn't the best job." Arriaga became a dairy farmer. If all Basques had done that, instead of herding sheep, "they'd own the Boise Valley several years" by then.[133]

Italians like James Bacca, born 1901 in Trento, migrated to America because the family hillside could support only the oldest son, and he already had three brothers and a sister in Wyoming. After three years he went home, found a wife, and returned, eventually to become a fireman in Potlatch, Idaho.[134] Mildred Battaglia, born in Italy in 1905, arrived in Portland, Oregon, with her mother, after her father had sent for them; he had first gone to New Orleans, "had a rough time there" with language problems, tried San

Francisco, worked on the railroad, and then "found quite a few friends that he knew from Italy" in Portland. Someone backed him in starting a feed store, which became the family business.[135] As with Mexicans and so many groups, family was crucial, both for psychic and economic support and as the matrix for gradual assimilation. In the Nicolavo family of Price, Utah, Italian opera and folk tunes mixed with cowboy songs, and the family name changed to Nick. Angelo Giordano, a mason in Italy, emigrated to America "because my brother was here" and became a coal miner in Utah and, like Tony Priano from Catanzaro in Calabria, found himself among Greeks, Croats, Japanese, and many others in the mountain mining towns.[136] Achille Reali, mining coal in Mount Harris, Colorado, became Archie Royal and sent a photo of himself in a cowboy costume to his intended, Albina, who was working at her parents' boardinghouse in Price.[137] It helped.

Jews kept coming to the West. Jacob Avshalomov, later conductor of the Portland Junior Symphony, was born in Tsingtao, China, where his father had migrated from Siberia, thence to China, then to San Francisco (where he married Jacob's mother), back to China again, then to Portland.[138] Jessie Bloom, born in Dublin, Ireland, in 1887 of Lithuanian parents, married a cousin who ran a store in Fairbanks, Alaska, and returned there with him in 1912. But she went back to Ireland in 1914 to have her second baby, stayed awhile, and thus "I was in the Sinn Fein Rebellion in 1916." She came back to Seattle ("so much like Dublin . . . the climate is the same . . . and the people were just as friendly in those days"), spent World War II in Dublin again, and finally settled in Seattle.[139]

Edith Feldenheimer, a New Yorker, arrived in Portland in 1925 with her husband, whose family had been wholesale jewelers in San Francisco. She "had never been west of the Hudson and Paul was in New York and we met there at a school dance actually. . . . He proposed the second time we were together. I thought it was ridiculous; I thought that was the way westerners made conversation." When he persisted for two years, she married him. Portland "has a sort of semi–New England background and I felt that having gone to Smith College, I was very much aware of what New England had to offer in the way of culture"; she later served on the boards of the Portland Museum and Reed College.[140] From a very different mold was "Scotty" Cohen's father, a German-born watchmaker, who brought his wife and nine children directly from Glasgow to Portland in 1911—"he had all his relations here"—and in 1919 the twenty-two-year-old Scotty became sportscaster for the Portland Pacific Coast League baseball games and remained so until 1955.[141]

By 1918 Seattle's Jewish community numbered 5,000.[142] Los Angeles counted 20,000 by 1917; the number rose to 70,000 by 1930, then to 130,000 by 1941. In contrast with San Francisco, where Jews had lived since 1850 and remained prominent in the city's power elite, Los Angeles Jewry included many tubercular health seekers as well as, typically, a midwesterner or "an acculturated European immigrant or his grown sons," heading west "in search of ampler opportunities and sunshine." Los Angeles boomed during the 1920s, and Jews contributed to that boom, most visibly in the new motion picture industry. While working-class Jews continued to live in Boyle Heights east of downtown, the new entrepreneurs were creating affluent neighborhoods westward along Wilshire Boulevard and in Hollywood. By 1929 Los Angeles was already a major Jewish city.[143]

It was not yet a major African-American city, nor was there one anywhere in the West. In truly sizable numbers, the Black West did not begin until the migrations of World War II. Yet communities did exist in Seattle, Portland, Denver, San Francisco, and Los Angeles, as well as smaller places. All of them were growing, but not always from natural increase.

Denver's black population rose from about 5,400 in 1910 to 7,000 in 1929, some from births but much more from in-migration. During the 1920s more African-Americans died in Denver than were born, but the community nevertheless kept growing from the addition of about 125 from out of state each year. Their proportion in Denver's population actually shrank slightly from 2.5 to 2.25 percent between 1910 and 1929. Housing was substandard, but 49 percent were homeowners. Men worked most often as railway porters or janitors, women as servants or laundresses.

During the six years from 1923 through 1928, Denver recorded 505 African-American births, but from 1924 through 1928, 734 deaths. The leading causes were tuberculosis (156), heart disease (105), and pneumonia (96). Cancer accounted for only 35 deaths, reflecting a young population. Auto accidents claimed only 2, homicides 15, figures well below those of the white population. Most unions refused to admit blacks; police arrested them at a rate almost four times their proportion of population but very often for "vagrancy," "for investigation," or in connection with "disorderly houses," seldom for crimes against person or property.[144] Denver was nonetheless regarded by African-Americans before 1940 as one of the cities more receptive to them.

Not so San Francisco, which blacks evaluated as "unfriendly." Its 2,414 in 1920 accounted for only one-half of 1 percent of its people. Oakland, the railroad terminus across the bay, had about 5,500, a third of them homeowners.[145] C. L. Dellums, later a leader of the Brotherhood of Sleeping Car Porters and uncle of Congressman Ron Dellums, headed for San Francisco from his home in Corsicana, Texas, in 1923. But a porter directed him to Oakland: "Let me give you some advice, young man. Get off in Oakland.

There are not enough Negroes in San Francisco . . . you will never find a job. The few Negroes around here in the Bay District are in Oakland, so you can make some contacts."[146]

If there was a black mecca in the West at that time, it was Los Angeles. From about 2,100 in 1900, the city's African-American population became 7,600 in 1910, 15,600 in 1920, and close to 40,000 in 1929. The bulk of the increase came from Texas and other southern states, escaping (like blacks moving north at that time) the worst of Jim Crow, following the Southern Pacific, generally seeking better climate and better jobs. By 1910 blacks were living near downtown, just east in Boyle Heights, just west near Pico and Vermont, and around Thirty-fifth and Normandie, with Central Avenue becoming "an eclectic mix of stately homes representing the cream of Black society, rentals and apartments that housed the new southern migrants, and the business and professional offices of the Black middle class." With the influx of the 1920s came increased resistance. Watts, for example, hitherto a separate town, voted for annexation to Los Angeles in 1926 in order to *avoid* becoming fully black.[147] It was, however, already 14 percent African-American by 1920, more than anywhere else in California, "an attractive, increasingly African American suburb whose reputation had reached the East."[148] Despite segregation, discrimination in housing, Klan attacks, and other insults, the black community developed vibrantly in 1920s Los Angeles.[149] Even in L.A., however, migration was nothing like what it would become after 1940. The entire West received only about 40,000 black migrants from other regions during the entire 1920s, and only 50,000 in the 1930s.[150]

Black migrants had their many stories to tell, not only as migrants to Los Angeles but across the West. Charlotta Spears came to Los Angeles in 1910 from Rhode Island, started selling subscriptions to an African-American newspaper, and, after the owner died two years later, bought it with fifty dollars lent her by a neighbor. She renamed it the *California Eagle* and made it the leading black newspaper in the West, fighting the Klan (once in 1925 shooing off Klansmen with her revolver), restrictive real estate covenants, and school segregation, until she sold it in 1951.[151]

Rosa Tigner's farm worker parents left east Texas about 1922 for Pocatello, Idaho, "where my grandfather had . . . settled due to working conditions there on the [Oregon Short Line] railroad. . . . We knew the places that didn't serve us and we just didn't go." Erma Hayman was born in Nampa, near Boise; her father came to Montana from the South for his health and a job in the copper mines, then moved on to Nampa, where her mother, "a real farmer," helped run their dairy farm. Real estate, pool halls, and restaurants all were segregated, "worse than the South for a while."[152] Marie Smith, granddaughter of slaves and later the first woman president of the National Association for the Advancement of Colored People in Portland, arrived at Toppenish, Washington, on the Yakima reservation, in 1910, after her mother and grandmother had died. Her father, already there mining coal, sent for her, and "I came all the way from Paris, Texas, clear across the country. They had Jim Crow cars. The Jim Crow car was the car where the men smoked and spit tobacco all over everything." When she married, it was to "a Pullman porter and he was frozen on the job," for that was the upper limit of mobility.[153]

Otto Rutherford, another future president of the Portland NAACP, was a native; his father and uncle, barbers from Columbia, South Carolina, moved to Portland in 1897. He later recalled that black people "lived all over the city," and although "until 1926 no. . . . Negro or no Oriental could buy property," his family knew a white lawyer who would buy property for them, and consequently "I have never lived in a rented house in my life." When Paul Robeson or Marian Anderson came to Portland, "the Benson [Hotel] would take them, but it was under their conditions, you know, eat in your room, ride the freight elevator." Segregated restaurants did not end until 1951, when "we had our first civil rights law, and bless his heart, Mark Hatfield, although he's a Republican and I'm something else, he sponsored that."[154]

Virginia Clark (Mrs. John Gayton) lived from her infancy in Spokane and then in Seattle. Her father had been born in Vancouver, British Columbia, the grandson of an American slave who made it to Canada via the Underground Railroad in the 1840s. An aunt was a clerk at the Library of Congress; an uncle (with a law degree from Howard University), a Patent Office examiner. Clark herself attended Howard for two years. Her father did "maintenance work," did railroad work, and, finally and more permanently, clerked at the Seattle post office. Everywhere these educated and respectable people bumped against job ceilings and segregated public places. She remembered ice-cream confectioneries in Tacoma, "but we didn't particularly want to go when you didn't know how it would be." In Spokane, where she lived as a child, blacks "didn't want to go to places where they were not wanted and would be insulted, although in several specific instances . . . it probably hindered their mode of living, like perhaps [not] buying property or getting a job that they thought they were qualified for."[155]

The common features of the lives of these people migrating and living in the West before 1929 are evident. Life and opportunity were better than in the Jim Crow South, though only in big cities like Seattle, Portland, or Los Angeles; smaller ones like Coos Bay or Tillamook became well-known Klan towns. Not to exculpate Los Angeles; the Klan was strong there too and briefly took over the Orange County government.[156] Job discrimination was everywhere. Clustering into neighborhoods existed, but segregation was not as rigid as it became after 1941, when much greater numbers arrived. No one could do much about it until the 1940s. In Oklahoma, African-Americans solved the problem earlier by creating towns of their own; Boley, with twenty-five hundred people in 1914, and seven others "conclusively demonstrat[ed] the Negro's capacity for self government and as a town builder," as the *Chicago Broad Ax* said.[157]

Despite the Chinese Exclusion Act of 1882 and its follow-ups, and the Gentlemen's Agreement of 1907 limiting Japanese migration, people from China, Japan, India, Korea, and the Philippines kept arriving during the 1910s and 1920s. Even the stringent restriction acts of 1921 and 1924 did not stop them entirely. Those acts had a much more severe impact on European immigration, which up to then had been practically unlimited. If Asian migration had been open all that time, California and other western destinations would likely have been much less Anglo-American much earlier. San Francisco continued to be the main port of entry for Asians, as New York was for Europeans, and as New York used Ellis Island for processing migrants, San Francisco used Angel Island, a hilly, wooded outcropping in the bay, five miles around, just inside the Golden Gate, a short ferry ride from Tiburon.

Angel Island was, however, only in the most superficial sense "the Ellis Island of the West." That label obscures the differences in how official America treated Europeans and Asians who knocked on the door. Most Europeans trudged through Ellis Island in a few hours. About 175,000 Chinese spent weeks or months at Angel Island between 1910 and 1940, proving they should be admitted; 90 percent eventually were,[158] after struggling to convince the immigration police that they had been born in the United States or were relatives of "merchants" or other groups privileged in the exclusion laws. The interrogation was most severe for Chinese, many of whom were impersonating relatives whose papers had been lost and who were questioned closely about minute details of their families and lives back in China. A small mistake—a year or two in a cousin's age, for example—could cost weeks of detention.[159]

By the 1920s about one in three Chinese-Americans was native-born. Males decreasingly outnumbered females (about five to one in 1920, three to one in 1930).[160] While far from being a demographically normal minority, with a balanced sex ratio, the Chinese were on their way, if glacially, to becoming one. Ben Woo, who became a butcher in San Francisco, arrived there in 1911 on a Japanese ship after thirty-one days. He got through Angel Island in three days, then joined his father and grandfather, who owned a Chinese grocery store in the city. He went to school, then to work as a cook, and married in 1925. Tony Woo, later a meat cutter, came over at age sixteen, spent six months on Angel Island, and was finally released to his brother in Winslow, Arizona. At that point he was sent to school; "they put me in third grade with all the small kids, and then so they don't give me a chance to study, seem to be most of time play around in school yard . . . so then I quit, everybody laugh at me." He learned English, accounting, and window display on his own, moved to San Francisco, and supported himself through the 1920s and the Depression. But he admitted that he did "face a lot of trouble" when he tried to "buy a house for myself."[161]

Not all Chinese lived in Chinatown. They could be found in every farming area in California except the Imperial Valley. The heaviest concentration in the 1910s and 1920s was in asparagus growing in the Sacramento River delta. By 1909 the Southern Pacific had built a rail spur and a packing shed at Walnut Grove, a village about twenty miles downstream from Sacramento, and by 1929 ten asparagus canneries were operating in or near there. In 1914 a Chinese merchant, Chan Tin San, opened a store and saloon a couple of miles away on land leased from the estate of George Locke. When the Walnut Grove Chinatown burned down in 1915, its residents moved to Locke, which was (and still is) an unincorporated Chinese town of several hundred people, some "semimigrant workers," but many living in families, producing Locke-born children over the next two or three decades. In the asparagus-growing years, single Chinese men worked ten hours a day, six days a week, and then descended on Locke, "which served the same function to these farm laborers as Dodge City did to cowpunchers," with whorehouses ("all staffed by white women"), gambling houses, and, more prosaically, markets, dry goods stores, and a post office.[162]

Nineteen-year-old Mabel Quong arrived from Hong Kong in 1923 and married a San Francisco man. They moved to Boise and became the first Chinese there to own their own farm (raising strawberries on twenty-eight acres), the first to send a daughter to college ("Straight A, my children"), the first to own a new truck. Mi Lew came from China in 1920, aged six, with his father, who had been in America before; they lived in Walla Walla's small Chinatown, then Spokane, and finally near Moscow, Idaho. He graduated from Washington State University in 1929, then returned to China for two years, and came back to marry and open a restaurant with his wife in 1932. Restaurants, laundries, and truck farming supported the hundreds of Chinese-Americans living in the Spokane–Moscow–Walla Walla area in the 1920s and 1930s.[163] In Seattle Chinese managed to establish a small Chinatown (later renamed the International District), but the exclusion laws kept them, except for fifteen or twenty families, a bachelor society.[164]

The Chinese-born living in the United States peaked at 107,000 in 1890 and fell to 46,000 in 1930, as the 1882 exclusion law gradually took effect, while Japanese-born reached 82,000 in 1920, then dropped to 71,000 in 1930, thanks to the Gentlemen's Agreement. Koreans, Filipinos, and Indians from India numbered only a few thousand each in these years—small but enough to begin group histories.[165] Indians, chiefly Sikhs, moved down from Vancouver (where they had been grudgingly admitted, for a time, as fellow British subjects) to the lumber mills of Washington and Oregon. They also later came up from Mexico, and some arrived through Angel Island.[166] Lumbering and railroading, their foothold occupations, gave way quickly to farming, first as workers, then as lessees, finally as owners insofar as the alien land laws permitted.

By 1919 Asian Indians were farming eighty-eight thousand acres in the Sacramento and San Joaquin valleys and thirty-two thousand more in the Imperial Valley. They were considered good tenants, "efficient at irrigation and picking," whether peach trees or cotton stalks. Men outnumbered women almost five to one, but the Indians formed families (sometimes with Mexican women) whenever possible. Lending each other funds on personal security, they bought farmland whenever they could until the Supreme Court ruled in 1923 that a Sikh farmer was not a "free white person" and thus could not become a citizen; under California law such a person, an "alien," could not own land either. Legal immigration stopped in 1924, and although at least three thousand Indians may have entered illegally from Mexico by 1940, the group was frozen in time, much like the Chinese and Japanese, until the laws changed after World War II.[167]

About 7,200 Koreans (6,000 adult males and a few hundred women and children) came to Hawaii as contract farm workers between 1903 and 1905, and about 2,000 proceeded to the mainland. The Korean government interdicted emigration in 1905, and no more than another 2,000 arrived until after World War II. Half were picture brides going to Hawaii and California, and the rest were students and farm workers.[168] From 1913 through the 1920s Koreans figured prominently in rice growing in the northern Sacramento Valley. On leased farms of a hundred to several hundred acres, Korean families worked hard and did well, achieving "the only prosperity they knew during their pioneer period of settlement in California," using oral agreements with landowners to circumvent the alien land laws. Others headed south from Angel Island to Fresno, Los Angeles, or Riverside County, working and living, getting along.[169]

Filipinos were in a unique category because their homeland became a dependency of the United States in 1898 as a prize of the Spanish-American War. To exclude them from full rights, the laws had to be drawn and interpreted deftly. The 1924 restriction law actually worked to the Filipinos' advantage. By cutting off other Asian immigration, it left jobs to be filled, and in the next five years about 50,000 Filipinos came to the American mainland, 24,000 to California (95 percent of them young men), supplementing the 6,000 or so already there. Stockton and stoop labor became the targets; nine blocks along El Dorado became Little Manila.[170] By 1929 Filipinos helped harvest potatoes, beets, apples, and hops in the Yakima Valley as well as in California. Fights and work stoppages broke out in several places in 1929–1930 over job competition or simple racial differences between whites and Filipinos or between Filipinos and other Asians or Mexicans.[171]

The first Filipinos, like the early Chinese and Japanese, were almost exclusively male, and by the late 1920s hundreds of young Filipino men in Seattle were living in the International District as a bachelor society.[172] Maria Beltran was one of the rare Filipinas who arrived in the 1920s. She was already a nurse in Baguio City (site of an American army base) and decided to emigrate when a major told her that "if you went to the United States you could improve yourself very much, Mary; you are doing very good, and you could be somebody else." She recalled, "Well, you know, when you are young and somebody talks to you like that, you know . . . he helped me a lot." She married a Filipino in 1931; the couple bought a house, chose to stay in Seattle, and raised their family there.[173]

The 1914–1929 years were preeminently the era of immigration restriction aimed at just about every group except Mexicans and Filipinos (whose turn came in the 1930s). It was also the era of the Ku Klux Klan and of Jim Crow at his most muscular. But just as not everyone joined the Klan, so not everyone detested other groups. Some people simply did not notice; a woman who remembered her childhood in Idaho City in the 1920s recalled many different Europeans, one "colored family," and the Chinese "pretty much gone"; she saw "no race discrimination in those days."[174] Others noticed and rejected the prevalent racism. Edna Dessery gave her master's thesis in psychology at Berkeley (1922) the rather unpromising title "A Study of the Mental Inferiority of the Italian Immigrant," but she concluded that the great majority whom the schools had classified as mental defectives had become "efficient, successful workers . . . leading normal and entirely satisfactory lives" and that the Italians were "not hopelessly inferior but potentially of great promise."[175] Wilma Robertson, who spent her girlhood on an Arizona ranch in the 1920s and 1930s, regarded Mexicans as "my friends. They lived with us—an everyday association," and when she became older, she thought that "if there was any real racist type thing, it was against the American Indian. . . . The Indian was the scum of the earth. You didn't trust an Indian because they were going to steal from you . . . [but] I remember in the sixth grade [about 1933] I had a very close friend that was a Mexican and all of the Anglo kids I remember were angry at me and the thing that you said then was 'you greaser lover' . . . racism was there. I just was not involved in it."[176]

But if not overtly racist, others could be patronizing. Social workers did their well-intentioned best to train Mexican and eastern European immigrant mothers in English and child-rearing practices.[177] The state of California, through an agency that opened in December 1913, tried to help immigrants cope with naturalization, housing, education, sanitation, labor camps, sexual harassment, and many other problems, hearing hundreds of cases in its first year.[178] Progressives split on immigration restriction; so did organized labor; so did organized capital. The end product of all the era's political forces, however, was restriction. The West was richly multicultural, as it had been since at least Gold Rush times. But the differences among groups escaped much of the white middle class, who evenhandedly discriminated against blacks, Asians, Mexicans, and European immigrants alike.

Los Angeles and the Metropolitan West

Of all the demographic developments in the West between 1914 and 1929, the most astonishing was the explosion, for the second time, of Los Angeles and southern California, making the boom of the 1880s look like a hesitant prequel. The new boom showed better than anywhere, a prominent sociologist declared, that "America is not finished, not static, not crystallized, but still evolving, still plastic, still pregnant with nobler form and richer content."[179] The city of Los Angeles was home to 439,000 in 1914; in 1929, three times that.[180] It had done what Chicago had done in the late nineteenth century, and it would keep going, in time and space, spreading through Los Angeles County and the neighboring counties of Ventura, San Bernardino, Riverside, and Orange. Around Los Angeles grew satellites between 1910 and 1930: Pasadena from 30,000 to 76,000; Glendale from 2,700 to 63,000; Long Beach from 18,000 to 142,000; Santa Monica from 8,000 to 37,000; and down the coast, San Diego from 40,000 to 148,000.[181]

By 1913 Los Angeles had almost completely submerged its Spanish and Mexican origins to become a famously Anglo-American city. Its high culture—the universities and soon Cal Tech and the Huntington Library—and institutions, such as the *Los Angeles Times* and the downtown power moguls, were Anglo-Protestant; Hispanics, blacks, Asians, and soon the wealthy but strongly Jewish west side motion picture community did not set the cultural pace. Anglo purity in culture was shored up undoubtedly by the city's many migrants from the Midwest, both the small towns and farms of Iowa and

Illinois and the Chicago area. Demographically Los Angeles was always much more complex than it was culturally, but until late in the twentieth century no other group softened the cultural clout of the Midwest-tinctured Anglos. Pasadena has been called, correctly, an "intensely Anglo-American city" in those days,[182] and from a distance the rest of Los Angeles seemed scarcely less so. Close up there was more to it.

The city grew in part from annexation, but the county's boundaries remained stable, so county figures are a better indicator of what was happening. It was this. Los Angeles County had 170,000 people in 1900, and 504,000 in 1910, an average annual increase of 33,000. In the next four years, to 1914, it accumulated 74,000 people a year, to become 790,000. The rest of the 1910s through 1920 were relatively slow, averaging 24,000 a year, so that in 1920 the total was 936,000. Then came the greatest boom yet. Through the 1920s the county added, on average, 124,000 people every year, the biggest single one being 1923–1924, when the net addition was immense, 283,000. By 1930 its population was 2,208,000. From 1914 to 1930, then, the county added 1,400,000 people, or an average of 90,000 a year, or 1,700 *a week*, for sixteen years. This had to slow; the first five years of the 1930s brought an average annual increase of only 36,000, including an actual net loss of 27,000 in 1932–1933, the only negative year since the American takeover of 1846. So the upward curve of Los Angeles County's population was steady except for the surges of 1910 to 1914 and 1920 to 1924.[183]

These increases were extraordinary, much more rapid than the growth rate of the entire region, indeed of the whole United States. They also account for an inordinate share of it. Between the censuses of 1910 and 1930 the United States added about 31,000,000 people, or 33.5 percent. The West grew faster; the region (as the census counts it, which does not include the Dakotas to Texas portion) added 3,538,000, or 53.8 percent. California aside, the West grew about 40 percent. Los Angeles County, in the same twenty years, increased 338 percent, or ten times the national rate and over six times as fast as the rest of the West. To hammer home the point one other way, the increase of 1,704,000 in the single county of Los Angeles from 1910 to 1930 was very close to the 1,772,000 gain of the entire ten western states other than California itself. Los Angeles's increase boosted California's share of regional growth to almost two-thirds (62.9 percent).[184]

PERCENT INCREASE, 1910–1930

U.S.	Census West	Calif.	L.A. County
33.5	53.8	138.7	338.1

Not that metropolitan growth was negligible in the West outside L.A. Between 1914 and 1930 Los Angeles overtook San Francisco, but the Bay Area—counting only the cities of San Francisco, Oakland, and Berkeley—rose from 684,000 to 1,000,000, a 46 percent increase. Trailing both California cities were Seattle, at 366,000 in 1930 (up 17 percent since 1914), Portland at 302,000 (up 16 percent), Denver at 288,000 (up 17 percent), and Salt Lake City at 140,000 (up 27 percent). Spokane (116,000), Tacoma (107,000), and El Paso (102,000) were the other cities over 100,000 in the census region by 1930.[185] Smaller cities also increased, from the plains through the mountain West to the Pacific. The West, long more urban than the national average, continued to be so in 1930 (58.4 percent for the West, 56.2 percent for the nation—and 73.3 percent for California).[186] From all these numbers, three things stand out: the more urban residence of westerners; the emergence of substantial regional cities amid the wide-open spaces; and the dominance of California, and especially Los Angeles, as the engine of western population development—and, by implication, economic and cultural development too.

Why was Los Angeles forging ahead of the nation and the region? Climate, as always. Water, assured after the Owens Valley aqueduct opened in 1913 and reassured by the Colorado River Compact of 1922. The Panama Canal. The harbor at San Pedro, which by 1924 handled more tonnage than San Francisco or any other West Coast port. Oil. Railroads connecting the city to a rich hinterland. Streetcars and interurban rails beyond the far ends of the county. In the 1920s more roads and more cars. The motion picture industry. The California Dream. Mexican and Asian dreams. Ample food, much grown locally. Boosterism, but beneath it, solidly based optimism. Opportunity, for investors, developers, white-collar and blue-collar people alike. The palpable, unquenchable air of success of the place. Two million individual stories and sets of hopes and expectations.

Other places had some of these elements, but only Los Angeles had all of them and more, along with a unique synergism that can never be fully explained. From Iowa retirees to movie moguls, everyone required real estate, and the flat land from downtown, west along Wilshire to Santa Monica, north through the San Fernando Valley, south toward Long Beach and eastward into the San Gabriel Valley, all began filling up. As a huckster entreated in 1929, "Los Angeles real estate stands like the Rock of Gibraltar for safety, certainty and profit. Don't be satisfied with six per cent on your money. Don't be satisfied with twelve per cent. Buy property like this and keep it, and as sure as the world moves it will pay you one hundred per cent to one thousand per cent."[187] Oddly enough, he was right.

"All the way through there is a record of 'balanced prosperity,' " observed a business editorialist in 1928.[188] Southlanders fought and won more water, as well as electric power, by getting a share of the Boulder Dam project harnessing the lower Colorado. Sierra snowmelt from the Owens River aqueduct assured water for the county's first million; the Colorado was to assure it for millions more. "Los Angeles is in the fight to win. She must have Colorado River water—and from Boulder Canyon dam-site, adequately and dependably to serve water and power to the people, to the industries and commerce of the city at cheapest cost, for all time," argued the physician and civic leader John R. Haynes.[189] She got it.

With it, the city and agriculture continued to flourish. The Southern Pacific kept advertising and selling land, but in small, capital-intensive plots. "Irrigation cuts down the number of acres we once thought necessary to provide an income," and twenty or even less would make a living: "Ask the Japanese, who estimate 8 acres intensively farmed are one man's constant task." Although "no settler should have less than $5,000 capital for equipment, buildings and incidental expenses during the first year," that and diligence would grant success to a neofrontiersman.[190] But it was a California Dream, not a homesteading dream, that invigorated the state, especially its southern part.[191]

Los Angeles's freeways are often credited or blamed for the city's decentralization. But the low density and sprawl came first, preceding cars, and cars preceded the freeways. The Pacific Electric system with its 1,164 miles of interurban tracks across four counties contributed significantly. The whole process was incremental, from the founding of Pasadena several miles northeast, to the annexation of the San Fernando Valley northward and the harbor area 15 miles south, to the inevitable beach communities from Malibu to Palos Verdes to the west. Planners sought to avoid, not emulate, the density of eastern cities and, with the help of first the interurbans and then automobiles, create a new kind of city entirely.[192] In 1915 every eighth resident owned a car, and in 1925, every second one, three times the rate of other Americans.[193]

By 1919 and through the 1920s California was the eighth-ranking state in value added by manufacture. In 1920 it far exceeded any other state in capital invested in irrigation with $195,000,000, which it proceeded to increase to $451,000,000 by 1930, five times more than Colorado, in second place, and it had almost three times as many irrigated farms as Colorado. In 1930 California was first in fruit farms and truck farms; second in stock ranches; first in poultry farms; first in citrus, olive, avocado, date, and grape production; and the clear leader in farms with electric lights and flush toilets.[194] Agriculture

in fact was still "the basic industry of the State," with income that "far out-
strips the combined income of oil and mining" and production costs that
"more than triple that of the motion picture industry."[195]

In Los Angeles "rural vs. urban" was not a real dichotomy, for agriculture
was part of the metropolitan boom. A business writer revealed a local secret
in 1929 that much of Los Angeles County was still farmland, but "because of
the particular type of Agriculture in Southern California, it is possible for
many business men to own lands in specialty crops, and farm them from
their city office."[196] (Or rather, hire Japanese and Mexicans to do it for
them.) Hype aside, masses of midwesterners and others kept coming, buying farm plots and city lots. Palos Verdes Estates, a distinctly upscale development on the southwest coast, recruited buyers on Sunday afternoons with
"free programs of music, Spanish dancing, stunt flying, athletic contests,
aquaplaning and yacht racing," orchestras, flag-raisings, and more.[197] Real
estate itself was a major industry. Word of mouth brought thousands from
"the snow-bound, blizzard-swept prairies" to "the orange-scented valleys of
their new home," as a real estate flack wrote in 1921. But he then came close
to the real explanation for the southland's continued expansion despite the
national recession of 1921–1922:

> The constant stream of people seeking new homes in a mild climate
> would [alone] be sufficient to keep Southern California prosperous.
> They must be housed, [which attracts] thousands of skilled mechan-
> ics; both the new residents and the house builders swell the trade of
> grocery, dry goods and furniture stores, of garages, cafeterias and
> bootleggers, of shoe dealers, chile-con-carne parlors, dairies and elec-
> tric lines. These enterprises, in turn need more employees to wait on
> their customers, more power to light the stores and run the cars, more
> paper to advertise, more lawyers to collect the bills, etc., until for every
> new resident drawing an income from the old farm in Iowa there are
> three or four workers to look after his needs.[198]

Motion pictures, Americans' new toy, and oil, their new necessity, were
not the only elements in Los Angeles's success, but they were key ones and
have remained so ever since the 1910s. From the standpoint of population
change, films brought in a diverse labor force, including artists, capitalists,
and stagehands, and took urban development west of downtown to Hollywood and beyond. The first of Los Angeles's studios opened in 1910, and
Cecil B. De Mille began shooting grandiose, "full-length" productions in
1913, a leap comparable in scope (nothing else, to be sure) from the chamber
symphonies of Haydn's day to Beethoven's *Eroica*. By 1917 filmmaking had

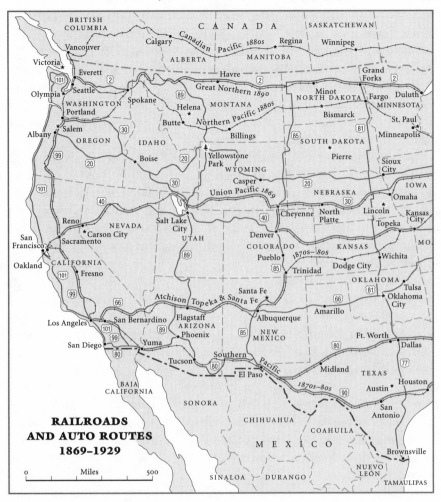

RAILROADS
AND AUTO ROUTES
1869–1929

become the country's fifth-largest industry (perhaps larger), and Los Angeles was its epicenter.

Oil had been part of the L.A. economy since Doheny's first wells of 1892. By the 1920s much of southwest Los Angeles was covered with a forest of oil derricks. California was the leading oil-producing state in the country during the mid-1920s, ahead even of Texas. Large fields opened up at Huntington Beach, Long Beach, Torrance, Dominguez, Inglewood, and Seal Beach between 1920 and 1926. Natural gas blew forth with the oil; "blowouts, gassers, rushers, fires, explosions, craters, geysers" described the Signal Hill field at Long Beach in 1921. The Gold Rush spirit overcame thousands of gawkers who paid ten dollars and up for shares, sometimes as small as 0.000008 percent, in a single well. Like the gold and silver fields of the nineteenth century, the oil fields of 1920s' Los Angeles occasionally dried up quickly but often paid off. Shacks, sheds, and shanties proliferated on the southwest edges of the city, transient as the drillers and drivers who briefly lived there.[199] But oil never moved great numbers of people, either in southern California or in Texas or Oklahoma. Los Angeles benefited as a metropolis, both from the immediate economic effect of selling tens of millions of barrels of crude every year and from the reinforcement of its image as the failure-free city of angelic opportunity.

Beverly Hills became the happy outcome of a failed oil speculation when three investors gave up after drilling thirty dry wells on their land, subdivided it (thus ending any more drilling), and sold it to high-end home seekers.[200] The Pacific Electric Railway Company's Big Red Cars, owned by Henry E. Huntington until he sold it to the Southern Pacific in 1910 so he could collect paintings and books, both spread the metropolis and tied it together. Between the high San Gabriels, abruptly jutting to over five thousand feet on the north edge of the basin, and the sea, no natural barriers impeded the expansion of the city except the ridge of hills separating the San Fernando Valley from Hollywood and the rest of the city, and these could easily be got around or across. Unlike Seattle or San Francisco, water did not confine Los Angeles; this city had everywhere to go. The interurban system by 1914, with its tracks covering Los Angeles County and pressing into Orange, San Bernardino, and Riverside, made the twenty-odd–mile trips from the Santa Monica beach or the port at Long Beach—or dozens of suburbs in between and eastward—in less than an hour from downtown. The horizontal sweep of Los Angeles did not begin with freeways and cars, as so often thought. It started with the overlay of street railways on an unresisting topography.

The street railways in fact were so successful that by the 1920s they (plus automobiles) began to choke the downtown center. Neither streetcar nor auto could turn or pass without threatening the other. From then until the 1980s "downtown" declined in significance, while outlying places like Pasadena, Santa Monica, Hollywood, Beverly Hills, Century City, and others increased, giving rise to the idea of L.A. as a "centerless," or "polycentric," metropolis, which easterners understood poorly, and regarded condescendingly, since it was so unlike Boston, New York, Philadelphia, or even Chicago. The streetcars themselves receded as automobiles took over. Wilshire Boulevard opened in 1924 as *the* high road from downtown to the Santa Monica Pier, lined with palm trees, replete with a shopping center, sequential traffic lights, department stores, and great hotels, all of them pacesetters.[201]

Planners were already thinking of a freeway system for autos. Los Angeles and Pasadena in 1922 bought land for a highway between the two cities along the Arroyo Seco, and the voters approved the plan in 1924. The first section opened in January 1939, and most of the rest in 1940, putting the fabled Los Angeles freeway system in operation.[202] The full reality came only after World War II, but the concept began in the 1920s. Even then Los Angeles was opting to remain, and to become, horizontal. In the 1930s its population density was half that of Denver or Seattle, one-sixth that of New York or Boston—a hoped-for result of earlier thinking.[203]

"Climate, scenery, and boosterism" contributed to the explosion of the car culture in southern California in the 1920s. The state's car registration soared from 77,000 in 1912 to 365,000 in 1918 to 1,900,000 in 1929, and every tenth car owner belonged to the Automobile Club of Southern California. A business writer proposed that "If California ever adopts a new State flower, the motor car is the logical blossom for the honor. . . . Whether commercially or socially . . . it is the same. . . . All Hail the Automobile!"[204] The city was still, much more than most, a city of migrants. It was also, in 1929, the city with nearly the fewest people under twenty and the most over forty-five of the country's ten largest cities.[205]

Migrants from Mexico or Asia did not bring much money with them, but those from New York, Illinois, Indiana, and Iowa did, and they spent considerable of it on homes and cars. They retained midwestern identity and culture. Observers often remarked on the native-born, middle-class, Protestant culture of much of Los Angeles—Hollywood and the barrios excepted, of course—and how different it therefore seemed from San Francisco. Many new residents clustered in state societies, which met from time to time. None was more famous than the Iowa State Picnics, held every winter on the last Saturday in February at Lincoln Park in east Los Angeles and every summer in Long Beach. As many as 150,000 expatriate Hawkeyes and their friends gathered beneath placards bearing the names of counties, emptying "countless baskets, boxes, and hampers" filled with "chicken fried, baked, and stewed, hams boiled and baked; great roasts of beef . . . deep bowls of potato salad," and all the fixings. After coffee and dessert, speeches and more talk. From this more than any other event, observers and promoters assured the reading public that Los Angeles was safely Anglo, a Midwest with climate, prosperity, and palm trees, an image that disguised the city's great ethnic and racial diversity.[206]

From wind-battered homesteads in Oklahoma and Montana to the Iowa picnic, through the barrios and the Little Tokyos, Manilas, and Chinatowns, along the irrigated latifundia of the Central Valley, from farm villages and mining towns to the great magnet of humankind that Los Angeles had become, the West developed between 1914 and 1929 both diversely within itself, yet convergently with the Midwest and Northeast in the national demography and economy. The West shared those other regions' spotty prosperity through the World War I years and the 1920s. It would also share in their Great Depression during the 1930s.

7

DUST BOWL AND DEPRESSION, 1929–1941

> *The wind wasn't so strong, but it come in from the north. . . . A lot of people thought the world was coming to an end. . . . That thing come in, and you can't imagine the birds and hawks flying in front of it. . . . A lot of people here died of dust pneumonia.*
> —Robert Kohler, Boise City, Oklahoma, on "Black Sunday," 1935

A Pause between Two Americas

A dwindling minority of Americans who have any personal memory of the Great Depression of the 1930s are still alive. The majority who are too young can never understand what it was like. But the Depression was without question the main story of those dozen years, from the stock market crash of October 1929 to Pearl Harbor in December 1941, because the economy affected everybody. The other side of that story was the response to it: Franklin D. Roosevelt's New Deal, which confronted the Depression from 1933 to 1938 with a panoply of federal initiatives. Much less noticed were several demographic changes. To begin with, birthrates continued their long-term downtrend, but more sharply down than ever before. The nativist immigration restriction laws of the 1920s took full effect in 1929 and compounded that slowdown; despite the murderous rise of Hitlerism in Europe and the Japanese war in Asia, few newcomers managed to enter the United States. In the case of Mexicans the migration flow reversed, as hundreds of thousands, citizens and noncitizens, were effectively deported. Less numerous, but particularly important for the population and culture of the West, an internal migration—often but oversimply called the Dust Bowl migration—brought to the region the first sizable cohorts of southern whites (and a few blacks).

How did the Depression and the New Deal affect the West? They brought the region more closely into the national misery yet simultaneously kept alive the traditional dream of the West as the region of hope, where starting over remained possible. From a later perspective, the years 1929 to 1941 appear as a hiatus between a pre-1929 America, when the settlement frontier closed, European migration ended, and Mexican and Asian migration tentatively began and when Los Angeles and the West started being truly metropolitan, and a post-1941 America of baby boom, another world war, and the Cold War, with their attendant population shifts.

The Urban West in the Depression

The West still attracted people in the 1930s, bedraggled though they often were, forced migrants instead of voluntary ones. The California Dream persisted, though homesteading had ended and the gold rush idea slept. Even blown-out farmers and out-of-work youths continued to imagine that just maybe the West would deliver a way out of the Depression. The result was almost a pure westward movement for once, with none of the other usual directional components: northward for Mexicans or eastward for Asians.

Most states in the region, and southern California above all, continued to grow well beyond the national average for the 1930s. California added 22 percent, or 1,230,000 people, huge by nearly any standard except for its 66 percent growth in the 1920s and 53 percent in the 1940s.[1] The western census region outside California managed to rise about 12.5 percent during the Depression decade, while the nation eked out only a 7 percent increase—not only the lowest ever but less than half the rate of any previously recorded decade. The cutting off of immigration, together with a historically low birthrate, accounted for the slow growth (death rates, the other component of population change, actually dropped slightly).[2] Because the West provided about 2,000,000 of the total national increase of 7,000,000, the region's share of national population inched up from 10 to 11 percent.

The West's cities did not change in size very differently from those in other regions during the 1930s. Everywhere the historic urbanizing trend—an ever-greater proportion of people living in cities—virtually halted.[3] (It resumed with a vengeance in the 1940s.) Outside the West only New York City kept pace with the nation, adding more than 500,000. Philadelphia, Cleveland, and Boston actually lost residents, while Chicago and Detroit barely held even. Washington, D.C., was the only other exception; all those

New Dealers made it a boomtown. In the West, while no major city lost population, only Denver and Los Angeles gained in double-digit percentages. Los Angeles (the city) added 266,000 to reach 1,504,000 in the 1940 census, and the county reached 2,786,000.[4]

Population shifts reflect what people think are possible or even desirable options, and during the Depression large cities (except New York, Washington, Denver, and Los Angeles) did not draw people. Nor, on the other hand, did rural counties in the West. In Montana, for example, the overhomesteaded Great Plains disgorged thousands. Except for Butte, where the copper-mining community was failing, Montana's small cities basically accounted for the state's 10 percent increase: Bozeman and Missoula, the university towns; Helena, the state capital; and the area around Glacier Park.[5] In Washington State, though the big cities did not gain, neither did the truly rural central and eastern farm counties, which lost people. Increases came in "rurbia," just outside major cities, where a modicum of industrial or seasonal farming jobs existed; in timber-lumber communities and irrigation districts; and around the large dam-building projects on the Columbia, from Grand Coulee (begun in 1933) to Bonneville.[6]

The twelve years of the Great Depression divide into three and a half years of downslide to early 1933, followed by eight and a half of stabilization and moderate improvement. The low point was the winter of 1932–1933, when thousands of banks failed, bringing the nation's financial system to virtual collapse, and unemployment reached an official 24.9 percent, a rise from 3.2 percent in 1929. It remained in double digits until the eve of war in 1941, when it was still 9.9 percent.[7] The West suffered too. Los Angeles and San Francisco business activity fell in September and October 1929, as did Boston's, Chicago's, and that of most eastern cities. The Bank of America business index for the West, in which 100 was "normal," dropped to 59 in December 1932. The California employment index, based on the 1926 level, slid to 59 in the oil industry, 36 in canning, and 35 in sawmills. A bushel of wheat that had brought $1.36 in 1925 sold for 36 cents in 1932. Bank deposits, construction starts, and department store sales all nosedived, and so did payrolls, by as much as 55 percent. In Los Angeles even tourism languished, despite the 1932 Olympics, and only the film industry did at all well (as did the public library, where circulation increased by a million books in 1932; if you could not get a job, you could at least read).[8]

Minorities lost jobs disproportionately. Not only were unemployment rates high, but many people who had struggled to join the middle class by earning professional credentials were forced into lower-level work, dentists transformed into chauffeurs and owners of businesses into messengers, for example. New Deal programs such as the National Youth Administration (NYA) and Works Progress Administration (WPA) employed many African-Americans in San Francisco, and it helped them when Harry Bridges integrated his dockside International Longshoremen's Association. In Seattle blacks lost service jobs all over the city—in hotels, on the docks, at the University of Washington.[9] Some rural southern blacks, just like whites, believed in some version of a California Dream sufficiently to flock to Los Angeles, whose black population climbed from 38,000 in 1929 to about 65,000 in 1941. But it was a desperate dream; if the Depression, as has been well said, "crippled White America . . . it devastated Black America."[10] As a percentage of the southern black population, however, the migration was still small.

All over the West the Depression reduced the hopeful to lives of quiet desperation.[11] To Phoenix came migrant seasonal farm workers, 54 percent from Oklahoma. Out-of-work copper miners from around Arizona also gravitated to Phoenix, where they lived in camps that "were wretched, disease-plagued places," south of the tracks, traditionally the poorest part of the city.[12] In Idaho, farming, mining, and lumbering all were in terrible shape; drought was so severe in 1934 that irrigation was impossible. A few desperate farmers tried to subsist on logged-over land in the far north of the state, and in southern Idaho others were suspected of setting fires in order to generate firefighter jobs.[13] Denver, although its population rose, stagnated economically: "Not a single new office building, not a hotel, nor any other structure of note was undertaken in the business district . . . until after World War II."[14]

Eugene, Oregon, an established New England–like city of 19,000 in 1930, rode out the Depression with less damage than most. Yet its banks, farmers, public agencies, retailers, lumber mills, and the University of Oregon suffered failures, cuts, or losses of income. Unemployment, and relief both private and public, expanded through 1932. But Eugene's Depression was comparatively bearable, and 57 percent of its voters supported Herbert Hoover's reelection, though that was lower than the city's usual Republican margin. Although federal programs (National Recovery Administration, Civilian Conservation Corps, WPA, and others) did much to resuscitate Eugene's economy in 1933, the voters were not bought off and continued to vote for anti–New Deal Republicans in 1934. Hardly through their efforts, banking stabilized, the Public Works Administration (PWA) pumped money into university construction, and tax payments returned almost to normal in 1935. Eugene gave Roosevelt a 60 percent majority in 1936, and its population grew 10 percent between 1930 and 1940.[15] About a hundred miles north Portland similarly survived, muddling through with most of its conservatism unsullied. As a contemporary observed, "To know how Portland,

Oregon, would act under the stress of any given circumstances, it is only necessary to imagine how Calvin Coolidge would act."[16]

Los Angeles hardly escaped the Depression untouched, but in many ways the city's luck held.[17] All the industries that helped it double during the 1920s—autos, aviation, and entertainment—held their own during the 1930s. Agriculture remained important. A Chamber of Commerce writer noted that plots of a half acre to two acres were becoming popular investments, "in no sense a place to make a living" but good for stashing nest eggs and growing some food.[18] The recently annexed port at Long Beach processed goods worth a billion dollars by 1930, and another new oil field appeared in 1936 beneath Long Beach Harbor. By the 1950s so much oil had been pumped out that the ground subsided as much as twenty-four feet in places. Solution: pump water back in, stop the subsidence, and (a "silver lining") deepen the port's channels.[19]

Though thousands of retirees and others lost their homes in the Depression, the city's economy began expanding again late in the 1930s. From Hoover Dam, completed in early 1936, came a 242-mile aqueduct to supplement the Owens Valley supply with Colorado River water. The Automobile Club of Southern California in 1937 brought out a comprehensive freeway plan, which quickly went forward. "The city's congenital optimism has not been destroyed," affirmed the WPA guidebook. "It finds solid ground for its hopes as homeseekers and tourists increasingly turn their eyes once again to the City of Angels."[20]

The Demographic Baseline

Births, deaths, diseases, and health shifted in the West in interesting ways in the 1930s, laying the groundwork for a very different demographic future, as yet wholly unpredicted. Not only were the 1930s a decade when migration touched a historic low, but so did birthrates. With homesteading behind it, and the baby boom ahead of it, American and western society paused in the 1930s between two enormous demographic phases.

The huge surprise after 1940 would be the baby boom. The eminent demographers Warren Thompson and P. K. Whelpton published in 1933 an authoritative study that projected the likely U.S. population in 1980 to be 155,000,000.[21] It turned out to be 226,542,203. Neither they nor anyone, extrapolating from the baby-scarce early 1930s, foresaw the upswing of the 1940s and 1950s. That boom was to serve as the foundation of American development well into the twenty-first century, determining where people would live and work, what shape their families and quality of life would take, and what their old age would be like. Migration and declining fertility had dominated American demographic history from the colonial period through the 1920s, but a sharp rise in fertility replaced them from the 1940s to the 1960s. In between, the 1930s were a comparative lull.

With the ebb of homesteading, mining, and lumbering, the age and sex structures that had always typified frontier populations reached nearly "normal" distributions by the 1930s, "normal" meaning similar to those of the Midwest and Northeast and of urban-industrial societies elsewhere. In Washington State, where there were 163 men to every 100 women in 1890, the ratio had gradually evened to 106:100 for the native-born by 1940 and was virtually balanced in Seattle, Spokane, and Bellingham.[22] It remained least balanced around settled farms and traditionally transient lumber camps and sawmills.[23] In California the once-lopsided sex ratios of gold rush days subsided to 108 males per 100 females in 1930, 104:100 in 1940. Across the state the range was wide: on farms around Stockton, where single Filipino and other migrants worked, the ratio was still 169:100, but urban California had fewer than 98 males to 100 females and Los Angeles County only 94.[24] In other western states the closest parities in 1940 appeared in the more urban Texas, Kansas, Nebraska, Oklahoma, Utah, and Colorado—all under 103— and the most skewed in rural Nevada (125), Wyoming, Montana, and Idaho—all at least 111.[25]

Age became more normally distributed as well. Migration always affected the size of age-groups, since teens to thirties people usually migrate more than older ones. Thus migrant-rich California through the 1930s continued to have a higher than normal cohort of twenty- and thirty-somethings, fewer children, and more than the usual proportion of over-sixty-fives than the country at large. But the discrepancies were narrowing.[26] In Kansas children became fewer and older people more numerous, proportionately; in that long-settled farm state, aging had well begun. Similarly, in Montana farmers' ages rose in such a definite pattern that clearly the same people were living and working in place, seldom leaving except when they died, not being replaced by new blood.[27]

Washington's population aged unusually fast in the 1930s. Its European and Japanese immigrants had arrived before 1930, and as they grew older and had no successors, they raised the median age. After 1920 more and more Washingtonians found themselves over forty-five.[28] Young farm men often did not marry; young farm women preferred towns and cities to their mothers' rural lives. By 1940, among Washington farmers in their twenties, men outnumbered women more than three to one, one reason for the low birthrate.[29] Nationally and locally it is easy to assign the fertility drop of the 1930s to the Depression, but in truth that was simply the exacerbator of other things: the long-term fertility decline coincident with rural to urban shifts; the comparative disadvantage of women on farms without electricity, running water, or medical care when towns and cities were getting them; the increase in mobility and awareness brought by cars and all-weather roads; the need to piece together part-time jobs to survive; in short a systemic set of chicken and egg factors reinforcing each other. Bad times made them exigent.

When westerners died, the causes were not radically different from those that killed Americans in other regions. Tuberculosis had subsided by the 1930s from its near-epidemic levels early in the century, and some parts of the West, like Idaho, Utah, and Nebraska, were as TB-free as anywhere. Arizona recorded about three times as many TB deaths in 1940 as the national average, but that reflected its many sanitaria, the last refuge of health seekers in that final preantibiotic time. California and Nevada led in deaths from cirrhosis of the liver, at rates about double the national average, and Nevada was first in suicides; as a region the West was ahead of the nation in traffic deaths but fell far behind the South in homicides. Otherwise westerners died from much the same killers—cancer, heart disease, stroke, diabetes, flu, and pneumonia—as other Americans did.[30]

Birthrates in the West, like everywhere else, fell during the 1930s. The American rate had been declining ever since records had been kept, from an estimated 55 births a year per 1,000 in the early 1800s, to 32 in 1900, to about 20 in 1931. This slippage resulted, most think, from the gradual closure of the frontier and the increasing proportion of Americans living in cities, where fertility has always been lower than on farms. From 1932 through 1940 the national birthrate fell below 20 for the first time ever. Again the Depression simply intensified a long-term downtrend. Avoiding parenthood was a survival device.

In 1933 the national birthrate bottomed out at 16.6, reflecting a child-avoiding behavior not equaled again until the very different mid-1960s.[31] Most of the Great Plains and mountain states held close to the national rate every year—Texas and the Dakotas slightly above, Kansas slightly below. Utah and Idaho kept their rates relatively high—in the low twenties—above region and nation, helped by Depression-proof Mormon fertility. At the low end anywhere in the country were Oregon's 12.5 and California's 12.6 in 1933, and the nation's least fertile city was San Francisco.[32] In other words, Californians and Oregonians were having 3 babies while the rest of Americans were having 4.

New Mexico was a special case, with the highest birthrates of the seventeen western states. Its lowest year was 1936, when its birth rate was 26.3 and the nation's was 16.7. But no population boom resulted, because the state's infant mortality remained over 10 percent, swelled by poor health care among its Hispano and Indian populations.[33] In Arizona, infant mortality in the mining town of Morenci—population about 2,300 in 1930, mostly Mexican—slightly exceeded the state average but about doubled the national average.[34]

Morenci, a Phelps Dodge company town, was unfortunately not untypical in its inadequate public health system. A company doctor supervised it, aided by one part-time nurse and a few Red Cross volunteers. They well realized the need for prenatal and postnatal care, as well as better diet; 40 percent of schoolchildren were underweight. Towels, soap, and showers were novelties. There was as yet no pasteurization of milk. The water supply, piped in from "both the Eagle River and deep wells," was not treated either, but the health officer tested it frequently and saw "practically no chance of contamination of any type in the rugged open country from which the water is secured."[35] In the early 1930s the campaign for cleanliness was just arriving in Morenci, and as elsewhere in the rural West, it would not be complete for another decade. Anglo officials in El Paso in 1936, claiming "that Mexicans could not be taught hygiene," tried to categorize the Mexican population as "nonwhite," in order to make the infant mortality rate and the public health program look better. The Mexican-American community fought this successfully.[36]

The Mexican Repatriations

The early 1930s, however, brought a massive expulsion of people, which was perpetrated by federal and local authorities. The victims were Mexican-Americans. During the Depression migration to, and within, the United States also fell, not only because many could not afford it but also because of fascism-nazism in Europe, war in eastern Asia, and the full implementation of the restrictive laws of the 1920s. The Depression itself discouraged all but the most desperate and determined. Economics also combined with racism and pressure from both employers and job seekers to bring about official deportations of Mexicans and Filipinos. Most Europeans and Asians could not enter; many Mexicans and Filipinos could not stay. Meanwhile the Depression virtually stopped all internal movement except westward out of the southern plains. Migration in the 1930s thus either did not happen as it had for centuries, or it happened for unpleasant reasons. In this way too the decade was a deathly calm before a huge storm of population growth and change beginning with World War II.

For Mexican-Americans the 1930s brought a reversal of the great influx of the preceding thirty years. By 1929 more than 1,500,000 Mexican-Americans were living in the United States, some native-born, some Mexican-born. Between 1929 and 1935 certainly no fewer than 450,000 and possibly as many as 1,000,000—one-third to two-thirds—left for Mexico. "Repatriation" was the official term, but it was a misnomer because many "repatriates" had been born in the United States, and most of them had never been in Mexico. Whatever the number, it was greater than the Indian removals of the nineteenth century and greater than the Japanese-American relocations soon to come in World War II. The Mexican repatriation of 1929–1935 was the largest involuntary mass migration under American auspices up to that time.[37] Perhaps 100,000 had arrived illegally,[38] but many more were here before the post-1924 border controls, or had come after 1924 legally, or were native-born Americans.

The departures resulted from "a systematic campaign against Mexicans by federal, state, and local authorities and private agencies."[39] Behind it were economics and politics. The economics of the repatriation were simple. Jobs and livelihoods began evaporating even before the crash of October 1929 and kept disappearing through 1933. Farm, factory, and service workers left in rising numbers. As neighborhoods emptied, small-business people—groceries and barbershops, cantinas and theaters—lost their customers and closed. Property values plunged in some places, forcing rapid sales at prices that wiped out years of hard work by immigrant families. (In this, as in other respects, the repatriation eerily presaged the problems of the Japanese-American community about a decade later.) Some of the migration to Mexico was "more or less voluntary" because business was bad and jobs were scarce north of the border, but much was "coercive repatriation."[40]

The politics were a little more complicated, a combination of much tighter control of immigration through enforcement of the restrictionist laws of 1924 and 1929 and the ways in which federal, state, and local officials responded to the declining economy and employment rates. Serious repatriation—over seventy-nine thousand people—began in 1929, before the stock market crash, as the Immigration Bureau cracked down for the first time on Mexicans without visas. Lengthening relief rolls from 1930 onward gave the policy more urgency and public support. The repatriation thus was not an inevitable outcome of the onset of the Great Depression. It was instead the result of how the public and many politicians related the Depression and rising unemployment to a minority group. Some Mexican-Americans required unemployment relief from local governments, and received it, though not out of proportion to their numbers. Nativist-inclined politicians and public, however, chose to think that great numbers of Mexicans were getting a free ride from their taxes, that they refused to work, and that those who did were taking jobs away from "real" Americans. Solution: move out the Mexicans, save tax and welfare money, open up jobs.[41]

Congress passed a Deportation Act in March 1929, setting forth grounds for deporting aliens, and another in May that made a returning deportee liable for felony charges.[42] Combined with the 1924 requirements, these laws gave the Hoover administration all the weapons it needed to keep out, and send out, great numbers of Mexicans. Secretary of Labor William N. Doak announced that through the Immigration Bureau he would get rid of "400,000 illegal aliens" and thus solve unemployment and the Depression. County officials in Los Angeles "were more than willing" to help and did much to organize over a dozen deportation trains that carried thousands from Los Angeles to El Paso and other border points.[43] While federal authorities led the way, public and private agencies in California and other border states cooperated with alacrity. The California legislature, in August 1931, passed an alien labor act against the hiring of "aliens" by companies contracting with the state and through it removed many hundreds of Mexicans "from construction sites, highways, schools, government office buildings, and other public works projects."[44] Unions did not mourn either. Charitable organizations and public relief units often preferred to help non-Mexicans first.[45] The church did not help; neither L.A.'s Archbishop John J. Cantwell nor his newspaper, the *Tidings*, spoke out against the deportations.[46]

With the cooperation of local law enforcement, the Immigration Bureau conducted "sweeps" in the San Fernando Valley and the Los Angeles Plaza in February 1931, arresting anyone who looked Mexican and could not produce proper identification papers. In March the first trains filled with repatriates and deportees started leaving L.A. for El Paso and the border. Deportations also took place in Texas. Of 45,000 Mexican workers in Phoenix, 6,400 voluntarily left in 1931, and over 5,000 left San Bernardino.[47] Deportation became a new tool for union busters in New Mexico, California, Arizona, and south Texas through the 1930s.[48] By the end of 1931, the heaviest year, 138,519 people were forced or persuaded to leave the United States for Mexico.[49] Some Americans protested the government's policy: the agricultural department of the Los Angeles Chamber of Commerce and growers who needed the workers, the Bank of America and other banks that watched Mexicans' deposits disappear, and ideological opponents of nativism. The Mexican consul in Los Angeles, Rafael de la Colina, and his colleagues in other cities did what they could to smooth the roughest edges from the process. But they did not try to reverse it, partly for lack of power and partly because the Mexican government had the idea that the repatriates would bring skills and assets that would help its agriculture and industry.

They did not often do so, for lack of jobs, and many repatriates, especially children born in the United States, found adjustment difficult. For many, leaving Mexico during the revolution or the Cristero revolt had been an upheaval—one very fresh in many minds—and so was the return.[50] When sweeps removed wage earners, wives and children had no recourse but public welfare. When a noncitizen family member faced deportation, the choice for spouses and children who were American citizens was wrenching. A rancher just north of El Paso recalled years later the sight of Mexican cars, loaded with furniture and mattresses, headed for the border: "This road up here would be lined clear up past Anthony [in New Mexico, about twenty miles north of the border in El Paso] with vehicles going back to Mexico, waiting to get across the bridges. Most of them, as they got across the bridges, were broke and didn't have anything. There were sharks over there; they gave them a little for what equipment they had; their car, truck, or whatever they'd take. Some of them had been farming up here, and [they had] a little bit of farm tools and what not. Juárez was swamped."[51] Many chose their own moment to leave because they were afraid the authorities would pick a worse one for them. Some returned in the late 1930s or the 1940s, when demand for workers soared again.[52] Some returned to villages they had not seen for years; for others, born and raised in Los Angeles or another American city, these villages they had never seen could be extremely disorienting.

Beginning in 1933, the worst was over. Though the Depression continued through the decade, it did not intensify, and New Deal relief and jobs made survival in the United States more likely. A few repatriates benefited from the Mexican government's development programs, but most of the Mexican-born "went home to familiar villages," with often disagreeable results. Los Angeles County officials kept harassing Mexicans to leave but were able to put together only three more repatriation trains after April 1933.[53] Repatriation figures, never below 70,000 annually during the Hoover years, fell to less than half that in 1933 and steadily declined to 8,037 in 1937.[54]

Some repatriates, who had never intended to stay, left voluntarily, and the Mexican government for its own reasons cooperated in the process. But it was a huge forced removal, much larger than the Indian removals of the 1830s, 1840s, and 1860s. An indeterminate number were U.S. citizens by birth, unable to document the fact because their birth registration was either not required or not done. The 1930s repatriation did not destroy the Mexican-American community; half to two-thirds remained. But it disproportionately removed business and professional people, many of whom left before the sweeps, so that Mexican America became more uniformly blue collar. In Los Angeles it eliminated any Mexican presence from downtown and segregated it into the East Los Angeles barrio for many years.[55] The repatriation was a gross social trauma for Mexican-Americans, as it had been for Indians and was soon to be for Japanese-Americans.

Asians, Europeans, and the Nativist Laws

The immigration laws of 1921 and 1924 succeeded in stopping most Europeans and Asians from coming to the United States and the West in the 1930s. Only one other group besides Mexicans—the Filipinos—had the distinction of becoming official repatriates. After the Philippine Islands became an American dependency, Filipinos had the right to come and go freely to Hawaii and the mainland United States, exempt from the immigration laws that virtually excluded other Asians. Many young men migrated first to Hawaii and then to California and other states as migrant farm workers. By the early 1930s somewhere between 45,000 and 80,000 Filipinos—male by a 14:1 ratio—were living and seeking work in the United States, most of them in the West.[56]

In 1934 Congress passed the Tydings-McDuffie Act, making the Philippines a semiautonomous commonwealth and promising full independence in 1946. The act also deprived Filipinos of the rights of citizenship and set a quota of fifty immigrants a year. A Repatriation Act followed in 1935: the federal government would pay for transportation back to the Philippines for anyone who wished to go; but such a person, like a Mexican who repatriated with public help, could never come back. Filipinos who initially supported the measure balked at the no-return clause. Though the bill passed with backing from church groups as well as nativists, only 7,400 chose to return by 1937, and many of those did so on their own or with private rather than government help.[57] Almost 10,000 had already paid for their own return fares in 1933–1935.[58]

Other Asian immigrants were exceedingly few. Official figures list a few hundred from China and a few dozen from Japan each year during the 1930s, but again, a true net figure might well be negative.[59] Chinese-Americans, whether born in China or the United States, increased in California, where more than half of them lived, by about 2,200 during the 1930s to nearly 40,000. Japanese-Americans, however, 95 percent of whom lived in the West, decreased by about 8,000 in the Pacific states and 3,000 in the mountain states. Their total, Issei and Nisei combined, fell from 131,669 to 120,927,[60] and a good part of the reason was their return to Japan during the 1930s to educate young Nisei in Japanese language and customs. War between China and Japan through much of the decade gravely disturbed conditions in China; the Depression further encouraged Chinese-Americans to stay in the States during the 1930s.[61]

Japan, on the contrary, seemed to be prospering, and enough Nisei were sent there for education in the 1930s that a new word, Kibei, developed to describe them. How many there were, how many remained in Japan, and how many returned to America are all mysteries; one estimate is eleven thousand going, fewer returning.[62] In any event, Issei males had clearly stopped arriving in significant numbers after 1908 and females after 1924. By then stable families were the norm—one that the male-skewed Chinese community had yet to achieve—and the Nisei began to be born, at relatively modest rates. By 1941 many were in their teens or twenties. Economically the community had done well, for example, controlling much of the wholesale and retail produce marketing at the Los Angeles City Market and Wholesale Terminal Market, leasing and otherwise farming over 220,000 acres in California alone.[63] The attack on Pearl Harbor by Japan in December 1941 was to shatter their hard-won demographic and economic successes.

The nativist national origins quota laws of the 1920s aimed primarily at the exclusion of southern and eastern Europeans. Asians and Mexicans were almost innocent bystanders in the anti-immigrant campaign that began in Congress in the 1890s and finally succeeded thirty years later. European migration resumed for about five years after World War I at something approaching prewar levels; but the 1924 law reduced the totals by about half, and the 1929 law (aided by the Depression and then World War II) kept official entries below 100,000, and in most years below 50,000, until 1946.[64] These are figures only for "immigrants" and do not reflect emigrants. Steamships in fact took more people away from the United States from 1931 through 1937 than they brought, a net loss of 288,550 in those seven years.[65] Add the Mexican departures, and the conclusion is that the United States underwent a substantial net out-migration in the 1930s for the only time in its history. For once the economic opportunities were not there.

Some Europeans who did arrive proceeded to the West. Among them were thousands of refugees from Germany and other European countries being threatened or overrun by the Nazis. Some were Jewish, some not, but most were "middle-aged and middle-class" and decidedly urban although their urbanity often was better suited to Vienna or Berlin than Los Angeles.[66] Perhaps ten thousand came to Los Angeles, half of them Jews,[67] the great majority not at all prominent, though a few were. Joseph Wechsberg, the writer, "used to walk from his home in Westwood village [in west Los Angeles] to the local post office, but as he finally realized, only the poor and very eccentric walked in southern California." Thomas Mann, the novelist, became "the towering figure of the German emigration" to Los Angeles, but his brother, Heinrich, who had also been a celebrated novelist in Germany, never adjusted and died a lonely death in 1950, six years after his wife had killed herself.[68] Heinrich Mann, according to Marta Feuchtwanger, wife of the novelist Lion Feuchtwanger, "always said his fame in America reposes on the legs of Marlene Dietrich—because she played in *The Blue Angel*," which was based on one of his novels.[69]

Many of the 1930s' refugees to the West were men and women of great and established talent, among them Alma Mahler, widow of Gustav Mahler and wife of Franz Werfel; the soprano Lotte Lehmann; Bertolt Brecht, the playwright; physicists such as Enrico Fermi, Leo Szilard, and Emilio Segre, who were soon working on the atomic project at Los Alamos; psychologists and social scientists such as Herbert Marcuse and Ernst Simmel; the conductor Otto Klemperer; and the composers Arnold Schoenberg and Igor Stravinsky.[70] This merely begins a long list of the refugee intellectuals who, however reluctantly, brought a tincture of *Mitteleuropa* to southern California.

The list could have been much longer but for the refusal of Congress and the State Department to relax the quota system and admit more refugees from the Nazi monstrosity. Repeated attempts failed. In 1940 the State Department purposely put "every obstacle in the way" to "postpone and postpone the granting of visas."[71] Amazingly and tragically, it filled just 47 percent of the German and Austrian visa quotas in 1941.[72] Led by Breckinridge Long, the assistant secretary for special problems, the State Department adamantly refused to budge, and even the War Refugee Board of the early 1940s, whose job was rescuing Jews, had meager success. The Roosevelt administration has enjoyed (and was careful to promote) a reputation for humanitarianism. But, as Henry Feingold writes, "The rescue story is replete with examples of indifference, sabotage of rescue initiatives, and seeming compliance with the goals of the [Nazis'] Final Solution."[73] Marta Feuchtwanger remembered "people standing in line for days and around the blocks at the American consulates [in France, where some German Jews had fled], and they didn't let them in. They didn't give them a visa. . . . [T]he consul general . . . told me, 'We don't want those émigrés or refugees; they only spoil our good relations with the Vichy government.' "[74]

One escapee was a young wine merchant from Bingen-am-Rhein, Alfred Fromm. The oldest son of an established Jewish wine making family, he arrived in New York "on December 5, 1933, the day Prohibition was repealed. . . . I was delegated to open the American market." With the Nazis already in power, he met sales resistance against German products. Told that Rabbi Stephen Wise was the "most prominent Jew in New York," Fromm got an appointment. Rabbi Wise told him, "Alfred, I will give you one piece of advice. All the Jews in Germany will leave with a pack on their back. This is just the beginning. Get out as fast as you can. Take out whatever money you can." Fromm's family resisted, but he got them out, selling the family business. After a time in New York, Fromm headed west. He became the worldwide agent for Christian Brothers Winery in the Napa Valley, built a house in San Francisco with a view of the Golden Gate Bridge, and lived out a solid bourgeois life, as his ancestors had done in the Rhineland.[75]

The Jewish community of San Francisco gained new blood from the migrations of the 1930s, which some, like the young rabbi Jacob Weinstein, later of Chicago's KAM Temple, thought it needed.[76] The enrichment of the Los Angeles community was even greater and more visible, as the Jewish population of the city increased from 70,000 in 1930 to 130,000 in 1941, several thousand of them refugees from Germany and Austria. Many came from Chicago; by no means all were prominent people, but the European refugees' well-publicized arrival may have encouraged others. From the older immigrant neighborhood of Boyle Heights, the center of Jewish life in Los Angeles moved westward along Wilshire Boulevard, with its magnificent new temple, where Rabbi Edgar F. Magnin presided, through Hollywood toward Beverly Hills. By the late 1930s the L.A. Jewish community ranked fourth largest in the country, behind New York, Chicago, and Philadelphia.[77]

Out of the Dust Bowl, Off the Farms

Another migration of the 1930s also brought refugees to the West, but they were decidedly not intellectuals and artists. The closing of the settlement frontier had already pushed hard-pressed homesteaders toward the West Coast in the 1920s, and drought and the Depression intensified small farmers' problems in the 1930s. Emigrant flows from the Great Plains to California and other western states actually shrank in the 1930s, compared with the 1920s—in that way too the decade brought a demographic pause—but the sheer misery of many of these unfortunates has been made legendary by John Steinbeck's novel *The Grapes of Wrath*, the film based on it, and Dorothea Lange's photographs for the Farm Security Administration.

In truth the Depression dampened migration, bringing "a precipitate decrease," in a demographer's words, in the nation's internal migration compared with any period since 1900. As was true of Europeans before World War I, the well-off did not migrate (except as tourists), and the utterly destitute never could relocate. It took a little *something*, in the 1930s, to be able to buy gas or a bus ticket. Thus many whose circumstances might have expelled them westward in the 1920s did not have that choice in the 1930s. Those who did, however, almost always headed west. The substantial flows

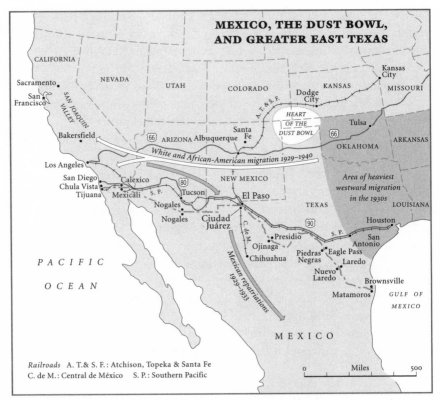

MEXICO, THE DUST BOWL,
AND GREATER EAST TEXAS

CALIFORNIA

Sacramento
San Francisco
NEVADA
UTAH
COLORADO
KANSAS
Kansas City
MISSOURI
Dodge City
HEART OF THE DUST BOWL
Tulsa
Bakersfield
66 ARIZONA Albuquerque
Santa Fe
66
OKLAHOMA
ARKANSAS
White and African-American migration 1929–1940
Los Angeles
San Diego
Chula Vista
Tijuana
Calexico
Mexicali
S. P.
80
Tucson
Nogales
NEW MEXICO
El Paso
TEXAS
Area of heaviest westward migration in the 1930s
LOUISIANA
Nogales
Ciudad Juárez
C. de M.
90
Houston
S. P.
Presidio
Ojinaga
Chihuahua
Piedras Negras
Eagle Pass
Laredo
Nuevo Laredo
San Antonio
Mexican repatriations 1929–1935
Brownsville
Matamoros
GULF OF MEXICO
PACIFIC
OCEAN
MEXICO

Railroads A. T.& S. F.: Atchison, Topeka & Santa Fe
C. de M.: Central de México   S. P.: Southern Pacific

0   Miles   500

of the 1920s from the plains states and the South to midwestern and eastern cities virtually stopped, while the westward migration, though reduced, included several hundred thousand. The Pacific Coast gained nearly four hundred thousand from the upper plains and another three hundred thousand from Texas, Oklahoma, Arkansas, and Louisiana between 1930 and 1940: fewer than before or after, but almost the only significant interregional migration that the depressed country experienced.[78]

The Dust Bowl was only part of it. The horrendous sky-blackening storms of the mid-1930s left the impression, ratified by Steinbeck's novel, John Ford's film of it, Lange's photos, and Woody Guthrie's songs, that the Dust Bowl was the sole locus of rural misery and migration. But the true Dust Bowl included only southwestern Kansas, the Oklahoma Panhandle, and adjacent counties in Texas, New Mexico, and Colorado, while the migrants came also from the prairie provinces of Canada all the way south into Texas and from parts of Louisiana and Arkansas that were not dusty at all except for what blew there from farther west. For that matter, the Lange-Steinbeck-Ford-Guthrie portrait of a victimized rural proletariat presented what those artists wished the migrants to be. It obscured what most of them really were and hoped to become: eventual winners, not losers, in the race for economic well-being.[79]

Migrants from the plains were in many cases honyocker-homesteaders who had managed to survive the 1920s but not the added problem of drought, who had kept trying dry farming until the climate became truly too dry, and who had been living at the rural margin and were getting pushed below it. Those from eastern Oklahoma, Arkansas, or Texas (which enjoyed wetter conditions through the 1930s than the plains did)[80] were often people who had begun appearing in statistics of increasing farm tenancy in those states in the 1920s. Mechanization and soil exhaustion, not dust storms, pushed them out; in fact fewer than 16,000 migrants to California came from the real Dust Bowl.[81] Many of them held tenaciously to the homesteading dream of individual and family achievement.

Only a minority of them became migrant farm workers in California, like Steinbeck's Joad family. Others kept searching for their own land or more or less willingly settled into factory and service jobs and bungalows in Los Angeles. Fewer but more visible, young families arrived in Central Valley farm areas around Fresno, Bakersfield, and Sacramento, often replacing blacks and Mexicans on farms and in cotton mills.[82] Many had not been farmers at all, but blue-collar or sometimes white-collar workers. As tenants they moved a lot: "Today's oil worker was yesterday's farmer and tomorrow's farm laborer . . . residence in Arkansas one year might lead to Oklahoma the next and then back to Arkansas the following. Everything depended on the winds of opportunity."[83] Where better than California for that?

As has always been true of mass migrations, individual stories can be counted in the millions, but through a great many of them runs the thread of economic and social self-improvement. Despite the Dust Bowl iconography and folklore, selfless class consciousness motivated few of the migrants. Like Europeans before them, they were reduced by circumstances such as low rainfall and low prices. But they were not helpless victims. They did something about it; they made lemons into lemonade, or so they hoped and tried to do. They helped themselves, though not without help; they got along and ahead as best they could, making use of such assistance as they could find.

The numbers, though reduced from the 1920s, remain impressive. Of the forty-eight states, only five lost population during the 1930s: the two Dakotas, Nebraska, Kansas, and Oklahoma.[84] Since births well exceeded deaths in all five, the out-migrations had to have been substantial to cause those losses. Oklahoma led the Union with 269,400 emigrants (11.2 percent of its entire population), while the Dakotas, Nebraska, Kansas, and Arkansas each lost over 100,000, and Texas 72,000. In the West the receivers were obvious: not the mountain states, which held about even, but Oregon and Washington, gaining roughly 100,000 migrants each, and California, at least 975,000.[85] Most of the movement was not only westward but also from farms to cities; from 1935 to 1941 American farms lost, net, more than 500,000.[86]

Much more of this migration happened in the second half of the 1930s than in the first. All but 100,000 of California's in-migrants arrived after 1934, the great majority of them not from the Dust Bowl but from north and east of it. The heaviest losses in percentage terms did come from Dust Bowl and other High Plains counties in the Dakotas, Nebraska, Kansas, and Oklahoma, the hardest hit being the Oklahoma Panhandle, down 28 percent. But nearly every part of Texas as well as Oklahoma City, Tulsa, Wichita, and Omaha gained, as did every place farther west except eastern Colorado and eastern Montana. The Los Angeles metropolitan area topped 2,900,000, while San Diego and the San Joaquin Valley led California's ubiquitous growth.[87]

Every state and county had its own story, but North Dakota's reflects them all. There the number of farms kept rising through the late 1920s and early 1930s, but in 1934 almost ten million acres of crops failed, producing almost nothing marketable. From 1935 to 1940 thousands of smaller farms (under five hundred acres) either were absorbed into large ones or simply went out of production. Tenancy rose from 35 to 45 percent. The average value of a North Dakota farm dropped from its peak in 1920 of $19,160 (or $41 per acre), to $12,199 ($25 an acre) in 1930, to $6,628 ($13 an acre) in 1940. Except for a few fortunate counties along the Minnesota border, the decline hit all parts of the state.[88] Thus the drought and Depression of the 1930s did not start any crushing new chapter in northern plains farm life but continued the reversal already evident before World War I from earlier overexuberant settlement.

The Dust Bowl migration, in short, whether from the Dust Bowl proper or from other parts of the Midwest and plains, did not begin in force until the mid to late 1930s. Earlier in the decade states like New Mexico continued to tout tourism and poured money into paving the still-graveled sections of Route 66, which were not finally blacktopped until the summer of 1938. Tourist camps, gas stations, and restaurants continued to seek and win the tourist (and migrant) dollar, and road-building jobs became the chief form of state-level unemployment relief.[89]

A few well-heeled visitors "motored" to the West and wrote books about their trips, in the tradition of Mrs. Massey and Emily Post. Lewis Gannett, a columnist for the *New York Herald Tribune*, drove a Ford V-8 to Los Angeles and back in the summer of 1933. He came to "love those cabins. . . . In the Far West they form impressive 'auto courts,' complete with modern plumbing, and sometimes even with cabin dance-halls. We had liked better the modest cabins of roadside farmers. Sometimes they were dirty; usually they were clean; we always took the precaution of sniffing at the outhouse, most reliable of quick tests, before even dickering about prices."[90] Cross-country driving had improved infinitely since 1915, but dependable plumbing, not to say credit cards, remained decades ahead. Migrants did not enjoy "auto courts" or even cabins very often; they lived differently, seeking jobs and the means of survival or a fresh start. Not many African-Americans were going west yet, but the poet Langston Hughes spoke for some of them in "West Texas":

Down in West Texas where the sun
Shines like the evil one
I had a woman
And her name
Was Joe.

Pickin' cotton in the field
Joe said I wonder how it would feel
For us to pack up
Our things
And go?

So we cranked up our old Ford
And we started down the road
Where we was goin'
We didn't know—
Nor which way.

But West Texas where the sun
Shines like the evil one
Ain't no place
For a colored
Man to stay![91]

Still another memoir begins, like Steinbeck's Tom Joad's migration, in Oklahoma, but its outcome is different and more typical of many actual migrants. Oca Tatham, a twenty-three-year-old odd-job man with a wife and two children, set out in August 1934 from Sallisaw, Oklahoma, near Fort

Smith, Arkansas, well east of the true Dust Bowl, with a dozen relatives and neighbors in a 1929 Chevy truck. A week later they arrived at the Santa Monica beach at the western end of Route 66. The Tathams were not seasonal migrant workers but people who "wanted permanent jobs and homes, and California simply seemed like the best opportunity for getting them." Others like the Tathams, like European immigrants, went home when they could. But the Tathams stayed in California's Central Valley.[92]

They were not class-conscious rural proletarians but intense individualists—economically, religiously, and politically. Their forebears had migrated from England to colonial Virginia, then through the Cumberland Gap to Kentucky, on to Missouri, and in 1902 to Indian Territory, each move accompanied by tens of thousands of others, all part of successive Upland South frontiers. To each they brought a broad Protestant culture, developing over time until by the late twentieth century, the Tathams were Pentecostal, Republican from Lincoln through Reagan except for FDR in 1932, fiercely family-oriented, and ultimately rich from a succession of real estate transactions and other entrepreneurship.

Driving up U.S. 99 past Bakersfield, they felt they were "in the kind of country that was familiar to them now: spindly oil towers hovered over cotton and alfalfa fields, just like Oklahoma." For a couple of seasons survival was just as chancy as in Oklahoma. Then Oca Tatham's talent as a horse trader began to gain economic traction, except that now he traded old cars, junk, and finally real estate. By the outbreak of war in 1941 he was operating several dump trucks as Oca Tatham Trucking, mostly on credit. When the defense buildup created hauling contracts galore, he was on his way to a solid fortune.[93] The war brought prosperity not just to workers at Lockheed and Kaiser.

No single place from which people departed for the West in the 1930s is entirely typical, including Sallisaw, Oklahoma. But amid the variety and nuance are common elements. On the northern wheat-growing plains, farm income in the Dakotas and Saskatchewan fell 60 to 65 percent in 1931–1935 compared with the late 1920s, and in Montana, Manitoba, and Alberta about 50 percent. Overfarming and oversettlement, exacerbated by dry farming methods, drove people off the land as soon as drought set in. Saskatchewan produced a miserable 2.6 bushels of wheat per acre in 1937, the worst ever for the province. But North and South Dakota (averaging 0.2 bushels per acre in 1934) produced even less.[94] More than 250,000 people abandoned their farms, and another 50,000 headed north to the edge of the boreal forest, 240 miles north of Regina, beyond good soil, once again pushing hope beyond realism. Like the Dakotas, Saskatchewan lost population during the decade, while Alberta and Manitoba only just kept pace with out-migration through high birthrates.[95] In 1929 one group of nineteen recently arrived families from Germany tried to homestead some burned-over poplar forest and swampland even farther north, became disgusted, and returned in 1939 to the Third Reich, which they admired. It put them to work making armaments.[96]

Dakota's sad statistics, recounted above, led Lorena Hickok to write to her friend Eleanor Roosevelt that there were "darned few traveling salesmen on the road out there anymore." Although she had lived in South Dakota as a child, she told Harry Hopkins, the federal relief administrator, "a more hopeless place I never saw."[97] West of the Missouri River in South Dakota, despite fading memories of the drought years of 1910–1911, settlers "maintained staunch hopes" through the 1920s. Reeling from drought in the early 1930s, they refused to accept the government's declaration that their area was "submarginal" and that they should relocate. But record heat in the summer of 1936 forced "a flood" of out-migration. Federal programs helped stabilize matters somewhat, but depopulation had begun. It angered and confused many who stayed and never stopped believing that hard work and faith would keep their communities going.[98]

Montana suffered severe droughts in 1931, 1933, 1934, 1936, and 1937. The state lost ten thousand of its farms (18 percent) over the decade.[99] In western Nebraska better-off farmers found in the late 1920s that combines made wheat a much more lucrative crop. They also benefited after 1933 from federal aid, and consequently wheat acreage actually increased. Production controls also lifted livestock prices, so that "plainsmen with good land holdings and good luck could do rather well, comparatively," through the Depression.[100] More marginal farmers, however, could not afford to lose income through production controls or spend money for combines. Thus the net effect was to stabilize or shrink the rural population and confirm, in the minds of those who stayed, their attachment to the land. Women, however, often lost faith in the family farm. One wrote in 1938 to a farm journal lamenting that her daughter, just out of high school, was about to marry a farmer: "When I think of the struggle ahead for her, I actually ache."[101] In the Dust Bowl counties of southwestern Kansas, young people left in droves from 1935 to 1940, 20 percent of them for California.[102]

In Oklahoma many who might have gone west managed to struggle along because of such federal programs as the WPA, NYA, and CCC, all of which built roads, schools, bridges, post offices, and other public works. By 1941 many young men were joining the armed forces, which together with defense factories became the nation's ultimate solution for the Depression. Russell Adams recalled later that the CCC north of Woodward built a park, housing many men in a "pretty good size barracks." He was driving down a road when one of the worst dust storms hit, pushed by a strong wind; we were "so scared we didn't know what to do" and backed off into a ditch; you "couldn't see twenty feet. . . . [It was] like being in the dark, or driving with your lights off." Another man from Woodward believed that the dust on "Black Sunday," April 14, 1935, was thick enough to choke anyone out in it; his family stayed inside and covered the windows with wet blankets. Robert Kohler recalled the Dust Bowl in his seventies, fifty years later: "a lot of fellers tell me we can never have a dust bowl again with the new machinery, but I don't agree with 'em. If it gets as dry and the wind blows like it did in the 'thirties, it'll get away from us. We've got to hold the vegetation on it." Fern Behrendt blamed deep plowing for topsoil blowing away; then "people just got up and left here in droves and went to California. Well, it wasn't over three years 'til the most of 'em come back. But we was too poor to get away." In El Reno even lawyers lived on turnips for weeks.[103]

From Saskatchewan to Texas people were operating under pressures that strongly encouraged moving: low crop prices, low incomes for those not in farming but dependent on farmers, abnormally low rainfalls, twenty to thirty years of ecologically unsuitable farming methods, and, on the other hand, cars, roads, railroads, and a West Coast that couldn't be worse and legendarily promised to be better. Many of course stayed put. Either they could not afford even an old truck like Oca Tatham's, or they had enough capital and luck to survive or do well, absorbing or buying up the homesteads of those who were leaving. In the demographic long term the 1930s marked, for the plains and neighboring states, a continuation of trends visible twenty years earlier: a population that was stabilizing in total numbers, growing older, exporting young people, and not attracting newcomers. By the late 1930s stabilization had turned into depopulation, which has been the story of the sixty years since.

The westward-bound migrants of the 1930s exhibited another perennial characteristic of all migrants, whether Texan-Okie-Arkie, European, Asian, or Mexican. They depended on information from family or friends already in the new place. Over a quarter million from Texas, Oklahoma, and Arkansas crowded into California and other Pacific states in the 1920s, and in typical chain fashion, they telephoned, visited, and wrote back "home" about where the best chances lay: Los Angeles, the oil fields, or the Central Valley. California wages continued to be higher in the 1930s than Texas or Oklahoma pay; even cotton picking paid much better. The news of this, sent home, explains why, though conditions were much the same, so few people east of the Mississippi went to California, while those from Arkansas and Texas very seldom went north or east.[104] The links of the chains were already in place: one led to Illinois, Indiana, and Michigan; the other to California.

A smaller stream from Oklahoma, Texas, and Arkansas—some tens of thousands—tried farming in northern Idaho and western Washington on logged-off timber lands. Attempts at such stump farming were not unknown in the 1910s, but larger numbers, at once hopeful and desperate, many with no farming experience even on good land (and this was extremely poor), resorted to it during the Depression. In the Idaho Panhandle those who tried it either lapsed within five years into migrant labor or managed to clear and crop only an acre or two. After their own growing season ended, hard-up migrant families picked first vegetables near Yakima, next ferns near Centralia, then clams along the ocean, followed by peas and cherries along the Columbia River, then, by late summer, irrigated crops along the Snake River to Twin Falls. In Washington more than twenty thousand new "self-sufficient" farms, the first since the 1850s, sprang up during the 1930s, but "self-sufficing was a census category, not an economic reality; in practice subsistence [meant] poverty." Such enterprises produced a net, and miserable, annual cash income of sixty-nine dollars in Idaho, seventy-five dollars in Washington.[105] The main significance of the stump farming movement was that some people would try anything if it carried the faintest glimmer of landownership. But nearly all failed and retreated; the demographic significance was slight.

Tramps and transients multiplied but, as always, left few records. Leo Smith, born on a ranch near Ketchum, Idaho, traveled by boxcar from Oregon to California in early 1934 and was arrested by officials trying to discredit Upton Sinclair's run for the governorship: "I should of known better. I got in there at the wrong time. . . . I got rounded up just like cattle, put in this jail and they'd taken our pictures. . . . It had big headlines. 'All the bums come to California! Sinclair runs for governor!' " Next stop was a labor camp near El Paso: "you had to deal out your clothes, take a shower, go in there and stay just one month then you're supposed to move on." He made it back to Boise "after traveling widely."[106]

California of course absorbed the great majority of migrants. A state report counted 293,400 in the five years 1930–1934—even after subtracting the Mexican repatriates—and 925,000 in the six years 1935–1940.[107] They merged easily into the latifundia system, filling field and harvest jobs (and living quarters) vacated by repatriated Mexicans and Filipinos. The new WPA guide to California matter-of-factly informed readers: "The old family-size farm, run by the farmer and his family and a few hired hands, is steadily declining in importance and in number. Those that remain are increasingly operated . . . as commercial enterprises. . . . Many are direct adjuncts of fruit and vegetable packing corporations. . . . Two percent of California farms control one-fourth of the acreage, nearly one-third of the crop value, and pay more than one-third of the bill for hired labor. . . . The bulk of the farm work in California today is performed, not by the independent farmer, but by a vast army of some 200,000 wage earners, most of them migrant laborers."[108] Efforts to organize farm workers were sporadic and ineffectual, for a series of reasons. Publicizing their plight did not produce legislative reform, revise growers' labor practices, or precipitate lasting unions.[109] However well Steinbeck's novel and Lange's photographs fixed themselves in the public mind, the Depression experience did not fundamentally change California's longstanding latifundist agriculture. It worked too well for too many people.

The westbound migrants themselves were hardly of a piece in origins, culture, or destination. Many, often with town or city backgrounds, turned left at Barstow and followed Route 66 to the Los Angeles metropolis, whose size absorbed and diluted their identities. A group almost as large turned right, into the San Joaquin Valley, where they southwesternized it to an audible degree, whether they remained marginal or in time became wealthy like the Tathams.[110] Many migrants to the valley parked for a while in camps run by the social reformer–minded Federal Security Administration, but they were not true proletarians or even good convert material. The New Dealers went away, while the migrants' Upland South conservative individualism remained.[111]

Did the New Deal Affect Western Population?

Despite deep cultural differences, the migrants voted—when they voted—for Roosevelt in 1932 and 1936 and for the Democrat Culbert Olson for governor of California in 1938.[112] The New Deal's impact on political culture was transitory. In three other areas, however—Great Plains agriculture and farm population, Indians, and the huge dams, bridges, and other public works it built throughout the mountain and Pacific West—the New Deal reverberated for many decades. These were by no means the first time that Washington changed the West: recall the Homestead Act and later land acts, the transcontinental railroad subsidies, mining subsidies, the Newlands Act, the Panama Canal, and immigration laws. But the New Deal considerably expanded federal activities, notably in transportation, the military, land use, and public works, and it started some important new ones.[113]

Its effect on agriculture, specifically in the Great Plains, was to stanch the outflow. The Agriculture Department under Secretary Henry A. Wallace of Iowa fought to preserve and revitalize the Midwest and Great Plains. As a result, farmers were paid by the Agricultural Adjustment Administration to keep land out of production, which horrified eastern nonfarmers. The Soil Conservation Service, new in 1936, helped farmers build shelterbelts—lines

of bushes and trees athwart the wind—in the hope of lessening wind erosion and dust storms. Home Loan Banks routed mortgage money and
underwriting to rural communities where credit had completely dried up.
The "bank holiday" of March 1933—and subsequent banking legislation,
including deposit insurance—stopped the domino effect of bank failures
that were wiping out savings and restored a battered banking system to
operational levels.

These structural changes lasted into the next decade and in some cases
longer. Shorter-term efforts to relieve want, joblessness, and poverty
included direct relief or, more important, jobs especially for young men: the
Public Works Administration (succeeded soon by the Works Progress
Administration), the armylike Civilian Conservation Corps, the National
Youth Administration (where Lyndon Johnson got his political start), and
the planners' delight, the Resettlement Administration. The Farm Security
Administration resettled over thirteen thousand families mostly on irrigation colonies around the mountain West; a minority of these held on to
their plots for some years.[114] Though these programs helped employ people
only for weeks or months, they were often enough to tide them over until
the economy recovered.

In Idaho, to take one state as an example, a dazzling array of New Deal
agencies preserved thousands of farmers and city dwellers. Outstanding
among them were the CCC ("fences, roads, trails, bridges, campgrounds,"
etc.); the WPA ("twenty-five airports, seventy-eight educational buildings,
numerous parks, and more than one hundred public buildings, sewer systems, waterworks, athletic fields, and fairgrounds"); the Rural Electrification
Administration; the Home Owners Loan Corporation and Federal Housing
Authority; the Reconstruction Finance Corporation; and others. Idaho
came out of the New Deal ranking eighth among the states in per capita federal investment.[115] Nevada, which ranked first, got 50 bridges, 142 miles of
new roads and improvements on another 900 miles from the WPA, as well
as 133 public buildings (hospitals, high schools, courthouses), water and
sewerage works, a municipal golf course for Reno, and much else.[116]

In the long run, perhaps the outstanding New Deal measure affecting the
West was the Taylor Grazing Act of June 1934. It both wrote into law the end
of homesteading and redirected High Plains economic life away from crop
monoculture to stock raising. Overgrazing as well as overhomesteading had
become obvious by the late 1920s. The homesteading problem had taken
care of itself by the defeat and retreat of people who abandoned their fences
and farms on the northern plains. The Taylor Act simply recognized that
fact and, by withdrawing almost all public lands from any further homesteading, reversed 150 years of land law, effectuated John Wesley Powell's

plan of 1878, and prevented any more stubborn dreamers from ruining themselves. The grazing problem required regulation; as Paul Gates observed, "Overgrazing, destruction of the better grasses and survival of poisonous plants, erosion of steep hillsides and silting up of reservoirs, all emphasized the need for control." Plunging livestock prices in the early 1930s pushed private herds farther onto the public lands.[117]

The Taylor Act, through a Grazing Service (whose duties shifted in 1946 to the Bureau of Land Management), authorized the formation of districts that would lease public land (with preference to local stock raisers) for a fee and limit the number of animals to be grazed. Stockmen and other local leaders sat on advisory boards to guide land allocations and grazing fees.[118] Thus the act firmed up the economic ground under the feet of ranchers (though less so for farmers) who still operated. It did not, at least, invite new people to the plains, as the homestead acts had done. Its intent was conservation, which to a degree it achieved; its effect also was to stabilize existing population and relieve pressure to emigrate. As a conservative economist later wrote (while advocating the privatizing of the public domain), "No longer was the range livestock industry viewed as a temporary restriction to inevitable, agricultural settlement of western lands. Further, ranchers were well organized in local, state, and national organizations [and thus] were influential among western politicians, [allowing them] to importantly determine the nature of the grazing privileges granted and the programs adopted under the Taylor Grazing Act."[119] The shift from farming to ranching, and the political clout of ranchers, went on through much of the century. Politically, in 1934, the rancher finally defeated the homesteader. But aridity had already decreed that. Agribusiness, which involves far fewer people than homesteading, continued producing all the food and fiber that an ever more urban public required.

Although the Indian population had been recovering since 1900 or 1910 from its historic low points, the "Indian New Deal" promoted this process. It also attempted, with less success, to revivify the reservations as places to live. John Collier and others had pushed all through the 1920s for radical changes in federal Indian policy. The Indian Reorganization Act of 1934 reversed the assimilationist objective of the Dawes Severalty Act of 1887, as far as federal policy went, and since severalty had failed anyway, it made reservation living a better option. In addition, the Indian Emergency Conservation Work, a kind of Indian CCC run by the Bureau of Indian Affairs, employed eighty-five thousand between 1933 and 1942.[120] Other New Deal agencies also provided relief, employment, and public health assistance. In 1936 another act extended economic coverage to Oklahoma Indians whose reservations had disappeared into severalty. Pueblos, Navajos, Zuñis, and Hopis in New Mexico and Arizona received support for soil and livestock conservation.

To Indians' intense objection, however, federal conservation required that Navajo, Zuñi, and others' sheep and goat herds be thinned because the land was overgrazed. The Navajos suffered "a grave and emotional" crisis; as Ray Yazzie put it, "I think the only thing we have trouble with long time ago was this one white man John Collier," the designer and administrator of the Indian New Deal.[121] Nevertheless federal agents shrank the Navajo, Zuñi, and other Pueblo sheep herds.[122] Public health improvements that cut contagious diseases and infant mortality and straight-out relief and employment measures had a more directly beneficial effect on Indian population than tribal reorganization did. Western Indian groups increased in number by 10 to 25 percent between the late 1920s and World War II.[123] By then American Indian numbers had recovered to about half a million.

Much more permanent than the Indian New Deal were the public works, great and small, that the Interior Department and other agencies constructed around the mountain and Pacific states during the 1930s. Some projects like Boulder (né Hoover) Dam, the California aqueduct system, and the numbered U.S. highways had begun in the 1920s. Others such as Arizona's Salt River Project and New Mexico's Elephant Butte Dam and Reservoir predated World War I and followed in the wake of the 1902 Newlands Act. But the 1930s continued, completed, or began many major works, and in that decade the practice of unemployment relief on public works projects became a habit and virtually a reflex.

Some of their effects on population change were indirect; others were immediate and visible. Fort Peck Dam on the upper Missouri River in Montana, the largest earth dam anywhere, and Grand Coulee on the Columbia in northern Washington, the largest concrete dam, both got under way in 1933 and 1934 and were essentially finished in 1940 and 1941. Neither generated any great population surges to their areas, except for worker communities that disappeared when the job was over. But well downstream from both, the results had real demographic impact: flood control, irrigation, electric power (Grand Coulee), and dependable water (Fort Peck).[124] Hoover Dam (1931–1936) required a substantial, though mostly temporary, federally built community, Boulder City, but it eventually contributed to the growth of Henderson and Las Vegas close by and Los Angeles in the distance, because L.A. came to depend on the Colorado River water that the dam released to it.[125]

In California a state water plan conceived in the 1920s became federalized in 1935, linking it directly through the Bureau of Reclamation to the Newlands Act of 1902. It was renamed the Central Valley Project, and soon included Shasta Dam (built between 1938 and 1944), channeling the Sacramento River in the north, and the Friant Dam on the San Joaquin in the south, built a little later. Throughout the 350 miles of Central Valley between the two dams emerged a network of aqueducts, canals, channelized rivers, and all manner of irrigation works. Donald Worster's "hydraulic society" had leaped from the rudimentary to the resplendent.[126] The demographic and economic development of the Central Valley from south of Bakersfield to north of Redding—with Sacramento, Stockton, Fresno, and many other towns between them, the world's most productive (and most thoroughly engineered) agricultural factory—could not have happened without the New Deal outburst of concrete pouring.

Two of the most famous public works projects of the 1930s, the great bridges over San Francisco Bay, owed very little to the New Deal. They began before it and were financed by local bond issues with only slight and indirect federal contributions. The Oakland-Bay Bridge, two spans of 2,310 feet each, opened in 1936, followed by the Golden Gate Bridge, with its 4,200-foot span, in 1937. The first tied San Francisco to Oakland, Berkeley, and the other East Bay cities, substituting a few minutes by car or bus for the traditional half hour ferry ride. It had a huge impact on population development in the East Bay, especially in the 1940s, when Alameda and Contra Costa counties soared from 613,000 to 1,039,000. The Golden Gate made Marin County much more accessible to the city, replacing a considerably longer ferry ride. Marin managed to remain relatively small and very upscale, but its population also increased.[127] The Golden Gate Bridge has evoked poetry, but to some it meant the triumph of efficiency over beauty. Bertram Dunshee, for many years a planner and engineer for Marin County, thought the bridge "was premature," and it would result in "hordes of people coming into Marin County and changing its character entirely."[128] But hordes never came to Marin; if the bridge brought anyone, it was hippies to Sausalito, professionals to Mill Valley, and retirees to Tiburon. From those places the Golden Gate Bridge cannot be seen. Far more people crossed the Oakland-Bay Bridge to the East Bay, from which the Golden Gate can be seen in the west.

Within five years after the bridge had started carrying people across the Golden Gate, thousands of others steamed under it on their way to the Pacific War. The Bay Area, and the West generally, were about to be transformed by World War II.

8

THE WAR, THE BABY BOOM, AND SLOUCHING TOWARD WATTS, 1941–1965

*If there is any part of the nation where Americans under-
stand that America is really at war, where America-at-
war has become a living, everyday reality to everybody,
that place is the Pacific Coast. . . . Three-fourths of these
boys from all parts of the land . . . say they intend when
the war is over to come back there to live.*

—*Fortune*, "The Westward Empire," July 1942

*My wife usually goes over to collect the rents, and lately
she's been coming back talking about how many pregnant women she sees there. I passed that off . . . for a
while, but the other day I happened to be over in Inglewood and decided to stand around a while and see. And
do you know that over half of the women that passed me
were* pregnant!

—Los Angeles businessman, quoted in *Fortune*,
July 1942

The War Stimulus

The Second World War triggered great changes in the American West, as it did everywhere else. Change was nothing new for the West, but from Pearl Harbor Day, December 7, 1941, the pace was explosive, as the war news, much of it bad, poured in. Victory, whatever it took, was the supreme prior-ity, with the side effects to be sorted out later.

Wartime accelerated what was already happening in the West, rather than divert the region along wholly new lines. For decades before 1941 westerners were more likely than other Americans to live in towns and cities. The sud-den creation of shipyards, plane factories, military bases, and intense demand for housing and services just concentrated them more. Some say that the war transformed the West from a sleepy outpost, an economic colony, to a region in its own right,[1] and certainly much was new and visible: the Liberty ships splashing down the ways every day; the huge Kaiser steel mill at Fontana, just east of Los Angeles, bigger than any mill the West had seen; air force bases newly built or expanded, from Wichita and Salina in Kansas, to San Antonio, to the coast and, of course, in Hawaii and Alaska; Lockheed, Consolidated, Boeing, and the other huge airplane plants; the shipyard cities at Richmond and Vallejo, near San Francisco, and Vanport,

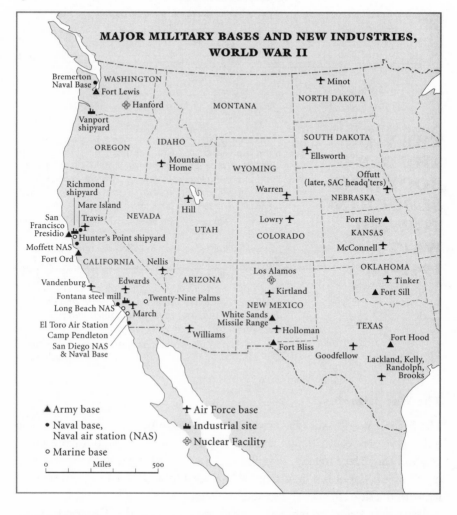

MAJOR MILITARY BASES AND NEW INDUSTRIES,
WORLD WAR II

Bremerton
Naval Base
WASHINGTON
Fort Lewis
Hanford
MONTANA
Minot
NORTH DAKOTA
Vanport
shipyard
OREGON
IDAHO
Mountain
Home
SOUTH DAKOTA
Ellsworth
WYOMING
Offutt
(later, SAC headq'ters)
Warren
NEBRASKA
Richmond
shipyard
Mare Island
San
Francisco
Presidio
Travis
NEVADA
Hunter's Point shipyard
Hill
UTAH
Lowry
COLORADO
Fort Riley
KANSAS
McConnell
Moffett NAS
Fort Ord
CALIFORNIA
Nellis
Los Alamos
OKLAHOMA
Tinker
Fort Sill
Vandenburg
Edwards
ARIZONA
Kirtland
Fontana steel mill
Twenty-Nine Palms
Long Beach NAS
March
NEW MEXICO
White Sands
Missile Range
Holloman
TEXAS
El Toro Air Station
Camp Pendleton
San Diego NAS
& Naval Base
Williams
Fort Bliss
Goodfellow
Fort Hood
Lackland, Kelly,
Randolph,
Brooks

▲ Army base
● Naval base,
Naval air station (NAS)
○ Marine base
✚ Air Force base
⚒ Industrial site
⊕ Nuclear Facility

0   Miles   500

just north of Portland, doomed to be destroyed by flood in 1948. These sig-
nified major change. But the West was ready for it in 1941; the war emergency built on what was already there.

The sheer scale of change, however, overwhelmed many personal landscapes, wrenching people from the Depression doldrums. The existing
African-American communities, small and unobtrusive in Denver and the
coastal cities, finally received their share of the Great Exodus that had come
to Chicago, New York, and other northern cities since 1915 as 279,000 black
migrants arrived from the South to settle in the West during the 1940s. The
Northeast and Midwest attracted even more, but for the first time Los Angeles and other western cities became a serious option for many young black
people. Whites, meanwhile, kept moving west, in the 1940s' largest interre-

gional shift: over 800,000 from the South, over 1,000,000 from the Midwest.[2]

Most, if not all, of these migrations would likely have happened without the war. The West's population increased three times as fast as the rest of the country's, rather than "only" twice as fast, as it had in the 1920s and 1930s, but again, this was acceleration, not novelty.[3] Yet the war made it happen, not least because this time the country faced enemies not only eastward but westward across the Pacific, with nothing but water and their own efforts to shield westerners from the Japanese Navy. Like the prospect of imminent hanging, this focused western minds intensely after December 7, 1941.

The West, especially its cities, gained *civilian* population, quite aside from men and women in uniform.[4] From early 1940 to late 1943 California alone (chiefly Los Angeles, the Bay Area, and San Diego) found itself with almost a million new civilians, despite the loss of Japanese-Americans to relocation camps and young people to the armed forces. By then California had become about 75 percent metropolitan and 80 percent urban.[5]

The rural-urban balance in the West had long since tipped toward cities, and the war stamped a heavy foot on the urban side of that balance. San Diego had been "capturing the Navy" since the Panama Canal opened. By 1941 it was positioned to become the main operating base for the Pacific Fleet and all the business and new population that went with it. Within a year after Pearl Harbor newcomers were living in twenty thousand new houses and apartments, with many more under construction.[6]

Los Angeles had virtually every advantage for plane building, including experience and nearly year-round flying weather; again, climate was destiny. Although one could argue that it was dangerous for the new "Detroit of the Air Age" to be within reach of Japanese carrier-based planes, the location there of the Big Six plane makers (Douglas, Lockheed, Vultee, North American, Vega, and Northrop)[7] and the success of Robert Millikan of the California Institute of Technology in securing aerodynamics contracts overwhelmed objections. By 1945 Los Angeles "had more defense contracts than it knew what to do with."[8] Nor was it just aircraft; L.A.'s shipyards reawakened, its clothing factories and food processing plants could hardly keep up,[9] and its oil wells pumped on and on. More than 550,000 new jobs opened between early 1940 and mid-1943, including 65,000 for women within aircraft plants alone.[10]

Many of them became the famous Rosie the Riveters, and Norma Cantrell was one of them. Seventeen in 1942, one of eleven children in a broken Texas farm family, she had already been a migrant date picker in the Imperial Valley. At the time of Pearl Harbor she was working at the post exchange at Fort Sill, Oklahoma. There "all hell broke loose on the 7th of December," and within days "everybody was leaving to go [to] Seattle or California." Norma went to Los Angeles, and after some odd jobs pinsetting and pumping gas, she became an assembler at Lockheed-Vega from July 1942 to late 1945. "I didn't even have to go for the job; people were coming to me for jobs. Not only just me, but everyone. They were recruiting workers and they didn't care whether you were Black, white, young, old." She made paychecks faster than she could cash them. "You were bombarded" with job offers. "They were begging for workers."[11]

Mexican Rosies also worked in the aircraft factories. Defense jobs required American citizenship, so Dolores Ortega de Sousa became a citizen, although she had already lived in California for more than fifteen years. From 1942 to 1944 she was a riveter on B-25s.[12] Lupe Romero had gone to El Paso from Guadalajara in 1922, when she was age four and her family lost their cotton hacienda after the revolution. She had married Bob Purdy, a railroad and electronics worker, in 1935; they had moved to Los Angeles the next year for the opportunities. She had been a garment worker for two years when Douglas Aircraft hired her as an assembler-riveter in 1942, and she worked in defense jobs until the war ended. "I didn't go to work because I wanted more money. I wanted to help my country," she declared when interviewed years later. She was not sad to leave the factory's incessant noise in 1945 and stayed at home for five years until her three children reached high school.[13]

Northward along the coast, the war channeled life, people, and dollars into the Bay Area, Portland, and Puget Sound. People remembered the Depression well, but they knew it was over. San Francisco Bay became encircled with shipyards (Mare Island, Hunter's Point, Bethlehem, Todd-Kaiser, Marinship, and others), airfields (Moffett Field, Alameda Naval Air Station), dry docks, and much else. Vallejo tripled to 100,000. Richmond quadrupled in population and went from 15,000 to 130,000 jobs. Outward from the city for fifty miles, the area became "a huge dormitory" for war workers, servicemen, and their families.[14] In Oakland and some other East Bay communities, the newcomers were often African-Americans, building on an existing community, not without friction with old-timers or meeting discrimination from segregated shipyard unions. After the war hundreds of thousands stayed.[15] By 1944 between 25 and 40 percent of the populations of the Bay Area, Los Angeles, and San Diego had arrived since 1940. California's migrants now nearly all came from outside the state, often from the same general area as those of the 1930s, but these newcomers got good jobs. More than half were young married women, many with husbands in the service, many with spouses—enough to produce "an unprecedented birthrate" for California[16]—and ushering in, unbeknownst as yet, the baby boom.

In Portland, Kaiser brought in "workers by the train load from Chicago and New York" early in the war, totaling over ninety thousand.[17] The upper Midwest predominated in the migration flow, but the stories of actual migrants, as always, told a lot more. The trail from Oklahoma and Arkansas was warm too. Mildred Secrest, for example, moved to Portland in 1942 to work at the Oregon Shipyard, which felt like a concentration camp compared with her country origins. Born in Tulsa, "I was a little sensitive about the 'Okie' and 'Arkie' bit. . . . My grandfather got his homestead by riding when they opened up the Cherokee Strip. My grandparents lived there until their family was full-grown, then they moved out to Vancouver, Washington. My dad had homesteaded in [Alberta,] Canada when he was a young man; that's where my father and mother met. . . . When they left the farm in Canada, they went back to Oklahoma, then out to Montana, then onto Vancouver where I lived until I moved to Portland in '42."[18]

In Seattle, Boeing led in job creation, soaking up people "from the farms, the forests, and the mines."[19] In the twelve months before Pearl Harbor, Seattle gained one and a half billion dollars in federal contracts and 42,000 new people; it had netted only 3,000 during the entire 1930s. By November 1943, defense employment in the area peaked at 385,000, greater than Seattle's entire population in 1940.[20] Boeing, employing tens of thousands, not only operated its main plant in south Seattle but opened others in Renton, Bellingham, Chehalis, Everett, and Aberdeen, all west of the Cascades.[21] The new hydroelectricity from Grand Coulee and Bonneville ran new aluminum mills at Spokane, Longview, and Tacoma, and Boeing made fuselages with that aluminum. Washington's economy changed from the lumber legacy of its early years to "aluminum, airplanes, and ships."[22] From rural Washington counties, young people swarmed to Seattle, Bremerton, Tacoma, Spokane, and Vancouver to take jobs in shipyards or at Boeing or to build airfields and bases. The rural-urban tilt became ever steeper, but as a sociologist observed, "Ten years ago few could have dreamed a time would come so soon when the labor of every able-bodied young man would be in demand, when a generation of youth would find the world waiting for them with jobs or with weapons of war."[23]

Certain obscure places leaped to immediate significance in the early 1940s. Among them was Las Vegas, a onetime railroad watering stop in the southern Nevada desert, which had been a support community for the Boulder Dam project in the 1930s. Its population in 1940 was eighty-four hundred. The war brought a huge magnesium plant and Nellis Air Force Base. After that followed the first entertainment resorts, which with atomic testing some miles to the north made Las Vegas's postwar future. The place had few natural advantages, but its unnatural ones included a highway to

Los Angeles (1935), Union Pacific streamliners, Nevada's legal gambling (since 1931), and easy divorce. The first big tourist hotel, El Cortez, opened in late 1941, and the first on the Strip, El Rancho Vegas, in 1942.[24]

A very different war-spawned place was Los Alamos, New Mexico. In a supersecret enclave, sequestered within their own county government, barbed wire, and sentries about thirty-five miles northwest of Santa Fe, physicists and engineers were building the atomic bomb. The town remained into the 1990s "a one-company town—100 percent dependent on Washington."[25] Hanford, Washington, was another secret site. In early 1943 the army chose it for making plutonium. After evicting the town's several thousand residents at knockdown prices, the army started operating its first reactor in September 1944. It then moved fifty-one thousand workers and their families into nearby Richland, creating practically overnight Washington's fifth-largest city. By early 1945 Hanford existed no longer as a town but as a 560-square-mile bomb factory. The Tri-Cities—Richland, Pasco, and Kennewick—were launched as federally dependent communities, sustained through the Cold War by the doctrine of nuclear deterrence. The downside appeared years later. The Atomic Energy Commission had not properly secured millions of gallons of nuclear waste, and by 1995 it had begun seeping into groundwater not far from the Columbia River.[26]

During the war itself no one counted the costs or side effects of moving people, machines, and money across the western landscape. Existing bases mushroomed, new ones appeared overnight, and all of them brought people. The Pacific Coast was covered with them. The interior West won its share as well—for example, in Idaho, Mountain Home Air Force Base, Farragut Naval Base on Lake Pend Oreille, a naval ordnance plant at Pocatello, and the Minidoka "relocation center" for Japanese-Americans;[27] in Utah, Hill Air Force Base (1938, the state's largest employer), Ogden Arsenal, and the Clearfield Naval Supply Depot at Ogden;[28] in New Mexico, Holloman Air Force Base near Alamogordo and others near Albuquerque and Roswell; Grand Forks and Minot air bases in North Dakota; Oklahoma's Fort Sill (artillery) and Texas's Fort Bliss and Fort Hood (armored) as well as the ring of air bases around San Antonio; the aircraft factories and bases at Wichita, Kansas; and others. After the armistice in 1945 many of them simply continued, expanded and electronified, jetted and nuclearized, through forty-four years of the Cold War.

"Relocating" the Japanese-Americans

An immediate demographic consequence of the war was the forced evacuation of more than 40,000 Japanese-born residents and more than 70,000 of their American-born children from California, Oregon, and Washington in early 1942. A law dating back to 1790 barring nonwhites (later ruled to include "Mongolians") from becoming citizens had prevented the Issei from ever naturalizing. Thus, when the war broke out, they automatically became "enemy aliens." As such, they were assumed to be saboteurs who would assist overtly or through espionage a Japanese invasion of the West Coast. Fears of attack or invasion were not completely hysterical. Several Japanese submarines were operating along the Pacific Coast, and one nearly sank a cargo ship in the Catalina Channel, off Long Beach, on December 24, 1941.[29] But to connect the resident (and two-thirds native-born) Japanese-Americans with the Japanese Imperial Navy required a leap beyond reality that only residual racism could make. The Federal Bureau of Investigation picked up hundreds immediately after Pearl Harbor and took them off without any notice at all. Others, after the army announced the general evacuation, had a few days to sell their stores and properties for whatever they could get. Then they were herded to "staging areas" like the stables of the Santa Anita racetrack and interned in places that even Mayor Fletcher Bowron of Los Angeles frankly called "concentration camps."[30]

After Germany and Italy had declared war on the United States on December 11, 1941, resident but noncitizen Germans and Italians also became liable to the hysteria over "enemy aliens" and "fifth columnists." Thousands in California, from the Italian-born fishermen of San Francisco to German Jews in Los Angeles (including, unbelievably, some who had just escaped the Nazis) had to move inland from a 150-mile-wide zone along the coast or were taken by the army to prison camps in Minnesota, North Dakota, and Montana. By late 1943 about ten thousand Italians and Germans had been arrested, and fifty-seven hundred were interned. But most restrictions on these nationalities were lifted between June and December 1942, not so much from any ebbing of hysteria as from the dawning realization, even by Secretary of War Henry Stimson, that the practical consequences were too great. Tens of thousands of Germans and Italians—"enemy aliens" in official parlance—lived on the West Coast. But millions lived on the East Coast, where any threat of invasion or naval bombardment by the Italian or German navies was presumably much more serious. Interning them all would have been impossible, physically and politically. For the same reason that Japanese were never interned on Hawaii—they were vital to the economy and too numerous to remove—Italians and Germans did not suffer internment for long or in great numbers, in California or elsewhere. Yet they were subjected to grievous insults and indignities.[31]

For the Japanese-Americans the loss of freedoms bore down much harder and lasted much longer. From above-the-store apartments in Little

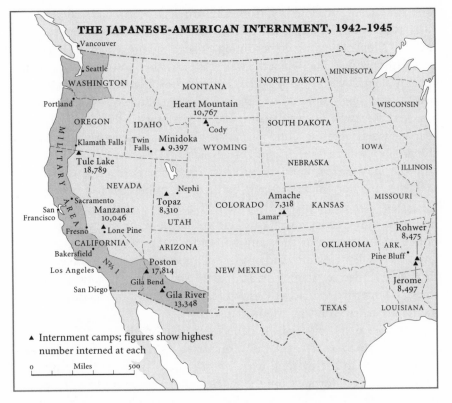

THE JAPANESE-AMERICAN INTERNMENT, 1942–1945

▲ Internment camps; figures show highest
number interned at each

0   Miles   500

Tokyo, the small specialty farms and wholesale food markets of Los Angeles
County, and their fishing boats came Issei and Nisei families, the immigrants in their forties and fifties, the children from their twenties down to
toddlers.[32] The largest group was from Los Angeles County, home to about
30 percent of the entire Japanese-American population, but Seattle contributed many. The order from Washington, vigorously enforced by the
army and local authorities, was to get "the Japs" away from the coast.

The deportations took place in early 1942. Releases came slowly, a few to
areas needing farm workers;[33] 22,000 into the army in 1943 and 1944; others
in late 1944 after court orders had reversed certain of the executive acts—
roughly 40,000 all told. Almost 80,000 still remained in custody as 1945
opened.[34] Most of them were expelled that year almost as abruptly as they
had been swept up in 1942. Fear fed this forcible uprooting. From Los Angeles Mayor Bowron wrote the director of civilian defense in Washington,
"Because of the large Japanese population here . . . it is apparent that the
Japanese Government is supplied with detailed information as to the location of every military objective."[35] Even California Attorney General Earl

Warren and Los Angeles County Supervisor John Anson Ford supported the evacuations at first, though Ford successfully persuaded the Federal Security Agency to provide for destitute internees and their families and helped as best he could his Nisei constituents in the Manzanar camp.[36] Warren exploded to an admiral, "Well, my God! We have thousands and thousands of Japanese here. We could have an invasion here." The future chief justice cooperated with the army and coordinated sheriffs and peace officers all over the state to carry out the evacuation.[37] Bowron, Ford, and Warren were later remorseful. Others were not, like the American Legionnaires who ostracized decorated Nisei veterans even after 1945.

The demographic story was expulsion, internment, and partial return. Ten large "relocation centers" were hurriedly tossed together, mostly in desert climates except for two in Arkansas swamplands and some secretive "isolation centers" at former CCC camps. Japanese-Americans from Los Angeles usually went to Manzanar, between the Sierras and Death Valley; those from Portland and Seattle to Minidoka, Idaho, or Heart Mountain, Wyoming; those from the Bay Area to Topaz, Utah.[38] Those who refused to forswear allegiance to Japan (because that would have made them stateless persons, citizens nowhere), or who had been educated in Japan (the Kibei), went to Tule Lake, just south of the California-Oregon border.[39] Some adult males went alone; others, with families.

Releases began in 1943 and continued until the last people left in 1946. Many were forced out because they had adjusted to the camps and had no homes to go back to. Nor were they particularly welcome if they tried to return before the war ended in August 1945. In Hood River, Oregon, where the American Legion in late 1944 struck the names of killed in action Nisei from the local honor roll, the returnees faced "intense antagonism" and "social intolerance," as did whites who helped them.[40] In California's Central Valley, the several hundred returnees of early 1945 met night riders shooting into their houses, arsonists, and many less violent but unmistakable racists.[41] After August the return flow increased. The new state attorney general, Robert W. Kenny, co-opted local law enforcement officials to prepare for the returnees. The all-Nisei 442d Regimental Combat Team, with its impeccable record of heroism, could not be gainsaid, and Kenny sent a few dozen veterans, wearing their Purple Hearts and Bronze Stars, around the state on "a brilliant public relations campaign."

By August 14, 1945—V-J Day—twelve thousand Japanese-Americans were back in California, with thousands more on the way.[42] Voters defeated an effort to write the alien land law into the California constitution in 1946, and the state supreme court voided the law itself in 1952. Even ex-Mayor Bowron, at a congressional hearing in 1954, condemned the "hysteria" that

removed the Japanese-Americans "too quickly to properly settle their business affairs"; he confessed in 1956 "that I was entirely wrong in ever entertaining a suspicion as to the local residents of the Japanese race."[43] Yet the
Native Sons of the Golden West continued to fight Asian immigration, "vigorously oppos[ing] . . . the immigration into the United States of additional
unassimilable aliens." Others continued a quieter racism.[44]

Reentry was difficult, and not everyone tried to go home. Fewer than half
the ninety-four hundred coming out of Topaz, Utah, in 1945 returned to the
West.[45] When the Poston, Arizona, camp shut down in late 1945, the War
Relocation Authority announced that 69 percent were "headed for California," although most released earlier had gone east.[46] In 1940 almost 90 percent of Japanese-Americans outside Hawaii lived in Washington, Oregon, or
California; in 1950, only about 70 percent. Denver, Chicago, Salt Lake City,
New York and New Jersey, and even some southern states gained ethnic Japanese in some numbers.[47] By 1965 well over 50 percent of Japanese, Chinese,
and other Asian-Americans lived in the three Pacific coastal states and
Hawaii, over a third of them in California.[48] The War Relocation Authority,
which had carried out the internments, helped resettle Issei and Nisei. While
the war was still on, some were shifted to defense industries and even the
Tooele Ordnance Depot in Utah, an ammunition base, the height of irony
considering the hysteria over sabotage that triggered the internments to
begin with.[49]

Not until the 1980s did federal courts overturn two of the decisions justi-
fying the wartime internment of the Japanese.[50] But many, Issei or Nisei, still
called the West home despite the bad memories and the racists. The Nisei
journalist Bill Hosokawa remembered that "for myself, there was nothing to
go back to in Seattle." He was "happy to remain in Des Moines" until he
received a letter from Minidoka that "made return a personal thing. My parents were going home." His Issei father wrote, "I helped to pioneer the American West. I have another opportunity to pioneer, for there are many people
in the camp who are afraid to return to the Coast. Since it became known
that we are going back, twelve other families decided to go back too."[51]

Jeanne Wakatsuki, praying for guidance in the Maryknoll chapel at Manzanar—Maryknoll nuns had operated missions in the Japanese-American
communities of Los Angeles and Seattle since 1920, and some young Nisei
women had joined the order[52]—doubted she could face racism in Los Angeles again, but she knew "that Papa would never move back east." The West
Coast was "still his home territory." She knew that he was "too old to start
over, too afraid of rejection in an unknown part of the world, too stubborn
and too tired to travel that far." He would never adjust to a factory job; "he
had run his own businesses, been his own man for too long." Back they

went, picked up what was left of their possessions in Boyle Heights, moved into a project in Long Beach, and started over.[53]

For Merry Masunaga, "a goodly number returned" to southern California "because they really had no place else to go." Her family, with a struggle, restarted their nursery business.[54] The stories are many, but in the Los Angeles of 1945 a California Dream, however misshapen by racism and recent events, still persisted: "When I came back [Riichi Satow recalled twenty-seven years later], I found the Japanese community was very different. Everybody was busy trying to earn a living. You see, we lost just about everything. Those who owned land were at least able to keep their land, but most of us were economically destroyed, completely uprooted.... When there was a job available somewhere, we went to get it quickly. That's how most of us made our comeback."[55]

Housing may have been the most difficult problem. County Supervisor Ford worked to solve it; the churches offered hostels; even the War Relocation Authority recognized some responsibility.[56] In one of the more bizarre twists in the story of minority groups in the West, the returnees from Manzanar and the other camps found they often could not go home again, at least to Little Tokyo. While they were away, as Los Angeles's war industries boomed and housing for new workers became incredibly hard to find, their homes had become home to thousands of African-Americans coming West for the first time.

The Great Exodus Heads West

Not all the new black Angelenos settled in Little Tokyo, nor did the district become entirely black. Many Japanese-Americans returned in 1945 and resettled, and it has remained the home of many of their important institutions, such as the Japanese-American National Museum. In the summer of 1942, however, a few weeks after the Japanese had been taken away, *Fortune* reported: "Row upon row of Japanese homes and stores and farms stand deserted (or newly occupied by whites and Chinese), while their former owners and their families . . . loll [!] or work in assembly points and inland concentration camps. The Coast is not formally under martial law, but whatever the Commander of the Fourth Army, at this writing Lieutenant General John L. De Witt, says goes."[57]

Very soon after that African-American newcomers moved in, with the tacit approval of the federal and local authorities. With only 5 percent of the city available to them because of real estate segregation, the majority settled in the South Central area. Watts, up to then divided among whites, blacks, and Latinos, became almost wholly black after twelve thousand migrants arrived.[58] From that time on it was overcrowded, weak on public services, an emerging ghetto.[59] Some families, however, as Bowron testified to a Senate committee, occupied "a section of Los Angeles formerly occupied by the Japanese and known locally as 'Little Tokyo.' "[60] By one estimate, Little Tokyo shifted from thirty thousand Japanese-Americans in 1940 to eighty thousand African-Americans by 1944.[61] The mayor created a Little Tokyo Committee with representatives from the police, housing, public health, and recreation departments to maintain health and order, not to evict the newcomers; the housing shortage was extreme, and there was nowhere else for them to go.[62] And they stayed, in formerly Japanese neighborhoods in other coastal cities as well as Los Angeles.[63]

By 1945 Bowron had begun worrying about what would happen when the Japanese returned. Little Tokyo, he wrote, "now embraces almost exclusively a colored population for whom other housing in this immediate area simply cannot be provided." The mayor "feared an adverse effect upon morale in this important war production area, disturbances, and possibly race riots." He therefore urged that several relocation centers be kept open "purely on a voluntary basis" because "not only are homes owned by American-born Japanese now occupied by others, but the housing problem in Los Angeles at the present time is, I believe, the most difficult of any large city in America. There are no vacant houses, apartments or hotel rooms."[64] By 1947 community leaders—Japanese, black, and white—cooperated sufficiently to defuse the frictions in Little Tokyo aside from a few stickups and other minor incidents.[65] It also helped greatly that many former residents headed instead to suburbs like Gardena and that black migrants preferred newer, better-equipped housing well south of downtown whenever they could get it.[66]

Black communities in Los Angeles, Oakland, Portland, Seattle, and elsewhere in the West before 1940 were fairly small and stable, developing quietly since the railroads started bringing people to them around 1900. Raymond Chandler, the novelist, opened his *Farewell, My Lovely* (set in Los Angeles and published in 1940, before the war industry migration) with the sentence "It was one of the mixed blocks over on Central Avenue, the blocks that are not yet all [N]egro." Fifty years later another writer, the African-American Walter Mosley, made a similar point when one of his characters recalled: "It must have been 1935 when I met Jop. . . . That was back before the war, before every farmer, and his brother's wife, wanted to come to L.A."[67] When they arrived, they found San Francisco and Portland unfriendly, Oakland and Los Angeles more welcoming. Serious bigotry sometimes surfaced.[68] Yet W. E. B. DuBois had declared in 1915, "Nowhere in the United States is the Afro-American so well and so beautifully housed" as in Los Angeles, and migrants hoped he was still correct.[69]

The greatest event in the history of African-America since Emancipation—the Great Exodus from the rural South to the urban North—had bypassed the West almost completely until World War II. Longer distances, lack of word of mouth encouragement, employer discrimination before 1942, and possibly the seeming exoticism and whiteness of the West kept southeastern black people moving toward New York, and southwestern ones toward Chicago and Detroit, during the first, 1915 to 1940, phase of the exodus. Not many African-Americans had ever shared in the Agrarian Myth,[70] nor, until 1940, in the California Dream either. Chicago's Bronzeville and New York's Harlem were dreams within closer reach. The onset of the war, which became also the end of the Depression, invited African-Americans to head out on Route 66, as whites had been doing for years, and by other roads, and by railroad. Most of these migrants bypassed interior cities, and 70 percent of them headed for the five major West Coast metropolises: Los Angeles, the Bay Area, Seattle, Portland, and San Diego.[71]

At the close of the war Carey McWilliams predicted that Los Angeles would become "one of the great centers of Negro life in America." From 1912, when in his view, "there were sufficient Negroes to constitute a real colony," numbers in Los Angeles County rose to about 75,000 by 1940.[72] Then came the war, with its sudden and enormous demand for workers. California's black population soared from about 125,000 in 1940 to nearly 300,000 by 1945 and 600,000 by 1950, with the heaviest concentrations in south Los Angeles and the eastern Bay Area.[73] In wartime alone, and mostly in 1943 and 1944, after the unions had started desegregating, the black population swelled from under 20,000 to 65,000 in the Bay Area and in Los Angeles from 75,000 to 135,000.

A great many were women in their late teens and twenties. They clearly outnumbered men among twenty to twenty-four-year-old wartime newcomers to the Bay Area and to Los Angeles. As in most modern migrations, the young predominated, but with so many men entering the armed forces, young women provided an unusually large share of this one.[74] Some followed servicemen stationed in the West. Others took advantage of federal antidiscrimination rules to find jobs in aircraft factories. Los Angeles also received some older migrants, male and female, going west with their children or seeking to retire, becoming the first group of African-Americans to have that choice, as their life expectancies began to lengthen.[75] By 1946 over 7 percent of L.A. was black.[76]

Most of the new black Californians left the same states that had supplied whites in the 1920s and 1930s: Texas, Louisiana, Arkansas, and Oklahoma (which lost one-seventh of its African-Americans), with some coming from as far as Georgia.[77] Longtime Congressman Augustus F. Hawkins recalled that the existing black community in South Central was "practically over-run" by newcomers from those states as well as Alabama and Mississippi. People migrated "because of a lack of civil rights" and a "very high rate" of lynchings where they came from, together with a California Dream of "orange groves and beautiful beaches." His own family arrived in the 1920s, having first moved to Denver, and then "they just simply moved westward." Hotels, drugstores, restaurants, and other black-owned businesses studded Central Avenue, shifting it from white to black; later, said Hawkins, it evolved from "black to brown" as it gained a Hispanic majority.[78]

Chain migration combined with accessible routes, usually the Southern Pacific Railroad or U.S. 66 from Oklahoma to either Los Angeles or California's Central Valley, U.S. 80 from Dallas, and U.S. 90 from Houston to El Paso and on to southern California and up the coast. Josephine Lamothe, born in 1909 near Lafayette, Louisiana, had lived in Los Angeles for about fifteen years when the war started, but she had never worked outside her home. During her nine years of school she "read a lot about California" and decided to live there when she married. "I just expected it to be beautiful, like I read about it. And it is." At seventeen she married a railroad worker, and his pass took them to Tucumcari, New Mexico. Two of his sisters had moved to Los Angeles in 1920, and the young couple made their way to the home of one of them, on East Forty-Eighth Place in Los Angeles. With a reference from a brother-in-law, her husband got a construction job and then became the janitor of a building he had worked on.

By early 1942 Josephine had eight children. But the youngest was already six, her mother was living with them, and her husband worked a split shift. So when a friend encouraged her to join her in trying for a defense job, she went, was hired, and spent the next three years as a driller-riveter at North American Aviation in El Segundo, one of many black men and women, "plenty of us," riding the "really wonderful" Big Red Cars. North American laid her off in 1945, then offered her another job in 1946, but since it was on the swing shift, she declined. In 1952 she became an aircraft assembler again, this time with Lockheed in Burbank, where she worked until 1972.[79] Tina Hill, another black Rosie, recalled her sister's saying that "Hitler was the one that got us out of the white folk's kitchen."[80]

Around San Francisco Bay employers and some unions kept black workers from good jobs until, in 1942 and 1943, the CIO and Harry Bridges's International Longshoremen's Association, the federal Fair Employment Practices Committee, and the California Supreme Court's decision in the case of *James* v. *Marinship* against the segregated boilermaker's union, opened them up.[81] C. L. Dellums recalled later that he and another union leader, Clarence Johnson, fought doggedly to open the Kaiser shipyards in

Richmond to blacks. "We had spent three days out there at that shipyard alone trying to get Negroes in there, and then in about two years they are launching a ship named for a Negro"—George Washington Carver—with Lena Horne swinging the champagne bottle. By then, according to Dellums, "there were about 10,000 Negroes working in the four shipyards."[82] After mid-1945 the shipyards cut back employment severely, but perhaps as many as 85 percent of the recently arrived black population remained in the area. Others kept coming, creating a community of some forty thousand people, about an eightfold increase over 1940, large enough to include both a professional and business class and a "proletariat,"[83] living in Oakland, San Francisco's Fillmore district, and certain industrial towns around the bay.

At the Kaiser shipyard in Richmond, the country's largest, ninety thousand workers turned out Liberty ships in a matter of days, and another forty-five thousand assembled and launched ships at the Mare Island Naval Shipyard just up the bay at Vallejo. Oakland, much larger than either and with an established black community, became home to thousands more. Kaiser recruiters in the South encouraged and even paid for many migrants' fares to Richmond, but most went on their own. Whites came first, from 1940 to 1943, but by then hiring discrimination had broken down and word of mouth job networks were in place, and the heaviest black migration followed from 1943 to 1945. It resembled, in many respects, the pre-1924 migration from the poorer parts of Europe to the United States: many came never intending to stay but wanting to accumulate cash to take home. The migrants were just the right age, from late teens to late twenties, averaging about twenty-three; in the southern context, they were just beginning to encounter "Jim Crow very keenly." Also, in the context of the places they left they were better educated and seldom the very poorest. Black men and women who left the South for the Bay Area "had more years of formal education and were more highly skilled and more likely to own property than were poorer black southerners." Young and vigorous, they "had fewer reasons to remain."[84]

One great difference between the black migrants to the 1940s West and European peasant migrants to the 1900s Northeast was their sex ratios. The Europeans had been mostly job-seeking young men, often with fiancées or wives back home. But almost two-thirds of the black migrants were female, and of those women, half were married with children. The war explains much of the difference; husbands were in the armed services. Between the Jim Crow South and the Bay Area's well-paying jobs and promise of a decent family life after the war, the migration decision was easy. Tens of thousands made that choice.[85]

In Portland, employment for African-Americans had been restricted to railroad and hotel work before 1940. Then the shipyards there and around Vancouver began hiring thousands (women as well as men), raising the area's black population from 1,900 to 25,000 by 1944.[86] Temporary housing for 44,000, about half of them black, was created outside the city along the Columbia and named Vanport. In May 1948 the river flooded, breaking through the levee and wiping out the entire jerry-built community. Thirty-nine people died, and thousands of homeless moved up the hill into Portland. There was a silver lining: when "all the children came into Portland, [it] needed 300 more teachers," and Portland desegregated its elementary schools, then its secondary schools, and finally its principals and administrators.[87] Housing, however, remained segregated.

In Seattle the African-American population expanded from 3,789 in 1940 to 5,400 in 1944 to 15,666 in 1950. The influx began with the demand for shipyard and aircraft workers, but it did not stop in 1945. Seattle's public housing (uniquely in Northwest cities) did not segregate blacks. Seattle Transit hired black drivers from 1945 on, and the school system hired black teachers beginning in 1947.[88]

In small Washington towns with new military bases, however, such as Bremerton, Yakima, and Walla Walla, African-Americans suffered discrimination in restaurants and other public places.[89] In Reno, Nevada, the local NAACP fought hard and successfully to end exclusion from restaurants, hotels, and casinos. Yet as late as the mid-1950s black performers in Las Vegas, including Sammy Davis, Jr., and Nat King Cole, could not stay at the hotels where they performed. This ended when Josephine Baker, playing El Rancho Vegas in 1956, asked why no blacks were in her audience and refused to perform until there were.[90]

The war, its extraordinary and sudden demand for labor on the West Coast, and the migration of African-Americans to meet that demand irrevocably changed the population of the coastal West—especially the largest cities, but many smaller places as well. Discrimination did not cease, but it eased in some places. Housing, schooling, and access to good jobs remained problematic always; the Watts upheaval was twenty years in the future, but many of its preconditions lay festering and unattended to when the war ended. In 1947 Horace Cayton, the Seattle writer who was to coauthor the classic study *Black Metropolis* with St. Clair Drake, named "America's 10 Best Cities for Negroes." Among them were Seattle (unsegregated, with a "topflight" educational system, but bring your own recordings if you like boogie), San Francisco ("the police will not bother you if you happen to walk down the street with a very light complexioned colored girl"), and Los Angeles ("overcrowded, tense, and tawdry" but civil liberties are "good, i.e.

by American standards"). Portland and San Diego he specifically excluded.[91] A new and ambiguous chapter in western history, the emergence of a multiracial, minority mosaic, was opening.

The Baby Boom

In its issue of December 1, 1941, a week before Pearl Harbor, *Life* magazine ran a story titled "Boom in Babies: In 1941 They Are Fighting a Birth Rate War with Hitler." With photos of crowded maternity wards, *Life* observed that "hundreds of parents are having babies for the first time in ten to fifteen years." Young couples were marrying and starting families earlier, older ones now had steady jobs, and "the 1940 draft marriages are producing a 1941 baby crop."[92] In the summer of 1948 the *Chicago Tribune* announced that developers had opened Park Forest on the far South Side, with "homes laid out in staggered clusters around a cul-de-sac" so that "every mother from her kitchen window can keep an eye on her youngster in centrally located and fenced-in 'tot yards.' "[93]

The baby boom, the most consequential demographic event in modern American history, was well under way. Contrary to the conventional wisdom that begins it in 1946, the boom actually started just before Pearl Harbor, when war-related employment was already ending the Depression. It is true that live births did not top 3,000,000 until 1946, but bedroom behavior was definitely changing in 1941, when birth*rates* rose above 20 (live births per 1,000 people) for the first time since 1931, when the Depression deepened. The boom peaked in 1954, when the birthrate reached 25.3 and live births topped 4,000,000. In 1965 the rate slipped below 20, and the number fell below 4,000,000 again; these events marked the end of the baby boom.[94]

The start-up year is conventionally given as 1946 because so many servicepeople (men *and* women) returned just then and marriages and births leaped upward. But the first reversal of the 1930s' low rates happened in 1941. In fact the baby boom was the first and only reversal of the downtrend in birthrates that had continued since colonial times. Why it started and why it ended—after 1965 birthrates never again touched 20, and seldom 17 or 18— have never been fully explained. A sense of personal confidence and economic security after more than a decade of the Depression, nationalistic gusto, and marriage and family becoming "the thing to do" no doubt all combined to start it. Postwar prosperity, fed in part by the Cold War, helped it continue. Twenty-five years later it stopped, for many reasons, among them sheer parental aging and fatigue; wartime babies deciding when they reached their twenties in 1962–1965 not to do as their parents had done but to seek education and employment; the marketing of oral contraceptives to reinforce the decision to limit family size; some subtle cultural changes associated with "the 1960s," all helped end the boom.[95]

It is impossible to understand American history in the twentieth century without realizing that the baby boom, despite its length, was an event, a historical happening. We usually think of events as brief, singular occurrences—like the attack on Pearl Harbor, or D-Day in Normandy on June 6, 1944, or the Hiroshima atomic bomb—or bracketed ones like World War II in its four-year entirety. We understand that these kinds of events had consequences. The baby boom was also an event, though of longer duration, and it had consequences and will continue to have them until the last baby boomer exits the Social Security system sometime late in the twenty-first century. World War II involved tens of millions of Americans, and its effects reverberated for decades. But the baby boom involved hundreds of millions, and its effects will last a century. As an event, it has been explained much less well than World War II. World war could happen again. So could another baby boom. For the history of society—American or western—the baby boom is the main event, the big story, from 1941 on.

The baby boom was nowhere more explosive than in the six farthest west states, where births together with migration made them the fastest-growing part of the country between 1940 and 1943, except for Washington, D.C.[96] *Fortune* magazine observed that 1941 "brought the greatest number of marriages ever recorded," nearly 1,700,000, with the consequent rise in births in 1942. But like virtually every analyst of population trends, it could not bring itself to predict that the boom would continue. "This wartime upswing, however, is probably only temporary, only a jog in the long-declining graph of the U.S. birth rate," which after the war "will resume its downhill trend." *Fortune* quoted several of the very best demographers, who were only letting history be their guide, and history certified nearly two hundred years of a falling American birthrate.[97] A survey by Metropolitan Life noted the rise in marriages in 1941, highest in cities "most affected by the war boom" (Los Angeles, up 10 percent over 1940, led the largest cities), and "the highest birth rate since 1930" as "Joe Stork got a lot more orders." It predicted that 1942 would "be even a bigger year for Cupid."[98] But the consensus of sober publications and soberer demographers was that "the current boom in birth and marriage rates will soon go into a tailspin."[99]

As late as the fall of 1943 one demographer kept expecting "an immediate decrease in births during the height of our activity in the war, when more than 10,000,000 men are away from home."[100] In the meantime the War Production Board kept having to authorize the manufacture of hundreds of thousands of baby carriages and strollers, while new mothers ingeniously bartered carriages, cribs, and clothes. By 1946 demand for triplet-size baby carriages surprised everybody, and in 1947 feature stories concerning the new profession of baby-sitting multiplied.[101]

"What no one foresaw was the postwar baby boom," wrote a sociologist years later.[102] Defense-related jobs continued after V-J Day. The GI Bill, with its subsidies for educating and housing veterans and their families, placed not a security blanket but a solid launching pad under millions of young people's hopes. Servicemen returned from Europe and the Pacific with war brides, whose countries' loss was America's baby boom's gain. Marriages at youthful ages not common since farm settlement days became the rule during the war for servicepeople and continued after 1945 because couples "looked toward a future whose many contingencies they believed could be controlled."[103] Through the 1950s television and the popular print media cemented the image of the commuting father, the homemaking mother, and three to five neat stepwise children, happily at home in a "Father Knows Best," "Leave It to Beaver" white suburbia. Marriage age rose and fertility started slipping after 1957, for reasons even less clear than why the boom started. Perhaps the assassination of John F. Kennedy in late 1963 and the first large troop movements to Vietnam helped end it, though it is not clear how. Prosperous times continued; no depression occurred to provide a convenient economic explanation. Whyever it was, the boom was over by 1965, and a new age of demographic behavior began.

Since then the baby boomers have aged through infancy, grade school, college, and on to middle age. At every point their huge cohort changed consumption for several years: new schools, then new colleges, then new houses and jobs. By the late 1990s they were contributing mightily to pension plans and the Social Security fund; by 2030, doomsayers predicted, they would be using them up. The dependency ratio (of unproductive youth and elderly versus productive eighteen to sixty-five-year-old adults) would soar, making their own retirements and health plans shaky. But the ratio was abnormal too in the 1950s and 1960s when the boomers were as yet supported by the rest of society, and that expense has long since been absorbed; society survived. The true crisis in the dependency ratio passed without comment when the baby boomers were still babies. The Census Bureau affirmed: "At no time through 2050 would the dependency ratio be as high as that which existed in the 1960s."[104]

The West eagerly participated in the baby boom. Its industrial recovery beginning in 1941; the migration of young people to it during and after the war; its permanent attractions for many servicepeople who traveled through it during the war; the ensuing Cold War economy in the region; the GI Bill, which not only educated millions into middle-class occupations but provided veterans' home loans to house millions of young families in middle-class lifestyles; its suburbs, houses, cars, and consumer credit; the Social Security and private pensions that for the first time liberated parents as they reached retirement age from dependence on their children, who could instead spend resources on themselves and their own families: all these made the postwar surge most intense in the West.

In California earlier marriage and earlier arrival of the first child began during the war and continued long afterward.[105] In Washington State the birthrate had been well below the national average during the Depression but exceeded it by 1949.[106] Of the sixteen states with the highest birthrates in 1961, twelve were western (seven mountain states plus Alaska, Hawaii, Texas, and the two Dakotas), while all the others except Oregon met or exceeded the national rate.[107] Beginning in 1965, parts of the West were to lead in the postboom fertility collapse.

Freeways and California Dreams, 1945–1960

In February 1945, anticipating American victory in the war, *Fortune* magazine looked ahead toward peacetime in the West. It polled "the country's leading businessmen" and discovered that among western executives, 34 percent believed their companies would provide more jobs than during the war, yet 34 percent also expected worse unemployment "during reconversion" than in 1937–1940. Executives from outside the West (73 percent) thought that the West would fare "not as well" as the Midwest and South and that their companies' activity in the West would not change much from before the war.[108] They were as mistaken as the demographers.

Fortune's "West" meant the three Pacific Coast states; only in passing did it mention the mountain or plains West. This myopia, however, allowed it to concentrate on the richest, fastest-growing, and most war-affected part of the West, from southern California to Puget Sound. Although *Fortune* pushed the thesis that the war had "radically changed" the coast, it admitted that even in 1939 the area had "the world's highest living standards," more cars per capita, lower living costs, more fresh air and sunshine and sports, and a "psyche" that "has not yet been scarred like that of the fatalistic East." Los Angeles County led the nation not only in the value of its agricultural output—"figs and almonds and olives and quinces and grapes and citrus fruit and truck"—but also in producing airplanes, oil well machinery, and of course motion pictures. In 1939 L.A. "assembled more autos than any other city except Detroit, made more furniture than Grand Rapids, manufactured almost as many tires as Akron, was third in food processing and oil refining, and fourth in clothing manufacture."

Problems lurked, however. How to absorb the new black population in Little Tokyo and avoid "an ominous anti-Negro feeling" and prejudice against Mexicans and Japanese? Also, what would happen to "the ephemeral shipyards at Portland and the overgrown plane factories in Seattle [which will] all but collapse" and to "the thousands who will be jobless immediately after the War"? Were the factory-farms of California's Central Valley a desirable system, dependent as they were on highly capitalized irrigation systems and low-paid migrant workers?[109] Yet such recent changes as the great new steel plants at Geneva, near Provo, Utah, and at Fontana, between Los Angeles and San Bernardino; the expanded seaports; the oil and waterpower; the new dams and other infrastructure all promised a good future. Getting by the postwar reconversion would be a "purgatory," but the longer term promised much. *Fortune*'s prognosis, in short, was that things would get worse, but then they would get much better.[110]

In fact the West between 1945 and 1960 exceeded the expectations of *Fortune* and virtually all other prognosticators, for good and for ill. It produced more babies, steel, psychiatrists, concrete, fruits and vegetables, suburbs with houses and cars (and jobs to build them), and more tension among races, ethnic groups, and economic classes than seemed plausible in 1945. It acquired, not coincidentally, commercial jets and major-league baseball. The postwar fifteen years were boom times, almost (figuratively) cloudless. They became, however, decreasingly smogless; smog was an unwelcome postwar by-product of population growth and industrial development most notoriously in Los Angeles, but elsewhere in the West too. (California's stringent emission laws succeeded later in reducing smog, however.) Building on its strong prewar urban base, the West became irrevocably metropolitan and exported its unique metropolitan forms far and wide. Los Angeles, always so differently horizontal from eastern cities, showed the way (for good or ill) for metropolis building elsewhere.

The coastal and mountain Wests shared in all important national trends between 1945 and 1960. Most prominent were sharp population growth and the explosion of modest insularities into major metropolises; the baby boom and the Cold War defense economy, synergistically producing population growth; the combination of suburbs, home and car ownership, and a democratization of middle-class lifestyle among many young whites, some Asians, and a very few Hispanics and African-Americans. Migrants from other parts of the United States and from Mexico kept coming; Europeans (other than refugees) and Asians did not.

The GI Bill (1944) and Social Security (1935) together fostered a whole new young middle class, the bill by financing higher education and low-interest guaranteed home loans, Social Security by relieving young couples of much of the burden of housing and caring for elderly relatives. Pensions from companies, in many cases the result of tough labor union bargaining, operated after 1945 as never before to ensure decent lives for retired workers. Unions of steel, auto, and other industrial workers gained their bargaining power from the 1935 Wagner Act. Thus three measures of the Roosevelt administration made America after 1945 much more secure and confident than after the armistice of 1918. This confidence underwrote the earlier marriages and larger families that were nowhere more evident than in the coastal and sunny West, and it also reassured a large share of the nation's new "senior citizens."

The despair of the Depression gave way to 1950s Baroque. The chaste little Fords and Chevies of the early postwar years gave way to fin-waving family chariots in the 1950s; people happy in 1940 to have indoor toilets were buying by 1955 the best tinted porcelain tubs and toilets that Kohler could produce; the meek seven-inch TV screens of 1949 metastasized gradually into twenty-five-inch black-and-white holes sucking into them the entire mental energies of families, and when color screens came on the market in 1959, the national addiction to television became irreversible. The thousand-square-foot GI Bill–financed box house of 1946, the veteran's dream come true, looked almost obsolete by 1960 next to four-bedroomed, family-roomed, two-and-a-half-bathed middle-class mansions. Not everybody had them, nor would everyone for some time, if ever. But emulation, if not ownership, set the new standards.

These phenomena were national—on Long Island, in Levittown near Philadelphia, in Park Forest, and in the truly New South, much of it adrenalized by defense contracts. The West, however, not only shared in the expansion but, in population terms, led it, growing by 40 percent in the 1940s and 39 percent in the 1950s, twice or three times the national rate.[111] For the first time western birthrates matched or exceeded national averages.

While the baby boom pushed young families into the San Fernando Valley and many another new suburb, migrants from states near and far kept arriving too. Route 66 in the postwar decade was never busier, a "crammed, cracking highway" that "truly lived up to the dreams of those who had cast their lot" building gas stations, tourist cabins, knickknack stores, and greasy spoons along its four lanes from Chicago and St. Louis to Santa Monica. The Interstate Highway Act of 1956 signaled the end of 66's romantic heyday, though interstates did not entirely bypass it until the mid-1980s.[112] But interstates made migration to California even easier, and signs appeared preserving the old road's dowager status for romantics and tourists as "Historic Route 66."

Essayist Calvin Trillin recalled how his father led his family from Kansas

City to California for several summers after 1945. He drove them most of the way on Route 66, and although he never managed to move there, he believed southern California was the most American part of America, with which his children needed to be familiar.[113] Simone de Beauvoir, the existentialist doyenne and familiar of Jean-Paul Sartre, who traveled the United States in 1947 (much of it by Greyhound bus), both loved and hated Los Angeles. Fifty years later one of her observations still fits many people: "None of the Americans that I've known in the East has ever set foot in California; when they take their leisure, Europe, near and close, attracts them more. And there are many people in this country [California] who have never seen New York." She could hardly believe that western people left their houses open: "I'm not even sure there are any locks. . . . I love this blithe carelessness." Driving north along the coast, Beauvoir was entranced by the wildness and lack of road signs: "In spite of its giant towns, its factories, its mechanized civilization, this country remains the most virgin in the world; man with his works and pomps is here a new and sporadic phenomenon, whose laborious efforts only scratch the earth's surface." Then, coming to "a village of implacable ugliness, we eat hamburgers stuffed with onions, squeezed between the two halves of a bun." But her motel made her "for one night . . . proprietor of a minuscule villa by the sea, [with] a balcony where we can look at the early stars."[114]

From southern California up the coast and back across the mountain West, an explosion of population, suburbs, machinery, and development unified the region more than ever with the rest of the nation. By 1960, in the view of many, the West had become the leading edge of American culture, economy, and society. In the nineteenth century the West captivated the American imagination by its exotic and nubile emptiness. After 1945 it did so by its ebullience and by fulfilling so many promises.

Each of its metropolises played the metropolitan symphony in its own rhythm and key. In Los Angeles employment lagged behind the national rate from late 1945 almost until 1950, when the Korean War boosted aircraft and metal products industries. Even so, the state's per capita income remained 20 to 25 percent higher than the nation's, even in 1949–1952.[115] The freeway era began in Los Angeles when the Arroyo Seco (soon to be the Pasadena) opened just before the war, with parts of the Hollywood Freeway opening during it. Then the 1950s became the great decade of freeway construction in both Los Angeles and the Bay Area. Roads, bridges, office buildings, and other public works often involved "slum clearance"—i.e., wiping out poorer neighborhoods without adequate thought to resettling residents or preserving ethnic enclaves like Los Angeles's Chinatown or Bunker Hill. The Hispanic leader Edward Roybal, then a city councilman, insisted that relocating

people into comparable or better housing would not work.[116] Yet the freeways extended L.A.'s characteristic low density in all four directions across
the basin.[117] Mayor Fletcher Bowron faced and fumed over a desperate
housing shortage in the late 1940s, and he oversaw the sprawl that began
solving it in the early 1950s.[118] By the end of the decade a critic could complain about "a legion of bulldozers gnawing into the last remaining tract of
green" between Los Angeles eastward to San Bernardino, but the city, led by
the San Fernando Valley, had pushed past Philadelphia by 1960 to become
the nation's third in population.[119]

In all this suburban surge, downtown L.A. seemed momentarily
neglected, "a snaggle-toothed city lacking in unity, shoving mismatched
buildings together without unity or style . . . streets without excitement
where even the pigeons seem poor in spirit." But by the early 1960s the 136-
acre Bunker Hill project had turned into the Civic Center, the cultural city
on a hill that boasted the Dorothy Chandler Pavilion and two other major
auditoriums. The city without a center was more than ever a city of several
centers—downtown, Pasadena, Beverly Hills, Westwood, Long Beach, and
others—not to mention northern Orange County, where the Irvine Ranch,
legatee of Spanish times, started calving off communities, developments,
and campuses, including the University of California at Irvine.[120] Bad news
for some, good news for others: a western story.

As the freeway system expanded, dispersing people more broadly
throughout the basin than the Pacific Electric system and the automobiles of
the 1920s had done, all Los Angeles took on the classic features of suburbia
except for lack of a dominant central "urb" and except for the white middle-
class homogeneity that marked American postwar suburbs elsewhere. Los
Angeles's suburbs were not of the same race and class. Watts was never
Brentwood or even Van Nuys, and never would be. Nor, since the 1920s, was
the center magnetic enough to have a periphery. The term "center-
periphery" had never fitted Los Angeles very well and certainly did not apply
in the freeway era. The Los Angeles of the freeways "was not so much a
departure from the past as a fulfillment of its basic structure."[121]

Many urbanologists could never understand or accept Los Angeles, smitten as they were by the 1920s-era Chicago-school model, which insisted that
all big cities must have a downtown core surrounded by concentric rings of
industries, warehouses, tenements, and finally single-family houses. In truth
southern California was all suburbia, decentralized, polycentric, equili-
brated, amorphous, where ranch-style houses, shopping malls large and
small, light industry, office high-rises, and public service facilities popped
up everywhere. It was not the end of suburbia, because it was not "sub" any-

thing.[122] It was the apotheosis of suburbia. Whatever else it was, Los Angeles after 1945 was the prototype, the cutting edge of American urbanism.[123]

Los Angeles's status as the nation's leading agricultural county rapidly became a casualty of population dispersal. It also changed Santa Clara County south of San Francisco from farmland into Silicon Valley in those years. But, said their defenders, other places would always grow enough food.[124] L.A. would be "the progenitor of urban change throughout the United States" and in fact the model for "the typical human ecological setting in this and other countries."[125]

How much it connected with long-term American traditions—the California Dream or the Homestead Ideal—is worth considering. Was the bungalow in the San Fernando Valley a makeover of the small family farm, with sun, smog, and freeway replacing lonely hardship? In the nineteenth century young couples went west to create, in an indivisible package, a family and a farm. After 1945 similar hopes and opportunities drew such people to the tract houses sprouting on the dwindling citrus groves of the Los Angeles Basin, there to assist strenuously in creating the baby boom and a new, post-suburban way of life.

Los Angeles's expansion between 1945 and 1965 was not classless, raceless, or without eastern connections. The writer Joan Didion has remembered it as "a peculiar and visionary time, those years after World War II to which all the Malls and Towns and Dales stand as climate-controlled Monuments."[126] The more rarefied communities may have seemed classless, thus leading the young Angeleno James Fallows into culture shock when he went to stratified Harvard.[127] But many newcomers remained working class, like the steelworkers whom Henry Kaiser imported from Pennsylvania to operate his giant new mill at Fontana, or the black defense workers who confronted white homeowner resistance and the Klan when they tried to find housing in Watts and South Central Los Angeles,[128] or the Mexican braceros arriving as contract workers.

Eastern money financed banks, savings and loans, and insurance companies; federal dollars made defense "California's most important manufacturing industry," employing nearly a fourth of the state's manufacturing workers. Los Angeles County received more than half, San Diego and Santa Clara counties most of the rest, of California's Pentagon contracts.[129] Defense plants required workers; workers needed housing; houses had to have streets and services. Racial discrimination never ended, but against strong resistance, it lessened. Often too, new suburbs, rather than mixing people, were for blacks *or* Latinos *or* whites. Separately or together, all rose in numbers.

The Minority Mosaic in Southern California

Minorities found their places in the southland's expansion and often per-force stuck to them. While the West's share of the American black popula-tion rose from less than 1.5 percent in 1940 to 5.9 percent in 1960, Los Angeles remained the chief magnet. As usually happens in migrations that are basi-cally labor-seeking, young adults were heavily represented. Coming either directly from Texas and the lower South or from northern cities after trying them for a while (nearly half made such double hops), African-Americans continued to migrate to Los Angeles.[130] The black component increased from about 3 percent (75,000) of the county's population in 1940 to about 8 percent (462,000) in 1960, but among all minorities they were the most con-fined and segregated.

Asians and Latinos moved into newly developed parts of the county twice as fast, and whites three times as fast, as blacks did.[131] Segregation in Los Angeles, though not as bad as Chicago's, was severe; the proportion of its population that was black increased faster between 1940 and the 1960s than the space it occupied.[132] But if Walter Mosley's fictional migrant Easy Rawlins can be believed, the California Dream lured young black men and women from Houston to Los Angeles after World War II as well as during it. When Easy walked into a south Los Angeles bar, "half the people in that crowded room had migrated from Houston after the war, and some before that. California was like heaven for the southern Negro. . . . Sitting there and drinking John's scotch you could remember the dreams you once had [in Houston] and, for a while, it felt like you had them for real. . . . In Houston and Galveston . . . people worked a little job but they couldn't make any real money no matter what they did. But in Los Angeles . . . the promise of get-ting rich pushed people to work two jobs in the week and do a little plumb-ing on the weekend."[133] The black community stretched from Little Tokyo, which it never wholly abandoned, southward to Inglewood, Watts, and beyond. It was crowded and segregated, but more hopeful than Texas or Louisiana, and truthfully better in many ways. Most of the migrants had had enough of tenant farming and farm labor and stayed in Los Angeles or other cities, even small ones.[134]

When Langston Hughes took the *California Zephyr* from Chicago to San Francisco in 1953, he found San Francisco "as attractive as ever," with many more "dark faces" than before the war. "In the Fillmore district there are sev-eral Negro night spots, a be-bop bar, and a hotel called the Booker T. Wash-ington. Which, me being a race man, makes San Francisco just about perfect."[135] The wartime migration of black people into Richmond, Oakland, and San Francisco (including the newly evacuated Japanese district, as in Los Angeles) continued after 1945. The Bay Area's overall population doubled from 1940 to 1960, but its black population became twelve times as large, rising from 19,759 (mostly in Oakland) to 238,754.

The pattern will surprise no one familiar with American cities. However large, the African-American population clustered in segregated, usually marginal or substandard, tracts. In the early 1960s these included Oakland, west and south Berkeley, North Richmond, and Vallejo east of the bay; Menlo Park and East Palo Alto south of it; and the Fillmore, Bayview, Hunter's Point, Western Addition, and Ingleside districts of San Francisco. Nearly everywhere Marin County's "housing industry" simply excluded them. Asians were also constricted in their housing choices, but, according to one survey, just one-third of all vacant rentals in San Francisco in 1961 were available to blacks, "and those were almost exclusively in existing Negro areas," while Asians were permitted to rent in two-thirds of the vacancies.[136] Despite higher than average unemployment (some of it because of white-only unions), restriction to often substandard housing, and low wages, black migrants continued to arrive.[137] African-American life around the bay had improved since 1939 and remained better than in many other places.

But a great many migrants left the South with upwardly mobile values. Either they or their parents had made the leap from sharecropping to wage earning, and they were convinced that education was the key to climbing higher. To them, the remaining and palpable barriers irritated, irked, and frustrated to the point of street riot by 1965, when the Watts uprising forever punctuated western and American black history.[138]

For Asians and Latinos, 1965 also marked a huge divide, because Congress finally ended the 1920s-era national origins quota limitations on immigrants. But even in the era of restricted foreign immigration of the 1940s and 1950s, Los Angeles and San Francisco actually gained in foreign-born population, while eastern cities fell back. In 1940 New York State was home to two and a half times as many foreign-born as California, but by 1960 California led in both residents and new arrivals. For Asian-Americans, the alien land laws and antimiscegenation laws went by the boards in 1948; Japanese and Korean war brides lived with their white ex-GI husbands all over the region.[139] Despite the tiny immigration quotas, seventy-eight thousand Chinese and Japanese arrived in the United States during the 1950s as war brides or refugees. In 1948, doing justice to Asians, blacks, and everyone, the California Supreme Court threw out laws banning interracial marriage, and most other western states followed suit.[140]

Chinese, Filipinos, East Indians, and Koreans arrived after 1945 to enlarge their still-small groups in the West, most of them in California. During the war the Chinese found themselves regarded favorably for the first time, because Kuomintang China was America's ally in the Pacific. The Angel Island immigration center burned down in 1940, an accident hardly unwelcome to many, symbolizing hoped-for change. One came in 1943, when Congress repealed Chinese exclusion, and although the new law formally admitted only 105 Chinese a year, it permitted naturalization. The War Brides Act of 1945 admitted 6,000 Chinese women, thus finally allowing the community to reproduce itself.[141] Old-country mores, particularly restrictions on women, began to loosen. Educated Chinese-Americans, both women and men, took white-collar and factory jobs during the war or joined the military.[142]

By the 1950s Chinese America included several generations. Mabel Tom Lee, born in Stockton in 1915, returned with her family to Guangdong about 1919, graduated from an American high school there, and, after surviving the Japanese occupation of China, came back to the United States in 1946 to a few difficult years raising her family and helping run their laundry business. By 1976 she was comfortably retired. Tony Woo, the meat cutter from Hong Kong, was drafted for World War II, returned to Hong Kong in 1947, and married. Back in San Francisco in 1949, his wife died. He remarried and by his sixties owned his home and some rental property: "My wife help a lot. She manages pretty good with money, so we doin' pretty good the last fifteen years."[143]

The newer generation often left the mainland, some before the 1949 Communist takeover, some after it. Several thousand moved to Seattle after the immigration law eased in 1943, usually settling not in the older Chinatown (renamed the International District) but north and east of it in Beacon Hill, Capitol Hill, and the University District.[144] Fay Wong, from Toisan near Guangdong, escaped the Japanese war by coming to Seattle in 1939, aged twenty-one. After a stint in U.S. Army intelligence, which sent him to the Philippines and Japan as an interpreter, he opened the Summit Grocery in Seattle. He and his wife lived in the back of the store and worked six ten- to twelve-hour days a week until they retired, thirty-one years later. In the process they brought up four children, saw them through college, and by 1990 prided themselves on their grandson who had become a chemical engineer, a profession Wong had aspired to, but for which he had lacked the necessary education, making him a failure in his own eyes.[145] San San Chen was a chemistry student in Nanjing when the Maoists took power in 1949. Married in 1959, she and her husband worked in research laboratories, had three children by 1972, and survived the Cultural Revolution. In 1980, after four years of applying, her husband and elder son entered the United States on student visas. She and a daughter followed in 1981 on a family visit; her second son completed the family journey in 1982. In Seattle she worked in Chinese restaurants, he studied, and gradually, working through difficulties, they established themselves.[146]

Native Americans underwent serious upheaval during the war and postwar years. Many of them left rural areas (in their case, reservations) for cities, like everyone else, especially southwestern cities and above all Los Angeles. California's once-numerous native Indians had dwindled to 15,000 by 1900 and recovered only to 20,000 by 1950. But during the 1950s migration nearly doubled Indian numbers in the state to 39,000 in 1960. Most settled in Los Angeles (32 percent of the state total), the Bay Area (10 percent), and San Diego (9 percent). From the 1930s to about 1955 the Oklahoma tribes predominated, arriving just as white Oklahomans did. Then the sources shifted to Arizona, New Mexico, and the northern plains, assisted by the relocation program of the Bureau of Indian Affairs (BIA). By 1965 the estimated 25,000 Indians in Los Angeles included several dozen tribal groups, with Navajo, Sioux, and Cherokee accounting for a third. (Groups native to California had become virtually invisible.)[147]

Native American migrants to Los Angeles and other western cities between 1945 and 1965 were more often male than female. Indian men in California, compared with whites, were a little younger, from more rural backgrounds, less educated (9.7 completed school years vs. 12), more often unemployed, less well paid, and doing more menial work. They migrated above all to find jobs, wages, and better living conditions, and they often did, though a sizable minority returned to reservations within a few months or a season. In these respects they resembled fairly closely the pre-1914 European immigrants and the young African-Americans of the Great Exodus. The Indians were less ghettoized, however. Though about 46 percent lived in low-rent central Los Angeles, the rest located in the southeast working-class suburbs or more generally throughout the metropolis, becoming "much more widely scattered" than blacks or Hispanics. The BIA's relocation program moved thousands to Los Angeles and was "a massive stimulant to the growth" of the area's Indian population.[148]

Even more, however, arrived on their own. The other federal Indian program of the time—"termination," or the severing of federal support for tribes—had little impact on Indian migration to California, although Indians hated and feared it.[149] Even relocation, though it shifted more than thirty-three thousand Indians between 1953 and 1960, many of them from Navajo, Hopi, or Sioux reservations to cities, simply intensified the rural to urban shift among Indians evident as early as the 1920s.[150] Like whites and blacks, they were taking part in the cityward migration that was happening all over the country in the postwar years. The rise of California from a distant sixth among states with Indians in 1940 to fourth in 1960 to first in 1980 is testimony, if anything, that the state's magnetism knew no color line.

Mexican Los Angeles, reinforced more by natural increase than by immigration, solidified its possession of Boyle Heights and Belvedere. East Los Angeles became the greater barrio, full of Spanish speakers born in the United States. Turf was constantly challenged. The most dramatic episode was the zoot suit or pachuco riots in Los Angeles in early June 1943, between Anglo servicemen and young Mexican-Americans. Zoot suits were a wartime clothing fad among young men, especially blacks and Latinos. A proper zoot suit had wide, padded shoulders, long lapels, pegged trousers, oxford shoes, a wide-brimmed porkpie hat, and a watch or key chain that hung from belt to shoes. It set the wearers apart. Unfortunately it set them all too far apart from Anglo servicemen in very different uniforms, the navy's, and farthest apart of all were Latino zoot suiters, or pachucos (the term arose in the late 1920s in El Paso and spread to other barrios, including Los Angeles's, to refer to certain youth gangs).[151] To beery sailors, the apartness of the zoot suiter/pachucos, who dressed weirdly, were dodging the draft, and racially did not measure up, was infuriating.

They attacked, in something close to "organized race warfare."[152] On the evening of June 7 about a thousand servicemen began marauding, pulling any "Mexicans" they could find from theaters, bars, and streetcars.[153] "For four nights" soldiers, sailors, and some civilians surged through the downtown and east side in an "outrageous display of mob violence . . . 'doing what the police have been unable to do,' as one serviceman put it."[154] The Los Angeles police let this go on at first but gradually became more evenhanded and admitted that sailors might have started it. Commentators drew parallels to Nazi mobs attacking Jews, belying the official wartime all-in-this-together rhetoric of class and racial equality. No one was killed, and damage was fairly minor. As a demographic event it was insignificant. But it was a harbinger, although only a few then predicted that race riots would eventually plague Los Angeles.[155]

For some Mexican-Americans, on the other hand, the war brought unhoped-for opportunity. The playwright Luis Valdez, born in Delano, California, in 1940 of American-born parents, recalled his earliest childhood. The army, after it removed Japanese-American farmers in 1942, replaced them with "Mexicans" like his father. "Suddenly we were *rancheros!* So World War II was a very prosperous time for my family. . . . The only *patrón* we had to deal with was the U.S. Army, which showed up occasionally. But a strange and tragic thing had happened on our ranch before we got it. The Japanese farmer who had lived on it refused to go to a concentration camp. So he hanged himself in the kitchen. . . . Then in 1945 . . . the G.I.s came back, and the Mexican farmers . . . began to lose their farms [and] my family fell to utter poverty. In 1946 we hit the road, and I got to pick those tomatoes next to Moffett Field, and watch the blimps go by. That is a California story."[156]

From about one hundred thousand in 1941, the city's Latino population grew to more than six hundred thousand by 1960, about a quarter of them living in East Los Angeles, others scattered throughout the basin, some displaced during the 1950s by urban renewal (as at Chavez Ravine, new home of the Dodgers) or by freeways. By the eve of the great changes about to come with the 1965 Immigration and Naturalization Act, they were a growing but politically quiet minority.[157]

"Spanish-surname" people—in California in this period, nearly all Mexican in origin—had for some time been the state's largest minority. In the 1950s they increased by 88 percent (over 100 percent in Los Angeles and Orange counties),[158] reaching 1,426,538 officially in the 1960 census and certainly more in actuality. The baby boom, not immigration, accounted for most of the increase. As of 1960, 80 percent of California's Latinos were American-born, 46 percent of parents also American-born. In other words, well over 500,000 were at least third generation (and a few could trace their California roots back 150 years or more). This diverse group made up 53 percent of California's minorities in 1960. African-Americans were 33 percent, the other 14 percent being Asians plus the 1.5 percent Native Americans.[159]

By 1965 over a million Mexican-Americans lived in southern California, most of them urban, under thirty-five, and born there. The stereotype of the peon, while it had some basis in migrant agricultural workers (truly part of the ongoing latifundia), fitted—if at all—a minority within the minority. By the early 1960s about one out of four Spanish-surname Californians was indeed a low-skilled worker (farm, factory, or domestic), but another fourth were in business, professional, or other white-collar positions. Half were working class to lower middle class, their subculture "probably best regarded and understood as a variant of American working-lower-class culture," like European immigrants in eastern cities twenty or thirty years earlier.[160]

In addition to the immigrants, Mexico provided the braceros, the seasonal farm workers—eventually 220,000 of them during the war—who arrived on contracts, with government approval, to remedy the labor shortage caused by the swollen armed forces. Only about 4,000 came in 1942, but in each year from 1943 through 1945, 50,000 to 60,000 brought in the harvests. They joined German prisoners of war, Japanese-American detainees, deferred farm boys, conscientious objectors, and convicts among the millions of workers placed on farms by the U.S. Department of Agriculture and other agencies to keep food and fabrics coming. For the migrant Mexicans, the government became their principal contractor, and remained so until 1964.[161]

As the Mexican population in Los Angeles moved east after the war, the older generation of Russian Jews still in Boyle Heights joined the younger Jewish community arising on the west side. Los Angeles Jewry, perhaps 130,000 in 1941, rose to 150,000 in 1945 and, with 1,000 or 2,000 a month coming throughout the late 1940s and beyond, to 496,000 in 1965. Historian Deborah Dash Moore recounts the tale of Eddie Zwern, a Jewish boy from the Bronx whose army stint took him to California. After mustering out, he returned, brought his wife, then brothers, sisters, and parents, and eventually more than 250 New York Jews.[162] The California Dream never worked better. All the elements of California-bound migration operated in Zwern's case: military service to acquaint him with a West he would never otherwise have seen, marriage and family (thus the baby boom), the GI Bill's educational and homeowning support, his own ambition and hard work, the chain migration of his family. This happened after 1945, but it "harks back to classic tales of Jewish immigration to the United States—or Italian or Irish or German before that. Films and the hotel business provided jobs for many, but in time so did "such typical Jewish occupations as retailing, real estate and construction, and the garment trades."[163]

Probably no more than 10,000 came from Europe or, before 1965, from Israel (though the sabras, the migrants born in Israel, were to expand later). The great majority came from Chicago, Cleveland, and other midwestern cities and secondarily from New York and New England. Many, about 120,000 by 1965, joined the exodus to the San Fernando Valley:[164] an inexact Zion, but one to which Calvin Trillin's father might have taken his family from Kansas City had he been younger. An important local motive was good education, the excellence of California's public colleges and universities. The miserably undeveloped public higher education systems in New York and the rest of the Northeast in the pre-SUNY 1950s were no longer the only choices (along with the City University of New York). Good climate, professional-level jobs, and the proliferation of temples and kosher delis did the rest. Newcomers started calling the San Fernando Valley "The Valley of the Shadow of Debt," and by the mid-1960s Los Angeles ranked in size behind only New York, exceeding even Tel Aviv, as a Jewish city.[165]

The Postwar West: A Brief Tour

Important as they were, minorities were not the whole story of the West's population in the twenty years following the war. The baby boom affected every group and locality. Metropolises proved inexorably magnetic, as ever

higher percentages of the people lived in them. Federal impact was ubiquitous, ranging from the military itself and Cold War–related industries and
careers (including nuclear weapons and missile systems), to interstate highways and other public works, to farm, mining, forest, fishing, financial, and
many other policies and laws. From the plains to the Pacific, these marked
the population patterns of the postwar West. A brief *tour d'horizon* will provide a few details to demonstrate.

By 1962 California had passed New York as the state with the most people.
New York in fact contributed to its own eclipse, providing (with Illinois) the
most new migrants to California, followed by Texas, Ohio, and Michigan.[166]
A majority of the people of the thirteen western states (since 1959 Alaska
and Hawaii had joined the mainland eleven) lived in California, and about
half the Californians lived in the Los Angeles area. The Bay Area came next,
but Santa Clara County, including San Jose and the Silicon Valley, were
catching up to it, as was San Diego. Sacramento, the capital, nearly doubled
in the 1950s and 1960s. Fresno and Stockton and a little later Modesto and
Bakersfield, the population centers of the Central Valley, each pushed
toward the hundred thousand that they reached in 1970 or 1980, pulling
people from California's rural areas and small towns.[167] Into the 1950s
migrants accounted for much of California's growth, but these were young
people, and their babies counted as native-born Californians, allowing natural increase to overtake migration by 1960 as the state's main source of new
people.

After the war more federal jobholders (313,400) lived in California than in
than any other state or the District of Columbia. Moreover, federal employees formed only part of the federal government's economic impact. Though
the shipyards around San Francisco cut back after 1945, aircraft, aerospace,
electronics, and other high-tech military procurement created hundreds of
thousands of jobs, hence families, around San Diego, Los Angeles, and San
Jose. California obtained more of this Pentagon-generated money than any
other state after 1945, and by 1965 it had absorbed 40 percent of all aerospace
research funds. Eleven percent of Californians' personal income came from
defense-related work. Despite occasional layoffs, the Cold War economy
appeared convincingly recession-proof, enough to justify cars, houses,
babies, and all the roads, schools, hospitals, and diaper services that went
with them.

The effects rippled almost everywhere.[168] In Sacramento, where more
than sixty thousand worked in government jobs (twenty-five thousand for
the state) by 1965, a guided missiles company called Aerojet-General
employed thousands more, who built and tested Polaris and Titan rockets,
bought components from an army of salespeople, all of whom "talk, eat, and

sleep rockets," clogged roads, shopped at malls, and raised families.[169] To the north and south of Sacramento the massive Central Valley Project (federal, completed 1951) and State Water Project (developed during the 1950s and 1960s), with their welter of dams, canals, power plants, and irrigation works that were only partially finished when the war ended, kept abuilding. Agriculture in California went "from partial to almost total reliance on irrigation"; latifundia continued to be the norm, with migrant workers performing stoop labor on land owned increasingly by oil companies, agribusiness, the Southern Pacific, and other large landowners.[170] Population grew moderately, by the standards of the coastal metropolises. The Central Valley's greater surge was to occur after 1965.

Oregon, almost by habit, shared but diffidently in the economic and population expansion of 1945–1965.[171] Workers, many of them women from rural Oregon, from the Dakotas, or other upper Midwest places, had flocked to Portland to work in the Kaiser shipyard in north Portland. The trains were crowded, according to Pearl Borg: "We got on at Grand Forks, North Dakota [with] the three kids, Keith was a baby six months old at the time. And we couldn't find a spot to sit so we sat in the rest room, the whole way out as far as Spokane." Like forty-four thousand others, she squeezed into the infant (and integrated) community of Vanport. She remarked, "You couldn't kill your kids, the walls were too thin." Thus, as an Oregon woman remembered, the flood "just splintered [the fabricated houses] like toothpicks." Afterward survivors sometimes faced a six-month wait for new housing. Shipyard workers "decided they liked it out here and were staying, boys were just home from the service, getting married, and looking for places to live—the housing situation was very bad."[172]

Immediately following World War II, Oregon attracted former servicemen like Arthur McCourt of Chicago. He recalled: "How I sort of happened to come to the Northwest was that our ship was being given to the Russians and we were sent back here and we arrived in Astoria, Oregon, on VJ day. . . . We were there about a month and a half. I was living at Seaside and going to the shipyard every day. I grew to like the Northwest." After a little time back home, "we all decided that Chicago wasn't a place to raise our families." He became an accountant for Weyerhaeuser and, with another man, founded the company's archive.[173]

Most of Oregon's population growth in the 1950s, however, came not from out of state but from boom babies. Only a tenth of its new citizens were migrants, about three-fourths of them women, mostly headed for Portland. Oregon's rural counties, like so many across the country, were losing people.[174] With their traditionally low birthrate, Oregonians were not likely to replenish the country villages, while youth marched off to Portland

and beyond. Where would the countryside of the future find people? In Eugene a prescient man remarked in 1963: "What really worries us is California. We live in constant dread of Californians' falling in love with Oregon. It will be a sad day when those people come up here and decide to stay."[175] But that time would come.

Washington was another scene entirely. Boeing and bases flooded the Puget Sound area with money and jobs; the Atomic Energy Commission shifted whole towns around the Tri-Cities section of the Yakima Valley as its plutonium production, and pollution, got under way; Grand Coulee and lesser dams on the Columbia River kept producing the cheapest electricity in the country. The 1960 census affirmed that Washington was sharing in the baby boom, while gaining in older people, African-Americans, Japanese-Americans, and suburbanites, especially around Seattle. The Pentagon gave, but sometimes it took away, as when Bremerton and Tacoma lost navy and national guard units in 1963. As a rule, at that time it pulled people into the area.[176]

Washington's population changes between 1945 and 1965 were much like California's, except on a smaller scale and without as many new migrants. The baby boom, the Cold War, and massive public works, stimulating both economic and demographic expansion, were striking features in both states, however. Washington grew 37 percent in the 1940s and 20 percent in the 1950s, becoming about two-thirds metropolitan. Half the population lived in the three counties from Everett south through Seattle to Tacoma, and only about a quarter in the much larger area east of the Cascades, most of them around Spokane or in the Yakima Valley. Migrants accounted for 19 percent of the state's growth in the 1950s, the baby boom for the other 81 percent. Males still slightly outnumbered females (the sex ratio in 1960 was 111:100), thanks mostly to the military and to older men (retired loggers or farmers) in some isolated areas. But the statewide trend was toward balance.

Washington remained ethnically but not racially diverse. By 1960 its old-line Scandinavians, Germans, Irish, and British had reached their third or fourth generations, and the state was still 96 percent white, well above the national average of about 87 percent. In the three Puget Sound counties, with half the state's population, only about 40,000 African-Americans, 13,000 Japanese-Americans, and 12,000 other Asians tinctured the whiteness.[177] In the 1950s, however, Latino families started replacing the lonely bracero, staying year-round, and forming the beginning of the minority that became the state's largest by 1980.[178] Washington rapidly diversified in the 1960s. By 1970 it held 71,000 blacks, 70,000 Latinos, 20,000 of Japanese ancestry, and it ranked fourth to seventh in numbers of Japanese, Filipinos, American Indians, and Chinese.[179]

Along the West Coast plane builders converted to peacetime more easily than shipbuilders did. Thus Los Angeles and Seattle expanded their wartime workforces, while San Francisco Bay had troubles. In Seattle, Boeing modified the B-29 bomber into the civilian Stratocruiser, raising its workforce from eighteen thousand in 1948 to thirty-one thousand in 1953.[180] Later in the 1950s it introduced the 707, the first of many hugely successful commercial jets, and despite some uncomfortable dips, Boeing, its workforce, and Seattle's population have expanded ever since.

Cheap and abundant electricity from the great dams along the Columbia helped the war effort and postwar growth, but the dams (including the greatest of them all, Grand Coulee) prompted only momentary population surges. The rough-and-ready construction worker town of Grand Coulee peaked at twelve thousand in 1935; by 1964 it had nearly emptied when a landmark café burned, "symbolically marking the end of the construction era."[181] Unlike Hoover Dam near Las Vegas, Grand Coulee remained magnificent but remote. The Army Corps of Engineers and the Bureau of Reclamation built hundreds of dams all over the West between the 1930s and 1960 and transformed the physical landscape.[182] However, of the great public works of the mid-twentieth century, dams seldom produced population centers. Bridges often did, most notably San Francisco's, or Seattle's, which cross Lake Washington eastward to Bellevue and the Cascade foothills. The vast interstate highway system, collectively the greatest public works of the time, linked the West as even the railroads had not done.

Nuclear and missile systems also required clusters of people. The government's wartime atomic development program centered in three places: Oak Ridge, Tennessee, with a uranium separation plant; Los Alamos, New Mexico, with the atomic scientists' laboratory; and Hanford, Washington, which made the plutonium. Hanford itself disappeared from the map by February 1945 because it was higher than top secret and only a few operating and security people kept it going. Twenty-five miles south, where the Yakima River joined the Columbia, Richland became the company town where Hanford workers lived. Nearby Kennewick (a farm supply community) and Pasco (blue collar, black, and Latino) joined Richland to form the Tri-Cities.[183] Hanford left an ominous residue, however: radiation between 1945 and 1951 that much later poisoned the thyroids of perhaps fourteen thousand persons, and groundwater pollution from five hundred thousand gallons of radioactive fluid leaking from poorly stored plutonium wastes.[184]

But these were not the problems of the 1950s and early 1960s, whose progressive spirit pervaded the Seattle World's Fair of 1962. Century 21 redeveloped a dilapidated area north of downtown, strengthened central Seattle as it was intended to do, but also publicized the city as a mature, suburbanized metropolis, no longer a well-kept secret.[185] By 1965 the plutonium problem was still underground in the figurative sense, and Puget Sound was on the verge of "being discovered."

In 1959 the offshore territories of Alaska and Hawaii finally became western states. Quiet outposts until World War II, both benefited greatly from it and from the Cold War. Hopes that Alaska would become the last farm frontier never materialized; small farming, even in places much closer to markets than Alaska, was succumbing to mechanization and consolidation. New Deal attempts to promote homesteads failed in the 1930s. But army and navy bases at Kodiak, Fairbanks, and Anchorage, started in 1939, were bellwethers.[186] Alaska jumped from 73,000 in 1940 to about 250,000 in 1965; Hawaii from 423,000 to over 750,000.[187] By 1965 the military presence was a fixture of Alaskan life, to be supplemented after 1968 by the opening of the Prudhoe Bay oil field and the construction of the Alaska pipeline southward to Valdez in the 1970s. Until then, from the end of the war to 1965, Alaska sported three principal cities: its tiny capital, Juneau (population 6,800 in 1965), where the summer Salmon Derby engaged its workforce of mostly state employees; boreal Fairbanks (then 23,000, if one includes nearby Eielson Air Force Base of the Strategic Air Command); and bustling Anchorage, still only about 45,000, where a Richter 8.4 earthquake in March 1964 managed to kill only 131 people.[188] The Alcan Highway, a by-product of the war, connected Fairbanks and Anchorage to Canada and the "lower forty-eight." But it was a long and lonely road, and commercial jets were just beginning to provide mass access.

The Japanese bombing of Pearl Harbor in December 1941 riveted American attention on Hawaii, and thousands of servicemen passed through the islands in the next several years. This traffic ensured a future resting not just on pineapples and sugar but also on the military, tourism, and, for some, long-term jobs and retirement homes. The Japanese and Filipino contract workers of earlier days had given way by the 1950s to young families of Chinese, Japanese, haoles (whites), and Hawaiians, often of mixed race, as reflected in the names of public figures like Fong, Ariyoshi, Inouye, Burns, Fasi, and (a bit later) Mink and Waihee. Uniquely in the United States, Hawaii had no ethnic majority. Roughly one-third was mainland Asian (chiefly Japanese, secondarily Chinese), one-third white, and one-third Filipino, Puerto Rican, or Hawaiian.[189] Portuguese and African-Americans, often ex-servicemen, completed the mix. By 1965 Honolulu verged on three hundred thousand population. Little Lahaina, on Maui, had just over three thousand, but locals were already claiming that "all Maui is entering its real-

estate phase. . . . There are great days ahead." And so there were. The Shera-
ton Maui and the Robert Trent Jones golf course at Kaanapali had already
begun operating, and they were far from the last.[190]

Geographically separate they may have been, but Alaska and Hawaii
shared enough with the mainland West—statehood, babies, the military, the
go-ahead spirit—to qualify for membership in the region by the early 1960s.
The mountain West followed a similar path between 1945 and 1965, though
more slowly. Hardly stagnant, its pace was nevertheless sufficiently slower
than Puget Sound or California to separate it further from the coastal West.
Montana, Idaho, and Wyoming gained people in the 1950s and 1960s, but all
from natural increase; their migration streams were definitely outbound. All
three states remained well below a million, despite military bases and irrigated agriculture. Great Falls and other towns across Montana and North
Dakota became ringed by Minuteman missiles planted in the ground, and
massive dam building punctuated the Missouri River in several places. The
construction phase aside, however, none of these brought people.[191] Nor, in
Idaho, did lumbering, mining, farming, food processing, or nuclear reactor
stations; people kept moving from farms to cities or out of the state.[192]
Those who defined their West by emptiness could continue to regard these
states, and much of Colorado, Utah, and Nevada just south of them, as
"deep West." Population concentrated in only two strips: one through
Ogden, Salt Lake City, and Provo on the west side of the Wasatch Front, and
the other from Greeley to Denver to Pueblo on the east side of the Front
Range in Colorado. Neither strip was solid by 1965, but the trend since 1945
pointed that way.

Utah and Colorado, with more people than the northerly mountain
states, also became more metropolitan. Along Utah's Wasatch Front, baby
booms had always been normal, and Mormon population virtually tripled
from 1945 to the late 1960s. Over a hundred thousand new migrants came to
Utah from 1950 to 1965, the great majority to defense industries, led by Hill
Air Force Base near Ogden, Tooele Army Depot, and Thiokol, with the
state's three largest payrolls.[193] The war brought the huge Geneva plant of
U.S. Steel to Orem, next to Provo. Defense accounted for almost 9 percent of
Utah's workers, third highest in the United States.[194] Colorado also benefited
from the Cold War, and (as in Utah) the great majority of its population
huddled in a few counties in the lee of the mountains.[195] Lowry Air Force
Base, the Rocky Mountain Arsenal, and NORAD (the North American Air
Defense Command) around Denver and the Air Force Academy, which
opened in Colorado Springs in the mid-1950s, all Cold War by-products,
helped boost the population of the Front Range strip. Denver, controlled by
sleepy oligarchs until the war, awakened to the bulldozers and hammers of

New York development mogul William Zeckendorf and the Texas oil money of the Murchison family after 1945. As elsewhere, "urban renewal" rearranged many of its neighborhoods in the 1950s.[196] By 1960 about half the population of Colorado, and more of Denver's, had been born elsewhere; migrants flocked to its new suburbs and new jobs.[197]

California and Alaska aside, the fastest-growing states in the West from 1941 to 1965 were Arizona, Nevada, and New Mexico: not coastal, not well watered, but warm and sunny. Besides the baby boom and the military-industrial impact, which swelled urban population all over the region, the Southwest battened on two other elements new to the 1940s: cheap, practical air conditioning and a leisure class founded on Social Security and private pensions. As better nutrition, medicine, and living conditions conquered tuberculosis, polio, and other killers, American life expectancy pushed beyond the normal retirement age, in effect creating an over-sixty age cohort enjoying dependable incomes and good health. Many decided to enjoy them in specially built communities like Sun City or Lake Havasu City, Arizona, or Leisure World south of Los Angeles, or cheek by jowl to baby-booming young families in new suburban developments.

Air conditioning lowered mortality and may have helped raise the birthrate; it certainly promoted migration to an otherwise impossibly hot climate.[198] "Central air" in homes, and in cars, went from luxury in the 1940s to novelty in the 1950s to necessity in the 1960s. Once a haven for tuberculars and other health seekers, the postwar Southwest and southern California after 1945 attracted seniors, the outdoor-oriented, and tourists who, like earlier visitors, often stayed on or spent their winters there.

Former servicemen and women who had passed through on their way to the Pacific or been stationed in the West were persuaded to stay by the now-manageable climate and the inviting opportunities.[199] Polio victims and others physically disabled but mentally fit learned that California could keep them vital and productive beyond the level of most other states.[200] In 1946 the Aspen (Colorado) Skiing Company opened the world's newest and longest chair lift; Taos began New Mexico's ski tourism in 1956; and in 1957 a veteran of the army's ski troops bought some ranchland for $125 an acre around Vail, Colorado, and started the most famous of postwar ski resorts.[201] Tourists were by definition transient, but the industries they supported were permanent and their workforces year-round (if, in those days, stratified, with whites in front offices and Latinos and African-Americans in livery).

Leisure-retirement communities sprouted in the 1950s, welcoming pensioners and others over fifty-two or so. Sun City, Arizona, just northwest of Phoenix, opened in 1960 with modest homes and amenities and soon proved highly successful, becoming more elaborate and upscale over the next two decades.[202] Only a tiny proportion of the country's elderly settled in retirement communities, and most were by no means wealthy, but such places gained attention as a new kind of suburb, an expression of the California Dream expanded across the Southwest. For the over-sixties, an expanding and now self-sufficient part of the population, the leisure-retirement home (whether in a planned and exclusively senior community or not) expressed once more, in a revamped way, the lure of the West. Many, like Sun City, did not express great affluence (as Scottsdale or Palm Springs later suggested) because their retirees were not especially affluent. But Social Security and better private pensions made relocating at retirement possible as it never had been before the Great Depression.

Like the rest of the country, the West was not simply urbanizing but metropolitanizing, its population concentrating more and more into cities that to eastern and traditionally trained eyes were sprawling limitlessly. Los Angeles was not exceptional but typical. In many places the cityscape abruptly descended from a small "downtown" with a few taller buildings to many blocks of one or two-story buildings extended in whatever direction the terrain permitted. The California bungalow or its variant became the norm from Seattle to Albuquerque, often capped (especially in schools, churches, and city halls) by red tile roofs suggestive of the mission style.[203] Crisscrossed by grids of freeways and boulevards, Denver, Phoenix, Salt Lake City, and other cities became navigable, understandable, and attractive. At least they were to a vigorous population: in 1950, 1960, and 1970 the West's metropolitan areas rated well above the nation and any other region in proportion of high school graduates and white-collar workers, average years of school completed, and median family income.[204]

The metropolises of New Mexico, Arizona, and Nevada exploded in the postwar decade in ways, and for reasons, like southern California. Albuquerque soared from 35,000 in 1940 to 97,000 in 1950 to 201,000 in 1960, from the baby boom, moderate migration, and the annexation of much of Bernalillo County, which reached about 300,000 by 1965. World War II brought branch offices of the Interior and Agriculture departments, as well as Kirtland Air Force Base, Sandia Laboratory, and other military bases, making Albuquerque "one of the most highly concentrated military training and weapons development complexes in the United States."[205] The University of New Mexico, with 1,800 students in 1940, had become ten times as large by the 1960s, thanks in part to the GI Bill. Its medical center served the entire state. Annexations kept the middle class within the city's boundaries.[206] Like Phoenix, Tucson, Denver, and Salt Lake City, Albuquerque was nourished on a combination of federal infusions (including the GI Bill and

1. On to California: the family of Wilbur
Jacobs, future historian of the West, in
Kansas en route to Pasadena, 1926.

2. The Jacobs family in western
Nebraska, 1926.

3. Ralph Bunche, future UN official and Nobel Peace Prize laureate, as a senior at UCLA, 1927.

4. Alice Wong, Mary Dunn, and Helen Wong at Venice Beach, Los Angeles, on the Fourth of July, 1931.

5. Midwives at Taos, New Mexico, late 1930s.

6. The Dust Bowl: children in an Oklahoma classroom, March 25, 1935.

7. The New Deal and the Depression: a Mormon woman, originally from Denmark, after receiving her first old-age assistance check, 1939.

8. Homesteader: the mother of John Lynch, in Williams County, North Dakota, October 1937. The storage battery powers the radio; rural electrification was yet to arrive.

9. Service station at Questa, New Mexico, September 1939. It did, or sought, a good business with pass-throughs from Oklahoma to California.

10. A migrant worker family from Texas, July 1940.

11. Wheeler, Montana, the boom-town of the Fort Peck Dam construction site, after the job ended. Public works projects did not always produce population.

12. The 1941 Crow Fair and Rodeo at Crow Agency, Montana. Indian onlookers share their expertise.

13. A town in ranch country: Sheridan, Wyoming, in August 1941, as the economy began to recover.

14. The baby boom, earliest stage: A migrant worker couple at a camp operated by the Farm Security Administration at Wilder, Idaho, in May 1941, with their infant twins.

15. Shigeru Shimoda, Nisei teenager, Seattle, late 1920s. Note the Lincoln photograph.

16. The internment of Japanese-Americans. Buses and property being loaded at 23rd and Vermont, Los Angeles, April 30, 1942.

17. The internment in process: Los Angeles, April 30, 1942.

18. The Fukuda family's effects, Los Angeles, April 30, 1942.

19. Nisei child awaiting evacuation and internment at Manzanar, April 1942.

20. Funeral at the Heart Mountain, Wyoming, internment camp, August 15, 1944.

21. A "Rosie the Riveter": union card of Helen Summers Brown, Los Angeles, April 1943.

22. The veterans' California Dream: Kaiser-built tract houses on sale in the San Fernando Valley, 1947.

23. The African-American migration: two "brothers" in Los Angeles, 1953.

24. Route 66 in its last days before the interstate superseded it, looking west into El Reno, Oklahoma, early 1950s.

Social Security), education, health care, public works, and smokeless high-tech (often defense-related) industry. The Army Corps of Engineers helped, with flood control and reservoirs.[207]

Elsewhere around New Mexico, Hispanics and Indians nearly kept pace with state growth. The white war against Germany and Japan included them too. Fred Johnson, a Navajo, was drafted in 1942, then about thirty and inno-cent of English. He later reminisced: "I didn't even know what I was doing, but I was trying to go and fight for my country and then finally I asked one of the Mexican boys . . . what are we doing, and he was educated and he said we are going to the draft for the army. There is a war going on in Germany." He served three years, saw action at Iwo Jima, and returned "with never a scratch on me."[208] Alfred Rael, governor of Picuris Pueblo in the 1950s, recalled how young men learned trades under the BIA relocation program, went off to Denver or the Van Nuys aircraft factories, and never came back: "it was a good place and they were making good money."[209] Hispanos also found their lives redirected by military service, and after the war some headed for Los Angeles or other defense-related jobs. World War II and its aftermath destabilized both Indians and Hispanos in New Mexico, but not without an upside, at least in their own eyes. The state's military volunteer rate was the nation's highest.[210]

Los Alamos and White Sands Proving Grounds remained central to the national nuclear program.[211] In the Four Corners area of the Colorado Plateau, where New Mexico, Arizona, Utah, and Colorado touch, mining booms scooped out uranium just south of Moab, Utah; uranium and vana-dium near Durango, Colorado; and natural gas and oil near Farmington, New Mexico. For about twenty years following 1945, new mines, smelters, gasoline refineries, and power generators dotted the plateau. Although no great population boom resulted around the Four Corners, its fuel output underpinned the growth of the Southwest's large cities.[212] Farmington became the fuel capital, and Durango (along with Mesa Verde) the tourist and skiing center of that remote area.[213] Santa Fe meanwhile was in the process of being discovered and developed as a cultural center, with summer opera and chamber music. By 1965 its Canyon Road already boasted perhaps the densest thicket of art galleries in the country.[214]

Arizona's postwar development outsped New Mexico's, and adjacent Las Vegas's was the most startling of all. Phoenix had 65,000 permanent resi-dents in 1940, augmented by 35,000 tourists a year visiting the newly opened Camelback Inn and less famous havens.[215] The 1940s brought air training centers, Goodyear and Alcoa, and aircraft electronics producers. Servicemen and defense workers stayed, tourists and health seekers kept coming (and staying). Sky Harbor Airport and Interstate 10 nullified the city's previous isolation, while air conditioning made the desert livable.[216] Subdivisions ate up thousands of acres of irrigated farmland as the city, constantly annexing, extended in all directions outward into Maricopa County. By 1960 three-fourths of the city's population of 439,000 had been annexed in the preceding decade, much of it in 1958–1960; the city of 9.6 square miles in 1940 had become 187 square miles and soon rose to nearly 300.[217] Manufacturing (three hundred new establishments between 1948 and 1960, besides the continuing large ones) edged ahead of agriculture and tourism as income generators in Phoenix.[218] In the middle of a desert Phoenix had become the manufacturing leader of the Southwest.

Sometimes metropolises annexed, sometimes not. Pragmatism prevailed, in the service of expansion. Some satellites of Phoenix, roughly coeval with it—places like Chandler, Glendale, Mesa (a Mormon establishment), and Tempe (home of growing Arizona State University)—maintained their identities. For retirees, Sun City opened in 1960, and Scottsdale rose along with the Dow Jones average somewhat later. As long as Phoenix had water—and its political leaders made sure of that, through federally bought public works—it expanded faster than any city in the Southwest, even Los Angeles.[219] Minorities sought and in some respects gained parity; desegregation for African-Americans came in 1953 to schools, barbershops, and restaurants, though in hiring, at Woolworth's and Motorola, not until the early 1960s.[220] To a black observer, Phoenix was "making a commendable effort to overcome the stigma of prejudice and segregation, long attached to the City and State."[221] The much larger Latino community—about 70,000 in Phoenix in 1965, mostly native-born citizens, constituting about 20 percent of Arizona's population—struggled with the usual minority problems of low wages and poor housing, compounded by the refusal of Anglos to distinguish among citizens, contract workers, and illegals.[222]

Tucson, about 120 miles to the southeast, also gained after 1945 from military-industrial infusions like Hughes Aircraft, employing two thousand, and from annexations.[223] Its growth rate approximated Phoenix's, but it remained about half the size.[224] In the other direction, just above Hoover Dam in Nevada, the wondrous boom of Las Vegas—America's only metropolis begun after 1900 that reached a million population before 2000—sprang forth from a combination of suddenly high wartime incomes, assured water, air and highway links to Los Angeles, Pentagon activity (the Nevada Test Site and air bases both known and top secret), and strategic metals mining. In addition, Las Vegas benefited from tolerant laws on gambling, marriage and divorce, and low taxes; entrepreneurship and investment from sources both legal and shady; and the spread of television, which made entertainment celebrities and the Strip known and envied across the country.

Like Pasadena in the 1870s, Las Vegas since the 1940s became a new urban phenomenon. It began as a Mormon colony in 1855 but collapsed in two years. During the Indian wars it was a forlorn and tiny outpost called Fort Baker, and then it was a private ranch. By the 1920s its population was less than 3,000, its function a watering and coaling stop on the Union Pacific. The construction of Hoover Dam in the 1930s created "more optimism than jobs." One of the last cross-country auto trekkers to write a book about the trip, Dorothy Hogner, drove through in early 1936 with her husband in a 1929 Ford roadster. To her, "The country was as empty as you could imagine, no agriculture, few filling stations even, until we came to Las Vegas, a small dusty city with bits of houses, and hotels, a mining center. But there were garages, and we had our noisy muffler fixed."[225]

In 1940 the divorce and gambling action of Nevada centered in Reno. Las Vegas received some stimulation from a defense-related magnesium plant and an air force gunnery center, but these were piddling installations. In that year, however, California hotelman Thomas Hull "triggered the process which eventually vaulted Las Vegas ahead": he built a "ranch-like resort . . . not in Las Vegas proper but across the city line on the southwest corner of Highway 91 (the Los Angeles Highway) and San Francisco Street." Hull's El Rancho Hotel was the first on what soon was known as the Strip. R. E. Griffith's Frontier Hotel followed in 1941, and the underworld figure Bugsy Siegel's Flamingo in 1946. Although Siegel did not long survive an argument with Lucky Luciano, the Flamingo "was the real turning point because it combined the sophisticated ambience of a Monte Carlo casino with the exotic luxury of a Miami Beach–Caribbean resort." The great Vegas watering holes of the 1950s—the Desert Inn, Thunderbird, Tropicana, and others—soon appeared.[226] Federal support, neither coordinated nor planned, was essential: Hoover Dam, providing electricity and water; the highway to Los Angeles (soon Interstate 15); the federally subsidized airport; and nuclear testing, for a quasi-industrial base and patriotic pride.[227] Vegas became a town of casino hotels and suburbs.

Anglos and Braceros on the Plains

The Great Plains, except for its cities, did not grow like the Southwest and the Pacific Coast after the war. Smaller places like Minot, Grand Island, and Salina and larger ones like Wichita, Oklahoma City, and Fort Worth did expand, fed, like their southwestern sisters, by air force and army bases and

defense-related industries. Wichita in the 1950s behaved like a smaller
Phoenix, its grid pattern racing across the flat prairie toward the edges of
Sedgwick County, its economy resting firmly on the tripod of wheat, oil and
gas, and aircraft. A plane-building town long before the war, because of its
blue skies and flat landscape, Wichita in the 1950s was producing Boeing
B-52s as well as Beech's and Cessna's corporate, commuter, and pleasure
craft.

While Wichita and the other cities of the plains prospered, doing their
share for the baby boom, the vast settlement frontier of 1870 to 1920 continued to empty and age. Where homesteaders had scrambled in 1910 to get in,
young people in the 1950s scrambled to get out, deserting farms and country
towns for cities near or far. Emigration was rife, as it had been, beginning in
the 1920s and continuing through the dusty 1930s, yet the 1950s saw the
broadest-scale flight of any decade, in terms of counties that lost people.[228]
Having seen California or Hawaii or Puget Sound, they were not eager to
return to western Kansas or the Dakotas, especially since agricultural economics seemed inexorably to be squeezing out small units. In imitation of
California, much of the Great Plains dispensed with live-in farm families,
turned to agribusiness, and hired seasonal harvest workers on contract,
many of them braceros from Mexico, or American-born Latinos.

Rural areas were stagnating and losing people all across the country, not
just in the Great Plains. In the late 1930s America's farm population finally
fell off its 1916–1936 plateau of about 32,500,000, and dropped to 23,000,000
in 1950, to 12,000,000 in 1965, and kept falling, even as the nation's nonfarm
population kept rising.[229] Farmers and other country dwellers grew ever
more rare, and the homestead ideal ever more mystically distant. The war
and its aftermath jolted many out of their homesteads, but the process was
longer running. In the same years that the baby boom swelled overall population, about half the nation's counties lost people.[230]

Pressures on family farms in the northern Great Plains were already
tightening in the 1920s and 1930s. But unlike much of the West, the northern
plains received only a small boost from the war and reconversion. Demand
for winter and spring wheat and other products profited those individuals,
families, and corporations able to keep up with new technology and effi-
ciencies of scale, but many could not or would not do so. North Dakota fell
from 681,000 in the 1930 census to 618,000 in 1970; South Dakota from
693,000 in 1930 to 666,000 in 1970.[231] In North Dakota private and state
agencies continued to promote tourism. The stayers and publicists clung to
the mythology of the settlement period: that hard work pays off in a decent
and dependable citizenry, free of social pathologies; that theirs was an "outward utopia" where living might not be easy but "puts iron in the soul of

those strong enough to face it," who "may, after all, have the last laugh."[232] The figures on out-migration showed that not even all Dakotans believed this. The faithless, however, slipped away quietly; boosterism remained orthodoxy.

The Ukrainians whose progenitors had settled in western North Dakota around Billings County between 1896 and 1912 were hard pressed during the Depression. By 1932 many of the second generation were migrating to sawmills and wood products factories in western Oregon and Washington. During and after World War II the young, often war veteran third generation were marrying other local ethnics such as Czechs and German-Russians; older farmers retired to town and deeded their land to the county as a kind of collateral for welfare; farm areas continued to depopulate. The Lebanese who had settled north of Williston beginning in 1905, if they stayed and lived to the 1950s, would have seen their descendants depart.[233] The old ethnic enclaves both homogenized and disintegrated.

Sometimes larger farms resulted not from abandonment or corporate buy-ups but from families consolidating their holdings and leasing them to active, younger relatives.[234] Increasingly expensive (and more efficient) fertilizers, harvesting machinery, and other capital costs forced many consolidations and, as farmers folded, the collapse of the county seats and other little towns that existed to serve and sell to them. Many Indians on Dakota reservations found themselves flooded out after Congress approved the Pick-Sloan Plan in 1944 authorizing the Army Corps of Engineers and the Bureau of Reclamation to build dams and control floods on the Missouri River. The dams had "a devastating impact," causing a third of the Indians to relocate, disrupting "long-standing communal and kinship ties."[235] Corps-built dams and reservoirs also put scores of farm communities, Anglo and ethnic, in Kansas and Nebraska, under deep water.

The two Dakotas and Iowa already led the nation in tractors per farm in 1940. Cars, trucks, combines, telephones, and electricity and the appliances it brought to both home and barn all improved efficiency as well as quality of life. A man could farm more acres, more quickly, with better output. The average size of farms rose steeply after 1935. These improvements took cash, but cash did not flow without them, squeezing farmers especially during the 1950s, when tractor prices about doubled while wheat actually brought in less than in 1946. The average size of a South Dakota farm, 157 acres, in 1910 reached 438 in 1930 and 674 in 1950. The number of farms dropped accordingly. By 1960, 70 percent of South Dakotans lived in towns or cities. More than half the smaller towns lost people too, and the depletion accelerated in the 1960s. "It was not so much a dramatic collapse as it was a steady and deadening attrition," depriving small places of the critical mass necessary to keep churches, schools, public agencies, health care, and commerce operating. These trends did not abate in the 1970s, 1980s, and 1990s.[236]

To the west and south, in Montana, Wyoming, Colorado, Nebraska, and Kansas, the story was similar. Montana's eastern farming counties generally lost people, though some larger towns (by Great Plains standards), including Havre, Glendive, and notably Billings, gained in the 1950s and 1960s. Similar urbanizing happened in Wyoming, where rural counties lost but Cheyenne and Casper expanded, and in Colorado, where the Fort Collins–Denver–Colorado Springs–Pueblo strip continued to grow while plains counties to the east lost people.[237] An economic historian of Colorado called 1900 to 1940 "the era of Agriculture" and 1940 to 1960 "the era of Defense," which helps account for the state's out-migration from farms from 1920 to 1940 and its in-migration to suburbs of the technically educated and skilled from 1940 to 1965.[238]

By 1950 Colorado was importing migrant workers to harvest beans, cucumbers, potatoes, and tomatoes (July to October) and sugar beets (until mid-November). Mostly *nuevomexicanos* and *tejanos*—i.e., American citizens who were Latinos—they traveled as families, earning very low incomes, living in "rural slums . . . makeshift quarters," the children receiving sporadic, much-interrupted schooling.[239] Juanita Salazar, born in 1950 in Edinburg, Texas, lived the migrant life in Colorado and several other states through the 1950s and 1960s. Contractors brokered their labor with growers; medical benefits were nonexistent; care was chancy. Salazar recalled that when she "got pregnant with my first daughter, I worked pretty much until my eighth month and I was pretty heavy, but I worked . . . with all three of my children." In the workers' camps "there was a lot of people . . . they had to share the bathrooms, the showers, we all had to share those and the showers didn't even have a door on them. . . . We had electricity [but] we didn't have water inside, we didn't have sinks to wash dishes or anything [or refrigerators]. You had to use a scrubbing board . . . they had like big tubs . . . that you also had to share with the other people."[240] In El Cerrito, an old *nuevomexicano* village, young men left for Pueblo, Colorado, to work at the army ordnance depot or the steel mills, and before long, wives and children and older relatives followed. After 1945 three-fourths of the people left, and El Cerrito became "a moribund community."[241] In eastern New Mexico, northeastern farming counties thinned, while southeastern counties, including atomic and air force Alamogordo and irrigated Carlsbad, had "continuous and at times vigorous growth."[242]

Technology spared western Kansas from becoming buffalo commons for at least a generation. Despite a mini–Dust Bowl that afflicted farmers and everyone else in the early 1950s, population loss was stanched in certain counties along the Arkansas River by a dam and reservoir built by the Army Corps of Engineers and a water agreement in 1948 between Kansas and Colorado. Garden City and Dodge City on the Arkansas both increased by several thousand between 1945 and 1965.[243]

Of much broader significance was exploitation of the Ogallala Aquifer through center-pivot irrigation. Agriculture in the Texas and Oklahoma panhandles, the western third of Kansas, and much of Nebraska received a new lease on life with the discovery of the huge aquifer, an underground water source as large as Lake Huron that had accumulated since the Pleistocene. The new technique of center-pivot irrigation, invented in 1949 by Frank Zybach, a tenant wheat farmer from Strasburg, Colorado, revived the profit-making possibilities of the High Plains. In the center of a quarter section of prairie, a well with a powerful pump drew water from the aquifer and showered 133 acres with it, enriched with herbicide or fertilizer, from a long, movable arm that crept in a circle around the axis, causing wheat and other crops to sprout in an abundance that completely eluded the underfunded homesteader of a generation or two earlier. This kind of agriculture took capital—perhaps twenty thousand dollars in the early 1950s for pump, well, and sprinkler—which many farmers could not afford. But in Nebraska alone, ten thousand center-pivots were in operation by the 1970s.[244]

The device "industrialized the landscape during the 1960s," and it sustained many a plains county's modest population. It will do so until the aquifer is mined to death. By the 1970s its shallow southern tip was already drying up, and the end of the rest was increasingly predicted.[245] The settlement frontier, begun in the late nineteenth century, was changing through marketing, technology, and the requirements of capital into a resource exploitation frontier after all, as depopulation and the depletion of the aquifer indicate. The process simply took longer than metal-mining frontiers did. Instead of a skewed sex ratio, the rural plains population of the postwar period took on a skewed age ratio, as the young left and those remaining kept getting older.

Oklahoma City, Tulsa, Norman (the university), and Lawton (next to the army's Fort Sill) kept Oklahoma's population from suffering more than minor losses in the 1940s, and the state gained slightly through 1965. The cities offset fairly general declines in western and other rural counties.[246] Regarding the aquifer and the future of the area, panhandle rancher Robert Kohler, appointed by the governor to the High Plains Council, said in 1983 that the water table had dropped about two feet a year, and springs that were there "when I was a kid have all dried up." The council examined the aquifer, and although it might not last, Kohler predicted that "they'll bring water to this country some day—it won't come from eastern Oklahoma, it will come from Alaska—that's my opinion."[247] Hope, if not water, was inexhaustible.

The Texas story was less straightforward for several reasons. Oil and natural gas, and the pipelines to ship them, kept expanding a string of communities from Fort Worth west through Abilene, Big Spring, Midland, and Odessa. Military bases and defense-related industries invigorated the demographic landscape of Texas as they did California's. Agriculture, which in west Texas increasingly meant cotton, mechanized after a practical cotton-picking machine became available, harvesting 18 percent of the nation's crop in 1952, 95 percent in 1967.[248] During those years harvest hands became redundant.[249]

Farm technology, consolidation of farms for market efficiency, and consequent depopulation were not the whole story in rural Texas in those days. The bracero program demands some paragraphs of its own, for two reasons relating to the history of population: one, it introduced hundreds of thousands of Mexican farm workers to Texas, California, and a few other places around the West, and two, although they arrived initially on short-term contracts and therefore had little immediate impact on population development, many returned to stay, often with their families, contributing to the rapid rise since the 1960s in the Latino population of the Southwest. During World War II only the emergency justified to proassimilationists like the educator George I. Sánchez or the League of United Latin-American Citizens (LULAC) the presence of so many imported Mexican workers. At any other time they undercut every effort at assimilation and better treatment in housing, education, and employment. Prejudice against Mexican-American veterans with distinguished combat records, like that against Nisei veterans, was outrageous in any case, but the braceros and especially the *espaldas mojadas*—the illegal migrants, denigrated as "wetbacks"—greased the slippery downward slope of stereotyping. To unscrupulous employers, the *mojados* were truly cheap labor because they were unregulated, unlettered, illegal, and defenseless.

From 1942 to 1947 and again from 1951 to 1964, the bracero program brought tens, then hundreds of thousands of Mexican contract workers into the United States almost every year—first to California, then also to Texas, New Mexico, Arizona, Arkansas, and Washington. Along with them, and in larger numbers after the wartime agreement ended in 1947, came the *mojados*. An undetermined number, estimated in 1965 at several hundred thousand, stayed in the United States, augmenting and often troubling the American-born Mexican heritage population. By 1945, returning servicemen and illegals (estimated by Mexican sources at a hundred thousand by

1947) began to obviate bracero contract workers. Contracts with braceros bound growers to minimal levels of wages and working conditions, but employment of *mojados* did not; thus, "as long as [growers] could obtain undocumenteds, they could ignore braceros."[250]

In the early 1950s the Immigration and Naturalization Service executed a draconian removal of illegals, under the name Operation Wetback. The campaign repatriated 3,500,000 people from 1950 to 1954, including more than 1,000,000 in 1954 alone.[251] Carried out by federal, state, and local agencies, "supported by aircraft, special units, and public sentiment," it ensured that "police surveillance and militarization became a part of labor regulation."[252] The McCarran-Walter Immigration Act of 1952 ratified deportations of noncitizens and legitimized harsh sweeps that ensnared citizens as well.[253] When the INS expelled, by its own count, more than 1,000,000 *mojados* in 1954, it took many Mexican-born but long-resident family members of American citizens along with them, wrecking families and businesses and raising nothing but the level of prejudice, repeating the scandal of 1929–1932.[254]

Counterbalancing the deportations, Mexican and American diplomats managed to agree in 1951 on a second bracero program that lasted until 1964. For growers in Texas, California, and nearby states the braceros provided a cheap, dependable labor force that disappeared after the harvest. For Mexico the program was a safety valve for its unemployed and an assist to its balance of payments.[255] In California the braceros became a continuing presence from 1942 to 1964. In Orange County, as elsewhere, they displaced local, often American-born labor in the citrus groves and depressed wages and housing conditions. Thus they inadvertently helped promote agribusiness because the profit on big units using cheap labor remained high.[256] Landowners and developers could keep their land in profitable production through bracero and *mojado* workers, while watching and waiting for even greater future profits as their land values soared.

The migrants who picked oranges and lemons sent or carried some of their wages back to Mexico, while the American-born "Mexicans" more often took factory or construction jobs and tried to raise families, living as best they could in Santa Ana (at that point starting to become largely Latino) or other California towns, picking their way through a labor market without a solid floor.[257] Every county in California employed at least a few braceros by the late 1950s, when 150,000 to 200,000 were coming to the United States each year to work in Central Valley agribusinesses.[258] Few probably stayed beyond their contracts, but after the program formally ended, illegal immigration increased,[259] including former braceros hoping to become permanent Californians.

From about 200,000 in 1951, the annual admissions of braceros crept up to 445,000 in 1956 and stayed at that level until 1960. They were still at 178,000 in 1964, when the program ended. About 19 percent (33,000) of the 1964 group became immigrants. Contract workers most often originated in central Mexico, undocumenteds closer to the border. The wartime braceros worked chiefly in California, but by 1953 they were providing 87 percent of the cotton pickers and 74 percent of the cowboys of Texas, 59 percent of all agricultural workers around Artesia, New Mexico, and 50 to 80 percent of the melon harvesters in Yuma, Arizona, and the Imperial Valley. In 1963, just before the close of the program, 39 percent were working in Texas, 25 percent in California, 11 percent in Arkansas, and the rest in New Mexico, Arizona, and a few other states, making up well over half the migrant labor force.[260]

Border towns, as paired ports of entry, benefited from the bracero traffic. The most active were Mexicali/Calexico, at the edge of the Imperial Valley; the twin Nogales in Arizona and Sonora; Ciudad Juárez and El Paso, the largest; and along the lower Rio Grande (called the Río Bravo in Mexico), Piedras Negras/Eagle Pass, and Nuevo Laredo/Laredo. In Texas the Mexicans supplemented and competed with Spanish-speaking Americans from San Antonio south to the border. The American-born migrants had the option of working in other states rather than for the fifty cents (raised in 1962 to seventy cents) an hour that the braceros earned, but the natives, traveling often with their families, still made only about a thousand dollars a year.[261] The story had at least three sides: the growers', the braceros', and the Texas-born Hispanics'. Each gives us one part of the picture.

"Cowboy" Boyd, a grower in Lubbock, was twenty-eight in 1951 and just out of the military. He formed the Lamesa Labor Association to help bring braceros from Mexico to the cotton harvest. After getting approval from the Dallas office of the U.S. Department of Labor, he and others proceeded to Chihuahua City and Monterrey and recruited workers at U.S. and Mexican government centers. The workers arrived in Juárez by Mexican transportation, walked across the river to El Paso, and then were signed up formally (thus getting around U.S. statutes against foreign contract labor). Hired buses took them to Lubbock or Lamesa, about 300 miles away. A grower paid fifteen dollars per worker to the Labor Department to cover transportation and other costs, half that if the worker was rehired to pick beets in Colorado. Boyd explained that his association also hired Mexican-Americans, but there were not "near enough to go around" because much more hand labor was needed in those days before cotton picking became mechanized. Braceros were supposed to be over fifteen years old, in order to comply with the 1949 U.S. Child Labor Law. Seldom, however, did anyone check the ages of children in American-born families.[262]

Armond Jackson, who farmed near the Rio Grande below El Paso, preferred bracero workers to wetbacks and hired five or six at a time:

> They were good simply because they were out here on contract. You had to have a place for them to stay. But they stayed there and did our work. They weren't chasing around to try to find grass over the fence that was greener. If they left, they had to go back to Mexico. You had to get them through the employment office down there, but that was fine. They worked good. They were the best we ever had. . . . The farmers, I think, would all like to see the *bracero* program come back. I liked them; in fact, when they took it out, farmers could help their *braceros* get their papers to stay over here, get what they called their green cards. I helped practically all of mine get over, but I discontinued that because as soon as they got their cards, they'd go off.

Treatment? "I think it was good. I don't know anyone of them maltreated anyplace." Wages? "They were paid good wages. They weren't starvation wages. They were paid good wages. Of course, they weren't paid the wages that we get now, nobody was. They were paid good wages."[263]

The braceros saw it differently. Francisco Sanchez, born in Zacatecas in 1924, became a bracero in 1945, signing up with American contractors in Mexico. He picked tomatoes and lemons near Merced, then San Jose, California, then Washington and Idaho. He got thirty, forty, occasionally fifty cents an hour, which he thought not bad; room and board cost fifty cents a night.[264] Bernardo Martínez, from Torreón, worked for American Smelting and Refining (ASARCO) in Mexico and then the United States, both as a bracero and a *mojado*. His father had come to the United States about 1911 as a refugee from the Villistas, worked in Arizona lead mines, and died of lung disease in 1933. Bernardo also mined lead, returned to Mexico, and went north again as a bracero from 1944 to 1946. He worked *a la chanza*—taking his chances without papers—in a Dodge City restaurant in 1946, in Garden City, Kansas, in 1947, and in Spokane, Fresno, Stockton, Chicago, and Seattle in the 1950s. Caught and deported, he returned after paying $300 for false papers.[265] Illegals were of course at greater and constant risk of discovery and deportation. Like Martínez, Federico Veloz first migrated from Mexico to the United States as a bracero and later reentered illegally; he retired at age sixty-five in Los Angeles. Alfonso Bernal Lucero entered illegally four times after 1954, paying $200 to $250 each time. In 1974 he was working as a cook in a Mexican restaurant in Los Angeles, looking as "straight" as he could to avoid police notice.[266]

A Berkeley public health analyst, surveying the bracero program in California, concluded that it "was simply a device for American agri-business to take selfish advantage of the poverty of Mexican peons (which comes from the same root as 'pawns'), to the devastation of U.S. farm workers, Mexican-Americans whether farm workers or not, small farmers, family life in rural Mexico, and every reasonable standard of social decency and honor."[267]

Dr. José Roman, Jr., a physician, remembered treating braceros. He himself was born in Marfa, Texas, two hundred miles southeast of El Paso, of refugees from the Mexican Revolution. After graduating from local schools, he earned a B.A. in biology from Texas Christian University in Fort Worth in 1948, and then an M.D. from the Texas Medical School in Galveston in 1956. He interned at El Paso General Hospital and then, since he "was in debt and poor and had a family," joined a clinic in Pecos "established by the cotton farmers of the area" for the braceros, of whom there were twenty-five to thirty thousand in season. He saw this as "an opportunity for me to start working right away . . . plus being able to do some good."

Roman believed that "perhaps 95 percent were common laborers from all over Mexico; hard workers, had a lot of physical endurance, uneducated. . . . Some of them didn't speak Spanish; instead, some peculiar (I would suspect) Indian dialects that no one but . . . their own group understood." They ranged in age from eighteen to their fifties, often had "large families back home," earned good money by Mexican standards—"several hundred dollars" in a few weeks. They lived in barracks, fitted with cots, heaters, showers, and outside toilets, and they ate "beans, potatoes, rice, bread and sometimes vegetables," although at the clinic they had three meals a day, one with meat. Work ran from "sunrise to sundown, six days a week. If they got an afternoon off, it was usually on a Saturday, and they would go into the city to window-shop and drink." The Mexican-American community, Roman believed, "tolerated" the braceros who spent a little money in their shops but "probably didn't hold them in very high esteem" because they "represented people who took jobs away from them." He considered the bracero program "an economic aid to both sides," also helping reduce illegal immigration. Why did it end? "Because of the invention of the cotton-picking machines; they were faster, and more economical . . . there was no further need for the braceros. . . . [Pecos] is not as active as it used to be."[268]

Frank Gonzalez was a bicultural broker. Born on the border at Nogales, Arizona, son of a cross-border freight expediter, he graduated from the American high school but then worked his way through the National University in Mexico City with a job at Air Mexicana. He stayed in Mexico City another ten years, but returned when his American draft board called him up during the Korean War. He served, then married, and his wife persuaded him that Lubbock was the land of opportunity (her parents lived there). He "came very poor to Lubbock" in 1956, but oil companies were leasing service stations to veterans without much capital. Frank's was on the edge of downtown, and he made a reputation among his businessmen customers for cleaning windshields better than anyone else in town. By 1959 he owned an automatic laundry, or "washateria," and had become a small businessman.

Lubbock, he reported later, was known as "a hell-hole for Mexico," though by the 1950s its cotton growers were hiring seventy-five thousand braceros as well as twenty thousand Mexican-Americans from south Texas. Gonzalez was shocked when he arrived to find people of "my race" shoeless, in "extreme poverty." "I saw right away there were great causes for misunderstandings—the language, the culture, the social scale—the whole thing was just made to create problems. . . . I was in a unique position to help because I was completely bilingual and had been brought up in both countries." In 1960, as a member of the South Plains Lions Club, he played the Cold War card, arguing that "if Russia were the next door neighbor to Mexico, instead of the United States, and if these farm workers were coming to Russia . . . do you think for a minute that the Russians would neglect these people—not take care of them, indoctrinate them with all the Communist ideas?" He proposed a plan whereby modest investment by the Anglo leadership would teach local Mexicans better farming methods and creditworthiness.

Whether his anti-Communist argument would have improved conditions is moot. At that point the Mexican government opened a consulate in Lubbock. The new consul was a young foreign service woman on her first assignment, and she did not like Gonzalez's plan to teach braceros how to raise better chickens. When she called a local beauty parlor for an appointment, the owner's husband heard her thick accent and hung up on her after shouting, "If you're the consul of Mexico, I'm President Eisenhower." To this insult on the national honor she replied with a cable to Mexico City to withdraw all 75,000 braceros from the area. It was three weeks from harvest. The terrified Chamber of Commerce asked Gonzalez what to do. He said, either write off your crop, or send your ten leading capitalists to Mexico City by tomorrow, apologize profusely, and hope. The business leaders and growers asked Frank to lead the delegation, and he did. The sackcloth and ashes expedition restored both the bracero program and his own plan. (When he was interviewed in 1973, however, Gonzalez believed the Mexican vs. Anglo problem in Lubbock had only become worse.)[269]

· · ·

From Texas to Canada, from 1941 to 1965, the Great Plains became an ever more efficient agricultural factory and, at the same time, home to ever fewer people. On the Canadian prairies the number of farms and farmers fell by half between 1941 and 1981, and a farm became "little different in kind from an urban enterprise of similar size."[270] The hard truth was that homesteads were simply not as efficient as large mechanized holdings. That had always been true in California's Central Valley, and it became clear on the Great Plains in the decades following World War II. Latifundia succeeded; homesteads failed. California agriculture was already 75 percent electrified by 1940, when only 35 percent across the nation and 20 percent in the mountain states had thus modernized, and West Coast farms also led after 1945 in efficiency of machines and labor.[271] At the same time, Great Plains family farms, even when irrigated, continued to be an enormous gamble, into the 1960s. Colorado ranch wife Vivian Hamburg recalled that hailstorms "wiped out the entire crop—a year's work"—seven seasons running, making farming "the biggest gamble of all."[272] Family farms, for all the folklore and, more important, despite the utter commitment and all the grinding work that people poured into them for decades, nearly disappeared. The Agrarian Myth was seldom uttered after 1965, its basis in reality long since cut off.

Another sustaining myth—that the West, as legatee of the American frontier, engendered social harmony and progress—was about to be shattered as well.

Slouching toward Watts, 1960–1965

In 1961 the Age of Eisenhower devolved into Camelot. The placid consensus, or conformities, of the 1950s appeared for the moment to be supplemented by a New Frontier through which a hard-nosed idealism would solve problems, like race and poverty, that the 1950s had tried to sweep under the rug. But the thousand-day interlude of renewed optimism was brief. After the assassination of John F. Kennedy in November 1963, blow after blow smashed the naive serenity of national culture. Lyndon Johnson's Great Society tried, and initially appeared, to carry social problem solving beyond anything seen since Roosevelt's New Deal. But acids of discontent ate away at the foundations of the Great Society even at its height in 1965. A crash impended, and its loudest sounds came from California, erstwhile land of so many dreams. Student protests at the University of California at Berkeley in 1964 were at first more titillating than ominous, just another California kookiness. But splits over the deepening Vietnam War, civil rights protests in the South and outrage at what "the white power structure" was doing to thwart the demise of Jim Crow, and growing refusal to put up with poverty and squalor concocted an explosive national climate. Across the country, large cities did explode in 1964 and 1965. Blown up with them were the confidence and optimism of the twenty postwar years.

By 1960 African-American communities in major western cities had grown far larger and more substantial than they had been in 1940. Migration, begun in wartime, did not stop in 1945 or 1955. Although western blacks remained second in minority size behind Latinos and shared minority status with Asians and Indians as they did not in the South, they had irreversibly rooted themselves in Denver, Phoenix, Seattle, the Bay Area, and many smaller places. Above all, they were a major presence in Los Angeles. Yet for the most part they remained poor, job-confined, and segregated.

The public and the media overlooked these conditions in the late 1950s and early 1960s. In Seattle nearly all of the city's twenty-seven thousand blacks (5 percent of the population) in 1960 crowded into the Central District and were ignored elsewhere; whites living in Queen Anne or Magnolia "might acknowledge in principle the existence of some racial grievance by blacks, but most felt justified in ignoring the issue."[273] Seattle voters defeated an open housing ordinance in 1963. The Congress of Racial Equality (CORE) conducted a boycott to correct job discrimination in downtown stores from October 1964 to January 1965, but it "produced no spectacular victory."[274] Job and housing problems also afflicted San Francisco's black community, which "made only marginal political progress between 1954 and 1965." The Fillmore District, which had pleased Langston Hughes a few years before, was a Chicago-style ghetto. A five-day race riot erupted in 1966 following a white cop vs. black teenager suspect shooting.[275]

In Los Angeles before 1965 complacency mingled with some real African-American successes, including the election of Tom Bradley and two other black candidates to the City Council in 1963. The city had become, by 1960, 14 percent African-American, with upward of five hundred thousand black people. They concentrated south of Olympic Boulevard to the city limit (Imperial Boulevard) and from Fairfax or Western, including Watts, beyond the city-county line into Compton and other suburbs.[276] In Watts itself lived twenty-seven thousand people in 1965, 43 percent of them below the poverty line, 39 percent of its families with a female head, 14 percent of its men unemployed. Median family income was $3,771, about $900 below the average for black south Los Angeles and $1,200 below the average for Latino east Los Angeles.[277] Since the war Watts had become 85 percent black, housing 9 percent of the L.A. community, and it had "steadily declined into a slum."[278]

Before 1965 observers saw problems but stressed progress. A newsmagazine reported in 1956 that although recent migrants from the South had less than ten years of education, "young Negro adults who had received their education in Los Angeles schools [averaged] 12.1 school years completed, a figure almost identical with that for the 'Anglo' whites in Los Angeles County." UCLA elected a black student body president. Although "Los Angeles still has Negro neighborhoods that are dilapidated and overcrowded," one also can "find middle-class neighborhoods where Negroes occupy neat stucco or frame houses that are graced by lawns and flowering shrubs" and shiny new cars; "at aircraft and automobile-assembly plants, as well as at other factories, you can now see Negroes working alongside whites at equal rates of pay." The result: "City officials claim, and many Negroes concede, that racial friction in Los Angeles is a less explosive problem than in Detroit and other northern cities." Black-Hispanic friction existed, but the magazine's overall judgment was optimistic that racial peace and progress lay ahead.[279]

In 1962 a reporter for *Los Angeles* magazine claimed that migrants continued to come because of job opportunities and good climate. "Instead of riots in Los Angeles, the Negro has heard about people, people that make him both proud and hopeful," like UCLA's Ralph Bunche.[280] A less boosterish publication related how Bob Liley, a twenty-nine-year-old black physicist with wife and child, met stiff resistance when they tried to buy a home in Monterey Park. But with the help of CORE and a new antidiscrimination ordinance from the City Council, they succeeded, and "if there will be no flags of greeting when the Lileys move in, at least there isn't likely to be a burning cross on their lawn either."[281]

But Watts blew up for four days in August 1965. The riot left thirty-four dead, over a thousand injured, and at least forty million, perhaps two hundred million dollars, in destroyed property.[282] Spreading from the epicenter around 103d and Central to over forty square miles of the city, the maelstrom sucked in about a hundred thousand rioters and "spectators" and sixteen thousand national guard, Los Angeles police, and other law enforcers. Most of the burned buildings were stores, not homes or schools. A recent history of the riot found that it touched off both black nationalism and also white backlash in California, helping elect Ronald Reagan governor in 1966.[283]

The Watts tragedy did not stop migrants from coming to Los Angeles. Undoubtedly, however, it marked the end of an era. Two months afterward a *Frontier* reporter blamed "bad, segregated housing" as the main cause, resting on the refusal in 1953 of Republican mayoral candidate Norris Paulson, Police Chief William H. Parker, "the *Los Angeles Times,* then rigidly conservative, and the real estate lobby," to support broad-scale public housing.[284] But blame was not theirs alone. A lot of voters elected Paulson, and a lot of citizens conspired in redlining. The federally appointed McCone Commission issued its report in 1966, calling for better schools, jobs, wages, and behavior from the LAPD, in order to avoid any further "formless, quite senseless, all but hopeless violent protest." But a psychiatrist pointed out that in fact black people "felt new joy" at the uprising, that it was "an alternative to despair" in places like Watts, whose "psychological climate last summer was one of apathy tangled with an acute sense of injustice."[285] Such grim assessments were far too discouraging to gain the wide acceptance that might have helped avoid the next great Los Angeles riot, which erupted in 1992.[286]

Across the West, as in the rest of the world, the size and shape of the population were very different in 1965 from 1941. The changes were not yet fully apparent in the official media; a reader of the *Los Angeles Times* could learn that the metropolis was about to become the nation's second city, that its freeways and new cultural center were magnificent, and that urban renewal meant progress. But the reader would also be reassured that the place remained overwhelmingly Anglo-American, the "west coast of Iowa," a manifestly midwestern, middle-class, Protestant society. Until Berkeley and until Watts. Even then the racial and ethnic diversity of Los Angeles—and many other western cities were scarcely less diverse by then—remained unappreciated. A new federal immigration law in 1965 would make it inescapable, but for the moment the truth was still hidden. On the Great Plains, where amid an enormously productive agricultural factory the people aged, shrank in numbers, and moved away, the Homesteading Ideal had nearly lost almost its entire basis in economic and social reality and was about to be discarded into the historical dustbin where old myths end up.

Los Angeles, Seattle, Phoenix, and other western cities continued to attract migrants and lead the nation in growth. But the postwar era was over. People born at the time of Pearl Harbor, the earliest baby boomers, were leaving college in 1965, having grown up in families where college and suburban homes, underwritten for many of their parents by the GI Bill, had been facts of life.

When the baby boom ended in 1965, America's postwar self-confidence ended with it. The boom stopped abruptly, but its consequences were to frame the social and economic lives of the region and nation for another life span, as the boomers grew up and grew old, on the way producing their own offspring, the echo generation. Under the new immigration law, and with baby making decreasing in favor, immigration soon replaced high birthrates as the generator of population growth, nowhere more than in the West, once again redrawing the region's demographic map.

9

"WHERE IT ALL STARTS," 1965–1987

> *The baby-boom generation was an anomaly, a blip on the demographic landscape, a boom time that we didn't suspect would bust, or even slide. Boomers now look back at their own childhoods with nostalgia and at their children's with concern.*
>
> —Ellen Goodman, 1995[1]

In the nineteenth century Americans often went east to get ahead—for example, Samuel Langhorne Clemens, William Dean Howells, William James, Josiah Royce, and T. S. Eliot, just to name a few intellectuals who began life in the then West. Since the 1920s, however, many originals went west: Georgia O'Keeffe settled at Abiquiu, New Mexico, northwest of Santa Fe; Frank Lloyd Wright built his home and studio, Taliesin West, outside Phoenix. Then there were all those Europeans, from Thomas Mann to Igor Stravinsky. And to Los Angeles from the Midwest also came national icons Marion Morrison (soon known as John Wayne) and Ronald Reagan. By 1965 the West had ceased to be a frontier in any traditional sense. Yet it seemed to be forever pioneering, originating, creating. In the next two decades it became the cockpit of several great national events, none of them momentary, all reflecting long-term, basic demographic change: the end of the baby boom, a wholly new immigration, environmental concerns, and inexorable metropolitanism.

The Collapse of the Baby Boom

In the mid-1960s the historic long-term decline in American fertility resumed. In 1965 live births, which topped 4,000,000 a year every year from 1954 through 1964, fell to 3,760,000 and kept falling;[2] the national fertility rate, which reached a modern peak in 1957 at 123, slid below 100 in 1965 (and fell to 65 in 1976, where it basically stayed through the 1990s).[3]

The rate bespoke stability, a "dim echo" of the boom,[4] but the numbers meant a more crowded future. Births rose again in the late 1980s. Female boomers born in the late 1940s or early 1950s often postponed having children, but as their biological clocks began running out in their thirties, many opted for motherhood. The "echo" did in fact happen—not from changes in individual behavior but from the sheer numbers of individuals. Despite the baby bust that began abruptly in 1964–1965 (when births *per woman* resumed their low pre-1941 pattern) and continued into the 1990s, the numbers of births *for all women* never dropped below 3,100,000 a year in those years.

If a society is simply to replace itself, its women must bear, on average, 2.1 children during their fertile years. In 1957 American women were bearing, on average, 3.7. Beginning in 1965, the rate fell sharply, and it reached 1.7 in 1976. Several European countries had already gone lower, Italy to 1.2. The American rate touched 2.1 again in 1990 and hovered near that for another decade.[5]

The shift in population behavior in 1965, for the country and the West, was as decisive as that of 1941. The baby boom that commenced abruptly also ended abruptly. Why? We know that women began marrying later after 1965, stopped at two children, and waited longer to have the first child. That suggests that they used more contraceptives and spent more time in higher education and/or in jobs. "The pill" did not end the baby boom; Enovid, the first contraceptive pill widely marketed, became available in 1960, three years after births had started dropping. But its use (along with the IUD and other methods) spread from then on, so that by 1975, when fertility rates were lowest, about three-fourths of couples were contraceiving compared with one-third of 1930s' couples.[6] For some set of reasons, couples began to prefer small families; the pill became one of several means to achieve that goal.[7]

Others attribute the bust to cultural changes. Undoubtedly the 1960s' steep rises in high school completion, college attendance, and jobs outside the home kept larger numbers of women from marrying and immediately having children. Very likely, people entering their twenties in 1965 faced a different set of choices from those of 1945, and parents who had been having children for a decade or so simply wanted no more. For one careful sociologist, the explanation for the sudden bust was the interaction of several factors that postponed not marriage and childbearing in general, but the timing of the first child, to the point in life where one or two, rather than the boom's three or four, became the norm. These factors were whether a woman attended college and whether her husband did also; contraceptive use; marrying at age twenty-two or later rather than at nineteen or twenty; Catholics ignoring the Vatican's proscription of contraceptives that earlier produced higher birthrates for their group; and above all, working after marriage.[8] Other factors, such as the political turmoil of the late 1960s, the Vietnam conflict and who did or did not have to go there, or the new environmental sensitivity reflected in Earth Day in 1970, may have operated to lower the birthrate. But none of these has been proved to have had any direct bearing.

Westerners behaved generally much like other Americans, except that they produced some of the highest birthrates of both boom and bust. Of the ten states with the highest in 1960, eight were western. The same was true in 1987.[9] (By 1997, although Utah continued to top the states in birthrate, the West hewed closely to the national average: about half the states above it, half below.)[10] This reflected migration. Migrants, as always, were young and therefore fertile; as the West continued to attract young people (baby boomers in this period), by that fact it ensured itself high birthrates. When migration slackened after 1987, western birthrates slowed to the national norm. And hordes of baby boomers went westward in the 1970s and 1980s.[11] One analyst of the boom generation saw them searching for "personal opportunity and space," "safety," and "meaning," which they regarded as the opposite of "self-interest."[12] If so, many boomers may have seen California and the West as the most likely place to reach these goals, for they fitted nicely into the California Dream and the myth of western self-fulfillment.

But even though birthrates in Washington, Oregon, and California fell sharply after 1965, the youthfulness of their populations kept most western states above the national average through the 1960s, 1970s, and 1980s, some exuberantly so. Alaska's led the nation up to 1970. Utah, with its many Mormons faithful to their "be fruitful and multiply" theology, scarcely budged during the bust; its birthrate in 1960 was 29.5 and in 1980 was still 28.6, while the country at large fell from 23.7 to 15.9. Contrasts within the region were great. Seattle and San Francisco lagged well below the national average for big cities, while Denver and Phoenix surpassed it. During the 1980s, however, rates converged around the national mean; Salt Lake City came down, and San Francisco rose.[13] As Utah's fertility rate closed toward the national average, an observer concluded that "economic reality is apparently winning out over Mormon ideology."[14] The West's youthfulness translated into more children. Utah still claimed the lowest median age in the country, with Alaska second. Of the western states (including the plains states), only Oregon's (32.6 years) was significantly above the national average of 31.7 in 1986, and its birthrate, not surprisingly, was low.[15]

As the huge baby boom cohort aged, its consequences shifted. Infants became schoolchildren, then college students (or a young working class, often Vietnam veterans) and, by the 1980s and 1990s, middle-aged adults in every category of sex, race, education, residence, and family status. The diaper services of the 1950s went bankrupt in the 1970s as boomers often shunned marriage (though many cohabited) and parenthood. Led by California's excellent higher education system, universities and colleges expanded enormously in the 1960s, then stabilized in the 1970s and 1980s. The baby bust of 1965 to 1987 was especially vivid in California because so many young people lived there. Its very large baby boom generation continued to mean that wherever and whatever the effects of the baby boom, the largest state would feel them most intensely.[16] By 1986 the oldest boomers moved into their forties, and the youngest into college. Many would probably not enjoy the quality of life that their parents did.[17]

The Immigrants' Return: The Act of 1965

For forty years following the national origins quota acts of 1921 and 1924, the United States let in few immigrants and limited those it did admit mainly to northern European "Anglo-Saxons." The only serious exceptions included refugees (far too few, from Hitler's Germany and Stalin's eastern Europe), braceros for a time, handfuls of Asians, and some family members. The next comprehensive immigration law, the 1952 McCarran-Walter Act, admitted some refugees but kept the national origins quotas. Real change—as it turned out, as radical and irreversible as the 1840s to 1920s open doors that transformed white Americans from predominantly British stock to pan-European—became possible in 1965.

Like most great measures, the new immigration law had consequences unintended as well as intended. National origins quotas purposely discriminated against eastern and southern Europeans. But until the early 1960s not enough of them voted. The 1965 act, named after Senator Philip Hart of Michigan and Representative Emanuel Celler of New York City, both with large ethnic constituencies, replaced national origins quotas with a preference system favoring family members of citizens and permanent residents

(74 percent of those to be admitted) and professional or skilled persons "of exceptional ability" or "in occupations for which labor is in short supply" (20 percent). Spouses, parents, and unmarried minor children of U.S. citizens could be admitted without regard for preferences and above and beyond the total annual number, set at 290,000, of whom 170,000 were to come from Europe and Asia (with a cap of 20,000 from any one country), and 120,000 from the Western Hemisphere (with no limit per country). Discrimination against Asians ended.[18]

The new law did succeed as intended in reuniting families and attracting skilled people. It also ended racial and ethnic quotas, in ways unsuspected by the legislators who passed it. Instead of Poles, Italians, Greeks, and other southern and eastern Europeans previously kept out, Asians and Latin Americans arrived in unprecedented numbers once the law became operational in 1968. From 1921 to 1960 about 58 percent of immigrants to the United States had come from Europe, and another 19 percent from Canada, making a three-fourths "Anglo" total. Latin America had sent 18 percent, and Asia 4 percent. During the 1970s, under the new act, the sources shifted radically. Latin America sent 40 percent, Asia 35 percent—a non-Anglo three-fourths—with Europe providing only 18 percent and Canada 4 percent.[19]

Moreover, these were only the people who arrived under the new preferences. Nonpreference family members and refugees from mainland China and Southeast Asia added significantly to them. In 1985, for example, the United States admitted 570,000 under various laws, and of them 46 percent came from Asia, 39 percent from Latin America (chiefly Mexico), and 11 percent from Europe.[20]

Sources within Asia also changed. Few Japanese arrived, so that Chinese and Filipinos outnumbered them by 1980. The Chinese bore little resemblance to the bachelor laborers of the past; women balanced men about equally, and the new Chinese were often students, professionals, and otherwise skilled persons, some wealthier than almost any previous immigrants. Koreans and the previously few Indians increased by more than 400 percent during the 1970s to about 360,000 each. Vietnamese, Cambodians, and Laotians, virtually unknown before 1968, totaled 262,000 by 1980.[21]

All this affected the West more than any other region. Geography assured that most Asians and Latinos would arrive not on the Atlantic coast, where immigrants had traditionally arrived, but along the Mexican border and especially in California, most especially in Los Angeles. The state by 1980 was home to one-fourth of all foreign-born Americans and more than half the Mexican-born. In another generation, because of these immigrants, their youth, and their children, California was poised to become the first state other than Hawaii where whites (of whatever ethnicity) were not the majority but were outnumbered by the combined Asians, African-Americans, and Latinos. Between 1960 and 1990 Los Angeles shifted from 80 percent non-Hispanic white to less than half, as Asians rose from 2 to 11 percent and Latinos from 11 to 36 percent.[22]

Across the West, not only in California but in some surprisingly remote parts, the texture of the new Latino and Asian migrations was enormously rich and varied. For Latinos the late 1960s and the 1970s were fast-moving times. The ending of the bracero program in 1964 did not stop migrant workers from coming to the United States. Many who earlier would have arrived under contract started adding instead to the flow of illegals. From 1968 the new immigration law admitted many thousands who were fully legal, especially family members of American citizens and residents. Many Mexican and Mexican-Americans faced intolerable labor conditions; Cesar Chávez answered with United Farm Workers militancy. To social discrimination, young Mexican-Americans responded with the Chicano movement, a more aggressive stance than the 1940s–1950s generation's assimilationism.

There was no single Latino experience. The law clearly distinguished American citizens of Mexican heritage (Mexican-Americans), legal immigrants from Mexico, and illegal or undocumented migrants from Mexico or Central America. Beyond that, class, occupation, property, and degree of ethnic and religious attachment, all present since the revolutionary migration of 1910–1921, divided people whom the Anglo majority lumped together as "Mexican" or "Chicano" or "Hispanic." Yet these majority attitudes forced this minority to unite, as happened earlier to "immigrants" or "Indians" no matter how different they really may have been. Richard Rodriguez wrote of his Sacramento childhood, "In the late 1960s, when Cesar Chavez made the cover of *Time* as the most famous Mexican American anyone could name, he was already irrelevant to Mexican-American lives insofar as 90 percent of us lived in cities and we were more apt to work in construction than as farmworkers. My mother, who worked downtown, and my father, who worked downtown, nevertheless sent money to Cesar Chavez, because the hardness of his struggle on the land reminded them of the hardness of their Mexican past."[23]

In El Paso, a forty-year-old lawyer and rising politician, Tati Santiesteban, told an interviewer in 1975 how his father escaped the Villistas and crossed the river illegally into west Texas about 1917. He grew up in Hudspeth County, downriver from El Paso, on a ranch owned by "Dave Gil [, who] was a colored gentleman that my dad's people crossed the river in order to tenant farm." The family moved to El Paso. His mother insisted he take classes in English, not Spanish, for which he was deeply grateful since he thus gained friends and lost his accent: "My home was completely Spanish speak-

ing . . . yet it's the impact [of] those early years . . . where you can pick up
the language just like all of us had to do." He became vice-president and the
"Cutie Boy" of the Ysleta High School student body, graduated from a military college in New Mexico, served as an army second lieutenant, attended
the University of Texas Law School at Austin, where he became student body
president, returned to practice law in El Paso, and was elected to the Texas
Senate.

He believed deeply in education—"bilingual, co-mingled with bicultural"—since Mexican-Americans miss full acceptance in both countries
"because of our language barrier, not our color." In the United States the
accent aroused all the predictable prejudices; in Mexico it marked the
Mexican-American as a *pocho,* who speaks bad Spanish, because he is (as
Rodriguez defines the word) "the child who wanders away, ends up in the
United States, among the gringos, where he forgets his true home."[24]

Santiesteban was born a citizen of the United States. "Juan García" (a
pseudonym) was born in Guadalajara in 1942 and entered illegally in a taxi
in Nogales, Arizona, in 1967. The Border Patrol caught him but gave him a
temporary work permit. With it he became a field hand, speaking very little
English, but by 1969 he signed on as a busboy in a Sizzler steak house in
Santa Monica. By then his wife had joined him, leaving one son in Mexico.
In the next three years they had two American-born children, and "Juan"
had worked his way up to assistant manager of the steak house. At that
point, thirty years old, he had hopes and plans: to learn better English,
become manager of his own steak house, buy a house, see his sons well educated even though that might change them. Elementary education was better in Mexico, he thought, but chances for life success were better in the
United States, although it was "too hard" for many Mexicans.[25]

The differences between people like Santiesteban, Rodriguez, "Juan García," Cesar Chávez, the illegal and legal farm workers, the angry Chicanos in
the barrios, and many others were great. Ralph Murilli, the district director
of LULAC (the League of United Latin American Citizens) in El Paso, an
assimilationist, nonconfrontational man, saw his main function as finding
financial aid to educate young Mexican-Americans. Conrad Ramirez, a
native of Alpine, Texas, who managed the Small Business Administration in
El Paso in the early 1970s, used several strategies to convince banks that
Mexican-Americans were creditworthy. Bonifacio Delgado, a second-
generation Texan, became a social worker and ran the Llano Estacado program for migrants around Lubbock.[26]

Migrant workers, whether in Texas or California or the Northwest, shared
media attention in the late 1960s, along with the nascent Chicano activists.
Until 1964, when the bracero program ceased, undocumented migrants

were unusual. As happened in west Texas in the 1950s, braceros or Mexican-Americans from south Texas amply filled the labor demand. But after 1964, "illegals" (often former braceros) kept coming because they were used to doing so and because the new hemispheric quota in the 1965 law fell well below earlier totals. The Border Patrol claimed to have apprehended 8,300,000 illegals during the 1970s. Many of them, however, were the same persons making repeat attempts. By 1980, though no one knew for certain, probably between 1,700,000 and 2,200,000 "illegals" were living in the United States, most of them in the Southwest.

Furthermore, they included not just young men, as the bracero program did, but family members, many of whom could claim quota preferences. Young men grew older and brought their brothers and sons to work with them. Then they sent for their wives and sisters. In settled migrant communities, women probably were as numerous as men by the early 1980s, and their U.S.-born children of course had a balanced sex ratio. As with European immigrant groups early in the century, women did not migrate as often as men, but when they arrived, they usually stayed, so that communities grew roots. Birthrates dropped from Mexican to American levels fairly quickly, partly because migrating was disruptive and partly to adapt to local norms. By the end of the 1970s, Mexican-American communities had become a mixture of American-born citizens of all ages, Mexican and Central American nationals who were legally resident, and illegals. One family might include all three categories. Fewer and fewer migrated to follow harvests. By 1980, whether citizens, legal migrants, or illegals, most worked in manufacturing, construction, tourist and travel positions, restaurants, domestic service, and other urban-located jobs. The 1965 act was meant to unite migrant families, and it succeeded in doing so for Mexican-Americans.[27]

Yet migrant farm labor continued. California's latifundist agribusiness absorbed it, as did cotton picking and construction in Texas, and irrigated farming in Arizona and the Northwest. A construction contractor in El Paso admitted in 1970 to not knowing whether he was hiring legals or illegals: "They come in, apply for a job. They speak pretty good English or maybe very good English. They have a Texas driver's license, a Social Security card. They have a birth permit. It may be somebody else's, but you don't know this. And you find out later that they're illegal aliens. . . . If I need fourteen pipelayers, I need fourteen pipelayers. . . . If I didn't just hire them and there's no others available, how am I going to complete this job? And if they have a five-hundred-dollar-a-day penalty if you don't complete that job, you're going to [hire these men] in the first place. In the second place, I know this man. I know he's a good worker, and I like him. So what do I care, I just give him a job." They came to work, not to steal, he said; he had to pay a competitive wage, or they would find one somewhere else. "You know, you have to look at the illegal alien. I don't blame him. Change my position with his and I'm coming across that bridge. That's all there is to it. The thing I think about most of, with the illegal aliens, is that here's a man that wants to work. If he'll take a chance on going to jail coming across that bridge, if he'll walk from here to Albuquerque, or here to Las Cruces or somewhere, that man just wants to work."[28]

On the other hand, Cesar Chávez fought growers, the American Farm Bureau Federation, and the rival Teamsters union through the 1960s and 1970s to get minimum wages and union contracts. He did so with work strikes, hunger strikes, and nonviolent protest in the manner of Gandhi and Martin Luther King.[29] The Los Angeles community also had its troubles: on August 29, 1970, 20,000 Chicanos marched in East Los Angeles to protest the Vietnam War and the disproportionate presence of Mexican-Americans in the U.S. forces there. More incidents followed, and in 1971 La Raza Unida emerged as a new political party in Los Angeles.[30]

Most Mexican-Americans typically lived in Los Angeles, El Paso, or another city near the border. By 1970 another 100,000 Mexicans and Mexican-Americans lived in Washington and Oregon, more often still doing farm work, which southern Californians had left by that time. Doubling in the 1970s, Latinos displaced African-Americans as Washington's largest non-white minority. Between 1970 and 1980 California's Hispanics rose from 2,400,000 to 4,500,000, Texas's from 1,800,000 to about 3,000,000. Of the entire Latino population of the United States, 46 percent lived in California and Texas in 1970, 51 percent in 1980. These counts underrepresented the undocumented. Mexican demographers estimated that 1,500,000 to 3,800,000 of them were living in the United States in 1980, while American demographers estimated 2,500,000 to 3,500,000. Besides the Mexicans, another 3,000,000 "other Hispanics" (census terminology) lived in the United States—over 750,000 in California, chiefly from El Salvador, Guatemala, and Nicaragua. Wherever their source, they were making homes, families, and lives in the United States, more than 2,000,000 in the L.A. metro area by 1980.[31]

Although Latinos were becoming the largest minority in the West, many others lived there too. Differences among European ethnics whose parents and grandparents had arrived before 1929 dissolved in the face of their differences from Latinos and Asians. A 1967 news story on Los Angeles ethnics was one of the last to observe a range of European stocks yet ignore Asians. It described Chileans, many with German names; 140,000 Germans reading their *California Staatszeitung;* 30,000 Norwegians and 45,000 Swedes; 6,000 Italians (amid 140,000 Italian-Americans) centering in Glendale; 140,000

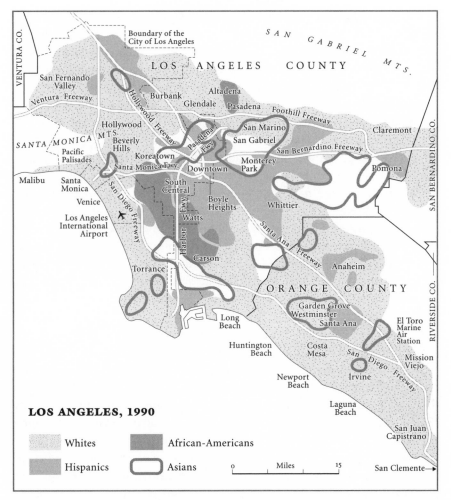

LOS ANGELES, 1990

Whites   African-Americans

Hispanics   Asians   0   Miles   15   San Clemente➤

Russians near Western Avenue; 70,000 Poles; west side Yiddish speakers; Czechs; Canadians; and others. Only a few lines described Chinese, Japanese, and Filipinos.[32] Not a word was said about Koreans, Vietnamese, or east Indians; their arrival and visibility began precisely in 1968, the effective date of the 1965 law and the wind-down of the Vietnam War. In class and occupation, sources, the wealth or poverty they brought with them, and many other ways, the new Asian-Americans were at least as varied as the new Latinos and indeed as the Europeans, recent or long established. The gulfs separating a merchant family from Hong Kong or Taiwan from a boatful of Vietnamese refugees, or an Indian anesthesiologist from a Cambodian peasant, were vast, certainly no less wide than those separating Polish Jews and Sicilians of a previous generation.

Of the traditional Asian minorities, the Japanese received little immigrant reinforcement. They proceeded quietly from the Nisei to the Sansei (third) generation after 1965, shaking off the wartime internment experience and achieving substantial educational and occupational advances. Chinese America, on the other hand, was rejuvenated by new arrivals from Taiwan, the People's Republic, and Hong Kong. The census counted 237,000 Chinese in 1960, 432,000 in 1970, and 806,000 in 1980, a virtual doubling each decade, a greater immigration than the nineteenth century's.[33]

A 1962 executive order by President John F. Kennedy, permitting mainland Chinese refugees in Hong Kong to come to the United States, brought in 15,000 during the next four years. By then the 1965 immigration law, which gave preference to family reunification and encouraged naturalization, made continuing migration possible. San Francisco received upward of 3,000 new Chinese a year in the late 1960s,[34] keeping it the foremost Chinese-American city with 88,000 and California the leading state with 322,340, or three-fourths the national total.[35] Seattle was another likely destination. Alan Lai came to it in 1984, a native of Macao who lived and went to school in Hong Kong; he typified the new Chinese immigrant in several ways. Well traveled in Europe and with a degree in social work, Lai married a Chinese-American, settled in Seattle, and became a U.S. citizen. As such he was able to bring over his parents and a brother and sister, "so that I can at least give them the opportunity." Asked in 1997 whether he would return, he reflected: "I'm settled in here . . . I don't want to see too much interruption in my child's education . . . but after that point would I still be staying here? I don't know, but . . . I'm happy with living in America still."[36]

Taking all Asians together, the 1965 act made an enormous difference. In that year Asians accounted for 7 percent of all immigration. Five years later they were 25 percent, and by 1975 over a third. Then Vietnamese began entering as refugees outside the preference quotas.[37] Both preferences, occupational and family, favored Asian migration; engineers and medical professionals and others "had a stunning impact on the size and ethnic composition of highly educated workers in the United States."[38] Family reunification, building on these initial entrants, took over as the preference of choice after the early 1970s.

In education and wealth, many Asians had no parallel except among the much less numerous Jewish refugees of the 1930s. Other post-1965 Asian immigrants were much less well off and more traditionally resourceless. Despite many exceptions, Hong Kong sent the best-educated, most skilled, and wealthiest immigrants of the 1960s and 1970s. Close behind were the nearly hundred thousand professionals and managers from India. Taiwanese, Japanese, and Koreans, including many brides of American servicemen, ranked next in these categories; then came Filipinos, and finally the Vietnamese, Cambodians, and Hmong from the former Indochina. To generalize, the post-1965 Asian migrants formed two streams: one professional and managerial, often speaking excellent English; the other, peasant-workers, often without English, experience, or skills.[39] Thus some of the new Asian-Americans were third world, others definitely first world.

Small numbers of Koreans and Filipinos had lived in the United States well before 1965. Several thousand Koreans reached Hawaii in 1902 as contract sugar workers, but few were seen on the mainland until the Korean War, when servicemen returned with brides, and after Hawaii gained statehood in 1959. When the 1965 act removed the racial restriction, Koreans began coming to Los Angeles and a few other places in California to grow rice or other intensive crops.[40] A student in 1969 correctly predicted a "tremendous" increase: Korean population grew from under 10,000 in 1970 to over 350,000 in 1980, then rose to almost 700,000 when the next major immigration law passed in 1986.[41] Less equipped than some other new Asian groups to enter professions, they preeminently became owner-operators of small shops, both in their own Koreatown, just west of downtown Los Angeles, and farther south in predominantly black and Latino areas. There they replaced Jewish shopkeepers both as providers of goods and services and as targets of neighborhood resentment, as the riots of 1992 in South Central later showed.[42]

Filipinos, freely admissible from 1898 to 1934, when their country was an American dependency, were reduced to a quota of 100 immigrants a year from then until 1965. Like the earlier Chinese, the pre-1934 Filipinos were a bachelor group, recruited for stoop labor in the Central Valley but prohibited by anti-Asian laws from landowning or marrying, though a few married Mexican women. Numbering about 50,000, they eventually formed an " 'old-timer' generation."[43] Then the 1965 law opened the door. In five years, 241,000 lived on the mainland (135,000 in California), and another 96,000 in Hawaii. By 1980, at 774,000, they outnumbered Japanese-Americans.[44] Together with Asian Indians, Filipinos quickly replaced Europeans as the main source of immigrant physicians, nurses, engineers, and other professionals. As with the Chinese, the sex ratio of the post-1965 Filipinos was balanced, promising a demographically solid future.[45] Also like other Asians, Filipinos used the professional skilled preferences for several years and then shifted chiefly to family preferences, creating a double chain of migration.[46]

Vietnamese, Cambodians, and Hmong could avail themselves of the 1965 act, but they were generally admitted as refugees. They came in stages: first, after Saigon fell on April 30, 1975, an initial 150,000 or so; second, the 450,000 "boat people," who desperately pushed off the Vietnamese shore in rickety crafts, and other refugees who arrived from 1977 to 1982; and finally, in the late 1980s and early 1990s, another 100,000 who had spent several years in prison for working with the Americans. By the end of the 1980s they had become the third-largest and latest Asian group in the United States, behind only the Chinese and Filipinos. In addition, they were parents of 200,000 children born in the United States. In Seattle, people from Vietnam, Laos, and Cambodia sewed outdoor clothes and gear. Others held janitorial or other service jobs.[47] In Fresno, Hmong from Cambodia petitioned the county planning commission in the early 1990s for permission to build a Buddhist pagoda-temple. Counted as one of eighty ethnic groups in the county, "they were the latest to arrive and the lowest on the totem pole." Their story—the repression of religion in Cambodia, their escape from the Khmer Rouge, and their plea to raise their children in Fresno "to be Americans—but to preserve our own culture, too"—earned them their building permit.[48]

Most of the early arrivals were true refugees rather than voluntary immigrants. A teacher in Oakland interviewed some of them and asked why they had left. "Most of them could not answer," she said, "because they had not in fact ever made such a decision. They were victims of a historical event. . . . They had almost all been refugees from the North in 1954 [when the French departed], and some of them had moved several times as a result of war during their lives." As one told her, "We are not immigrants, we are refugees . . . nostalgia is very deep."[49] After the initial wave of 1975 and the first boat people, however, the U.S. government's Orderly Departure Program controlled the migration, and family reunification became the norm.[50]

Many arrived in California, often at military bases like Camp Pendleton in San Diego County, and about half settled in the state. The federal government strove to resettle them, and local churches, both Protestant and Catholic, "adopted" Vietnamese families; like the Catholic parish in Laguna Hills, near Pendleton, they became way stations toward nearby Westminster, soon to be known as Little Saigon. By 1992 about sixteen thousand of Westminster's eighty thousand residents were Vietnamese. Enclaves also developed in Merced, Fresno, Stockton, and San Jose and in the East Bay. Some became fishermen in Monterey. Boat people arrived under sponsorship of governmental and charitable organizations and then moved to inland locations like Oklahoma City. In Garden City, Kansas, two large beef-packing plants opened in 1980 and required about four thousand workers. Mexicans and Vietnamese met that demand, radically changing the size and ethnic composition of the town.[51]

Southeast Asians looked similar only to outsiders. They differed in religion (they might be Buddhist or Catholic); in occupation, from exprofessors of engineering and army brass from Saigon to peasants from the deepest heart of Laos; and in English and business skills (some had worked with Americans, had contacts and credit, and became successful business-people quickly, while others took years training for low-paying jobs). Politically they tended to be conservative, fiercely anti-Communist, and promilitary. In 1992 a Vietnamese refugee was elected (as a Republican) to the Westminster City Council. But "Viet Democrats" already existed, based on "a growing class of educated, professional young Vietnamese-Americans."[52] Finally they differed, according to their disparate origins, in birthrates. The hundred thousand Hmong maintained a fertility rate of nearly ten children per family, about as high as biologically possible. But their American-born children planned on only two or three,[53] just like middle-class professionals from Saigon.

Preferences for family reunification or for the highly skilled under the 1965 act, and the admission of refugees and their families under subsequent legislation, changed the size and composition of Asian America. While some settled around New York or Chicago, metropolitan Los Angeles and other California cities received the bulk. In virtually every group the sex ratio was balanced, the arrivals were of family-forming age, and a substantial fraction spoke English, were educated, and had some money. Most married and reproduced at something like white American rates. Many among them became middle class much faster than previous immigrants, certainly faster than earlier Asians. Between 1970 and the mid-1980s more than 1,500,000 Asians arrived, most of them under the 1965 preferences—about three hundred thousand for their skills and over a million as family members. Additional hundreds of thousands entered as Vietnam refugees.[54]

The fallout from the 1965 act and other immigration laws through the 1970s changed many a local population, probably none more than California's Orange County. Because it was also becoming metropolitan with almost unparalleled speed, Orange County gives us a prime example of how the new immigration operated in context with other profound social changes. Few places were whiter in 1965, and few became more mixed in color and ethnicity by 1987. For a long time much of the county consisted of the Irvine Ranch, the lineal descendant of large Mexican-era land grants of Juan Bandini and his son-in-law Don Abel Stearns.[55] Imitating Los Angeles's explosive growth, Orange reached 30,000 in 1910, 100,000 in the 1920s, 216,000 in 1950, 1,000,000 by 1970, and about 2,000,000 by 1980.

The Santa Ana Freeway (Interstate 5) flowed through it by 1955, tying it to Los Angeles to the north and San Diego to the south. Half of its three million citrus trees disappeared during the 1950s, replaced by houses, offices, and factories. Aerospace and other manufacturing jobs went from none to fifty thousand. Disneyland opened in Anaheim in 1955, the Irvine campus of the University of California and the Fullerton campus of California State University started classes in 1957, and the Los Angeles Angels arrived in 1966.[56] Orange County suddenly had lots of people, as well as major-league baseball, higher education, manufacturing, the military (Seal Beach Navy Station and El Toro Marine Air Station, with Camp Pendleton just to the south), huge shopping malls in Costa Mesa and Newport Beach, of course miles of beaches, including Huntington, Newport, and Laguna, and the world's most famous amusement park.

Then Orange County became ethnically very interesting. Driving through Anaheim, Santa Ana (the county seat), Irvine, or along the Pacific Coast Highway in the early 1970s, travelers saw only the old-stock communities so typical of Los Angeles before 1940. Anaheim, which began as a German colony in the 1880s, had long since lost any such ethnic character, and indeed none of any kind was visible save occasional Cantonese restaurants, also relics of an older immigration.

By the mid-1980s Santa Ana had become a Latino city. Westminster by then had fine Vietnamese restaurants. Signs in Korean and Vietnamese festooned Westminster and Garden Grove. Laguna Beach, where summer seldom ended, continued to sport its surf crowd but also had developed a visible gay community. Mission Viejo, an upper-middle-class suburban kind of place whose ordinances required building in a faux-mission style, "in keeping" with Serra's Mission San Juan Capistrano a couple of miles away, had a high baby boom birthrate that in combination with local educational advantages produced a long succession of pubescent swimming champions. Next to it, Laguna Hills was filled chiefly by the Leisure World retirement community, where the birthrate was nil. Gated communities sprang up through the hills above the beaches, and on the beach, between Capistrano and Richard Nixon's San Clemente, the opulent Ritz-Carlton invited the public to cross its pink marble floors. Orange County had become (by various accounts) an indefinite suburb, a postsuburb, an edge city, a cutting edge.[57]

America's oldest "minority," the Native Americans, were of course not affected by the changes in immigration law, but they assuredly became part of the metropolitan mix after 1965 as they rebounded in size. A phenomenal rise in Indian population began in the 1950s, far greater than biology could explain. Increasing numbers of people told census takers that they were Indians, whether in fact they were full bloods, part Indian, spouses of Indians, children of Indians, or only wanna-be Indians. The birthrate among Indians was higher than among whites (43 in 1964, dropping to 26.7 in 1980), but self-reporting added many more.[58] Across the United States, Indian population had held steady at roughly 350,000 from the late 1920s to 1950. Then it soared to 793,000 in 1970 and to nearly 2,000,000 in 1990,[59] not far from its probable level before European diseases began devastating it. Despite the rise, Indians had become the smallest "major" minority, constituting only 0.8 percent of the total population in 1990, far fewer than blacks (30,400,000), Latinos (24,000,000), or Asians (8,000,000).

In parts of the West, however, Indians formed a visible presence. Oklahoma, New Mexico, Arizona, and California were each home to over 100,000; Texas, Oregon, Washington, Montana, and South Dakota each had more than 25,000.[60] Like everyone else, Indians urbanized during and after World War II. From 7 percent in 1940, they became 45 percent urban by 1970, and 62 percent by 1990. California became the state with the most Indians by 1980, and Los Angeles the largest Indian city, with 47,000.[61] By 1990, although Indian leaders claimed they were undercounted (and they probably were), Los Angeles may have had as many as 100,000, particularly from the larger southwestern groups such as the Navajos, Hopis, and Apaches.[62] As early as 1969, some reports put the Indian population of Los Angeles, Riverside, and Orange counties above 65,000. If so, the metropolitan area included almost one-fourth of the entire American Indian population. Clusters formed in the towns of Bell, Cudahy, and Santa Ana, where the city line meets Orange County.[63] Some 1960s militancy spilled over among Los Angeles Indians, but never as feistily as in South Dakota, in part because of tribal divisions. South Dakota was mostly Lakota, while many groups lived in Los Angeles, including enough Navajos to set them apart from others. Calvin Trillin learned on a visit in 1970 that "young Navajos can't resist country and western," but "Sioux and other Plains Indians are interested strictly in rock."[64]

Many Indians continued to live on reservations. Of the 220,000 Navajos, the largest group, 40,000 had gone to cities by the early 1980s, but 180,000 remained on their large reservation in eastern Arizona, southern Utah, and western New Mexico. Despite mineral and livestock resources and some income from tourism, they were hardly rich. In the 1970s and 1980s some Indians opened bingo games and casinos on reservations. Others won lawsuits over land and fishing rights. The Puyallups, near Tacoma, gained $162,000,000 ($20,000 apiece) in 1988.[65] As always, the "fit" of Native Americans on the North America that had once been exclusively theirs, with the now-overwhelming non-Indian majority, involved mixed signals: reservation or city? Keep the land or sell it? Stay traditional or outcapitalist the whites? At any rate, after 1965, nobody any longer told Indians they should become just like white homesteaders, as the Dawes Act of 1887 had done. White homesteaders were even scarcer.

Alternatives and Countercultures

Another "minority" shed its traditional invisibility after 1965. Orange County's Laguna Beach has been mentioned as having had a gay scene by then, but it was by no means the principal gay community in the West. It was, however, one of many that were part of an unprecedented mass "outing" starting in the late 1960s, though gay men had taken part in the Gold Rush. They lived in northern California, invisibly, in the following decades. Certainly they were present in San Francisco during World War II, and many remained after the war, with more arriving in the 1950s. San Francisco proved to be a port of embarkation during the war not only for ships but also for many previously closeted small-town young people. The first visible organization for gay men, the Mattachine Society, appeared in Los Angeles in late 1950, and by 1952 it had chapters in Laguna, San Diego, Fresno, Bakersfield, and San Francisco.[66] The Bay Area became the epicenter of the movement, "a special place" for gays, both male and female.[67] The Daughters of Bilitis, for lesbians, formed there in 1955.[68]

The 1960s' revolutions in mores permitted gay communities to become much more public, particularly in the rapidly changing West. After 1965 gay people in San Francisco and elsewhere experienced a new openness and a major new migration from all over the country and beyond. In the Castro District (which became the nation's best-known gay area except possibly New York's Greenwich Village) and other San Francisco neighborhoods, gay people probably numbered 90,000 by 1972 and 150,000 by 1978.[69] San Francisco "had become, in comparison to the rest of the country, a liberated zone for lesbians and gay men" and contained the most elaborate and probably the largest gay population anywhere.[70]

The Castro, like much of San Francisco, was changing from blue collar to white, from manufacturing to service occupations and professions. Its enclaves of "old" ethnics—Chinese, Italian, and Irish—carried on somewhat beleaguered existences. But younger, ethnically unidentified men and women, many of them gay, added to the city's rainbow of groups. Working-class Castro developed in the 1970s into a gentrified community of Victorian houses, shops, and delicatessens. On the hills southwest of Market Street and downtown, a true community emerged of a demographically novel type: young people, with few children, or over-sixties, with a somewhat male-skewed sex ratio that, for once, was of cultural but not biological significance. San Francisco had other gay neighborhoods, all older—the Tenderloin, Polk Gulch, and Folsom Street—and gay people lived in the East Bay and Marin County too. But "the Castro, by contrast, was a neighborhood," a creation of the 1970s, "the first gay settlement, the first true gay community, and as such it was a laboratory for the movement. It served as a refuge for gay men and a place where they could remake their lives; now it was to become a model for the new society—a 'gay Israel.' It had an ideology rather different from that of gay groups on the East Coast. . . . It was something new under the sun."[71]

These several hundred thousand young men, and a considerable number of women, migrating to the Bay Area and other western cities—Los Angeles, Seattle, Boise, Denver, and others—believed they could live in ways forbidden in their less tolerant hometowns. Head counts and oral histories remain to be done on just who arrived, and from where, as well as why San Francisco became their destination. As a demographic phenomenon, distinct from its much-written-about cultural and political aspects, the gay migration is still underresearched. But clearly what happened was a new expression of the California Dream—opportunity and liberation, this time gay liberation. Gay liberationists in the 1970s had often been involved in antiwar or student protests. The Beat Generation poets, the Mattachine Society, and the Daughters of Bilitis of the 1950s, followed by the hippies, who coalesced in another San Francisco neighborhood, Haight-Ashbury, in the 1960s, provided historical backdrops for gay liberation in the 1970s.[72]

In a disastrous way the gay communities shrank in the 1980s. AIDS infected and killed females and straight males too, but gay behavior undeniably could transmit the disease. Gay men ran a high incidence of it, and gayness was mistakenly, but often, blamed entirely for it. In the mid-1980s San Francisco's gay population was no larger, and was certainly older, than it had been at its peak in 1978. "Vibrant" no longer best described the Castro. The city reported 634 AIDS cases by mid-1984, fewer than New York but many more proportionately. Starting in 1981 with 24 cases, AIDS found fertile ground in San Francisco, a city with both a gay community and intravenous drug users.[73]

The double demographic consequence was a suddenly high death rate among a by-then thirtyish and fortyish male population and a nearly complete turnoff to further immigration of outlanders to the gay community. By the late 1980s the rate of new cases had fallen sharply, but the death rate among the already infected rose further because of AIDS's long gestation. The chief AIDS officer of the San Francisco Health Department, Dr. George Rutherford, said that "the epidemic is having a huge economic impact on the city, and it will have a huge demographic impact as well, because a large proportion of the population is going to die."[74] Thus ended a major mass migration.

The 1960s brought other expressions of "different" social organization, notably the hippie drug culture of San Francisco's Haight-Ashbury and the reawakened ghost town of Jerome, Arizona, as well as communes and ashrams.[75] Communes came and went, mostly oblivious of the long history of American communitarian societies. How many there were in the 1960s and 1970s will never be known, nor will the numbers who participated. A few achieved national notoriety, particularly a colony known as Rajneesh-puram, in remote north-central Oregon about halfway between Bend and The Dalles. Founded by a charismatic Indian, Bhagwan Shree Rajneesh, it flourished from 1981 to 1985. Several thousand cultists, visitors, and students lived there or passed through in 1984–1985. They ranged from young urban professionals seeking religious revelation to social dropouts, looking, as one writer put it, for "a year-round summer camp." They were not local people or surplus Oregon farm kids, but more akin to the "countercultural com-munes, survivalist enclaves, and protofascist settlements" that popped up in isolated parts of the postwar Pacific Northwest. They also presaged the larger, more bourgeois migration from the metropolitan to the interior West of the later 1980s. Rajneeshpuram collapsed in 1985, for several reasons not uncommon to earlier communitarian colonies.[76]

Cults and communes were not new in the post-1965 West. The tradition of California bohemians traces back to Bret Harte in the Gold Rush, Jack London and Mary Austin at Carmel around 1900, Henry Miller at Big Sur in the 1940s, and the Beat Generation poets of 1950s San Francisco.[77] The unravelings of the 1960s and 1970s produced a much larger number of com-munes, enclaves, dropout dens, and the like, of numbers uncounted, and of short life spans. Opposition to the Vietnam War fed such activity, a common feature of which was a suspicion of authority and social rules.

Such pervasive counterculturalism had never happened before. But nei-ther had the baby boom.

The 1973 Oil Crisis, Slow Growth, and Environmental Demography

Concerns about environmental protection took off in the 1960s as never before. Significant numbers of Americans began to question openly whether unregulated growth—of the population, of cities, or of the economy—rep-resented progress and a better society, as traditionally assumed. With regard to the history of population, environmentalism took the form of slow-growth measures, channeling or limiting where people went. In the 1970s political crises overseas led to grave shortages of oil and soaring prices for it, in turn triggering a race to develop fossil fuel resources in the mountain West. Environmentalism, on the one hand, a new resource exploitation frenzy, on the other: this polarity joined environment to population in new but opposing ways.

No one has ever proved a causal relationship between the end of the baby boom and the rapid spread of the modern environmental movement, but it seems more than coincidental that both happened in the 1960s. The abrupt decline in birthrates after 1964 paralleled surging public support for environmental improvement and new laws to bring it about. In one peculiar and sharp case the office of Mayor Wes Uhlman of Seattle issued a staff paper in 1970 recommending "environmental goals" that Seattle should reach by 1975. Besides calling for more green space, taxes on big cars, and lower density, the paper urged a tax on third children. Physicians would collect the tax on "each child born to a family beyond the first two," and additional children "would bear larger taxes." The proceeds would "support planned-parenthood activities and eventually subsidize flat-rate abortion fees."[78]

The idea proved a bit extreme, but its linkage of population control with environmental improvement was not. Western communities from Boulder to Petaluma were beginning to implement slow-growth ordinances by 1970.[79] Portland later led large cities in growth controls; a 1980 poll found that 59 percent of Oregon residents agreed that the state's population was enlarging too fast.[80] Of all the western states in the postwar period, Oregon consistently had the lowest birthrate and some of the strongest environmental politics, a major shift from the 1930s when chambers of commerce, the State Planning Board, and the Army Corps of Engineers—a fairly routine combination of forces in those days—joined to build the irrigation and flood control system called the Willamette Valley Project. By 1969 the legislature was requiring localities to devise planning ordinances, and in 1973 it enacted a statewide land use planning law, shrinking the average home-building lot in Portland from 12,800 to 8,500 square feet in a decade.[81] To fight "sprawl" like southern California's, the same law created a Land Conservation and Development Commission to ensure that growth would be "up, not out"—i.e., that it would take place within "urban growth boundaries" around cities. Voters approved the law in three statewide referenda.[82]

Along the Pacific Coast the low point of the baby bust undoubtedly coincided with the high tide of environmentalism. From 1973 to the late 1980s, however, environmentalism either never took firm hold in the interior West or retreated in the face of the international oil crisis. The OPEC oil embargo against the United States and other industrial countries in 1973–1974, reinforced in 1979 by the revolution in Iran, set off a frenzied search for energy alternatives. The mountain West, possessing immense deposits of coal and oil shale, became more than ever a prime target of development. The energy crisis revitalized boomer boosterism and environmental exploitation.

Once again, as in the gold and silver rushes of the nineteenth century and the oil booms of the early twentieth, a new spate of firecracker communities popped up all over the West. Wyoming, which had scarcely been growing at all, and those parts of Colorado, Utah, Idaho, and Montana with fossil fuel deposits boomed. The Alaska pipeline, another 1970s creation, gave that new state a long-term boost. Northwestern Colorado and adjacent parts of Utah, which lost population during the 1960s, nearly doubled in the 1970s from oil shale development. Coal strip mines sprinkled boomtowns over western North Dakota, Wyoming, and Montana. Examples abound and say much about the volatile mix of international fuel demand, eagerness for jobs in the oil patch, and decisions by corporations remote from the communities they affected.

Craig, Colorado, up to then a stable county-seat town of about eight thousand, did not handle the rush of construction workers and coal miners very well. Schools and the town hospital became overcrowded, while drug use, suicide, and crime rates soared.[83] Gillette, Wyoming, became notorious for the "Gillette syndrome," "social unrest and population impact [that] became a generic label applied to western boomtowns," very much like the mining places of the late nineteenth century. Farmington, New Mexico, near the huge Four Corners power plant whose sulfurous smoke threw haze all over the Grand Canyon and the Southwest, was another locale where dysfunction became ordinary. In Rock Springs, Wyoming, the population doubled in the early 1970s; but calls to police quadrupled, and mental health cases increased nine times over.[84]

The town of Rifle, Colorado, about ninety miles south of Craig on Interstate 70, went through even worse boom and bust dislocations. Since World War I the existence of vast deposits in the surrounding mountains of shale suffused with oil had been common knowledge, but no one had devised a way to extract it at a price that could compete with drilled oil. By 1974, with oil at embargo-high prices, several companies decided it was worth a try and spent $210,000,000 on leases. Soon roads, apartment buildings, schools, and excavating equipment appeared.

Oil prices leaped again in 1979 with the Iranian crisis, and in 1980 Exxon rumbled into western Colorado. It issued a "white paper" in July 1980, promising an investment of five hundred billion dollars; six strip mines each bigger than Utah's Bingham Canyon, the largest then existing; twenty-two thousand workers at each mine; and thousands more at each of dozens of new processing facilities. Exxon then began building a pilot town of twenty-five thousand, dwarfing nearby Rifle's twenty-two hundred. Workers, many of them young men with new families, poured into its prefab housing and devoured its groceries and services at ballooning prices.

In early May 1982, after investing almost a billion dollars, Exxon suddenly decided oil shale would not be competitive and pulled out. More than two thousand jobs evaporated, and further thousands of people were soon out of work. Many were stuck there. Like an Indian tribe of the 1800s suddenly infected from the outside with guns and whiskey and then abruptly deprived of them, Rifle could not revert to the quiet farming and ranching place it had been before. It settled into long-term stagnation.[85]

The Department of Labor reported in early 1986 that mining and smelting jobs in the seven Rocky Mountain states had plummeted from 94,000 in 1981 to 24,000 by October 1985, with a loss of two billion dollars in wages. The bust in oil shale was only part of it. Copper mining was disappearing too: from 94 mines in the region in 1981, 32 remained at the end of 1985. Montana, the onetime leading producer, no longer had any active copper mines at all. Atlantic Richfield (ARCO), by then the owner of the Anaconda smelter, shut it down in 1980, and in 1983 it closed its Butte operations, snuffing out 3,325 Montana jobs between 1970 and 1983. Across the mountain states, oil rigs closed too, from 568 in early 1982 to 254 four years later.

It was not the spotted owl or tree huggers that cost the interior West so many of its jobs in these years. Price competition from elsewhere in the world, as well as mechanization of these industries, lay fundamentally at the root of these changes. Small farms and metals mining had been contracting for years; the roller coaster of the 1970s and 1980s, touching many localities, dramatized long-term trends. By 1988 only Unocal operated anything related to oil shale around Rifle, a "research plant." Although (thanks to Exxon's inconstancy) the go-stop cycle was particularly severe around Rifle and Craig, they were hardly unique.[86]

Environmental concerns reinforced world market price squeezes and technological demands to modify long-standing western attitudes about development. President Jimmy Carter canceled many a dreamed of public works project in the West in 1977. Even in the Reagan years, when the president and his interior secretary, James Watt, took care to protect ranchers, developers, agribusiness, and the giveaway 1872 mining law, federal agencies drew back from further great projects in the West. The Bureau of Reclamation announced in 1987 that "the most gigantic projects are already done" or "being built or already rejected on economic or environmental grounds." The massive Garrison Diversion Project in North Dakota, which with bipartisan support would have spent an estimated seven hundred thousand dollars for each farm it irrigated, died along with other projects that in the Roosevelt era would likely have sailed on.[87] The Bureau of Reclamation would henceforth concentrate on "managing existing projects, conserving water, and assuring good water quality and environmental protection."[88]

Mining, logging, and ranching continued in the West, but they occupied steadily declining numbers of people. A "latter-day gold rush" might still take an Elko, Nevada, from eight thousand in 1980 to sixteen thousand by 1988; Deadwood, South Dakota, might still earn a living from open-pit gold mining; some towns fought to *acquire* nuclear waste dumps. Environmentalism did not conquer all.[89] Yet by the 1990s a newspaper as conservative as the *Chicago Tribune* swung its weight behind environmentalism and against federal subsidies to ranchers and mining companies. *Sports Illustrated,* read by a good many hunters and fishermen, damned the 1872 mining law, the U.S. Forest Service's "below-cost sales of trees from national forests," and lax enforcement of grazing guidelines by the Reagan and Bush administrations.[90]

By the late 1980s environmentalism pervaded much of the coastal West. Slow-growth campaigns touched southern California. The Los Angeles suburbs of Alhambra, Monterey Park, Sierra Madre, and San Gabriel limited new apartment construction; Riverside County, then the fastest growing in the Los Angeles Basin, made developers pay "impact fees" for roads, sewers, and other municipal services. By 1987 in Orange County slow growth "forged an unlikely alliance between leftist Democrats and rightist Republicans," all of them sick of heavy traffic.[91] San Diego's City Council in 1987 restricted new housing units to eight thousand a year.[92] Northward, Seattle imposed caps on the size of office buildings (though not until after the seventy-six-story Columbia Center had materialized in 1985).[93] Although office parks sprawled east of Seattle from Redmond to Issaquah, producing serious rush-hour congestion, environmentalists in Seattle, Portland, and Denver kept pressing for slow growth, regional zoning, and light rail to reduce commuter traffic.[94] Nowhere probably was the change in mood before and after 1970 more evident than in Colorado. In May 1970, after the usual competition, Denver was chosen as the site for the 1976 Winter Olympics. The local argument was that "people coming for the games will return." However, an anti-Olympics movement, critical of crowds, density, and new settlers, had already begun at Evergreen. By 1972 Democratic state legislators Robert Jackson in Pueblo and Richard Lamm in Denver led the antis. The Sierra Club and other groups climbed on board; John Denver wrote a slow-growth song; and the Olympics were banished.[95] By the 1990s environmentalists and cattle ranchers had joined to preserve mountain meadows and vistas from the creep of subdivisions.[96]

In polar-opposite ways, environmental concerns affected western population from the 1960s through the 1980s, the slow-growth movement suppressing it, the search for minerals and new energy sources promoting it. The West could still suffer from economic decisions made far away, like Exxon's devastation of Rifle. But new migrants were often far from development-minded. Seeking their own environmentalist agenda, hoping to keep the West (or their corner of it) "as it was," they were ready to prevent any Gillette syndromes from arising around their new homes.[97]

Older residents were not always doormats of distant boardrooms either. Town officials in Meeker, Colorado (1980 population: 2,356), exactly halfway between Craig and Rifle, "told the oil companies that the town and county wanted no part of the oil shale construction camps and the problems that went with them."[98] If Meeker could opt for slow growth in the midst of the oil shale boom, other towns could resist the meretricious goodies too.

Metropolises and Leading Edges

In the years following 1965, people continued to migrate to the West and, more than before, to move within it. The interior and coastal Wests continued to grow at different rates and to attract whites and minorities differently. In general, Latinos, African-Americans, Asians, and American Indians increasingly preferred the coastal and metropolitan West, but so did whites, and the West led all other regions, even in most years the Sunbelt South, in attracting migrants, whether American-born or foreign-born, white or otherwise. The South's newcomers, however, were preponderantly American-born (plus Cubans), while the West took in the lion's share of Asians and non-Cuban Latinos.[99] The West also led all regions in natural increase because its people were young, and a young age structure almost always translates into high birth and low death rates. As in most migrations, the twentyish and better educated moved in greater proportion than the very young or the elderly, and thus the Great Plains lost educated and energetic youth to the coast and metropolises.[100] California, Arizona, and other coastal and border states received many retirees, but young migrants more than balanced them, so that the region's median age, the Great Plains aside, remained below the level of other regions.

While people flocked to the border and coastal states, others fled the northern plains and Rockies, particularly Kansas, Nebraska, the Dakotas, Wyoming, Montana, and Idaho. The fuel frenzy of the late 1970s temporarily sucked people into Montana, Wyoming, Utah, and Colorado, but otherwise they lost people from the 1960s through 1987.[101] Texas benefited much more and much longer from the oil crisis, attracting tens of thousands from the Midwest and even gaining more than it lost to California into the mid-1980s, when the westward migration resumed, but thereupon Texas overextended itself, and the fossil fuels slump finally reached it.[102]

Put together, the West's in-migration and age and sex structure gave it an exceptionally balanced and attractive climate for expanding its population and its economy. It did so, during the 1970s and 1980s, in the form of large— and, to the eastern mind-set, "sprawling"—metropolises whose shape was becoming visible in the 1940s and in certain places, Los Angeles in particular, well before then. Since 1940 most of the nation's fastest-growing metropolitan areas have been in the West.[103] Elsewhere the trend has been for core cities to stabilize or shrink, suburbs to gain, and smaller cities to grow faster than large ones. While not all western core cities grew—San Francisco and Denver, politically hemmed in, shrank a little—others did, notably Los Angeles, Seattle, and Phoenix. In 1950 the West contained only two of the country's fourteen million–plus metropolitan areas (Los Angeles and San Francisco). By the late 1980s it had twelve of the country's thirty-seven, if we include Texas in the West, and Denver, San Francisco, Colorado Springs, Las Vegas, Houston, and Austin crowded the top ten destinations of mobile baby boomers.[104]

None of this should have been surprising. The West had been the most *urban* region since the late nineteenth century, and by the late twentieth it was becoming the most *metropolitan,* which is what old-style urbanism was metamorphosing into. Its suburbs and edges were making previously rural and distant counties metropolitan, while its largest core cities completely outstripped those elsewhere.[105]

By 1987 commuting was changing. Instead of the traditional suburb to center trip, more workers were traveling suburb to suburb, and their distances averaged 50 percent less. The many-centered metropolis was replacing the city-plus-suburb format of urban life. Of the two dozen fastest-growing cities in the country during the 1980s, eighteen were in California, most of them part of the Los Angeles complex, and all but two of the others were in Arizona, Texas, Nevada, and Colorado.[106] The suburb to suburb commuting and living pattern, avoiding the core city, emerged in these years most definitively in greater Los Angeles because it was already decentralized. The prime case, once again, was Orange County, which after 1960 became "in the minds of many . . . the quintessential post-suburban metropolis," governmentally fragmented, without an obvious center, but multiplying ten times over from 1950 to 1980.[107]

The old categories of rural vs. urban did not fit California or much else of the West by 1987, though they lingered strongly in parts of the interior, in self-perception perhaps more than in reality. "Rural" suggests agricultural, cultivated, farmed. But most of the West's enormous agricultural activity took place in *metropolitan* counties. Los Angeles County before 1950, after all, had been the country's premier agricultural county as well as the fastest-growing large city. After 1965 metropolitan agriculture described places like

Bakersfield, Fresno, Napa, and Sonoma and almost all of California except the Sierra Nevada and the far north. Irrigated, mechanized, capital-intensive agriculture, staffed by migrant workers, was metropolitan rather than rural in any traditional sense. A rural area next to a metropolis had to fight hard to keep its farms and traditional character, usually through various low-growth techniques, as Marin County did just north of the Golden Gate Bridge. Parts of Marin turned into affluent suburbs of San Francisco anyway. Some family farms were preserved, but real estate prices tempted older residents to sell, traffic worsened, and Marin County became "a commuter target for people from Sonoma County" just north or the city just south.[108] Those large areas in the West that continued to be nonfarmed, nonmined, and even nonlogged were not truly rural, but wilderness; people neither lived in them nor subsisted on their products.

After 1965—actually after 1950 on the plains—what might best be called the unpeopled West expanded. A reverse frontier process took place: young people did not seek homesteads or small towns; they left the family farms, where technology and consolidation obviated farmhands, either from the family or hired. Instead of peopling county seats and railroad whistle-stops, Westerners aggregated in medium-size cities like Billings, Boise, Logan, Bend, Yakima, or Yuma (to pick some at random) and, more often, in the rings surrounding truly large places.

As a geographer pointed out in 1988, in the entire vast region—almost a quarter of the United States—from a line just north of Las Vegas, Phoenix, and Albuquerque all the way to Canada, except around Denver and Salt Lake City, fewer than four million lived. That was truly the interior West, the mythic West that romantic conservatives insisted on regarding as the "real West."[109] Much more "real," in terms of where people chose to live, was the metropolitan West. In the 1980s over 85 percent of population expansion happened there, and every western state except Wyoming and North Dakota gained people, most spectacularly Nevada (by 49 percent), California (23 percent), and Texas (18 percent).[110] After the oil shale collapse, places in the interior West whose economies relied on resource extraction took heavy hits. The unpeopled West grew in size, as Americans abandoned it, and in romantic fabulosity; the peopled West, however, grew in numbers and wealth.

Purple Mountains and Fruited Plains: The Interior West

The full story of internal migration, baby bust, immigrants, minorities, and Anglos across the interior West after 1965 would be impossibly detailed. Only under a statistician's green eyeshade could we see the precise differences and trend lines among the dozens of metropolitan areas and the 777 counties west of the ninety-eighth meridian. But some generalizations are possible and called for; a few bellwether communities reveal the larger tale.

On the Great Plains from Texas to Canada and west to the Rockies, the populations of the majority of farm and ranch counties slowly and unremittingly attrited, decade by decade. Small farms increasingly could not compete with larger units, whether run by families or agribusiness companies. Farms consolidated; young men and women either were not needed to run them or preferred not to and left for cities. Small businesses in county seat towns dried up for want of customers, and so did the towns. As their median age rose, some counties verged on geriatric status, yet physicians and hospitals thinned out too. Rarely was there an exception. Among them were Garden City and Dodge City, Kansas, with their newly arrived Vietnamese and Mexican packinghouse workers; Bismarck and Pierre, the Dakota state capitals; Rapid City and Lead, tourist centers for the Black Hills. A few outposts like Scottsbluff and Minot held their own. In Oklahoma, farm counties lost, while the sprawl of Oklahoma City ran for forty miles or more west to El Reno and south past Norman. In Texas, the panhandle and High Plains mechanized, driving people from the wheat and cotton fields, while oil towns like Odessa and Midland and the cotton and college mecca of Lubbock, the largest city on the plains west of the ninety-eighth, kept growing. New to the 1990s (thanks to the 1986 immigration law) was the sudden surge in the border towns, big ones like El Paso and the smaller ports of entry of Presidio, Del Rio, Eagle Pass, and Laredo, reflecting more border traffic, more migrants, more trade, and more *maquilas,* the American-owned factories south of the border.

Parts of the plains had been losing people ever since homesteading peaked in 1913, but the shrinkage became serious in the 1950s and 1960s. Since settlement days the plains saw towns come and go; Kansas by itself may have gained and lost as many as six thousand.[111] In western Oklahoma several counties lost population steadily starting early in the century, almost as soon as they were created.[112] In all Texas west of the Pecos except El Paso, an area as large as South Carolina, only fifty-five thousand were left in 1987, thirteen thousand of them in Pecos, its largest town. With dozens of substantial mountain peaks, the University of Texas's McDonald Observatory, the border towns like Presidio, and the "Republic of Texas" secessionists of 1997 near Fort Davis, the area was not really depopulated but never populated.[113] Depopulation more accurately described land a few score miles to the northeast, where the southern tip of the Ogallala Aquifer had been mined sufficiently by the mid-1980s to force a comeback of dryland farming. In southwestern Kansas, around Sublette, estimates fell rapidly on how long the aquifer would last—some believed no longer than 2000—though despite rising concern and much official hand wringing, the center-pivot pumps kept mining the groundwater to grow feed for a million head of cattle.[114]

The baby boom produced a hefty cohort of farm kids in the 1950s and 1960s and hence a swelling supply of potential young farmers twenty-some years later. But the baby bust after 1964 and a series of crunches that beset farming in the 1980s—the high cost of fuel, inflation, unusually poor crop and livestock prices, and finally a scorching drought in 1988—depressed farm population to the lowest level since settlement. Between 1960 and 1985 the ratio of farm children (the pool from which future farmers would come) to farm adults dropped by almost half. When owner-operators aged, some leased their farms to children or nieces or nephews. Others who held on until they died would often have seen their land absorbed through estate sales into larger units. As the demographer Calvin Beale pointed out in the late 1980s, "The decline of the farm population from nearly 25 percent of all Americans in 1940 to just 2 percent by the mid-1980s is surely one of the most profound and dramatic changes in our national life. Agriculture is larger than ever in output, but only one-sixth as many people are on farms now (5 million) as were at the beginning of World War II (30 million)."[115] In 1987 the national farm population in fact dipped below 5,000,000, a flat 2 percent of the population, to 4,986,000. Once before it had been exactly that. But that had been in 1800, when farmers and their families were 94 percent of the American people.[116]

For young people, several routes led away from the farm or the small town. The armed forces remained the same efficient mixer and mover of young people through the Cold War that it had been in World War II. Many left home for the state universities in Manhattan, Stillwater, Lubbock, or other such way stations to professional or business careers, and they never came back. A very few became rodeo riders, leaving "dying small towns" to relive a nostalgic myth. The countryside even produced homeless people: an Erie, North Dakota, farm woman took her three children to a homeless shelter in Fargo in 1989 because local farmers could no longer afford her husband's tree care service and the family had gone broke.[117]

Yet some areas held steady or even gained. Center-pivot irrigation from the Ogallala Aquifer preserved a few and made others prosper. The 184 counties lying over the aquifer gained over 87,000 people (about 4 percent) between 1960 and 1990. Southwestern Kansas, parts of the Texas Panhandle, and the Platte River valley in Nebraska were minor growth spots. Oklahoma, Nebraska, North Dakota, Montana, and Wyoming lost residents between 1985 and 1988, but Texas, Kansas, South Dakota, Colorado, and New Mexico increased moderately.[118]

The tales of two cities, Garden City in Kansas and Miles City in Montana, contrast what happened to plains people from the late 1960s to the late 1980s. One grew; the other, much more typically, did not. Garden City and its surrounding county actually doubled from 16,093 in 1960 to 33,070 in 1990, when most counties in western Kansas dropped by 10 to 50 percent. In a sea of plains counties from Texas to Canada, few escaped population decline. People wondered whether southwestern Kansas, the center of the 1930s Dust Bowl and the early 1950s mini–Dust Bowl, would ever grow again. It did so, unexpectedly, by combining technology, the economics of beef production, and immigrants. After traditional sugar beet farming had died out along the Arkansas River in the 1950s, center-pivot technology[119] introduced plenty of water to grow alfalfa and wheat. Alfalfa fattens cattle. Feedlots multiplied in southwestern Kansas, and on them, six-hundred-pound yearlings devoured the alfalfa, marbled their way to about twelve hundred pounds, and then took a final train ride to slaughterhouses in Kansas City.

In 1980 this economy changed. A company called IBP Inc. (formerly Iowa Beef Processors) built a packing plant, the largest anywhere, at Garden City. Three years later another packinghouse opened there, while nearby Dodge City and Liberal gained three more. By 1987 the two Garden City companies, with four thousand workers, killed and packed 2,400,000 cattle. Kansas was outmeatpacking even Texas and California.[120]

Pre-1980 Garden City resembled other Kansas towns and cities by having a white majority and a 10 or 15 percent Latino minority that dated back to 1905–1910, when the Santa Fe, Missouri-Kansas-Texas, and other railroads were bringing workers up from Mexico. To this stable mix came two new groups after 1980: fresh contingents of Mexicans (and a few Central Americans) and about two thousand Vietnamese, Cambodians, Laotians, and Chinese, to work in the packinghouses. The Asians formed 8 percent of Garden City's population by 1987. They were young, mostly single men, although some women and children arrived too. Turnover was fairly high, but replacements kept coming from California or other new enclaves in a typical chain migration pattern. The Vietnamese were second-wave migrants—not the first group that exited with American forces but boat people. Of those in Garden City, nearly half were from one fishing village. Some of the first to arrive had previously worked in the aircraft plants in Wichita, about two hundred miles east, but had been laid off. The original chain often ran from California refugee camps to aircraft factories—first in southern California, then in Wichita—to Garden City. The packinghouses also attracted job-seeking young whites, along with Latinos and Asians. Each of these groups numbered about two thousand by 1985. The host community displayed some prejudices, but in general it coped fairly well.[121]

Miles City, Montana, enjoyed no such infusion of capital or people. The largest town in the Yellowstone Valley east of Billings, it barely held its own from the 1920s to the 1980s. Its population peaked at ninety-six hundred in 1980, then fell to eighty-five hundred in 1990; another three thousand dotted the rest of Custer County. Cattle ranching had always been its economic life. With no Ogallala Aquifer and therefore no alfalfa, its cattle ate prairie grass, which requires rainfall and, even in rainy years, many acres to supply a herd large enough to support a family. In the 1980s drought struck repeatedly, the worst summer being 1988. A rancher named John L. Moore then reported that "in the last 11 months we have received only two inches of moisture. I can look at the reservoirs and count the days before they will be finished."[122] Cattle prices stayed low; land values sank while mortgages and machinery remained costly. Many ranchers were forced out of business. Young men went to work for large, often corporate ranches or left the area. Land worth $135 an acre in the 1970s fell below $50 in the 1980s. Even a large, prudently run spread faced over $600,000 a year in interest payments, and its foreman observed that "there's no way to make that kind of money running cattle." Country hamlets folded, and larger towns like Miles City retained what business there was in supplying ranchers. New ranches became "as rare as two-headed calves," and "young rancher" by 1988 was "a contradiction in terms."[123]

From the 1920s through the 1980s the trend line in Great Plains population hardly deflected at all. Southwestern Kansas was a rare case of growth. It combined fortunate geology (the aquifer) with expanding market demand (those billions of Big Macs and Whoppers) with an available immigrant labor force (the Latinos and Vietnamese). Miles City, and most of the plains, had none of the above.

The Rockies and Great Basin, in contrast, sprouted a few metropolises. At the northern end sat Boise, like an oasis, and about three hundred miles southeast of it lay Utah's population crescent extending from Ogden to Salt Lake City to Provo. A leap five hundred miles eastward across the mountains found another crescent along Colorado's Front Range from Fort Collins south through Denver and its sprawling suburbs to Colorado Springs and Pueblo. Another three hundred miles south lay Santa Fe and Albuquerque. A good day's drive southwest, in Arizona, were Tucson and the sprawl of Phoenix. Las Vegas formed another oasis, almost equidistant from Phoenix, Salt Lake City, and Los Angeles. Here were truly America's wide-open spaces, now with metropolises scattered throughout them.

Smaller places expanded, in ways often strange to western traditions. On the downside, Gillette gave its name to the "syndrome of social pathologies" shared by Rock Springs and Evanston in Wyoming and the oil shale towns of Colorado.[124] On the upside, yuppiedom flocked to the skiing, golf, and condos of Vail and Aspen, Colorado; Jackson Hole, Wyoming; Big Sky, Montana; and Park City, Utah. Santa Fe and Taos led the nation in art galleries per capita; Lake Havasu City, Arizona, became famous as a community for retirees. In their contemporary forms, all these were creations of the 1960s, 1970s, and 1980s. Except for isolated spots like Elko, Nevada (a new gold rush), or Moab, Utah (uranium), and the short-lived synthetic fuels boomtowns, mining languished. Along with ranching it occupied an ever-smaller niche in mountain state economies, yielding in economic muscle (though not yet in political strength) to the defense and tourist industries and to service jobs in restaurants, motels, land mortgage-insurance companies, and state and local government.

Throughout the intermountain West from the Rockies to the Sierras and Cascades, several keys to success buoyed local growth. Transportation of course was essential; just as pre-1920 settlement required railroads, so post-1965 mobility required jet planes and interstate highways. Package tours to Las Vegas, direct flights between Aspen and La Guardia, and ever-simpler long-distance flying and driving shrank the West and made it accessible. The keys were tourism and resorts; metropolitan spread; environmental ruthlessness, spiced with an occasional sense that historic preservation pays; federal impact; new, especially high-tech manufacturing; higher education; and capitalizing on the retirement proclivities of a population growing older and wealthier.

Tourism and resort activity seemed to emerge everywhere, from Coeur d'Alene south to Tombstone, from Denver across to Reno, in small towns and large. Here the mountain states had an insuperable advantage. The Great Plains have a wonderful beauty, but their subtlety escapes almost anyone who was not raised on them. The mountains, parks, and forests need no such introduction. While population stagnated on the plains, it kept rising amid the mountains.

Metropolitan development, whose many aspects included concentration of governmental and private services, assured every state except Wyoming and Montana, even Alaska, of at least one hundred thousand–plus city by the 1980s. In Oklahoma and Kansas, metropolises accounted for all the net growth. Sometimes annexation inflated a city's numbers, but most did very well whether they formally absorbed their suburbs or not. Phoenix, for example, did some annexing, but its metropolitan area included several places like Mesa, Tempe, Sun City, Chandler, and Glendale that not only

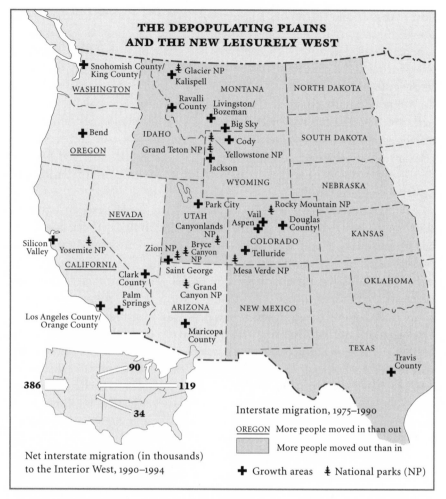

THE DEPOPULATING PLAINS
AND THE NEW LEISURELY WEST

Snohomish County/
King County
WASHINGTON

Glacier NP
Kalispell
MONTANA
NORTH DAKOTA

Ravalli
County
Livingston/
Bozeman

Big Sky

Bend
IDAHO
OREGON
Grand Teton NP
Cody
Yellowstone NP
SOUTH DAKOTA

Jackson

WYOMING
NEBRASKA

Park City
Rocky Mountain NP

NEVADA
UTAH
Canyonlands
NP
Vail
Aspen
Douglas
County

Silicon
Valley
Yosemite NP
Zion NP
Bryce
Canyon
NP
COLORADO
Telluride
KANSAS

CALIFORNIA
Clark
County
Saint George
Mesa Verde NP
OKLAHOMA

Palm
Springs
Grand
Canyon NP
ARIZONA
NEW MEXICO

Los Angeles County/
Orange County

Maricopa
County

TEXAS
Travis
County

90

386   119

34

Interstate migration, 1975–1990

OREGON More people moved in than out

More people moved out than in

Net interstate migration (in thousands)
to the Interior West, 1990–1994

✚ Growth areas   🌲 National parks (NP)

kept their independence but themselves each approached or passed a hundred thousand during the 1970s and 1980s.

Phoenix deserves special notice because it exemplifies in high style both metropolitan development and environmental ruthlessness. Bruce Babbitt, a descendant of pioneer ranchers who became a Democratic governor and U.S. secretary of the interior, recalled in 1977 how Newlands Act water projects made Phoenix subdivisions possible, some fraudulently. "Prior to 1950 Arizona was really a cowtown, start to finish," he remarked. "Phoenix was really a backwater." But it changed "overnight; became a big, dynamic, urban state in the '50s."[125]

Zig Kalnitz, an ex-marine whose father arrived from New York and bought a bar in Tempe in 1956, remembered the changes on Mill Avenue,

near Arizona State University. In the 1950s Tempe "was an old, rather traditional community, a small college town." Arizona State had about ten thousand students, and the bar clientele was "pinochle players sitting around at
the great big old oak tables that were probably about eighty years old. Most
of the guys were from sixty to eighty, and they'd sit for hours." In the 1960s
the scene gradually changed. The pinochle gerontocracy gave way to students by 1965, and the university expanded to more than twenty thousand,
mixing (Kalnitz thought) kids avoiding service in Vietnam and returning
veterans on marijuana, hash, and by 1970 LSD. Then bikers arrived. He had
to hire uniformed and armed security guards to keep them out, and finally
his father sold the bar.[126]

Another businessman on Mill Avenue, Victor Linoff, ran an antiques
shop and furniture-refinishing store with his wife from 1973 to the late 1980s,
and they too saw changes. Businesses of "a bohemian nature" catering to
"college-aged people" gave way to stores attracting "yuppies, demographically young adults and young professionals, people in their mid-twenties up
to probably their mid-forties" (in other words, baby boomers reaching
adulthood). Linoff hated urban renewal, which "just literally tore out the
heart of old Scottsdale and redid it completely to build that civic plaza," he
recalled. Tempe, envying Scottsdale's success, brought in a gung ho federal
redevelopment director who was "of the school of literally what's called slash
and burn; let's just tear it all out, and we'll put something else new in there."
Linoff and his wife "tried to purchase nearly every historical building down
here" to preserve and rehabilitate them. He believed they had failed, but so
had the crowded sterility of "renewal." Ignoring Arizona State, Tempe
"steamrolled their redevelopment in deference to the developer, with no
regard for either the community as a whole, nor the people who have lived
and worked in this area."[127] Such was one merchant's opinion. Many agreed,
however, that "urban renewal" raised profits more than population.

In the 1980s western communities more often avoided slash-and-burn
renewal and tried to make all they could from whatever history they had
(and some "history" they never had). From "forts" and "cowtowns" along
the interstates in the Great Plains to Denver's Sixteenth Street mall and in
scrubbed-up historic districts all the way from Austin, Texas, to Calgary to
Old Sacramento, the 1980s and 1990s brought a decided shift of emphasis.
Environmentalism frequently appealed to the same people who supported
historic preservation, and the aging of those born from the 1920s through
the baby boom provided a more affluent and nostalgic demographic base.

In Phoenix there seemed to be room for all: the retirees of Scottsdale; the
leisure seekers who first vacationed at the Biltmore, the Wigwam, or the
Hyatt Regency at Gainey Ranch and then decided to stay; the old-timers, like

"the dean of Arizona four-wheelers," Ed Fouts, who knew every rock within a hundred miles;[128] the yuppies and historic preservationists; the corporate executives at Dial Inc. and elsewhere. Among them too were slow-growth advocates, upset by 1987 with "foul air and mounting traffic congestion" and fond of pointing out that Phoenix had gone from seventeen square miles in the 1950s to over four hundred, re-creating Los Angeles's "problems" of "a weak downtown district surrounded by miles of low-density sprawl poorly served by public transportation, oriented to the automobile and the freeway and requiring workers to commute long distances." In their view, developers—for whom it was cheaper to build on the ever-expanding outskirts than redevelop near the center or in Latino or black neighborhoods south of Van Buren—were the culprits, aided by ineffective "master zoning." As home prices and land taxes began comparing favorably with southern California's, migrants from there started arriving. Whatever its problems (and where it would get enough water was certainly one of them), Phoenix continued to absorb enormous quantities of cement, lumber, wires, desert, and people.[129] Rather like Los Angeles, though that would not have been considered a compliment, Phoenix was pioneering, becoming a prime case of a late-twentieth-century "frontier," the metropolitan one, sharing few things with the traditional, romanticized West except its undeniably anarchic, untrammeled, free-for-all expansiveness.

Another element of mountain state growth was federal investment: the interstate system, mostly in place by 1980, military bases, and defense plants. Las Vegas's enthusiasm in the 1960s for the nuclear test site a few dozen miles north rested in part on the seven thousand jobs it provided, nearly as many as all private manufacturing in Nevada. A huge gunnery range, with "bombs in the backyard," was the trade-off. By the time the testing went underground, casinos and entertainment had picked up the slack. When a federal installation closed, as Walker Air Force Base did near Roswell, New Mexico, in 1967, the town lost thousands of its people, perhaps a third. Recovery came slowly. But twenty years later the Walker site had been made over into an Industrial Air Center, including an airport, a college campus, and a regional medical center.[130]

New manufacturing meant jobs and thus the arrival of people. Manufacturing payrolls quadrupled in the mountain states between 1950 and 1970 and continued to rise through the 1980s.[131] Higher education and high-tech industry were especially sought after as desirable multipliers of population and prosperity. Postsecondary education in the West, like the Midwest before it, had traditionally come from public rather than private institutions, with a few prominent exceptions like Stanford, Caltech, or Reed College. In the post-*Sputnik* and baby-booming 1960s, western public education enjoyed a brief golden age. Tempe, Austin, Lawrence, Norman, Albuquerque, Missoula, Provo, Pullman, and Moscow, and others in the mountain and plains states, paralleled the expansion of Madison, Bloomington, and Ann Arbor farther east. So did Pacific Coast universities within large cities, such as Berkeley, UCLA, and the University of Washington. California built its three-tier system of research universities, state colleges, and community colleges, the widest-reaching system of quality public education ever achieved. Silicon Valley infused people and money into the area between San Francisco and San Jose as computers began covering the nation in the 1970s, but it was only eponymous of other high-tech enclaves emerging in or near cities and campuses all around the West.

University and technology-oriented places nearly always developed unusually fast in these years. Young people who first passed through them as students often stayed or returned. Art, music, and lectures attracted retirees and leisure seekers. Research brought federal funds, which created jobs for the trained. Not every college town became another Berkeley, but even the second- and third-level institutions made life in their towns more attractive than in neighboring places without them.

As the West left behind its traditional mining and agriculture, with mining towns like Bisbee and Clifton losing nearly half their people, other places built motels, spas, ski slopes, golf courses, and anything else that might loosen the pocketbooks of every age-group from teens to the retired. To localities that could grasp one, and preferably several, of these keys, people and prosperity would come. Many places succeeded in doing so. Consequently, not one mountain state failed to grow in double digits in the two decades following 1965, even Montana, Idaho, and Wyoming, while Alaska, Nevada, and Arizona paced the nation.

In specific and concrete cases, novelty competed with tradition. Colorado, for example, displayed many of the region's demographic complexities. It was both urban and rural; plains and mountain; Anglo, Hispanic, and black; liberal in places (Boulder) and conservative in others (Colorado Springs); at once high tech and primary extractive. By the 1980s several hundred ghost towns dotted Colorado, and over a hundred post offices closed between 1941 and 1987. Yet suburbia thrived; "subdivisions popped up as rapidly as Russian thistles in the Front Range strip." In a rectangle 10 to 30 miles wide, bisected vertically by Interstate 25, running 125 miles from Fort Collins through Denver and past the Air Force Academy to Colorado Springs, lived (and still live) the great majority of Coloradans, the rest of them strung out among a few mining towns, boutique-laden resorts like Telluride and Vail, some farm and ranchland, and the oases of the western slope. A new edition of the 1941 *WPA Guide to Colorado* appeared in 1987, and it summarized the most visible changes:

> Huge circles now dot homestead grids, where half-mile-long center-pivot sprinklers have replaced irrigation ditches. In the mountains, forty-five ski and winter-sports areas have been carved from engelmann spruce forests. . . . Even the most remote nooks and crannies of Colorado are scarred with tire tracks. Cities and towns are no longer compact oases huddled around town halls. Rather they are sprawling clusters of suburbs that have invaded the countryside. It is hard to tell where Denver stops and Boulder, Aurora, Littleton, Golden, and other Front Range municipalities begin. . . . Old Denver City and Auraria, the two pioneer settlements of 1858, have been largely obliterated by urban-renewal projects. . . . Wheat fields, ranches, and dairies that once surrounded the Mile High City are now sprawling subdivisions, with shopping-center nuclei.[132]

The people of Utah hugged the western face of the Rockies as Colorado's hugged the eastern. The Thiokol missile factory paired with Denver's Rocky Flats, Orem's software companies with Boulder's, and the ski racks in the Salt Lake City airport with Denver's. Salt Lake City differed in its ethnic homogeneity; it remained the core of Mormonism, doubling its numbers through births and evangelism. The Latter-day Saints' exclusion of African-Americans from full priesthood earned Brigham Young University's all-white basketball team a series of protests in the late 1960s, but the church leadership reversed the policy in the 1970s. This did not produce a surge of black migration to Utah, but then, not many others surged there either; instead of in-migrants, Utah exported people in the 1970s, but it still grew because its birthrate remained high.[133]

The newest West that arose from the mid-1970s through the 1980s combined tourism with leisure and retirement. In one place, at least, the 1960s counterculture presaged yuppification. At Arroyo Seco, New Mexico, a few miles north of Taos Pueblo, "hippies" created communes in 1968–1970, uniting both Anglo businessmen and the old Spanish-Americans in resentment. But as hippiedom aged and withered, the area successfully promoted skiing, summer tourism, and handicrafts.[134] From Taos south to Santa Fe, tourism blossomed. In Wyoming rancher-farmer traditionalists objected to a Stanford Research Institute study and a statewide conference that put tourism as the state's top goal, with ranching and mining last. But with thousands of cattle ranches and farms going broke, the new jobs in tourism and services assured a future that would rest, ironically, on the myth of the Old West, of cowboys and wide-open spaces, rather than on real ranching and mining. The more the imagined and mythified history was propagandized, the more people came to Wyoming to "experience" it.[135]

In Moab, Utah, two young brothers whose uranium prospecting played out early in the 1980s opened the Rim Cyclery to sell and service mountain bikes. The gassy bikes made environmentalists retch, but they drew ten thousand bikers a year to the area, even though Moab itself shrank from fifty-three hundred in 1980 to under four thousand in 1990. In even tinier Blanding, Cedar Mesa Products began making hand-painted ceramics for tourists in 1982, and by 1987 it employed thirty Navajo and Ute craftspeople and grossed half a million dollars. New golf courses decorated the desert at Moab, Kanab, and Springdale.

None of this occurred without conflict, either mental or material. A local writer concluded that with "the collapse of the mining economy and the rise of the environmental movement . . . the Colorado Plateau is up for grabs."[136] Southern Nevada was less ambivalent about developer Don Laughlin. Across the Colorado River from Bullhead City, Arizona (population: about five hundred), downstream from Hoover Dam, Laughlin bought an old motel on six acres in 1966 for $235,000. By 1988 it had become a $167,000,000 casino, amid eight others almost as large. Three thousand people resided in the town of Laughlin, previously nonexistent, and across the bridge another twenty-two thousand lived in Bullhead City. By then they all were part of the Las Vegas area, the fastest-growing metropolis in the United States.[137]

As farmers fought development of condominiums in Driggs, Idaho, just across the Tetons from Jackson Hole, western Colorado towns along Interstate 70, like Parachute and Glenwood Springs, advertised for retirees and got some. The weather was cooler than Arizona's, and the homes were much less pricey than southern California's. In Tucson middle-class migrants who sought to escape hay fever brought their familiar houseplants with them, and allergies shot up to twice the national rate.[138] But so did Tucson's population.

Farther west, in Washington, Oregon, Alaska, and Hawaii, as in the plains and mountain states, growth and stagnation fell into time zones—not mountain and Pacific zones on the clock, but historic zones starting with the 1950s. Places that boomed in the 1950s and early 1960s often did so because agricultural technology was enriching them or because Pentagon infusions created jobs. By the later 1960s and into the 1980s suburbanization and synthetic fuels accounted for much of the growth, with many western communities soaring from the "new-new West" combination of high tech, tourism, leisure, and baby boomer maturation. Anchorage took off in the 1960s and kept expanding. Other places leaped forward beginning in the later 1970s or 1980s: Bullhead City, Florence, Sedona, and the Phoenix area in Arizona; Boise and Coeur d'Alene in Idaho; Las Cruces and Chimayo, New Mexico; a host of Portland suburbs, as well as Eugene and Salem; the San Juan Islands of Washington and almost anywhere around Seattle; Kihei on Maui, Mililani on Oahu near Wheeler Air Force Base, and Kailua-Kona on the Big Island of Hawaii.

Hawaii also gained in special ways from the 1965 immigration law, which allowed thousands of Filipinos and Koreans to enter, together with Vietnamese. Simultaneously mainlanders turned tourism into Hawaii's chief industry, and many tourists either stayed permanently or kept returning as snowbirds. The Hawaiian climate and lifestyle enriched the migration of young professionals as well.[139]

In Washington State the 1970s opened with both a low birthrate and an exodus of laid-off workers as Boeing and other aerospace employers for a time slumped.[140] Receding in population, Seattle seemed to be moving to the suburbs.[141] But that changed after 1980. The city and everything around it surged. Loathing California's sprawl, civic leaders warned that "we could have a Los Angeles type boom [or] another San Fernando Valley, complete with choking smog and wall-to-wall development." Seattle housing prices took off; a post-Victorian house on Capitol Hill, fifteen minutes' walk east of downtown, bought in 1983 for $150,000, sold in 1988 for $450,000—truly a Californiaesque happening.

West of Puget Sound, in the villages of the Olympic Peninsula, another phenomenon occurred. So many retirees came for the peace and climate that 50 percent of the population was receiving Social Security checks—"former teachers, firefighters, police officers, Foreign Service officers, and airline pilots" among them, said the director of the Sequim Chamber of Commerce, himself a former L.A. policeman.[142] The military presence also continued to fasten people around Puget Sound. In the Yakima Valley and the Tri-Cities of central Washington, more and more Spanish-speaking migrants produced everything from lettuce to sauvignon blanc grapes. Well-founded fears of plutonium leaks from waste buried at Hanford did not inhibit population growth.[143]

Everywhere the story was similar: metropolises surging, rural areas slipping. Portland, in its controlled way, continued to grow, while Washington and Oregon east of the Cascades edged slowly along, with a few faster-paced exceptions like the irrigated Yakima Valley and the secluded, attractive city of Bend, Oregon. In California in the 1970s and 1980s the metropolis spread dozens of miles from central Los Angeles into Riverside County, the Central

Valley was turning into a continuous ribbon of hundred thousand–plus cities, "Silicon Valley" entered an envious nation's vocabulary, and San Jose suddenly had more people than San Francisco.

In no other region was the spirit of "the 1960s" as culturally pervasive as in the West. The 1965 immigration law and the arrival of Asians and Latinos of new kinds and in great numbers "browned" the West as nowhere else. The end of the baby boom, the continuing Sunbelt migrations, and the shifts in economic life from ranching and mining to tourism and leisure "grayed" it as well. (The depopulating interior West underwent more graying than browning.) From 1965 to 1987 irrevocable change came in unforeseen ways. The rest of the century brought some surprises too.

10

THE LEADING EDGE, 1987–1998

> The urban character of the West truly alarmed the critics. However, few of them ever paused to ask why, if the western city was such a miserable place, so many thousands of people continued to flock to it.
>
> —John M. Findlay, 1992[1]

> Don't Californicate Oregon
>
> —Bumper sticker, ca. 1991

Trends Probable and Trends Problematic

Certain elements in the demographic panorama of the West at the close of the 1990s have accumulated such magnitude, depth, and force over the last two, three, ten, or twenty decades that we may have some confidence that they will continue. Others we can be less sure of. Among the longer lived and therefore more certain are these. Homesteading ended decades ago, and few family farms still exist on the Great Plains or westward other than huge, commercial, computerized operations; or fugitive countercultural hideouts from modernity; or ranchettes for the rich or comfortable.

Second, the West grows increasingly multiracial, multiethnic, and multicultural, especially in California and along the Mexican border and most especially in southern California, whose eighteen-plus million people now outnumber New York State.[2] The West has always been diverse, often more so than the rest of the country (certainly since 1965), and its high proportion of non-Anglo native-born citizens—Latino, black, Asian—would remain high even if immigration were abruptly and completely cut off.

Third, the West, not only the archetypal southern California, has become irrecoverably metropolitan and, in its own late-twentieth-century fashion, marked most visibly by freeway systems, many centers (or what were tradi-

WHERE THE MINORITIES LIVED, 1990

● African-Americans

■ Mexican and Central Americans

▲ Asians, Pacific Islanders

▮ American Indians, Aleuts, Eskimos

Symbols indicate major concentrations, mainly in urban areas

tionally called downtowns), and of course dispersion across large spaces (once known as sprawl).

Among the less certain and possibly transient are birthrates. Will "minority" birthrates fall to Anglo levels? Will anyone's birthrates fall further below replacement levels, or could another baby boom erupt? As for the economic health of the region and its role in the Pacific Rim, will economic involvement tie the West to Asian disruptions just as political-military involvement tied the eastern United States to Europe and its twentieth-century wars? Not that they were avoidable; they were world conflicts; but new and Asian-originating involvements might also be. Is the shift of western communities permanent, from traditional extractive activity (mining, fishing, lumbering, ranching, farming) to more service-oriented activities catering to a mobile and affluent population at several strata—youth, parents and families, seniors—resulting in a ski resort here, a Shakespeare festival there, outlet malls, casinos, state and national parks, and all the small businesses around them? Will they last? Tourist cabins and railroad tours did not. Will California slump and will people migrate out of it, as happened from 1989 to 1996, or will it continue to grow faster than the rest of the West and the nation, as it resumed doing? Will the globalization of communications wipe out regionalism altogether?

In the years from 1987 through the 1990s, the depopulating of rural areas, the continuing size and diversity of immigration, and metropolitanization all proceeded. So did the less certain trends just mentioned. We look at both sorts of changes here: first immigration, redirected once more by a federal law in 1986; the apparent fall, but then resurrection, of California; and a last *tour d'horizon* of the West, a few examples of how it looked in the late 1990s, the superficial changes cluttering like static the significant, long-term signals. Finally and briefly, a few words of retrospect and prospect.

The late 1980s brought some perturbations, but they proved transitory. Another baby boom threatened, but it was only a brief echo. By late 1997 the birthrate in the nation and the West fell to 14.4, lower than ever, much lower than during the 1929–1941 Depression.[3] The end of the Cold War shut many defense plants in California, hitting the aerospace and aircraft industries hardest, but proclamations of California's demise were greatly exaggerated. Inexorably California reinvented itself once more. Los Angeles became the most complex mélange of ethnicities any American city had ever seen, and other western metropolises, often despite themselves, emulated it. Southern California again was the economic locomotive of the West, and by the close of the 1990s the nation's fastest-growing metropolises all were western: Phoenix, Los Angeles, and Las Vegas. Growth, to be sure, was no more a self-evidently good thing than it ever was, but for better or worse the West continued to outgrow the rest of the nation. From mid-1996 to mid-1997 the nation's population rose 0.9 percent, the West's 1.6 percent, the fastest of any region; California picked up another 410,000, more than any other state, and Nevada soared 4.8 percent, keeping it the fastest-growing state for the twelfth year in a row.[4]

Immigration "Reform and Control," 1986

The Immigration Reform and Control Act (IRCA) of 1986 did not revamp and redirect the 1965 act so much as it perfected and extended it. In 1965 no one had foreseen the massive shift away from European toward Latino and Asian immigration, or what Mexicans and Central Americans might do after the bracero program terminated in 1964. What did happen was a sharp rise not only in legal migration but also in "undocumenteds" who continued to migrate seasonally and often remained in California and other border states.

Undisputed figures for undocumented migrants do not exist. Low estimates came from those who favored immigration, high ones from opponents. The Border Patrol and other law enforcement agencies knew how many illegals they caught and sent back: 1,800,000 in the year preceding passage of IRCA in October 1986.[5] How many stayed is another question. One expert, using Census Bureau figures, estimated 100,000 to 300,000 a year, as of 1980–1983; the Border Patrol's "educated guess" in 1986 was 500,000.[6] The most reliable figures, from the Binational Study on Migration created by the presidents of the United States and Mexico and carried out by a team of American and Mexican demographers in 1995–1997, placed the net increase in the population of undocumenteds from 1990 through 1995 at 630,000, or 105,000 a year on average. Many more than that entered, as immigration restrictionists claimed, but most of them also went back.[7]

During the 1970s and 1980s population expanded in northern Mexico, more from improvements in public health than from births (the birthrate in fact fell). This growth concentrated in cities all along the border from Matamoros, opposite Brownsville, Texas, west to Tijuana, just south of San Diego. In the fifty years from 1940 to 1990, while southern California from Santa Barbara to the border multiplied in population about five times, from 3,600,000 to 17,400,000, the two *municipios* of Tijuana and Ensenada, by the border in Baja California, multiplied thirty-eight times, from 35,000 to 1,007,000.[8]

A great many Mexican and Central American migrants never crossed the U.S. border and instead lived and worked in northwestern Mexico, often in American-owned companies called *maquiladoras*, which produced electronics, toys, furniture, and other goods from U.S.-made components. Mexican workers assembled the components, which returned duty-free ("in bond") for sale in the United States. The *maquiladoras* expanded contacts but not, its defenders insisted, illegal migration.[9] For one thing, the North American Free Trade Agreement increased jobs in northern Mexico (220,000 at the *maquiladoras* from 1994 to 1997) but reduced them in El Paso and other border cities. By 1997 unemployment was lower among Ciudad Juárez's 1,300,000 than among El Paso County's 701,000; 20,000 were commuting *from* El Paso *to* jobs in Juárez; lower wages were better than no wages.[10] Even more of the *maquiladoras*—about three hundred, or nearly half—were in Baja California, just south of San Diego, directed from offices on the American side.

Legal border crossings, whether to work in the *maquiladoras* or on the American side or for other reasons, were vastly more numerous than illegal ones, as anyone could see who watched the flow of people and traffic at the San Ysidro end of I-5 into Tijuana or across the bridges between El Paso and Ciudad Juárez. At Tijuana alone, over 100,000 people a day, 38,000,000 a year, crossed the border legally *before* IRCA became law.[11] The border was not only the line itself, certainly a legal and political barrier, but also an economic and social zone of contact for the roughly 3,000,000 people who lived twenty miles on either side of the line in 1986.

How to control illegal entries became the controversial question. Although they were a small fraction of all entries, politicians and media raised them high in popular consciousness as the national mood swung to the right in the Reagan years. The 1965 law did not address illegals, although many braceros who had habitually signed on for summer jobs in Texas and California kept coming after the program ended. When the law was amended in 1976 to limit family preferences to twenty thousand a year, undocumented entries rose again.[12]

IRCA was to have corrected this situation. After several years of work by special commissions and extensive congressional debate, the law provided three things. It sanctioned employers with fines and possible prison terms if they hired people who could not produce proper documents. It granted "amnesty" to illegals who had arrived before 1982, giving them temporary residence and the opportunity to apply in 1988 for permanent residence and citizenship in 1992 if they wished. Finally it bestowed temporary status to illegal farm workers of the preceding three years and provided for more workers if growers needed them.[13] In short, IRCA instituted employer sanctions (but who would check the documents?), amnesty (because deporting millions of undocumented but often longtime residents would have been impossible), and a kind of bracero program ("lite"). How many would choose amnesty was obviously as unknown as the number who immigrated every year. The 1965 act, soon amended, had capped the number at 270,000, but family members, refugees, and asylees—all legal—doubled the annual totals from 1982 through 1986.[14]

Did IRCA work? Note first that it meant to address illegal Mexican immigration, not immigration from Asia or anywhere else. Some Asians arrived illegally, under the sibling preference in the 1965 act, but efforts by restrictionists to rescind that provision were kept out of IRCA,[15] and this problem was not large; other Asians could and did enter under the Amerasian Homecoming Act of 1987, for children of American servicemen and Vietnamese women, and other statutes. To judge by the drop in Border Patrol apprehensions, IRCA reduced illegal crossings by about a third in early 1987 compared with 1986.[16]

By May 4, 1988, the cutoff date for amnesty applications, about 2,100,000 illegal residents had paid the filing fees ($185 for adults, $50 for children, a bargain $420 for families of three or more), and when the counting was done, the total stood at 2,655,000. Of these, 55 percent (almost 1,500,000) lived in California, 15 percent in Texas, and the rest chiefly in other western states.[17] About 1,800,000 (45 percent of them female) applied for amnesty because they had resided in the United States since before 1982, and another 800,000 (16 percent female) applied under the farm worker provisions. Three out of four were Mexican, and most of the others Salvadoran, Guatemalan, Colombian, or Filipino.[18]

As of 1987, when IRCA was about to take effect, about 19,000,000 Americans were Latinos, 4,000,000 of them foreign-born, 34 percent living in California and another 21 percent in Texas.[19] Under IRCA, between 2,000,000 and 3,000,000 Mexican temporary residents became legal, and after the waiting period, nearly 3,000,000 applied for citizenship. Mexicans, even those living in the United States more or less permanently, had traditionally held back from naturalizing. A likely reason is that American law requires a person to renounce any prior citizenship. (Mexico permits dual citizenship.) For a Mexican, often moving back and forth across the border, or expecting to, renunciation was much less convenient than for a Cambodian or Russian, for whom going back was not an attractive option. Even after IRCA, Mexicans became citizens at a slower rate than Asians, although more Mexicans, especially those with higher educations, white-collar jobs, and higher incomes, naturalized than any other group in 1994. The all-or-nothing character of assuming American citizenship no doubt caused misgivings. As one woman said after taking the oath, "You are proud to become an American, but that doesn't mean that you don't want anything to do with your native country."[20] While an Irish immigrant in 1900 had little difficulty renouncing allegiance to Queen Victoria, it was another matter for a Mexican living in east Los Angeles to renounce a native land that was just a couple of hours south on I-5.

IRCA wrought revolutionary changes in communities in both countries. Granjenal, for example, a village a hundred miles west of Mexico City in Michoacán, shrank from about three thousand to five hundred or fewer. Most of its people went to Santa Ana in Orange County, where they had been going for twenty years for construction jobs; some had been braceros as far back as the 1950s. IRCA allowed them to stay legally, and with that status, family members could join them and be legal too. Santa Ana, still a mostly Anglo town in the early 1970s, became overwhelmingly Latino, mostly Mexican but also Salvadoran and Guatemalan, by the 1990s. A former *granjenaleño* named Francisco Lopez, who reached Santa Ana as a twenty-four-year-old in 1962, was one of the construction workers who created Leisure World, Mission Viejo, and other monuments of the Orange County boom. Still working in his late fifties, he saw his eight American children graduate from high school and college, own homes, and start businesses.[21] The California Dream, in its *El Norte* version, continued to operate. If for Lopez it meant more hard work than success, that too followed in the next generation. It almost certainly would never have been possible in Granjenal.

In 1994, Californians passed the anti-immigrant Proposition 187, which aimed to deprive large classes of noncitizens of education and health care. It was, however, a strong inducement to naturalize and resulted in a record number of new applications.[22] IRCA thus very likely cut the number of people illegally residing in the United States. It certainly did not end illegal migration, nor did Proposition 187 or federal restrictions in 1996 on welfare and educational benefits for noncitizens. Mexicans seldom migrated simply for these benefits, or even for higher wages alone; social networks, families on both sides of the border, and the ability to accumulate capital to send or take home motivated them more, as they had motivated Europeans before 1924.[23] Many eligible for amnesty did not trust the administration of the act or feared mistreatment by law enforcement, mistakenly or accurately. Although women, children, and first-time migrants initially appeared as undocumenteds in lower numbers than before, by 1989 they were back to pre-IRCA levels. Some migrated in the hope of joining spouses who were qualifying for amnesty; others came for wage-paying jobs of their own (93 percent of migrant Mexican women, with or without spouses, earned wages). In some lines of work, such as domestic service, papers were less likely to be checked.[24]

The amnesty period of one year may have been too short to educate some who had lived in the United States for some time and had had negative experiences with law enforcement. The farm worker provision did not work well; illegals with false or unchecked documents kept getting employed.[25] Over 1,300,000 immigrants arrived in 1990 and 1991 under the 1965 preferences. Further changes in 1990 admitted more people with desirable skills or from the Soviet Union and Ireland, where pressure to come to the United States was vocal and high. But the Hispanic and Asian flows continued.[26] The 1990 law also reinforced family reunification, offering legal residence to tens of thousands of spouses and children of men whom IRCA had amnestied.[27] The undocumenteds still probably numbered between 3,500,000 and 4,000,000 in 1994, 1,500,000 (about 40 percent) of them in California.[28]

In California by 1992 more Hispanic babies were born than non-Hispanic white ones, far more than African-American or Asian, both because Latino numbers rose from 500,000 in 1970 to 2,100,000 in 1992 and because their fertility rate was higher.[29] Mexican-American women bore 18 percent of the country's babies in 1995. If their fertility continued, each woman would have 3.3 children in her lifetime, a baby boom level more than twice that of other

American women.[30] Although minority group birthrates have usually converged down toward the national mean, the high Hispanic rate of the mid-
1990s assured that their proportion of the population would grow for some
time even if immigration stopped cold. Because Latinas' median age would
remain several years below non-Hispanic whites' well into the twenty-first
century, the Census Bureau projected that Latinas would average 3.0 children each through the year 2050.[31]

By no means all—in fact not even half—the undocumented immigrants
in the United States were Mexicans or other Latinos. The majority were
Europeans who arrived on legal visas and then overstayed them. Of the illegal *entrants,* however, most were Mexicans, Salvadorans, and Guatemalans,
and they received most of the attention from the media and the Immigration and Naturalization Service.[32] By the mid-1990s, especially in California,
the irony was that IRCA's amnesties, together with the 1965 and 1990 family
preferences, had invited women and children, who became major users of
public health, education, and other services. They thus also became major
targets of resentment from non-Latino taxpayers, even though illegal immigrants nationally absorbed only 6 percent of welfare money.[33] Backlash triggered the stringent federal welfare law of 1996 threatening even legal
immigrants—including nearly four hundred thousand living in California—with losing Social Security and other benefits.[34] A 1997 study of immigration by the National Research Council found that impacts differed:
entrants with little education did compete for jobs with disadvantaged residents and did drain welfare resources; entrants who arrived or became
skilled made net contributions. Perceptions were frequently not that accurate; sound bites smothered sociological accuracy; ballot initiatives like
Proposition 187 manifested a new xenophobia.[35]

IRCA thus seriously affected the West's Latino community by providing
increased legal status and by adding women and children, but it did not rev-
olutionize it. Latinos were increasingly metropolitan, decreasingly agricultural. Traditional stoop labor became less and less desirable, more poorly
paid and worse treated in 1996 than in 1976, more than ever the lower tier in
a two-tiered economy of propertied and nonpropertied.[36] As more naturalized Latinos voted, political muscle began to bulge, notably in the 1996
defeat of Orange County's Congressman Robert Dornan, a right-wing
Republican, by Loretta Sanchez, a Latina Democrat. By 1990 Latinos outnumbered African-Americans in Los Angeles, Phoenix, San Francisco, Las
Vegas, and some smaller western cities. Both IRCA and the anti-immigrant
clamor of the 1990s promoted citizenship and Latino political cohesion.[37]

Assimilation continued to be difficult and ambivalent. Latinos could be
many things, from migrant Indians from remote villages to fourth-

generation upper-middle-class Americans of Mexican ancestry or even blue-blooded *nuevomexicanos*.[38] The 1990 census counted four hundred thousand Guatemalans and Salvadorans in Los Angeles, most of them west of downtown and the University of Southern California.[39] San Francisco was nearly as diverse. By the late 1990s Latinos lived and worked all over the West, in Alaska, Idaho, South Dakota, Hawaii, as well as, more traditionally, in Washington and the border states.[40]

Asians who arrived in the wake of the 1965 law were at least as diverse in origin, class, occupation, mode of arrival, and level of success. Koreans, Chinese, Indians, and Filipinos particularly increased in numbers after 1986, and Asians made up almost 50 percent of the newly naturalized citizens of the early 1990s.[41] Of the foreign-born Chinese in the Los Angeles metropolitan area in 1990, the largest group came from the People's Republic, followed by Taiwanese, Vietnam Chinese (by then running 60 percent of the businesses in Chinatown), and Hong Kong people.[42] Many arrived with professional educations or money, unlike any earlier immigrant groups, enough to change the wealthy Los Angeles suburb of San Marino from very Anglo-American to 30 percent Chinese by 1987.[43]

San Marino's shifts were symptomatic of a great many throughout the Los Angeles metropolis. In San Gabriel, site of Serra's mission and still home to many Latinos, a shopping plaza by 1987 already included "a Filipino grocery and sandwich shop, a Vietnamese cafe, a Japanese bakery, an Indonesian deli and restaurants offering Taiwanese, Chinese and Japanese cuisine." Monterey Park, advertised by a Taiwanese developer in the 1970s as the Chinese Beverly Hills, became Little Taipei and 50 percent Asian by 1988, amid much resistance from the older white residents, who in many cases had arrived in the 1950s seeking "an innocent, small-town pleasantness" but could not read the new Chinese signs on shops.[44] Except for New York City, Monterey Park was the most popular destination for newly arrived Asians in the mid-1980s. Alhambra, next door, changed in the 1980s from chiefly Anglo to 26 percent Chinese. While the eastern part of the city of Los Angeles remained strongly Mexican, several towns just beyond it in the San Gabriel Valley became strongly Asian.

So also did Koreatown just west of downtown Los Angeles. Stretching south toward black South Central and still the largest community of Koreans, it had turned half Latino by 1990.[45] Korean shopkeepers replaced Jewish ones in some black neighborhoods, resulting unhappily in Korean-black animosity in the South Central disturbances of early 1992.[46] Beyond in Orange County, Westminster's Bolsa Avenue was known as Little Saigon, the commercial and community center for (by 1997) seventy thousand Vietnamese, a good part of the three hundred thousand admitted after 1981 in the Orderly Departure Program for political prisoners, children of American servicemen and Vietnamese women, and family members of refugees who had already arrived since 1975.[47]

A few miles away in Long Beach, in a several-block district split by Route 1, lived most of the area's twenty-five or thirty thousand Cambodians (as of 1990), many of them survivors of incredible journeys from the killing fields of Pol Pot.[48] Many had dodged rocket attacks, been driven from their homes by the Khmer Rouge, spent months or years in squalid refugee camps, and watched the murders of parents and siblings and the mass slaughter of others, and they stoically bore up under racial slurs (from both whites and blacks) and problems with English in schools and on jobs once they arrived in Long Beach. One young man remembered Cambodia as "sometimes a dream or sometimes a nightmare." Meanwhile he had begun his upward climb in America.[49]

At the other end of the Asian scale, a few with corporate and high-tech experience had returned to Taipei or Seoul by 1995.[50] They scarcely formed a mass movement, more likely reflecting the cosmopolitan transpacific character of the upper economic echelons of southern California. Segregation was declining in American suburbs; Orange County had become the ninth most integrated place in the country, just ahead of Honolulu. Degrees of segregation differed greatly, however. Of the large minorities, African-Americans remained remarkably contiguous in their concentrated residence from the Crenshaw District west of downtown southeastward through Inglewood, Watts, and Compton to Carson, with an outlying black district in northwest Pasadena. The less numerous Cambodians and Salvadorans were even more segregated. Asian Indians and Pakistanis, on the other hand, scattered widely partly because they were of diverse religions, partly because they usually arrived with good English, and partly because many worked in dispersed health care or engineering occupations. Least segregated of all minorities were the nearly hundred thousand American Indians living all over the five-county area, 60 percent of them with white spouses.[51]

Immigrants from the Near East—Israelis, Arabs, Armenians, and Iranians—spread explosively in Los Angeles from 50,000 in 1970 to 300,000 in 1990, concentrating on the west side and in parts of the San Fernando Valley.[52] When Mikhail Gorbachev allowed Armenians to emigrate in 1987, thousands headed for East Hollywood. Arabs—Palestinians, Syrians, Lebanese, and others—scattered from the San Fernando Valley east through Glendale and north Pasadena to San Dimas in the San Gabriel Valley. Los Angeles's 639,000 Jews ranged from descendants of the Germans who arrived in the nineteenth century to refugees of the 1930s to newly landed

Israelis, most of them living on the west side between the Fairfax District (where Yiddish signs abounded in the 1990s) and the beach.[53]

Although Poles, eastern European Jews, Irish, and Scandinavians still peopled California and the rest of the West, the ethnic divisions of the early twentieth century had functionally disappeared after three or four generations of intermarriage. The geographer authors of a remarkable book on what the 1990 census revealed about Los Angeles concluded by asking whether it was "a multiethnic society—a single society whose people simply vary in their ethnic heritage"—or just a "collection of separate ethnic societies." Using as their basis the rarity of intermarriage and shaky English among many groups, they reluctantly decided it was only "a set of separate societies."[54]

But time may change that. The once apparently "unmeltable ethnics" of Europe merged in West Coast cities by the close of the twentieth century into a fairly homogeneous Anglo group. Edges between Irish, Poles, Germans, Swedes, and other white Europeans may have remained sharp in Chicago or New York, but along the coastal West, at least, they had almost disappeared. They had become as insignificant as distinctions among villages and provinces that once separated Polish or Italian immigrants from each other, before they discovered that Americans did not care and treated them all as Poles or Italians. In the context of Asians and Latinos, themselves very diverse, European ethnicities had mostly melted in the West. As for Los Angeles, its people had always been a mixture, but after 1965 it was more diverse than New York. Its northern European–stock majority became, in effect, a single Anglo group, still dominant in pockets like Pasadena and the Palos Verdes peninsula but in most of the metropolis only one group among many.

The Bay Area and Seattle also have seen a merger of European ethnicities, where an O'Brien may hide grandparents who were German, Italian, and Croatian or where someone named Lee may look Swedish but be partly Chinese. As European ethnic differences largely evaporated in the metropolitan West over time, so may the newer distinctions over further time. If the American future brings "a new hybrid ethnic group," then it may well be that "the future has already arrived" in southern California.[55] Or at least that the elements are there.

The hope, or fear, that Asians, Latinos, whites, and blacks would eventually mix as thoroughly as Europeans have was not idle; 9.7 percent of the American people in 1997 were foreign-born, the highest proportion since 1945, and the actual numbers (officially 25,800,000, plus perhaps 2,000,000 or 3,000,000 more undocumented) were higher than ever before. Nationally, nearly one-third of the foreign-born had become naturalized; half, by birthplace, were Latino, a quarter Asian, a fifth European. California led the states in foreign-born percentage (24.9). Los Angeles (including Orange and Riverside counties) attracted more immigrants than anywhere else in the early 1990s, followed by New York, with the San Francisco Bay Area third.[56] The new immigration, post-1965 and post-IRCA, continued to change the West as Europeans had changed the East Coast and Great Lakes states earlier in the century. Even interior places, like Garden City and Dodge City, Kansas, felt the impact. California, however, received by far the most. Coupled with the end of the Cold War, the California Dream was undergoing dramatic revision, ambivalently for Asians, Latinos, and Anglo-Americans alike.

The Fall and Rise of California

It depended on who was doing the California dreaming. The California economy sagged badly for five or six years beginning in 1989. It roared back, but during the downturn much soul-searching in western media (along with schadenfreude in eastern and midwestern media), and substantial out-migration for the first time, belied the traditional dream. "White flight," mostly to the interior West, balanced Hispanic and Asian arrivals and was often motivated by the desire to escape them. Driven by another western myth, that of nostalgic individualism, some Anglos retreated to the interior West. Perhaps the most pessimistic assessment came from a westerner, Philip Fradkin, who wrote in 1995: "Much has been written about the California Dream, but little . . . about the California nightmare. I believe the future will be a dark, chaotic time."[57] In my opinion, this assessment was too gloomy, but some evidence undoubtedly supported it. California's demographic and economic experience of 1987 to 1998 was volatile; it included economic insecurity and social disgruntlement, by no means all of it xenophobic, and hardening class divisions along with much movement of people in and out of the state. The universally lower-middle-class society described 150 years before by Tocqueville, with much equality of opportunity and property, was not the California of the 1990s.

The tiers of haves and have-nots, latifundists and migrant workers, citizens and excludeds, were not new in California's history. Contrasts sharpened vividly. Within months in 1965, the Watts riot erupted, while both the downtown Music Center and the Los Angeles County Museum of Art on Wilshire Boulevard opened.[58] In 1961 the Big Red Cars finally stopped running, yet the freeway system was mostly in place. Good often balanced bad. Even Watts and South Central had their amenities; they did not make sense as ghettos in New York or Philadelphia terms because they did not look bad enough to qualify as such. As Calvin Trillin wrote in 1970, "to someone familiar with Eastern slums Watts still has a quiet, open look—superficially the kind of place that people in Bedford-Stuyvesant have in mind when they talk about getting a little bungalow somewhere with its own front yard."[59] But housing deteriorated, unemployment rose, tranquillity deceived.

Nevertheless, Los Angeles and the rest of California boomed along until the late 1980s. In every year except two from 1978 to 1987, the state gained over 2 percent in population, more of that from migration than from natural increase. In 1986, 355,000 people—net—migrated to California, a greater surge than in any year except the extraordinary wartime 1943.[60] By the late 1980s, however, destinations were shifting.

In Los Angeles County, over 70 percent of the new people were Latinos. Asian population increased 15 percent, African-American 10, and non-Hispanic whites very little. Whites were heading for the Central Valley, from Bakersfield north through Fresno, Stockton, Sacramento, and Redding. Housing was cheaper than on the coast by perhaps a third, and commutes were much shorter. The state demographer Elizabeth Hoag reported having "this picture in my head of people streaming into Los Angeles, staying there for a while, then streaming out," heading for the interior. Arizona and Nevada already were netting more people from California than they were sending. A book-writing couple who had been in 1970 among the first to move to Laguna Niguel, in southern Orange County, for its openness and natural beauty decided it had become overgrown by 1984 and moved to southwestern Colorado, where, they said, "the West still lives. Real Louis L'Amour country."[61] (In fact L'Amour lived there.) Many cries about "white flight" from California were heard from 1989 on, but the pattern—attracting Asians and Latinos, exporting whites—had already begun by the mid-1980s.

Neither then nor later was white flight an avalanche, nor economic downturn a disaster. California remained comfortably the leading state in cash farm receipts (almost $14,000,000,000 in 1985, 10 percent of the country's), and Fresno, Tulare, and Kern counties in the Central Valley led California.[62] The greatest concentration of the nation's largest and richest farms were there, many of them corporate, and operated from city skyscrapers. Directed from offices on Wilshire Boulevard in Los Angeles, the Tejon Ranch Company sold $22,000,000 in livestock and other farm products in 1978. Tenneco West, from Bakersfield, farmed over a million acres in California and Arizona. Chevron and the Southern Pacific Company joined it as major "farmers."[63] Above San Francisco, the revivified California wine industry emerged in the Napa and Sonoma valleys during the 1970s and 1980s. San Jose, with a $1,400,000,000 public-private downtown redevelopment project, made itself the capital of Silicon Valley, with a population up tenfold between 1945 and 1987. San Diego, gaining migrants from Los Ange-les while it condemned "Los Angelization," outran even San Jose.[64]

Not everyone participated in the 1980s boom, however; not those on the lower tier, wherever they were. In 1987 Los Angeles had a homeless problem, and not just downtown in Pershing Square. In Venice and Santa Monica about 2,500 were without shelter, some 356 living on the towns' famous beaches. Irvine in Orange County considered putting its homeless families into the city's animal shelter. The homeless in Orange County were "largely a problem of once-middle-class families thrown unexpectedly awry by a job layoff, serious illness or other common life misfortune," wrote one reporter. A median-priced home in Los Angeles and Orange counties ($175,600 and $204,000 respectively) rose beyond the reach of 75 percent of households in 1988. San Diego County's median home cost $249,000 in 1989. Developers pushed eastward into Riverside County, distant and dusty, but around Coachella and away from the resorts like Palm Springs and Palm Desert, an intrepid commuter could still buy a home for under $150,000.[65]

The boom peaked in 1987. A think tank projected that forty-six counties across the United States would contain most of the new jobs by 2000, with Los Angeles County topping them all with 805,000.[66] But the *Los Angeles Times* was already announcing that the "bloom is off the boom." The 623,000 gross increase in people in the preceding fiscal year, heaviest in Riverside and San Bernardino counties east of Los Angeles, was hardly an unmixed blessing. The state, said the *Times,* was not ready to provide the needed services, nor could it because of the anti–property tax Proposi-tion 13 of 1978. "Only through more aggressive regional planning and gov-ernance, with strong state participation, can California welcome more millions of residents and still maintain an attractive and affordable envi-ronment," it warned.[67] Planning and governance of that kind, however, did not materialize.

By early 1989 the "star of the American economy" faced too-expensive housing, too-distant commutes, and too little tax revenue—or so the media and much of the public perceived. Compared with Portland, Seattle, or the interior West, houses in Los Angeles had become too expensive, drives to work too much of a hassle, schools gasping for money but filling with immi-grants. The end of the Cold War in 1989 and the collapse of the Soviet Union in 1991 did not bring a hoped-for peace dividend, releasing money for infra-structure and services. Instead it abruptly shrank federal contracts for aero-space and electronics and thus jobs at Hughes Aircraft, Rockwell International (the B-1 bomber), Northrop (the B-2 stealth bomber), Lock-heed, and other defense contractors in southern California and Silicon Val-ley.[68] How bad would things get, and how long would bad times last?

Bad enough and long enough, but not disastrous. The impact of the slump on California's population was chiefly a shift in patterns of migration. It combined a new white flight, in which the state continued to import people from Latin America and Asia but exported whites to Arizona, Nevada, Washington, and the distant interior West of Idaho and Montana. This shift, and talk that the California Dream had died, became conventional wisdom in the media.

The downside and the flight were real enough. An analysis by the Southern California Association of Governments concluded that as early as 1975–1980 more native-born people were leaving southern California than were arriving; whiter and older residents, born in Los Angeles or themselves earlier migrants, were heading for northern California or elsewhere in the West.[69] This movement continued through the 1980s. By 1990 Washington State (often the Seattle area) attracted the most Californians, with Nevada, Arizona, and Oregon close behind.[70] So the shift out of California, especially out of southern California, was old news by the late 1980s. Before then, however, it was such a small net figure, and so overshadowed by the boom following the 1979–1982 national recession, that no one paid attention until the exodus increased and the mood changed drastically from morning of America to fretfulness. In California a baby boom echo produced 40 percent more preschool children in 1990 than in 1980, promising a further strain on tax-starved school and health systems.[71]

Realtors claimed correctly that people were leaving for affordable housing as often as for better jobs. Median house prices doubled between 1986 and 1989 (repeating the late 1970s experience) to over $200,000 statewide. By 1993 the Los Angeles and San Francisco medians were $220,000 to $240,000. The leading ten cities to which Californians emigrated in 1991–1992 all had lower median home prices, led by Phoenix in the number of ex-Californians and in the lowest price (then $87,200). It was still possible to leave San Francisco for a place like Santa Rosa, in Sonoma County, or Los Angeles for Palmdale, over the San Gabriel Mountains. But slow growth was closing those options, and they required very long commutes.[72]

At about the time that home prices soared, rainfall fell off drastically. From 1986 through 1992 a drought worse than any since the 1930s dried out the state, reducing agricultural output and jobs and forcing water rationing in Santa Barbara and elsewhere. At the same time Pentagon cutbacks cost engineers, skilled workers, and middle-level managers their jobs. Unemployment reached 9.5 percent in mid-1992, higher than in any other industrial state.[73] Until 1989 what was unpleasant was merely curious, but from that point the mood truly soured; 58 percent of respondents in a *Los Angeles Times* poll agreed that the quality of life had declined since the mid-1970s.

"Everybody I know is now talking about how to get out of here," commented native Anne Taylor Fleming.[74]

Besides these structural problems of drought, housing inflation, long commutes, and job losses after the end of the Cold War, California in those years suffered momentary but jarring disasters. Bad enough were natural ones, such as the Richter 7.1 earthquake that disrupted the 1989 World Series in San Francisco, the Richter 6.7 at Northridge in the San Fernando Valley in 1994, and the fire that burned out three thousand in the hills above Berkeley and Oakland in November 1991. Worse, because humanly made, was the sequence of race conflicts that began with the police beating of Rodney King in Los Angeles on March 3, 1991, the acquittal of those police in April 1992, and the resulting riot that erupted in Los Angeles, "a maelstrom of rage," with whites, blacks, and this time Asians and Latinos involved.[75] Black Congressman Augustus F. Hawkins remarked later that the 1992 riot was "more widespread" than the 1965 Watts riot; 1992 "was countywide [with] more involvement of other ethnic groups."[76] Conviction of some of the police officers in a second trial in April 1993 had a quieting effect. But danger from youth gangs had become chronic, as had cultural friction among races and immigrants.[77]

Well before 1992 African-Americans had been replaced by Latinos and Asians as the principal minority migrating to the West. The Great Exodus out of the South ended in the late 1960s and by 1975 mildly reversed; on balance, more blacks headed south than west. Many came nevertheless. Nevada, California, Arizona, and Texas remained magnet states for college-educated blacks; Silicon Valley, Sacramento, Phoenix, and Las Vegas became attractive. Seattle desegregated in the 1960s and in 1989 elected a black city councilman, Norm Rice, as mayor although only 10 percent of the people were black. Los Angeles, however, lost a few thousand after 1987, far fewer than New York or Chicago, but another indication of southern California's economic slump at the end of the Cold War.

Military bases, including Fort Ord near Monterey and the El Toro Marine Air Station in Orange County, closed in 1993. All told, eighteen bases shut down in California between 1988 and 1993, a painful weaning away from Pentagon dependency. Streets and buildings in Koreatown and South Central damaged in the 1992 riots were restored slowly, if at all.[78] Yet the mood hid some silver linings. Bad as the military build-down was, it directly involved only 1 or 2 percent of the state's economy. Output never fell more than half a percentage point, and not until 1993. When population growth slowed, the rate still kept within 0.1 percent of the nation's. Trade with Asia pushed the port of Los Angeles past New York in 1989 in volume. In the early 1990s, as the national economy began a long upswing, entertainment and tourism more than made up for California's losses in aerospace and military bases.[79] Were the gloom and doom exaggerated? Yes, in the media and in the perceptions of many citizens. The class and income structure, as always, favored some and squeezed others, and around 1990 more than usual were being squeezed, but the state was hardly shutting down. California itself was an exaggerated, out-in-front case of the sour mood of the whole country.

Who were the real migrants in this ill-reputed period? Most analyses concentrated on race and ethnicity, but the class dimension sheds another light on California's migrations of 1987–1997. The state, from 1985 to 1990, led in immigrants (1,499,000), but it also gained more than 150,000 people from elsewhere in the United States. The whites who left it had, on average, lower incomes and less education than the people it kept or got from other states or from Hong Kong, Taiwan, and Japan. High school dropouts were twice as frequent among its out-migrants as among the general population.[80] These people headed north or into the interior West. White emigrants from California also included older people, a net 37,000 of them, sunbelters looking elsewhere as the state grew too expensive for them. In short, wrote demographer William Frey, California's "net migration is positive for higher-income whites and negative for lower-income whites."[81]

Taking "education" to mean college degrees, California benefited there too. In the late 1980s, over a hundred thousand white and many minority college graduates arrived. The state gained, then, at both ends of the income and education spectra: non-Hispanic whites and Asians of above-average education and income, as well as poorer and less educated Latinos and Asians. The latter, competing with less educated and lower-income non-Hispanic whites and some African-Americans, were encouraged to go elsewhere.

California undoubtedly lost people in the late 1980s to 1996. The Department of Motor Vehicles, which counted registrations of formerly out-of-state cars, found that California gained from every western state except Nevada in 1988–1989 but lost to each of them in 1992–1993. Yet a 5 percent sample of the 1990 census, a much broader base, suggests that throughout the gloomy years the people departing were not the Silicon Valley or Caltech types, or those in motion pictures or television, or those who kept California and the coast ahead of the country in per capita book buying.[82] Instead they were displaced aircraft workers, families struggling to find affordable housing large enough and close enough to jobs, or hard-pressed retirees whose fixed incomes forced a move to Oregon or Arizona.

Gloomsayers also underestimated the resilience of the world's seventh-largest economy. Senator Bill Bradley presciently predicted as early as 1990 that California "will become far stronger in the 1990s," and if it could conquer its environmental and racial problems, its "influence will be difficult to overstate" in the nation and in the post–Cold War world.[83] It did not conquer those problems, but it prospered anyway. Despite the tragicomic bankruptcy of Orange County in late 1994, signs of better times and a better mood kept appearing: the Century Freeway, the last of them all, opened in late 1993, a postscript to the postwar era. Latinos as well as Asians earned more and became more often self-employed the longer they lived in southern California. Chinese-American real estate agents made sure houses and offices for their clients had the proper *feng shui,*[84] or harmonious siting; the smog situation improved; new suburbs once more devoured farmland up and down the Central Valley; homes in Los Angeles County began selling again as the median price fell to $170,000, not that far from the other Pacific states' $153,000; Fort Ord became California State University at Monterey Bay.[85]

By 1994 the moving companies were showing net in-migration, and by 1995–1996 driver's license changes again favored California.[86] International immigration and natural increase kept the state total climbing toward thirty-five million, ten million in Los Angeles County, the country's largest by far.[87] Providing the most new jobs through the 1990s were construction, foreign trade, technology, tourism, and entertainment. Small businesses flourished: textiles, toys, food processing, freelance services, and software, among others. The state, it was said, "is again becoming a magnet for the young, adventurous, entrepreneurial types who have flocked here for more than 150 years."[88] The *New York Times* admitted that "it is not hard to find good news in California these days," and London's *Economist* reported that despite some strains, "California is beaming down on the rest of the country again."[89]

People suffering cutbacks in welfare and many agricultural workers had less to applaud.[90] Television coverage on the fifth anniversary of the violence at Florence and Normandie Avenues, the epicenter of the April 1992 episode, reported depressingly little change. Some small businesses reopened, but many lots remained vacant and many people unemployed. Los Angeles, like much of the United States, maintained its two-tiered economy—or rather, a several-tiered economy, labor force, society, and culture.

Mayor Richard Riordan announced in 1997, accurately, that the city was doing as well as or better than in 1992. But too many in it were not. Ever since missionaries first met Indians, California always had a social structure divided between owners or incipient owners and a fairly permanent wage labor class. The Midwest, with its homesteads, at least for a time provided a shot at something like Tocquevillian equality. In the long run, however, homesteads proved less market-effective than the latifundia of California. By the late twentieth century, on the Great Plains, homesteads ultimately folded into corporate or family agribusiness. The two-tiered economy produced more for less (especially less for the wage laborers) than the homesteads did. It was just more efficient capitalism. Whether it was better and safer socially—whether it could provide avenues of mobility to deflect the resentment generated by the inequality, urban danger, and poverty that have accompanied it—would become more urgent when whites ceased to be the majority. For all its real achievement and magnificence, California at century's close was a long way from Tocqueville's America.

Last Tour of the Century

As California fell and recovered in the 1990s, the rest of the West absorbed its emigrants and led in the national boom. The mountain and Pacific states increased about 10 percent in population from 1990 to 1995, about twice the rate of the rest of the country, with Nevada, Idaho, Arizona, Colorado, Utah, Washington, and New Mexico fastest.[91] The (net) 1,100,000 who left California in the first half of the 1990s went largely to those states.[92] Growth was seldom unambiguously healthy. Rapid development—"an acre an hour" around Phoenix, whole once-timbered mountainsides east of Seattle, vast pasturelands south of Denver—clashed with ever-louder demands to slow it down. Californian "equity exiles" drove up real estate prices in the small towns and suburbs they invaded (although the new dollars often revitalized their economies). Between 1990 and 1993 median household income fell in thirty-seven of the fifty states at a national rate of 6 percent. But of the thirteen where household income rose, twelve were in the West, from South Dakota, Nebraska, and Oklahoma through the mountains to Oregon and Washington.[93]

Across the entire West, rural counties that were close to metropolitan centers, but not yet officially part of them, invariably gained people. These "incipiently metropolitan" counties were the growth centers of the 1990s, the targets of migration. Counties on the Great Plains distant from metropolises were not.[94] In some ways besides the scenery, life in the West improved upon life elsewhere in the country: contrary to legend (or past history), the region employed *fewer* migrant farm workers than the South or Northeast; poverty and infant mortality rates held slightly below the nation's in nearly every western state.[95] Of the nation's twenty counties with the highest per capita aftertax income in 1995, seven were western, and twelve were predicted to crowd the top twenty by 2000. Pitkin County, Colorado, led the entire country in 1995 with an income of $34,861 for each of its 13,900 residents, who included the "resident sheiks and movie stars" in and around its county seat, Aspen, and its ski slopes. In summers, golf and music festivals beckoned. The manager of a new development called Aspen Glen (town houses from $450,000, detached houses to $1,100,000) remarked: "You could almost say Colorado is a resort in itself."[96] Two districts in Alaska were in the top five; Marin County, California (Sausalito, Tiburon, Mill Valley) was seventh; Esmeralda County, Nevada (precious metals mining again) eighth; Teton County, Wyoming (Jackson Hole, also a resort area, where gift shops and galleries "relentlessly peddle variations on the cowboy theme") twelfth; and Sully County, South Dakota, fourteenth, its 1,600 residents each enjoying more than $24,100 from fine wheat crops harvested by very few hands.[97]

Other comparisons could be surprising, as revealed by Joel Garreau's "edge city database," which ranked the "top tens" of many facts of metropolitan existence. The infamous long commutes of Los Angeles actually ranked well behind New York's, while among the nation's shortest commutes (under fifteen minutes) were Silicon Valley, Austin (Texas), Portland, and Las Vegas. All the ten top places in bars per worker were in Texas, but all the top ten in restaurants per worker were in California. San Francisco, Los Angeles, and Seattle led the country in workplaces with fewer than fifty employees, the West often preferring innovative entrepreneurship to large corporate bureaucracy.[98] Another survey found the West's major cities to be more racially mixed, older (especially Honolulu and San Francisco), with more college graduates, higher household incomes, and costs of living than cities elsewhere.[99]

Little of this applied to the Great Plains, where gravely different social and economic forces operated. Although farm income improved somewhat in the 1980s, depopulation continued. Onetime homesteads consolidating into larger units led occasionally, and briefly, to statistical freaks like the several Dakota counties among the nation's highest per capita incomes— because wheat farms prospered without needing many farmers. But as American farms of all sizes continued to disappear (from 2,700,000 in 1969 to 1,900,000 in 1992), large ones became almost the norm and earned most of the income.[100] Wheat prices fell again after Congress curtailed subsidies in 1996. Farmers who got through the 1980s finally sold out to expanding neighbors hoping to survive on volume, more often than to corporations (in fact corporate farming was outlawed in Nebraska). The sellers moved to their state's larger cities or out of state; the expanding farms became large-scale, completely commercialized, and fully computerized in managing feed, fertilizer, and "every conceivable element of agriculture."[101]

Great Plains communities prospered to the extent that they were tied to metropolitan markets. Garden City, Dodge City, and Liberal, in southwestern Kansas, became growth spots amid a depopulating area because the beef from their new packing plants sold on national markets. Lexington, Nebraska, on the Platte River between Kearney and North Platte, added about three thousand because IBP, the same meatpacking company that reinvigorated Garden City, opened a plant there in 1990. Kearney grew by two thousand, thanks largely to a company that sold outdoor gear through mail-order catalogs. But Lexington and Kearney were virtually the only places in western Nebraska to expand; others lost people.[102]

In North Dakota, ten counties (all west of the ninety-eighth meridian) suffered double-digit percentage losses between 1990 and 1995. Only Fargo and Bismarck grew appreciably. A few small places tried hard. The North American Bison Cooperative, a packinghouse producing buffalo meat from ten thousand homegrown head a year, opened in 1995 at New Rockford, north of Jamestown.[103] A few miles away at Carrington, durum wheat growers started the Dakota Pasta Factory, and in Linton, nine miles north of Lawrence Welk's hometown of Strasburg, Rosenbluth Travel used fiber optics to book reservations from all over the country. At Minot the national Quality Inns reservation center handled six million calls in 1996.

But Minot's population hardly changed, and the town remained dependent on its air base and college. Carrington and Linton still lost people, while Strasburg attracted tourists but not residents to the Welk birthplace. Other attempts to resuscitate prairie towns simply flopped. United Van Lines reported two moves out of North Dakota in 1996 for each one into it.[104] Young male farmers resorted to a singles directory published by *Farm Journal* to advertise for wives; young women did not seem eager to "listen to the blue jays and watch the sunsets," as one young man did, or to share in the hard work. Plainsmen were suffering "an epidemic of bachelorhood," which further sped depopulation.[105]

In South Dakota, Sioux Falls became a major credit card clearinghouse and added almost 12,000 people in the early 1990s, over a third of the whole state's growth. The new casino on the Sioux's Pine Ridge Reservation raised Shannon County by 18 percent, to 11,675.[106] But more often the story was also rural reduction. West of the Missouri, where twenty-one thousand farms existed in 1930, eight thousand remained in 1992, averaging fewer than 2 people on each farm; nearly everybody was living in town.[107] The plains participated in the baby boom with less gusto than other parts of the country, and the baby boom echo of the 1980s barely registered on the vital indicators meter. A Nebraska county that averaged about 25 births a year during the boom produced but 1 newborn in 1995; other places in Kansas, Nebraska, and the Dakotas had nowhere near enough births to sustain themselves. Who, an essayist asked, will "do the reaping" in the twenty-first century?[108]

Just to the west, on the High Plains of Montana and Wyoming, regional centers like Billings and Gillette added people. But ranching and farming areas, where depletion had begun decades earlier, changed little.[109] In those states the gainers were resort and tourist areas like Jackson, Cody, Bozeman, Livingston, or Ravalli County south of Missoula. Jackson and Gillette had virtually nothing in common but growth, and not even that with the rest of Wyoming; already the smallest state in population, it fell further in 1997, to 481,000.[110] Bozeman became ringed with the estates of Hollywood celebrities, and the average home price rose from $65,000 in 1990 to $101,000 in 1994, but salaries at Montana State University (or anywhere else in town) did not swell accordingly.[111] "Modem cowboys," reputedly all from California, running consulting businesses out of ranchettes, forced up real estate prices at Kalispell, just outside Glacier Park; almost uniquely in Montana and Wyoming, such places gained modestly.[112] Where mining and smelting were traditional (and dying in the 1980s), the modem cowboys and Aspenizing phenomena turned around their demographic declines. Anaconda and Butte may have become history, but Bozeman, Livingston, and Kalispell were transforming into a "new-new" Montana.

In the mountains of Idaho and Utah and in Oregon east of the Cascades, tourism, leisure, and cyber-aided employment also promoted such places as Park City, Utah (a ski resort and home of Sundance's rustic merchandise), Coeur d'Alene, Idaho, and Bend and Ashland in Oregon. Dilapidated Kellogg, in the Idaho Panhandle, replaced smelting with skiing; Vail turned grazing into golf.[113] St. George and surrounding Washington County, in the southwestern corner of Utah, became a retirees' heaven, sporting forty new subdivisions in 1995, and soaring 49 percent (from forty-nine to seventy-one thousand) in the first half of the 1990s.[114] In Nevada, Elko provided a rare element of demographic nostalgia with its boomlet in precious metals mining. But the future lay in the edge citification of the Lahontan Valley, between Fallon and the Reno–Carson City corridor.[115]

Nevada's (and the nation's) greatest growth exploded in southernmost Clark County, home of Las Vegas. By 1990 every month brought a thousand new single-family houses, and each year nearly a dozen new schools.[116] The metropolitan area added over 26 percent from 1990 to 1994, giving it over 1,000,000 people. Henderson, which began as a dormitory for workers on Boulder Dam, was the fastest-growing large city in the United States, up 57 percent to 101,000.[117] By 1997 Las Vegas's hubris had reached the point at which it openly challenged New York's Times Square as the best place to welcome in the New Year.[118] How to provide enough water for all these people, indefinitely, remained an ill-answered question. The Colorado River was already overtaxed as the main supply for Las Vegas, Phoenix, San Diego, Los Angeles, and all the irrigated cropland in between.

The modem cowboys might better have been called transistor tramps, because their ability to leave California for the interior also allowed them to move freely within the region, and many did. Transience also typified Las Vegas for thousands who came for construction work, casino jobs, services, looking for "a city where the living was affordable and the taxes were low."[119] Whatever the condition of the California Dream by the mid-1990s, there never was a Nevada Dream to match it. The attractions were utilitarian and unromantic. Las Vegas in the 1990s was not a replay of Los Angeles in the 1920s.

The transistor tramps were not the only equity exiles from California. The California emigration sent "a far greater number [of] workaday technicians and corporate middle managers" to the interior West. Boise attracted businesses, jobs, and people (about a third of them from California) with low housing costs, low taxes, low crime rates, despite low wages as well. From 1987 through 1993 and beyond, new jobs sprouted in Boise as fast as anywhere in the country; the city of 34,000 in 1960 passed 215,000 in the early 1990s. Hewlett-Packard (laser printers) and Micron Technology led in job development, each with payrolls of about 5,000—many more than the 3,000 miners still active around the state.[120] Boise became the nation's fourth–fastest-growing metropolitan area between 1990 and 1996, many of its newcomers on the run from California.

They did not, however, make Idaho more culturally complex. Confirming what some California observers had begun to suspect, the migrants to Boise and elsewhere in the interior West were not bringing California free-spiritedness with them but were "fleeing more racially and politically diverse states."[121] Acting out their myth-based convictions, they moved in part to prove that the "real West," individualistic and monochrome, could still exist for them. They intensified Idaho's conservatism, rather than dilute it. In Utah, natural increase combined with migration. Salt Lake City, like Boise, attracted high technology firms, claiming 850 by the early 1990s. Provo matched Boise in creating new jobs, with Utah the leading new-job state (Idaho was fourth) in 1993.[122]

The novel phenomenon of incipiently metropolitan counties—not officially part of the metropolis but no longer rural either—surfaced strongly around Denver. The city peaked in 1970 at 515,000 and then lost people for the next twenty years, like many core cities around the country. In the first half of the 1990s the core rebounded, while all the counties around it expanded in double digits. Douglas County, just south, added 109 percent from 1990 to 1996, topping the nation, with Park and Elbert counties fourth and sixth.[123] Highlands Ranch, founded in 1981 fifteen miles south of downtown, went from 15,000 in 1990 to 30,000 in 1994, the "fastest-growing planned community in the nation," full of corporate transferees and equity exiles. Castle Rock, a little farther south on Interstate 25, also exploded with tract housing and commuters. "Too far from the urban sprawl to be considered a suburb, yet too suburban-like to be considered a traditional small town," Castle Rock exemplified the new exurbia, the incipiently metropolitan edge.[124]

Federal impact continued to stimulate population shifts. Colorado Springs, a center of the religious right and with more than half its economy "related to the military," grew from 45,000 in 1950 to over 280,000 in 1990, spurred by the Air Force Academy's locating there. Pueblo, at the southern end of the Front Range metropolitan strip, battened on several new federal agencies. About thirty miles west of Pueblo, Florence and Fremont County increased by more than 7,000 as they built a complex of thirteen state and federal prisons. Denver, winding down its arms depot and air bases, became the vibrant center by the mid-1990s of the nation's largest cable TV companies, a base for mutual fund dealers and for international trade.[125] Yet while the Denver area and the rest of the Front Range strip boomed and became home to 80 percent of Coloradans, the plains east of it for three hundred miles into Kansas lost most of its hospitals and physicians, compounding rural depopulation.[126]

Across the West empty spaces usually remained federal property—military, Indian, or public domain. As in California's aerospace industry, so famously riddled by the reduction of Cold War contracts in the late 1980s, other places felt the supporting hand of the Pentagon pull away. Several thousand were laid off in 1988 and again in 1994 at the Hanford Nuclear Reservation in Washington when it ceased making plutonium and began cleaning up its decades of nuclear waste. High school students at Richland loyally voted to keep their mushroom cloud symbol, but by the mid-1990s home prices had plunged in the Tri-Cities.[127] Occasionally Cold War messes promoted growth; west of Salt Lake City, Tooele City and County doubled in population in the 1990s around a $650,000,000 incinerator built to destroy the army's chemical weapons arsenal.[128]

On a much larger scale, Seattle throve on federal impact. Growth Management Acts in 1989 and 1994 seemed only to whet builders' appetites, and they moved east beyond Issaquah, fifteen miles into the mountains, to erect new gated communities with homes in the $300,000 to $600,000 range. The median home price around Seattle in 1997 was lower than that, $169,000, but the city was a landlord's dream, with occupancy rates of up to 99 percent for rental properties in desirable neighborhoods.[129] Californians, about 20 percent of the new migrants to Washington around 1990, complained of the insults they bore from natives resentful of their portable home equities,[130] but they kept coming to the Puget Sound area, the home of Microsoft and other computer companies as well as Boeing, America's largest exporter. Portland, with Intel and other cybertech firms, also drew migrants. The coastal Northwest would never again be a well-kept secret, supposedly too remote to visit.

As southwestern cities spread into their surrounding deserts, always seeking water, Seattle and (most successfully) Portland sought to cope with deteriorating air quality, stifling traffic (Interstate 5 in both cities always seemed jammed), and ever-increasing numbers. Portland perhaps fared best, but what it would do if and when it gained another million people could not be predicted optimistically.[131] Citizens' initiatives continued to defeat annexation moves, confronting and stifling growth pressures through the 1990s.[132] Some of the richest of the newly rich communities, like Aspen, Vail, and Jackson, became too expensive for their own workers, forcing them down the road and out of the county or, in Jackson's case, across the state line to Driggs and Victor in Idaho. In Texas the border cities led the state's early-1990s growth of 10 percent, along with Dallas–Fort Worth and Houston, but the North American Free Trade Agreement did not benefit everyone; El Paso suffered 12 percent unemployment in early 1997.[133]

Thus went the new West at the close of the 1990s and the century. From 1990 to 1996 Las Vegas led the country in rate of growth, 41 percent, while the Los Angeles metropolitan area gained the most people, 964,000 (with Atlanta second at 582,000). Foreign immigration produced that huge rise despite the departure of over 1,000,000 from Los Angeles in those same years—a good many to Las Vegas.[134] A region of vibrant, rapid, and diverse growth, it also contained many downsides. The emptying of farms and small towns, and the disappearing economic significance of mining and ranching, turned much of the region 180 degrees from what it had been early in the century. Always more urban than the rest of the country, at least statistically, the West by the end of the 1990s was emphatically metropolitan—in its central cities, its suburbs, and its "incipiently metropolitan" rings. Migration from southern California to the Pacific Northwest and the interior accounted for the most highly visible changes in both the sending and receiving places.

But the exodus from California was never that great, and it lasted only a few years. More significant was the absorption of the large majority of the West's people into the metropolitan maelstrom everywhere from the High Plains to Honolulu. Isolated areas hardly existed anymore, and those that did depopulated. In Arizona, for example, incipiently metropolitan Cochise

County, on Interstate 10 not far from Tucson, rose from 31,000 people in 1950 to 110,000 in 1995, while neighboring Greenlee County, with no major highway, languished.[135]

The historic western myths all have been transformed. One, the Home-steading Ideal, has not survived, succumbing to economic and climatic real-ity by 1929 and evaporating as myth by the 1970s. The California Dream has taken a beating from time to time, not least from 1989 to the mid-1990s, but it continues to motivate people, certainly the Latino and Asian migrants whose versions of it are very much alive. The Gold Rush itch reincarnated itself in hunts for exotic minerals in places like Moab, Utah, in the 1950s and in the great energy scramble—for oil shale, natural gas, and coal—of the late 1970s and early 1980s. Headlong development of real estate and resources has been modified in part and in some places by slow-growth efforts. The myth of the cowboy and of ranches persists despite their disappearing num-bers, because television, advertisements of the Marlboro Man, and motor vehicles with ranch-redolent names, keep reinforcing it; it also promotes tourism, recreation, and real estate.

When I was a boy in New York State in the 1940s, I knew I lived in the Empire State. The parts of the United States that seemed to produce any-thing worthwhile, like cars, clothes, or baseball, were the Northeast and the Midwest. The South was sleepy, and the "Far" West remote. The country's significant cities were the sixteen with major-league baseball teams, located within a parallelogram whose corners were Boston, Washington, St. Louis, and Chicago.

This mental geography has shifted strikingly in the past fifty years. The urban colossi of that time have stagnated or flat-out shrunk, while others, in the West, once hardly heard of, have surpassed them. Five pairs of cities, now next or close to one another in the population rank order, reveal the story. In each pair the western one in 1950 was tiny compared with the well-established metropolis in the Midwest and Northeast. But by the mid-1990s the upstarts outpopulated their withered elders:[136]

CITY & RANK	1950 (NOT 1850)	1994
52. Mesa, Ariz.	16,790	313,649
53. Buffalo, N.Y.	580,132	312,965
58. Anaheim, Calif.	14,556	282,133
60. Louisville, Ky.	369,129	270,308

41. Sacramento, Calif.	137,572	373,964
43. St. Louis, Mo.	856,796	368,215
11. San Jose, Calif.	95,280	816,884
14. Baltimore, Md.	949,708	702,979
7. Phoenix, Ariz.	106,818	1,048,949
10. Detroit, Mich.	1,849,568	992,038

Decade after decade of western growth rates, steadily exceeding every other region's, accumulated by the end of the twentieth century into a West continuing to outstrip the traditional regions of the dominant core American culture east of it. The population figures were unassailable.

Some Postmillennial Projections

At the same time, the West appeared by many indicators to be separating into two subregions: coastal/border and interior. Their twenty-first-century future can hardly be *predicted* with certainty. But the national, and regional, futures can be *projected* to some degree, on the basis of the size and shape of the population already in place in the late 1990s.

In 1995 the Census Bureau laid out a high, middle, and low estimate of what the nation's people might look like between then and 2050. By that time, according to the middle estimate, the United States would contain 394,000,000 people. That would mean only a 50 percent increase in the fifty-five years since 1995, when the total was 263,000,000—much slower than the 99 percent, or virtual doubling, that took place in the preceding fifty-five years between 1940 and 1995.[137]

Total growth, however, would not take place evenly. The elderly (the very last of the baby boomers and many of their children) and, in much larger numbers, the Latino or Hispanic population would increase faster than other people. Hispanics[138] by 2010 might outnumber African-Americans as the largest minority and by 2050 would constitute over 24 percent of the total. Hispanics would also be the youngest group, with their median age of twenty-six in 1995 rising only to thirty-one by 2050, while non-Hispanic whites, at thirty-seven in 1995, would have an average age of forty-four in 2050. The census's middle series foresaw the major groups changing positions between 2000 and 2050. Non-Hispanic whites would drop from 72 percent of the total to 53 percent; African-Americans would rise from 13 to 15; Asians and Pacific Islanders from 4 to 9; and Hispanics from 11 to 25 percent. Indians, Eskimos, and Aleuts would remain about stable around 1 percent, though rising in numbers. Asians would gain most from immigration, at 2.5 percent per year, while Hispanic increase would come not from immigration but from higher fertility, which was expected to stay about 2.98 children per woman compared with 2.4 for blacks, 1.9 for Asians, and 1.8 for non-Hispanic whites.[139]

If the white birthrate kept on dropping, life spans lengthening, and immigrants arriving at the 1990s' volume of about 820,000 a year, these projections would come true. California, by these estimates, would be home to 63,000,000 by 2040, equal to the entire American population in 1890, half of them Latino. The other major gainers in the next several decades should be Florida, Arizona, Washington, and Colorado. (All ten of the fastest-growing counties from 1996 to 1997 were in Arizona, California, Nevada, Texas, and one in Florida; all but three, in percents, were also western.)[140] In the shorter term, from 2000 to 2020, every western state except for the Great Plains states and Montana—and no others except Florida and Georgia—was projected to increase by double-digit percentages. The West will—not would—almost certainly continue to lead the Midwest, Northeast, and South in the first quarter and half of the twenty-first century, as it led them throughout the twentieth.[141] Whether the coastal and border West would keep on declining in native white proportions, while interior western states rose, was unclear; estimates disagreed.

The weighting westward of the American population, however, seems beyond doubt in the first ten, twenty-five, or fifty years of the twenty-first century. Projections of course can always shift abruptly. A new baby boom as unanticipated as the last one might inundate resources. A drastic surge of nativist laws might exclude immigrants and deport the nonnaturalized. Water might become unavailable or severely limited; the Columbia and the Colorado, the only major rivers in the West, both are vulnerable. An uncontrolled virus or other plague, a volcano, or nuclear war might erupt. Historians, your author included, are poor at prediction. But we can affirm with certainty that everything changes—borders, customs, languages, and all else—and in unexpected ways. If trends apparent in the 1990s (in fact, for several decades) remain, the West and above all California will gain further weight—demographic, and therefore economic, political, and cultural—and will continue to become grayer and browner. The sea changes of just the past fifty years, spotlighted by the reshuffling of the rank order of the nation's leading cities since 1950 (the five pairs above, for example) will almost certainly go on.

Consider, then, that we are in the middle of a century that began in 1950 and will end in 2050. The projected outlines of population change in the West are as just described. But consider also that we are in the middle of a millennium that began in 1500 and will end in 2500. The development of the people of what has become the West of the United States, in the five hundred years since 1500 or so, has been the subject of this book. What will they do in the next half millennium?

Projections into such a distance would be absurd, but some speculations may be at least entertaining. The coastal and border West may become the dominant region of North America, facing an East Asia whose economies at last match its huge populations. Demography matters, and demographic movements in large enough numbers can decide cultural and political arrangements. That has happened in North America since 1500. Europeans marginalized Native Americans. Anglo-Americans overwhelmed the resi- dent Mexican provincials in Texas between 1821 and 1836, leading directly to the acquisition of California and the Southwest by the United States in 1848. It seems likely that "non-Hispanic whites," as the census calls them, will maintain their majority status nationally for some time, but likely not in the coastal and border West. The major groups—non-Hispanic whites, Hispan- ics, African-Americans, and Asian-Americans—are trending toward equal size. In the next half millennium Hispanic people may become the West's majority. It would be a delicious irony if the demographic dominance of 1848 reversed.

Also, in time, will a new language, perhaps combining Spanish, English, and Chinese, develop? English did not take its modern shape until centuries after the Normans had enriched Anglo-Saxon. Will the cultural groups in the West and Southwest ultimately syncretize? Or, culturally and linguisti- cally, will the West become a Beirut or Belfast or Bosnia writ large, splitting into an Anglo interior and a multicultural coastal and border rim, at swords' points with each other and, along class lines, within themselves?

The national center of gravity has shifted and continues to shift. The worldview westward, from Manhattan to vagueness, no longer suffices. The myth of homesteading has already been consigned to the past, and gold rushing, California dreaming, and the macho cowboy are overdue for over- haul. A new national story, one that must include all the American people, whatever their ancestors' origins, is also overdue. Where they will take them- selves in the next century or the next half millennium is anyone's guess. Where they came from in the past is the story we have been telling you here.

NOTES

A few newspaper titles are abbreviated here: *NYT* for *New York Times*, *LAT* for *Los Angeles Times*, *PI* for *Seattle Post-Intelligencer*, and *HCN* for *High Country News*. "OH" stands for Oral History interview; see the bibliography for the list and location. Only author and short title appear here; full references and other abbreviations are in the bibliography.

1: *Where the West Is and Why People Have Gone There*

1. The classic history of the California Dream is Kevin Starr's multivolume work (see bibliography).
2. Schwartz, *From West to East*, 14–15 (the Queen Califia legend), 72 ("Child of Indian and European hallucinations; of Bourbon reform, Franciscan millenarianism and the Enlightenment; of English piracy and smuggling, Mexican federalism, and American commerce, the new California was uniquely modern"). See below, chapter three, on the creation of Pasadena and Anglo Los Angeles as a new form of American city life.
3. Starr, *The Dream Endures*, 4.
4. Allen, "Cowboyphobia," 3, 5, 6.
5. On employment-seeking migration prior to mass transatlantic trips, see Hoerder and Moch, *European Migrants;* on labor- and land-seeking migration across the Atlantic to North and South America, see Nugent, *Crossings*.
6. For a discussion of Cody, Roosevelt, and Turner as mythmakers, see Slotkin, *Gunfighter Nation*. Also, White, "Frederick Jackson Turner and Buffalo Bill;" also Nugent, "Happy Birthday, Western History."
7. The Census Bureau has long divided the country into four regions: East, South, Midwest (until recently North Central), and West. This census West included, until 1959, eleven states: Montana, Wyoming, Colorado, New Mexico, Arizona, Utah, Nevada, Idaho, Washington, Oregon, and California. Hawaii and Alaska were added when they became states in 1959.
8. Nugent, "Where Is the American West? Report on a Survey."
9. Barone and Ujifusa, *Almanac of American Politics 1994*, 775.
10. Scott, *Time* (Aug. 7, 1989).
11. Survey response from Betty Braddock of Dodge City.
12. U.S. Census, *State and Metro Area Data Book 1997–98*, 10.
13. Lodge, *Paradise News*, 174–75.
14. Godfrey, "Departing Correspondent Looks at Western Culture," *Toronto Globe and Mail*, Aug. 6, 1988.
15. The eight California districts (in descending order of opulence) centered in Beverly Hills, Silicon Valley, Los Angeles from Venice south to San Pedro, San Mateo County, Malibu, Pasadena, Santa Clara, and Newport Beach. The other two in the top ten were Honolulu and part of Westchester County just north of New York City. Barone and Ujifusa, *Almanac of American Politics 1994*.

16. Jefferson, *Notes on Virginia,* Query XIX, and letter to J.-B. Say, Washington, February 1, 1804, in Koch and Peden, *Life and Selected Writings of Thomas Jefferson,* 280, 575.
17. Joseph J. Ellis's words in *American Sphinx,* 205, 212–13.
18. Wills, *John Wayne's America,* 35, 38, 45.
19. Leroux, "It's the End of the Trail for the Marlboro Man," *Chicago Tribune,* June 27, 1997; obituary of John Benson, *Chicago Tribune,* March 16, 1995; obituary of David McLean, *Chesterton* (Ind.) *Tribune,* Oct. 19, 1995.
20. April 5, 1993.
21. *USA Today,* Oct. 14, 1993.
22. *Montana,* 42 (Autumn 1992), 93.
23. Nancy Shoemaker, "Teaching the Truth about the History of the American West," *Chronicle of Higher Education,* Oct. 27, 1993.
24. Popper, "Strange Case of the Contemporary American Frontier," 101; Anne Matthews, "The Poppers and the Plains," *NYT Magazine,* June 24, 1990; Lang, Popper, and Popper, 229–308.
25. Goldstein, "Many Wests: A Review Essay," 148.

2: *From Time Immemorial to 1848*

1. Fiedel, *Prehistory of the Americas;* Dixon, *Quest for the Origins of the First Americans;* Schlesier, *Plains Indians,* A.D. *500–1500.*
2. For one Native American's views, see Vine Deloria, Jr., *Red Earth, White Lies.* Deloria has "difficulty taking scientific doctrines seriously" (p. 10). He rejects the Beringia explanation of Indian origins, human overkills of the large mammals, and the accuracy of carbon dating; dismisses the absence of long-term human evolutionary evidence; and argues that many orally transmitted creation stories had historical bases.
3. Josenhans et al., "Early Humans and Rapidly Changing Holocene Sea Levels in the Queen Charlotte Islands–Hecate Strait, British Columbia, Canada," 71–74; Wallace, "Mitochondrial DNA in Aging and Disease," and "What Mitochondrial DNA Says about Human Migrations," 40–47.
4. Dickason, *Canada's First Nations,* 49.
5. Gutiérrez, *When Jesus Came, the Corn Mothers Went Away,* xxviii.
6. *NYT,* July 19, 1994, April 23, 1995, and June 1, 1995.
7. Gutiérrez, *When Jesus Came,* xxi.
8. Collins, "Prehistoric Rio Grande Settlement Patterns," 321; George Johnson, "Social Strife May Have Exiled Ancient Indians," *NYT,* Aug. 20, 1996.
9. White, "Winning of the West: The Expansion of the Western Sioux," 319–43, describes this process vividly.
10. Schlesier, *Plains Indians,* 361–81; Norris, *Dakota,* 127.
11. Brooks and Bell, "Last Prehistoric People," 316–17.
12. Dickason, *Canada's First Nations,* 69.
13. Ubelaker, "North American Indian Population Size." His estimate is lower than (for the same area) Russell Thornton's in 1987 of seven million, and Henry Dobyns's of 1983 of eighteen million. None of these is frivolously arrived at, but I prefer Ubelaker's. For a convenient summary of nearly two dozen such estimates since 1910, as well as breakdowns by region and timespan, see Ubelaker, "North American Indian Population Size: Changing Perspectives," in Verano and Ubelaker, 169–76. For an extensive discussion of all estimates and how they were arrived at, see Daniels, "The Indian Population of North America in 1492."
14. Ubelaker, "North American Indian Population Size," 291.

15. Declines in numbers: Arikaras, 16,000 (contact) to 380 (1904); Pawnees, 20,000 (1750) to 650 (1910); Crows, 6,000 (1805) to 1,799 (1910); Arapahos, 2,500 (1805) to 1,419 (1910).

16. West, *The Way to the West,* 14–18, and 88–91 for the impact of smallpox, tuberculosis, venereal diseases, malaria, alcoholism, cholera, and others, as well as reduced fertility and resistance contrasted with white settlers' high fertility.

17. West, *The Contested Plains,* 67.

18. Bray, "Teton Sioux Population History, 1655–1881," 167–70, 174–75, 177, 179.

19. Simmons, *Last Conquistador,* 100, 111.

20. Braudel, *Civilization and Capitalism,* III:403–05, 420–22.

21. Boyd-Bowman, "Patterns of Spanish Emigration to the Indies until 1600," 582–84, 587, 596–99, 601–02.

22. Simmons, *Last Conquistador,* 96, gives "somewhere above 500 for the total"; Bowden, "Spanish Missions, Cultural Conflict, and the Pueblo Revolt of 1680," 97, gives "an initial force of 400 persons."

23. Taylor, *In Search of the Racial Frontier,* 27–30. Isabel de Olvera, a servant but the first free black woman in northern New Spain, joined the settlement in 1600. The first black person in the region was the slave Esteban, a member of the Narváez expedition of 1528 (an effort at exploration, not settlement).

24. Simmons, *Last Conquistador,* 96–97.

25. Riley, *Rio del Norte;* Simmons, *Last Conquistador;* and (throughout these pages) Weber, *Spanish Frontier,* the standard work.

26. Riley, *Rio del Norte,* 4.

27. Reff, *Disease, Depopulation, and Culture Change in Northwestern New Spain, 1518–1764,* 130–38.

28. Riley, *Rio del Norte,* 18, 224. Bowden gives "30 to 40 thousand" in "an estimated 75 or 80 permanent towns," 97. Oñate himself estimated 60,000; a friar in 1638 estimated 40,000; another friar in 1679 estimated 17,000; another in 1706 estimated 6,440 in eighteen pueblos (Knaut, *Pueblo Revolt,* 154–55).

29. Goodman, *Navajo Atlas,* 54–55. Gutiérrez, *When Jesus Came,* xxvi–xxvii, summarizes current anthropological opinion: "Athapaskan nomads" appeared "just east of the Pueblos" about 1525, then moved westward. Those "who would become known as the Navajo and Jicarilla Apaches" entered northern New Mexico and Arizona (the San Juan Valley and past Four Corners). The "ancestral Lipan, Mescalero, Chiricahua, and Western" Apaches entered southern New Mexico and Arizona. Coronado mentions meeting some in 1541, Oñate more in 1598; there were at least tens of thousands of them. They snuffed out some pueblos, raided and traded with others.

30. Riley, *Rio del Norte,* 250.

31. Schilz and Worcester, "Spread of Firearms," 2.

32. Riley, *Rio del Norte,* 268, and Bowden, "Spanish Missions," 98, both give 380 killed, while Bowden provides the 2,500 total. Knaut, *Pueblo Revolt,* 134–35, estimates that "the number of people of European background residing in New Mexico on the eve of the revolt stands near one thousand," the great majority born there, "never having seen Mexico, much less Spain." Also Bronitsky, "Indian Assimilation in the El Paso Area," 151–68; Timmons, *El Paso,* 17–19.

33. Riley, *Rio del Norte,* 269.

34. Reff, *Disease, Depopulation . . .* 16, 202, 236, 275–76; Nostrand, "The Spread of Spanish Settlement in Greater New Mexico: An Isochronic Map, 1610–1890," 82–87.

35. Jones, *Los Paisanos,* 13, 123–28.

36. Ibid., 129, gives 27,200 Spanish and mestizos, and 9,400 Indians, in 1818, and total populations of Albuquerque 8,200, and Santa Fe 6,700. Gutiérrez, *When Jesus Came,* gives

slightly different figures, 167, and populations of individual pueblos, 173; their fluctuations add weight to the need to regard all these numbers as approximations.

37. Hordes, "The Inquisition and the Crypto-Jewish Community in Colonial New Spain and New Mexico," 106–18; Hordes, "The Sephardic Legacy in New Mexico," 82–90; *NYT*, Nov. 11, 1990.

38. Weber, *Spanish Frontier*, 209; Jones, *Paisanos*, 193.

39. Reff, *Disease, Depopulation . . .*, 232–34.

40. Jackson, *Indian Population Decline*, 57.

41. Alonzo, *Tejano Legacy*, 1–7: "Later Anglo arrivals have appropriated the history of the pioneer effort for themselves. . . . For some newcomers from the United States, the history of the region starts with the founding of the ranches of Richard King and Mifflin Kenedy in the 1850s." But to the contrary, "Tejanos continue to see land loss as a result of wholesale Anglo thievery accomplished through various means, such as lawsuits, intimidation, and violence, including the use of the Texas Rangers and other law-enforcement officers" (6–7).

42. The foregoing is indebted to Jones, *Paisanos*, 38–44, and Weber, *Spanish Frontier*, 153–55, 161–63, 186–91.

43. Weber, *Spanish Frontier*, 194, 230–35.

44. Schuetz, "Indians of the San Antonio Missions, 1718–1821," 375–76.

45. Weber, *Spanish Frontier*, 195; Jones, *Paisanos*, 47–48.

46. Hackel, "Land, Labor, and Production," 117–18, 122–23, 127–28, 136.

47. Cook, *Population of the California Indians, 1769–1970*, 43 (310,000); Ubelaker, "North American Indian Population Size," 173 (221,000); Hurtado, *Indian Survival on the California Frontier*, 1 (quote).

48. Jones, *Paisanos*, 204–06; Weber, *Spanish Frontier*, 263; Nunis, "Alta California's Trojan Horse: Foreign Immigration," 300.

49. Sandos, "Between Crucifix and Lance," 204, 210–13, 215–16.

50. Hackel, "Land, Labor, and Production," 122.

51. González, " 'The Child of the Wilderness Weeps for the Father of Our Country,' " 151: "At the height of the mission period in 1830, the neophytes [Indians on missions] and gentiles [Indians in settlements] totaled 98,000 souls and outnumbered the priests, soldiers, and settlers nearly ten to one." The estimate of a drop from seventy-two to eighteen thousand in 1830 is Sherburne Cook's, cited in Sandos, "Between Crucifix and Lance," 222.

52. Cook, *Conflict between the California Indian and White Civilization*, 210–16 (quote, p. 210).

53. Cook, *Population of the California Indians*, 199. Elsewhere, Cook (*Conflict*, 255) points out: "To a certain extent in the missions and predominantly in the aboriginal habitat the Indian had retained his primitive social and religious character and, indeed, had appropriated a few features of the white civilization . . . [but] when the Indian was forced to withstand the shock and impact of the Anglo-Saxon invasion . . . his social structure was not only utterly disorganized, but almost completely wiped out."

54. In the 1990s the world's highest death rates are in parts of Africa, with twenty or twenty-two; the United States' is about eight. Unknown is the death rate among California Indians *not* on the missions in the early nineteenth century.

55. Jackson, "Dynamic of Indian Demographic Collapse in the San Francisco Bay Missions," 145.

56. Ibid., 150, says that "few epidemics attacked the Alta California missions," but elsewhere he notes "a severe smallpox outbreak in 1838" (*Indian Population Decline*, 52). Walker and Johnson, "Effects of Contact on the Chumash Indians," 133–35, indicate several epidemics including diphtheria, measles, influenza, and smallpox.

57. Engstrand, "Enduring Legacy," 36–39.

58. Lothrop, "Rancheras and the Land," 61.

59. *Realty Blue Book of California,* 1924, 13.

60. Jorge Vera Estanol, in *Realty Blue Book,* 21.

61. Engstrand, "Enduring Legacy," 36–47; Liebman, *California Farmland,* 6–8. For Pío Pico's efforts as the last Mexican governor to keep California Mexican, see *Don Pío Pico's Historical Narrative,* 98–147. "Anglo Californios" refers to Americans who assimilated; see below, pp. 51–52.

62. Walker and Johnson, "Effects of Contact," 136. On secularization and its effects, see Weber, *Mexican Frontier,* 60–68, 186. Also, Jackson, *Indian Population Decline,* 44–53, and Jackson, "The Changing Economic Structure of the Alta California Missions," 387–415.

63. Meighan, "Indians and California Missions," 189.

64. Tibesar, *Writings of Junípero Serra,* I:249; further quotations are on I:353, II:249, III:355, and III:413–14.

65. Taylor, *In Search of the Racial Frontier,* 34.

66. Hernandez, "No Settlement without Women," 208–12, 217.

67. Lothrop, "Rancheras," 61; Castañeda, "Engendering the History of Alta California, 1769–1848," 241, 244.

68. Weber, *Spanish Frontier,* 260, 264–65, 322, 327.

69. Jones, *Paisanos,* 213–21.

70. Weaver, *Los Angeles: The Enormous Village,* 17–20.

71. Wittenburg, "Three Generations of the Sepulveda Family," 198, 207–08.

72. Jones, *Paisanos,* 129, assuming this census of 1817 is accurate; it may be an undercount but close to the true figure.

73. Nugent, "Frontiers and Empires in the Late Nineteenth Century," 393–408.

74. Frost, "Vitus Bering Resurrected," 91–92, 96–97; Gibson, "Russian Expansion in Siberia and America," 33–34; Hunt, *Alaska: A Bicentennial History,* 21–23.

75. Gibson, "Russian Expansion," 34.

76. For the Russian-Tlingit conflict see Chevigny, *Russian America: The Great Alaskan Venture, 1741–1867,* 93, 96–97, 101–03.

77. Webb, *Last Frontier,* 22–28.

78. Boyd, "Population Decline from Two Epidemics on the Northwest Coast," 249–53; Gibson, "Russian Expansion," 38.

79. Webb, *Last Frontier,* 42.

80. Hunt, *Alaska,* 30.

81. Sandos, "Between Crucifix and Lance," 213, and Nunis, "Alta California's Trojan Horse," 304.

82. Tikhmenev, *History of the Russian American Company,* 133–42; Bunje, "Russian California, 1805–1841," 3–7, 35–36; Caughey, *California,* 180–81, 208–11; Rolle, *California,* 81–84.

83. Near present Vancouver, Washington, not Vancouver, British Columbia, three hundred miles north.

84. Scott and De Lorme, *Historical Atlas of Washington,* plates 23 and 24 and text.

85. Morton, *Canadian West to 1870–71,* 500, 505, 718–20, 730.

86. Billington and Ridge, *Westward Expansion,* 472.

87. Faragher, *Daniel Boone,* 276–81.

88. Sandoval, "Gnats, Goods, and Greasers," 22–31; Clapsaddle, "West and Dry Routes of the Santa Fe Trail," 98–115.

89. Utley, *A Life Wild and Perilous: Mountain Men and the Paths to the Pacific.*

90. Unruh, *Plains Across,* 20.

91. Benson, "Texas as Viewed from Mexico, 1820–1834," 220–30. On the Catholic requirement, Miller, "Stephen F. Austin and the Anglo-Texan Response to the Religious Establishment in Mexico, 1821–1836," 283–316.

Notes to Chapter 3

92. Weber, *Mexican Frontier*, 1, 4; De León, *Tejano Community*, 4; Jones, *Paisanos*, 48.
93. Billington and Ridge, *Westward Expansion*, 428–32; Weber, *Mexican Frontier*, 213. The Americans also brought a thousand slaves, defined as "contract labor" to get around the Mexican law against slavery.
94. Benson, "Texas as Viewed from Mexico," 252, 264–66, passim.
95. Epperson, "1834 Census—Anahuac Precinct, Atascosito District," 437–47.
96. Taylor, *In Search*, 37–45, 60: the "empire for liberty," in Texas, was really an "empire for slavery," 39.
97. Hoerig, "Relationship between German Immigrants and the Native Peoples in Western Texas," 423–51; Anderson, "Delaware and Shawnee Indians and the Republic of Texas, 1820–1845," 231–60.
98. De León and Stewart, *Tejanos and the Numbers Game*, 15, 20–22, 27.
99. Billington and Ridge, *Westward Expansion*, 461; Utley, *Life Wild and Perilous*, 213–14.
100. Boag, *Environment and Experience*, 20–22, 140.
101. Bowen, *Willamette Valley*, 11–12, 25.
102. Lamar, *The Far Southwest*, 39. For the northern New Mexico fur trade, see Weber, *The Taos Trappers*.
103. Ubelaker, "North American Indian Population Size," 173 (table 3), estimates 215,950 Southwest Indians in 1800, 176,740 in 1850; 180,000 is a very rough interpolation.
104. Bogue, "Agricultural Empire," in Milner, et al., 282–83.
105. Alonzo, *Tejano Legacy*, 12.
106. Utley, *Indian Frontier of the American West 1846–1890*, 1–2.
107. West, *Way to the West*, 58–71.
108. Weber, *Mexican Frontier*, 228–29.
109. Engstrand, "Enduring Legacy," 42–43.
110. Blumenson, *Patton*, 25–26. Wilson's son, his son-in-law James deB. Shorb, and Henry E. Huntington later owned much of the area around Pasadena and created San Marino, the site of the Huntington Library.
111. Woolsey, "A Capitalist in a Foreign Land: Abel Stearns in Southern California before the Conquest," 108.
112. Caughey, *California*, 242–44; McWilliams, *Southern California*, 53.
113. "Father McNamara's Letter 1846" and "To Pío Pico (Application for a grant of land)," July 3, 1846, in Abel Stearns mss., Huntington Library.
114. Caughey, *California*, 248–55; Rolle, *California*, 135–42; Munkres, "The Bidwell-Bartleson Party," 64–66; Hackel, "Land, Labor, and Production," 136; Nunis, "Alta California's Trojan Horse," 317.
115. Rolle, *California*, 153–60; Utley, *Life Wild and Perilous*, 228–39, for the American conquest of northern California and the roles of John C. Frémont and Kit Carson in it.
116. On cultural prejudice consequent upon Manifest Destiny, Gutiérrez, *When Jesus Came*, 337–40. Sundquist, 131, points out that "many accounts by explorers and settlers were very sympathetic to native inhabitants, but much of the writing was imbued with fatalistic notions of the inevitable demise of 'savage' life or the corruption and degeneration of Hispanic culture."

3: The United States Captures Its West, 1848–1889

1. Loosley, "Foreign Born Population of California, 1848–1920," 1–2.
2. Rohrbough, *Days of Gold*, 8; this is the best and most recent history.
3. Loosley, "Foreign Born Population," 4–5, 9. U.S. Census, *Historical Statistics*, I:25, series A195.
4. Sylva, "Foreigners in the California Gold Rush," chap. 2.
5. Ubelaker, "North American Indian Population Size," 173; Hurtado, *Indian Survival*, 100.

6. *Cork Examiner,* July 21, 1852.
7. McEntire, *Population of California,* 191.
8. Riley, "Women on the Panama Trail to California, 1849–1869," 531–48; Levy, *They Saw the Elephant.*
9. McEntire, *Population of California,* 192; Beesley, "From Chinese to Chinese-American," 168–79.
10. Petrik, "Capitalists with Rooms," 29–30.
11. U.S. Census, *Historical Statistics,* series A195–209, I:25–35.
12. Communities where both mining and farming took place—"agri-mining," as Dean May calls them in *Three Frontiers*—muddy these distinctions.
13. McEntire, *Population of California,* 88–93.
14. Hudson, "Who Was 'Forest Man'?," 69–83, especially 70, 81–82.
15. McEntire, *Population of California,* 74–75; Loosley, "Foreign Born Population," 10. The others included 2,000 Central and South Americans, 1,700 Swiss, 1,500 Portuguese, 896 Australians, 730 Poles, and hundreds of smaller groups. Also, Hardaway, *Narrative Bibliography of the African-American Frontier,* 91.
16. Taylor, *In Search of the Racial Frontier,* 82, 88.
17. Chen, "Internal Origins of Chinese Emigration to California Reconsidered," 521–46.
18. Chan, *This Bitter-Sweet Soil,* xx, 8, 17, 27–28, 38, 41, 46, 79.
19. McEntire, *Population of California,* 138–39, 146–47; Chu, "Chinatowns in the Delta," 27. For an overview, see Roger Daniels, *Asian America,* chaps. 1 and 2; on Chinese women migrants, see Tong, *Unsubmissive Women.*
20. Peterson, *Idaho,* 60; Wunder, "The Courts and the Chinese," *IdY,* 24.
21. Tipton, "Men Out of China," 347; Fong, "Sojourners and Settlers," 238.
22. Chan, "Chinese in Nevada," 267–68, 282, 303.
23. Laurie, "Civil Disorder and the Military in Rock Springs, Wyoming," 44–59.
24. Little, *Excerpts of Marin History; Don, Old St. Hilary's.*
25. Burchell, *San Francisco Irish,* 3–14, 49.
26. Hoy, "The Journey Out," 68–69; Dwyer, *Condemned to the Mines,* 80.
27. Dwyer, *Condemned to the Mines,* 90, 156–57.
28. Clar and Kramer, "The Girl Rabbi of the Golden West: The Adventurous Life of Ray Frank in Nevada, California and the Northwest," 99–111, 223–36.
29. Weissberg, "Gold Rush Merchants in Shasta County, California," 291–305; Zarchin, *Glimpses of Jewish Life in San Francisco,* 60–64.
30. McEntire, *Population of California,* 36–37.
31. Park, "German Associational and Sporting Life in the Greater San Francisco Bay Area, 1850–1900," 47–64; Madden, *German Travelers in California.*
32. Palmer, "Italian Immigration and the Development of California Agriculture," 297; Gumina, *Italians of San Francisco 1850–1930,* 5, 11–13, 29; Baily, "Adjustment of Italian Immigrants in Buenos Aires and New York"; Klein, "Integration of Italian Immigrants into the United States and Argentina."
33. Rohrbough, *Days of Gold,* 223.
34. California's 1850 Act for the Government and Protection of Indians remained in effect until the Civil War and "led to virtual Indian slavery"; Sandos, "Between Crucifix and Lance," 220.
35. Hurtado, introduction to Heizer, *Destruction of California,* vi, 41, 243; Heizer and Almquist, *The Other Californians,* 27, 38–40, 48 (on vagrancy laws), 57 (indenture "was a legalized form of slavery of California Indians").
36. Kevin Starr minces no words: "The murderous rage that drove the white settlers of Lassen County to exterminate the Yahi like so much vermin, to destroy whole villages, to stab and shoot women and children to death as if they were clearing a field of rabbits, had its parallels in the massacre of the Armenians prior to World War I, the Great War

itself, which raised the slaughter to new levels of efficiency, and, by the 1930s, the first stages of the Holocaust." Starr, _The Dream Endures,_ 340.

37. Rohrbough, _Days of Gold,_ 229.
38. McEntire, _Population of California,_ 15–16, 23–25; Lapp, _Blacks in Gold Rush California._
39. In 1880 Los Angeles County had 33,000 people; San Francisco, 234,000.
40. Powell, "Labor's Fight for Recognition in the Western Coalfields," 20.
41. Emmons, _The Butte Irish,_ 83.
42. Ashcroft, "Miner and Merchant in Socorro's Boom Town Economy," 103–17.
43. Wyman, _Hard Rock Epic,_ 5.
44. Hurtado, _Indian Survival,_ 101.
45. Ubelaker's estimates, from "North American Indian Population Size," 292.
46. Torrez, "The San Juan Gold Rush of 1860," 257–72.
47. West, _Contested Plains,_ 145–47. The fifty-niners were almost entirely young men; males outnumbered females even more than among the forty-niners.
48. Schwantes, _Pacific Northwest,_ 122.
49. Schwartz, "Sick Hearts: Indian Removal on the Oregon Coast, 1875–1881," 228–64.
50. Doyle, "Journeys to the Land of Gold: Emigrants on the Bozeman Trail, 1863–1866," 54–67.
51. On the frontier rural mode of life, see Nugent, _Structures of American Social History,_ 54–64.
52. Gates, "Public Land Issues in the United States," 368.
53. Wishart, "Dispossession of the Pawnee," 382, 386, 389–401.
54. Socolofsky and Self, _Historical Atlas of Kansas,_ map and text 35.
55. Owens and Owens, "Buffalo and Bacteria," 65–67.
56. Socolofsky and Self, _Historical Atlas of Kansas,_ map and text 41.
57. Shortridge, "People of the New Frontier: Kansas Population Origins, 1865," 166–67, 179.
58. Emigrant promotional literature is voluminous. For a valuable analysis, see Turk, "Selling the Heartland," 150–59.
59. Taylor, _In Search,_ 107, 136; 138–41 (on Nicodemus); 141–43 (on the Exodusters).
60. Taylor, "From Esteban to Rodney King," 6.
61. Hamilton, "Origins and Early Promotion of Nicodemus," 221–42.
62. Haywood, "The Hodgeman County Colony," 210–21.
63. Douglas, "Forgotten Zions," 108–19.
64. Riley, "Kansas Frontierswomen Viewed through Their Writings," 2–9; quotations from 6, 8.
65. Riley, "Kansas Frontierswomen . . . Allen," 83–95; quotations from 87, 93, 94.
66. Riley, "Kansas Frontierswomen . . . Robbins," 138–45; quotation from 140.
67. Gates, _History of Public Land Law Development,_ 799.
68. Harris, _Long Vistas,_ 5, 20.
69. Hoover, "Sioux Agreement of 1889," 58–59. A minority, including Sitting Bull, refused to agree. Their resistance culminated in his assassination, and two weeks later, on December 29, 1890, the misnamed "Battle" (actually, massacre by the army) of Wounded Knee; for that, see Utley, _Lance and the Shield,_ 291–312.
70. Hoover, "Sioux Agreement," 71–75, 84–87.
71. Hudson, "The Study of Western Frontier Populations," 35–60.
72. Hutton, " 'Fort Desolation,' " 20–30.
73. Nelson, " 'All Well and Hard at Work': The Harris Family letters," 24–37.
74. Richter, "Heritage of Faith," 155–72; Nelson, " 'Everything I Want Is Here!,' " 105–35.
75. Burns, "Collapse of Small Towns on the Great Plains," 6–8.
76. Robbins, " 'At the End of the Cracked Whip': The Northern West, 1880–1920," 4.
77. Roeder, "A Settlement on the Plains: Paris Gibson and the Building of Great Falls," 6–10.

78. Studness, "Economic Opportunity and Westward Migration of Canadians," 570–74.

79. Parley, "Moffat, Assiniboia," 32–36; McDougald, "Cypress Hills Reminiscences," 27–29.

80. Friesen, *Canadian Prairies*, 137, 149, 181–86, 201–04.

81. Thomas, "The Rancher and the City: Calgary and the Cattlemen, 1883–1914," 203.

82. West, "Scarlet West," 16–27.

83. Older authorities put the number of black cowboys at five to nine thousand (Hardaway, *Narrative Bibliography*, 143–44, 152–53; Porter, "Negro Labor in the Western Cattle Industry, 1866–1900," 346–74); but Taylor, *In Search* (156–58, 164) notes that the 1890 census counted only sixteen hundred (probable) black cowboys, though there were twenty-five thousand buffalo soldiers (blacks) in the army in the West between 1866 and 1917.

84. Dykstra, *The Cattle Towns,* and for Abilene particularly, Dykstra's "The Last Days of 'Texan' Abilene," 107–19. Wichita grew from 4,911 in 1880 to 23,853 by 1890, with another 20,000 in the surrounding county. Dodge City rose from 996 in 1880 to 1,763 in 1890, with another 3,500 in the county (U.S. Census, 1930, I:400–03).

85. Barnes, *Western Grazing Grounds and Forest Ranges,* 25.

86. Wheeler, "The Blizzard of 1886," 415–32; quotation from 427.

87. Nostrand, "Century of Hispanic Expansion," 361–86.

88. Lister and Lister, "Chinese Sojourners in Territorial Prescott," 1–4.

89. Ruffner OH, 3–6.

90. Lamb, "Jews in Early Phoenix, 1870–1920," 301.

91. Stern and Kramer, "Who Was Isaacson, Arizona Named For?," 121–24.

92. Stern, "The Tombstone, Arizona Jewish Saga," 217–30.

93. Lang, "New Mexico Bureau of Immigration, 1880–1912," 195, 206, 209.

94. Bakken, "Mexican and American Land Policy," 237.

95. Knowlton, "The Mora Land Grant: A New Mexican Tragedy," 59–73; also, Tyler, "Ejido Lands," 24–35, and Hall, "Land Litigation and the Idea of New Mexico Progress," 48–58.

96. Tigges, "Santa Fe Landownership in the 1880s," 153–80, especially 154, 163–64, 178–79.

97. May, *Three Frontiers,* passim.

98. Neunherz, " 'Hemmed In,' " 101–11, especially 102.

99. MacDonald, "Population Growth and Change in Seattle and Vancouver, 1880–1960," 300.

100. Schwantes, *Pacific Northwest,* 186; Brown, "The Promotion of Emigration," 3–17.

101. *Hist. Stats.,* A195, I:33, I:36.

102. Schwantes, *Pacific Northwest,* 187.

103. Laurie, " 'The Chinese Must Go,' " 24–29.

104. *NYT,* August 20, 1995. Professor David H. Stratton of Washington State University uncovered and investigated this episode.

105. Morrissey, *Mental Territories,* 23, 26, 42–48, 60.

106. Johansen and Gates, *Empire of the Columbia,* 317–32.

107. Edwards, "Walla Walla: Gateway to the Pacific Northwest Interior," 28–43.

108. *Atlas of Washington Agriculture,* 4 (map).

109. Morrissey, *Mental Territories,* 75–76, 86–92.

110. Stern, "Jewish Community of Eureka, Nevada," 95–97, 114; Olson, "Pioneer Catholicism in Eastern and Southern Nevada 1864–1931," 168.

111. Douglass and Bilbao, *Amerikanuak,* 208, 215, 242–44, 260–61; Etulain, "Basque Beginnings in the Pacific Northwest," 27–29; Bieter, "Reluctant Shepherds," 12–13.

112. May, *Three Frontiers,* 93, 128, 253.

113. Meinig, "Mormon Culture Region," 197n.

114. Hulmston, "Mormon Immigration in the 1860s," 32–48.

115. *Hist. Stats.,* series A195; Skolnick et al., "Mormon Demographic History," 10. "Apostolic age" is Jan Shipps's phrase, in *Mormonism.*

116. Arrington and May, " 'A Different Mode of Life', " 3–20.

117. Arrington and Wilcox, "From Subsistence to Gold Age," 340–69.

118. Skolnick, "Mormon Demographic History," 13–14.

119. May, "Stability Ratio," 141–58.

120. May, "People on the Mormon Frontier: Kanab's Families of 1874," 187.

121. Belshaw, "High, Dry, and Lonesome," 364, 376.

122. Meinig, "Mormon Culture Region," 204, 208; West, "Cardston," 162–69.

123. Arrington, "Mormon Settlement of Cassia County, Idaho," 36–41; Bitton, "Peopling the Upper Snake," 47–52; Boyce, "Mormon Invasion and Settlement of the Upper Snake River Plain," 50–58.

124. May and Cornell, "Middleton's Agriminers," 2–11.

125. Emmons, *The Butte Irish*; May, *Three Frontiers*.

126. Gates, "Public Land Disposal in California," 177.

127. Engstrand, "Enduring Legacy," 46.

128. Monroy, *Thrown among Strangers*, 227.

129. Cleland, *The Irvine Ranch*, 35–37, 59, 132.

130. Bogue, "An Agricultural Empire," 291.

131. Gates, *History of Public Land Law Development*, 116; Gates, *Land and Law in California*, 157–58, 179–80.

132. Bakken, "Mexican and American Land Policy," 247; Gates, *Land and Law*, 251.

133. White, "Animals and Enterprise," 242, 254.

134. Rolle, *California*, 269–70; Paul, *Far West and the Great Plains in Transition, 1859–1900*, 226–27; Jelinek, *Harvest Empire*, 38–41; Bean, *California*, 271–72; Liebman, *California Farmland*, 20–51.

135. Thompson, "Insalubrious California," 50.

136. Nadeau, "Wheat Ruled the Valley," 18–20.

137. Bakken, "Mexican and American Land Policy," 258.

138. Rolle, *California*, 257–64.

139. Gates, *History of Public Land Law Development*, 378, 456–57. Montana received 263,000 acres or about 10 percent more than California, mostly in the lavish Northern Pacific grant, a checkerboard *sixty* miles on *each* side of the track (Gates, 374).

140. Ibid., 385.

141. Orsi, "*The Octopus* Reconsidered," 198, 206. The reference is to Frank Norris's novel of 1901 *The Octopus*, wherein the Southern Pacific strangles helpless ranchers.

142. Gilmore, *Gender and Jim Crow*, 12.

143. Fresno, *Centennial Almanac*, 5, 20–21, 31, 35.

144. Reps, *Cities of the American West*, 187, 192.

145. Jelinek, *Harvest Empire*, 60.

146. Gates, *History of Public Land Law Development*, 413, 441.

147. Gates, *Land and Law in California*, 252.

148. Monroy, *Thrown among Strangers*, 238–40. Also, on Indians and Hispanics in Orange County, see Haas, *Conquests and Historical Identities in California, 1769–1836*.

149. Rader, " 'So We Took Only 120 Acres': Land and Labor in the Settlement of Southern California," 3, 5–9, 11.

150. U.S. Works Progress Administration, *California*, 247.

151. Elliott, "Pasadena. History of the San Gabriel Orange Grove Association," in Elliott-Berry mss., Huntington Library, 1; Madison, "Taking the Country Barefooted: The Indiana Colony in Southern California," 236–49.

152. Berry to Thomas B. Elliott, San Francisco, August 21, 1873, Elliott-Berry mss.

153. Berry to Elliott, San Diego, September 1, 1873, same (HM 24551).

154. Berry to Elliott, Los Angeles, September 9, 1873, same (HM 24555).

155. Berry to Elliott, Los Angeles, September 18, 1873, same (HM 24559).

156. Berry to "Sis Helen," Los Angeles, September 23, 1873, same (HM 24676).

157. Calvin Fletcher to Elliott, Los Angeles, December 31, 1873, same.

158. Elliott, "Pasadena. History . . . ," 3.

159. Berry to "Sister Helen," ca. January 1, 1874, same (HM 24614).

160. Elliott, "Pasadena. History . . ." same. The word is likely a corruption of a Chippewa term. Altadena, the name of its unincorporated neighbor farther up the mountainsides, is a corruption of a corruption. The twenty-five-thousand-dollar figure is from *California: A Guide to the Golden State,* 247.

161. Berry to Elliott, Los Angeles, February 3, 1874; Berry to "E. W. B.," Muscatel, California, April 9 and 18, 1874, same.

162. Hayden, "Power of Place," 7.

163. Woolsey, "Rites of Passage," 82–83 and passim.

164. Jaher, *Urban Establishment,* 584.

165. Dumke, "Boom of the 1880s," 100; for a more elaborate picture, consult Dumke's book.

166. McEntire, *Population of California,* 41–42.

167. McWilliams, *Southern California,* 118–19.

168. Lothrop, "Boom of the '80s Revisited," 268.

169. Starr, "Oligarchs, Babbitts & Folks," 28–30, 32 (Garland quote).

170. Reps, *Cities of the American West,* 265, 270; Dumke, "Boom of the 1880s," 105–06; Lothrop, "Boom of the '80s Revisited," 268.

171. Lothrop, "Boom of the '80s Revisited," 283.

172. Reps, *Cities of the American West,* 281.

173. Dumke, "Boom of the 1880s," 201–02.

174. Lothrop, "Boom of the '80s Revisited," 263.

175. McWilliams, *Southern California,* 121–23.

176. Post, "America's Electric Railway Beginnings," 206–09.

177. Parker, "Southern Pacific Railroad and Settlement," 103–19.

178. Santa Ana Assn., *The Santa Ana Valley,* 34.

179. Wood, *Over the Range to the Golden State,* 168–69.

180. Baur, *Health Seekers of Southern California,* viii–ix; Baur, "The Health Seeker in the Westward Movement, 1830–1900," 105, 107.

181. Fitch, "Colony Life in Southern California," 151–58; Hine, *California's Utopian Colonies,* 6–7 and passim.

182. Davis, "From Oasis to Metropolis," 363.

183. Los Angeles Chamber of Commerce, *Los Angeles City and County,* 1–8, 39.

184. Winther, "Rise of Metropolitan Los Angeles," 404–05.

185. I adapt here seven themes from Dumke (1994), 102–03.

186. Monroy, *Thrown among Strangers,* 252.

187. Lothrop, "Boom of the '80s Revisited," 272. Davis, *City of Quartz,* 27, makes a somewhat similar point.

188. "Cities" here meaning places of tens or hundreds of thousands, not the census's twenty-five hundred.

189. Abbott, "Building Western Cities: A Review Essay," *Colorado Heritage,* 1984:1, 40.

190. Cronon, *Nature's Metropolis: Chicago and the Great West,* best discusses this.

191. Abbott, "Boom State and Boom City," 207; Leonard, "The Irish, English, and Germans in Denver, 1860–1890," 126; Tank, "Mobility and Occupational Structure," 191–212; "Denver: The Old Bulls Retreat," 245.

192. Reps, *Cities of the American West,* 477–82; Rohrbough, *Aspen.*

193. Luckingham, "Southwestern Urban Frontier, 1880–1930," 40–41.

194. Bufkin, "From Mud Village to Modern Metropolis," 63–64, 72.

195. Luckingham, "Urban Development in Arizona," 197–98.

196. *Seattle City Directory for 1890*, 65.

197. Turner, "Significance of the Frontier in American History," 47.

4: Defying the Depression, 1889–1901

1. *Life*, (April 5, 1993), as discussed in chapter one.

2. U.S. Census, *Historical Statistics*, I:135 (series D86). The highest rate ever recorded was 24.9 percent in 1933, also lower than the reality.

3. Although the Democrats won control of one or both houses of Congress in elections from 1910 to 1916, and the Democrat Woodrow Wilson was elected president in 1912 and 1916, it was only because the majority Republicans split between conservative and progressive factions.

4. The nation increased from 62,948,000 to 75,995,000, or 20.8 percent. The West (the census region, which does not include the Great Plains) increased from 3,134,000 to 4,309,000, or 38.7 percent. U.S. Census, *Historical Statistics*, I:8 (series A2), I:22 (series A172).

5. "Oklahoma" is a Choctaw word for "red people."

6. Prucha, *American Indian Treaties*, 319–20, 353–55.

7. Dale and Wardell, *History of Oklahoma*, 231; Gibson, *Oklahoma*, 173.

8. Hoig, *Oklahoma Land Rush of 1889*, x.

9. "Unassigned" to any Indians.

10. Hoig, *Land Rush*, 44–48, 58–60, 77, 90, 116, 124–25.

11. Gibson, *Oklahoma*, 176.

12. Morgan and Morgan, *Oklahoma: A Bicentennial History*, 53.

13. Green, "Oklahoma Land Rush of 1889," 120–30.

14. Morris et al., *Historical Atlas of Oklahoma*, text for map 48.

15. The Cherokee Outlet was the land due west of the Cherokee area proper. Theoretically the Cherokees had first option to occupy it if they ever needed to.

16. Gibson, *Oklahoma*, 180. Tonkawas and Pawnees living there negotiated allotments for themselves rather than cash.

17. McReynolds, *Oklahoma*, 299–301; Gibson, *Oklahoma*, 180.

18. Carman, *Historical Atlas of Kansas*, II:33.

19. Shortridge, *Peopling the Plains*, 143.

20. McReynolds, *Oklahoma*, 304–05.

21. Tinker, Jr., OH, Nov. 15, 1982, Pawhuska.

22. Lookout, Jr., OH, Aug. 22, 1983, Tulsa.

23. McReynolds, *Oklahoma*, 307.

24. Brown, *Italians in Oklahoma*, chap. 2; Bernard, *Poles in Oklahoma*, chap. 2.

25. Lovett, "The Levites of Apache, Oklahoma," 299–307.

26. Littlefield and Underhill, "Divorce Seeker's Paradise," 21–34.

27. Taylor, *In Search of the Racial Frontier*, 146–48.

28. Franklin, *Journey toward Hope*, 11.

29. Morgan and Morgan, *Oklahoma*, 62; Franklin, *Journey toward Hope*, 27–28.

30. Thornton, *American Indian Holocaust and Survival*, entitles his chapter 5 "Decline to Nadir: 1800 to 1900."

31. Utley, *Indian Frontier of the American West*, 84–85, 120.

32. Spicer, *Cycles of Conquest*, 222–23.

33. Hoover, "Sioux Agreement of 1889," 57–59, 65–69.

34. Bray, "Teton Sioux Population History," 179.

35. Utley, *Indian Frontier*, 170–72; Peterson, *Idaho*, 20, 88–89; Lamar, *Far Southwest*, 473–74; Spicer, *Cycles*, 254–57, 261.

36. Spicer, *Cycles,* 350.
37. Fuss, "Riding Buffaloes and Broncos."
38. Ubelaker, "North American Indian Population Size," 173, gives 547,000 for North America, of whom 466,000 lived in the United States, including 287,000 in the West. Thornton, *American Indian Holocaust,* 160, gives the census figure of 237,000.
39. Campbell, "Changing Patterns," 339–40, 352–55; Thornton, 120.
40. Frost, "Pueblo Indian Smallpox Epidemic," 418, 422–28, 432–35, 437, 442–45.
41. Spicer, *Cycles,* 261.
42. Snider OH, transcript 14, 18.
43. Brock OH, transcript pp. 6–7.
44. Wetherill OH, 1953, tape 424, transcript 17–21; tape 432, transcript 19.
45. Powell, *Report,* 8, 22, 24.
46. Ibid., 6.
47. Rusinek, "Western Reclamation's Forgotten Forces," 29–35.
48. Gates, *History,* 646–54; Worster, *Rivers of Empire,* chap. 4.
49. Gates, *History,* 654; Opie, *Law of the Land,* 116.
50. Mormon historians have described this system in detail. Also see Worster, *Rivers of Empire,* 75, 80–82; Wilson, "How the Settlers Farmed," 333–56; Hundley, "Great American Desert Transformed," 32.
51. Den Otter, "Irrigation in Southern Alberta, 1882–1901," 127, 129, 132–35; Arrington, "Irrigation in the Snake River Valley," 3–4; Thomas, *Development of Institutions under Irrigation,* 214, 237, 245; Opie, *Ogallala,* 75–85; Ehrlich, "My Childhood on the Prairie," 116–18.
52. Opie, *Ogallala,* 65; Bogue, "Agricultural Empire," 300.
53. Opie, *Law of the Land,* 103–04.
54. Kelley, *Battling the Inland Sea,* 58–63 (quotes, 62).
55. Paul, *Far West and Great Plains in Transition,* 241.
56. Hundley, *Great Thirst,* 98 (quote); Opie, *Law of the Land,* 142.
57. Hundley, *Great Thirst,* 100–01.
58. Opie, *Law of the Land,* 142. Italics author's.
59. Adams, *Irrigation Districts in California, 1887–1915,* 8–9, 19, 34–37, 46–47, 79, 115.
60. Rolle, *California: A History,* 280.
61. Hundley, "Great American Desert Transformed," 32.
62. Gates, *History,* 651.
63. Bogue, "Agricultural Empire," 301; Opie, *Law of the Land,* 119.
64. Wood, *Over the Range to the Golden Gate,* 58–59, 104.
65. Porter, Gannett, and Hunt, "Progress of the Nation 1790 to 1890," xxxiv. This statement was Turner's basis for his thesis that the frontier, which had made Americans who they were, was over.
66. Schwantes, *Coxey's Army,* x, 10, 57–59, 195.
67. Lewelling, "The Tramp Circular," reprinted from *Topeka Daily Capital,* Dec. 5, 1893, in Tindall, *A Populist Reader,* 166–68.
68. Flynt, *Tramping with Tramps,* 107–08.
69. Schwantes, "Images of the Wageworkers' Frontier," 41–42.
70. Northern Pacific, *Great Northwest,* 185, 189, 194, 195, 332.
71. Missouri Pacific, *A Description of the Summer and Winter Health and Pleasure Resorts,* 82.
72. Schwantes, "Varieties of Early Railroad Tourism"; Schwantes, *Railroad Signatures.*
73. Fitzgerald, " 'We Are All in This Together,' " 18–21.
74. Clark and Roberts, *People of Kansas,* 35–39, 46, 64, 161.
75. Nelson, " 'Everything I Want Is Here!,' " 108–09.
76. Turner, "Pioneer Farming Experiences," 41; Rodwell, "Saskatchewan Homestead Records," 10–29; Jones, *Empire of Dust*; Friesen, *Canadian Prairies,* 186, 204. On specific

groups, see Leonoff, "Jewish Farmers of Western Canada," 100, 201, 303, 310; Schwieder, "Frontier Brethren," 4, 8, 13; Yuzyk, "75th Anniversary of Ukrainian Settlement," 247; Royick, "Ukrainian Settlements," 278–79, 285; Kaye, "Ruthenians," 97; Ward, "Trek of the Doukhobors," 17, 19, 24; Rock, "Vasya Pozdnyakov's Dukhobor Narrative," 153; "Sect that Fled Czarist Russia Looks Homeward," *NYT,* Oct. 19, 1992.

77. Moffat, *Population History of Western U.S. Cities and Towns,* 127–31.

78. Hardaway, *Narrative Bibliography,* 196–97, citing Lang, "The Nearly Forgotten Blacks on Last Chance Gulch, 1900–1912," 50–57.

79. Petrik, "Capitalists with Rooms," 30, 36; Butler, *Daughters of Joy,* xvii, chaps. 1, 6; Barnhart, *Fair but Frail.*

80. Emmons, *Butte Irish,* chaps. 1, 3; Malone, "Collapse of Western Metal Mining," 459; *NYT,* July 26, 1993.

81. Livermore Papers, Box 1, diary for July 13, 1898. Also, Smith, "A Land unto Itself," 197–99.

82. White, "*It's Your Misfortune,*" 341–42, puts this episode in the context of anti-Chinese violence across the West in the 1870s and 1880s.

83. Barth, *Instant Cities,* 187, 198, 224–25.

84. U.S. Census, *Population,* 1890, I:lxvii; Abrams, "Chasing an Elusive Dream," 204, 212–13, 217.

85. Rohrbough, *Aspen,* 193, 195.

86. Mahar, *Economic Forces,* 10, 22.

87. Perilli, *Colorado and the Italians,* 27–29, 36–39.

88. Jameson, "Imperfect Unions," 166.

89. Powell, "Labor's Fight for Recognition," 20.

90. Jameson, "Imperfect Unions," 169. Cripple Creek's women also included four physicians and twenty-five nurses in 1902.

91. Meinig, *Southwest,* 41–42, 50–51. On El Paso, see De León and Stewart, *Tejanos and the Numbers Game,* 12, 87; M. Agatha, "Catholic Education and the Indian," 14–15. Drexel had also, by 1889, built Indian schools in Dakota Territory, California, Wyoming, Indian Territory, Oregon, and Montana.

92. Bufkin, "From Mud Village to Modern Metropolis," 73; Luckingham, "Urban Development in Arizona," 199.

93. "Arizona as a Health Resort," (Chicago) *New World,* Oct. 20, 1897.

94. Peterson, "The 'Americanization' of Utah's Agriculture," 110–12, 122; Peterson, Foreword to Goldberg, xii–xiii.

95. Austin, "Desert, Sagebrush, and the Northwest," 133.

96. Mason OH, transcript 6, 9–10, 12, 19.

97. Slavin OH, transcript 7, 9.

98. Hervin OH, transcript 1–3.

99. Brounstein OH, transcript 1–3, 7, 11.

100. Settle OH, transcript 3, 7, 8, 12, 18, 20, 22, 24, 33.

101. Sims, "Japanese American Experience in Idaho," 2; Jensen, "Apartheid: Pacific Coast Style," 335–40.

102. Adair OH, transcript 38.

103. Mercier, "Women's Economic Role," 52.

104. Nasi, Gwilliam, Hallberg, Bottinelli OH. The IWW, Industrial Workers of the World, was a more ideologically radical union than the Western Federation of Miners, despite some overlap between the two.

105. Schoenburg, "Jews of Southeastern Idaho," 291.

106. Olcott, *State of Oregon Blue Book,* 174–75.

107. Liebman, *California Farmland,* 79.

108. Hill, "Shaping of California's Industrial Pattern," 66.

109. U.S. Census, *Population,* 1890, I:lxvii; McEntire, *Population of California,* 25.

110. McWilliams, *Southern California*, 128–29.

111. Spano, "Making Sense of Elusive Malibu," *NYT,* Jan. 5, 1992.

112. Starr, *Americans and the California Dream,* 46, 417.

113. Southern Pacific, *California for Health, Pleasure, and Profit,* 3.

114. Hine, *California's Utopian Colonies,* chaps. 3, 6, 8; Orth, "Ideality to Reality," 195–210.

115. Romo, *East Los Angeles,* 28–33; Jaher, *Urban Establishment,* 584; Hayden, "Power of Place," 7.

116. Hayden, "Power of Place," 7; DeGraaf, "City of Black Angels," 327–28.

117. Jaher, *Urban Establishment,* 636.

118. Kramer, "Herman Silver of Silver Lake," 3, 5, 7, 9–11; same, Part II, 129, 135.

119. Vorspan and Gartner, *History of the Jews of Los Angeles,* 91, 109.

120. Toll, "Fraternalism and Community Structure," 380–85, 403.

121. Eisenberg, "To New York or . . . Oregon?"

122. Franks and Lambert, *Early California Oil,* 73–74.

123. McEntire, *Population of California,* 21, 75, 138–39.

124. Article IV, sections 3 and 4.

125. When they finally became states, their populations were more than sufficient: Oklahoma, entering in 1907, held the record with 1,414,177; New Mexico (1912) had 330,000; Arizona (also 1912), well over 200,000.

126. The United States also acquired the Philippines, Puerto Rico, and some Pacific islands as a result of the 1898 war with Spain, but since these never became "western," they are not part of this story.

127. U.S. Census, *Population,* 1890, I:cci.

128. MacDonald, *Distant Neighbors,* 47.

129. Much of the foregoing rests on Webb, *Last Frontier,* 133–41, 269.

130. Shortridge, "Collapse of Frontier Farming in Alaska," 583.

131. Stannard, "Disease and Infertility," 325–50, describes the Hawaiian case, not minimizing epidemic and endemic diseases but stressing the suppression of fertility, so that deaths soon outnumbered births. The comparison with the California missions is apt. Hawaii also suffered volcanic eruptions, earthquakes, tsunamis (all no doubt before European arrivals as well as after), and shipwrecks; see Schmitt, "Catastrophic Mortality," 217–27.

132. Tabrah, *Hawaii,* 5, 7, 93; Almeida, *Portuguese Immigrants,* 15–17.

133. U.S. Census, *Historical Statistics,* series A195–A201, I:26.

5: The Golden Twilight of the Settlement Frontier, 1901–1913

1. From 1863 through 1900 an average of thirty-seven thousand a year; from 1901 through 1913, seventy-eight thousand a year. Gates, *History,* 799–800.

2. Ibid., 800.

3. Moffat, *Population History of Western U.S. Cities and Towns,* various pages.

4. U.S. Census, *Historical Statistics,* series A195, I:24–37.

5. Henderson OH, August 4, 1970.

6. Revier and Fluke OH, July 24, 1958.

7. Richardson, *Texas,* 390, 392.

8. It was estimated to be the size of Lake Huron. But Lake Huron is constantly replenished, and the aquifer is not. Green, "History of Irrigation Technology," 29–39.

9. Meinig, *Imperial Texas,* 82–83, 103–07.

10. Migration from Mexico to the United States will be discussed in chapter six.

11. Alley OH, August 28, 1985.

12. Russell Adams OH.

13. Behrendt OH, January 5, 1983; Kohler OH.

14. Parman, *Indians and the American West,* 9–10 (see chaps. 1 and 2 for an overview of how the Dawes Act operated); Hoxie, *A Final Promise,* 157, 187; and case studies by William T. Hagan, Donald J. Berthrong, and Frederick E. Hoxie on the administration of the Dawes Act, in Iverson, *Plains Indians.*
15. Shortridge, *Peopling the Plains,* 143–50.
16. Clark and Roberts, *People of Kansas,* 36, 161.
17. Schlebecker, "Agriculture in Western Nebraska," 253, 259.
18. Census; also Riney-Kehrberg, "In God We Trusted, in Kansas We Busted . . . Again," 190–92.
19. Fink and Carriquiry, "Having Babies or Not," 158.
20. U.S. Census, *Historical Statistics,* series C42–C43, I:94.
21. U.S. Census, *Population,* 1910. West of the ninety-eighth meridian the largest towns in South Dakota were Aberdeen, 10,753; Mitchell, 6,515; Huron, 5,791; and Rapid City, 3,854; in North Dakota, Minot, 6,188; and Bismarck, 5,443.
22. Colorado Promotion and Publicity Committee, *Colorado: Its Agriculture, Its Horticulture,* 18, 23–25.
23. Denver Reservoir Irrigation Company, "Call of the West." This and other promotional pamphlets cited here may be found in the Beinecke Library of Yale University.
24. Big Horn Basin Development Co., 1908.
25. Heileman, *Klamath,* 10, 11 (quote), 15 (quote), 19, 21.
26. "The Wheatland Colony," 16–19, 21.
27. Clark, *Water in New Mexico,* 87–90.
28. Chicago, Burlington & Quincy Railroad, *Irrigation Bulletin No. 1, 1905.*
29. Hargreaves, *Dry Farming . . . 1900–1925,* 3.
30. Hargreaves, *Dry Farming . . . 1920–1990,* 3.
31. Hargreaves, *Dry Farming . . . 1900–1925,* 85–109, 140–41, 179–82, 220–22, 224–59. The Campbell quote is on p. 93. Hargreaves concludes, "The essence of the dry-farming movement was not the discovery and promulgation of new techniques or new crop varieties which assured successful cultivation of the semiarid lands, but rather the organized effort to attract settlers into the region" (220).
32. Nugent, *Crossings,* 145; Hargreaves, *Dry Farming . . . 1900–1925,* 440–47.
33. Hudson, *Plains Country Towns,* 56.
34. Ridgley, "Railroads and Rural Development," 165–87.
35. Hudson, "Two Dakota Homestead Frontiers," 443–44, 454–61.
36. Henke, "Settlement Process," 14–33 (quote, 23–24). On the Poppers and a "Buffalo Commons," see chapter one.
37. Hampsten, "The Nehers and the Martins in North Dakota," 175–229 (quotes, 206, 224, 226).
38. Sherman and Thorson, *Plains Folk,* 338–42.
39. Trupin, *Dakota Diaspora,* 56, 64, 76, 91–93, 150, 152.
40. Rikoon, *Rachel Calof's Story,* 21–22, 24–25, 69, 85, 90–91, 100. Rachel died in 1952, aged seventy-six. Rikoon notes that probably fewer than 2 percent of the homesteads continued into a second generation (125).
41. This procedure was called commutation. If after filing for a homestead you decided you did not want to live there for the prescribed five years, you had the option of buying the land for $1.25 an acre, the minimum price for public land before the 1862 Homestead Act and for much of it long after.
42. Schulte, " 'Proving Up and Moving Up,' " 228–29, 234–35, 238–42.
43. Waltz, "West River Pioneer," 42–77; part two, 140–69; parts three and four, 1987, 241–95, (quotes, 141–42, 151–52). For other accounts of women as homesteaders, see Lindgren, *Land in Her Own Name,* and for a comprehensive treatment, Riley, *The Female Frontier.*

44. Nelson, " 'Everything I Want Is Here!,' " 122–23.
45. Fletcher, "End of the Open Range," 188–211, especially 208–10.
46. Murray and Murray, "Herding Sheep," 68–71.
47. Great Northern Railway, "Great Judith Basin," 3, 5, 12.
48. MacDonald, "Honyockers."
49. "Honyocker" is a term of arguable origin, but Carol Bryan, of California State University in Fresno, reported on the Internet (H-West), Dec. 2, 1997, that the *Independent* (a popular magazine) of July 1913 included an essay on "The Lady Homesteader." It explained that "honyocker" is a Russian term "borrowed by the people who already lived in the Western country before it was thrown open for settlement, and applied facetiously to the homesteaders with the meaning perhaps of 'one new at his business,' therefore 'a blunderer.' But far from considering it a reproach our merry enterprising young people on the homesteads claim it as a title of honor and respect."
50. Two excellent studies of High Plains community formation are Myers, "Homestead on the Range" and Bennett and Kohl, *Settling the Canadian-American West,* based on hundreds of local histories.
51. Lux, "Honyockers of Harlem," 2–14, especially 6. For the context of federal land policy, see Gates, "Homesteading the High Plains"; for Northern Pacific land operations, see Cotroneo, "Colonization of the Northern Pacific Land Grant" and "Selling Land on the Montana Plains." Also, Melcher, " 'Women's Matters': Birth Control, Prenatal Care, and Childbirth in Rural Montana, 1910–1940."
52. Wyoming, *The State of Wyoming,* 8, 46, 77, 81, 128.
53. Harris, *Long Vistas,* 46–47, 59, 69–70, 74.
54. The well-known case of Elinore Pruitt Stewart, which she serialized in the *Atlantic Monthly* and which became the basis for the film *Heartland,* involved not only her own attempt to homestead, but manipulation of the laws to add to her husband's tract. See Smith, "Single Women Homesteaders."
55. Harris, *Long Vistas,* 163.
56. Ernie Betasso, in Rogers, *In Other Words,* 78.
57. Rio Grande Home Co., "There's a Home for You in the Sunny San Luis Valley, Colorado."
58. Clason, *Free Homestead Lands of Colorado Described,* 5, 7.
59. Fleming, " 'Sockless' Jerry Simpson: The New Mexico Years," 49–69, especially 64; also, Meinig, *Southwest,* 56–62, 66–70.
60. New Mexico Bureau of Immigration, *Colfax County,* 17, 19, 47; same, *Union County,* 3, 4; same, *Eddy County,* 1, 4–5, 11, 19, 41.
61. Frost and Walter, *Land of Sunshine,* I, 40–41, 53, 119, 121.
62. Wells, *The New Nevada,* 3, 5, 11.
63. Norcross, "Nevada: Fifty Years Asleep."
64. Goldberg, *Barry Goldwater,* 20–21.
65. Timmons, *El Paso,* 196–201.
66. Babbitt, "History of Land Fraud," 3–4. On speculation and the Salt River, see also Worster, *Rivers of Empire,* 171–74.
67. Poster in the Beinecke Library, "Fortunes Made from Imperial Valley Farms Present Opportunities Even Bigger and Better."
68. (Yuma County Commercial Club), *Land of Promise.*
69. Peterson, Foreword to Goldberg, *Back to the Soil,* xii–xiii, xv–xvii, xx.
70. Ibid., xiii, xv.
71. Stathis, "Utah's Experience with the Desert Land Act," 191.
72. Goldberg, *Back to the Soil,* 64, 123–24, 134.
73. Stowell OH, March 1970.

74. Armond Jackson OH.
75. Harmsworth, *Sixty Years of Population Growth*, 15–16, 29–35.
76. Harkness, "Basque Settlement in Oregon," 273–75; Paquette, *Basques to Bakersfield*, 1, 5, 87–88.
77. Etulain, "Basque Beginnings," 29–30; Bieter, "Reluctant Shepherds," 14–15; Douglass and Bilbao, *Amerikanuak*, 263, 299–300, 342–45.
78. Uberuaga OH, Jan. 1986.
79. Peterson, *Idaho*, 126–34.
80. Arrington, "Irrigation in the Snake River Valley," 3–6.
81. Rexburg Commercial Club, *Great Upper Snake River Valley*, cover, 15–17.
82. Glaser, "Migration in Idaho's History," 23; Hitt OH, Allan OH.
83. Washington, *Atlas of Washington Agriculture*, 4–5, 10, 51; numbers of farms rose from thirty-three thousand in 1900 to about sixty-five thousand in 1915.
84. Edwards, " 'The Early Morning of Yakima's Day of Greatness,' " 78–89.
85. Johansen and Gates, *Empire of the Columbia*, 374.
86. Ficken and LeWarne, *Washington*, 65, 67.
87. Johansen and Gates, *Empire of the Columbia*, 372, 374.
88. Landis, *Rural Population Trends*, 13, 20–21, 26–27.
89. Limbaugh, "From Missouri to the Pacific Northwest," 229–57.
90. Bertha Marston OH, quoted in Boag, "Ashwood on Trout Creek," 144; also 117, 122–23, 136–39, 143–45.
91. U.S. Census, *Historical Statistics*, series K1, K4, K5, I:457, show that from 1900 to 1913 the United States gained seven hundred thousand new farms, covering sixty-one million acres, on which lived 2,395,000 people. Farm population in the Great Plains, mountain, and Pacific states rose between 1900 and 1920 by 1,963,000; the rest of the country by only another 137,000.
92. Ibid., series K17, K41–K44, K64–K66, I:458–63.
93. Mellinger, *Race and Labor in Western Copper*, chaps. 2, 6; Schwantes, *Bisbee*, 125–26.
94. Zanjani, "To Die in Goldfield," 47–53, 56, 60, 62–64, 66 (quote).
95. Lillard, *Desert Challenge*, 293–94.
96. H. Papanikolas, "Toil and Rage," 122, citing the *Report 1911–1912* of the Utah Bureau of Immigration.
97. Notarianni, "Utah's 'Ellis Island,' " 180–81; Saloutos, "Cultural Persistence and Change," 89; H. Papanikolas, "Toil and Rage," 121.
98. Petrakis, "Memories: Reflections on the Lives and Deaths of Two Mothers," *Chicago Sunday Tribune Magazine*, May 14, 1995.
99. Z. Papanikolas, *Buried Unsung*.
100. Mellinger, "Frontier Camp to Small Town," 259–60, 264–66.
101. Lang, "The Nearly Forgotten Blacks on Last Chance Gulch, 1900–1912," 50–57.
102. Emmons, *Butte Irish*, 63.
103. Ibid., 398–400, 407–09; Mercier, " 'The Stack Dominated Our Lives,' " 40–57; Farling, "Legacy of Montana's Pioneers," *HCN*, March 14, 1988.
104. The North Star Mining Company and Associated Records are in the Beinecke Library of Yale University. Quoted and referred to here are items from Boxes 40, 41, and 42.
105. Scamehorn, "In the Shadow of Cripple Creek," 225, 228.
106. Moran, "Marble: The Tale of a Colorado Town," *HCN*, Aug. 29, 1988.
107. Mahar, *Economic Forces*, 5.
108. Daskarolis, "San Francisco's Greek Colony," 114–17.
109. Scott, "Greek Community in Pocatello," 30, 32–33.
110. Demus OH.
111. Cofone, "Themes in the Italian Settlement," 116, 120–26.

112. Zellick, "Men from Bribir," 44, 46, 50–51.
113. Kohs, "Jewish Community of Los Angeles," 90, 113.
114. Baganha, "Social Mobility of Portuguese Immigrants," 279, 282, 286–89, 294–95; Vaz, *Portuguese in California,* 45, 63, 64, 68; Almeida, *Portuguese Immigrants,* 10, 15.
115. Palmer, "Italian Immigration," 141–43, 146, 151, 297.
116. Scherini, "Italian American Community of San Francisco," 19–23 (quotes 21–22).
117. Gumina, *Italians of San Francisco,* 79, 96.
118. Cofone, "Reno's Little Italy," 97–110; Martinelli, "Italy in Phoenix," 319–25, 326; Gould, "Portland Italians, 1880–1920," 246, 250–51, 253–54; Toll, "Ethnicity and Stability: The Italians and Jews of South Portland," 162, 166, 167 (quote), 174, 180, 181–83.
119. From the *B'nai B'rith Messenger* of Los Angeles, Sept. 13, 1907, reprinted in "Organized Jewish Life Begins in Pasadena—1907," *WSJH,* 20 (Oct. 1987), 93–94.
120. Marinbach, *Galveston: Ellis Island of the West,* xiv, 12–14, 18, 112–15, 173, 190–91.
121. (Dublin) *Irish Catholic,* Sept. 16, 1893, Sept. 28, 1901, Sept. 9, 1905 (quote), Aug. 1, 8, 1908, Feb. 11, 1911, Apr. 15, 1911, May 13, 1911 (quote), June 24, 1911, Oct. 7, 1911, Dec. 16, 1911. See also Hoy, "The Journey Out."
122. Thomas, *The Lord May Be in a Hurry,* 70–71, 116, 123, 127, 138–43.
123. Hardaway, *Narrative Bibliography,* 162, 164–69, 178–80, 188; Wayne, "Negro Migration and Colonization in Colorado;" Taylor, *In Search,* 153–55.
124. Cuba, "Polish Community in the Urban West," 33–36, 44, 46, 51–54, 61, 68–74.
125. Wakatsuki, "Japanese Emigration," 447; Modell, "Tradition and Opportunity," 165.
126. Murase, *Little Tokyo,* 6; Wakatsuki, "Japanese Emigration," 416–17; Daniels, *Asian America,* 103. There may have been more than twenty-five thousand; Shimpo, "Indentured Migrants from Japan," 48, gives thirty-five thousand.
127. Wakatsuki, "Japanese Emigration," 463.
128. Modell, "Tradition and Opportunity," 182.
129. Wakatsuki, "Japanese Emigration," 478–79, 487.
130. U.S. Census, 1920, I:75–76; Daniels, *Asian America,* 115, 135.
131. Modell, *Economics and Politics of Racial Accommodation,* 17.
132. Smith, "A Day in the City: Sights and Scents Celestial," 23–25. "Celestial" was a Gold Rush–vintage reference to China's Celestial Empire.
133. Kato OH, Jan. 3, 1976.
134. Kanegai OH, Dec. 6, 1975.
135. Kasai OH, Nov. 26, 1975, and autobiography.
136. Tamura, "Gender, Schooling and Teaching, and the Nisei in Hawai'i," 3; Murase, *Little Tokyo,* 8; Mason and McKinstry, *Japanese of Los Angeles,* 16, 32; Daniels, *Asian America,* 152. Ichioka, *The Issei,* 164–75, explains the picture brides.
137. Mason and McKinstry, 13–14, 31; Ichioka, *The Issei,* 3.
138. Ichioka, *The Issei,* 150.
139. Azuma, "Oregon's *Issei,*" 316–18, 328, 330, 332, 338.
140. Higgs, "Wealth of Japanese Tenant Farmers," 492.
141. Olin, "European Immigrant and Oriental Alien," 313; Daniels, *Asian America,* 138–45; Ichioka, *Issei,* 153–56, 233–43; Modell, *Economics and Politics of Racial Accommodation,* 38–43; Iwata, "Japanese Immigrants in California Agriculture," 31.
142. Ichioka, "Japanese Immigrant Response to the 1920 California Alien Land Law," 157–78.
143. White, "Race Relations in the American West," 400, 405, 411 (quote).
144. (San Francisco) *Grizzly Bear,* May 1907, Aug. 1907, May 1921. The May 1920 issue carried an anti-Japanese lead editorial concluding. "The Good Lord never intended that there should be a mixture of the different colored races, else He would not have created some of white, some of black, some of yellow, and some of red." Someone should explore how all this connects with the magazine's masculine boosterism, as in its first issue in May

1907: "Boost! Boost everything that will aid city, county or State. Throw away your hammer and boost—don't be a 'Sissy Fuss' and follow every ism. Be manly, courageous—join in the effort to secure better conditions—help build a better and more prosperous State. But wherever you are, whatever you do, don't growl—but Boost! Boost!! Boost!!!"

145. Marquis, "Inter-Racial Amity in California," 138–42. See also John P. Irish, "Japanese Farmers in California."

146. Fujii OH.

147. Smith, " 'Japanese' in Utah (Part I)," 135; Ulibarri, "Utah's Ethnic Minorities," 222; Stearns, "Settlement of the Japanese in Oregon," 262–69.

148. Reisner, *Cadillac Desert*, 106. He goes on to say: "The Owens River made Los Angeles large enough and wealthy enough to go out and capture any river within six hundred miles, and that made it larger, wealthier, and a good deal more awful. It is the only megalopolis in North America which is mentioned in the same breath as Mexico City [which is not in North America?] or Djakarta. . . ." What Reisner condemns, of course, others applaud.

149. Starr, *The Dream Endures,* 159.

150. Kahrl, *California Water Atlas,* 29–32.

151. Crenshaw, *Salt River Valley Arizona,* 3, 9, 13, 23; "Water for Phoenix: Building the Roosevelt Dam," 279–94; Luckingham, "Southwestern Urban Frontier, 1880–1930," 47.

152. Foote, "Redemption of the Great Valley of California," 229–30, 232–35, 245.

153. California's urban percentage in 1910 was 61.7; the Northeast's, 71.8; the Midwest's, 45.1. U.S. Census, *Historical Statistics,* series A178–A179, A202–A203, I:23, I:25.

154. MacDonald, *Distant Neighbors,* 59–60; Taylor, "Black Urban Development," 433–34, 448 (quote); Abbott, "Boom State and Boom City," 221–22.

155. Taylor, *In Search,* 192–93, 196–202, 206–08.

156. *Chicago Sunday Record-Herald,* May 14, 1911; "The Growth of Los Angeles," *Out West,* 19 (Nov. 1903), 534–35; Charles F. Lummis, "A Lesson in the Census," *Land of Sunshine,* 14 (Jan. 1901), 61; American Express advertisement in *New Yorker,* May 20, 1987, 53.

157. Newton, *Jottings from a Shoemaker's Diary,* 22–26, 38–39, 45.

158. Nadeau, "Wheat Ruled the Valley," 21.

159. Foster, "Western Response to Urban Transportation," 33; densities of Seattle and Denver were close to four thousand.

6: Tourists, Honyockers, Mexicans, and More, 1914–1929

1. Lotchin, "Metropolitan-Military Complex," 19–30 (quotes, 24); Greb, "Opening a New Frontier," 405–24.

2. Starr, *Americans and the California Dream,* 295–306 (especially 303, "the frontier was lost forever"); 402–13.

3. See the many local "Review of Health Conditions and Needs" published from 1909 through the 1910s by the Metropolitan Life Insurance Company in cooperation with the General Federation of Women's Clubs.

4. Military censors on both sides covered up the flu epidemic among their own troops. Spain, not being a belligerent, published its case numbers. In thanks the world called the disease "Spanish" influenza. On the pandemic, see Patterson and Pyle, "Geography and Mortality of the 1918 Influenza Epidemic," and Crosby, *America's Forgotten Pandemic,* esp. 207 for totals. Also, Taubenberger et al., "Initial Genetic Characterization of the 1918 'Spanish' Influenza Virus," 1793, 1795, and *Chicago Tribune,* "Devastating 1918 Flu Is Linked to U.S. Pigs," March 21, 1997.

5. Champion OH.

6. In 1870 the nation was 24.8 percent urban, the West 25.8; in 1880, nation 28.2 and West 30.0; in 1890, nation 35.1 and West 37.0. After that:

PERCENT URBAN	1900	1910	1920	1930
U.S.	39.7	45.7	51.2	56.2
West	39.9	47.9	51.3	58.4
Northeast	66.1	71.8	75.5	77.6
Midwest	38.6	45.1	52.3	57.9
South	18.0	22.5	28.1	34.1

U.S. Census, *Historical Statistics,* series A57, A172, A178, I:11, I:22.

7. For example, in Colorado, the counties containing Aspen, Telluride, Leadville, and Vail—all future resorts—lost two-thirds or more of their 1900 populations by 1930. Roskelley, *Population Trends in Colorado,* 8.

8. U.S. Census, *Population,* 1930, pp. 22, 128.

9. Same, esp. pp. 84, 90, 92, 107–08. Mexicans were classified as nonwhite in 1930 but not in other years.

10. California continued to be more foreign-born than the national average: 14.7 for the United States, 24.6 for California, in 1910; 13.2 for the United States, 22.1 for California, in 1920; and 11.6 for the nation, 18.9 for California, in 1930. See censuses, and McEntire, *Population of California,* 75–76, 92. Despite Iowa's reputation as the main supplier of California's people, only about 3.3 percent of Californians at that time were Iowa-born (U.S. Census, *Population,* 1930, 116, 118–25).

11. *Railroad Age Gazette,* Dec. 4, 1908, quoted in Schwantes, *Railroad Signatures,* 241.

12. Morris, "Indian Detours," 73–74.

13. Now known as the Camino Real Hotel. The bar continues to serve prizewinning margaritas beneath the Tiffany dome.

14. Klein, "Frontier Products," 44.

15. James Murray Forbes Papers, Box 7, "Log. Black Hawk. 1903."

16. Pomeroy, *In Search of the Golden West,* 126–27, quoting one traveler.

17. Ramsey, *Veil, Duster, and Tire Iron,* 39, 52–53, 67, 71. In 1959 the Automobile Club of America justly named Ramsey the "woman driver of the century." For more on the early auto trips, see Nugent, "The 'Finding' of the West."

18. Post, *By Motor to the Golden Gate,* 6–8, 82–83, 99, 119–20, 149, 160, 183–84, 196–97.

19. Massey, *It Might Have Been Worse,* 2–7, 11–12, 49, 77, 106, 129.

20. Lewis, "Adventures in Automobumming," Dec. 20, 1919, and Jan. 3, 1920.

21. Van de Water, *The Family Flivvers to Frisco,* 12, 16, 49, 173 (quote), 195, 233; McGill, *Diary of a Motor Journey;* Flagg, *Boulevards All the Way—Maybe;* Hokanson, *Lincoln Highway.*

22. Belasco, *Americans on the Road,* esp. chap. 6.

23. Carolan, *Motor Tales and Travels,* xiii, 20, 63, 68.

24. Gates, *History of Public Land Law Development,* 800.

25. U.S. Census, *Historical Statistics,* series K1, I:457.

26. Adams OH and Alley OH, 1980s.

27. U.S. Census, *Historical Statistics,* series Q289, II:728; series Q329, II:732.

28. Jones, "Strategy of Railway Abandonment," 141–42.

29. Bosley, "Coburg: A Montana Town That Is No More," 38–51.

30. Bennett and Kohl, *Settling the Canadian-American West,* chap. 11, "Rudyard: A Railroad-Homestead Town as Seen by Contemporaries," 156–81; quote, 178; they stress the similarity of homesteading and small-town building on both sides of the Canadian-American border in the prairie-plains West.

31. Fair OH, July 6, 1979.
32. In the 1920s Dallas County rose 55 percent from 210,551 to 325,691; Harris County (Houston), 93 percent from 186,667 to 359,328; El Paso County, 29 percent from 101,877 to 131,597, and Tarrant County (Fort Worth), 41 percent from 108,572 to 152,800. U.S. Census, *Population,* 1930, I:1055–59; U.S. Census, *Population of States and Counties,* 154, 160.
33. Morrison, *A Taste of the Country,* 153. Beale was writing in 1983.
34. MacDonald, "The Honyockers: Dryland Pioneers," 4.
35. Ibid., 7–10.
36. Schlebecker, "Agriculture in Western Nebraska," 254–61.
37. Shortridge, *Peopling the Plains,* 150.
38. Clark and Roberts, *People of Kansas,* 37, 57, 61, 106–07, 132, 150, 161, 183, 192.
39. Sherman et al., *Plains Folk,* 26.
40. Ibid., 301–02, 307.
41. Sankary OH, transcript 1–15.
42. Ankli, "Farm Income," 92–93.
43. Friesen, *Canadian Prairies,* 272, 329.
44. Hudson, "Two Dakota Homestead Frontiers," 461.
45. Duncan, *Out West,* 125.
46. Nelson, *After the West Was Won,* xiv.
47. Ibid., especially chap. 8–11; quotation, 177.
48. Allen, *Homesteading the High Desert,* xiv–xv, 86, 97–98, 102–116, 140–41, 144–45 (quotes, 116, 144).
49. Bowen, "A Backward Step," 233, 238–39.
50. Blevins OH, Nov. 1979.
51. Barnes, "Home on a Canadian Rockpile," 18–22.
52. McPhee, *Rising from the Plains,* 100–01.
53. Raban, "The Unlamented West," 60, 70–72, and *Bad Land: An American Romance.*
54. Ward, "Wheat in Montana," 18–19, 25.
55. Gates, "Homesteading the High Plains," 126–29.
56. Davis, *Honey in the Horn,* 367–68, 370.
57. Doig, *Dancing at the Rascal Fair,* 259–60, 350–52.
58. Hargreaves, *Dry Farming . . . 1920–1990,* 4.
59. Hargreaves, *Dry Farming . . . 1900–1925,* 481 (quote), 484, 502.
60. Jones, " 'We'll All Be Buried Down Here in This Dry Belt . . . ,' " 42–43, 46–47, 49–50.
61. Jones, *Empire of Dust.*
62. Barrett and Arrington, "The 1921 Depression," 12.
63. Brower OH, transcript 41.
64. Bramer OH, transcript 4.
65. Fink, *Agrarian Women,* 191.
66. Kittredge, "Desire and Pursuit of the Whole," 10.
67. Lux, "Honyockers of Harlem," 13.
68. Rolle, *California,* 367–68.
69. Rundell, *Early Texas Oil,* 11–12, 23, 31, 37.
70. Ibid., 94–190; Lynch, *Roughnecks, Drillers, and Tool Pushers.*
71. U.S. Census, *Population of States and Counties,* 158; Griffin, *Land of the High Sky,* 53, 68–69, 147–56.
72. Champion OH.
73. Bruce OH, Nov. 26, 1976.
74. Moffat, *Population History of Western U.S. Cities and Towns,* 282.
75. Feis, "Tulsa," 22.
76. Franks, Lambert, and Tyson, *Early Oklahoma Oil,* 20, 36, 37, 40–41, 55–58, 110, 234.
77. Cook, "The Oil Patch," 121.

78. Gómez-Quiñones, *Mexican-American Labor,* 70; Longmore and Hitt, "Demographic Analysis," 140–41. The 1930 census reported a total "Mexican" population of 1,422,533, which included 616,998 born in Mexico, 541,197 born in the United States of one or two Mexican parents, and 264,338 born in the United States of U.S.-born parents of Mexican stock. The third group is certainly an underenumeration by at least 200,000 in New Mexico alone. Numbers are imprecise because of unusual difficulties the census had with undercounting and defining Mexicans and including second-, third-, and older-generation people who were born in the United States among "Mexicans," which it did not do with purely European-stock people. In addition, no one counted border crossings with any precision before 1924, and at that point the law illegalized many entrants so that to this day head counts are arguable and have to be arrived at by a combination of demographic devices.

79. This paragraph summarizes research in the public use microsamples of the 1910 census recently conducted at the Population Research Center of the University of Texas by Myron P. Gutmann et al., in "A New Look at the Hispanic Population of the United States in 1910."

80. Gómez-Quiñones, *Mexican-American Labor,* 70; same, "Mexican Immigration," 24.

81. Longmore and Hitt, "Demographic Analysis," 143; Foley, *White Scourge,* 42.

82. Foley, *White Scourge,* 43. This was a Bureau of Labor estimate. Flight from the Mexican Revolution likely increased the proportion of women and children too.

83. Longmore and Hitt, "Demographic Analysis," 143, 145, 146.

84. Nostrand, "Hispano Homeland in 1900," 382–92, 396; Hansen, "Commentary," 280–83.

85. Nieto-Phillips, "Colonists and Hispanophiles"; he has since completed his dissertation at UCLA: " 'No Other Blood': History, Language, and Spanish American Ethnic Identity in New Mexico, 1880s–1920s."

86. George I. Sánchez, *Forgotten People,* 11.

87. Carlson, "Seasonal Farm Labor in the San Luis Valley," 97–100.

88. McLean, "Spanish-Americans in Colorado," 87.

89. Ibid., 88–89.

90. Roskelley, *Population Trends in Colorado,* 46, 79.

91. Eckles OH. Eckles was the first woman to be graduated from the state normal school and the first woman elected to state office, becoming state superintendent of public instruction in 1921, as a Democrat.

92. Foley, *White Scourge,* 41.

93. González Navarro, *Población y Sociedad en México,* I:34–35, II:131–33, II:151–52.

94. For revolutionary factionalism in a small town (San Juan del Río, Durango) around 1910, especially between Villistas and Carrancistas, see Miguel Martinez OH.

95. G. Chavez OH.

96. Richard Garcia, *Rise of the Mexican American Middle Class.*

97. OHs of Barrionuevo, Zayas, Ponce, Kim, and de la O.

98. Gates OH (quotes from transcript 21–22) and De Riddle OH.

99. Maria de la O. OH.

100. Gamio, *Quantitative Estimate Sources and Distribution,* 13–14.

101. Ibid., 18; George J. Sanchez, *Becoming Mexican American,* 41, 46–47; Mario Garcia, *Desert Immigrants,* 36; Womack, "Mexican Revolution, 1910–1920," V:80–82, 113–22, 140–53; Meyer, "Mexico: Revolution and Reconstruction in the 1920s," V:155–60, 174–75. Some land reform did take place—180,000 hectares were redistributed to peasants between 1915 and 1920—but not until the Lázaro Cárdenas regime (1934–1940) did it really happen; Cárdenas redistributed 18,000,000 hectares (Meyer, 188).

102. Cardoso, *Mexican Emigration to the United States,* 39.

103. Rodriguez, *Days of Obligation,* 215–16.

104. Pace, "Mexican Refugees in Arizona, 1910–1911," 5–16.

105. Timmons, *El Paso,* 217.
106. Cardoso, *Mexican Emigration,* 40.
107. Richmond, "Mexican Immigration and Border Strategy," 272–83 (quote).
108. Balderas OH; Candelaria OH.
109. Cardoso, *Mexican Emigration,* 71, 77–78, 82, 89–90.
110. And away from Texas during the 1920s. Hernández Álvarez, "Demographic Profile," 472.
111. Loosley, "Foreign Born Population of California," 29, 76.
112. Rochin and Ballenger, "Labor and Labor Markets," 179.
113. Gordon, *Employment, Expansion, and Population Growth,* 21.
114. Romo, "Work and Restlessness," 157, gives 97,000 and 250,000. Gutiérrez, *Walls and Mirrors,* 57, gives 190,000.
115. Romo, "Work and Restlessness," 166–67.
116. Cardoso, *Mexican Emigration,* 93.
117. Reisler, "Always the Laborer, Never the Citizen," 254 (quote).
118. The irony is pointed out by Guerin-Gonzales in *Mexican Workers and American Dreams,* chaps. 1 and 2. She says, for example: "At the same time that California farmers tried to promote and protect an image of California as a place where farming was a family affair, where neighbors contributed their labor during harvest season as part of a communal project, and where the American Dream held out the promise of land ownership and economic independence, they created an agricultural society in which farming was a business, labor was constituted by an army of migrant and impoverished workers, and access to their American Dream was determined by race" (23).
119. Gómez-Quiñones, "Mexican Immigration," 24–25.
120. Alvarez, "Familia: Migration and Adaptation," 132.
121. Ibid., 65–66.
122. García, "The Chicana in American History," 317, 321, 324–25; also, Dolan and Hinojosa, *Mexican Americans and the Catholic Church.*
123. Smith, *The Mexicans in Oklahoma,* 10.
124. McBane, "What Is Whiteness," and "The Role of Gender in Citrus Employment, 68–81; Gómez-Quiñones, *Mexican American Labor,* 77; Samuel Gompers, head of the AFL, told the Oxnard local never to accept Mexican or Japanese members.
125. *The Survey* (Sept. 15, 1920), 715.
126. "Spanish-American Population of Denver," 5–8 (mimeo in the Western History Department, Denver Public Library); McCormick, "1992 Secession Movement in Southwest Kansas," 249.
127. Oppenheimer, "Acculturation or Assimilation," 431–41; for a first-rate community study, see Laird, "Argentine, Kansas: The Evolution of a Mexican-American Community, 1905–1940."
128. Taylor, *Mexican Labor in the . . . Imperial Valley,* 2, 15; Taylor, *Mexican Labor . . . Migration Statistics,* II:2–6; III:6–9, 12–15.
129. Romo, *East Los Angeles,* 4, 61–64, 71–83, 160. The principal employers between 1917 and 1930 were the Southern Pacific, the Santa Fe, two freight transfer railroads, and the Pacific Electric streetcar system (71).
130. As in Rodriguez's *Hunger of Memory.*
131. Saloutos, "The Immigrant in Pacific Coast Agriculture, 1880–1940," 201.
132. Miller, "Changing Faces of the Central Valley," 174–89, details all these.
133. Arriaga OH.
134. Bacca OH.
135. Battaglia OH.
136. OH of Giordano, Priano, and others.
137. "Why Italian-Americans in the West?"
138. Avshalomov OH.

139. Bloom OH.
140. Feldenheimer OH.
141. Cohen OH, Aug. 31, 1976.
142. Winn, "Seattle Jewish Community," 69.
143. Vorspan and Gartner, *History of the Jews of Los Angeles,* 113–27.
144. Reid, *Negro Population of Denver,* 1, 7, 11–12, 17–18, 20–22, 25.
145. Broussard, "Organizing the Black Community," 336–37. Population figures for cities are from the 1920 census, vol. I, tables 16–18.
146. Dellums OH, transcript 3–4.
147. DeGraaf, "City of Black Angels," 330–32, 344, 347.
148. Taylor, *In Search of the Racial Frontier,* 234.
149. Bunch, *Black Angelenos,* 21, 30–36.
150. Price, *Changing Characteristics of the Negro Population,* 39.
151. *LAT,* Feb. 22, 1993, B3.
152. Tigner OH; Hayman OH.
153. Smith OH.
154. Rutherford OH.
155. Gayton OH, transcript 1–4, 6, 9.
156. Letter to author from Professor William Deverell, Pasadena, July 25, 1997.
157. (Chicago) *Broad Ax,* "Race Progress in Southwest," Aug. 29, 1914; "The Negro Makes Good in Business," Sept. 12, 1914.
158. Tsai, *Chinese Experience in America,* 100; *NYT,* Nov. 11, 1990.
159. For a description of the immigration process at Angel Island from the viewpoint of two Chinese who went through it, see OHs of Yuen and Chow.
160. Light, "From Vice District to Tourist Attraction," 376–77.
161. OHs of Jang See Chan, Ben Woo, Tony S. Woo.
162. Chu, "Chinatowns in the Delta," 22, 28, 31, 33; Gillenkirk and Motlow, *Bitter Melon,* 10, 13–14, 18–24.
163. OHs of Quong and Mi and Marie Lew.
164. Lee, "Sojourners, Immigrants, and Ethnics," 54–56.
165. U.S. Census, *Historical Statistics,* series C273–C277, I:117.
166. McWilliams, *Factories,* 117–19; Hess, "Forgotten Asian Americans," 576–80; Tatla, "Sikh Free and Military Migration during the Colonial Period," 71–72; Jensen, *Passage from India,* 16.
167. Jensen, *Passage from India,* 34–40, 269–71; she writes of the post-1924 situation, "Excluded from immigration, prosecuted for their political activities [for Indian independence from the British], excluded from citizenship, denaturalized, excluded from land ownership, and regulated even in the choice of a mate in the states where most of them lived [by antimiscegenation laws], Indians now formed a small band of people set apart from Americans by what truly must have seemed a great white wall," 269; Hess, 588–90; Tatla, 72; Wenzel, "Rural Punjabis of California," 245–50, 252–53.
168. Houchins and Houchins, "Korean Experience," 548, 554, 563, 575; Sucheng Chan, "Koreans in America," 11.
169. Lee, *Quiet Odyssey,* xxix, xlvii, 14–15, 173–76.
170. Melendy, "Filipinos in the United States," 523–25; Hemminger, "Little Manila," 21–27; McWilliams, *Factories,* 131.
171. Lasker, *Filipino Immigration,* 13–21, 324. Lasker's figure for Filipinos in the U.S. mainland in 1929 is 56,000 (plus another 75,000 in Hawaii); others estimated them between 25,000 and 80,000. Pido, *The Pilipinos in America,* 65, gives 80,000 on the mainland in 1929, 125,000 in 1940. Restrictions did not apply until 1935, when, ironically, Congress passed a law that limited annual immigration to 50, while also promising future Philippine independence (Pido, 65).

172. Bergano OH.
173. Beltran OH.
174. Halley OH.
175. Dessery, "Study of the Mental Inferiority of the Italian Immigrant," 59, 61.
176. Robertson OH.
177. See, for example, a description of how the California home teachers' law operated in Los Angeles, in Amidon, "Home Teachers in the City," *Survey Graphic,* 56 (June 1, 1926), 304–07.
178. California, *First Annual Report of the Commission of Immigration and Housing,* esp. 61–70.
179. Day, "Races and Cultural Oases," 327.
180. U.S. Census, *Statistical Abstract,* 1914, 42; U.S. Census, *Statistical Abstract,* 1942, 27.
181. U.S. Census, *Statistical Abstract,* 1942, 26–28.
182. Starr, *The Dream Endures,* 65, 72.
183. Rolle, *Los Angeles,* 144.
184. U.S. Census, *Historical Statistics,* series A195, I:24–37.
185. U.S. Census, *Statistical Abstract,* 1914, 42–43; 1942, 26–28. Omaha, the two Kansas Cities, Wichita, Tulsa, Oklahoma City, Dallas, Fort Worth, and San Antonio had also passed a hundred thousand, most by 1920, but they are all east of the ninety-eighth meridian except San Antonio.
186. U.S. Census, *Historical Statistics,* series A57, A69, I:11; A178–179, I:22; A202–03, I:25.
187. Robinson, "The Southern California Real Estate Boom of the Twenties."
188. "A City's Seven League Boots," *Southern California Business,* 7 (Feb. 1928), 21.
189. Haynes, "A Canyon and a City," *Survey Graphic* (June 1, 1924), 283.
190. Southern Pacific Company, *California for the Settler,* 43–44.
191. Starr, *Material Dreams,* 177.
192. Bottles, *Los Angeles and the Automobile,* 18–21 and elsewhere; also, 29–31 for the interurbans and street railways.
193. Ibid., 92.
194. U.S. *Census of 1930,* I:599, 694, 710, 722–23, 759.
195. U.S. Works Progress Administration, *California: A Guide to the Golden State,* 67.
196. Holloway, "Southwest Agriculture Centers in Los Angeles," *Southern California Business,* 8 (March 1929), 12–13, 46.
197. Robinson, "Southern California Real Estate Boom," 27.
198. Woehlke, "The Corn Belt in California," 30.
199. Franks and Lambert, *Early California Oil,* 101–07.
200. Ibid., 106.
201. Starr, *Inventing the Dream,* 71; same, *Material Dreams,* 78–82.
202. Goodwin, "The Arroyo Seco: From Dry Gulch to Freeway," 73–94.
203. Foster, "Western Response to Urban Transportation," 32–33.
204. Brilliant, "Social Effects of the Automobile in Southern California," 11, 29.
205. McWilliams, *Southern California,* 229.
206. Moate, "Iowa State Picnic."

7: Dust Bowl and Depression, 1929–1941

1. U.S. Census, *Historical Statistics,* series A195, I:25.
2. Ibid., 1975, series A172, I:22, the West; A195, I:25, California; series B167, I:59, overall death rate. The national population increased by 7.2 percent between 1930 and 1940; the previous low for a decade was 14.9 percent, between 1910 and 1920.
3. Ibid., 1975, series A57 and A69, I:11, population in urban and rural territory; series A178–A179, I:22, urban-rural population by region. Between the 1930 and 1940 censuses,

the urban proportion of U.S. population increased from 56.2 to 56.6 percent; of the West, from 58.4 to 58.5 percent. The other three regions changed from 77.6 to 76.6 percent urban (Northeast); 57.9 to 58.4 percent urban (Midwest); 34.1 to 36.7 percent urban (South).

4. Denver increased 11.8 percent, from 288,000 to 322,000. The Bay Area (San Francisco, Berkeley, and Oakland) increased 2.1 percent; Portland, 1 percent; Seattle, 0.5 percent.

5. Browder and Hoflich, *Population and Income in Montana,* 2–3 (Table 1).

6. Reuss, *Back to the Country: The Rurban Trend,* 4–5; Armstrong, Robinson, and Hoy, *History of Public Works in the United States,* 356–58.

7. U.S. Census, *Historical Statistics,* series D85–86, I:135.

8. Mullins, *Depression and the Urban West Coast,* 3–6, 13, 87–89, 136.

9. Broussard, *Black San Francisco,* 113, 118–19, 121, 129–30; Berner, *Seattle 1921–1940,* 218–19; Taylor, *Forging of a Black Community,* 63–64.

10. Bunch, *Black Angelenos,* 36.

11. Thoreau, in *Walden* (1854), wrote: "The mass of men lead lives of quiet desperation." If the West had escaped this generalization, it finally applied in the 1930s.

12. Roberts, "Minority-Group Poverty in Phoenix," 353–59.

13. Arrington, "Idaho and the Great Depression," 3, 7; Pomeroy, *Pacific Slope,* 294–95.

14. "Denver: The Old Bulls Retreat," *Fortune* (April 1958), 245.

15. Shinn, "Eugene in the Depression, 1929–1935," 341–69, esp. 343, 347–51, 353–55, 359, 363–65.

16. Tilden, "Portland, Oregon," 35; Mullins, *Depression and the Urban West Coast,* 111–13, portrays Portland's relief measures as still halfhearted by 1932.

17. Between the 1930 and 1940 censuses, Los Angeles grew from 1,238,048 to 1,504,277—i.e., 266,229, or 21.5 percent—New York from 6,930,446 to 7,454,995—i.e., 524,549, or 7.6 percent—Washington 486,869 to 663,091—i.e., 123,778, or 36.1 percent. U.S. Census, *Statistical Abstract,* 1942, 27, table 25.

18. Gast, "Why People Seek Small Farm Homes," 18–19.

19. Miller, "Port of Los Angeles–Long Beach in 1929 and 1979," 349.

20. U.S. Works Progress Administration, *California: A Guide to the Golden State,* 214 (quote); Rolle, *California,* 384–85; Bottles, *Los Angeles and the Automobile,* 216–18. The sheer area of Los Angeles—441 square miles—became a talking point in itself; the San Fernando Valley, at 204 square miles, nosed out Chicago (202); West Los Angeles's 60, Denver's 58; Venice-Palms equaled Akron's 38; and the other eight statistical districts matched Nashville, Richmond, Easton (Pa.), Schenectady, Elizabeth (N.J.), Utica, and Syracuse, according to Chamber of Commerce; "Los Angeles—a City of Cities," 26.

21. Thompson and Whelpton, *Population Trends in the United States,* 318–19.

22. U.S. Census, *Population,* 1940, vol. 2, part 7 (Utah-Wyoming), 304.

23. Landis, *Fifty Years of Population Growth in Washington,* 18.

24. Thompson, *Growth and Changes in California's Population,* 49.

25. U.S. Census, *Statistical Abstract,* 1942, 14, Table 15. The U.S. ratio at that time was 100.7:100, with six northeastern and eight southern states below 100—i.e., fewer males than females.

26. Thompson, *Growth and Changes,* 57.

27. U.S. Census, *Population,* 1940, vol. 2 part 3 (Kansas-Michigan), 21 (table 8); *Agriculture,* vol. 1, part 6, Montana, 10 (table 10).

28. Landis, *Fifty Years,* 24.

29. Davies, *Farm Population Trends in Washington,* 21, 24–26, 33–35.

30. U.S. Department of Commerce, *Vital Statistics of the United States 1940,* part 2 (Natality and Mortality Data), 18–19 (table 1).

31. These and the following birthrates by state are in U.S. Department of Commerce, *Vital Statistics 1946,* part 1 (Natality and Mortality Data), 2–3.

32. Mirkowich, "Recent Trends in Population Distribution in California," 303.
33. The three Pacific states, conversely, had the lowest infant mortality in the region. Harmsworth, *Sixty Years of Population Growth in Idaho*, 59 (table 26), 68 (table 33).
34. The strict meaning of "infant" mortality is death before the first birthday.
35. "Review of Health Conditions and Needs in Morenci, Arizona."
36. Garcia, "Mexican Americans and the Politics of Citizenship," 187–204 (quote 188). White Americans had no deeply embedded traditions of public or private hygiene either; see Hoy, *Chasing Dirt*.
37. Responsible figures vary. Hoffman, *Unwanted Mexican Americans in the Great Depression*, the first historical treatment of these events, says: "Between 1929 and 1939 approximately half a million Mexicans left the United States. Many of the departing families included American-born children to whom Mexico, not the United States, was the foreign land" (2); his Appendix D (174–75) tabulates the flow month by month from January 1929 through December 1937, giving figures in the U.S. National Archives "collected by the Mexican Migration Service" and totaling 458,039. Guerin-Gonzales, *Mexican Workers and American Dreams*, 94, states: "In all, more than three hundred and sixty-five thousand Mexican immigrants and Mexican Americans left the United States for Mexico between 1929 and 1932." David Gutiérrez, *Walls and Mirrors*, 72, says: "Although repatriation statistics . . . are highly unreliable, scholars estimate that at least 350,000, and perhaps as many as 600,000, persons of Mexican descent returned to Mexico during the depression decade" (technically, of course, children born in the United States were not "returning" but encountering). Cortés, "Mexicans," 703, writes that "about 500,000 persons were shuttled to Mexico, most of them from the Southwest, but some 10 percent from the Midwest, particularly Illinois, Michigan, Indiana, and Minnesota." At the high but still credible end, Balderrama and Rodriguez, *Decade of Betrayal*, state that while "[i]n all honesty, it is virtually impossible to cite a specific figure" for many reasons (120), nonetheless, "Taking the conservative middle ground, it is reasonable to estimate that the total number of repatriates was approximately one million" (122).
38. Fogel, *Mexican Illegal Alien Workers*, 12.
39. Gómez-Quiñones and Maciel, " 'What Goes Around, Comes Around,' " 39.
40. Ibid.
41. Balderrama and Rodriguez, *Decade of Betrayal*, 99.
42. Samora, *Los Mojados*, 40–41.
43. Balderrama and Rodriguez, *Decade of Betrayal*, 58–60, say that Doak was "acting under President Hoover's orders to create a diversion to counteract organized labor's hostile attitude toward his administration" (the American Federation of Labor favored reducing the Mexican labor force). See George J. Sánchez, *Becoming Mexican American*, 214–15.
44. George J. Sánchez, *Becoming Mexican American*, 211.
45. Ibid., 212.
46. Engh, " 'A Multiplicity and Diversity of Faiths,' " 471.
47. Cardoso, *Mexican Emigration to the United States, 1897–1931*, 145.
48. Dinwoodie, "Deportation," 193–206; Wollenberg, "Race and Class," 155–64.
49. Balderrama and Rodriguez, *Decade of Betrayal*, 56–60; Hoffman, *Unwanted Mexican Americans*, 174.
50. As late as mid-1932, the exiled archbishop of Guadalajara dedicated a new church in Brawley, California, for refugees, thousands of whom were living in the Imperial Valley. (Chicago) *New World*, July 8, 1932.
51. Jackson OH, Feb. 1975, transcript 14–15.
52. Cruz Burciaga OH, February 1974, transcript 40–41.
53. George J. Sánchez, *Becoming Mexican American*, 217–23.
54. Hoffman, Appendix D, 174–75.

55. George J. Sánchez, *Becoming Mexican American,* 225.
56. Melendy, "Filipinos," 361, gives the figure of forty-five on the mainland in 1935; Bogardus, "Filipino Repatriation," 68, gives 70,000 in 1935; Pido, *Pilipinos in America,* 65, gives 80,000.
57. Melendy, "Filipinos," 360–61.
58. Bogardus, "Filipino Repatriation," 69.
59. U.S. Census, *Historical Statistics,* series C104, C106, I:107.
60. U.S. Census, *Statistical Abstract,* 1942, table 16, 16–17.
61. Daniels, *Asian America,* 98.
62. Ibid., 176.
63. Iwata, "Japanese Immigrants in California Agriculture," 34.
64. U.S. Census, *Historical Statistics,* series C89, I:105.
65. U.S. Census, *Historical Statistics,* series C299, I:119, "total departures," subtracted from series C296, "total arrivals." The biggest loss came in 1932, when 471,590 passengers arrived and 585,561 departed, for a net minus 113,971.
66. Goren, "Jews," 591.
67. Starr's figure in *The Dream Endures,* 367.
68. Jackman, "Exiles in Paradise," 193–94, 196–97.
69. Feuchtwanger, "An Emigre Life," OH transcript 1199.
70. Jackman, "Exiles in Paradise," and Fermi, *Illustrious Immigrants.*
71. Goren, "Jews," 591.
72. Feingold, *Politics of Rescue,* 296.
73. Ibid., x, 15.
74. Feuchtwanger, "An Emigre Life," 1239–40.
75. Fromm OH. He died in San Francisco in 1998.
76. See the remarkably frank letter from Weinstein to Horace M. Kallen, Nov. 30, 1938, in Weinstein Papers, Chicago Historical Society.
77. Vorspan and Gartner, *History of the Jews of Los Angeles,* 104, 197; Kramer and Clar, "Rabbi Edgar F. Magnin," 346–62; Kohs, "Jewish Community of Los Angeles," 92, 96.
78. Eldridge and Thomas, *Population Redistribution and Economic Growth,* 119–22.
79. Shindo, *Dust Bowl Migrants in the American Imagination,* 1–10, and elsewhere. The book contains successive chapters on Lange, Steinbeck, Ford, Guthrie, and others, and concludes with "The Ghost of Tom Joad," on how the icons have "completely displaced the dust bowl migrant of historical circumstances" (216).
80. Skaggs, "Drought in the United States, 1931–40," 402.
81. Gregory, *American Exodus,* 11; also, on mechanization and soil exhaustion, Worster, *Rivers of Empire,* 223–24.
82. Mirkowich, "Recent Trends in Population Distribution in California," 306–07.
83. Gregory, *American Exodus,* 31.
84. U.S. Census, *Historical Statistics,* 1975, series A195, I:24–37. The percentage losses were 7.2 for South Dakota, 5.7 for North Dakota, 4.5 for Nebraska, 4.3 for Kansas, and 2.5 for Oklahoma.
85. Ibid., series C42–C73, I:93, "Estimated Net Intercensal Migration."
86. Ibid., series C78–C80, I:96, "Estimated Annual Movement of the Farm Population."
87. Bogue, Schryock, and Hoermann, *Subregional Migration,* 11, cxciv–ccxi, 313–18.
88. U.S. Census *Agriculture, 1940,* vol. I, part 2, 370–71, 382.
89. Tydeman, "New Deal for Tourists," 208–13; Kelly and Scott, *Route 66,* 161.
90. Gannett, *Sweet Land,* 199.
91. Rampersad, *Collected Poems of Langston Hughes,* 252.
92. Morgan, *Rising in the West,* xvii.
93. Ibid., 5, 8, 21–22, 42, 84, 98, 105, 140–41.
94. Ankli, "Farm Income on the Great Plains and Canadian Prairies," 94–96.

95. Friesen, *Canadian Prairies,* chap. 15, esp. 386–89, 392; Powell, "Northern Settlement," 81, 85.

96. Wagner, "*Heim ins Reich:* The Story of Loon River's Nazis," 41–50. Wagner writes that "they blamed their economic plight on Canada's supposedly 'Jewish dominated government' "; he does not know if they survived the war.

97. Beasley, "Lorena Hickok to Harry Hopkins, 1933," 63, 65.

98. Nelson, *The Prairie Winnows Out Its Own,* 2, 149–50, 156, 162–63, 167–77.

99. Ward, "Wheat in Montana: Determined Adaptation," 25, 28.

100. Schlebecker, "Agriculture in Western Nebraska," 262–64.

101. Quoted from *Nebraska Farmer* in Schwieder and Fink, "Plains Women," 86.

102. Riney-Kehrberg, "In God We Trusted," 194–99; also, Riney-Kehrberg, *Rooted in Dust.*

103. OHs of Adams, Alley, Kohler, Armold, and Behrendt.

104. Gregory, *American Exodus,* 26–27. Besides Gregory's excellent book, which has been the most useful for my present purposes, several other histories of the Dust Bowl and its migrants are Stein, *California and the Dust Bowl Migration,* focusing on Oklahoma emigrants and their experience in California's migrant camps and farm workers' union, finding they were more often strikebreakers than strikers; Worster, *Dust Bowl: The Southern Plains in the 1930s,* a prizewinning history of the Dust Bowl proper; Bonnifield, *The Dust Bowl: Men, Dirt, and Depression,* as much on those who did not migrate as on those who did; Hurt, *The Dust Bowl,* a brief and balanced treatment that includes discussion of the 1950s' mini–Dust Bowl. For a rather unforgiving critique of the literature, see McDean, "Dust Bowl Historiography," 117–26.

105. Glaser, "Migration in Idaho's History," 26–28; White, "Poor Men on Poor Lands," 122–30; see also Rajala, "Bill and the Boss," 168–79.

106. Leo Smith OH, Sept. 1973.

107. McEntire, *Population of California,* 54. This eleven-year total is about 240,000 higher than the federal calculation for ten years noted earlier. They are probably equally approximate.

108. WPA, *California,* 68–69. Latifundia in California have been discussed in earlier chapters. For another description of migrant labor, see Chambers, *California Farm Organizations,* and for a vivid portrayal of how the "farm hand . . . has been supplanted by an agricultural proletariat" and how corporate California agriculture had become, see McWilliams, *Factories in the Field,* 48 and elsewhere.

109. For detailed analysis, see Daniel, *Bitter Harvest,* esp. chaps. 5 to 8, and 280–85.

110. How the migrants divided into two streams, urban and rural, and how they were received are best described in Gregory, *American Exodus,* chap. 2.

111. The imperviousness of the southwestern migrants to New Deal ideals is discussed by Shindo, *Dust Bowl Migrants in the American Imagination,* 33–34.

112. Starr, *Endangered Dreams,* 223.

113. The best overview of the New Deal and the West, especially the departments of Agriculture and Interior and some others, is Lowitt, *New Deal and the West.* Excellent for what it essays, the book is not chiefly concerned with population changes.

114. Cannon, *Remaking the Agrarian Dream,* chaps. 1, 9, 10.

115. Arrington, "Idaho and the Great Depression," 3–9; Peterson, *Idaho,* 150–57.

116. Moehring, "Public Works and the New Deal in Las Vegas," 107–29.

117. Gates, *History of Public Land Law Development,* 607. Congress refused to repeal the 1862 Homestead Act and its successors outright, so "land-hungry people continued . . . the search, hopeless as it was," but few filings were granted; Gates, "Homesteading in the High Plains," 133.

118. Gates, *History,* 613–22; Lowitt, *New Deal and the West,* 64–71.

119. Libecap, *Locking Up the Range,* 47. He continues: the director of the Grazing Service "called for the election of advisory boards of ranchers . . . only ranchers qualified to use

Taylor lands were eligible to vote. The local advisory boards importantly determined the assignment of the initial grazing permits. . . . The recommendations of the advisory board were almost always followed," 49; since then local ranchers have been confirmed in these roles.

120. Ourada, "Indians in the Work Force," 52.

121. Yazzie OH, 1968, transcript 7.

122. Lowitt, *New Deal and the West*, 129; Perlman, "New Deal at Zuñi," 63–74.

123. Ubelaker, "North American Indian Population Size," my interpolations from table 3, 173.

124. Swain, "Bureau of Reclamation and the New Deal," 144–46; Saindon and Sullivan, "Taming the Missouri," 34–57.

125. Stevens, *Hoover Dam*, 50, 140–41, 222–23. For the racially segregated nature of the project, its labor force, and nearby towns, see Fitzgerald, "Blacks and the Boulder Dam Project," 255–60.

126. Swain, "Bureau of Reclamation and the New Deal," 142; Worster, *Rivers of Empire*, 239–43, 256; Reisner, *Cadillac Desert*, 158.

127. From forty-two thousand in 1930 to eighty-six thousand in 1950; U.S. Census, *Population of States and Counties*, 20.

128. Dunshee OH, transcript 11–13.

8: The War, the Baby Boom, and Slouching toward Watts, 1941–1965

1. Gerald D. Nash sees World War II as a critical turning point in the history of the West in *American West Transformed*, viii–ix, 17, chap. 11. Rhode, "Nash Thesis Revisited," dissents.

2. Eldridge and Thomas, *Population Redistribution and Economic Growth*, 119, 122–25.

3. The West's share of the U.S. total rose from 10.9 to 13.4 percent during the 1940s. U.S. Census, *Historical Statistics*, series A172, I:22.

4. Abbott, *New Urban America*, 99.

5. McEntire, *Population of California*, 17–20.

6. Lotchin, *Fortress California*, chap. 2, "Capturing the Navy: San Diego." Lotchin concludes that San Diego "got the prize of the fleet because of the brokerage of an urban congressman, the drive of its boosters, and the political and military calculations of a civilian politician, the Secretary of the Navy"—not from geographic or geological advantages. On housing, Abbott, *New Urban America*, 115. Also, Shragge, " 'A New Federal City,' " 333–62.

7. Verge, *Paradise Transformed*, 22.

8. Lotchin, *Fortress California*, 134 (quote) and chap. 4.

9. Verge, "Impact of the Second World War on Los Angeles," 289–314, esp. 301–06.

10. Ibid., 301–02.

11. Cantrell OH, typescript viii, 24, 26–32.

12. Ortega de Sousa OH, transcript 1–7.

13. Purdy OH, viii, 2, 33–38.

14. Abbott, *New Urban America*, 109–10; "Richmond Took a Beating," *Fortune* (Feb. 1945), 262–69.

15. Johnson, "War as Watershed," 2; Johnson, *Second Gold Rush*, esp. "Conclusion," 235–40.

16. McEntire, *Population of California*, 119–25.

17. Abbott, *New Urban America*, 108–09.

18. Secrest OH.

19. Janeway, "Trials and Errors," 24.

20. MacDonald, *Distant Neighbors*, 144–46.

21. Johansen and Gates, *Empire of the Columbia*, 529.

22. Ficken and LeWarne, *Washington*, 130–32, 142.

23. Landis, *Loss of Rural Manpower*, 5 (quote), 12–13, 20–21.

24. Nash, "Planning for the Postwar City," 108–10.

25. Fred Brueggeman, county development director, quoted in "Atomic City Ponders Its Future After Bomb," *NYT*, Nov. 29, 1995.

26. Ficken and LeWarne, *Washington*, 140, 146–47; Geranios, "The First Casualties of Nuclear Age," *South Bend* (Ind.) *Tribune*, March 14, 1993; *NYT*, Aug. 5, 13, 1990; *PI*, Aug. 11, 1997; Steele, "Radioactive Waste from Hanford Is Seeping toward the Columbia," *HCN*, Sept. 1, 1997.

27. Peterson, *Idaho*, 158.

28. Alexander, "Ogden, A Federal Colony in Utah," 291–310.

29. Verge, *Paradise Transformed*, 23.

30. Mayor Fletcher Bowron to Drew Pearson, Oct. 23, 1942, in Bowron mss. Bowron was incensed that camp authorities at Manzanar had released a woman named Miya Kikuchi to give a lecture tour for the YWCA, and he wrote the Federal Bureau of Investigation and Drew Pearson about it.

31. Fox, *Unknown Internment*, xii–xiii, 62–63, 71, 118, 136, 139, 147, 163–64, 186; Fox, "General John DeWitt and the Proposed Internment," 407–38; Lothrop, "Untold Story," 7–14; Gumina, *Italians of San Francisco*, 199. German and Italian prisoners of war who were interned in the West sometimes stayed or returned after 1945; see Busco and Alder, "German and Italian Prisoners of War," 55–72, and Spidle, "Axis Invasion," 93–122. "After Silence, Italians Recall the Internment," *NYT*, Aug. 11, 1997.

32. Thomas et al., *Japanese American Evacuation and Resettlement*, 4. Fifty percent of the Issei were over forty-nine; two-thirds of the Nisei were under twenty. Of the West Coast Japanese-Americans in 1941, 45 percent farmed, with the rest mostly in trade and personal services.

33. Seabrook, "The Spinach King," *NY* (Feb. 20/27, 1995), 222–35, includes the story of a Japanese-American fisherman's family from Los Angeles whose boat was confiscated and who went to Manzanar and then, among several hundred others, to New Jersey as farm workers. They never returned to the West, though others did in the late 1940s. Riichi Satow, from Sacramento, interviewed in 1974, was interned for ten months at Poston, Arizona, and then paroled to a sugar beet farm near Denver, owned by a German-Russian (Satow OH, 63).

34. Daniels, *Asian America*, 241, 254, 274–80; Smith, " 'Japanese' in Utah," 129–44 and 208–30; Azuma, "A History of Oregon's *Issei*, 1880–1952," esp. 341–55; for western Canada, where internment also took place (and did not end until 1949), see Lee, "Road to Enfranchisement," 44–76, and Daniels, "Japanese Relocation and Redress," 2–14; in Mexico, which ordered all Japanese removed 100 km inland from the Pacific Coast, see Mathes, "Two Californias during World War II," 323–31.

35. Bowron to James M. Landis, Los Angeles, Apr. 18, 1942, in Bowron papers.

36. Wayne Allen to (County Supervisor) John Anson Ford, Washington, Jan. 31, 1942; Ford to Kay Sugahara, Los Angeles, May 26, 1942; Ford to Director, War Relocation Authority, Los Angeles, Jan. 22, 1943; Sugahara to Ford, Santa Anita Reception Center, Arcadia, Calif., May 20, 1942; Sugahara to Ford, Amache, Colo., Camp, Feb. 24, 1943; Ford to Sugahara, Los Angeles, March 9, 1943; Fred M. Tayama to Ford, Santa Anita Reception Center, May 8, 1942 (with Ford's penned reply); Tayama to Ford, Manzanar, Sept. 15, 1942; and others (all from Ford papers, Huntington Library).

37. Jahnsen OH, transcript 122. Jahnsen continued: "The California attorney general's office went down and helped the FBI and others to pick these Japanese people up, who we felt were ready to help the Japanese invasion of California. We had to segregate the sheep from the goats, the locals from the foreigners. . . . I remember one little Japanese girl pleading with us. She appeared to be a very nice little girl. I think it was in Paso Robles, or down at King City. She pleaded with me, and said, 'Please don't take me. I'm not a

Buddhist. I'm not for this. I'm a Christian—I'm not a Buddhist. I'm not for this—I'm a Christian,' I said, 'Well, I can't do anything about it. Orders are orders and I'm just here to help out.' We got them all together in this little community of Paso Robles. . . . They were taken in and sent to Tule Lake. The federal agencies were under the orders of the commanding general, as we were at war. Then the Internal Revenue come in and took over all the property, which I think was poorly handled, in a lot of ways. Some of their property was lost or stolen; never could be properly identified or returned. Some of these people were heavily invested. Their property was more or less confiscated and later sold. . . . Some people managed to be able to buy some of these vineyards and orchards. They later made lots of money on the sale of these properties. This was unfair. It was guaranteed that these things would be returned. I remember serving some of the search warrants and taking property and giving receipts for this property. Everything they had we gave them a receipt for, under the limited period of time and the speed with which you were operating. These people were just taken right off their property, men, women, and children. Well, it would be like Hitler putting the Jews in the freight car. . . . It's a helluva way to handle these things, but they weren't gassed like the Jews were." Jahnsen transcript, 126–27. For a fictional account of the evacuation and return of a fisherman and family from Washington's San Juan Islands, read Guterson, *Snow Falling on Cedars;* another novel, Leffland's *Rumors of Peace,* is the story of an Anglo schoolgirl from "Mendoza" (based on Martinez, east of San Francisco Bay), who begins the war period with strong anti-Japanese stereotypes but by 1945, after exposure to the university at Berkeley, achieves more mature understanding.

38. Many descriptions of the camps exist. See for example Arrington, *Price of Prejudice,* 15–37; Kasai OH and "bicentennial history" transcripts; Hoover OH.
39. Wax, "In and out of the Tule Lake Segregation Center," 12–25.
40. Azuma, "Oregon's *Issei,*" 354–55.
41. Leonard, " 'Is that What We Fought For?,' " 468.
42. Stevenson, "Return of the Exiles," 96–99.
43. "Bowron Says Nisei Evacuated Too Suddenly Here in Last War," unidentified clipping, Sept. 3, 1954, and Bowron to John P. Benjamin, Los Angeles, Sept. 28, 1956, in Bowron mss.
44. Mimeographed resolution from Eldred L. Meyer, chairman, Grand Parlor Americanism Committee, Native Sons of the Golden West, Apr. 19, 1948, in Ford papers.
45. Arrington, *Price of Prejudice,* 40–41.
46. News release, "W.R.A. Centers Closing on Schedule," Oct. 2, 1945, in Ford mss.
47. Daniels, *Asian America,* 288; Hata and Hata, *Japanese Americans and World War II,* 21.
48. Daniels, *Asian America,* 288, 306, 313; U.S. Bureau of Labor Statistics, "Minority Groups in California," 980; Mathison, "The Many Faces of L.A.," 41, observed that "returning Japanese-Americans spread out to settle everywhere in the city."
49. Taylor, "Leaving the Concentration Camps," 169–94, esp. 178, 182.
50. A federal district court in San Francisco in 1984 overturned the 1944 decision against Fred Korematsu for refusing to evacuate, and the U.S. Court of Appeals for the Ninth Circuit in 1987 overturned the 1943 decision against Gordon Hirabayashi for violating curfew and internment orders. *NYT,* Sept. 25, 1987.
51. Hosokawa, *Thirty-five Years in the Frying Pan,* 49–50.
52. Dries, *Missionary Movement in American Catholic History,* 77–78; Lernoux, *Hearts on Fire,* 102–04.
53. Houston and Houston, *Farewell to Manzanar,* 114, 132–34.
54. Masunaga OH, Feb. 17, 1979, transcript 175.
55. Satow OH.
56. "Notes on Conference in office, March 21, 1946 re Japanese Housing"; letter, Newell Steward to Senator Sheridan Downey, Los Angeles, Apr. 8, 1946; and "Evergreen Hostel:

A Hostel for Returning Japanese Americans," American Friends Service Committee and the Presbyterian Church in U.S.A. booklet, Dec. 19, 1944, in Ford papers. For extended treatments of the resettlement, see Thomas et al., *Japanese American Evacuation and Resettlement,* part 2, life histories; Bloom and Riemer, *Removal and Return,* chiefly on property losses; Daniels, *Concentration Camps North America,* 157–70; Girdner and Loftis, *Great Betrayal,* chap. 15.

57. *Fortune,* 26 (July 1942), 89.
58. Taylor, *In Search of the Racial Frontier,* 268; DeGraaf, "Significant Steps," 24–33.
59. Collins, *Black Los Angeles: The Maturing of the Ghetto, 1940–1950,* 38–76.
60. Verge, *Paradise Transformed,* 52.
61. DeGraaf, "Significant Steps," 30.
62. Bowron to "Hon. Sheridan Downey, Chairman, and Members of Sub-Committee of Military Affairs Committee, United States Senate," Apr. 27, 1943, 11–12: "A serious, even a tragic situation, exists with respect to the great need of housing facilities for racial minorities, particularly Negroes. Private housing has not offered sufficient relief for Negro families. Public war housing, which has a stated policy of no discrimination because of race, color or creed, has attempted to relieve the situation but the demand is too great. It is estimated that some 25,000 to 30,000 Negroes have moved into the Los Angeles area during the past two years, most of them within the last ten months. The migration from out of state is continuing at the rate of from 350 to 500 families a week. Investigators of the Housing Authority report many instances of Negro families living under not only sub-standard but unhealthy conditions. One Negro family of seven persons was found living in a garage back of a church. There was no toilet or running water, five children slept in one bed and the parents slept on the garage floor. Cooking was done in a bucket over an open fire. The father was employed in a shipyard and earned sufficient wages to pay reasonable rent, but was unable to find a place where his family could live." Also, Bowron to Irl D. Brett (special assistant to the attorney general), Los Angeles, Nov. 4, 1942; "Meeting on War Housing for Negroes, Board of Public Works Session Room," Aug. 10, 1943, 5–6; George M. Uhl, M.D. (health officer, city of Los Angeles) to Bowron, Los Angeles, Sept. 15, 1943; all in Bowron mss.
63. Taylor, *In Search of the Racial Frontier,* 272–73.
64. Bowron to William H. McReynolds (administrative assistant to President Roosevelt), Los Angeles, Jan. 26, 1945 (F. Bowron Collection, Box 1); Harold L. Ickes (secretary of the interior) to Bowron, Washington, Feb. 9, 1945; Bowron to President Roosevelt, Los Angeles, March 5, 1945 (F. Bowron Collection, Box 1).
65. Press release, "Pilgrim House District Assembly of Rotary District 107," July 9, 1947, Bowron mss; Collins, *Black Los Angeles,* 29, mentions several incidents from late 1944 to 1946.
66. Daniels, *Asian America,* 294. Housing shortages produced a similar situation in San Francisco, where "by 1943 about 9,000 blacks were crowded into an area [the Fillmore District] previously occupied by 5,000 Japanese Americans" (Wollenberg, "James vs. Marinship," 266).
67. Chandler, *Farewell My Lovely,* 767; Mosley, *Devil in a Blue Dress,* 2.
68. For example, a broadside from A. J. Davis of Los Angeles, 1912, urging boycotts of any banks or restaurants that hired the "black monsters;" Davis to Meyer Lissner, Lissner mss., Dept. of Special Collections, Stanford University (thanks to William Deverell for this reference).
69. "California People Make Marvelous Record in Ten Years," *Chicago Defender,* Jan. 30, 1915.
70. Because slavery, which was the condition of 90 percent of African-Americans during the frontier period before 1865, and the restrictions of the first decades of emancipation,

absolutely contradicted the freedom at the essence of the Agrarian Myth. Nugent, *Structures of American Social History*, 78–79.

71. Taylor, *In Search of the Racial Frontier*, 254, provides a table with numbers and percent changes in the black populations of these five areas in 1940 and 1950. Los Angeles accounted for more than the others combined (171,209, or 8.7 percent of the metropolitan area in 1950); San Francisco and Portland together came in second with 91,064 by 1950 (9.7 percent of the area) but made the largest percentage gains over 1940.

72. McWilliams, *Southern California*, 324–25.

73. Ong and Chapa, *Socio-Economic Trends in California*, 9.

74. McEntire, *Population of California*, 126. The sex ratio (males per 100 females) of the age twenty to twenty-four cohort, April 1944, moving into the Bay Area, was 43.3; into Los Angeles, 36.8: exceedingly female-skewed. Also, Broussard, *Black San Francisco*, 139.

75. Smith, "Changing Number and Distribution of the Aged Negro Population," 352–54.

76. Williams, "Negro's Migration to Los Angeles," 102, 112–13.

77. McEntire, *Population of California*, 126–27; Broussard, *Black San Francisco*, 138; Taylor, *In Search of the Racial Frontier*, 251.

78. Hawkins OH, "Black Leadership in Los Angeles," 13–14.

79. Houston OH, transcript vii, 4, 27–31, 41–53, 92–93.

80. Tina Hill OH, vii, ix, 12–13, 24–39, 46–48, 110–14; also, Gluck, *Rosie the Riveter Revisited*, 22–49.

81. DeGraaf, "Significant Steps," 26–27; Wollenberg, "James vs. Marinship," 263, 274–76; Broussard, *Black San Francisco*, chaps. 8 and 9, has an extensive treatment of employment, discrimination, and housing.

82. Dellums OH, 98–99.

83. Wollenberg, "James vs. Marinship," 277–78.

84. Lemke-Santangelo, *Abiding Courage*, chap. 2 (quote, 54).

85. Ibid.

86. Davis, "Sources for History of Blacks in Oregon," 207, 209.

87. Shelton Hill OH, transcript 1, 3, 9, 39. Mrs. Marie Smith OH, 7, also recalled: "We had a small group of black people here for awhile until the shipyards. When the shipyards came in, everybody became frantic. The whites and blacks too didn't want new people in here. So we had to get adjusted to that. . . . I think the thing that caused the most segregated housing pattern was after the flood in Vanport."

88. Taylor, "Great Migration," 109–13, 121–22. As in Los Angeles and San Francisco, formerly Japanese housing became home to African-Americans (125).

89. Droker, "Seattle Race Relations," 166.

90. Pittman OH No. 1, Dec. 1973, 139–46; Patrick, "Black Experience in Southern Nevada," 209–12, recounting an interview with William F. Bailey; he continued, "What they did to get her [Baker] to go on for the second show, they picked up some maids and porters that were working in the hotel and told them to hurry up and go home and change clothes and come back. Otherwise there wouldn't have been a second show. . . . She really was the first one that shook things up. Of course, she never played Vegas since then. She said she didn't need it."

91. Cayton, "America's Ten Best Cities for Negroes," 7, 9–10.

92. "Boom in Babies," *Life* (Dec. 1, 1941), 73–74.

93. "Park Forest Becomes a Model for Suburbs: Postwar Growth Takes Off with a 'GI Town' for Middle-Income Families," *Chicago Tribune*, July 24, 1997.

94. U.S. Census, *Historical Statistics*, series B1, B5, I:49.

95. Betty Friedan's *The Feminine Mystique*, which first appeared in 1963 (New York: W. W. Norton), both discussed the boom (in chap. 8, "The Mistaken Choice," which correctly noted early marriage as a prime cause) and warned its readers from echoing it. May,

Homeward Bound, stresses cultural factors, notably the ongoing nuclear threat from outside, and the media's glorification of motherhood (140–43); she sees that "affluence alone cannot explain the baby boom" (158). See also May's sequel, *Barren in the Promised Land,* on what followed the baby boom.

96. "War Forces Population Shifts," *Business Week* (Aug. 7, 1943), 42.
97. "Preview of the Postwar Generation," *Fortune,* 27 (March 1943), 116ff.
98. "Cupid and Stork Working Overtime during War Boom," *Science News Letter* (Jan. 17, 1942), 40.
99. "More Babies But—," *Business Week* (Oct. 10, 1942), 62. Conservative predictions came from demographers Philip M. Hauser in *Science;* William Fielding Ogburn, whose views were more hedged but still suggestive of a postwar downturn, "Marriages, Births, and Divorces," 20–29; Wilson H. Grabill, who admitted to a "wartime 'baby boom' " but hoped it would not "lull us with a false sense that the problems of a declining birth rate have been solved," in "Effect of the War on the Birth Rate and Postwar Fertility Prospects," 107–11.
100. Ogburn in *American City.*
101. *NYT,* Aug. 21, 1943; Dec. 11, 1943; Dec. 18, 1946.
102. Cherlin, "Explaining the Postwar Baby Boom," 57.
103. Modell, "Normative Aspects of American Marriage Timing since World War II," 210–34 (quote, 213).
104. U.S. Census, *Current Population Reports,* P25-1130 (Feb. 1996), 7; this report projected (9) that the ratio would rise only from 63.7 (dependents per 100 producers) in 1995 to 79.9 in 2050.
105. Thompson, *Growth and Changes,* 28–29.
106. Landis, *People of Washington, 1890–1950,* 21.
107. U.S. Department of Commerce, *Vital Statistics 1961,* I:1–16, 1–17, 1–29.
108. "Fortune Management Poll," *Fortune* (Feb. 1945), 270–74.
109. "The Golden West," *Fortune* (Feb. 1945), 113–20, 250–55; "all but collapse," 181.
110. The same issue includes "The El Solyo Deal" (how a forty-four-hundred-acre irrigated ranch, and thus Central Valley agriculture, work), 147ff; "Steel in the West," 130ff; "Ports of the Pacific," 124ff; "The Sinews of the West" (natural resources), 134ff; "Power to Burn," 141ff; "After the Battle" (on labor unions and employer associations), 176ff; "Richmond Took a Beating" (on the shipbuilding town with its many multiracial migrants), 262ff.
111. During the 1940s and 1950s the Northeast grew most slowly of the four great regions, the Midwest and South somewhat faster, and the West decidedly the fastest:

REGION	POP. GROWTH 1940–1950	POP. GROWTH 1950–1960
Northeast	9.7%	13.2%
Midwest	10.8%	16.1%
South	13.3%	16.5%
West	40.4%	38.9%
United States as a whole	14.4%	18.4%

Source: U.S. Census, *Historical Statistics,* series A172, I:22.

112. Kelley and Scott, *Route 66,* 161. The interstates that replaced and parallel Route 66 have no single number; they are I-55 from Chicago to St. Louis, then I-44 to Oklahoma City, I-40 to Barstow, Calif., I-15 down to San Bernardino, and I-10 to Santa Monica.
113. Trillin, "Messages from My Father," esp. 68–71.
114. Beauvoir, *L'Amérique au jour le jour,* 114, 118–19, 128–29; translations mine.
115. Gordon, *Employment Expansion,* 110–11, 129, 181.

116. Marine, "Bunker Hill," 15. Marine notes that the City Council and Planning Commission approved the project in 1951 and again in 1956; it was thus a brainchild of the early 1950s, like so many "urban renewal" projects around the nation. Marine concludes, "The present owners and residents will be [moved] somewhere else, whether they like it or not, and the power that moves them will put the land in the hands of other private entrepreneurs. There will be no housing for those who need it most. Redevelopment in other parts of Los Angeles, which need it as much or worse, will have to wait.... But Bunker Hill will be pretty—tall buildings, grassy slopes, planned streets, trees, a shopping mall. And the titans of downtown Los Angeles, watching their land values go up without investment on their part, will bask smiling in the warm glow of civic pride" (16). *Frontier* ceased publishing a short time later.

117. Schiesl, "City Planning and the Federal Government in World War II," 130–41; Rolle, *California,* 454–57.

118. Bowron to Ray L. Chesebro (city attorney), Los Angeles, March 12, 1945; Bowron to J. B. T. Campbell (managing editor, *Herald-Express*), Los Angeles, Aug. 17, 1945; Los Angeles Housing Authority, "Informational Bulletin," Aug. 1948, all in Bowron papers; "Bowron's Boom Town," *Time* (Oct. 11, 1948). Bowron's support of federally subsidized public housing in 1952 may have cost him reelection in 1953; see Donovan, "The Great Los Angeles Public Housing Mystery," 25–29; Lillard, "Problems and Promise in Tomorrowland," 79.

119. Whyte, "Urban Sprawl," 103; City of Los Angeles, "Bulletin 1959: Population Estimate by Communities," and same for each year through 1963, in Bowron papers. The city proper added over 1,100,000 between 1940 and 1963, while more than sixty other municipalities in the county became highly visible; some random examples, with 1940 and 1959 populations, are Van Nuys (11,266 to 110,200) and Reseda (1,805 to 67,400) in the San Fernando Valley (total, from 54,217 to 680,400); in West Los Angeles, Westwood (2,612 to 30,500) and Pacific Palisades (2,868 to 36,300); in southern Los Angeles, Gardena (1,623 to 12,000); in central Los Angeles, Watts (15,266 to 34,400). Pasadena rose from 81,864 in 1940 to 120,114 in 1958. The entire San Fernando Valley swelled from 150,000 in 1945 to 739,000 in 1960 (Findlay, *Magic Lands,* 23).

120. Duncan, "Painful Rejuvenation of Downtown," 31, 33, 70; Cleland, *Irvine Ranch,* 101ff; Marine, "Bunker Hill," 5–8, 16; Ebner, "Transforming Irvine," 13–26.

121. Fishman, *Bourgeois Utopias,* 178. For differences between Los Angeles's suburbia and others, see "Living atop a Civic Mushroom," *Newsweek* (Apr. 1, 1957), 36–42.

122. Fishman, *Bourgeois Utopias,* 184.

123. Jackson, *Crabgrass Frontier,* 265–66: "The numbers were larger in California, but the pattern was the same on the edges of every American city" by the 1980s.

124. Gregor, "Urban Pressures on California Land," 311–25.

125. Grey, "Los Angeles: Urban Prototype," 232–42 (quote, 242).

126. Didion, *The White Album,* 180.

127. Fallows, *More like Us.*

128. Davis, *City of Quartz,* 164, 387–408.

129. Doti and Schweikart, "Financing the Postwar Housing Boom in Phoenix and Los Angeles," 173–94; Clayton, "Defense Spending: Key to California's Growth," 280–93 ("In short, the cold war of the fifties has had the same effect on the population growth of California's defense-oriented counties as did the hot war of the forties," 291).

130. Taeuber, "Change and Transition in the Black Population of the United States," 122, 126, 130.

131. Van Arsdol and Schuerman, "Redistribution and Assimilation of Ethnic Populations," 464–67, 469, 471, 476–78.

132. McQuiston, *Negro Residential Invasion,* 151–52: "relatively few tracts become available to them in proportion to the increase in their population."

133. Mosley, *Devil in a Blue Dress*, 27, 49.
134. Lapp, *Afro-Americans in California*, 59.
135. Hughes, "Westward by Vista Dome, through the Lands Where Coyotes Roam," *Chicago Defender,* June 20, 1953.
136. Record, *Minority Groups and Intergroup Relations in the San Francisco Bay Area*, 4, 6, 7, 10–11, 14 (quote). Record gives the black rise in the six principal Bay Area counties as follows:

COUNTY	1940 POP	1950 POP	1960 POP
Alameda	12,335	69,442	111,000
Contra Costa	582	22,023	25,294
Marin	very small	3,257	4,070
San Francisco	4,846	43,502	74,000
San Mateo	very small	2,395	10,800
Solano	very small	6,604	12,741
TOTAL	<20,000	147,223	238,000

137. Broussard, *Black San Francisco*, chap. 12, "Postwar Employment: Gains and Losses," and 239–42.
138. Lemke-Santangelo, *Abiding Courage*, 181.
139. Rischin, "Immigration, Migration, and Minorities in California," 77–78, 81, 83.
140. The U.S. Supreme Court finally did so in *Loving v. Virginia* in 1967; see Pascoe, "Race, Gender, and Intercultural Relations," 11, 23.
141. Sucheng Chan, *Asian Californians*, 105.
142. Yung, *Unbound Feet*, 6, 279, 283.
143. OHs of Lee (Tom Kim Ping), 228–33; Tony S. Woo, 47–54; Bagaman, 318–23.
144. Chin, *Golden Tassels*, 105–09.
145. Wong OH, Dec. 3, 1990.
146. Chen OH, July 10, 1997.
147. U.S. Bureau of Labor Statistics, "Minority Groups in California," 980; Price, "Migration and Adaptation of American Indians to Los Angeles," 169–70.
148. Price, "Migration and Adaptation," 169, 170, 172.
149. The commissioner of the Bureau of Indian Affairs beginning in May 1950 was Dillon S. Myer, the same man who conducted the Japanese-American evacuations in 1942. Dippie (336–39, 343–44) writes: "Myer's managerial approach to Indian affairs, unrelieved by idealism or any special affection for Indians, was in tune with the times"; termination and relocation were "a direct repudiation of the New Deal's reservation-based program of tribal revitalization and the principle of choice." Harold L. Ickes, Roosevelt's secretary of the interior, called Myer in 1951 "a Hitler and Mussolini rolled into one" (in an article in *New Republic,* quoted in Prucha, *The Great Father,* II:1030). The Kennedy, Johnson, and Nixon administrations, in the civil rights era, backed away from the termination policy.
150. Thornton, *American Indian Holocaust and Survival*, 229; Parman, *Indians and the American West,* 142–43. Fixico, *Termination and Relocation* (184) writes: "Relocation . . . remembered for its negative impact, was overshadowed by the enormity of the fears surrounding the termination program. Termination was seen as an all-inclusive destroyer of Indian life-styles." For a judicious definition and history of termination and relocation, consult Prucha, *Great Father,* 1013–84 (the figure of 33,000 is from 1082).
151. D. Gutiérrez, *Walls and Mirrors*, 123; Schwartz, *From West to East*, 364.
152. "Pachuco Troubles," *Washington Inter-American*, 2 (Aug. 1943), 5.

153. McWilliams, "The Zoot-Suit Riots," 818–20.

154. McCarthy, "Report from Los Angeles," 243.

155. Leonard, "Pachucos and the Spanish Press;" Mazon, *Zoot-Suit Riots,* 1–2; "Portent of Storm," *Christian Century* (June 23, 1943), 735–36.

156. Valdez, "Envisioning California," 162, 165, 167–68 (quote).

157. Acuña, *Community under Siege,* 13, 43, 105, etc.

158. Peñalosa, "Changing Mexican-American in Southern California," 406.

159. Bureau of Labor Statistics, "Minority Groups in California," 979–80.

160. Peñalosa, "Changing Mexican-American," 410, 415.

161. Elac, "Employment of Mexican Workers in U.S. Agriculture, 1900–1960," 28–36; Wells, "Twentieth-Century Migrant Farm Labor," 68–69; Gamboa, "Mexican Migration into Washington State," 121–31; Timmons, *El Paso,* 242; Gilmore and Gilmore, "Bracero in California," 269.

162. Moore, *To the Golden Cities,* 21–23.

163. Ibid., 22, 35.

164. Vorspan and Gartner, *History of the Jews of Los Angeles,* 226, 230, 276–77. Moore, *Golden Cities,* 265, gives 440,000 in the city (1970); the Vorspan-Gartner figure is for the county.

165. Roberts, "Our Crowd—West," 35, 37, 70.

166. Morrison, "Role of Migration in California's Growth," 38–40.

167. Nugent, "People of the West since 1890," 66; Findlay, *Magic Lands,* Morrison, "Role of Migration," 41.

168. Gunther, *Inside U.S.A.,* 41; Bean, *California,* 524–25; Clayton, "Impact of the Cold War," 450–52, 460–62; Lotchin, "City and the Sword," 87–124, and same, *Fortress California.*

169. Hamburger, "Notes . . . Sacramento, Calif.," 81–87.

170. Liebman, *California Farmland,* 129 (quote), 144–73; Roos, *Thirsty Land,* 7–8, 89–90; Koppes, "Public Water, Private Land," 607–36; Kahrl, *California Water Atlas,* 49–56.

171. Consider the tale, related by Dorothy O. Johansen, "that in December, 1941, when practice emergency black-outs were ordered at a designated hour, the gay cosmopolites of San Francisco ignored the order and the lights, though dim in the bars, burned bright on the hills. Seattle's citizens so successfully blacked out that shops were looted, everyone had a riotous time, and, when the lights came on, life went on as usual. In Portland, the citizens turned out their lights and went to bed as they always did." Johansen, "Working Hypothesis," 1.

172. Pearl and Ing Borg OH, May 28, 1976, and Cates OH, 1976. For an extended discussion, based largely on oral histories, see Kesselman, *Fleeting Opportunities.*

173. McCourt OH, March 1979.

174. Oregon Board of Census report, cited in *Portland Sunday Oregonian,* Sept. 29, 1963.

175. Hamburger, "Notes . . . Eugene, Ore.," 96.

176. *Seattle Times,* April 16, 1961; *Seattle Sunday Times,* Sept. 1, 1963.

177. Erickson, *Selected Population Characteristics in Washington, 1950–1960,* 1–2, 8–11.

178. Ficken and LeWarne, *Washington,* 156–57; Gamboa, "Mexican Migration into Washington State," 121–24, 127, 129, 131.

179. Shepherd, *Demographic and Socioeconomic Profiles,* 1, 19, 63, and tables.

180. MacDonald, *Distant Neighbors,* 154.

181. Pitzer, *Grand Coulee,* 192.

182. Reisner, *Cadillac Desert,* 171–72, lists dozens of the major ones.

183. Ficken and LeWarne, *Washington,* 138–42, 146–47.

184. On the thyroid victims, see *NYT,* March 22, 1997; on leakage, see *NYT,* April 17, 1988.

185. Findlay, *Magic Lands,* chap. 5 ("The Seattle World's Fair of 1962: Downtown and Suburbs in the Space Age"), esp. 256–64.

186. Shortridge, "Collapse of Frontier Farming in Alaska," 583–604, esp. 597–98.

187. U.S. Census, *Historical Statistics,* series A195, I:24, I:26.

188. Hamburger, "Notes . . . Juneau, Alas.," 170–78; Hamburger, "Notes . . . Fairbanks, Alas.," 219–28 (quote, 225); Moffat, *Population History,* 1–4; *World Almanac 1997,* 303.

189. Tabrah, *Hawaii,* esp. chap. 16, "Statehood," 191–202.

190. Hamburger, "Notes . . . Liv-Lahaina, Hawaii," 166–74 (esp. 166, 170).

191. Vale and Vale, *Western Images, Western Landscapes,* 135, for map of missiles around Great Falls; Welsh, "Western Historians, U.S. Army Corps of Engineers, and the Rivers of Empire," 5–12.

192. Arrington, *History of Idaho,* chap. 26, II:123–44.

193. Clayton, "Impact of the Cold War," 463–70; Clayton, "An Unhallowed Gathering," 240–41.

194. Peirce, *Mountain States,* 207.

195. Ibid., 34, lists Lowry Field, Rocky Mountain Arsenal, the Air Force Academy, Fort Carson, and "more government offices than any city outside of Washington, including regional headquarters for virtually every important federal agency," as well as the private contractor Martin Marietta, then building Titan missiles at Denver. Malone and Etulain, *The American West,* 224–25, add the North American Air Defense Command (NORAD) and in 1980, over thirty-three thousand federal employees.

196. "Denver: The Old Bulls Retreat," *Fortune* (April 1958), 245–46; Abbott, *New Urban America,* 125–26, 156.

197. "Population, Denver Metro Area;" Abbott, "Boom State and Boom City," 224–25.

198. Arsenault, "The End of the Long Hot Summer," 611–13, 617–18, 628.

199. Malone and Etulain, *American West,* 129.

200. Author's conversation with Paul K. Longmore, June 15, 1987, Pasadena.

201. Coleman, "Unbearable Whiteness of Skiing," 583–614, esp. 589.

202. For a perceptive dissection, see Findlay, *Magic Lands,* chap. 4: "Sun City, Arizona: New Town for Old Folks," 160–213.

203. Abbott, "Southwestern Cityscapes," 69–78, explains why easterners find southwestern cities "incomprehensible."

204. Abbott, *New Urban America,* 49.

205. Metzgar, "Guns and Butter," 121.

206. Rabinowitz, "Growth Trends in the Albuquerque SMSA, 1940–1978," 62–66.

207. Welsh, "United States Army Corps of Engineers in the Middle Rio Grande Valley, 1935–1955," 295–318.

208. Fred Johnson OH, Nov. 1968, 4, 20. Leslie Marmon Silko's acclaimed novel *Ceremony* describes the problems of a former GI from Laguna Pueblo who also fought on Iwo Jima.

209. Rael OH, Nov. 1968, 8–9.

210. Metzgar, "Guns and Butter," 121, 125–26.

211. Rothman, *On Rims and Ridges,* chap. 11.

212. Gómez, *Quest for the Golden Circle;* Ringholz, *Uranium Frenzy.*

213. Gómez, "Urban Imperialism in the Modern West: Farmington . . . vs. Durango," 145.

214. Hamburger, "Notes . . . Santa Fe, N.M.," 206–12.

215. Luckingham, "Urban Development in Arizona," 214.

216. Ibid., 216–19, 222, 224; Konig, "Phoenix in the 1950s: Urban Growth in the 'Sunbelt,' " 19–24.

217. Luckingham, "Urban Development," 224, 226; Konig, "Phoenix in the 1950s," 33; Marvin Andrews (Phoenix City manager) OH, 9.

218. Luckingham, "Urban Development," 219; Konig, "Phoenix in the 1950s," 29.

219. Sheridan, *Arizona: A History,* 219–27, 280–81; Central Arizona Project Assn., "Water for Arizona: Key to Progress"; Dean, " 'Dam Building Still Had Some Magic Then,' " 81–98.

220. Sheridan, *Arizona,* 282–84; Andrews OH, 21–22.

221. Albert Barnett, "Future Looks Bright for Negroes in Arizona's 'Valley of the Sun,'" *Chicago Defender*, Dec. 12, 1953.
222. Sheridan, *Arizona*, 284–86; Luckingham, *Minorities in Phoenix*, esp. chaps. 2 and 8.
223. Hollon, *Great American Desert*, 222.
224. Sheridan, *Arizona*, 278–81; Bufkin, "From Mud Village to Modern Metropolis," 82–90.
225. Hogner, *Westward, High, Low, and Dry*, 276.
226. Laxalt, *Nevada*, 105, 116–17; Moehring, "Suburban Resorts and the Triumph of Las Vegas," 202–07.
227. Moehring, "Suburban Resorts," 207–10; "Policy Perspective: Las Vegas and Public Works," 3; Moehring, *Resort City in the Sunbelt: Las Vegas, 1930–1970*, esp. chaps. 7 and 8. Regarding nuclear testing, "the vast majority of citizens strongly supported further development and stockpiling of nuclear weapons, and implicitly endorsed continued testing in Nevada. Those few who did not were routinely accused of ignorance, hysteria, or involvement in communist plots. . . . [Tourists] flocked to Las Vegas . . . to see the mushroom clouds and watch history in the making" (Titus, "A-Bombs in the Backyard," 244, 246).
228. Gutmann et al., "Migration, Environment, and Economic Change in the U.S. Great Plains, 1930–1990," 3.
229. U.S. Census, *Historical Statistics*, series K1, I:457.
230. Morrison, *A Taste of the Country*, 97.
231. U.S. Census, *Historical Statistics*, series A195, I:34.
232. Sherman and Thorson, *Plains Folk*, 34–35.
233. Ibid., 268, 361.
234. Smith, "North Dakota's Prairie Communities," 51–53.
235. Parman, *Indians and the American West*, 130–31; Worster, *Rivers of Empire*, 267.
236. This follows Fite, "Transformation of South Dakota Agriculture," 278–305 (quote, 302).
237. Nugent, "People of the West since 1890," 54–55, 62–63.
238. Mahar et al., *Economic Forces behind Colorado's Growth*, 8, 30, 42–48.
239. Thoams and Taylor, *Migrant Farm Labor in Colorado*, 2–9.
240. Salazar OH, Feb. 1986; quotes, transcript 2, 4, 15.
241. Frumkin, "Rural Families in an Urban Setting," 495, 497.
242. Meinig, *Southwest*, 82–83.
243. Hurt, *Dust Bowl*, chap. 9; Hurt, "Return of the Dust Bowl," 85–93; Sherow, *Watering the Valley*, 150–60.
244. Ebeling, *Fruited Plain*, 251–53.
245. Worster, *Rivers of Empire*, 313; Opie, *Ogallala*, chaps. 1, 4.
246. Morris et al., *Historical Atlas of Oklahoma*, map 75.
247. Kohler OH, 1983.
248. Ebeling, *Fruited Plain*, 137.
249. Fite, *American Farmers*, 111.
250. Scruggs, "Texas and the Bracero Program," 251–64 (quote, 263).
251. Fogel, *Mexican Illegal Alien Workers*, 16. Further detail appears in Samora, *Los Mojados*, 51–55.
252. Gómez-Quiñones, "Mexican Immigration to the United States and the Internationalization of Labor," 26.
253. D. Gutiérrez, *Walls and Mirrors*, 134–36, 151, 157–67; Elac, "Employment of Mexican Workers," 36–45.
254. D. Gutiérrez, *Walls and Mirrors*, 164.
255. González Navarro, *Población y Sociedad en México*, II:161.
256. Haas, *Bracero in Orange County*, 4, 13. The program also favored large producers because, she writes, "the smaller grower was the last to be allocated Bracero labor," 18.
257. Ibid., 32, 40, 47.

258. Gilmore and Gilmore, "Bracero in California," 272–73.
259. Liebman, _California Farmland,_ 163–64.
260. González Navarro, _Población y Sociedad,_ II:141, 145–48.
261. Cox, "Problems of Texas Migrant Farm Workers Surveyed," _Chicago New World,_ May 18, 1962.
262. Wright "Cowboy" Boyd OH, July 13, 1973.
263. Jackson OH, Feb. 1975.
264. Sanchez OH, Nov. 1976.
265. Bernardo Martínez OH, Dec. 1974.
266. OHs of Veloz and Bernal Lucero.
267. Anderson, _Bracero Program in California,_ [xvii]. Sponsored by the American Friends Service Committee beginning in 1958, and originally written in 1961, Anderson's work at Berkeley, he states, was stopped and his report destroyed ("Introduction to the 1976 Edition").
268. Roman OH.
269. Gonzalez OH, July 4, 1973.
270. Friesen, _Canadian Prairies,_ 429, 431–32.
271. Fabry, "Agricultural Science and Technology in the West," 170, 180.
272. Hamburg, "Gambling," 216.
273. Taylor, _Forging of a Black Community,_ 190, 193.
274. Ibid., 200, 205–06. The City Council did pass an open housing ordinance in 1968, after the King assassination (208).
275. Broussard, _Black San Francisco,_ 241–42.
276. Sonenshein, _Politics in Black and White,_ 14–15, 46.
277. Valien, "Overview of Demographic Trends and Characteristics by Color," 33.
278. Taylor, _In Search of the Racial Frontier,_ 301; on the Watts episode, 299–303.
279. "West Coast, Too, Has Its Race Problems," _U.S. News & World Report_ (June 29, 1956), 36–43.
280. Marx, "The Negro Community: 'A Better Chance,' " 37–41.
281. Ward, "A Man Buys a Home, and Monterey Park Won't Ever Be Quite the Same Again," 7–9.
282. Lillard, "Problems and Promise in Tomorrowland," 84–85.
283. Horne, _Fire This Time,_ 3, 16.
284. Wilkinson, "And Now the Bill Comes Due," 10–12.
285. Hacker, "What the McCone Commission Didn't See," 10–15.
286. For another assessment that found widespread "alienation and anomia" among middle-class blacks living in Baldwin Hills and the San Fernando Valley in the late 1960s, see Bullough, "Alienation among Middle Class Negroes."

9: "Where It All Starts," 1965–1987

1. _Chicago Tribune,_ July 25, 1995.
2. U.S. Census, _Historical Statistics,_ series B1 and B5, I:49.
3. "The Future Population of the United States," _PopBull,_ 8. The "fertility rate" means the number of live births in a year per thousand women aged fifteen to forty-four in a population. It is more precise than the "birthrate," the number of live births in a year per thousand—male, female, of whatever age. For post-1970s data, U.S. Department of Commerce, _Vital Statistics of the United States 1987,_ I:1; _Population Today,_ 24 (March 1996), 6, and 25 (Feb. 1997), 6. Because so many girl baby boomers had matured into childbearing age, however, births per year touched four million again in 1988 and remained at or just below that level through the 1990s.
4. "New Baby Boom? No, Just a Dim Echo," _NYT,_ March 30, 1988.

5. Bouvier and De Vita, "The Baby Boom—Entering Midlife," 4, 9; Mitchell, "The Next Baby Boom," 24; U.S. Census "Population Profile," news release CB95-137 (Aug. 1, 1995).

6. Jones, *Great Expectations*, 198.

7. Masnick and McFalls, "A New Perspective on the Twentieth-Century Fertility Swing," 224; "Future Population of the United States," 26.

8. Pillai, "Postwar Rise and Decline of American Fertility," 429–34.

9. U.S. Department of Commerce, *Vital Statistics of the United States 1970*, I:41; *Vital Statistics 1979*, I:70; *Vital Statistics 1987*, 79. The highest ten (in downward rank order) in 1960 were Alaska, New Mexico, Utah, Arizona, Louisiana, Hawaii, North Dakota, the District of Columbia, Texas, Montana, and Delaware; in 1970, Utah, Alaska, Mississippi, New Mexico, Hawaii, Arizona, Georgia, Texas, Louisiana, and Idaho; in 1977, Utah, Idaho, Alaska, Wyoming, New Mexico, Louisiana, Mississippi, Hawaii, Arizona, and Texas; in 1987, Alaska, Utah, Arizona, New Mexico, California, Texas, Hawaii, Nevada, Louisiana, and Georgia. Thus Utah, Alaska, New Mexico, Arizona, Hawaii, and Texas stayed in the top ten throughout the 1960–1987 period.

10. U.S. Census, *State and Metropolitan Area Data Book 1997–1998*, 8.

11. Plane and Rogerson, "Tracking the Baby Boom, the Baby Bust, and the Echo Generations," 417–21.

12. Light, *Baby Boomers*, 12–13.

13. U.S. Department of Commerce, *Vital Statistics,* 1970, 1979, 1987; U.S. Census, *Pocket Data Book USA 1967*, 57, and same, *Pocket Data Book USA 1979*, 69.

14. "Fertility Rate Declines in Utah amid a Slump," *NYT*, Dec. 29, 1988.

15. *NYT*, Oct. 2, 5, 1987: Utah's median age was 25.5, Alaska's 28.4. At 31.9, Nevada and Washington were insignificantly older than the national average, California at 31.3 insignificantly younger. Besides Utah and Alaska, other western states averaging younger than 30.0 were Idaho, New Mexico, Wyoming, and Texas.

16. Dobbert, "Aging of Californians; Interstate Comparisons as of April 1, 1980," 1.

17. "Growing Pains at 40," *Time* (May 19, 1986), 23.

18. Bouvier and Gardner, "Immigration to the U.S.," 13–15; Bernard, "Immigration: History of U.S. Policy," 495. In 1976 the family and occupational preference system was applied to Western Hemisphere migrants, and the 1980 Refugee Act admitted more refugees while lowering the general total under preferences from 290,000 to 270,000.

19. Bouvier and Gardner, "Immigration to the U.S.," 16–17.

20. Ibid., 17; Patterson, *Grand Expectations*, 577–79.

21. Roger Daniels, *Asian America*, 321–22; Bouvier and Gardner, "Immigration to the U.S.," 21.

22. Bouvier and Gardner, "Immigration to the U.S.," 20–21; Sabagh and Bozorgmehr, "Population Change: Immigration and Ethnic Transformation," 87.

23. Rodriguez, *Days of Obligation*, 67. See also Rodriguez's *Hunger of Memory: The Education of Richard Rodriguez, An Autobiography*. The variety of Mexican-American experiences appears in Davis, *Mexican Voices/American Dreams*.

24. Santiesteban OH, by Richard Estrada, June 1975; Rodriguez, "Go North, Young Man," *Mother Jones* (July–Aug. 1995), 34.

25. Interview by Frances A. Cox, May 2, 1972, transcript 13.

26. OHs of Murillo and Ramirez; of Delgado, 1976.

27. Espenshade, "Short History of U.S. Policy toward Illegal Immigration," 7; D. Gutiérrez, *Walls and Mirrors*, 182–83; Stephen and Bean, "Assimilation, Disruption and the Fertility of Mexican-Origin Women in the United States," 67–88; Hondagneu-Sotelo, *Gendered Transitions*, 23–26; Mines and Massey, "Patterns of Migration to the United States from Two Mexican Communities," 105–06, 111, 118; "In a Village in Mexico, the Best Harvest Is Dollars," *NYT*, May 18, 1986.

28. Paschall OH, Aug. 1978, 9, 17.

29. Liebman, *California Farmland*, 171–73; Rolle, *California*, 474–77, 512–14; Wells, "Twentieth-Century Migrant Farm Labor," 69–71.
30. Lillard, "Problems and Promise in Tomorrowland," 85; Acuña, *Community under Siege*, 138–40, 175–77, 227–28, 262–70.
31. *Seattle Times*, Aug. 16, 1982; Slatta, "Chicanos in the Pacific Northwest," 155–62; Slatta and Atkinson, "The 'Spanish Origin' Population of Oregon and Washington," 108–16; D. Gutiérrez, *Walls and Mirrors*, 182–83; Bean and Tienda, *Hispanic Population of the United States*, 119; Passel and Woodrow, "Change in the Undocumented Alien Population in the United States, 1979–1983," 1320–21; Davis et al., "U.S. Hispanics: Changing the Face of America," 12–15.
32. Roberts and Thomas, "City of Ethnics," 45–50, 70–71.
33. Yung, *Unbound Feet*, 289.
34. Bay Area Social Planning Council, *Chinese Newcomers in San Francisco*, 60, 63.
35. Tsai, *Chinese Experience in America*, 140–41, 153, 156–57. In 1970 New York was second with 77,099, Honolulu third with 48,897, and Los Angeles/Long Beach fourth with 41,500. In 1980 San Francisco/Oakland continued to lead with 169,016; New York/Newark was second with 157,237; Los Angeles/Long Beach by then in third with 94,521; Honolulu fourth with 52,301. By 1980 San Jose, Sacramento, Seattle/Tacoma, and Anaheim/Santa Ana/Garden Grove (just south of Los Angeles) had joined the top eleven.
36. Lai OH, June 17, 1997.
37. Ong and Liu, "U.S. Immigration Policies and Asian Migration," 52.
38. Ibid., 58.
39. Liu and Cheng, "Pacific Rim Development," 74–94; Jensen, *Passage from India*, 280–82.
40. Lee, *Quiet Odyssey*, esp. Introduction, Appendix B, Appendix C.
41. Sucheng Chan, "Koreans in America," 11; Kyung Lee, "Settlement Patterns of Los Angeles Koreans," 61, 70.
42. Deutsch et al., "Contemporary Peoples/Contested Places," 657.
43. Guyotte, "Generation Gap," 64.
44. Melendy, "Filipinos in the United States," 520–21; "Last of the Manongs: Again Voices of a Farm-Labor Fight Find an Audience," *NYT*, May 11, 1993; Pido, *Pilipinos in America*, 33.
45. Pido, 77–82.
46. Consult Liu et al., "Dual Chain Migration," 487–513; their data come from Hawaii and the New York area, rather than California.
47. "Sewing for the American Dream," *Seattle Times*, Aug. 25, 1996.
48. Barich, "Hmong Temple," in Yogi, *Big Dreams*, 394–96.
49. Eleanor Swent interview of "Vietnamese Refugees in the East Bay," 1980; Swent, "They Still Dream of Vietnam," *San Francisco Sunday Chronicle & Examiner Magazine*, Aug. 21, 1977.
50. Muzny, *Vietnamese in Oklahoma City*, 30.
51. "New Immigrants Test Nation's Heartland," *NYT*, Oct. 18, 1993.
52. "A Vietnamese-American Becomes a Political First," *NYT*, Nov. 16, 1992. Also, on politics and demography, "Refugees Press on with Vietnam War," *NYT*, Aug. 3, 1987; "Vietnam War and Its Casualties Continue for Refugees in the U.S.," *NYT*, Aug. 25, 1989; "Old Soldiers: Last of the Refugees Who Are Free to Leave Vietnam," *NYT*, Sept. 14, 1992.
53. "Hmong Refugees Resist Adopting Birth Control," *NYT*, Aug. 27, 1989.
54. Sucheng Chan, *Asian Californians*, 113–14.
55. As described above in chapters two and three.
56. Ebner, "Transforming Irvine," 1997, 15–16; Teaford, *Post-Suburbia*, 46–48.
57. Kling et al., *Postsuburban California*, 22–23; Teaford, *Post-Suburbia*, 94–95.
58. Indian birthrates were higher than white or black in part because Indian women, especially those on reservations, married and began families young (nearly half in their teen

years). Death rates held around 22, compared to about 9 for whites at that time, with alcohol-related illnesses and suicide abnormally high as causes. Improving health care to Indians raised overall life expectancy above 71 by 1980, compared with 69.5 for black Americans and 74.4 for whites. Snipp, *American Indians,* 68; Snipp, "Demographic Comeback," 4–5.

59. Thornton, *American Indian Holocaust and Survival,* 168, 220–21; Snipp, *American Indians,* 64; Snipp, "Demographic Comeback," 4.
60. Snipp, *American Indians,* 78.
61. Followed by Tulsa (38,500), Oklahoma City (24,700), Phoenix (22,800), and Albuquerque (20,700).
62. Parman, *Indians and the American West,* 149; Thornton, *American Indian Holocaust and Survival,* 228–29; "Census Finds Many Claiming New Identity: Indian," *NYT,* March 5, 1991; Bahr, *From Mission to Metropolis,* 14; O'Hare, "America's Minorities," 10.
63. Gosting, "Red Power Struggle," *Los Angeles* (Oct. 1969), 42.
64. Trillin, "U.S. Journal: Los Angeles: New Group in Town," 92–104.
65. *Economist,* June 8, 1991, 31–32; "Tribe to Receive $162 Million in Settlement of a Land Suit," *NYT,* March 26, 1990; "150 Years Later, Indians Cope with the Bitter Results of Settlement," *NYT,* June 1, 1993.
66. Timmons, *The Trouble with Harry Hay,* xiv, 170–71.
67. D'Emilio, *Making Trouble,* 75.
68. Ibid., 53.
69. Stryker and Van Buskirk, *Gay by the Bay,* 64–65. Rolle, *California: A History,* 515, estimated gay people at one-sixth of San Francisco's population in 1970. Another estimate as of 1978 put gay people at one-eighth of the city's population and one-fifth of adults, or 75,000 to 150,000; Deutsch et al., "Contemporary Peoples/Contested Places," 651, 654. The doubling of gay population between 1970 and 1978 is asserted in FitzGerald, "The Castro—I," 34. She also states that New York and Los Angeles may have had higher gay populations, but San Francisco clearly led proportionately and in visibility (35). For gays in World War II America, with some mention of San Francisco and other places in the West, see Bérubé, *Coming Out under Fire.*
70. D'Emilio, *Making Trouble,* 87. This book, by a careful historian, supplies much detail on gay history from the 1950s through the 1970s, 74–95.
71. FitzGerald, "Reporter at Large; The Castro—I," 38, 43, 54.
72. Ibid., 44–53.
73. FitzGerald, "A Reporter at Large; The Castro—II," 49.
74. "Spread of AIDS Abating, but Deaths Will Still Soar," *NYT,* Feb. 14, 1988.
75. "Ghost Town that Was Restored to Life Is Now in Uproar over Raid for Drugs," *NYT,* Jan. 21, 1986.
76. Abbott, "Utopia and Bureaucracy," 77–78, 90, 92, 98, 99.
77. The standard work on early examples is Hine, *California's Utopian Colonies.* See also Rather, *Bohemians to Hippies.*
78. *Seattle Sunday PI,* April 12, 1970.
79. Hays, *Beauty, Health, and Permanence,* 225.
80. *Portland Sunday Oregonian,* Jan. 13, 1980.
81. "Confronting Sprawl, the Big Issue of the '90s," *NYT Real Estate Supplement,* Sept. 10, 1989, 16.
82. The strongest support came from Portland, Salem, and Eugene; strongest opposed were southeastern ranching and southwestern lumbering counties. Robbins, "The Willamette Valley Project of Oregon," 585–605; Abbott and Howe, "Politics of Land-Use Law in Oregon," 5–35.
83. Fradkin, *A River No More,* 99; Forstall, *Population of States and Counties,* 24.
84. Gulliford, *Boomtown Blues,* 2, 3, 90, 91–92.

85. Ibid., 12, 149–51, 193.

86. "Energy Price Drop Mars Mountain States' Hopes," *NYT*, Feb. 4, 1986; "Old Claims Fuel Dispute over Colorado Oil Shale," *NYT*, July 31, 1988. On Montana and copper, see Malone, "Historical Commentary—the Close of the Copper Century," 69–72; Malone, "The Collapse of Western Metal Mining: An Historical Epitaph," 455–64. Other copper towns that closed, or went nonunion and much scaled back, include Clifton, Ajo, Douglas, and Morenci (all not far from Tucson) in Arizona, Kellogg and Wallace in northern Idaho, and Leadville, Colorado: see "Copper's Plunge Is Pushing Mining Towns to the Brink," *NYT*, March 23, 1986; "Mom-and-Pop Mining Is Stirring in the Rockies," *NYT*, Aug. 17, 1986.

87. *Economist* (Feb. 25, 1984), 25–26 (which estimated the cost per irrigated acre at $3,787, of which "the lucky farmer" would be obliged to pay back only $77); "The Death of a Dinosaur," *NYT* (editorial), June 11, 1984; "Dakota Water Project: Giveaway or Blessing?," *NYT*, Aug. 18, 1984.

88. "After 85 Years, the Era of Big Dams Nears End," *NYT*, Jan. 24, 1987; "Water Projects Bureau Shifting to Conservation," *NYT*, Oct. 2, 1987.

89. "Gold Divides Dakotans as River Did," *NYT*, Oct. 9, 1988; Robbins, "Gripped by Gold Fever," *NYT Magazine*, Dec. 4, 1988.

90. "Peril in the West: Enforcing Environment Laws Gets Scary," *Chicago Tribune*, Nov. 24, 1994; "A GOP Test in the West for Taxpayers," *Chicago Tribune* (editorial), Jan. 29, 1995; "Ruinous Giveaways," *Sports Illustrated* (Apr. 19, 1993), 9.

91. "Where Growth Is King, A Move to Rein It In," *NYT*, Aug. 9, 1987.

92. "Sunny San Diego Acts to Slow Its Rapid Growth," *NYT*, June 28, 1987.

93. "The New California Dream: Closing the Door," *NYT*, June 12, 1988; "Seattle: Project Tailored to Space Limits," *NYT*, Nov. 26, 1989; "Impact Fees Re-examined in California," *NYT*, Apr. 4, 1993.

94. "So Long Cars, Hello People," *NYT*, May 31, 1987; "Seattle Has a Plan: Urban Renewal for Fun," *NYT*, Apr. 4, 1993; "Builders Scrambling to Meet Eastside Office Demand," *Seattle Times*, Sept. 3, 1997; "Seattle and Portland in Struggle to Avert Another Paradise Lost," *NYT*, Nov. 1, 1997; "For Denver's Future, a Battle of the Car vs. the Train," *NYT*, Nov. 3, 1997.

95. Philpott, "Turning against Tourists." Wayne Aspinall, the pro-Olympic, prodevelopment Democratic congressman from western Colorado, lost the 1972 primary; Lamm won the governorship in 1974. Philpott points out that though the antis were ostensibly antitourist, they were themselves often newcomers, year-round tourists who became quality-of-lifers.

96. "Rare Alliance in the Rockies Strives to Save Open Spaces," *NYT*, Aug. 14, 1998.

97. Ed Marston, "Coming into a New Land," *HCN*, Oct. 10, 1988, 7–9, 11.

98. Ed Marston, "The West Lacks Social Glue," *HCN*, Sept. 26, 1988, 8.

99. Albert et al., *The Dynamic West*, 6–8; U.S. Census, "Geographical Mobility: March 1987 to March 1990," table E.

100. Gober, "Americans on the Move," 24–26.

101. U.S. Census, *Historical Statistics*, series C42–C45, C61–C75 (net intercensal migration, 1960–1970), I:93; Gober, "Americans on the Move," 17–20; Albert et al., *Dynamic West*, 7. Because of the synfuels boom, Wyoming (with its small population base) had the highest in-migrant rate, 11 percent, of all the affected states between 1975 and 1980 (Gober, 19).

102. Gober, "Americans on the Move," 21–24; "Can Planning Rein in a Stampede?" (with migration illustrations based on California Department of Motor Vehicle license transfers), *HCN*, Sept. 5, 1994, 6.

103. Abbott, *Metropolitan Frontier*, 191.

104. Frey, "Metropolitan America: Beyond the Transition," 7–15, 18–19, 27–28; Population Reference Bureau, "Metro U.S.A. Data Sheet," 1987 edition.

105. Between the 1980 and 1990 censuses, the core cities of Los Angeles grew to 3,500,000, up 17.4 percent; San Diego to 1,100,000, up 27 percent; Phoenix to just under 1,000,000, up 14.5 percent. San Jose and El Paso also increased over 20 percent. Exceptions—from intent, tight boundaries, or reluctance to annex—were San Francisco, Seattle, Denver, and Portland, up 5 percent or less in the core city, although adjacent municipalities expanded. "The Census Bureau's Report on Cities," *NYT*, Jan. 27, 1991; on stable core vs. expanding suburbs in Denver and Portland from 1960 to 1975, see Abbott, *New Urban America*, 187–96.

106. "Suburb-to-Suburb Commuting Now National Pattern," *LAT*, June 26, 1987; "Census Bureau's Report on Cities," *NYT*, Jan. 27, 1991.

107. Teaford, *Post-Suburbia*, 5 (quote), 153–60. Joel Garreau introduced the term "edge cities" and explored the concept in *Edge City: Life on the New Frontier*. It has been criticized for overemphasizing commerce above other aspects of the "fundamentally de-centered or multicentered nature" of Orange County and for not giving enough consideration to its new Asian immigrants (see Kling et al., *Postsuburban California*, xiii–xv), but Garreau's handy phrase has absorbed the wider meaning these authors apparently desire.

108. Hart, *Farming on the Edge*, 1–14, 157–68 (quote, 167).

109. This area includes, but is even larger than, the "Empty Quarter" described by Garreau in *The Nine Nations of North America*.

110. Brownridge, "The Rural West Is Actually Very Urban," *HCN*, Sept. 12, 1988, 14–15, 18; "People Moving Back to Cities, U.S. Study Says," *NYT*, Apr. 13, 1986; "On the Trail of the White-Collar Settlers," *Economist* (Nov. 8, 1986), "Some Say Frontier Is Still There, and Still Different," *NYT*, Dec. 12, 1987; "Urban Areas Grew in 80's, Reversing a Trend," *NYT*, Aug. 8, 1989; "Census Data Show Sharp Rural Losses," *NYT*, Aug. 30, 1990.

111. Burns, "Collapse of Small Towns on the Great Plains: A Bibliography," 23.

112. Morris et al., 2d ed., 75; same authors and title, 3d ed., 75.

113. Applebome, "Out Where Texas Is, Well, Texas Sized," *NYT*, Oct 25, 1987.

114. Opie, "100 Years of Climate Risk Assessment on the High Plains," 268; Lacewell and Lee, "Texas High Plains," 127, 131.

115. Morrison, *A Taste of the Country*, 162–70.

116. U.S. Census, "Rural and Rural Farm Population: 1987," 1; *Historical Statistics.*, series A69, I:12.

117. David Rieff, "Ride 'Em, Cowboy! Rodeos and Reality," *NYT*, Sept. 13, 1994; "As Farms Falter, Rural Homelessness Grows," *NYT*, May 2, 1989.

118. Kromm and White, *Groundwater Exploitation in the High Plains*, 10–14; "Midwest Population Bouncing Back," *NYT*, Dec. 30, 1988.

119. Described in chapter eight; an expensive but effective irrigation technique using groundwater, usually from the Ogallala Aquifer.

120. By 1997 Dodge City's packing plants employed another four thousand, "Hispanic Workers Revitalize a Town," *NYT*, Jan. 29, 1998.

121. Stull, "I Come to the Garden,' " 303–12.

122. John L. Moore, "Bad Days at Big Dry," *NYT Magazine*, Aug. 14, 1988, 27.

123. Jim Robbins, "Discouraging Words in Montana," *HCN*, Sept. 26, 1988, 11–13; "Drought of '88 Spurs Comparisons to Dust Bowl Era, but Differences Abound," *NYT*, July 7, 1988.

124. *HCN*, July 7, 1997.

125. Babbitt, "History of Land Fraud in Arizona," 10–11.

126. Kalnitz OH, 1988, 1–8, 11–15, 19–23.

127. Linoff OH, 1988, 1–13.

128. On Ed Fouts, see "Traumatic Travel into History," *Arizona Republic* (Apr. 9, 1996), and

stories about him in the same newspaper, May 9, 1995, Oct. 31, 1995, Nov. 17, 1995, Oct. 10, 1996, Feb. 23, 1997, May 22, 1997 (my thanks to Ruth Hardin for these references).

129. "Alarm Raised on Growth of Phoenix," *NYT*, March 12, 1987; "Home Buyers Are Calling the Tune around Phoenix," *NYT*, March 5, 1989.

130. "Home of Closed Base Flies High Once Again," *South Bend Tribune*, July 7, 1993.

131. On Nevada: Peirce, *Mountain States*, 182.

132. Noel, intro., *The WPA Guide to 1930s Colorado*, x–xii.

133. Peirce, *Mountain States*, 212–13; Meinig, "Mormon Culture Region," 191–220; Trillin, "U.S. Journal: Provo, Utah," 121–25.

134. Trillin, "U.S. Journal: Arroyo Seco, New Mexico," 103–10.

135. "Wyoming Is Trying to Widen Its Horizon," *NYT*, Apr. 6, 1986.

136. Ray Wheeler, "Whither the Colorado Plateau?," *HCN*, Oct. 24, 1988, 15, 18–19.

137. "A Tiny Nevada Town Expands as Casinos Multiply," *NYT*, Aug. 28, 1988; Moffat, *Population History of Western U.S. Cities and Towns*, 9, 156; U.S. Census, "State and County Population 1990 and 1995," 29.

138. "New Fight in Old West: Farmers vs. Condo City," *NYT*, Oct. 3, 1989; "Rocky Mountain Towns Rejuvenated by Retirees," *NYT*, Feb. 15, 1987; "Tucson's Grass-Roots War against Allergies," *NYT*, March 23, 1987.

139. Nordyke, *Peopling of Hawai'i*, 130–33.

140. "City's Population in Major Shifts," *PI*, Jan. 26, 1976; Washington, *Forecasts of the State Population by Age and Sex 1987–2010*, 29–30.

141. "Humanity Heads for the Hills," *Tacoma News-Tribune*, Sept. 6, 1977; "Census: 41,000 Leave Seattle for the Suburbs," *PI*, Oct. 9, 1980.

142. "The California Crunch: Ready or Not, Here It Comes," *Seattle Times*, March 26, 1978; "Seattle's Surprise Population Surge," *PI*, April 16, 1987; "Upside-Down Climate in Washington," *NYT*, Sept. 4, 1987.

143. Washington, *Fiscal Impact of the Trident Submarine Support Base*, "Plutonium Leak in Idaho Symptom of Atomic Ills," *NYT*, April 17, 1988; "U.S. Sees a Danger in 1940's Radiation in the Northwest," and "Report Warns of Hanford's Radiation," *NYT*, July 13, 1990; H. Jack Geiger, "Generations of Poison and Lies," *NYT*, Aug. 5, 1990; "The First Casualties of Nuclear Age," *South Bend Tribune*, March 4, 1993; "Admitting Error at a Weapons Plant," *NYT*, March 23, 1998.

10: *The Leading Edge, 1987–1998*

1. Findlay, *Magic Lands*, 49.

2. As of July 1, 1997, the Census Bureau (*State and Metropolitan Area Data Book 1997–1998*) reported that the six California counties of Los Angeles, Orange, Riverside, San Bernardino, Ventura, and San Diego had a total population of 18,331,536 (130, 135). California led the states with 32,268,000; Texas was second with 19,439,000; and New York third with 18,137,000 (2). Thus Texas was the only *state* with more people than southern California.

3. *Population Today* (July/August 1998), 6.

4. "Nevada Fastest Growing State in Nation 12th Straight Year, Census Bureau Reports," U.S. Census news release. Of the country's ten fastest-growing counties in 1997, Douglas County near Denver led, at 12.9 percent in a year and 109.1 percent since 1990; Park and Elbert counties, also near Denver, were fourth and sixth; Lincoln, South Dakota (Sioux Falls), second; Nye, Nevada, fifth; three near Atlanta, one in northern Virginia, and one near Dallas filled out the top ten counties in rate. In numbers, the top five gainers were Maricopa, Arizona (Phoenix); Los Angeles; Clark, Nevada (Las Vegas), Orange and San

Diego; Riverside County (east of Los Angeles) was seventh. U.S. Census news release, "Fastest-Growing Counties Predominantly Southern, Western and Metropolitan, Census Bureau Reports."

5. Espenshade, "Short History of U.S. Policy toward Illegal Immigration," 7.
6. Bouvier and Gardner, "Immigration to the U.S.," 36–38.
7. "U.S.-Mexico Study Sees Exaggeration in Migration Data," *NYT,* Aug. 31, 1997.
8. Rubin-Kurtzman et al., "Population in Trans-Border Regions: The Southern California-Baja California Urban System," 1023, 1025.
9. Stoddard et al., *Borderlands Sourcebook,* 144–48, 179, 233, 238–40; Stoddard, *Maquila,* 27–30, 38–41, 70.
10. "Benefits of Free-Trade Pact Bypass Texas Border Towns," *NYT,* June 23, 1998.
11. Murray, "A Reporter at Large: Twins," 63–75.
12. Hondagneu-Sotelo, *Gendered Transitions,* 26.
13. Bouvier and Gardner, "Immigration to the U.S.: The Unfinished Story," 39–40.
14. Ibid., 44.
15. Sucheng Chan, *Asian Californians,* 114–15.
16. "Amnesty—Aliens Start Getting Their Red Cards," *Population Today* (July/Aug. 1987), 4.
17. "Immigration Door Closes," *Population Today* (June 1988), 4; Albert et al., *The Dynamic West: A Region in Transition,* 17.
18. Singer, "IRCA Aftermath," *Population Today* (Oct. 1988), 5, 9.
19. After California and Texas, the New York–New Jersey metro area contained 14 percent; Arizona, New Mexico, and Colorado followed. "Hispanic Growth Up 34% in Nation," *NYT,* Sept. 7, 1988; Winsberg, "America's Foreign Born," *Population Today* (Oct. 1993), 4.
20. Mogelonsky, "Natural(ized) Americans," 45–47, 49.
21. "Granjenal's Life Ebbs with Exodus," *LAT,* Aug. 3, 1997; "In Santa Ana, Mexican Villagers Re-Created Community," *LAT,* Aug. 4, 1997; both stories by Nancy Cleeland.
22. "The Latest Big Boom: It's Citizenship," *NYT,* Aug. 11, 1995.
23. Massey, "March of Folly: U.S. Immigration Policy after NAFTA," 22–33, esp. 27–32; Rubin-Kurtzman et al., "Population in Trans-Border Regions," 1037.
24. Hondagneu-Sotelo, *Gendered Transitions,* 26–27.
25. Martin and Midgley, "Immigration to the United States," 29.
26. Kalish, "Immigration: IRCA Tops Out, 1990 Law's Impact Yet to Begin," *Population Today* (Nov. 1992), 4.
27. Donato, "Current Trends and Patterns of Female Migration: Evidence from Mexico," 748, 750–53, 763–68.
28. "Population Update," *American Demographics* (May 1997), 20.
29. Burke, "Mexican Immigrants Shape California's Fertility, Future," *Population Today* (Sept. 1995), 4–5.
30. "Hispanic Births in U.S. Reach Record High," *NYT,* Feb. 13, 1998.
31. Day, *Population Projections of the United States by Age, Sex, Race, and Hispanic Origin: 1995 to 2050:* fertility rates for Hispanics and Asian/Pacific Islanders "are no longer projected to slowly decrease," 3; "No convergence of birth rates by race and Hispanic origin is assumed," 4.
32. "Greeted at Nation's Front Door, Many Visitors Stay on Illegally," *NYT,* Jan. 3, 1995.
33. "80's Policies on Illegal Aliens Are Now Haunting California: Politicians Wincing after Getting Their Wish," *NYT,* Oct. 15, 1994; "Fear and Self-Loathing in America," *Scientific American* (Jan. 1995), 27.
34. "In Danger: Benefits," *NYT,* Feb. 6, 1997.
35. For an intelligent analysis of several books, pro and con, on the new immigration, see Reimers, "The Immigration Debate," 86–93. Major media did not do justice to the books or the debate.

36. "Migrants Facing Oregon Hardship," *NYT*, April 16, 1988; "A New Wave of Immigrants on Lowest Rung in Farming," *NYT*, Aug. 24, 1995; Richard Estrada, "Declining Wages of Migrant Farmworkers Result of Labor Oversupply and Not Racism," *Chicago Tribune*, April 8, 1997; "Farm Workers Earn Less than in '76, Data Show," *Chicago Tribune*, April 12, 1997.

37. "Hispanic Voters Girding for New Tests," *NYT*, June 6, 1990; "More Mexicans Come to U.S. to Stay," *NYT*, Jan. 21, 1991; "Census Reveals a Surge in Hispanic Population: Blacks Are Surpassed in Four Major Cities," *NYT*, Oct. 9, 1994; "The Expanding Hispanic Vote Shakes Republican Strongholds," *NYT*, Nov. 10, 1996; "Hispanics Claim Win in Defeat of Dornan," *Chicago Tribune*, Nov. 14, 1996.

38. "Clash of Cultures Grows amid American Dream," *NYT*, Mar. 26, 1990; "They're in a New Home, but Feel Tied to the Old," *NYT*, June 30, 1991; "Poll Finds Hispanic Desire to Assimilate," *NYT*, Dec. 15, 1992.

39. Allen and Turner, *The Ethnic Quilt*, 78; Lopez, "Language: Diversity and Assimilation," 144; for a survey see del Pinal and Singer, "Generations of Diversity: Latinos in the United States."

40. Winsberg, "Specific Hispanics," 44–49, 52–53; "Job Search Lures Mexicans to Far Corners of U.S.," *NYT*, Feb. 4, 1997.

41. Mogelonsky, "Natural(ized) Americans," 46. Ong and Azores, "Asian Immigrants in Los Angeles: Diversity and Divisions," 100–29, is a useful brief survey, including numbers (104): in Los Angeles County during the 1980s, Chinese rose 159 percent, to 245,000; Filipinos by 188 percent, to 220,000; Koreans by 141 percent, to 145,000; Vietnamese by 130 percent, to 63,000; Asian Indians by 134 percent, to 44,000; Cambodians to 28,000, Thais to 19,000. Nationally the Asian-American population by 1997 numbered 9,600,000; of them, 24 percent were Chinese, 21 percent Filipino, 13 percent from India, 11 percent Vietnamese, 11 percent Korean, 5 percent Cambodian-Hmong-Laotian, and 7 percent other Asians. In 1990 the largest group in California and Washington was the Filipinos; in Texas, Vietnamese (Sharon Lee, "Asian Americans," 6, 13, 16).

42. Allen and Turner, *Ethnic Quilt*, 122. The numbers were 77,600 from the PRC ("mainland China"), 66,000 from Taiwan, 33,500 from Vietnam, 22,900 from Hong Kong, and then a drop to 4,300 Chinese from Cambodia, and smaller groups (120).

43. On San Marino, *NYT*, Nov. 19, 1987; "U.S. Asian Population Up 70% in 80's," *NYT*, March 2, 1990.

44. Lemann, "Growing Pains," 58–59.

45. "Asian Impact . . . Life in Suburbia," *LAT*, April 5, 1987; for a book-length study, see Horton, *The Politics of Diversity*.

46. "Tenuous New Alliances Forged to Ease Korean-Black Tensions," *LAT*, July 20, 1987; "L.A. Koreans and Blacks: Violence at Bottom Rung," *International Herald Tribune*, Oct. 7, 1991; "Flight Response by Korean-Americans: Fallout of 1992 Riots in South-Central Los Angeles Is Continuing," *NYT*, Jan. 6, 1997.

47. Allen and Turner, *Ethnic Quilt*, 155; "One Man's Vision for Little Saigon," *LAT*, Aug. 5, 1997.

48. The number is lower than the media's usual forty thousand and is the informed estimate of Professor Sherna Berger Gluck of California State University—Long Beach; letter to author, July 20, 1998.

49. The Oral History Collection in Special Collections/University Archives at California State University—Long Beach interviewed a number of Cambodians in 1988–1989. The transcripts remain somewhat restricted but are open for consultation and may be quoted pseudonymously.

50. "Skilled Asians Leaving U.S. for High-Tech Jobs at Home," *NYT*, Feb. 21, 1995.

51. Allen and Turner, *Ethnic Quilt*, 62, 90, 92, 152, 231. Los Angeles in 1990 led the nation's

metropolitan areas with eighty-seven thousand Indians in 1990, according to the census (up from forty-seven thousand counted in 1980); none of the next three, Tulsa, Oklahoma City, and New York, had as many as fifty thousand.

52. Sabagh and Bozorgmehr, "Population Change: Immigration and Ethnic Transformation," 89; Allen and Turner, *Ethnic Quilt*, 55–60.
53. Allen and Turner, *Ethnic Quilt*, 49, 57, 73.
54. Ibid., 230, 252–53.
55. Some of the foregoing relies upon Waldinger and Lichter, "Anglos: Beyond Ethnicity?," 413–41 (quotes, 413). On pockets of "English" ethnics, see Allen and Turner, *Ethnic Quilt*, 48, 54.
56. Marshall, "Quiet Integration of Suburbia," 9; U.S. Census, "Foreign-Born Population: 1994"; Frey, "Immigrant and Native Migrant Magnets," 37–40, 53; Cassidy, "Melting-Pot Myth," *NY* (July 14, 1997), 41; U.S. Census, "Foreign-Born Population Reaches 25.8 Million."
57. Fradkin, *Seven States of California*, xviii.
58. Peirce, *Pacific States of America*, 154.
59. Trillin, "U.S. Journal: Watts: The Towers," 140.
60. Of those 355,000 migrants, 40 percent came from ten states, led by depressed Texas, then Illinois, New York, and Florida; another 40 percent came from Mexico, Asia, and other foreign countries.
61. *California Statistical Abstract 1987*, 13; California, *Economic Report of the Governor 1987*, 3; California Department of Finance, "Population Estimates of California Cities and Counties, Jan. 1, 1986 to Jan. 1, 1987," 1 (for description of "The Driver License Address Change Composite Migration Estimating Method [DLAC]"); "Rush Is to Interior as California Growth Shifts," *NYT*, Jan. 16, 1986; "Cars, Pavement and People Are New Vista of Rural California," *NYT*, March 5, 1987. The émigrés from Laguna Niguel are described in Garreau, *Edge City*, 275–78 (quote, 278).
62. California Department of Food and Agriculture, *California Agriculture 1985*, 18, 19.
63. E. Smith, "America's Richest Farms and Ranches," 529–31, 540; Peirce, *Pacific States*, 84.
64. "Sonoma Journal: Time to Crush Grapes and Burst Wine Legend," *NYT*, Sept. 9, 1987; "San Jose, That Upstart in Hinterland, Takes on San Francisco," *NYT*, Feb. 8, 1989; "San Diego Eyes Its Big Bad Neighbor," *NYT*, July 9, 1989.
65. "Venice Journal: Sympathy and Ire as the Homeless Take to the Beach," *NYT*, Sept. 25, 1987; "A Division on Shelter in the West," *NYT*, Oct. 13, 1987; "California Home Buyers Squeezed," *NYT*, Aug. 16, 1988; "Frustrated San Diego Builders Looking Eastward," *NYT*, Nov. 5, 1989.
66. "In Sun Belt, New Predictions of Boom in Jobs and People," *NYT*, Sept. 22, 1987.
67. "Bloom Is off the Boom," *LAT* (editorial), March 16, 1987.
68. "California, Star of Economy, Sees Short-Term Prospects Dim," *NYT*, Jan. 11, 1989.
69. "Los Angeles Dream Is Dying for Some, Thriving for Others," *NYT*, Aug. 28, 1989.
70. "Poor Seekers of Good Life Flock to California, as Middle Class Moves Away," *NYT*, Dec. 29, 1991.
71. "Census Shows New Baby Boom in California," *San Francisco Chronicle*, May 9, 1991.
72. "California Dreaming, on a Rainy Day," *Economist* (June 23, 1990); "California, Here I go," *LAT* (Real Estate), Feb. 21, 1993; Anne Taylor Fleming, "Seeing the Future and Wanting No Part of It," *NYT*, Oct. 26, 1988; "Palmdale Journal: Where City Meets Desert Somewhat Awkwardly," *NYT*, Feb. 3, 1988. The ten destinations (with median home prices in 1991–1992, where available) were Phoenix, $87,200; Reno, $118,300; Seattle, $146,000; Dallas; Portland, $97,000; Denver, $96,900; Sarasota, $93,900; Queens and Brooklyn, New York, about $170,000; Chicago, $138,400; and Atlanta.
73. *NYT* reports: "Slump Catches Up with Once-Booming California," Feb. 24, 1991; "Cali-

fornia Painfully Faces Grim Truth of Drought," Feb. 26, 1991; "Stung by Reality, California Mingles Despair and Hope," July 31, 1992.

74. Fleming, "A Collective Yearning: Leaving Paradise Behind," *NYT,* Aug. 30, 1989.

75. Taylor, *In Search of the Racial Frontier,* 311 (quote), 313.

76. "Black Leadership in Los Angeles: Augustus F. Hawkins," OH, transcript 122–23.

77. Dunne, "Law & Disorder in Los Angeles," part 1, *New York Review of Books,* Oct. 10, 1991; "This City Is Not for Burning," *APWA Reporter* (Sept. 1992), 15–16; "Fleeing Los Angeles: Quake Is the Last Straw," *NYT,* Feb. 18, 1994; "As Cultures Meet, Gang War Paralyzes a City in California," *NYT,* May 6, 1991; "Girl [Hmong] Flees after Clash of Cultures on Illness," *NYT,* Nov. 12, 1994.

78. "Life after Base Closures Often Turbulent, Communities Find," *LAT,* April 12, 1993; "Rebuilding Lags in Los Angeles a Year after Riots," *NYT,* May 10, 1993.

79. "Study: California to Grow 23% in '90s," *Chicago Tribune,* Dec. 8, 1989; "New York's Port Loses No. 1 Title to Los Angeles as Asian Trade Eludes It," *NYT,* June 12, 1990; "Rise in California Population Slows to Trail Nation's Rate," *NYT,* Dec. 29, 1993.

80. Cassidy, "Melting-Pot Myth," 41.

81. Frey, "New White Flight," 40–48 (quote, 44).

82. "Book Buyers," *American Demographics* (March 1997), 42.

83. Bill Bradley, "California: Giant of the Future . . . ," *NYT,* May 22, 1990.

84. Literally, wind and water; siting a house in proper harmony with nature.

85. *NYT* reports: "Orange Country Loss Unlikely to Derail a Basic Prosperity" and "Local Investors Demand Some Funds Back," Dec. 13, 1994; "Final Freeway Opens, Ending California Era," Oct. 14, 1993; "Coptic Church in U.S. Receives a Bishop," Jan. 3, 1996; "Homes in Los Angeles Target Asians," Aug. 27, 1995; "Alarm Bells Ring as Suburbs Gobble Up California's Richest Farmland," June 20, 1996; "Charleston Bounces Back after Closing of Base," June 12, 1997; "California Homes Are Selling Again," March 28, 1996; "Housing Sales Show New Life with Good Year," Dec. 25, 1996. Also, "Suburbia Sprouts in California's Valley of Plenty," *Chicago Tribune,* Nov. 18, 1996; Lents and Kelley, "Clearing the Air in Los Angeles," 32–39; Carl Tucker, "Southern California's Immigrants Progress Rapidly," *Population Today* (May 1996), 5.

86. Fost, "California Comeback," 53; *California Economic Growth,* 3–18.

87. "California's Population Increases by 320,000," *NYT,* April 8, 1997.

88. *California Economic Growth,* 3–19; "How to Remake a City," *Economist* (May 31, 1997), 25; "California's Economy Shows Signs of Regaining Its Glitter," *NYT,* Dec. 19, 1995 (quote).

89. "A Resurgent California Finds All That Glitters Is Its Future," *NYT,* Sept. 3, 1997; "The West Is Best Again," *Economist* (Aug. 9, 1997), 19.

90. "California's Rural Job Woes Mount," *Chicago Tribune,* Aug. 9, 1997.

91. DeVita, "United States at Mid-Decade," 6.

92. Francese, "America at Mid-Decade," 28.

93. Edmondson, "The Lucky Thirteen," 2.

94. O'Malley, "The Rural Rebound," 24–29; Johnson and Beale, "The Rural Rebound Revisited," 46–50; Longino, "From Sunbelt to Sunspots," 22–31.

95. "Harvest of Shares: One Farm's Stock Plan Gives Its Migrant Workers a Stake," *NYT,* June 26, 1997; "America's Poor Showing," *Newsweek* (Oct. 18, 1993); "1997 Kids Count Data Sheet," Annie E. Casey Foundation and Population Reference Bureau publication.

96. "High in Rockies, a Golf-Housing Complex," *NYT,* Aug. 18, 1996, Aug. 9, 1997.

97. Dortch, "Counties with Full Pockets," 6–7; "Tourists Win Cultural Shootout in Jackson, Wyo.," *NYT,* Aug. 14, 1996 (quote).

98. Garreau, "Edge Cities in Profile," 27–28. The database's information is for 1990.

99. *America's Top-Rated Cities: A Statistical Handbook,* 287–301.

100. U.S. Census Bureau, Report CB96-131, Aug. 5, 1996.

101. Greg Burns, "Harvest of Despair," *Chicago Tribune,* June 21, 1998; "Growth of Factory-Like Hog Farms Divides Rural Areas in the Midwest," *NYT,* June 24, 1998; "For Amber Waves of Data," *NYT,* May 4, 1998; "New Kind of Farm Crisis Pummels Northern Plains," *NYT,* July 19, 1998.

102. O'Malley, "Rural Rebound," 28; U.S. Census, "State and County Population 1990 and 1995," 28–29; "Life on the Great Plains: A Test of Survival Skills," *NYT,* Dec. 12, 1993.

103. "North Dakota Ranches Riding High on the Return of Buffalo," *NYT,* Aug. 19, 1996.

104. U.S. Census, "State and County Population 1990 and 1995," 33–34; "Life on the Great Plains," *NYT,* Dec. 12, 1993, Jan. 1, 1995, Feb. 3, 1997.

105. "Home on the Range (and Lonely, Too)," *NYT,* Dec. 12, 1995.

106. U.S. Census, "State and County Population 1990 and 1995," 39–40; "Life on the Great Plains," *NYT,* Dec. 12, 1993; "Telemarketing Finds a Ready Labor Market in Hard-Pressed North Dakota" *NYT,* Feb. 3, 1997.

107. Nelson, *The Prairie Winnows Out Its Own,* 202.

108. Hyde, "Slow Death in the Great Plains," 44.

109. Billings's Yellowstone County rose 9.9 percent from 1990 to 1995, to about 125,000; Gillette increased about 8 percent, to 32,000.

110. "Wyoming Is Left Out of the Rockies' Boom," *NYT,* May 23, 1998.

111. "Montana Town Puts Out Unwelcome Mat," *HCN,* Jan. 24, 1994.

112. U.S. Census, "State and County Population 1990 and 1995," 27, 51–52; "Commuter Homes Rise in Montana Valley," *NYT,* June 19, 1994; "Ranches Add Tourism to Raising Cattle," *NYT,* Dec. 11, 1994; "Small Towns Under Siege," *HCN,* April 5, 1993; "Montana Town Puts Out Unwelcome Mat," *HCN,* Jan. 24, 1994; Robbins, "Creating a 'New' West," 66–72.

113. Robbins, "Creating a 'New' West," refers to a number of these places; *NYT,* May 29, 1988 (Anaconda); March 14, 1991 (Kellogg, Coeur d'Alene); Sept. 16, 1995 (Vail); Jan. 31, 1996 (Park City); Coleman, "Unbearable Whiteness of Skiing," 583–614.

114. *Newsweek* (July 17, 1995); "State and County Population 1990 and 1995," 46.

115. *HCN,* Apr. 3 and Nov. 27, 1995.

116. "In Las Vegas, Sands Bloom with Growth," *NYT,* Sept. 17, 1990.

117. U.S. Census Report CB95-179, Oct. 1, 1995.

118. "Las Vegas Casting a Shadow over New York's New Year," *NYT,* Dec. 28, 1996.

119. "A Booming Vegas Reinvents Itself," *NYT,* May 4, 1997.

120. "Boomtown U.S.A.," *NYT,* Nov. 14, 1993; "The West at War," *Newsweek* (July 17, 1995).

121. U.S. Census, "Las Vegas Metro Area Leads Nation in Population Growth," Dec. 31, 1997. Only Las Vegas and two Texas border areas (Laredo and around McAllen) had faster metro area growth rates than Boise, 1990–1996. Also, "In Idaho, the Poor Fear They Will Go the Way of State's Democrats," *NYT,* Apr. 16, 1998.

122. "An Open-Door Policy in Salt Lake City," *NYT,* Dec. 6, 1992; "The State of Jobs: High-Tech Utah," *Chicago Tribune,* May 15, 1994.

123. Moffat, *Population History,* 69; "State and County Population 1990 and 1995," 5–6; U.S. Census news release, "Fastest-Growing Counties."

124. "Discovered, at the Edge of Known Civilization, the Sub-Suburb," *NYT,* April 28, 1991.

125. Moffat, *Population History,* 68; "The Suburban Cowboys of the Mild, Mild West," *NYT,* Jan. 25, 1995; "Colorado Booms, and Some Worry," *NYT,* July 20, 1996; Elazar et al., *Cities of the Prairie Revisited,* 75, 80–81; "Rise in Christian Right Divides a City," *NYT,* Feb. 14, 1993; *NYT,* April 28, 1991, on Castle Rock; "Prisons: A Growth Industry for Some," *NYT,* Nov. 1, 1997, on Florence; "Denver Sheds Cowtown Image for Big League Aura," *NYT,* June 12, 1991; "Now that Denver Has Abdicated," *HCN,* May 3, 1993; "Heartland Needs No Ships to Win Global Trade Game," *NYT,* May 28, 1997.

126. "Colorado Danger Signs on Medical Emergency," *NYT,* Apr. 12, 1988.

127. "Students Learn Under a Cloud," *NYT*, Feb. 25, 1988; "Housing Cools Off in a Northwest Area," *NYT*, Oct. 29, 1995; "Hanford Cleanup Stalled for 10 Years," *PI*, Aug. 11, 1997; "Caught between Risks of Haste and Hesitation," *NYT*, Sept. 29, 1997; "Radiation Leaks at Hanford Threaten River, Experts Say," *NYT*, Oct. 11, 1997.
128. "Next Door to Danger, a Booming City," *NYT*, Oct. 6, 1996.
129. "Seattle Builders Turn to Farms and Forests," *NYT*, April 11, 1993; "Many Seek Security behind Walls and Guards of Private Communities," *NYT*, Sept. 3, 1995; "Seattle's in the Grip of a Rental Squeeze," *NYT*, March 2, 1997; conversation with Attorney S. D. Nugent, Seattle, April 1, 1997.
130. "Californians Find No Welcome Wagon upon Moving to Seattle," *South Bend Tribune*, Jan. 21, 1990.
131. "Northwest Fortunes, Once Grim, Thrive amid Nation's Recession," *NYT*, March 14, 1991; "Battle Lines Drawn in Sand: Las Vegas Seeks New Water," *NYT*, April 23, 1991; "Urban Sprawl Strains Western States," *NYT*, Dec. 29, 1996; "Drawing the Hard Line on Urban Sprawl: Portland Leads the Way," *NYT*, Dec. 30, 1996; "To Support Growth, Albuquerque Will Shift Source for Water," *NYT*, May 25, 1997.
132. "Oregon Growing, and So Is Backlash," *USA Today*, May 19, 1998.
133. "Borderline Working Class: Texas Labor is Feeling Trade Pact's Pinch," *NYT*, May 8, 1997.
134. "Immigration Fueling Cities' Strong Growth," *NYT*, Jan. 1, 1998.
135. Edmondson, "Where Are the Boonies?," 60; U.S. Census, *Population of States and Counties . . . 1790–1990*, 14; "State and County Population 1990 and 1995," 2.
136. "Population of 100 Largest U.S. Cities, 1850–1994," *World Almanac* 1997, 386.
137. In the fifty-five years between 1940 and 1995 (according to the Census Bureau), the U.S. population increased from 132,000,000 to 263,000,000, or 99.2 percent: call it a doubling. That was only slightly slower than the fifty years before that—i.e., 1890 to 1940—thanks to the baby boom; between 1890 and 1940 the total rose from 63,000,000 to 132,000,000, or 110 percent. Before 1890, when frontiers of settlement were opening up, rates of increase were much greater: from 1840 to 1890, from 17,000,000 to 63,000,000, or 271 percent; from 1790 to 1840, from 4,000,000 to 17,000,000, or 325 percent; from 1740 to 1790, from under 1,000,000 to about 4,000,000, or 400 percent. U.S. Census, *Historical Statistics*, series A2, I:8.
138. The census continues to use the term "Hispanic" rather than "Latino." It defines "Hispanic" as "A person of Mexican, Puerto Rican, Cuban, Central or South American or other Spanish culture or origin, regardless of race." A Hispanic can therefore be white, black, Asian, or Native American. Filipinos and Filipinas, though they may speak Spanish, are in the census's "Asian and Pacific Islander" category.
139. Day, *Population Projections*, 1–3, 5, 13, 15, 19, 31; U.S. Census, "How We're Changing; "The Minority Majority in 2001," *American Demographics* (Oct. 1996), 17.
140. U.S. Census, "Fastest-Growing Counties Predominantly Southern, Western, and Metropolitan," March 17, 1998.
141. Tom Morganthau, "The Face of the Future," *Newsweek* (Jan. 27, 1997), 57–60; Ambry, "States of the Future" (esp. state-by-state estimates), 39; U.S. Census, *Statistical Abstract . . . 1995*, 34–38.

BIBLIOGRAPHY

This bibliography includes only those items cited in footnotes, though I consulted and benefited from a number of others. Since the time span of this book makes primary and secondary sources difficult to segregate (some items are really both), I have instead just separated unpublished and published sources. Unpublished include manuscript collections; theses, conference papers, and various unpublished reports; and oral histories, mostly transcribed but some on tape, listed by where they were collected and deposited. Published sources here listed include books and shorter pieces (chiefly articles and essays).

Manuscript Collections

Bowron, Fletcher. Manuscripts. Henry E. Huntington Library, San Marino, Calif.
Elliott-Berry manuscripts. Huntington Library
Forbes, James Murray. Manuscripts. Massachusetts Historical Society, Boston, Mass.
Ford, John Anson. Manuscripts. Huntington Library
Livermore, Robert. Manuscripts. Massachusetts Historical Society
North Star Mining Company Records. Beinecke Library, Yale University
Stearns, Abel. Manuscripts. Huntington Library
Weinstein, Jacob. Manuscripts. Chicago Historical Society, Chicago, Ill.

Dissertations, Theses, Conference Papers, Miscellaneous Reports

Alvarez, Robert Richard, Jr. "Familia: Migration and Adaptation in Alta and Baja California, 1800–1975." Dissertation, Stanford University, 1979.
Babbitt, Bruce. "History of Land Fraud in Arizona." Speech to Scottsdale Westerners, Sept. 21, 1977, in Arizona State University Archives, Tempe.
Brilliant, Ashley Ellwood. "Social Effects of the Automobile in Southern California during the Nineteen-Twenties." Dissertation, University of California—Berkeley, 1964.
Bullough, Bonnie Louise. "Alienation among Middle Class Negroes: Social-Psychological Factors Influencing Housing Desegregation." Dissertation, University of California—Los Angeles, 1968.
Carman, J. Neale. "Historical Atlas of the Foreign-Language Units of Kansas." Vol. II. Microfiche. Lawrence: University of Kansas [ca. 1963].
Chin, Art. "Golden Tassels: A History of the Chinese in Washington, 1857–1977." Typescript in Wing Luke Asian Museum, Seattle.
Collins, Susan M. "Prehistoric Rio Grande Settlement Patterns and the Inference of Demographic Change." Dissertation, University of Colorado, 1975.
Denver Area Welfare Council, Inc. "The Spanish-American Population of Denver: An Exploratory Survey." Mimeo in Western History Department, Denver Public Library, 1950.
Denver Inter-County Regional Planning Commission. "Population, Denver Metro Area: Cur-

rent Estimates and Projections of Future Population." Third ed., Sept. 1965. Denver Public Library.

Dessery, Edna Lucile. "A Study of the Mental Inferiority of the Italian Immigrant." Thesis, University of California—Berkeley, 1922.

Ebner, Michael H. "Transforming Irvine: From Ranch to Masterplanned City." Paper read at Western History Association meeting, Oct. 1996, and revised version, June 1997.

Eisenberg, Ellen. "To New York or . . . Oregon? Patterns of Migration among East European Jews." Paper read at Western Jewish Studies Association meeting, spring 1997.

Elac, John Chala. "The Employment of Mexican Workers in U.S. Agriculture, 1900–1960: A Binational Economic Analysis." Dissertation, University of California—Los Angeles, 1961.

Fuss, Allison S. "Riding Buffaloes and Broncos: Rodeo as a Twentieth-Century Northern Plains Indian Family, Tribal, and Inter-Tribal Tradition, 1890–1996." Dissertation, University of Notre Dame, 1998.

Gutmann, Myron P.; W. Parker Frisbie; and K. Stephen Blanchard. "A New Look at the Hispanic Population of the United States in 1910." Paper read at Population Association of America meeting, May 1996.

Gutmann, Myron P.; Andrés Peri; and Glenn D. Deane. "Migration, Environment, and Economic Change in the U.S. Great Plains, 1930–1990." Paper read at Population Association of America meeting, April 1998.

Irish, John P. "Japanese Farmers in California." Unpublished pamphlet, Beinecke Library, Yale University.

Issei Oral History Project. "Issei Christians: Selected Interviews from the Issei Oral History Project." Sierra Mission Area, Synod of the Pacific, United Presbyterian Church USA, 1977. Typescript in Beinecke Library, Yale.

Johnson, Marilynn S. "War as Watershed: The East Bay and World War II." Paper read at the Western History Association meeting, Oct. 1992.

Laird, Judith F. "Argentine, Kansas: The Evolution of a Mexican-American Community, 1905–1940." Dissertation, University of Kansas, 1975.

Lee, Kyung. "Settlement Patterns of Los Angeles Koreans." Thesis, University of California—Los Angeles, 1969.

Leonard, Kevin Allen. "The Pachucos and the Spanish Press." Paper read at the meeting of the Pacific Coast Branch, American Historical Association, Aug. 1993.

Loosley, Allyn Campbell. "Foreign Born Population of California, 1848–1920." Thesis, University of California—Berkeley, 1927.

Los Angeles, City of. "Bulletin 1959: Population Estimate by Communities." Typescript in Bowron mss., Huntington Library.

MacDonald, Marie. "The Honyockers: Dryland Pioneers." Paper read at the Western History Association meeting, Oct. 1986.

McBane, Margo. "What Is Whiteness: The Creation of a Citrigrowers World, 1893–1934." Paper read at meeting of the Social Science History Association, Oct. 1994.

Moate, John. "Iowa State Picnic." Typescript, Dec. 31, 1941, in RG 91, Works Progress Administration, Arizona Writers Project mss., Arizona Division of History and Archives.

Nieto-Phillips, John. "Colonists and Hispanophiles: The Spanish American Ethos in New Mexico's Struggle for Statehood, 1874–1910." Paper read at meeting of the Social Science History Association, Oct. 1994.

Palmer, Hans Christian. "Italian Immigration and the Development of California Agriculture." Dissertation, University of California—Berkeley, 1969.

Philpott, William. "Turning against Tourists? Coloradans and the Environmentalist Outburst of the 1970s." Paper read at meeting of Pacific Coast Branch, American Historical Association, Aug. 1998.

Putney, Diane T. "Fighting the Scourge: American Indian Morbidity and Federal Policy, 1897–1928." Dissertation, Marquette University, 1980.

Rader, Emily. " 'So We Took Only 120 Acres': Land and Labor in the Settlement of Southern California." Paper read at Social Science History Association meeting, Oct. 1994.

Scherini, Rose Doris. "The Italian American Community of San Francisco: A Descriptive Study." Typescript, 1976, in University of California—Berkeley library.

Schuetz, Mardith K. "The Indians of the San Antonio Missions, 1718–1821." Dissertation, University of Texas—Austin, 1979.

Schwantes, Carlos A. "Varieties of Early Railroad Tourism in the Pacific Northwest." Paper read at Western History Association meeting, Oct. 1992.

Washington, State of. "Population of Cities and Towns 1890–1900–1910–1920." Mimeo, n.p., n.d., University of Washington Pacific Northwest Collection.

Oral History Interviews

ABBREVIATIONS:

ASA	Arizona State Archives, Phoenix
ASU	Arizona State University, Special Collections, Tempe
CSULB	Special Collections, California State University—Long Beach
Idaho	Idaho State Historical Society, Boise
Okla	Oklahoma Historical Society, Oklahoma City
Oregon	Oregon Historical Society, Portland
ROHO	Regional Oral History Office, University of California—Berkeley
TexTech	Southwest Collection, Texas Tech University, Lubbock
UCLA	Special Collections, University of California—Los Angeles
UNM	Center for Southwest Research, University of New Mexico, Albuquerque
UTEP	Special Collections, University of Texas—El Paso
Utah	Utah State Historical Society, Salt Lake City
U Wlib	Special Collections, University of Washington Library
U Warch	Archives and Manuscripts, University of Washington
WSA	Washington State Archives, Olympia
Wing Luke	Wing Luke Asian Museum, Seattle
Yale	Issei Christians Oral History Project, Beinecke Library, Yale University

Adams, Russell. Okla
Allan, Jessie Ettles. Idaho
Alley, C. L. Okla
Andrews, Marvin. ASU
Anonymous Cambodian. CSULB
Anonymous Pueblo Indian. UNM
Anonymous undocumented Mexican
    immigrant. CSULB (interview by
    Frances Cox)
Armold, Edna May. Okla
Arriaga, Juan. Idaho
Avshalomov, Jacob. Oregon
Bacca, James. Idaho
Bagaman, Mary. ROHO
Balderas, Guillermo. UTEP
Barrionuevo, Maria. UTEP
Battaglia, Mildred. Oregon
Behrendt, Fern. Okla
Beltran, Maria Abastilla. WSA
Bergano, Fabian. WSA

Blevins, Luia (Louie). Idaho
Bloom, Jessie. U Warch
Borg, Pearl and Ing. Oregon
Bottinelli, Frank. Idaho
Boyd, Wright "Cowboy." TexTech
Bramer, Henry. Idaho
Brock, Henry. UNM
Brounstein, Edward Tretiak. Oregon
Brower, Hazel and William. Idaho
Bruce, Lloyd. TexTech
Burciaga, Jose Cruz. UTEP
Calleros, Cleofas. UTEP
Candelaria, Rodolfo. UTEP
Cantrell, Norma. CSULB
Cates, Ida C. Oregon
Champion, Frank. TexTech
Chan, Mrs. Jang See. ROHO
Chavez, G. UTEP
Chen, San San. Wing Luke
Chow, Chris. ROHO

Cohen, William "Scotty." Oregon
Deiz, Mercedes Frances Lopez. Oregon
Delgado, Bonifacio. TexTech
Dellums, C. L. ROHO
Demus, Gus. Idaho
Dunshee, Bertram K. ROHO
Eckles, Belle. UNM
Fair, Mr. and Mrs. D. C. TexTech
Feldenheimer, Paul and Edith. Oregon
Feuchtwanger, Mara. UCLA
Fromm, Alfred. ROHO
Fry, Daniel. Idaho
Fujii, Henry. Idaho
Gates, Louise. UTEP
Gayton, Virginia Clark. U Warch
Giordano, Mr. and Mrs. Angelo. Utah
Gluck, Sherna Berger. Rosie the Riveter
    interviews by, typescripts, CSULB
Gonzalez, Frank. TexTech
Gwilliam, Frank. Idaho
Hallberg, Bill. Idaho
Hallie, Nellie. Idaho
Hawkins, Augustus F. UCLA
Hayman, Erma. Idaho
Henderson, Annie. TexTech
Hervin, Mrs. Israel E. Oregon
Hill, Tina. CSULB
Hitt, Betty. Idaho
Hoover, Lila Wilson. Idaho
Houston, Josephine Lamothe. CSULB
Jackson, Armond. UTEP
Jahnsen, Oscar. ROHO
Johnson, Fred. UNM
Kalnitz, Zig. ASU
Kanegai, Michiyo. Utah
Kasai, Alice. Utah
Kato, Ise. Utah
Kim, Sidney. UTEP
Kohler, Robert. Okla
Lai, Alan. Wing Luke
Lee, Mabel Tom. ROHO
Lew, Mi and Marie. Idaho
Linoff, Victor. ASU
Lookout, Frederick Morris, Jr. Okla
Lucero, Alfonso Bernal. CSULB
Martinez, Bernardo. UTEP
Martinez O, Miguel. UTEP
Mason, Howard. Idaho
Masunaga, Merry. ASU
McCourt, Arthur. Oregon

Murillo, Ralph. UTEP
Nasi, John. Idaho
O, Maria de la. UTEP
Ortega de Sousa, Dolores. CSULB
Paschall, Jim. UTEP
Pittman, Tarea. ROHO
Ponce, Fred. UTEP
Priano, Tony. Utah
Purdy, Lupe. CSULB
Quong, Mabel. Idaho
Ramirez, Conrad. UTEP
Rael, Alfred. UNM
Revier, Lucy Tubbs, and Flake, Olive
    Tubbs. TexTech
Riddle, Beatrix V. de, UTEP
Robertson, Wilma. ASU
Roman, Jose. UTEP
Rudisill, William Xavier. WSA
Ruffner, Lester W. "Budge." ASU
Rutherford, Otto. Oregon
Salazar, Juanita. Idaho
Sanchez, Francisco. UTEP
Sankary, Wanda. ROHO
Santiesteban, H. Tati. UTEP
Satow, Riichi. Yale
Schoeffler, Ada O. Idaho
Secrest, Mildred. Oregon
Settle, Eugene. Idaho
Simons, Mrs. Gertrude. WSA
Slavin, Virginia. Idaho
Smith, Leo. Idaho
Smith, Mrs. Marie. Oregon
Snider, Mrs. Agnes Meader. UNM
Stowell, Eugene and Lillian. Idaho
Taylor, Charles W. WSA
Tigner, Rose. Idaho
Tinker, Sylvester. Oklahoma
Uberuaga, Philip and Marie. Idaho
Veloz, Federico. CSULB
Vietnamese refugees, interviewed by
    Eleanor Swent, ROHO
Wetherill, Marietta. UNM
Wong, Allan Fay. Wing Luke
Woo, Ben. ROHO
Woo, Tony S. ROHO
Wyatt, Mary. Oklahoma
Yazzie, Ray. UNM
Yuen, Mr. ROHO
Zayas, Abigail de. UTEP

Books, Booklets, Government Documents, Bound Pamphlets

Abbott, Carl. *The Metropolitan Frontier: Cities in the Modern American West.* University of Arizona Press, 1995.

———. *The New Urban America; Growth and Politics in Sunbelt Cities.* University of North Carolina Press, 1981.

Acuña, Rodolfo F. *A Community under Siege: A Chronicle of Chicanos East of the Los Angeles River.* Chicano Studies Research Center, University of California—Los Angeles, Monograph No. 11, 1984.

Adams, Frank. *Irrigation Districts in California, 1887–1915.* Sacramento: California State Printing Office, 1916. ("State of California, Department of Engineering, Bulletin No. 2.")

Albert, Katherine M.; William B. Hull; and Daniel M. Sprague. *The Dynamic West: A Region in Transition: A Guide for State Policy Makers on the Top Ten Trends Transforming the West.* Council of State Governments, 1989.

Allen, Barbara. *Homesteading the High Desert.* University of Utah Press, 1987.

Allen, James P., and Eugene Turner. *The Ethnic Quilt: Population Diversity in Southern California.* California State University—Northridge, 1997.

Almeida, Carlos. *Portuguese Immigrants: The Centennial Story of the Portuguese Union of the State of California.* Supreme Council of União Portuguesa do Estado da California, 1978.

Alonzo, Armando C. *Tejano Legacy: Rancheros and Settlers in South Texas, 1734–1900.* University of New Mexico Press, 1998.

America's Top-Rated Cities: A Statistical Handbook. 2d ed.; vol. 2, *Western Region.* Universal Reference Publications, 1993.

Anderson, Henry P. *The Bracero Program in California.* Arno Press, 1976.

Annals of the Propagation of the Faith. Dublin: Society for the Propagation of the Faith [various years; vol. 31, 1868; vol. 33, 1870; vol. 34, 1871; vol. 38, 1875; vol. 43, 1880].

Armstrong, Ellis L.; Michael C. Robinson; and Suellen Hoy. *History of Public Works in the United States, 1776–1976.* American Public Works Association, 1976.

Arrington, Leonard J. *History of Idaho.* Vol. 2. University of Idaho Press, and Idaho State Historical Society, 1994.

———. *The Price of Prejudice: The Japanese-American Relocation Center in Utah during World War II.* Utah State University Faculty Association, 1962.

Bahr, Diana Meyers. *From Mission to Metropolis: Cupeño Indian Women in Los Angeles.* University of Oklahoma Press, 1993.

Balderrama, Francisco E., and Raymond Rodriguez. *Decade of Betrayal: Mexican Repatriation in the 1930s.* University of New Mexico Press, 1995.

Barnes, Will C. *Western Grazing Grounds and Forest Ranges.* The Breeder's Gazette, 1913.

Barnhart, Jacqueline Baker. *The Fair but Frail: Prostitution in San Francisco, 1849–1900.* University of Nevada Press, 1986.

Barone, Michael, and Grant Ujifusa, eds. *Almanac of American Politics 1994.* National Journal, 1994.

Barth, Gunther. *Instant Cities: Urbanization and the Rise of San Francisco and Denver.* Oxford University Press, 1976.

Baur, John E. *The Health Seekers of Southern California, 1870–1900.* Huntington Library, 1959.

Bay Area Social Planning Council. *Chinese Newcomers in San Francisco: Report and Recommendations of the Study Committee.* BASPC, 1971.

Bean, Frank D., and Marta Tienda. *The Hispanic Population of the United States.* Russell Sage Foundation, 1987.

Bean, Walton. *California: An Interpretive History.* 2d ed. McGraw-Hill Book Company, 1973.

Beauvoir, Simone de. *Amérique au jour le jour.* Gallimard, 1954.

Belasco, Warren James. *Americans on the Road: From Autocamp to Motel, 1910–1945*. MIT Press, 1979.

Bennett, John W., and Seena B. Kohl. *Settling the Canadian-American West, 1890–1915: Pioneer Adaptation and Community Building, an Anthropological History*. University of Nebraska Press, 1995.

Bercovitch, Sacvan, ed. *Cambridge History of American Literature*. Vol. 2: 1820–1865. Cambridge University Press, 1995.

Bernard, Richard M. *The Poles in Oklahoma*. University of Oklahoma Press, 1980.

Berner, Richard C. *Seattle 1921–1940: From Boom to Bust*. Charles Press, 1992.

Bérubé, Allan. *Coming Out under Fire: The History of Gay Men and Women in World War Two*. Free Press, 1990.

Bethell, Leslie, ed. *Cambridge History of Latin America*. Vol. 5. Cambridge University Press, 1986.

Big Horn Basin Development Co. (promotional booklet), 1908.

Billington, Ray Allen, and Martin Ridge. *Westward Expansion*. 5th ed. Macmillan, 1982.

Bloom, Leonard, and Ruth Riemer. *Removal and Return: The Socio-Economic Effects of the War on Japanese Americans*. University of California Press, 1949.

Blumenson, Martin. *Patton: The Man behind the Legend 1885–1945*. William Morrow and Company, 1985.

Boag, Peter G. *Environment and Experience: Settlement Culture in Nineteenth-Century Oregon*. University of California Press, 1992.

Bogue, Donald J.; Henry S. Schryock, Jr.; and Siegfried A. Hoermann. *Subregional Migration in the United States, 1935–1940*. Vol. 1: *Streams of Migration between Subregions: A Pilot Study of Migration Flows between Environments*. Scripps Foundation, Miami University, [1957].

Bonnifield, Paul. *The Dust Bowl: Men, Dirt, and Depression*. University of New Mexico Press, 1979.

Bottles, Scott. *Los Angeles and the Automobile: The Making of the Modern City*. University of California Press, 1987.

Bowen, William A. *The Willamette Valley: Migration and Settlement on the Oregon Frontier*. University of Washington Press, 1978.

Braudel, Fernand. *Civilization and Capitalism 15th–18th Century*. Vol. III: *The Perspective of the World*. Harper & Row, 1984.

Broussard, Albert S. *Black San Francisco: The Struggle for Racial Equality in the West, 1900–1954*. University Press of Kansas, 1993.

Browder, W. Gordon, and Harold J. Hoflich. *Population and Income in Montana*. "Regional Study No. 5." Montana State University Bureau of Business and Economic Research, 1953.

Brown, Kenny L. *The Italians in Oklahoma*. University of Oklahoma Press, 1980.

Buell, Paul D., et al., eds. *Annals of the Chinese Historical Society of the Pacific Northwest*. The Society, 1984.

Bunch, Lonnie G., III. *Black Angelenos: The Afro-American in Los Angeles, 1850–1950*. California Afro-American Museum, 1988.

Bunje, Emil Theodore Hieronymus; H. Penn; and Frederick Josef Schmitz. *Russian California*. R and E Research Associates, [1939] 1970.

Burchell, R. A. *The San Francisco Irish, 1848–1880*. University of California Press, 1980.

Butler, Anne M. *Daughters of Joy, Sisters of Misery: Prostitutes in the American West, 1865–90*. University of Illinois Press, 1985.

California. Commission of Immigration and Housing. *First Annual Report*. State Printing Office, 1915.

California. Department of Finance, Population Research Unit. *Population Estimates of California Cities and Counties, Jan. 1, 1986 to Jan. 1, 1987*, Report 87 E-1.

California. Department of Food and Agriculture. *California Agriculture: Statistical Review 1985*. State of California, 1986.

California. *Economic Report of the Governor 1987.* State of California, 1987.

California Statistical Abstract 1987. State of California, 1987.

Cannon, Brian Q. *Remaking the Agrarian Dream: New Deal Rural Resettlement in the Mountain West.* University of New Mexico Press, 1996.

Cantor, Milton, and Bruce Laurie, eds. *Class, Sex, and the Woman Worker.* Greenwood Press, 1977.

Cardoso, Lawrence A. *Mexican Emigration to the United States, 1897–1931: Socio-Economic Patterns.* University of Arizona Press, 1980.

Carolan, Herbert. *Motor Tales and Travels in and out of California.* G. P. Putnam's Sons, 1936.

Caughey, John W. *California.* Prentice-Hall, 1940.

———, and Laree Caughey. *Los Angeles: Biography of a City.* University of California Press, 1976.

Center for Continuing Study of the California Economy. *California Economic Growth.* CCSCE, 1997.

Chambers, Clarke A. *California Farm Organizations: A Historical Study of the Grange, the Farm Bureau, and the Associated Farmers 1929–1941.* University of California Press, 1952.

Chan, Sucheng. *This Bitter-Sweet Soil: The Chinese in California Agriculture, 1860–1910.* University of California Press, 1986.

———. *Asian Californians.* MTL/Boyd & Fraser, 1991.

Chandler, Raymond. *Farewell My Lovely.* Library of America, 1995.

Chevigny, Hector. *Russian America: The Great Alaskan Venture, 1741–1867.* Viking Press, 1965.

Clark, Carroll D., and Roy L. Roberts. *People of Kansas: A Demographic and Sociological Study.* Kansas State Planning Board, 1936.

Clark, Ira G. *Water in New Mexico: A History of Its Management and Use.* University of New Mexico Press, 1987.

Clason, George S. *Free Homestead Lands of Colorado Described: A Handbook for Settlers.* Clason Map Co., 1915.

Cleland, Robert Glass. *The Irvine Ranch.* Huntington Library, 1962.

Cohen, Robin, ed. *Cambridge Survey of World Migration.* Cambridge University Press, 1995.

Collins, Keith E. *Black Los Angeles: The Maturing of the Ghetto, 1940–1950.* Century Twenty One Publishing, 1980.

Colorado Promotion and Publicity Committee. *Colorado: Its Agriculture, Its Horticulture.* Denver: [n.p.], 1904.

Cook, Sherburne F. *The Conflict between the California Indian and White Civilization.* University of California Press, 1976.

———. *The Population of the California Indians, 1769–1970.* University of California Press, 1976.

Crenshaw, J. W. *Salt River Valley Arizona. A Land of Sunshine, Health and Prosperity. A Soil Unsurpassed in Productiveness. A Country of Wonderful Opportunities.* J. W. Crenshaw, 1907.

Cronon, William. *Nature's Metropolis: Chicago and the Great West.* Norton, 1991.

Crosby, Alfred W. *America's Forgotten Pandemic: The Influenza of 1918.* Cambridge University Press, 1989.

Dale, Edward Everett, and Morris L. Wardell. *History of Oklahoma.* Prentice-Hall, 1948.

Daniel, Cletus E. *Bitter Harvest: A History of California Farmworkers, 1870–1941.* Cornell University Press, 1981.

Daniels, Roger. *Concentration Camps—North America: Japanese in the United States and Canada during World War II.* Robert E. Krieger, 1981.

———. *Asian America: Chinese and Japanese in the United States since 1850.* University of Washington Press, 1988.

Davies, Vernon. *Farm Population Trends in Washington.* State College of Washington Agricultural Experiment Station, Bulletin No. 507, 1949.

Davis, Marilyn P. *Mexican Voices/American Dreams: An Oral History of Mexican Immigration to the United States.* Henry Holt, 1991.

Davis, Mike. *City of Quartz.* Vintage Books, 1992.

Davis, Kingsley, and Frederick G. Styles, eds. *California's Twenty Millions: Research Contributions to Population Policy.* University of California Population Monograph Series, No. 10, 1971.

Davis, H. L. *Honey in the Horn.* Harper & Brothers, 1935.

Day, Jennifer Cheeseman. *Population Projections of the United States by Age, Sex, Race, and Hispanic Origin: 1995 to 2050.* U.S. Census Bureau Current Population Reports, P25-1130. Government Printing Office, 1996.

De León, Arnoldo. *The Tejano Community, 1836–1900.* University of New Mexico Press, 1982.

———, and Kenneth L. Stewart. *Tejanos and the Numbers Game: A Socio-Historical Interpretation from the Federal Censuses, 1850–1900.* University of New Mexico Press, 1989.

Deloria, Vine, Jr. *Red Earth, White Lies: Native Americans and the Myth of Scientific Fact.* Scribner's, 1995.

DeMark, Judith Boyce. *Essays in Twentieth-Century New Mexico History.* University of New Mexico Press, 1994.

D'Emilio, John. *Making Trouble: Essays on Gay History, Politics, and the University.* Routledge, 1992.

Denver Reservoir Irrigation Company. *Call of the West; Denver & Dollars. . . . Irrigated Farms and Homes for One Hundred Thousand People at the Doors of Denver. The Best Investment in the West.* Denver: [n.p.], 1907.

Dickason, Olive Patricia. *Canada's First Nations: A History of Founding Peoples from Earliest Times.* University of Oklahoma Press, 1992.

Didion, Joan. *The White Album.* Simon and Schuster, 1979.

Dippie, Brian W. *The Vanishing American: White Attitudes and U.S. Indian Policy.* University Press of Kansas, 1982.

Dixon, E. James. *Quest for the Origins of the First Americans.* University of New Mexico Press, 1993.

Dobbert, Gwendolyn, comp. *The Aging of Californians: Interstate Comparisons as of April 1, 1980.* California Department of Health Services, Center for Health Statistics, Report 82-03049, June 1982.

Doig, Ivan. *Dancing at the Rascal Fair.* Atheneum, 1987.

Dolan, Jay P., and Gilberto M. Hinojosa, eds. *Mexican Americans and the Catholic Church, 1900–1965.* University of Notre Dame Press, 1994.

Don, Hillary. *Old St. Hilary's: The First One Hundred Years from Mission Church to Historic Landmark, 1888–1988.* Belvedere-Tiburon Landmarks Society, 1988.

Douglas, William A., and Jon Bilbao. *Amerikanuak: Basques in the New World.* University of Nevada Press, 1975.

Dries, Angelyn, OSF. *The Missionary Movement in American Catholic History.* Orbis Books, 1998.

Dumke, Glenn. *The Boom of the Eighties in Southern California.* Huntington Library, 1944.

Duncan, Dayton. *Out West: An American Journey.* Viking Press, 1987.

Dwyer, John T. *Condemned to the Mines: The Life of Eugene O'Connell 1815–1891, Pioneer Bishop of Northern California and Nevada.* Vantage Press, 1976.

Dykstra, Robert R. *The Cattle Towns.* University of Nebraska Press, 1968.

Ebeling, Walter. *The Fruited Plain: The Story of American Agriculture.* University of California Press, 1979.

Echevarria, Evelio, and Jose Otero. *Hispanic Colorado: Four Centuries: History and Heritage.* Centennial Publications [n.d.].

El-Ashry, Mohamed T., and Diana C. Gibbons, eds. *Water and Arid Lands of the Western United States.* Cambridge University Press, 1988.

Elazar, Daniel J., et al. *Cities of the Prairie Revisited: The Closing of the Metropolitan Frontier.* University of Nebraska Press, 1986.

Eldridge, Hope T., and Dorothy Swaine Thomas. *Population Redistribution and Economic Growth: United States, 1870–1950.* Vol. 3: *Demographic Analyses and Interrelations.* American Philosophical Society, 1964.

Ellis, Joseph J. *American Sphinx: The Character of Thomas Jefferson.* Alfred A. Knopf, 1997.

Emmons, David M. *The Butte Irish: Class and Ethnicity in an American Mining Town, 1875–1925.* University of Illinois Press, 1989.

Erickson, Eugene C. *Selected Population Characteristics in Washington, 1950–1960.* Washington Agricultural Experiment Station, Bulletin 661, 1965.

Fairbanks, Robert B., and Kathleen Underwood, eds. *Essays on Sunbelt Cities and Recent Urban America.* Texas A&M Press, 1990.

Fallows, James. *More like Us: Making America Great Again.* Houghton Mifflin, 1989.

Faragher, John Mack. *Daniel Boone: The Life and Legend of an American Pioneer.* Henry Holt, 1992.

Feingold, Henry L. *The Politics of Rescue: The Roosevelt Administration and the Holocaust, 1938–1945.* Rutgers University Press, 1970.

Fermi, Laura. *Illustrious Immigrants: The Intellectual Migration from Europe, 1930–41.* University of Chicago Press, 1968.

Ficken, Robert E., and Charles P. LeWarne. *Washington: A Centennial History.* University of Washington Press, 1988.

Fiedel, Stuart J. *Prehistory of the Americas.* 2d ed. Cambridge University Press, 1992.

Findlay, John M. *Magic Lands: Western Cityscapes and American Culture after 1940.* University of California Press, 1992.

Fink, Deborah. *Agrarian Women: Wives and Mothers in Rural Nebraska, 1880–1940.* University of North Carolina Press, 1992.

Fishman, Robert. *Bourgeois Utopias: The Rise and Fall of Suburbia.* Basic Books, 1987.

Fite, Gilbert C. *American Farmers: The New Minority.* Indiana University Press, 1981.

Fixico, Donald L. *Termination and Relocation: Federal Indian Policy, 1945–1960.* University of New Mexico Press, 1986.

Flagg, James Montgomery. *Boulevards All the Way—Maybe; Being an Artist's Truthful Impression of the U.S.A. from New York to California and Return, by Motor.* George H. Doran, 1925.

Flynt, Josiah. *Tramping with Tramps: Studies and Sketches of Vagabond Life.* Century, 1899.

Fogel, Walter. *Mexican Illegal Alien Workers in the United States.* UCLA Institute of Industrial Relations, 1979.

Foley, Neil. *The White Scourge: Mexicans, Blacks, and Poor Whites in Texas Cotton Culture.* University of California Press, 1997.

Forstall, Richard L., comp. *Population of States and Counties of the United States: 1790–1990.* U.S. Department of Commerce National Technical Information Service, 1996.

Fox, Stephen. *The Unknown Internment: An Oral History of the Relocation of Italian Americans during World War II.* Twayne, 1990.

Fradkin, Philip L. *A River No More: The Colorado River and the West.* Alfred A. Knopf, 1981.

———. *The Seven States of California: A Natural and Human History.* University of California Press, 1995.

Franklin, Jimmie Lewis. *Journey toward Hope: A History of Blacks in Oklahoma.* University of Oklahoma Press, 1982.

Franks, Kenny A., and Paul F. Lambert; *Early California Oil: A Photographic History, 1865–1940.* Texas A&M University Press, 1985.

Franks, Kenny; Paul Lambert; and Carl N. Tyson. *Early Oklahoma Oil: A Photographic History, 1859–1936.* Texas A&M University Press, 1981.

Fresno County Centennial Committee. *Fresno County Centennial Almanac.* Fresno: [n.p.,] 1956.

Friedan, Betty. *The Feminine Mystique*. Norton, 1963.

Friesen, Gerald. *The Canadian Prairies: A History*. University of Nebraska Press, 1984.

Frost, Max, and Paul A. F. Walter, comps. and eds. *The Land of Sunshine: A Handbook of the Resources, Products, Industries and Climate of New Mexico*. New Mexico Bureau of Immigration, 1906.

Gamio, Manuel. *Quantitative Estimate Sources and Distribution of Mexican Immigration into the United States*. Talleres Graficos Editorial y "Diario Oficial," 1930.

Gannett, Lewis [Stiles], *Sweet Land*. Doubleday, Doran, 1934.

Garcia, Mario. *Desert Immigrants: The Mexicans of El Paso, 1880–1920*. Yale University Press, 1981.

Garcia, Richard A. *Rise of the Mexican American Middle Class: San Antonio, 1919–1941*. Texas A&M University Press, 1991.

Garreau, Joel. *Edge City: Life on the New Frontier*. Doubleday, 1991.

———. *The Nine Nations of North America*. Houghton Mifflin, 1981.

Gates, Paul W. *Land and Law in California*. Iowa State University Press, 1981.

———. *History of Public Land Law Development*. Arno Press, [1968] 1979.

Gibson, Arrell Morgan. *Oklahoma: A History of Five Centuries*. 2d ed. University of Oklahoma Press, 1981.

Gillenkirk, Jeff, and James Motlow. *Bitter Melon: Stories from the Last Rural Chinese Town in America*. University of Washington Press, 1987.

Gilmore, Glenda Elizabeth. *Gender and Jim Crow: Women and the Politics of White Supremacy in North Carolina, 1896–1920*. University of North Carolina Press, 1996.

Girdner, Audrie, and Anne Loftis. *The Great Betrayal: The Evacuation of the Japanese-Americans during World War II*. Macmillan, 1969.

Gluck, Sherna Berger. *Rosie the Riveter Revisited: Women, the War, and Social Change*. Twayne, 1987.

Goldberg, Robert A. *Back to the Soil: The Jewish Farmers of Clarion, Utah, and Their World*. University of Utah Press, 1986.

———. *Barry Goldwater*. Yale University Press, 1995.

Gómez, Arthur R. *Quest for the Golden Circle: The Four Corners and the Metropolitan West, 1945–1970*. University of New Mexico Press, 1994.

Gómez-Quiñones, Juan. *Mexican-American Labor, 1790–1990*. University of New Mexico Press, 1994.

González Navarro, Moisés. *Población y Sociedad en México (1900–1970)*. 2 vols. Universidad Nacional Autonoma de México, 1974.

Goodman, James M. *The Navajo Atlas: Environments, Resources, People, and History of the Diné Bikiyah*. University of Oklahoma Press, 1982.

Gordon, Margaret S. *Employment, Expansion, and Population Growth: The California Experience: 1900–1950*. University of California Press, 1954.

Great Northern Railway. *The Great Judith Basin Montana*. [n.p.], 1908.

Gregory, James N. *American Exodus: The Dust Bowl Migration and Okie Culture in California*. Oxford University Press, 1989.

Griffin, John Howard. *Land of the High Sky*. First National Bank of Midland, 1959.

Grossman, James R., ed. *The Frontier in American Culture: An Exhibition at the Newberry Library, August 26, 1994–January 7, 1985*. Newberry Library and University of California Press, 1996.

Guerin-Gonzales, Camille. *Mexican Workers and American Dreams: Immigration, Repatriation, and California Farm Labor, 1900–1939*. Rutgers University Press, 1994.

Gulliford, Andrew. *Boomtown Blues: Colorado Oil Shale, 1885–1985*. University Press of Colorado, 1989.

Gumina, Deanna Paoli. *The Italians of San Francisco 1850–1930/Gli Italiani di San Francisco 1850–1930*. Center for Migration Studies, 1978.

Gunther, John. *Inside U.S.A.* Harper & Brothers, 1947.

Guterson, David. *Snow Falling on Cedars.* Harcourt Brace, 1994.

Gutiérrez, David. *Walls and Mirrors: Mexican Americans, Mexican Immigrants, and the Politics of Ethnicity.* University of California Press, 1995.

Gutiérrez, Ramón. *When Jesus Came, the Corn Mothers Went Away: Marriage, Sexuality, and Power in New Mexico, 1500–1846.* Stanford University Press, 1991.

——, and Richard J. Orsi. *Contested Eden: California before the Gold Rush.* University of California Press, 1998.

Haas, Lisbeth. *Conquests and Historical Identities in California, 1769–1836.* University of California Press, 1995.

——. *The Bracero in Orange County: A Work Force for Economic Transition.* University of California—San Diego Program in United States–Mexican Studies, Working Paper No. 29, 1981.

Hardaway, Roger D. *A Narrative Bibliography of the African-American Frontier: Blacks in the Rocky Mountain West, 1535–1912.* Edwin Mellen Press, 1995.

Hargreaves, Mary Wilma M. *Dry Farming in the Northern Great Plains, 1900–1925.* Harvard University Press, 1957.

——. *Dry Farming in the Northern Great Plains: Years of Readjustment, 1920–1990.* University Press of Kentucky, 1993.

Harmsworth, Harry C. *Sixty Years of Population Growth in Idaho, 1890–1950.* University of Idaho Department of Social Sciences, 1952.

Harris, Katherine. *Long Vistas: Women and Families on Colorado Homesteads.* University Press of Colorado, 1993.

Hart, John. *Farming on the Edge: Saving Family Farms in Marin County, California.* University of California Press, 1991.

Hasselstrom, Linda; Gaydell Collier; and Nancy Curtis, eds. *Leaning into the Wind: Women Write from the Heart of the West.* Houghton Mifflin, 1997.

Hata, Donald T., and Nadine I. Hata. *Japanese Americans and World War II.* Forum Press, 1974.

Hays, Samuel P. *Beauty, Health, and Permanence: Environmental Politics in the United States, 1955–1985.* Cambridge University Press, 1987.

Heileman, W. H. *Klamath: The California-Oregon Irrigation District Created by the United States Government.* [n.p.], ca. 1908.

Heizer, Robert F., and Alan J. Almquist. *The Other Californians: Prejudice and Discrimination under Spain, Mexico, and the United States to 1920.* University of California Press, 1971.

Hine, Robert V. *California's Utopian Colonies.* University of California Press, [1953] 1983.

Hoerder, Dirk, and Leslie Page Moch, eds. *European Migrants: Global and Local Perspectives.* Northeastern University Press, 1996.

Hoffman, Abraham. *Unwanted Mexican Americans in the Great Depression: Repatriation Pressures 1929–1939.* University of Arizona Press, 1974.

Hogner, Dorothy Childs. *Westward, High, Low, and Dry.* Dutton, 1938.

Hoig, Stan. *The Oklahoma Land Rush of 1889.* Oklahoma Historical Society, 1984.

Hokanson, Drake. *The Lincoln Highway: Main Street across America.* University of Iowa Press, 1988.

Hollon, W. Eugene. *The Great American Desert: Then and Now.* Oxford University Press, 1966.

Hondagneu-Sotelo, Pierrette. *Gendered Transitions: Mexican Experiences of Immigration.* University of California Press, 1994.

Horne, Gerald. *Fire This Time: The Watts Uprising and the 1960s.* University Press of Virginia, 1995.

Horton, John. *The Politics of Diversity: Immigration, Resistance, and Change in Monterey Park, California.* Temple University Press, 1995.

Hosokawa, Bill. *Thirty-five Years in the Frying Pan.* McGraw-Hill, 1976.

Houston, Jeanne Wakatsuki, and James D. Houston. *Farewell to Manzanar.* Houghton Mifflin, 1973.

Hoxie, Frederick E. *A Final Promise: The Campaign to Assimilate the Indian, 1880–1920.* University of Nebraska Press, 1984.

Hoy, Suellen. *Chasing Dirt: The American Pursuit of Cleanliness.* Oxford University Press, 1995.

Hudson, John C. *Plains Country Towns.* University of Minnesota Press, 1985.

Hundley, Norris, Jr. *The Great Thirst: Californians and Water, 1770s–1990s.* University of California Press, 1992.

Hunt, William R. *Alaska: A Bicentennial History.* Norton, 1976.

Hurt, R. Douglas. *The Dust Bowl: An Agricultural and Social History.* Nelson-Hall, 1984.

———. *The Rural West since World War II.* University Press of Kansas, 1988.

Hurtado, Albert J. *Indian Survival on the California Frontier.* Yale University Press, 1988.

———, and Peter Iverson. *Major Problems in American Indian History.* D. C. Heath, 1994.

Ichioka, Yuji. *The Issei: The World of the First Generation Japanese Immigrants, 1885–1924.* Free Press, 1988.

Iverson, Peter, ed. *The Plains Indians of the Twentieth Century.* University of Oklahoma Press, 1985.

Jackson, Kenneth T. *Crabgrass Frontier: The Suburbanization of the United States.* Oxford University Press, 1985.

Jackson, Robert H. *Indian Population Decline: The Missions of Northwestern New Spain, 1687–1840.* University of New Mexico Press, 1994.

Jaher, Frederic Cople. *The Urban Establishment: Upper Strata in Boston, New York, Charleston, Chicago, and Los Angeles.* University of Illinois Press, 1982.

Jefferson, Thomas. *Notes on the State of Virginia.* In Adrienne Koch and William Peden, eds., *The Life and Selected Writings of Thomas Jefferson.* Modern Library, 1944.

Jelinek, Lawrence J. *Harvest Empire: A History of California Agriculture.* Boyd & Fraser, 1979.

Jensen, Joan M. *Passage from India: Asian Indian Immigrants in North America.* Yale University Press, 1988.

Johansen, Dorothy O., and Charles M. Gates. *Empire of the Columbia: A History of the Pacific Northwest.* 2d ed. Harper & Row, 1967.

Johnson, Marilynn S. *The Second Gold Rush: Oakland and the East Bay in World War II.* University of California Press, 1993.

Jones, David C. *Empire of Dust: Settling and Abandoning the Prairie Dry Belt.* University of Alberta Press, 1987.

Jones, Oakah L., Jr. *Los Paisanos: Spanish Settlers on the Northern Frontier of New Spain.* University of Oklahoma Press, 1979.

Jones, Landon Y. *Great Expectations: America and the Baby Boom Generation.* Coward, McCann & Geoghegan, 1980.

Kahrl, William L., ed. *The California Water Atlas.* State of California, 1979.

Kelley, Robert. *Battling the Inland Sea: American Political Culture, Public Policy, and the Sacramento Valley, 1850–1986.* University of California Press, 1989.

Kelly, Susan Croce, and Quinta Scott. *Route 66: The Highway and Its People.* University of Oklahoma Press, 1988.

Kesselman, Amy. *Fleeting Opportunities: Women Shipyard Workers in Portland and Vancouver during World War II and Reconversion.* State University of New York Press, 1990.

Kling, Rob; Spencer Olin; and Mark Poster, eds. *Postsuburban California: The Transformation of Orange County since World War II.* University of California Press, 1991.

Knaut, Andrew L. *The Pueblo Revolt of 1680: Conquest and Resistance in Seventeenth-Century New Mexico.* University of Oklahoma Press, 1995.

Kromm, David E., and Stephen E. White. *Groundwater Exploitation in the High Plains.* University Press of Kansas, 1992.

Lamar, Howard Roberts. *The Far Southwest, 1846–1912: A Territorial History.* Norton, 1970.

Landis, Paul H. *Fifty Years of Population Growth in Washington.* State College of Washington Agricultural Experiment Station Bulletin 419, 1942.

———. *The Loss of Rural Manpower to War Industry through Migration.* State College of Washington Agricultural Experiment Station Bulletin 427, 1943.

———. *The People of Washington, 1890–1950.* Washington Agricultural Experiment Station Bulletin 535, Washington State College, 1952.

———. *Rural Population Trends in Washington.* State College of Washington Agricultural Experiment Station Bulletin 333, 1936.

Lapp, Rudolph. *Afro-Americans in California.* Boyd & Fraser, 1979.

———. *Blacks in Gold Rush California.* Yale University Press, 1977.

Lasker, Bruno. *Filipino Immigration to Continental United States and to Hawaii.* Arno Press, [1931] 1969.

Laxalt, Robert. *Nevada: A Bicentennial History.* Norton, 1977.

Lee, Mary Paik. *Quiet Odyssey: A Pioneer Korean Woman in America.* Introduction by Sucheng Chan. University of Washington Press, 1990.

Leffland, Ella. *Rumors of Peace.* Harper & Row, 1979.

Lemke-Santangelo, Gretchen. *Abiding Courage: African-American Women and the East Bay Community.* University of North Carolina Press, 1996.

Lernoux, Penny. *Hearts on Fire: The Story of the Maryknoll Sisters.* Orbis Books, 1993.

Levy, Joann. *They Saw the Elephant: Women in the California Gold Rush.* Archon Books, 1990.

Libecap, Gary D. *Locking Up the Range: Federal Land Controls and Grazing.* Ballinger Publishing Company, 1981.

Liebman, Ellen. *California Farmland: A History of Large Agricultural Holdings.* Rowman & Allenheld, 1983.

Light, Paul C. *Baby Boomers.* Norton, 1988.

Lillard, Richard G. *Desert Challenge: An Interpretation of Nevada.* Alfred A. Knopf, 1942.

Limerick, Patricia Nelson. *Legacy of Conquest: The Unbroken Past of the American West.* Norton, 1987.

Lindgren, H. Elaine. *Land in Her Own Name: Women as Homesteaders in North Dakota.* University of Oklahoma Press, 1996.

Little, Lucretia Hanson. *Excerpts of Marin History.* Belvedere-Tiburon Landmarks Society, 1983.

Little, William A., and James E. Weiss. *Blacks in Oregon: A Statistical and Historical Report.* Portland State University, Black Studies Center and Center for Population Research and Census, 1978.

Lodge, David. *Paradise News: A Novel.* Viking Press, 1991.

Los Angeles Chamber of Commerce. *Los Angeles City and County: Resources, Growth and Prospects.* Los Angeles, 1890.

Lotchin, Roger W. *Fortress California 1910–1961: From Warfare to Welfare.* Oxford University Press, 1992.

Lowitt, Richard. *The New Deal and the West.* Indiana University Press, 1984.

Luckingham, Bradford. *Minorities in Phoenix: A Profile of Mexican American, Chinese American, and African American Communities, 1860–1992.* University of Arizona Press, 1994.

Lynch, Gerald. *Roughnecks, Drillers, and Tool Pushers: Thirty-Three Years in the Oil Fields.* University of Texas Press, 1987.

MacDonald, Norbert. *Distant Neighbors: A Comparative History of Seattle and Vancouver.* University of Nebraska Press, 1987.

Maciel, David R., and Maria Herrera-Sobek. *Culture across Borders: Mexican Immigration and Popular Culture.* University of Arizona Press, 1998.

Madden, Henry Miller. *German Travelers in California.* Roxburghe Club, 1958.

Mahar, James F.; Dean C. Coddington; and John S. Gilmore. *Economic Forces behind Colorado's Growth, 1870–1962, with Projections to 1970.* Colorado State Department of Employment, 1963.

Malone, Michael P., and Richard W. Etulain. *The American West: A Twentieth-Century History.* University of Nebraska Press, 1989.

Malone, Michael P.; Richard B. Roeder; and William L. Lang. *Montana: A History of Two Centuries.* Rev. ed. University of Washington Press, 1991.

Marinbach, Bernard. *Galveston: Ellis Island of the West.* SUNY Press, 1983.

Mason, William M., and John A. McKinstry. *The Japanese of Los Angeles.* Los Angeles County Museum of Natural History, History Division, 1969.

Massey, Beatrice Larned. *It Might Have Been Worse: A Motor Trip from Coast to Coast.* Harr Wagner, 1920.

May, Dean L. *Three Frontiers: Family, Land, and Society in the American West, 1850–1900.* Cambridge University Press, 1994.

May, Elaine Tyler. *Barren in the Promised Land: Childless Americans and the Pursuit of Happiness.* Basic Books, 1995.

———. *Homeward Bound: American Families in the Cold War.* Basic Books, 1992.

Mazon, Mauricio. *The Zoot-Suit Riots: The Psychology of Symbolic Annihilation.* University of Texas Press, 1984.

McEntire, Davis. *The Population of California.* Parker Printing Company (for the Commonwealth Club of California), 1946.

McGill, Vernon. *Diary of a Motor Journey from Chicago to Los Angeles.* Grafton, 1922.

McPhee, John. *Rising from the Plains.* Farrar Straus & Giroux, 1986.

McQuiston, John Mark. *Negro Residential Invasion in Los Angeles County.* McQuiston Associates, 1969.

McReynolds, Edwin C. *Oklahoma: A History of the Sooner State.* University of Oklahoma Press, 1954.

McWilliams, Carey. *Factories in the Field: The Story of Migratory Farm Labor in California.* Little, Brown, 1939.

———. *Southern California: An Island on the Land.* Gibbs M. Smith, Peregrine Smith Books, [1946] 1983.

Meinig, D. W. *Imperial Texas: An Interpretive Essay in Cultural Geography.* University of Texas Press, 1969.

———. *Southwest: Three Peoples in Geographical Change, 1600–1700.* Oxford University Press, 1971.

Mellinger, Philip J. *Race and Labor in Western Copper: The Fight for Equality, 1896–1918.* University of Arizona Press, 1995.

Milner, Clyde A., II; Carol A. O'Connor; and Martha A. Sandweiss. *The Oxford History of the American West.* Oxford University Press, 1994.

Missouri Pacific Railway. *A Description of the Summer and Winter Health and Pleasure Resorts and Points of Interest Located on and Reached by the Missouri Pacific Railway. . . .* Woodward & Tiernan, 1890.

Modell, John. *The Economics and Politics of Racial Accommodation: The Japanese of Los Angeles, 1900–1942.* University of Illinois Press, 1977.

Moehring, Eugene P. *Resort City in the Sunbelt: Las Vegas, 1930–1970.* University of Nevada Press, 1989.

Moffat, Riley. *Population History of Western U.S. Cities and Towns, 1850–1990.* Scarecrow Press, 1996.

Monroy, Douglas. *Thrown among Strangers: The Making of Mexican Culture in Frontier California.* University of California Press, 1990.

Moore, Deborah Dash. *To the Golden Cities: Pursuing the American Jewish Dream in Miami and L.A.* Free Press, 1994.

Morgan, Dan. *Rising in the West: The True Story of an "Okie" Family from the Great Depression through the Reagan Years.* Alfred A. Knopf, 1992.

Morgan, H. Wayne, and Ann Hodges Morgan. *Oklahoma: A Bicentennial History.* Norton, 1977.

Morris, John W.; Charles R. Goins; and Edwin C. McReynolds. *Historical Atlas of Oklahoma.* 2d ed. University of Oklahoma Press, 1976.

Morrison, Peter A., ed. *A Taste of the Country: A Collection of Calvin Beale's Writings.* Pennsylvania State University Press, 1990.

Morrissey, Katherine. *Mental Territories: Mapping the Inland Empire.* Cornell University Press, 1997.

Morton, Arthur S. *The Canadian West to 1870–71, Being a History of Rupert's Land (the Hudson's Bay Company Territory) and of the North-west Territory (Including the Pacific Slope).* 2d ed., by Lewis G. Thomas. University of Toronto Press "in co-operation with University of Saskatchewan," [1939] 1973.

Mosley, Walter. *Devil in a Blue Dress.* Pocket Books, 1990.

Mullins, William H. *The Depression and the Urban West Coast, 1929–1933.* Indiana University Press, 1991.

Murase, Ichiro Mike. *Little Tokyo: One Hundred Years in Pictures.* Visual Communications/Asian American Studies Central, 1984.

Muzny, Charles C. *The Vietnamese in Oklahoma City: A Study in Ethnic Change.* AMS Press, 1989.

Nash, Gerald D. *The American West Transformed.* Indiana University Press, 1985.

———, and Richard W. Etulain. *The Twentieth-Century West: Historical Interpretations.* University of New Mexico Press, 1989.

Nelson, Paula M. *After the West Was Won: Homesteaders and Town-Builders in Western South Dakota, 1900–1917.* University of Iowa Press, 1986.

———. *The Prairie Winnows Out Its Own: The West River Country of South Dakota in the Years of Depression and Dust.* University of Iowa Press, 1996.

New Mexico Territory Bureau of Immigration. *Colfax County New Mexico. One of the Richest Counties in the Territory.* New Mexican Printing, 1902.

———. *Eddy County New Mexico. The Most Southeastern County in the Territory, the Great Irrigation System in the Southwest, Almost Limitless Range, Mild and Salubrious Climate, A Haven for Healthseekers, An Ideal Agricultural, Horticultural and Stock County.* Bureau of Immigration, [ca. 1905].

———. *Union County New Mexico. A Prosperous and Growing Section: Leading in the Sheep Industry, Possessing an Ideal Climate and Many Varied Resources and Attractions.* New Mexican Printing, 1902.

Newton, J. R. *Jottings from a Shoemaker's Diary.* [n.p., ca. 1910].

Norcross, Charles A. *Nevada: Fifty Years Asleep; Awakening 1915.* Nevada Bureau of Industry, Agriculture and Irrigation, 1915.

Nordyke, Eleanor C. *The Peopling of Hawai'i.* 2d ed. University of Hawaii Press, 1989.

Norris, Kathleen. *Dakota: A Spiritual Biography.* Houghton Mifflin, 1993.

Northern Pacific Railroad. *The Great Northwest: A Guide-Book and Itinerary for the Use of Tourists and Travelers over the Lines of the Northern Pacific Railroad, Its Branches and Allied Lines.* W. C. Riley, 1890.

Nugent, Walter. *Crossings: The Great Transatlantic Migrations, 1870–1914.* Indiana University Press, 1992.

———. *Structures of American Social History.* Indiana University Press, 1981.

Olcott, Ben W., comp. *State of Oregon Blue Book and Official Directory, 1919–1920.* State Printing Department, 1919.

Ong, Paul; Edna Bonacich; and Lucie Cheng. *The New Asian Immigration in Los Angeles and Global Restructuring.* Temple University Press, 1994.

————, and Jorge Chapa. *Socio-economic Trends in California: 1940 to 1980.* California Employment Development Department, 1986.

Opie, John. *The Law of the Land: Two Hundred Years of American Farmland Policy.* University of Nebraska Press, 1987.

————. *Ogallala: Water for a Dry Land.* University of Nebraska Press, 1993.

Papanikolas, Zeese. *Buried Unsung: Louis Tikas and the Ludlow Massacre.* University of Utah Press, 1982.

Paquette, Mary Grace. *Basques to Bakersfield.* Kern County Historical Society, 1982.

Parman, Donald L. *Indians and the American West in the Twentieth Century.* Indiana University Press, 1994.

Patterson, James T. *Grand Expectations: The United States, 1945–1974.* Oxford University Press, 1996.

Paul, Rodman W. *The Far West and the Great Plains in Transition, 1859–1900.* Harper & Row, 1988.

Peirce, Neal R. *The Mountain States of America: People, Politics, and Power in the Eight Rocky Mountain States.* Norton, 1972.

————. *The Pacific States of America: People, Politics, and Power in the Five Pacific Basin States.* Norton, 1972.

Perilli, Giovanni. *Colorado and the Italians in Colorado/Il Colorado e gl'Italiani nel Colorado.* Denver, [n.p.], 1922.

Peterson, F. Ross. *Idaho: A Bicentennial History.* Norton, 1976.

Pico, Pío. *Don Pío Pico's Historical Narrative.* Arthur H. Clark, 1973.

Pido, Antonio J. A. *The Pilipinos in America: Macro/Micro Dimensions of Immigration and Integration.* Center for Migration Studies, 1986.

Pitzer, Paul C. *Grand Coulee: Harnessing a Dream.* Washington State University Press, 1994.

Pomeroy, Earl. *In Search of the Golden West: The Tourist in Western America.* Alfred A. Knopf, 1957.

————. *The Pacific Slope: A History of California, Oregon, Washington, Idaho, Utah, and Nevada.* Alfred A. Knopf, 1965.

Post, Emily. *By Motor to the Golden Gate.* D. Appleton, 1916.

Powell, John Wesley. *Report on the Lands of the Arid Region of the United States, with a More Detailed Account of the Lands of Utah.* (Originally: U.S. Congress, 45th Congress 2d Session, House Executive Document 73, April 3, 1878.) Harvard Common Press, 1983.

Price, Daniel O. *Changing Characteristics of the Negro Population.* Bureau of the Census, 1960.

Prucha, Francis Paul. *The Great Father: The United States Government and the American Indians.* 2 vols. University of Nebraska Press, 1984.

————. *American Indian Treaties: The History of a Political Anomaly.* University of California Press, 1994.

Raban, Jonathan. *Bad Land: An American Romance.* Pantheon Books, 1996.

Rampersad, Arnold, ed. *The Collected Poems of Langston Hughes.* Alfred A. Knopf, 1995.

Ramsey, Alice Huyler. *Veil, Duster, and Tire Iron.* Castle Press, 1961.

Rather, Lois. *Bohemians to Hippies: Waves of Rebellion.* The Rather Press, 1977.

Record, Wilson. *Minority Groups and Intergroup Relations in the San Francisco Bay Area.* Institute of Governmental Studies, 1963.

Reff, Daniel T. *Disease, Depopulation, and Culture Change in Northwestern New Spain, 1518–1764.* University of Utah Press, 1991.

Reid, Ira De A. *The Negro Population of Denver, Colorado: A Survey of Its Economic and Social Status.* National Urban League "for the Denver Interracial Committee," 1929.

Reisner, Marc. *Cadillac Desert: The American West and Its Disappearing Water.* Viking Penguin, 1986.

Reps, John W. *Cities of the American West: A History of Urban Frontier Planning.* Princeton University Press, 1979.

Reuss, Carl F. *Back to the Country: The Rurban Trend in Washington's Population.* Washington State College Agricultural Experiment Station, Bulletin 426, 1942.

Rexburg (Idaho) Commercial Club. *The Great Upper Snake River Valley.* [n.p., n.d.; ca. 1913–1915.]

Richardson, Rupert N. *Texas: The Lone Star State.* Prentice-Hall, 1943.

Riebsame, William E., gen. ed. *Atlas of the New West: Portrait of a Changing Region.* Norton, 1997.

Rikoon, J. Sanford, ed. *Rachel Calof's Story: Jewish Homesteader on the Northern Plains.* Indiana University Press, 1995.

Riley, Carroll L. *Rio del Norte: People of the Upper Rio Grande from Earliest Times to the Pueblo Revolt.* University of Utah Press, 1995.

Riley, Glenda. *The Female Frontier: A Comparative View of Women on the Prairie and the Plains.* University Press of Kansas, 1988.

Riney-Kehrberg, Pamela. *Rooted in Dust: Surviving Drought and Depression in Southwestern Kansas.* University Press of Kansas, 1994.

Ringholz, Raye C. *Uranium Frenzy: Boom and Bust on the Colorado Plateau.* Norton, 1989.

Rio Grande Home Co. *There's a Home for You in the Sunny San Luis Valley, Colorado.* Rio Grande Home Co., [1911].

Rios-Bustamante, Antonio, ed. *Mexican Immigrant Workers in the U.S.* UCLA Chicano Research Center, 1981.

Ritchie, Robert C., and Paul Andrew Hutton. *Frontier and Region: Essays in Honor of Martin Ridge.* Huntington Library Press and University of New Mexico Press, 1997.

Robbins, William G., et al. *Regionalism and the Pacific Northwest.* Oregon State University Press, 1983.

Rodriguez, Richard. *Days of Obligation: An Argument with My Mexican Father.* Viking, 1992.

———. *Hunger of Memory: The Education of Richard Rodriguez, an Autobiography.* Bantam, 1983.

Rogers, Maria M. *In Other Words: Oral Histories of the Colorado Frontier.* Fulcrum Publishing, 1995.

Rohrbough, Malcolm J. *Aspen: The History of a Silver Mining Town, 1879–1893.* Oxford University Press, 1986.

———. *Days of Gold: The California Gold Rush and the American Nation.* University of California Press, 1997.

Rolle, Andrew. *California: A History.* 4th ed. Harlan Davidson, 1987.

———. *Los Angeles: From Pueblo to City of the Future.* 2d ed. MTL, 1995.

Romo, Ricardo. *East Los Angeles: History of a Barrio.* University of Texas Press, 1983.

Roos, Robert de. *The Thirsty Land: The Story of the Central Valley Project.* Stanford University Press, 1948.

Roskelley, R. W. *Population Trends in Colorado.* Colorado Agricultural Experiment Station, Colorado State College, 1940.

Rothman, Hal K. *On Rims and Ridges: The Los Alamos Area since 1880.* University of Nebraska Press, 1992.

Rundell, Walter, Jr. *Early Texas Oil: A Photographic History, 1866–1936.* Texas A&M University Press, 1977.

Samora, Julian. *Los Mojados: The Wetback Story.* University of Notre Dame Press, 1971.

Sánchez, George I. *Forgotten People: A Study of New Mexicans.* University of New Mexico Press, [1940] 1996.

Sánchez, George J. *Becoming Mexican American: Ethnicity, Culture and Identity in Chicano Los Angeles, 1900–1945.* Oxford University Press, 1993.

Santa Ana Valley Immigration Association. *The Santa Ana Valley of Southern California: Its Resources, Climate, Growth and Future.* Santa Ana, Calif.: [n.p.], 1885.

Schlesier, Karl H., ed. *Plains Indians, A.D. 500–1500: The Archeological Past of Historic Groups.* University of Oklahoma Press, 1994.

Schlissel, Lillian; Byrd Gibbens; and Elizabeth Hampsten. *Far from Home: Families of the Westward Journey.* Schocken Books, 1989.

Schmid, Calvin F. *Suicides in Seattle, 1914 to 1925: An Ecological and Behavioristic Study.* University of Washington Press, 1928.

Schwantes, Carlos A., ed. *Bisbee: Urban Outpost on the Frontier.* University of Arizona Press, 1992.

———. *Coxey's Army: An American Odyssey.* University of Nebraska Press, 1985.

———. *The Pacific Northwest: An Interpretive History.* University of Nebraska Press, 1989.

———. *Railroad Signatures across the Pacific Northwest.* University of Washington Press, 1993.

Schwartz, Stephen. *From West to East: California and the Making of the American Mind.* Free Press, 1998.

Scott, James W., and Roland L. De Lorme. *Historical Atlas of Washington.* University of Oklahoma Press, 1988.

Seattle City Directory for 1890. Polk's Seattle Directory Co., 1890.

Shepherd, George. *Demographic and Socioeconomic Profiles of the American Indian, Black, Chinese, Filipino, Japanese, Spanish Heritage, and White Populations of Washington State in 1970.* State Superintendent of Public Instruction, 1974.

Sheridan, Thomas E. *Arizona: A History.* University of Arizona Press, 1995.

Sherman, William C., and Playford V. Thorson, eds. *Plains Folk: North Dakota's Ethnic History.* North Dakota State University, 1988.

Sherow, James Earl. *Watering the Valley: Development along the High Plains Arkansas River, 1870–1950.* University Press of Kansas, 1990.

Shideler, James, ed. *Agriculture in the Development of the Far West.* Agricultural History Society, 1975.

Shindo, Charles J. *Dust Bowl Migrants in the American Imagination.* University Press of Kansas, 1997.

Shipps, Jan. *Mormonism: The Story of a New Religious Tradition.* University of Illinois Press, 1985.

Shortridge, James R. *Peopling the Plains: Who Settled Where in Frontier Kansas.* University Press of Kansas, 1995.

Silko, Leslie Marmon. *Ceremony.* Penguin Books, 1977.

Simmons, Marc. *The Last Conquistador: Juan de Oñate and the Settling of the Far Southwest.* University of Oklahoma Press, 1991.

Slotkin, Richard. *Gunfighter Nation: The Myth of the Frontier in Twentieth-Century America.* Atheneum, 1992.

Smith, Michael M. *The Mexicans in Oklahoma.* University of Oklahoma Press, 1980.

Snipp, C. Matthew. *American Indians: The First of This Land.* Russell Sage Foundation, 1989.

Socolofsky, Homer E., and Huber Self. *Historical Atlas of Kansas.* 2d ed. University of Oklahoma Press, 1988.

Sonenshein, Raphael J. *Politics in Black and White: Race and Power in Los Angeles.* Princeton University Press, 1993.

Southern Pacific Company. *California for the Settler.* Southern Pacific Company, (1922).

———. *California for Health, Pleasure, and Profit: Why You Should Go There.* Southern Pacific Railway, (1894).

Spicer, Edward H. *Cycles of Conquest: The Impact of Spain, Mexico, and the United States on the Indians of the Southwest.* University of Arizona Press, 1962.

Starr, Kevin. *America and the California Dream, 1850–1915.* Oxford University Press, 1973.

———. *Inventing the Dream: California through the Progressive Era.* Oxford University Press, 1985.

———. *Material Dreams: Southern California through the 1920s.* Oxford University Press, 1990.

———. *Endangered Dreams: The Great Depression in California.* Oxford University Press, 1996.

———. *The Dream Endures: California Enters the 1940s.* Oxford University Press, 1997.

Starr, S. Frederick, ed. *Russia's American Colony.* Duke University Press, 1987.

Steffen, Jerome O., ed. *The American West: New Perspectives, New Dimensions.* University of Oklahoma Press, 1979.

Stein, Walter J. *California and the Dust Bowl Migration.* Greenwood Press, 1973.

Stevens, Joseph E. *Hoover Dam: An American Adventure.* University of Oklahoma Press, 1988.

Stoddard, Ellwyn R.; Richard L. Nostrand; and Jonathan P. West, eds. *Borderlands Sourcebook: A Guide to the Literature on Northern Mexico and the American Southwest.* University of Oklahoma Press, 1983.

———. *Maquila: Assembly Plants in Northern Mexico.* Texas Western Press, 1987.

Stryker, Susan, and Jim Van Buskirk. *Gay by the Bay: A History of Queer Culture in the San Francisco Bay Area.* Chronicle Books, 1996.

Suwol, Samuel M. *Jewish History of Oregon.* S. M. Suwol, 1958.

Sylva, Seville A. *Foreigners in the California Gold Rush.* R & E Research Associates, 1972.

Tabrah, Ruth. *Hawaii: A Bicentennial History.* Norton, 1980.

Taylor, Paul S. *Mexican Labor in the United States Imperial Valley.* University of California Press, 1928.

———. *Mexican Labor in the United States. Migration Statistics.* University of California Press, 1933.

Taylor, Quintard. *The Forging of a Black Community: Seattle's Central District from 1870 through the Civil Rights Era.* University of Washington Press, 1994.

———. *In Search of the Racial Frontier: African Americans in the American West, 1528–1990.* Norton, 1998.

Taylor, Robert M., Jr., and Ralph J. Crandall, eds. *Generations and Change: Genealogical Perspectives in Social History.* Mercer University Press, 1986.

Teaford, Jon C. *Post-Suburbia: Government and Politics in the Edge Cities.* Johns Hopkins University Press, 1997.

Thernstrom, Stephan, ed. *Harvard Encyclopedia of American Ethnic Groups.* Belknap Press of Harvard University Press, 1980.

Thoams, Howard E., and Florence Taylor, eds. *Migrant Farm Labor in Colorado: A Study of Migratory Families.* National Child Labor Committee, 1951.

Thomas, Dorothy Swaine, et al. *Japanese American Evacuation and Resettlement: The Salvage.* Part 2: "Life Histories." University of California Press, 1952.

Thomas, George. *The Development of Institutions under Irrigation, with Special Reference to Early Utah Conditions.* Macmillan, 1920.

Thomas, Sister Mary, OP. *The Lord May Be in a Hurry: The Congregation of Dominican Sisters of St. Catherine of Siena of Kenosha, Wisconsin.* Bruce, 1967.

Thompson, Warren S. *Growth and Changes in California's Population.* Haynes Foundation, 1955.

———, and P. K. Whelpton. *Population Trends in the United States.* McGraw Hill, 1933.

Thornton, Russell. *American Indian Holocaust and Survival: A Population History since 1492.* University of Oklahoma Press, 1987.

Tibesar, Antonine, ed. *Writings of Junípero Serra.* 3 vols. Academy of American Franciscan History, 1955.

Tikhmenev, P. A. *A History of the Russian American Company,* trans. and ed. Richard A. Pierce and Alton S. Donnelly. University of Washington Press, [1861–1863] 1978.

Timmons, W. H. *El Paso: A Borderlands History.* University of Texas at El Paso, 1990.

Timmons, Stuart. *The Trouble with Harry Hay: Founder of the Modern Gay Movement.* Alyson Publications, 1990.

Tindall, George B. *A Populist Reader: Selections from the Works of American Populist Leaders.* Harper & Row, 1966.

Tong, Benson. *Unsubmissive Women: Chinese Prostitutes in Nineteenth-Century San Francisco.* University of Oklahoma Press, 1994.

Trupin, Sophie. *Dakota Diaspora: Memoirs of a Jewish Homesteader.* University of Nebraska Press, 1984.

Tsai, Shih-shan Henry. *The Chinese Experience in America.* Indiana University Press, 1986.

United States. Bureau of the Census. Censuses of Population, 1880–1990. Publisher and dates vary; usually published by Government Printing Office.

————. Census. *Statistical Abstract of the United States.* 1914, 1942, 1965, 1970, 1995. Government Printing Office [dates vary].

————. Census. *Historical Statistics of the United States, from Colonial Times to 1970.* 2 vols. Government Printing Office, 1975.

————. Census. *Pocket Data Book USA 1967,* and same, *1979.* GPO, 1966, 1979.

————. Census. *Rural and Farm Population: 1987.* Current Population Reports, Series P-27, No. 61, June 1988. Washington, 1988.

————. Census. *Population of States and Counties of the United States: 1790–1990.* Washington, 1996.

————. Census. *Current Population Reports,* P25-1130, Feb. 1996. Washington, 1996.

————. Census. *Geographical Mobility: March 1987 to March 1990.* Current Population Reports, Series P-20, No. 456, Dec. 1991. Washington, 1991.

————. Census. *The Foreign-Born Population: 1994.* Current Population Reports, P20-486, Aug. 29, 1995. Washington, 1995.

————. Census. *How We're Changing: Demographic State of the Nation: 1997.* Current Population Reports, Special Studies, Series P23-193, March 1997. Washington, 1997.

————. Census. "State and County Population 1990 and 1995." Internet http://www.census.gov/population/estimate-extract/county/co95_US.txt

————. Census. *State and Metropolitan Area Data Book 1997–98.*5th ed. Washington, 1998.

————. Department of Commerce. *Vital Statistics of the United States 1940.* Part II: Natality and Mortality Data. Government Printing Office, 1943.

————. Department of Commerce. *Vital Statistics of the United States 1946.* Part I: Natality and Mortality Data. Government Printing Office, 1948.

————. Department of Health, Education, and Welfare. *Vital Statistics of the United States 1961.* Vol. I: Natality. Washington, 1963.

————. National Center for Health Statistics. *Vital Statistics of the United States 1970.* Vol. I: Natality. Rockville, Md., 1975.

————. National Center for Health Statistics. *Vital Statistics of the United States 1979.* Vol. I: Natality. Hyattsville, Md., 1984.

————. National Center for Health Statistics. *Vital Statistics of the United States 1987.* Vol. I: Natality. Hyattsville, Md.: U.S. Department of Health and Human Services, 1989.

————. Works Progress Administration. Federal Writers' Project. *California: A Guide to the Golden State.* Hastings House, 1939.

Unruh, John D., Jr. *The Plains Across: The Overland Emigrants and the Trans-Mississippi West, 1840–60.* University of Illinois Press, 1979.

Utley, Robert M. *The Indian Frontier of the American West, 1846–1890.* University of New Mexico Press, 1984.

————. *The Lance and the Shield: The Life and Times of Sitting Bull.* Henry Holt, 1993.

————. *A Life Wild and Perilous: Mountain Men and the Paths to the Pacific.* Henry Holt, 1997.

Vale, Thomas R., and Geraldine R. Vale. *Western Images, Western Landscapes: Travels along U.S. 89.* University of Arizona Press, 1989.

Van de Water, Frederic F. *The Family Flivvers to Frisco.* Appleton, 1927.

Vaz, August Mark. *The Portuguese in California.* Irmandade do Divino Espirito Santo Supreme Council, 1965.

Verano, John W., and Douglas H. Ubelaker, eds. *Disease and Demography in the Americas.* Smithsonian Institution Press, 1992.

Verge, Arthur C. *Paradise Transformed: Los Angeles during the Second World War.* Kendall/Hunt Publishing Company, 1993.

Vorspan, Max, and Lloyd P. Gartner. *History of the Jews of Los Angeles.* Huntington Library, 1970.

Waldinger, Roger, and Mehdi Bozorgmehr, eds. *Ethnic Los Angeles.* Russell Sage Foundation, 1996.

Washington State. Department of Agriculture. *Atlas of Washington Agriculture.* [n.p.], 1963.

————. Office of Community Development. *Fiscal Impact of the Trident Submarine Support Base on the State of Washington.* Olympia, 1977.

————. Office of Financial Management. *Forecasts of the State Population by Age and Sex 1987–2010.* Olympia, 1986.

Weaver, John D. *Los Angeles: The Enormous Village, 1781–1981.* Capra Press, 1980.

Webb, Melody. *The Last Frontier: A History of the Yukon Basin of Canada and Alaska.* University of New Mexico Press, 1985.

Weber, David J. *The Mexican Frontier, 1821–1846: The American Southwest under Mexico.* University of New Mexico Press, 1982.

————. *The Taos Trappers; The Fur Trade in the Far Southwest, 1540–1846.* University of Oklahoma Press, 1971.

————. *The Spanish Frontier in North America.* Yale University Press, 1992.

Wells, A. J. *The New Nevada; The Era of Irrigation and Opportunity.* Southern Pacific Company, 1908.

West, Elliott. *The Contested Plains: Indians, Goldseekers, & the Rush to Colorado.* University Press of Kansas, 1998.

————. *The Way to the West: Essays on the Central Plains.* University of New Mexico Press, 1995.

White, Richard. *"It's Your Misfortune and None of My Own": A History of the American West.* University of Oklahoma Press, 1991.

Wills, Garry. *John Wayne's America: The Politics of Celebrity.* Simon & Schuster, 1997.

Wood, Stanley. *Over the Range to the Golden State, A Complete Tourist's Guide to Colorado, New Mexico, Utah, Nevada, California, Oregon, Puget Sound and the Great Northwest.* R. R. Donnelley & Sons, 1889.

World Almanac and Book of Facts, 1997. World Almanac Books, 1996.

Worster, Donald. *Dust Bowl: The Southern Plains in the 1930s.* Oxford University Press, 1979.

————. *Rivers of Empire: Water, Aridity and the Growth of the American West.* Pantheon Books, 1985.

————. *An Unsettled Country: Changing Landscapes of the American West.* University of New Mexico Press, 1994.

WPA Guide to 1930s Arizona, The. University of Arizona Press, 1989.

Wyman, Mark. *Hard Rock Epic: Western Miners and the Industrial Revolution, 1860–1910.* University of California Press, 1979.

Wyoming. Secretary of State. *The State of Wyoming: An Official Publication Containing Reliable Information concerning the Resources of the State.* S. A. Bristol Co., 1901.

Yogi, Stan, ed. *Highway 99: A Literary Journal through California's Great Central Valley.* Heyday Books, "in conjunction with California Council for the Humanities," 1996.

Yuma County Commercial Club. *Land of Promise: U.S.R.S. Premier Project, Yuma, Queen City of the Colorado.* Press Morning Sun, (1915).

Yung, Judy. *Unbound Feet: A Social History of Chinese Women in San Francisco.* University of California Press, 1995.

Zarchin, Michael M. *Glimpses of Jewish Life in San Francisco.* Judah L. Magnes Memorial Museum, 1964.

Articles in Journals, Essays in Books

Newspaper articles are cited by author and/or title only in the footnotes and not here. For books in which essays appear, see above (items marked "q.v.") for the full citation. Oft-cited journals are referred to by abbreviations, as follows:

AAAG	*Annals of the Association of American Geographers*
AmDemog	*American Demographics*
AgH	*Agricultural History*
BullHistMed	*Bulletin of the History of Medicine*
CalHist	*California History*
CalHSQ	*California Historical Society Quarterly*
ChronOk	*Chronicles of Oklahoma*
ColoMag	*Colorado Magazine*
GPQ	*Great Plains Quarterly*
IdY	*Idaho Yesterdays*
IMR	*International Migration Review*
JAH	*Journal of American History*
JarizH	*Journal of Arizona History*
JsoH	*Journal of Southern History*
JW	*Journal of the West*
KH	*Kansas History*
Montana	*Montana: The Magazine of Western History*
NMHR	*New Mexico Historical Review*
NebrH	*Nebraska History*
NevHSQ	*Nevada Historical Society Quarterly*
NY	*New Yorker*
OHQ	*Oregon Historical Quarterly*
PHR	*Pacific Historical Review*
PNWQ	*Pacific Northwest Quarterly*
PopBull	*Population Bulletin*
SaskHist	*Saskatchewan History*
SoCalQ	*Southern California Quarterly*
SWHQ	*Southwest Historical Quarterly*
UHQ	*Utah Historical Quarterly*
WHQ	*Western Historical Quarterly*
WSJH	*Western States Jewish History*

Abbott, Carl. "Boom State and Boom City: Stages in Denver's Growth." *ColoMag* 50, summer 1973, 207–30.

———. "Building Western Cities: A Review Essay." *Colorado Heritage* 1984:1, 39–46.

———. "Southwestern Cityscapes: Approaches to an American Urban Environment." In Fairbanks and Underwood, q.v., 69–78.

———. "Utopia and Bureaucracy: The Fall of Rajneeshpuram, Oregon." *PHR* 59, Feb. 1990, 77–103.

———, and Deborah Howe. "The Politics of Land-Use Law in Oregon: Senate Bill 100, Twenty Years After." *OHQ* 94, spring 1993, 5–35.

Abrams, Jeanne. "Chasing an Elusive Dream: Charles Spivak and the Jewish Agricultural Settlement Movement in America." *WSJH* 18, Apr. 1986, 204–17.

Agatha, Mother M. "Catholic Education and the Indian." In Roy J. Deferrari, ed., *Essays on Catholic Education in the United States* (Washington: Catholic University, 1942), 14–15.

Alexander, Thomas G. "Ogden, A Federal Colony in Utah." *UHQ* 47, summer 1979, 291–310.

Allen, Michael. "Cowboyphobia: A Diagnosis and Cure, or . . . The Emperors Wear No Duds." *JW* 36, Oct. 1997, 3–6.

Ambry, Margaret K. "States of the Future." *AmDemog*, Oct. 1994, 39.

American Express advertisement. *NY*, May 20, 1987, 53.

Amidon, Beulah. "Home Teachers in the City." *Survey Graphic* 56, June 1, 1926, 304–07.

Anderson, H. Allen. "The Delaware and Shawnee Indians and the Republic of Texas, 1820–1845." *SWHQ* 94, Oct. 1990, 231–60.

Ankli, Robert E. "Farm Income on the Great Plains and Canadian Prairies, 1920–1940." *AgH* 51, Jan. 1977, 92–103.

Armitage, Sue; Theresa Banfield; and Sarah Jacobus. "Black Women and Their Communities in Colorado." *Frontiers: A Journal of Women's Studies* 1, 1977, 45–51.

Arrington, Leonard J. "Idaho and the Great Depression." *IdY* 13, summer 1969, 2–8.

———. "The Influenza Epidemic of 1918–1919 in Southern Idaho." *IdY* 32, fall 1988, 19–29.

———. "Irrigation in the Snake River Valley: An Historical Overview." *IdY* 30, spring–summer 1986, 3–6.

———. "The Mormon Settlement of Cassia County, Idaho, 1873–1921." *IdY* 23, summer 1979, 36–41.

———, and Dean L. May. " 'A Different Mode of Life': Irrigation and Society in Nineteenth-Century Utah." *AgH* 49, Jan. 1975, 3–20.

———, and Linda Wilcox. "From Subsistence to Gold Age: Cache Valley Agriculture, 1859–1900." *UHQ* 57, fall 1989, 340–69.

Arsenault, Raymond. "The End of the Long Hot Summer: The Air Conditioner and Southern Culture." *JsoH* 50, Nov. 1984, 597–628.

Ashcroft, Bruce. "Miner and Merchant in Socorro's Boom Town Economy, 1880–1893." *NMHR* 63, Apr. 1988, 103–17.

Austin, Judith. "Desert, Sagebrush, and the Northwest." In Robbins, q.v., 129–47.

Azuma, Eiichiro. "A History of Oregon's *Issei*, 1880–1952." *OHQ* 94, winter 1993–94, 315–67.

Baganha, Maria Ioannis Benis. "The Social Mobility of Portuguese Immigrants in the United States at the Turn of the Century." *IMR* 25, summer 1991, 277–302.

Baily, Samuel L. "The Adjustment of Italian Immigrants in Buenos Aires and New York, 1870–1914." *American Historical Review* 88, Apr. 1983, 281–305.

Bakken, Gordon Morris. "Mexican and American Land Policy: A Conflict of Cultures." *SoCalQ* 75, fall–winter 1993, 237–62.

Barich, Bill. "Hmong Temple." In Yogi, q.v., 394–96.

Barnes, J. A. "Home on a Canadian Rockpile." *Canadian Geographical Journal*, 68, 18–21.

Barrett, Gwynn, and Leonard Arrington. "The 1921 Depression: Its Impact on Idaho." *IdY* 15, summer 1971, 10–15.

Baur, John E. "The Health Seeker in the Westward Movement, 1830–1900." *Mississippi Valley Historical Review* 46, June 1959, 91–110.

Beasley, Maurine Hoffman. "Lorena Hickok to Harry Hopkins, 1933: A Woman Reporter Views Prairie Towns." *Montana* 32, spring 1982, 58–66.

Beesley, David. "From Chinese to Chinese-American: Chinese Women & Families in a Sierra Nevada Town." *CalHist* 67, Sept. 1988, 168–79.

Belshaw, Michael. "High, Dry, and Lonesome: The Arizona Strip and Its People." *JarizH* 19, winter 1978, 359–78.

Benson, Nettie Lee. "Texas as Viewed from Mexico, 1820–1834." *SWHQ* 90, Jan. 1987, 219–91.

Bernard, William S. "Immigration: History of U.S. Policy." In Thernstrom, q.v., 486–95.

Bieter, Pat. "Reluctant Shepherds: The Basques in Idaho." *IdY* 1, summer 1957, 11–15.

Bitton, Davis. "Peopling the Upper Snake: The Second Wave of Mormon Settlement in Idaho." *IdY* 23, summer 1979, 47–52.

Boag, Peter G. "Ashwood on Trout Creek: A Study in Continuity and Change in Central Oregon." *OHQ* 91, summer 1990, 117–53.

Bogardus, Emery S. "Filipino Repatriation." *Sociology and Social Research* 21, 1936, 67–71.

Bogue, Allan G. "An Agricultural Empire." In Milner et al., q.v., 275–313.

Bosley, Donald R. "Coburg: A Montana Town that Is No More." *Montana* 25, Oct. 1975, 38–51.

Bouvier, Leon F., and Carl J. De Vita. "The Baby Boom—Entering Midlife." *PopBull* 46:3, Nov. 1991, 1–34.

———, and Robert W. Gardner. "Immigration to the U.S.: The Unfinished Story." *PopBull* 41:4, Nov. 1986, 3–50.

Bowden, Henry Warner. "Spanish Missions, Cultural Conflict, and the Pueblo Revolt of 1680." In Hurtado and Iverson, q.v., 96–104.

Bowen, Marshall E. "A Backward Step: From Irrigation to Dry Farming in the Nevada Desert." *AgH* 63, spring 1989, 231–42.

Boyce, Ronald R. "The Mormon Invasion and Settlement of the Upper Snake River Plain in the 1880s: The Case of Lewisville, Idaho." *PNWQ* 78, Jan.–Apr. 1987, 50–58.

Boyd, Robert. "Population Decline from Two Epidemics on the Northwest Coast." In Verano and Ubelaker, q.v., 249–53.

Boyd-Bowman, Peter. "Patterns of Spanish Emigration to the Indies until 1600." *Hispanic American Historical Review* 56, Nov. 1976, 580–604.

Bray, Kingsley M. "Teton Sioux Population History, 1655–1881." *NebrH* 75, summer 1994, 165–88.

Bronitsky, Gordon. "Indian Assimilation in the El Paso Area." *NMHR* 62, Apr. 1987, 151–68.

Brooks, Robert L., and Robert Bell. "The Last Prehistoric People: The Southern Plains Villagers." *ChronOk* 67, fall 1989, 296–319.

Broussard, Albert S. "Organizing the Black Community in the San Francisco Bay Area, 1915–1930." *Arizona and the West*, 23, winter 1981, 335–54.

Brown, Arthur J. "The Promotion of Emigration to Washington, 1854–1909." *PNWQ* 36, Jan. 1945, 3–17.

Bryan, Carol. Internet (H-West) communication regarding honyockers, Dec. 2, 1997.

Bufkin, Don. "From Mud Village to Modern Metropolis: The Urbanization of Tucson." *JarizH* 22, spring 1981, 63–98.

Burke, B. Meredith. "Mexican Immigrants Shape California's Fertility, Future." *Population Today*, Sept. 1995, 4–5.

Burns, Nancy. "The Collapse of Small Towns on the Great Plains: A Bibliography." *Emporia State Research Studies* 31, summer 1982.

Busco, Ralph A., and Douglas D. Alder. "German and Italian Prisoners of War in Utah and Idaho." *UHQ* 39, winter 1971, 55–72.

Campbell, Gregory R. "Changing Patterns of Health and Effective Fertility among the Northern Cheyenne of Montana, 1886–1903." *American Indian Quarterly* 15, summer 1991, 339–58.

Carlson, Alvar M. "Seasonal Farm labor in the San Luis Valley." *AAAG* 63, March 1973, 97–108.

Cassidy, John. "The Melting-Pot Myth." *NY*, July 14, 1997, 40–43.

Castañeda, Antonia I. "Engendering the History of Alta California, 1769–1848; Gender, Sexuality, and the Family." In Gutiérrez and Orsi, q.v., 230–59.

Cayton, Horace R. "America's Ten Best Cities for Negroes." *Negro Digest* 5, Oct. 1947, 4–10.

Central Arizona Project Association. "Water for Arizona: Key to Progress." Flyer. Phoenix, 1954.

Chan, Loren B. "The Chinese in Nevada: An Historical Survey, 1856–1970." *NevHSQ* 25, winter 1982, 266–314.

Chan, Sucheng. "Koreans in America, 1902–Present: A Selected Bibliography." *Immigration History Society Newsletter* 20, Dec. 1988, 11–15.

Chen, Yong. "The Internal Origins of Chinese Emigration to California Reconsidered." *WHQ* 28, winter 1997, 521–46.

Cherlin, Andrew J. "Explaining the Postwar Baby Boom." *Items* 35, Dec. 1981, 57–63.

Chicago, Burlington & Quincy Railroad. "Irrigation Bulletin No. 1, 1905." [n.p.]

Chu, George. "Chinatowns in the Delta: The Chinese in the Sacramento–San Joaquin Delta, 1870–1960." *CalHSQ* 49, March 1970, 21–37.

Clapsaddle, David K. "The West and Dry Routes of the Santa Fe Trail." *KH* 15, summer 1992, 98–115.

Clar, Reva, and William M. Kramer. "The Girl Rabbi of the Golden West: The Adventurous Life of Ray Frank in Nevada, California and the Northwest." *WSJH* 18, Jan. 1986, 99–111; Apr. 1986, 223–36.

Clayton, James L. "Defense Spending: Key to California's Growth." *Western Political Quarterly* 15, June 1962, 280–93.

———. "The Impact of the Cold War on the Economies of California and Utah, 1946–1965." *PHR* 36, Nov. 1967, 449–74.

———. "'An Unhallowed Gathering': The Impact of Defense Spending on Utah's Population Growth, 1940–1964." *UHQ* 34, summer 1966, 227–42.

Cofone, Albin J. "Reno's Little Italy: Italian Entrepreneurship and Culture in Northern Nevada." *NevHSQ* 26, summer 1983, 97–110.

———. "Themes in the Italian Settlement of Nevada." *NevHSQ* 25, summer 1982, 116–30.

Coleman, Annie Gilbert. "The Unbearable Whiteness of Skiing." *PHR* 65, Nov. 1996, 583–614.

Cook, Jimmie. "The Oil Patch: A Part of the Passing Parade." *Journal of American Culture* 14, summer 1991, 121–24.

Cortés, Carlos E. "Mexicans." In Thernstrom, q.v., 697–719.

Cotroneo, Ross R. "Colonization of the Northern Pacific Land Grant, 1900–1920." *North Dakota Quarterly* 38, summer 1970, 33–48.

———. "Selling Land on the Montana Plains, 1905–1915: Northern Pacific Railway's Land-Grant Sales Policies." *Montana* 37, spring 1987, 40–49.

Cuba, Stanley L. "A Polish Community in the Urban West: St. Joseph's Parish in Denver, Colorado." *Polish American Studies* 36, spring 1979, 33–74.

Daniels, John D. "The Indian Population of North America in 1492." *William and Mary Quarterly*, 3d series, 49, April 1992, 298–320.

Daniels, Roger. "Japanese Relocation and Redress in North America: A Comparative View." *Pacific Historian* 25, spring 1982, 2–14.

Daskarolis, George P. "San Francisco's Greek Colony: Evolution of an Ethnic Community, 1890–1945." *CalHist* 60, summer 1981, 114–33.

Davis, Cary; Carl Haub; and JoAnne Willette. "U.S. Hispanics: Changing the Face of America." *PopBull* 38:3, June 1983, 3–43.

Davis, Clark. "From Oasis to Metropolis: Southern California and the Changing Context of American Leisure." *PHR* 61, Aug. 1992, 357–85.

Davis, Lenwood G. "Sources for History of Blacks in Oregon." *OHQ* 73, Sept. 1972, 197–211.

Day, George M. "Races and Cultural Oases." *Sociology and Social Research* 18, March–Apr. 1934, 326–39.

Dean, Robert. "'Dam Building Still Had Some Magic Then': Stewart Udall, the Central Arizona Project, and the Evolution of the Pacific Southwest Water Plan, 1963–1968." *PHR* 66, Feb. 1997, 81–98.

DeGraaf, Lawrence B. "The City of Black Angels: Emergence of the Los Angeles Ghetto, 1890–1930." *PHR* 39, Aug. 1970, 323–52.

———. "Significant Steps on an Arduous Path: The Impact of World War II on Discrimination against African Americans in the West." *JW* 35, Jan. 1996, 24–33.

Den Otter, Andy A. "Irrigation in Southern Alberta, 1882–1901." *Great Plains Journal* 11, spring 1972, 125–37.

Deutsch, Sarah; George J. Sánchez; and Gary Y. Okihiro. "Contemporary Peoples/Contested Places." In Milner et al., q.v., 639–69.

De Vita, Carol J. "The United States at Mid-Decade." *PopBull* 50:4, March 1996, 1–48.

Dinwoodie, D. H. "Deportation: The Immigration Service and the Chicano Labor Movement in the 1930s." *NMHR* 52, July 1977, 193–206.

Donato, Katherine M. "Current Trends and Patterns of Female Migration: Evidence from Mexico." *IMR* 27, winter 1993, 748–71.

Donovan, Richard. "The Great Los Angeles Public Housing Mystery." *Reporter,* 6, March 4, 1952, 25–29.

Dortch, Shannon. "Counties with Full Pockets." *AmDemog* 18, Sept. 1996, 6–7.

Doti, Lynne Pierson, and Larry Schweikart. "Financing the Postwar Housing Boom in Phoenix and Los Angeles, 1945–1960." *PHR* 58, May 1989, 173–94.

Douglas, Donald M. "Forgotten Zions: The Jewish Agricultural Colonies in Kansas in the 1880s." *KH* 16, summer 1993, 108–19.

Doyle, Susan Badger. "Indian Perspectives of the Bozeman Trail, 1864–1868." *Montana* 40, winter 1990, 56–67.

———. "Journeys to the Land of Gold: Emigrants on the Bozeman Trail, 1863–1866. *Montana* 41, autumn 1991, 54–67.

Dumke, Glenn. "The Boom of the 1880s in Southern California." *SoCalQ* 76, spring 1994, 99–114.

Duncan, Ray. "The Painful Rejuvenation of Downtown." *Los Angeles,* Nov. 1963, 28–33, 68–71.

Dunne, John Gregory. "Law & Disorder in Los Angeles, Part I." *New York Review of Books,* Oct. 10, 1991.

Dykstra, Robert R. "The Last Days of 'Texan' Abilene: A Study in Community Conflict on the Farmer's Frontier." *AgH* 34, July 1960, 107–19.

Edmondson, Brad. "The Lucky Thirteen." *AmDemog* 16, Dec. 1994, 2.

———. "Where Are the Boonies?" *AmDemog* 17, Feb. 1995, 60.

Edwards, G. Thomas. " 'The Early Morning of Yakima's Day of Greatness': The Yakima County Agricultural Boom of 1905–1911." *PNQ* 73, Apr. 1982, 78–89.

———. "Walla Walla: Gateway to the Pacific Northwest Interior." *Montana* 40, summer 1990, 28–43.

Ehrlich, Clara Hilderman. "My Childhood on the Prairie." *ColoMag* 51, spring 1974, 116–18.

Engh, Michael E., SJ. " 'A Multiplicity and Diversity of Faiths': Religion's Impact on Los Angeles and the Urban West, 1890–1940." *WHQ* 28, winter 1997, 463–92.

Engstrand, Iris H. W. "An Enduring Legacy: California Ranchos in Historical Perspective." *JW* 28, July 1988, 36–47.

Epperson, Jean L. "1834 Census—Anahuac Precinct, Atascosito District." *SWHQ* 92, Jan. 1989, 437–47.

Espenshade, Thomas J. "A Short History of U.S. Policy toward Illegal Immigration." *Population Today* 18, Feb. 1990, 6–8.

Estanol, Jorge V. In *Realty Blue Book of California: A Compilation of Statewide Authorities on California Real Estate.* Los Angeles: Keystone Publishing Co., 1924, 13.

Etulain, Richard W. "Basque Beginnings in the Pacific Northwest." *IdY* 18, spring 1974, 26–32.

Fabry, Judith. "Agricultural Science and Technology in the West." In Hurt, q.v., 169–89.

Feis, Herbert. "Tulsa." *Survey Graphic,* Oct. 1, 1923, 22.

Fink, Deborah, and Alicia Carriquiry. "Having Babies or Not: Household Composition and Fertility in Rural Iowa and Nebraska, 1900–1910." *GPQ* 12, summer 1992, 157–68.

Fitch, George H. "Colony Life in Southern California." *The Cosmopolitan: A Monthly Illustrated Magazine* 2, Sept. 1886–Feb. 1887, 151–58.

Fite, Gilbert C. "The Transformation of South Dakota Agriculture: The Effects of Modernization, 1939–1964." *South Dakota History* 19, fall 1989, 278–305.

Fitzgerald, Daniel C. " 'We Are All in This Together'—Immigrants in the Oil and Mining Towns of Southern Kansas, 1890–1920." *KH* 10, 1987, 18–21.

FitzGerald, Frances. "A Reporter at Large: The Castro—I." *NY*, July 21, 1986, 34–70.

———. "A Reporter at Large: The Castro—II." *NY*, July 28, 1986, 44–63.

Fitzgerald, Roosevelt. "Blacks and the Boulder Dam Project." *NevHSQ* 24, fall 1981, 255–60.

Fleming, Elvis E. " 'Sockless' Jerry Simpson: The New Mexico Years, 1902–1905." *NMHR* 69, Jan. 1994, 49–69.

Fletcher, Robert S. "The End of the Open Range in Eastern Montana." *Mississippi Valley Historical Review* 16, Sept. 1929, 188–211.

Fong, Lawrence Michael. "Sojourners and Settlers: The Chinese Experience in Arizona." *JarizH* 21, autumn 1980, 227–56.

Foote, A. D. "The Redemption of the Great Valley of California." *Transactions* [of the American Society of Civil Engineers] 66, 1910, 229–45.

Fost, Dan. "The California Comeback." *AmDemog* 17, July 1995, 53.

Foster, Mark S. "The Western Response to Urban Transportation: A Tale of Three Cities, 1900–1945." *JW* 18, July 1979, 31–39.

Fox, Stephen C. "General John DeWitt and the Proposed Internment of German and Italian Aliens during World War II." *PHR* 57, Nov. 1988, 407–38.

Francese, Peter. "America at Mid-Decade." *AmDemog* 17, Feb. 1995, 28.

Frey, William H. "Immigrant and Native Migrant Magnets." *AmDemog* 18, Nov. 96, 37–40, 53.

———. "Metropolitan America: Beyond the Transition." *PopBull* 45:2, July 1990, 1–51.

———. "The New White Flight." *AmDemog* 16, April 1994, 40–48.

Frost, O.W. "Vitus Bering Resurrected: Recent Forensic Analysis and the Documentary Record." *PNWQ* 84, July 1993, 91–97.

Frost, Richard H. "The Pueblo Indian Smallpox Epidemic in New Mexico, 1898–1899." *BullHistMed* 64, fall 1990, 417–45.

Frumkin, Robert W. "Rural Families in an Urban Setting: A Study in Persistence and Change." *Journal of Human Relations* 9, summer 1961, 494–503.

"Future Population of the United States, The." *PopBull* 27:1 (Feb. 1971).

Gamboa, Erasmo. "Mexican Migration into Washington State: A History, 1940–1950." *PNWQ* 72, July 1981, 121–31.

Garcia, Mario T. "The Chicana in American History: The Mexican Women of El Paso, 1880–1920—A Case Study." *PHR* 49, May 1980, 315–37.

———. "Mexican Americans and the Politics of Citizenship: The Case of El Paso, 1936." *NMHR* 59, April 1984, 187–204.

Gast, Ross H. "Why People Seek Small Farm Homes." *Southern California Business* 12, April 1933, 18–19.

Gates, Paul W. "Homesteading the High Plains." *AgH* 51, Jan. 1977, 109–33.

———. "Public Land Disposal in California." In Shideler, q.v., 158–78.

———. "Public Land Issues in the United States." *WHQ* 2, Oct. 1971, 363–76.

Gibson, James R. "Russian Expansion in Siberia and America: Critical Contrasts." In Starr, q.v., 32–40.

Gilmore, N. Ray, and Gladys W. Gilmore. "The Bracero in California." *PHR* 32, Aug. 1963, 265–82.

Glaser, David. "Migration in Idaho's History." *IdY* 11, fall 1967, 22–31.

Gober, Patricia. "Americans on the Move." *PopBull* 48:3, Nov. 1993, 1–40.

Godfrey, Stephen. "Departing Correspondent Looks at Western Culture." *Toronto Globe and Mail*, Aug. 6, 1988.

Goldstein, Daniel. "Many Wests: A Review Essay." *Annals of Iowa* 53, spring 1994, 147–56.

Gómez, Arthur R. "Urban Imperialism in the Modern West: Farmington, New Mexico, vs. Durango, Colorado, 1945–65." In DeMark, q.v., 133–48.

Gómez-Quiñones, Juan. "Mexican Immigration to the United States and the Internationalization of Labor, 1848–1980: An Overview." In Rios-Bustamante, q.v., 13–34.

———, and David R. Maciel. " 'What Goes Around, Comes Around': Political Practice and Cultural Response in the Internationalization of Mexican Labor, 1890–1997." In Maciel and Herrera-Sobek, q.v., 27–65.

González, Michael J. " 'The Child of the Wilderness Weeps for the Father of Our Country': The Indian and the Politics of Church and State in Provincial California." In Gutiérrez and Orsi, q.v., 147–72.

Goodwin, H. Marshall, Jr. "The Arroyo Seco; From Dry Gulch to Freeway." *SoCalQ* 47, Mar. 1965, 73–94.

Goren, Arthur A. "Jews." In Thernstrom, q.v., 571–98.

Gosting, Ken. "The Red Power Struggle." *Los Angeles*, Oct. 1969, 42–44, 72–79.

Gould, Charles F. "Portland Italians, 1880–1920." *OHQ* 77, Sept. 1976, 239–60.

Grabill, Wilson H. "Effect of the War on the Birth Rate and Postwar Fertility Prospects." *American Journal of Sociology* 50, Sept. 1944, 107–11.

Greb, G. Allen. "Opening a New Frontier: San Francisco, Los Angeles and the Panama Canal, 1900–1914." *PHR* 47, Aug. 1978, 405–24.

Green, Donald E. "A History of Irrigation Technology Used to Exploit the Ogallala Aquifer." In Kromm and White, q.v., 29–39.

———. "The Oklahoma Land Rush of 1889: A Centennial Re-Interpretation." *ChronOk* 67, summer 1989, 120–30.

Gregor, Howard F. "Urban Pressures on California Land." *Land Economics* 33, Nov. 1957, 311–25.

Grey, Arthur L., Jr. "Los Angeles: Urban Prototype." *Land Economics* 35, Aug. 1959, 232–42.

Guyotte, Roland L. "Generation Gap: Filipinos, Filipino Americans and Americans, Here and There, Then and Now." *Journal of American Ethnic History* 17, fall 1997, 64–70.

Hackel, Stephen W. "Land, Labor, and Production: The Colonial Economy of Spanish and Mexican California." In Gutiérrez and Orsi, q.v., 111–46.

Hacker, Frederick J. "What the McCone Commission Didn't See." *Frontier*, March 1966, 10–15.

Hall, G. Emlen. "Land Litigation and the Idea of New Mexico Progress." *JW* 27, July 1988, 48–58.

Hamburg, Vivian. "Gambling." In Hasselstrom et al., q.v., 216.

Hamburger, Philip. "Notes for a Gazetteer: Eugene, Ore." *NY*, June 1, 1963, 95–99.

———. "Notes for a Gazetteer: Fairbanks, Alas." *NY*, Nov. 5, 1966, 219–28.

———. "Notes for a Gazetteer: Juneau, Alas." *NY*, March 13, 1965, 170–78.

———. "Notes for a Gazetteer: Liv-Lahaina, Hawaii." *NY*, Sept. 18, 1965, 166–74.

———. "Notes for a Gazetteer: Sacramento, Calif." *NY*, Feb. 2, 1963, 81–87.

———. "Notes for a Gazetteer: Santa Fe, N.M." *NY*, Oct. 17, 1964, 206–12.

Hamilton, Kenneth Marvin. "Origins and Early Promotion of Nicodemus: A Pre-Exodus, All-Black Town." *KH* 5, 1982, 221–42.

Hampsten, Elizabeth. "The Nehers and the Martins in North Dakota, 1909–1911." In Schlissel et al., q.v., 175–229.

Hansen, Nils. "Commentary: The Hispano Homeland in 1900." *AAAG* 71, June 1981, 280–83.

Harkness, Ione B. "Basque Settlement in Oregon." *OHQ* 34, Sept. 1933, 273–75.

Hauser, Philip M. (untitled comment on baby boom). *Science* 96, supplement 8, Aug. 21, 1942, 8.

Hayden, Dolores. "The Power of Place: A Proposal for Los Angeles." *Public Historian* 10, summer 1988, 5–18.

Haynes, John R. "A Canyon and a City." *Survey Graphic,* June 1, 1924, 283.

Haywood, C. Robert. "The Hodgeman County Colony." *KH* 12, winter 1989–90, 210–21.

Hemminger, Carole. "Little Manila: The Filipino in Stockton—Prior to World War II." *Pacific Historian* 24, spring 1980, 21–27.

Henke, Warren A. "The Settlement Process: Official State Promotional Activities." In Sherman and Thorson, q.v., 14–33.

Hernandez, Salomé. "No Settlement without Women: Three Spanish California Settlement Schemes, 1790–1800." *SoCalQ* 72, fall 1990, 203–33.

Hernández Álvarez, José. "A Demographic Profile of the Mexican Immigration to the United States, 1910–1950." *Journal of Inter-American Studies* 8, July 1966, 471–96.

Hess, Gary. "The Forgotten Asian Americans: The East Indian Community in the United States." *PHR* 43, Nov. 1974, 576–96.

———. "The 'Hindu' in America: Immigration and Naturalization Policies and India, 1917–1946." *PHR* 38, Feb. 1969, 59–79.

Higgs, Robert. "The Wealth of Japanese Tenant Farmers in California, 1909." *AgH* 53, April 1979, 488–93.

Hill, Forest G. "The Shaping of California's Industrial Pattern." *Proceedings of the Thirtieth Annual Conference of the Western Economic Association, Stanford, Sept. 1–2, 1955.* [n.p.] Western Economic Association, 1956, 63–68.

Hoerig, Karl A. "The Relationship between German Immigrants and the Native Peoples in Western Texas." *SWHQ* 97, Jan. 1994, 423–51.

Holloway, B. R. "Southwest Agriculture Centers in Los Angeles." *Southern California Business* 8, March 1929, 12–13, 46.

Hoover, Herbert T. "The Sioux Agreement of 1889 and Its Aftermath." *South Dakota History* 19, spring 1989, 56–94.

Hordes, Stanley. "The Inquisition and the Crypto-Jewish Community in Colonial New Spain and New Mexico." *WSJH* 24, Jan. 1992, 106–18.

———. "The Sephardic Legacy in New Mexico: A History of the Crypto-Jews." *JW* 35, Oct. 1996, 82–90.

Houchins, Lee, and Chang-su Houchins. "The Korean Experience in America, 1903–1924." *PHR* 43, Nov. 1974, 548–75.

Hoy, Suellen. "The Journey Out: The Recruitment and Emigration of Irish Religious Women to the United States, 1812–1914." *Journal of Women's History* 6, winter/spring 1995, 64–98.

Hudson, John. "Two Dakota Homestead Frontiers." *AAAG* 63, Dec. 1973, 442–62.

Hudson, John C. "The Study of Western Frontier Populations." In Steffen, q.v., 35–60.

———. "Who Was 'Forest Man'? Sources of Migration to the Plains." *GPQ* 6, spring 1986, 69–83.

Hughes, Langston. "West Texas." In Rampersad, q.v., 252.

Hulmston, John. "Mormon Immigration in the 1860s: The Story of the Church Trains." *UHQ* 58, winter 1990, 32–48.

Hundley, Norris, Jr. "The Great American Desert Transformed: Aridity, Exploitation, and Imperialism in the Making of the Modern American West." In El-Ashry and Gibbons, q.v., 21–83.

Hurt, R. Douglas. "Return of the Dust Bowl: The Filthy Fifties." *JW* 18, Oct. 1979, 85–93.

Hurtado, Albert. Introduction to Heizer, q.v., v–xi.

Hutton, Paul Andrew. "'Fort Desolation': The Military Establishment, The Railroad, and Settlement on the Northern Plains." *North Dakota History* 56, spring 1989, 20–30.

Hyde, Harlow A. "Slow Death in the Great Plains." *Atlantic Monthly* 279, June 1997, 42–45.

Ichioka, Yuji. "Japanese Immigrant Response to the 1920 California Alien Land Law." *AgH* 58, April 1984, 157–78.

Iwata, Masakazu. "The Japanese Immigrants in California Agriculture." *AgH* 36, Jan. 1962, 25–37.

Jackman, Jarrell C. "Exiles in Paradise: German Emigres in Southern California, 1933–1950." *SoCalQ* 61, summer 1979, 183–205.

Jackson, Robert H. "The Changing Economic Structure of the Alta California Missions—A Reinterpretation." *PHR* 61, Aug. 1992, 387–415.

Jameson, Elizabeth. "Imperfect Unions: Class and Gender in Cripple Creek, 1894–1904." In Cantor and Laurie, q.v., 166–202.

Janeway, Eliot. "Trials and Errors: Trouble on the Northwest Frontier." *Fortune* 26, Nov. 1942, 24–32.

Jensen, Joan M. "Apartheid: Pacific Coast Style." *PHR* 38, Aug. 1969, 335–40.

Johansen, Dorothy O. "A Working Hypothesis for the Study of Migration." *PHR* 36, Feb. 1967, 1–12.

Johnson, Judith R. "Kansas in the 'Grippe': The Spanish Influenza Epidemic of 1918." *KH* 15, spring 1992, 44–55.

Johnson, Kenneth M., and Calvin L. Beale. "The Rural Rebound Revisited." *AmDemog* 17, July 1995, 46–50.

Jones, David C. "The Strategy of Railway Abandonment: The Great Northern in Washington and British Columbia, 1917–1935." *WHQ* 11, April 1980, 141–58.

———. " 'We'll All Be Buried Down Here in This Dry Belt. . . .' " *SaskHist* 35, spring 1982, 41–54.

Josenhans, Heiner; Daryl Fedje; Reinhard Pienitz; and John Southon. "Early Humans and Rapidly Changing Holocene Sea Levels in the Queen Charlotte Islands–Hecate Strait, British Columbia, Canada." *Science* 277, July 4, 1997, 71–74.

Kalish, Susan. "Immigration: IRCA Tops Out, 1990 Law's Impact Yet to Begin." *Population Today*, Nov. 1992, 4.

Kaplan, Bernard M. "An Historical Outline of the Jews of Sacramento in the Nineteenth Century." *WSJH* 23, April 1991, 256–67.

Kaye, V. J. "The Ruthenians." *Canadian Slavonic Papers* 10, 1968, 96–99.

Kittredge, William. "Desire and Pursuit of the Whole: The Politics of Storytelling." *Montana* 42, winter 1992, 2–13.

Klein, Herbert S. "The Integration of Italian Immigrants into the United States and Argentina: A Comparative Analysis." *American Historical Review* 88, April 1983, 306–29.

Klein, Kerwin L. "Frontier Products: Tourism, Consumerism, and the Southwestern Public Lands, 1890–1990." *PHR* 52, Feb. 1993, 39–71.

Knowlton, Clark S. "The Mora Land Grant: A New Mexican Tragedy." *JW* 27, July 1988, 59–73.

Kohs, Samuel C. "The Jewish Community of Los Angeles." *Jewish Review* 2, July–Oct. 1944, 87–126.

Konig, Michael. "Phoenix in the 1950s: Urban Growth in the 'Sunbelt.' " *Arizona and the West* 24, spring 1982, 19–24.

Koppes, Clayton R. "Public Water, Private Land: Origins of the Acreage Limitation Controversy, 1933–1953." *PHR* 47, Nov. 1978, 607–36.

Kramer, William M. "Herman Silver of Silver Lake: Civic Leader and Lay Rabbi of Denver and Los Angeles." *WSJH* 20, Oct. 1987, 3–14, and Jan. 1988, 129–38.

———, and Reva Clar. "Rabbi Edgar F. Magnin and the Modernization of Los Angeles Jewry, Part II." *WSJH* 19, July 1987, 346–62.

———, and Norton B. Stern. "Letters of 1852 to 1864 Sent to Rabbi Isaac Leeser of Philadelphia from the Far West." *WSJH* 20, Oct. 1987, 43–59.

Lacewell, R. D., and J. G. Lee. "Texas High Plains." In El-Ashry and Gibbons, q.v., chap. 4.

Lamb, Blaine. "Jews in Early Phoenix, 1870–1920." *JarizH* 18, August 1977, 299–320.

Lang, Herbert H. "The New Mexico Bureau of Immigration, 1880–1912." *NMHR* 51, July 1976, 193–214.

Lang, Robert E.; Deborah Epstein Popper; and Frank J. Popper. " 'Progress of the Nation': The Settlement History of the Enduring American Frontier." *WHQ* 26, autumn 1995, 229–308.

Lang, William L. "The Nearly Forgotten Blacks on Last Chance Gulch, 1900–1912." *PNWQ* 70, April 1979, 50–57.

Laurie, Clayton D. " 'The Chinese Must Go': The United States Army and the Anti-Chinese Riots in Washington Territory, 1885–1886." *PNWQ* 81, Jan. 1990, 24–29.

———. "Civil Disorder and the Military in Rock Springs, Wyoming: The Army's Role in the 1885 Chinese Massacre." *Montana* 40, summer 1990, 44–59.

Lee, Carol F. "The Road to Enfranchisement: Chinese and Japanese in British Columbia." *BC Studies* 30, summer 1976, 44–76.

Lee, Douglas W. "Sojourners, Immigrants, and Ethnics: The Saga of the Chinese in Seattle." In Buell, q.v., 51–58.

Lee, Sharon M. "Asian Americans: Diverse and Growing." *Population Bulletin* 53:2, June 1998, 1–40.

Lemann, Nicholas. "Growing Pains." *Atlantic Monthly* 261, Jan. 1988, 58–59.

Lents, James M., and William J. Kelley. "Clearing the Air in Los Angeles." *Scientific American* 269, Oct. 1993, 32–39.

Leonard, Kevin Allen. " 'Is That What We Fought For?': Japanese Americans and Racism in California, the Impact of World War II." *WHQ* 21, Nov. 1990, 462–82.

Leonard, Stephen J. "The Irish, English, and Germans in Denver, 1860–1890." *ColoMag* 54, spring 1977, 126–53.

———. "The 1918 Influenza Epidemic in Denver and Colorado." *Essays and Monographs in Colorado History* 9, 1989, 1–24.

Leonoff, Cyril Edel. "The Jewish Farmers of Western Canada." *WSJH* 16, Jan. 1984, 99–117; April 1984, 200–26; July 1984, 303–35.

Levenson, Rosaline. "Chico's Jewish Community in the Twentieth Century, Part II." *WSJH* 20, July 1988, 339–59.

Lewelling, Lorenzo D. "The Tramp Circular [Dec. 5, 1893]." In George Brown Tindall, *A Populist Reader* q.v., 166–68.

Lewis, Sinclair. "Adventures in Automobumming." *Saturday Evening Post*, Dec. 20, 1919, and Jan. 3, 1920.

Life. Special issue on the West, Apr. 5, 1993.

Light, Ivan. "From Vice District to Tourist Attraction: The Moral Career of American Chinatowns, 1880–1940." *PHR* 43, Aug. 1974, 367–94.

Lillard, Richard G. "Problems and Promise in Tomorrowland." *CalHist* 60, spring 1981, 76–97.

Limbaugh, Ronald H. "From Missouri to the Pacific Northwest: Pioneer Families in the 20th Century." *OHQ* 91, fall 1990, 229–57.

Lister, Florence C., and Robert H. Lister. "Chinese Sojourners in Territorial Prescott." *Journal of the Southwest* 31, spring 1989, 1–4.

Littlefield, Daniel F., Jr., and Lonnie E. Underhill. "Divorce Seeker's Paradise: Oklahoma Territory, 1890–1907." *Arizona and the West* 17, spring 1986, 21–34.

Liu, John M., and Lucie Cheng. "Pacific Rim Development and the Duality of Post-1965 Asian Immigration to the United States." In Ong et al., q.v., 74–94.

———; Paul M. Ong; and Carolyn Rosenstein. "Dual Chain Migration: Post-1965 Filipino Immigration to the United States." *IMR* 25, fall 1991, 487–513.

Longino, Charles F., Jr. "From Sunbelt to Sunspots." *AmDemog* 16, Nov. 1994, 22–31.

Longmore, T. Wilson, and Homer L. Hitt. "A Demographic Analysis of First and Second Generation Mexican Population of the United States: 1930." *Southwestern Social Science Quarterly* 24, fall 1943, 138–49.

Lopez, David E. "Language: Diversity and Assimilation." In Waldinger and Bozorgmehr, q.v., 139–63.

Lotchin, Roger W. "The City and the Sword through the Ages and the Era of the Cold War." In Fairbanks and Underwood, q.v., 87–124.

———. "The Metropolitan-Military Complex in Comparative Perspective: San Francisco, Los Angeles, and San Diego, 1919–1941." *JW* 18, July 1979, 19–30.

Lothrop, Gloria Ricci. "The Boom of the '80s Revisited." *SoCalQ* 75, fall–winter 1993, 263–301.

———. "Rancheras and the Land: Women and Property Rights in Hispanic California." *SoCalQ* 76, spring 1994, 59–84.

———. "The Untold Story: The Effect of the Second World War on California Italians." *JW* 35, Jan. 1996, 7–14.

Lovett, John R. "The Levites of Apache, Oklahoma." *WSJH* 24, July 1992, 299–307.

Luckingham, Bradford. "The Southwestern Urban Frontier, 1880–1930." *JW* 18, July 1979, 40–50.

———. "To Mask or Not to Mask: A Note on the 1918 Spanish Influenza Epidemic in Tucson." *JarizHist* 25, summer 1984, 191–204.

———. "Urban Development in Arizona: The Rise of Phoenix." *JarizHist* 22, summer 1981, 197–234.

Lummis, Charles F. "A Lesson in the Census." *Land of Sunshine* 14, Jan. 1901, 61.

Lux, Mabel. "Honyockers of Harlem, Scissorbills of Zurich: A Personal Account of the Harsh Challenges Met by Homesteaders Who Answered Jim Hill's Siren Call." *Montana* 13, fall–winter 1963, 2–14.

MacDonald, Norbert. "Population Growth and Change in Seattle and Vancouver, 1880–1960." *PHR* 39, Aug. 1970, 297–322.

Madison, James H. "Taking the Country Barefooted: The Indiana Colony in Southern California." *CalHist* 69, fall 1990, 236–49.

Malone, Michael P. "The Collapse of Western Metals Mining: An Historical Epitaph." *PHR* 55, Aug. 1986, 455–64.

———. "Historical Commentary—The Close of the Copper Century." *Montana* 35, spring 1985, 69–72.

Marine, Gene. "Bunker Hill: Pep Pill for Downtown Los Angeles." *Frontier: The Voice of the New West,* Aug. 1959, 5–8, 16.

Marquis, Neeta. "Inter-racial Amity in California: Personal Observations on the Life of the Japanese in Los Angeles." *Independent* 75, July–Sept. 1913, 138.

Marshall, Alex. "The Quiet Integration of Suburbia." *AmDemog* 16, Aug. 1994, 9–11.

Martin, Philip, and Elizabeth Midgley. "Immigration to the United States: Journey to an Uncertain Destination." *PopBull* 49:2, Sept. 1994, 1–47.

Martinelli, Phyllis Cancilla. "Italy in Phoenix." *JarizHist* 18, autumn 1977, 319–40.

Marx, Wesley. "The Negro Community: 'A Better Chance.' " *Los Angeles,* March 1962, 37–41.

Masnick, George S., and Joseph A. McFalls, Jr. "A New Perspective on the Twentieth-Century American Fertility Swing." *Journal of Family History* 1, winter 1976, 216–44.

Massey, Douglas S. "March of Folly: U.S. Immigration Policy after NAFTA." *American Prospect* 37, March–Apr. 1998, 22–33.

Mathes, Michael. "The Two Californias during World War II." *CalHSQ* 44, Dec. 1965, 323–31.

Mathison, Dick. "The Many Faces of L.A." *Westways* 57, June 1965, 40–41.

May, Dean L. "People on the Mormon Frontier: Kanab's Families of 1874." *Journal of Family History* 1, winter 1976, 169–92.

———, et al. "The Stability Ratio: An Index of Community Cohesiveness in 19th-Century Mormon Towns." In Taylor and Crandall, q.v., 141–58.

———, and Jenny Cornell. "Middleton's Agriminers: The Beginnings of an Agricultural Town." *IdY* 28, winter 1985, 2–11.

McBane, Margo. "The Role of Gender in Citrus Employment: A Case Study of Recruitment, Labor, and Housing Patterns at the Limoneira Company, 1893 to 1940." *CalHist* 74, spring 1995, 68–81.

McCarthy, Thomas J. "Report from Los Angeles." *Commonweal,* June 25, 1943, 243.

McCormick, Peter J. "The 1992 Secession Movement in Southwest Kansas." *GPQ* 15, fall 1995, 247–58.

McDean, Harry C. "Dust Bowl Historiography." *GPQ* 6, spring 1986, 117–26.

McDougald, Mrs. James. "Cypress Hills Reminiscences." *SaskHist* 23, 27–30.

McLean, Robert. "Spanish-Americans in Colorado: Education, Health and Recreation." In Echevarria and Otero, q.v., 77–81.

McWilliams, Carey. "The Zoot-Suit Riots." *New Republic* 108, June 21, 1943, 818–20.

Meighan, Clement W. "Indians and California Missions." *SoCalQ* 69, fall 1987, 187–201.

Meinig, D. W. "The Mormon Culture Region: Strategies and Patterns in the Geography of the American West, 1847–1964." *AAAG* 55, June 1965, 191–220.

Melcher, Mary. " 'Women's Matters': Birth Control, Prenatal Care, and Childbirth in Rural Montana, 1910–1940." *Montana* 41, spring 1991, 47–56.

Melendy, H. Brett. "Filipinos." In Thernstrom, q.v., 354–62.

———. "Filipinos in the United States." *PHR* 43, Nov. 1974, 520–47.

Mellinger, Phil. " 'The Men Have Become Organizers': Labor Conflict and Unionization in the Mexican Mining Communities of Arizona, 1900–1915." *WHQ* 23, Aug. 1992, 323–47.

Mellinger, Philip J. "Frontier Camp to Small Town: A Study of Community Development." *Annals of Wyoming* 43, fall 1971, 259–69.

Melzer, Richard. "A Dark and Terrible Moment: The Spanish Flu Epidemic of 1918 in New Mexico." *NMHR* 57, July 1982, 213–36.

Mercier, Laurie K. " 'The Stack Dominated Our Lives': Metals Manufacturing in Four Montana Communities." *Montana* 38, spring 1988, 40–57.

———. "Women's Economic Role in Montana Agriculture: 'You Had to Make Every Minute Count.' " *Montana* 38, autumn 1988, 50–61.

Metzgar, Joseph V. "Guns and Butter: Albuquerque Hispanics, 1940–1975." *NMHR* 56, April 1981, 117–40.

Meyer, Jean. "Mexico: Revolution and Reconstruction in the 1920s." In Bethell, q.v., 155–96.

Miller, Howard. "Stephen F. Austin and the Anglo-Texan Response to the Religious Establishment in Mexico, 1821–1836." *SWHQ* 91, Jan. 1988, 283–316.

Miller, Sally M. "Changing Faces of the Central Valley: The Ethnic Presence." *CalHist* 74, summer 1995, 174–89.

Miller, Willis H. "The Port of Los Angeles–Long Beach in 1929 and 1979: A Comparative Study." *SoCalQ* 65, winter 1983, 341–78.

Mines, Richard, and Douglas S. Massey. "Patterns of Migration to the United States from Two Mexican Communities." *Latin American Research Review* 20:2, 1985, 104–23.

Mirkowich, Nicholas. "Recent Trends in Population Distribution in California." *Geographical Review* 31, April 1941, 300–07.

Mitchell, Susan. "The Next Baby Boom." *AmDemog* 17, Oct. 1995, 22–31.

Modell, John. "Normative Aspects of American Marriage Timing since World War II." *Journal of Family History* 5, summer 1980, 210–34.

———. "Tradition and Opportunity: The Japanese Immigrant in America." *PHR* 40, May 1971, 163–82.

Moehring, Eugene P. "Public Works and the New Deal in Las Vegas, 1933–1940." *NevHSQ* 24, summer 1981, 107–29.

———. "Suburban Resorts and the Triumph of Las Vegas." *Halcyon* [Reno] 10, 1988, 202–07.

Mogelonsky, Marcia. "Natural(ized) Americans." *AmDemog* 19, March 1997, 45–49.

Morganthau, Tom. "The Face of the Future." *Newsweek,* Jan. 27, 1997, 57–60.

Morris, Juddi. "Indian Detours: Turn-of-the-Century Travelers Discover a Brave New World." *Southwest Passages Magazine,* March 1995, 73–74.

Morrison, Peter A. "The Role of Migration in California's Growth." In Davis and Styles, q.v., 33–60.

Mullen, Pierce C., and Michael L. Nelson. "Montanans and 'The Most Peculiar Disease': The Influenza Epidemic and Public Health, 1918–1919." *Montana* 37, spring 1987, 50–61.

Munkres, Robert L. "The Bidwell-Bartleson Party: The Beginning of the Great Migration." *JW* 30, Oct. 1991, 64–66.

Murray, Henry T., and John A. Murray. "Herding Sheep in the Judith Basin at the Turn of the Century." *Montana* 38, spring 1988, 68–71.

Murray, William. "A Reporter at Large: Twins." *NY*, Dec. 29, 1986, 63–75.

Myers, Rex C. "Homestead on the Range: The Emergence of Community in Eastern Montana, 1900–1925." *GPQ* 10, fall 1990, 218–27.

Nadeau, Remi. "Wheat Ruled the Valley." *Westways* 55, April 1963, 18–20.

Nash, Gerald D. "Planning for the Postwar City: The Urban West in World War II." *Arizona and the West* 27, summer 1985, 99–112.

Nelson, Paula M., ed. " 'All Well and Hard at Work': The Harris Family Letters from Dakota Territory, 1882–1888." *North Dakota History* 57, spring 1990, 24–37.

———. " 'Everything I Want Is Here!': The *Dakota Farmer's* Rural Ideal, 1884–1934." *South Dakota History* 22, summer 1992, 105–35.

Neunherz, Richard E. " 'Hemmed In': Reactions in British Columbia to the Purchase of Russian America." *PNWQ* 80, July 1989, 101–11.

Noel, Thomas J. Introduction to *WPA Guide to 1930s Colorado,* q.v., x–xii.

Nostrand, Richard L. "The Century of Hispanic Expansion." *NMHR* 62, Oct. 1987, 361–86.

———. "The Hispano Homeland in 1900." *AAAG* 70, Sept. 1980, 382–96.

———. "The Spread of Spanish Settlement in Greater New Mexico: An Isochronic Map, 1610–1890." *JW* 34, July 1995, 82–87.

Notarianni, Philip F. "Utah's 'Ellis Island': The Difficult Americanization of Carbon County." *UHQ* 47, spring 1979, 178–93.

Nugent, Walter. "The 'Finding' of the West." In Ritchie and Hutton, q.v., 3–26.

———. "Frontiers and Empires in the Late Nineteenth Century." *WHQ* 20, Nov. 1989, 393–408.

———. "Happy Birthday, Western History." *JW* 32, July 1993, 3–4.

———. "The People of the West since 1890." In Nash and Etulain, q.v., 35–70.

———. "Where Is the American West? Report on a Survey." *Montana* 42, summer 1992, 2–23.

Nunis, Doyce B., Jr. "Alta California's Trojan Horse: Foreign Immigration." In Gutiérrez and Orsi, q.v., 299–330.

Ogburn, William Fielding. "Marriages, Births, and Divorces." *Annals* 229, Sept. 1943, 20–29.

———. [untitled comment] *American City* 58, Sept. 1943, 83.

O'Hare, William P. "America's Minorities—The Demographics of Diversity." *PopBull* 47:4, Dec. 1992, 1–47.

Olin, Spencer C., Jr. "European Immigrant and Oriental Alien: Acceptance and Rejection by the California Legislature of 1913." *PHR* 35, Aug. 1966, 303–15.

Olson, James S. "Pioneer Catholicism in Eastern and Southern Nevada, 1864–1931." *NevHSQ* 26, fall 1983, 159–71.

O'Malley, Sharon. "The Rural Rebound." *AmDemog* 16, Dec. 1994, 2.

Ong, Paul, and Tania Azores. "Asian Immigrants in Los Angeles: Diversity and Divisions." In Ong et al., q.v., 100–29.

———, and John M. Liu. "U.S. Immigration Policies and Asian Migration." In Ong, et al., q.v., 45–73.

Opie, John. "100 Years of Climate Risk Assessment on the High Plains: Which Farm Paradigm Does Irrigation Serve?" *AgH* 63, spring 1989, 243–69.

Oppenheimer, Robert. "Acculturation or Assimilation: Mexican Immigrants in Kansas, 1900 to World War II." *WHQ* 16, Oct. 1985, 431–41.

Orsi, Richard J. "*The Octopus* Reconsidered: The Southern Pacific and Agricultural Modernization in California, 1865–1915." *CalHSQ* 54, fall 1975, 197–220.

Orth, Michael. "Ideality to Reality: The Founding of Carmel." *CalHSQ* 48, Sept. 1969, 195–210.

Ourada, Patricia K. "Indians in the Work Force." *JW* 25, Apr. 1986, 52–58.

Owens, Kenneth N., and Sally L. Owens. "Buffalo and Bacteria." *Montana* 37, Sept. 1987, 65–67.

Pace, Anne. "Mexican Refugees in Arizona, 1910–1911." *Arizona and the West* 16, spring 1974, 5–16.

Papanikolas, Helen Zeese. "Toil and Rage in a New Land: The Greek Immigrants in Utah." *UHQ* 38, spring 1970, 100–204.

Park, Roberta J. "German Associational and Sporting Life in the Greater San Francisco Bay Area, 1850–1900." *JW* 26, Jan. 1987, 47–64.

Park, Susan B. "Memories of My Parents: Henry U. and May Colman Brandenstein." *WSJH* 19, Oct. 1986, 44–54.

Parker, Edna Monch. "The Southern Pacific Railroad and Settlement in Southern California." *PHR* 6, 1937, 103–19.

Parley, Kay. "Moffat, Assiniboia, North-west Territories." *SaskHist* 20, 1967, 32–36.

Pascoe, Peggy. "Race, Gender, and Intercultural Relations: The Case of Interracial Marriage." *Frontiers* 12, 1987, 5–17.

Passel, Jeffrey S., and Karen A. Woodrow. "Change in the Undocumented Alien Population in the United States, 1979–1983." *IMR* 21, winter 1987, 1304–34.

Patrick, Elizabeth Nelson. "The Black Experience in Southern Nevada." *NevHSQ* 22, summer 1979, 128–40.

Patterson, K. David, and Gerald F. Pyle. "The Geography and Mortality of the 1918 Influenza Pandemic." *BullHistMed* 65, spring 1991, 4–21.

Peñalosa, Fernando. "The Changing Mexican-American in Southern California." *Sociology and Social Research* 51, July 1967, 405–17.

Perlman, Susan E. "New Deal at Zuni: Livestock Reduction and the Range Management Program." In DeMark, q.v., 63–74.

Peterson, Charles S. Foreword to Robert A. Goldberg. *Back to the Soil*, q.v., xi–xxi.

———. "The 'Americanization' of Utah's Agriculture." *UHQ* 42, spring 1974, 108–25.

Peterson, Martin. "The Swedes of Yamhill." *OHQ* 76, March 1975, 5–28.

Petrik, Paula. "Capitalists with Rooms: Prostitution in Helena, Montana, 1865–1900." *Montana* 31, April 1981, 28–41.

Pillai, Vijayan K. "The Postwar Rise and Decline of American Fertility: The Pace of Transition to Motherhood among 1950–1969 Marital Cohorts of White Women." *Journal of Family History* 12:4, 1987, 421–36.

Pinal, Jorge del, and Audrey Singer. "Generations of Diversity: Latinos in the United States." *PopBull* 52, Oct. 1997, 1–48.

Plane, David A., and Peter A. Rogerson. "Tracking the Baby Boom, the Baby Bust, and the Echo Generations: How Age Composition Regulates US Migration." *Professional Geographer* 43, Nov. 1991, 417–21.

Population Reference Bureau. "1995 World Population Data Sheet."

———. "1987 Metro U.S.A. Data Sheet."

———. "1997 Kids Count Data Sheet."

Popper, Frank J. "The Strange Case of the Contemporary American Frontier." *Yale Review* 76, autumn 1986, 101–21.

Porter, Robert P.; Henry Gannett; and William C. Hunt. "Progress of the Nation 1790 to 1890." In 1890 Census, vol. 1, *Population*, xxxv–cxxvii.

Porter, Kenneth W. "Negro Labor in the Western Cattle Industry, 1866–1900." *Labor History* 10, summer 1969, 346–74.

Post, Robert C. "America's Electric Railway Beginnings: Trollers and Daft Dummies in Los Angeles." *SoCalQ* 69, fall 1987, 202–21.

Powell, Allan Kent. "Labor's Fight for Recognition in the Western Coalfields." *JW* 25, April 1986, 20–26.

Powell, T. J. D. "Northern Settlement, 1929–1935." *SaskHist* 30, autumn 1977, 81–98.

Price, John A. "The Migration and Adaptation of American Indians to Los Angeles." *Human Organization* 27, summer 1968, 168–75.

Raban, Jonathan. "The Unlamented West." *NY*, May 20, 1996, 60–81.

Rabinowitz, Howard N. "Growth Trends in the Albuquerque SMSA, 1940–1978." *JW* 18, July 1979, 62–66.

Rajala, Richard A. "Bill and the Boss: Labor Protest, Technological Change, and the Transformation of the West Coast Logging Camp, 1890–1930." *Journal of Forest History* 33, Oct. 1989, 168–79.

Reimers, David. "The Immigration Debate." *Journal of American Ethnic History* 17, spring 1998, 86–93.

Reisler, Mark. "Always the Laborer, Never the Citizen: Anglo Perceptions of the Mexican Immigrant during the 1920s." *PHR* 45, May 1976, 231–54.

Rhode, Paul. "The Nash Thesis Revisited: An Economic Historian's View." *PHR* 63, Aug. 1994, 363–92.

Richmond, Douglas W. "Mexican Immigration and Border Strategy during the Revolution, 1910–1920." *NMHR* 57, July 1982, 272–83.

Richter, Anthony A. "A Heritage of Faith: Religion and the German Settlers of South Dakota." *South Dakota History* 21, summer 1991, 155–72.

Ridgley, Ronald. "The Railroads and Rural Development in the Dakotas." *North Dakota History* 36, spring 1969, 165–87.

Riley, Glenda. "Kansas Frontierswomen Viewed through Their Writings." *KH* 9, spring 1986, 2–9; also summer 1986, 83–95; also autumn 1986, 138–45.

———. "Women on the Panama Trail to California, 1849–1869." *PHR* 55, Nov. 1986, 531–48.

Riney-Kehrberg, Pamela. "In God We Trusted, In Kansas We Busted . . . Again." *AgH* 63, spring 1989, 187–201.

Rischin, Moses. "Immigration, Migration, and Minorities in California: A Reassessment." *PHR* 41, Feb. 1972, 71–90.

Robbins, William G. " 'At the End of the Cracked Whip': The Northern West, 1880–1920." *Montana* 38, autumn 1988, 2–11.

———. "Creating a 'New' West: Big Money Returns to the Hinterland." *Montana* 46, summer 1996, 66–72.

———. "The Willamette Valley Project of Oregon: A Study in the Political Economy of Water Resource Development." *PHR* 47, Nov. 1978, 585–605.

Roberts, Glenys, and Gilbert Thomas. "City of Ethnics." *Los Angeles*, Jan. 1967, 45–50, 70–71.

Roberts, Myron. "Our Crowd—West." *Los Angeles*, April 1968, 35–37, 70–74.

Roberts, Shirley J. "Minority-Group Poverty in Phoenix: A Socio-Economic Survey." *JArizHist* 14, winter 1973, 353–59.

Robinson, W. W. "The Southern California Real Estate Boom of the Twenties." *Historical Society of Southern California Quarterly* 24, March 1942, 25–30; reprinted in Caughey and Caughey, q.v., 279.

Rochin, Refugio I., and Nicole Ballenger. "Labor and Labor Markets." In Stoddard, et al., q.v., 176–86.

Rock, Peter. "Vasya Pozdnyakov's Dukhobor Narrative." *Slavic and East European Review* 43, Dec. 1964, 152–63.

Rock, Kenneth W. " 'Unsere Leute': The Germans from Russia in Colorado." *ColoMag* 54, spring 1977, 155–83.

Rockafellar, Nancy. " 'In Gauze We Trust': Public Health and Spanish Influenza on the Home Front, Seattle, 1918–1919." *PNWQ* 77, July 1986, 104–13.

Rodriguez, Richard. "Go North, Young Man." *Mother Jones*, July–Aug. 1995, 34.

Rodwell, Lloyd. "Saskatchewan Homestead Records." *SaskHist* 18, autumn 1965, 10–29.

Roeder, Richard B. "A Settlement on the Plains: Paris Gibson and the Building of Great Falls." *Montana* 42, autumn 1992, 6–10.

Romo, Ricardo. "Work and Restlessness: Occupational and Spatial Mobility among Mexicanos in Los Angeles, 1918–1928." *PHR* 46, May 1977, 157–80.

Royick, Alexander. "Ukrainian Settlements in Alberta." *Canadian Slavonic Papers* 10, 1968, 278–97.

Rubin-Kurtzman, Jane R.; Robert Ham-Chande; and Maurice Van Arsdol, Jr. "Population in Trans-Border Regions: The Southern California-Baja California Urban System." *IMR* 30, winter 1996, 1020–45.

Sabagh, Georges, and Mehdi Bozorgmehr. "Population Change: Immigration and Ethnic Transformation." In Waldinger and Bozorgmehr, q.v., 79–107.

Saindon, Bob, and Bunky Sullivan. "Taming the Missouri and Treating the Depression: Fort Peck Dam." *Montana* 27, July 1977, 34–57.

Saloutos, Theodore. "Cultural Persistence and Change: Greeks in the Great Plains and Rocky Mountain West, 1890–1970." *PHR* 49, Feb. 1980, 77–104.

———. "The Immigrant in Pacific Coast Agriculture, 1880–1940." In Shideler, q.v., 182–201.

Sandos, James A. "Between Crucifix and Lance: Indian-White Relations in California, 1769–1848." In Gutiérrez and Orsi, q.v., 196–229.

Sandoval, David A. "Gnats, Goods, and Greasers: Mexican Merchants on the Santa Fe Trail." *JW* 28, April 1989, 22–31.

Scamehorn, H. Lee. "In the Shadow of Cripple Creek: Florence from 1885 to 1910." *ColoMag* 55, spring–summer 1978, 205–29.

Schiesl, Martin J. "City Planning and the Federal Government in World War II: The Los Angeles Experience." *CalHist* 59, summer 1980, 130–41.

Schilz, Thomas F., and Donald E. Worcester. "Spread of Firearms among the Indian Tribes on the Northern Frontier of New Spain." *American Indian Quarterly* 11, winter 1987, 1–10.

Schlebecker, John T. "Agriculture in Western Nebraska, 1906–1966." *NH* 48, 1967, 249–66.

Schmitt, Robert C. "Catastrophic Mortality in Hawai'i: An Update." *Hawaiian Journal of History* 23, 1989, 217–27.

Schoenburg, Nancy. "The Jews of Southeastern Idaho." *WSJH* 18, July 1986, 291–304.

Schulte, Janet E. " 'Proving Up and Moving Up': Jewish Homesteading Activity in North Dakota, 1900–1920." *GPQ* 10, fall 1990, 228–44.

Schwantes, Carlos A. "Images of the Wageworkers' Frontier." *Montana* 38, autumn 1988, 38–49.

Schwartz, E. A. "Sick Hearts: Indian Removal on the Oregon Coast, 1875–1881." *OHQ* 92, fall 1991, 228–64.

Schwieder, Dorothy. "Frontier Brethren: The Hutterite Experience in the American West." *Montana* 28, Jan. 1978, 2–15.

Scott, Mary Katsilometes. "The Greek Community in Pocatello, 1890–1941." *IdY* 28, fall 1984, 29–35.

Scruggs, Otey M. "Texas and the Bracero Program, 1942–1947." *PHR* 32, Aug. 1963, 251–64.

Seabrook, John. "The Spinach King." *NY,* Feb. 20 and 27, 1995, 222–35.

Shimpo, Mitsuru. "Indentured Migrants from Japan." In Cohen, q.v., 48–50.

Shortridge, James R. "The Collapse of Frontier Farming in Alaska." *AAAG* 66, Dec. 1976, 583–604.

———. "People of the New Frontier: Kansas Population Origins, 1865." *KH* 14, autumn 1991, 162–85.

Shragge, Abraham. " 'A New Federal City': San Diego during World War II." *PHR* 63, Aug. 1994, 333–62.

Sims, Robert C. "The Japanese American Experience in Idaho." *IdY* 22, spring 1978, 2–10.

Singer, Audrey. "IRCA Aftermath." *Population Today,* Oct. 1988, 5, 9.

Skaggs, Richard H. "Drought in the United States, 1931–40." *AAAG* 65, Sept. 1975, 391–402.

Skolnick, M.; L. Bean; D. May; V. Arbon; K. DeNevers; and P. Cartwright. "Mormon Demographic History: I. Nuptiality and Fertility of Once-Married Couples." *Population Studies* 32, March 1978, 5–19.

Slatta, Richard W. "Chicanos in the Pacific Northwest: A Demographic and Socioeconomic Portrait." *PNWQ* 70, Oct. 1979, 155–62.

———— and Maxine P. Atkinson. "The 'Spanish Origin' Population of Oregon and Washington." *PNWQ* 75, July 1984, 108–16.

Smith, Duane A. "A Land unto Itself: The Western Slope." *ColoMag* 55, spring–summer 1978, 181–204.

Smith, Elmer R. "The 'Japanese' in Utah." *Utah Humanities Review* 2, Apr. 1948, 129–44, and July 1948, 208–30.

Smith, Everett G. "America's Richest Farms and Ranches." *AAAG* 70, Dec. 1980, 528–41.

Smith, Jack. "A Day in the City: Sights and Scents Celestial." *Westways* 62, June 1970, 23–25.

Smith, J. Patrick. "North Dakota's Prairie Communities: The Journey from Twilight to a Dawn." *North Dakota History* 56, winter 1989, 48–56.

Smith, Sherry L. "Single Women Homesteaders: The Perplexing Case of Elinore Pruitt Stewart." *WHQ* 22, May 1991, 163–83.

Smith, T. Lynn. "The Changing Number and Distribution of the Aged Negro Population of the United States." *Phylon* 18, 1957, 339–54.

Snipp, C. Matthew. "A Demographic Comeback for American Indians?" *Population Today*, Nov. 1996, 4.

Spidle, Jake W. "Axis Invasion of the American West: POWs in New Mexico, 1942–1946." *NMHR* 49, April 1974, 93–122.

Stannard, David E. "Disease and Infertility: A New Look at the Demographic Collapse of Native Populations in the Wake of Western Contact." *Journal of American Studies* 24, 1990, 325–50.

Starr, Kevin. "Oligarchs, Babbitts & Folks: The Wasp in L.A." *The Californians* 8, Nov./Dec. 1990, 27–37.

Stathis, Stephen W. "Utah's Experience with the Desert Land Act." *UHQ* 48, spring 1980, 175–94.

Stearns, Marjorie R. "The Settlement of the Japanese in Oregon." *OHQ* 39, Sept. 1938, 262–69.

Stephen, Elizabeth Hervey, and Frank D. Bean. "Assimilation, Disruption and the Fertility of Mexican-Origin Women in the United States." *IMR* 26, spring 1992, 67–88.

Stern, Norton B. "The Jewish Community of Eureka, Nevada." *NevHSQ* 25, summer 1982, 95–115.

————. "The Pioneer of Sacramento Jewry." *WSJH* 21, July 1989, 345–49.

————. "The Tombstone, Arizona Jewish Saga." *WSJH* 19, April 1987, 217–30.

————, and Kramer, William M. "Who Was Isaacson, Arizona Named For?" *WSJH* 19, Jan. 1987, 121–24.

Stevenson, Janet. "The Return of the Exiles." *American Heritage* 20, June 1969, 96–99.

Stopanovich, Joseph. "South Slav Settlements in Utah, 1890–1935." *UHQ* 43, spring 1975, 155–71.

Studness, Charles M. "Economic Opportunity and the Westward Migration of Canadians during the Late Nineteenth Century." *Canadian Journal of Economics and Political Science/Revue Canadienne d'Économique et de Science Politique* 30, Nov. 1964, 570–84.

Stull, Donald D. " 'I Come to the Garden': Changing Ethnic Relations in Garden City, Kansas." *Urban Anthropology* 19, winter 1990, 303–12.

Sundquist, Eric J. "Exploration and Empire," in Bercovitch, q.v., 127–74.

Swain, Donald C. "The Bureau of Reclamation and the New Deal, 1933–1940." *PNWQ* 61, July 1970, 137–46.

Taeuber, Irene B. "Change and Transition in the Black Population of the United States." *Population* Index 34, Jan.–March 1968, 121–51.

Tamura, Eileen H. "Gender, Schooling and Teaching, and the Nisei in Hawai'i: An Episode in

American Immigration History, 1900–1940." *Journal of American Ethnic History* 14, summer 1995, 3–26.

Tank, Robert M. "Mobility and Occupational Structure on the Late Nineteenth-Century Urban Frontier: The Case of Denver." *PHR* 47, May 1978, 191–212.

Tatla, Darshan Singh. "Sikh Free and Military Migration during the Colonial Period." In Cohen, q.v., 576–80.

Taubenberger, Jeffery K.; Ann H. Reid; Amy E. Krafft; Karen E. Bijwaard; and Thomas G. Fanning. "Initial Genetic Characterization of the 1918 'Spanish' Influenza Virus." *Science* 275, March 21, 1997, 1793–96.

Taylor, Quintard. "Black Urban Development—Another View: Seattle's Central District, 1910–1940." *PHR* 58, Nov. 1989, 429–48.

———. "From Esteban to Rodney King: Five Centuries of African American History in the West." *Montana* 46, winter 1996, 2–23.

———. "The Great Migration: The Afro-American Communities of Seattle and Portland during the 1940s." *Arizona and the West* 23, summer 1981, 109–26.

Taylor, Sandra C. "Leaving the Concentration Camps: Japanese American Resettlement in Utah and the Intermountain West." *PHR* 60, May 1991, 169–94.

Thomas, L. G. "The Rancher and the City: Calgary and the Cattlemen, 1883–1914." *Transactions of the Royal Society of Canada* 6, June 1968, 203–15.

Thompson, Kenneth. "Insalubrious California: Perception and Reality." *AAAG* 59, March 1969, 50–64.

Tigges, Linda. "Santa Fe Landownership in the 1880s." *NMHR* 68, April 1993, 153–80.

Tilden, Freeman. "Portland, Oregon: Yankee Prudence on the West Coast." *World's Work*, Oct. 1931, 34–40.

Tipton, Gary P. "Men Out of China: Origins of the Chinese Colony in Phoenix." *JarizHist* 18, autumn 1977, 341–56.

Titus, A. Costandina. "A-Bombs in the Backyard: Southern Nevada Adapts to the Nuclear Age, 1951–1963." *NevHSQ* 26, [winter 1983], 235–54.

Toll, William. "Ethnicity and Stability: The Italians and Jews of South Portland, 1900–1940." *PHR* 54, May 1985, 161–90.

———. "Fraternalism and Community Structure on the Urban Frontier: The Jews of Portland, Oregon." *PHR* 47, Aug. 1978, 369–403.

Torrez, Robert J. "The San Juan Gold Rush of 1860 and Its Effect on the Development of Northern New Mexico." *NMHR* 63, July 1988, 257–72.

Trillin, Calvin. "Messages from My Father." *NY,* June 20, 1994, 56–78.

———. "U.S. Journal: Arroyo Seco, New Mexico." *NY,* Sept. 18, 1971, 103–10.

———. "U.S. Journal: Los Angeles: New Group in Town." *NY,* Apr. 18, 1970, 92–104.

———. "U.S. Journal: Provo, Utah." *NY,* March 21, 1970, 121–25.

———. "U.S. Journal: Watts: The Towers." *NY,* Dec. 4, 1971, 139–43.

Tucker, Carl. "Southern California's Immigrants Progress Rapidly." *Population Today,* May 1996, 5.

Turk, Eleanor L. "Selling the Heartland: Agents, Agencies, Press and Policies Promoting German Emigration to Kansas in the Nineteenth Century." *KH* 12, autumn 1989, 150–59.

Turner, Allan R. "Pioneer Farming Experiences." *SaskHist* 8, spring 1955, 41–55.

Turner, Frederick Jackson. "The Significance of the Frontier in American History." In Martin Ridge, ed., *Frederick Jackson Turner: Wisconsin's Historian of the Frontier.* State Historical Society of Wisconsin, 1986, 26–47.

Tydeman, William E. "A New Deal for Tourists: Route 66 and the Promotion of New Mexico." *NMHR* 66, April 1991, 208–13.

Tyler, Daniel. "Ejido Lands in New Mexico." *JW* 27, July 1988, 24–35.

Ubelaker, D. H. "North American Indian Population Size, A.D. 1500 to 1985." *American Journal of Physical Anthropology* 77, Nov. 1988, 289–94.

————. "North American Indian Population Size: Changing Perspectives." In Verano and Ubelaker, q.v., 169–76.

Ulibarri, Richard O. "Utah's Ethnic Minorities: A Survey." *UHQ* 40, summer 1972, 210–32.

Valdez, Luis. "Envisioning California." *CalHist* 68, winter 1989–1990, 162–71.

Valien, Preston. "Overview of Demographic Trends and Characteristics by Color." *Milbank Memorial Fund Quarterly* 48, April 1970, 21–45.

Van Arsdol, Maurice D., Jr., and Leo A. Shuerman. "Redistribution and Assimilation of Ethnic Populations: The Los Angeles Case." *Demography* 8, Nov. 1971, 459–80.

Verge, Arthur C. "The Impact of the Second World War on Los Angeles." *PHR* 63, Aug. 1994, 289–314.

Waddell, Karen. "Dearfield . . . A Dream Deferred." *Colorado Heritage,* no. 2, 1988, 2–12.

Wagner, Jonathan F. "*Heim ins Reich,* the Story of Loon River's Nazis." *SaskHist* 29, spring 1976, 41–50.

Wakatsuki, Yasuo. "Japanese Emigration to the United States, 1866–1924: A Monograph." *Perspectives in American History* 12, 1979, 389–516.

Waldinger, Roger, and Michael Lichter. "Anglos: Beyond Ethnicity?" In Waldinger and Bozorgmehr, q.v., 413–41.

Walker, Philip L., and John R. Johnson. "Effects of Contact on the Chumash Indians." In Verano and Ubelaker, q.v., 127–39.

Wallace, Douglas C. "Mitochondrial DNA in Aging and Disease" and "What Mitochondrial DNA Says about Human Migrations." *Scientific American* 277, Aug. 1997, 40–47.

Waltz, Anna Langhorne. "West River Pioneer: A Woman's Story, 1911–1915." *South Dakota History* 17, spring 1987, 42–77; summer 1987, 140–69; fall/winter 1987, 241–95.

Ward, Betty. "Trek of the Doukhobors." *SaskHist* 35, 1982, 17–24.

Ward, Mike. "A Man Buys a Home, and Monterey Park Won't Ever Be Quite the Same Again." *Frontier,* June 1962, 7–9.

Ward, Ralph E. "Wheat in Montana: Determined Adaptation." *Montana* 25, autumn 1975, 16–37.

"Water for Phoenix." [By "The Editors"] *JarizHist* 18, Aug. 1977, 279–94.

Wax, Rosalie H. "In and Out of the Tule Lake Segregation Center: Japanese Internment in the West, 1942–1945." *Montana* 37, spring 1987, 12–25.

Wayne, George H. "Negro Migration and Colonization in Colorado 1870–1930." *JW* 15, Jan. 1976, 102–20.

Weissberg, Muriel. "Gold Rush Merchants in Shasta County, California." *WSJH* 20, July 1977, 291–305.

Wells, Merle. "Twentieth-Century Migrant Farm Labor." *JW* 25, April 1986, 65–72.

Welsh, Michael. "The United States Army Corps of Engineers in the Middle Rio Grande Valley, 1935–1955." *NMHR* 60, July 1985, 295–318.

————. "Western Historians, the U.S. Army Corps of Engineers, and the Rivers of Empire." *North Dakota History* 59, summer 1992, 5–12.

Wenzel, Lawrence A. "The Rural Punjabis of California: A Religio-Ethnic Group." *Phylon* 29, 1968, 245–56.

West, Elliott. "Scarlet West: The Oldest Profession in the Trans-Mississippi West." *Montana* 31, April 1981, 16–27.

West, Karen. "Cardston, The Temple City of Canada." *Canadian Geographical Journal* 71, Nov. 1965, 162–69.

Wheeler, David L. "The Blizzard of 1886 and Its Effect on the Range Cattle Industry in the Southern Plains." *SWHQ* 94, Jan. 1991, 415–32.

White, Richard. "Animals and Enterprise." In Milner et al., q.v., 237–73.

————. "Frederick Jackson Turner and Buffalo Bill." In Grossman, q.v., 7–65.

————. "Poor Men on Poor Lands: The Back-to-the-Land Movement of the Early Twentieth Century—A Case Study." *PHR* 49, Feb. 1980, 122–30.

————. "Race Relations in the American West." *American Quarterly* 38, autumn 1986, 396–416.

————. "The Winning of the West: The Expansion of the Western Sioux in the Eighteenth and Nineteenth Centuries." *JAH* 65, Sept. 1978, 319–43.

Whyte, William H., Jr. "Urban Sprawl." *Fortune* 52, Jan. 1958, 103–09, 194–200.

Wilkinson, Frank. "And Now the Bill Comes Due." *Frontier,* Oct. 1965, 10–12.

Williams, Robert Lewis, Jr. "The Negro's Migration to Los Angeles, 1900–1946." *Negro History Bulletin* 19, Feb. 1956, 102/112–13.

Wilson, John P. "How the Settlers Farmed: Hispanic Villages and Irrigation Systems in Early Sierra County, 1850–1900." *NMHR* 63, Oct. 1988, 333–56.

Winn, Karyl. "The Seattle Jewish Community: A Photographic Essay." *PNWQ* 70, April 1979, 69–73.

Winsberg, Morton D. "America's Foreign Born." *Population Today,* Oct. 1993, 4.

————. "Specific Hispanics." *AmDemog* 16, Feb. 1994, 44–49, 52–53.

Winther, Oscar O. "The Rise of Metropolitan Los Angeles, 1870–1900." *Huntington Library Quarterly* 4, Aug. 1947, 391–405.

Wishart, David J. "The Dispossession of the Pawnee." *AAAG* 69, Sept. 1979, 382–401.

Wittenburg, Mary Joanne, SND. "Three Generations of the Sepulveda Family in Southern California." *SoCalQ* 73, fall 1991, 197–250.

Woehlke, Walter V. "The Corn Belt in California: How Climate Is Moving the Middle West to the Shores of the Pacific." *Sunset* 47, Aug. 1921, 29–32.

Wollenberg, Charles. "James vs. Marinship: Trouble on the New Black Frontier." *CalHist* 60, fall 1981, 262–79.

————. "Race and Class in Rural California: The El Monte Berry Strike of 1933." *CalHSQ* 51, summer 1972, 155–64.

Womack, John, Jr. "The Mexican Revolution, 1910–1920." In Bethell, q.v., 79–154.

Woolsey, Ronald C. "A Capitalist in a Foreign Land: Abel Stearns in Southern California before the Conquest." *SoCalQ* 75, summer 1993, 101–17.

————. "Rites of Passage? Anglo and Mexican-American Contrasts in a Time of Change: Los Angeles, 1860–1870." *SoCalQ* 69, summer 1987, 81–102.

Wunder, John. "The Courts and the Chinese in Frontier Idaho." *IdY* 25, spring 1981, 23–32.

Yuzyk, Paul. "75th Anniversary of Ukrainian Settlement in Canada." *Ukrainian Quarterly* 23, spring 1967, 247–54.

Zanjani, Sally S. "To Die in Goldfield: Mortality in the Last Boomtown on the Mining Frontier." *WHQ* 21, Feb. 1990, 47–69.

Zellick, Anna. "The Men from Bribir: The Croatian Stonemasons of Lewistown, Montana." *Montana* 28, Jan. 1978, 44–55.

INDEX

The author gratefully acknowledges and credits the following for permission to reprint photographs:

El Paso Public Library
Henry E. Huntington Library
Jacobs, Wilbur
Kansas State Historical Society
Library of Congress
Los Angeles Public Library
Oklahoma Historical Society
Sisters of the Blessed Sacrament
United States Archives II
University of Texas—El Paso

A Note About the Author

Walter Nugent spent his childhood years near the St. Lawrence River in upstate New York, and most of his teens in Kansas. In 1961, he finished a Ph.D. at the University of Chicago and became a history professor, briefly at Kansas State, then at Indiana University for twenty-one years, and since 1984 at Notre Dame. As a visiting professor he has also taught and lived in England, Israel, Germany, Poland, and Ireland. He has published eight previous books and well over a hundred essays and reviews on American and comparative history. He lives with his wife, the historian Suellen Hoy, in Chesterton, Indiana.

A Note on the Type

This book was set in Minion, a typeface produced by the Adobe Corporation specifically for the Macintosh personal computer and released in 1990. Designed by Robert Slimbach, Minion combines the classic characteristics of old-style faces with the full complement of weights required for modern typesetting.

Composed by North Market Street Graphics,
Lancaster, Pennsylvania
Printed and bound by Quebecor Printing,
Fairfield, Pennsylvania
Designed by Anthea Lingeman